# EXCEPTIONAL CHILDREN in the SCHOOLS

# EXCEPTIONAL CHILDREN
## in the SCHOOLS

Edited by LLOYD M. DUNN
George Peabody College for Teachers

*Contributing Authors*

SAMUEL C. ASHCROFT

LLOYD M. DUNN

FORREST M. HULL

LEONARD J. LUCITO

JOHN E. PATE

MARGUERITE WILSON

HARLEY Z WOODEN

HOLT, RINEHART AND WINSTON, INC.
NEW YORK • CHICAGO • SAN FRANCISCO • TORONTO • LONDON

# PREFACE

This is a book about exceptional children — the handicapped and the gifted — and the specialized school programs they need. As a text, it is intended for senior college undergraduates and beginning graduate students, preferably those who have had some background in general education and psychology. However, it was written not only for general and special educators but for all who serve exceptional children in any capacity in the schools. We hope that the book will prove useful as (1) a comprehensive overview for general educators, including classroom teachers who work with large numbers of cases of exceptionality, (2) an introduction for teachers planning to specialize in the field, and (3) a ready reference for those outside of education who are associated with school programs for exceptional children.

We believe this to be the first survey text in special education written by a number of authorities who have contributed chapters on their own specialities and who, at the same time, have served as an editorial committee, cooperating to plan a uniform format and to edit not only their own but the other authors' chapters. We have striven to arrive at a compatible philosophy, consistent format, and succinct total text while at the same time allowing each specialist to write authoritatively in his own field. It is our belief that we have achieved a successful compromise between, on the one hand, the sort of book in which one person attempts to write with equal authority on all of the diverse areas that the field includes and, on the other, the multiple-authored text in which each writer develops separately his own philosophy, style, and content, with resulting

v

overlap and inconsistency. Thus, we hope that our procedure has eliminated repetition, provided good cross-reference, and avoided the gaps and inadequate treatment of topics that might otherwise have resulted.

The book has been organized into 10 chapters, providing 10 logical units for a course offered over a quarter, semester, or trimester. This organization should lend itself to the teaching of a survey course by one instructor, or as a series by seven or eight specialists. Chapter 1 is a general overview. Chapter 10 deals with a problem common to all types of exceptionality — that of adjustment. Chapters 2 to 9, which cover the various areas of exceptionality in detail, follow a similar format, with sections in each on definitions, prevalence, identification, characteristics, educational procedures, and resources. References are listed at the end of each chapter, along with selected book references for professionals and parents and lists of films and resources.

Chapters 2 to 5 deal with the psychologically exceptional and 7 to 9 with the physically impaired. Chapter 6, on the speech impaired, falls between these chapter groupings, since it is relevant to both areas of exceptionality. Chapters 2 and 3 treat, respectively, the "educable" and the "trainable" mentally retarded. This field has been emphasized because it presents a major concern to educators. Chapter 4 is an extensive one devoted to the gifted and contains a discussion of creative and critical thinking. Chapter 5 deals with the emotionally disturbed and the socially maladjusted somewhat separately because children with these two sorts of handicaps are different in many ways. Chapter 6 is labeled "the speech impaired"; it covers a number of different kinds of speech disorders, including stuttering, organic speech disorders, and articulation problems. The deaf and the hard of hearing are incorporated into Chapter 7 because improved amplification and changes in educational provisions have brought these two fields together. Similarly, Chapter 8 discusses both the blind and the partially seeing because low-vision optical aids and other technological advances have lowered the barriers separating these two groups of children. Chapter 9 covers the crippled, the chronically ill, and the neurologically impaired. These three somewhat divergent areas are discussed in one chapter because children in these groups are frequently served together in homebound, hospital, and special school and class programs.

Arthur H. Hill, a pioneer special educator and former Chief, Exceptional Children and Youth in the U.S. Office of Education, has said: "The walls between the various areas of exceptionality have often been higher than between general and special education." In grouping together related areas in this book, we have attempted to lower such barriers.

We wish to express our gratitude to the many people who contributed to the preparation of this volume. More than two hundred students at George Peabody College for Teachers used early drafts of the manuscript, and their reactions have had a constructive influence upon its final version. Authors and publishers have been very generous in permitting us to quote their materials. We are sincerely grateful to the scholars who reviewed all or portions of our manuscript and made invaluable suggestions for its improvement: Professors Stanley Ainsworth, Maurice H. Fouracre, Miriam Goldberg, Norris G. Haring, Merrill Hollinshead, Samuel A. Kirk, Berthold Lowenfeld, Jerome H. Rothstein, and Alice Streng. And we are finally happy to acknowledge our debt of gratitude to Mrs. Leota M. Dunn, the editor's wife, for the endless copy and research skills that made her, in effect, managing editor of the book as it moved from plan to publication.

L. M. D.

NASHVILLE, TENNESSEE
*February 1963*

# CONTRIBUTING AUTHORS

**SAMUEL C. ASHCROFT, Ed.D.,** is associate professor of special education and director of the program for preparing educators of the visually limited, George Peabody College for Teachers. He was the first director of educational research at the American Printing House for the Blind. He is past-president of the Middle Tennessee Chapter, the Council for Exceptional Children. He has served as a consultant to the U.S. Office of Education, the American Foundation for the Blind, United Cerebral Palsy and other special education agencies. He serves as an associate editor of the International Journal for the Education of the Blind. He is a member of the American Association of Instructors of the Blind, the Council for Exceptional Children, and other professional education associations. Ashcroft is the senior author of the book *Programmed Instruction in Braille* and his writings on the education of the blind appear in the special education literature in his field. He taught, served as guidance counselor and assistant principal in Michigan Public Schools, and principal of the Iowa Braille and Sight Saving School. He was a consultant on the education of blind and other exceptional children in the Republic of the Philippines.

**LLOYD M. DUNN, Ph.D.,** is Chairman of the Department of Special Education, George Peabody College for Teachers. He is a past-president of the Council for Exceptional Children and present editor of the CEC Research Monographs. He was Associate Director of the U.S. Office of Education study "Qualification and Preparation of Teachers of Exceptional Children," and directed studies of special educator needs for the Southern Regional Education Board, and the Western Interstate Commission on Higher Education. He is the author of the Peabody Picture Vocabulary Test. He is a fellow of the American Association on Mental Deficiency, and advisor to the NEA Educational Policies Commission. Dunn holds membership in the American Educational Research Association, and the American

Psychological Association. He has served on President Kennedy's Panel on Mental Retardation, and has studied services for the retarded in many countries of Europe. For a number of years he taught regular and special education in Canada and the United States.

**FORREST M. HULL,** Ph.D., is associate professor of speech pathology and associate director, speech clinic, Colorado State University in Fort Collins. He formerly held joint appointments as associate professor of special education and speech science at George Peabody College for Teachers, and Vanderbilt School of Medicine, while serving in the capacity of coordinator of student training and director at the Bill Wilkerson Hearing and Speech Center. He holds advanced certification in speech in the American Speech and Hearing Association and is a charter member and former president of the Tennessee Speech and Hearing Association. He is presently an associate member, professional services board of the American Board of Examiners in Speech Pathology and Audiology for the American Speech and Hearing Association. Hull has taught courses in speech science and speech pathology for a number of years, and has been consultant in speech pathology for the Veterans Administration. He is presently a consultant in speech pathology for Sewall Rehabilitation Center, Denver, Colorado.

**LEONARD J. LUCITO,** Ed.D., is associate professor of special education and director of the gifted program, George Peabody College for Teachers. He is a member of the American Association for the Advancement of Science, the American Academy of Political and Social Science, the American Psychological Association, the Council for Exceptional Children, and Phi Delta Kappa. In addition, he is a member of the Association for the Gifted (a division of CEC) and of the Research Committee of CEC. Lucito has taught in the public schools of California, been a research fellow of the National Institute of Mental Health while at the Institute for Research on Exceptional Children, University of Illinois. His major interests are in the educational and psychological aspects of the gifted and mentally retarded.

**JOHN E. PATE,** Ed.D., is assistant professor of human behavior, Department of Psychiatry, Vanderbilt University School of Medicine. He directs the Wills Center School for emotionally disturbed children. As a former classroom teacher, supervising teacher, and elementary supervisor, Pate has a varied background in teaching and administration in several states. He has participated in school surveys and workshops in a number of school districts and served as consultant to the Southern Regional Education Board and the National Institute of Mental Health. He is a member of Phi Delta Kappa, Kappa Delta Pi, and other professional associations. Pate taught and supervised classes of disturbed children in a mental health clinic setting before joining the Vanderbilt University Department of Psychiatry.

MARGUERITE WILSON, M.A., is assistant professor of special education, in charge of the program of preparation for teachers of the physically impaired, and coordinator of the undergraduate program in special education, Brigham Young University, Provo, Utah. Her advanced graduate work was in the education of orthopedically handicapped children and other exceptional children. Prior to her appointment to Brigham Young University, she was an elementary teacher, a teacher of the physically handicapped, and director of the Junior League program for shut-ins in Salt Lake City. Her doctoral studies were pursued at George Peabody College for Teachers. Miss Wilson is a life member of the NEA, a member of AAUW, American Association on Mental Deficiency, Delta Kappa Gamma, and a member and past-president of the Utah Chapter of CEC.

HARLEY Z WOODEN, M.A., is past executive secretary, and a past president of the Council for Exceptional Children. He is past publisher and editor of the CEC journal, *Exceptional Children*. He has served Michigan in such roles as superintendent of the Michigan School for the Deaf; principal of the Ann J. Kellogg School, Battle Creek; state consultant for special education; and first assistant superintendent of public instruction in charge of administration. He is a past board member and treasurer of the American Hearing Society, and a present advisory board member to the Michigan Association for Better Hearing. He is a member of Phi Delta Kappa and holds an honorary M.Ed. from Eastern Michigan University. Wooden is presently engaged in free-lance activities in education of exceptional children.

# CONTENTS

## CHAPTER 1

# An Overview

LLOYD M. DUNN

An important key to excellence in teaching is an understanding and acceptance of all children and their individual differences. Consequently, educators are making more provisions than ever before for pupils who deviate from the average. Courses of study are becoming more varied, thus providing a challenge for both slow and rapid learners. Multitrack programs are in common use in the regular grades, especially in the medium- and large-sized high schools. Better diagnostic, guidance, and counseling services are in greater evidence. Learning through the use of programmed instruction, including automated teaching machines, is receiving increased consideration and trial. However, the trend to provide for individual differences is best illustrated through the efforts being made to open the door of educational opportunity to those who deviate most, namely, our exceptional children and youth. Increasing numbers of teachers now recognize the extremes by which students differ from one another either in their special abilities, or in their unusual limitations —physical, intellectual, social, and emotional. In fact, many exceptional pupils vary so far from the average that even such programs, procedures, and devices as those just cited do not provide adequately for their educational needs. Instead, they require special education services, ranging from a short period of time to a full school life, if they are to be supplied with suitable opportunities.

1

## Exceptional Pupils and Special Education Defined

The term "exceptional"- is used to describe those pupils whose patterns of educational needs are very different from those of the majority of children and youth. In other words, only those possessing deviations that require special-teaching competence or unusual school services are included. For example, many students possess hearing losses, but they are not considered exceptional unless the loss is great enough to produce a need for special instruction in communication skills. Similarly, many pupils have impaired vision, but most cases can be corrected by glasses; only the very few who need such special help as the use of large print, magnifiers, or braille materials are classified as exceptional. By definition then, exceptional pupils are those (1) *who differ from the average to such a degree in physical or psychological characteristics* (2) *that school programs designed for the majority of children do not afford them opportunity for all-round adjustment and optimum progress,* (3) *and who therefore need either special instruction or in some cases special ancillary services, or both, to achieve at a level commensurate with their respective abilities.*

It should be pointed out that the above expression "commensurate with their respective abilities" implies more than their abilities in academic pursuits. Included are their abilities to overcome certain limitations, such as a speech impairment; abilities to compensate for certain limitations, such as acquiring skills in speech reading for a hearing loss; and abilities to understand and accept a personal limitation or a giftedness and adjust to the problems associated with it. For example, cerebral palsied pupils may have problems in gaining social acceptance. Similarly, gifted children may encounter difficulties in finding common interests with their playmates, or in being challenged and interested in school.

It should also be pointed out, for emphasis, that a school program is considered by the authors of this text as special education only when it is conducted under adequately trained personnel using all the essential, special materials and facilities for the task. Whether a child who comes to school to receive an ancillary service only, such as physical therapy, should be considered as enrolled in special education must be left to local tradition and organization to determine. In some instances these services are offered neither in the school nor by it. In other instances, they are offered in the school, but not by it. In still others, the physiotherapist, while receiving instructions from an orthopedic surgeon for the treatments she administers, is on the school payroll and functions in the same general manner as any other member of the special education team.

Special education services embody three elements worthy of note. The first is composed of *trained professional personnel* possessing special competencies for serving a certain type or types of exceptional children. These personnel may include teachers, teacher educators, administrators, consultants, and as just mentioned, other such professional persons as the physiotherapist and speech therapist. The second element of special education services is special *curricular content* for certain areas of exceptionality, particularly for the mentally retarded, the gifted, and the deaf. Areas usually requiring some modifications in curriculum include the emotionally disturbed, the socially maladjusted, the severely hard of hearing, and the blind. Children who require little or no curriculum adjustment as a result of their handicap include the speech impaired, the not too severely hard of hearing, the partially seeing, and the nonsensory handicapped. The third element involved in special education services is that of *facilities* including such special building features as ramps, such special equipment as group hearing aids and braille books; and such extra library materials as technical books for the gifted and low-vocabulary–high-interest books for the retarded.

## The Educator's Challenge

Informed educators are vital to the future of the exceptional children found in every school system. Some such pupils are served exclusively by special educators. A much larger number are under the complete or partial direction of the regular classroom teacher but also receive instruction from special teachers and therapists who function on an itinerant, resource room, or other basis. Thus, children formerly excused from school, enrolled in special day or residential schools, or on a homebound instruction program are now more nearly in the general stream of education. The effectiveness of these integrated programs depends on the competence of all staff members concerned. If a team approach is to be meaningful, school administrators, visiting teachers, psychologists, and public health nurses, as well as regular classroom teachers need orientation in the education of the various types of exceptional children. Multiple exceptionalities make it equally necessary for specialists in one area of exceptionality to possess a working knowledge about the other areas. Mental retardation accompanied by either blindness or deafness, or a crippling condition accompanied by giftedness are cases in point.

Multiple disabilities appear to be on the increase. Wishik (1956) found one third of a sample of handicapped children in Georgia to have one disability, one third to have two, and one third to have three or more. This increase in multiple disabilities is attributed primarily to two factors. First, certain medical advances are preventing or ameliorating many infectious diseases, thus averting certain types of single disabilities, such as postpolio and tuberculosis. Second, other medical advances have resulted in preserving life in more and more babies with impairments that often occur in multiples. Thus, a child may possess any combination of either physical disabilities, or psychological exceptionalities, or both. So teachers who instruct exceptional children in one area need knowledge in the others.

If each exceptional pupil is to realize his full potential, there is no single factor more important than the availability of broadly prepared general and special educators. They must be informed, not only about the characteristics of these various types of children, but also about present-day educational practices and the underlying experimentation upon which such practices are based (Mackie et al., 1960). The central purpose of this text of ours is to provide an overview of the problems involved and some of their solutions.

## Special Education Requirements

A large percentage of persons now support the concept of equality of educational opportunity for all children, but such was not always the case. For example, school attendance in the early days of public education in the United States was only a *privilege* for those who met the requirements. Courts upheld school boards for expulsions based on a child's acts of negligence, carelessness of posture while sitting or reciting, or for other equally innocuous causes. Under such circumstances it is easy to understand how such a policy resulted either in the neglect of so many exceptional children of that day, or in their enrollment in separate programs of education. Somewhat after the turn of this century, the courts began to rule that the *right* to attend public school was fundamental, and that it could not be denied "except for the general welfare." This placed the burden of proof on the school board to justify its case. However, the child still had to accept what was offered him whether it met his needs or not. The next and last phase in this progress of democracy in opportunity has come in very recent years. Today the courts are tending to rule that the exceptional child not only has a right to an education, but the right to an *education somewhat in keeping with his needs* (Zedler, 1953).

Unfortunately not all people have caught up with the courts in their concepts of what constitutes equality of educational opportunity. There are people who fail to appreciate the full extent of the individual differences which exist among school children. There are those who believe the regular classroom teacher is capable of dealing with even extreme pupil deviations. There are those who fail to recognize that negative personal attitudes toward exceptional children on the part of educators result in many of these pupils being rejected and stigmatized in school. And, finally, there are the extreme environmentalists who think that identical school programs for all children help to overcome economic and social inequalities and, therefore, are more democratic than differentiations in programming. These are some of the philosophical problems and challenges with which the education of exceptional children is faced. Nevertheless, gains are being made today at a more rapid rate than ever before.

Equality of educational opportunity, the author believes, is achieved through enabling each pupil to develop at his own pace and, as nearly as possible, to the maximum of his potentialities. Therefore, the true meaning of equality of opportunity lies in diversified rather than similar school programs. Even with excellent opportunities, few pupils fully develop to the upper limits of their capabilities. However, their chances of nearing such a goal are enhanced when varied teaching, curricula, and facilities are provided—geared to the level, capacity, limitations, and characteristics of each individual child. Under this plan, different expectancies are set for different children. The goal for the educable mentally retarded is social competence, and economic independence in the unskilled and service occupations. The goal set for the trainable mentally retarded is the achievement of self-care, socialization, and oral communication in a sheltered environment. The goal for the gifted child is to move him to high accomplishment, by providing him with outstanding opportunities and stimulation. Thus the guiding principle for the educative process becomes one of devising a school program where each child has opportunity to work at his own level, and to progress as far and as fast as his learning characteristics will permit.[7]

Through regular school provisions for individual differences, most pupils have a reasonably good chance of achieving satisfactorily by remaining entirely in the main stream of education. This leaves about 8 percent of school children who, at any given time, would need to be classified as exceptional because they need one or more special services. Many will develop best in some type of program involving services both from regular and special personnel. A few will need separate school programs for their optimum progress. These facts constitute the challenge to all educators of the elementary and secondary schools, namely that of deciding what can best be done for each child. Improper diagnostic services, guidance, or placement can lose years for a child—years which will be difficult if not impossible to reclaim. Failure to challenge the gifted can result in the development of poor work habits and mediocre achievement in life, as well as in a definite loss to society. Failure to assist the handicapped to reach their optimum potentials may constitute not only a grave personal loss to them, but a lifetime, welfare burden on society. Given a special education program geared to their abilities, the likelihood that exceptional children will become successful, contributing, independent adult members of our society, is greatly enhanced. Thus, in addition to the humanitarian reasons, it is a good economic investment to provide proper services for exceptional children.

# Exceptional Children Classified

Considered in this publication are seven broad categories which include twelve types of exceptional children.

Pupils with intellectual limitations: (1) the educable and (2) the trainable mentally retarded.

Pupils with superior intellect: (3) the gifted.

Pupils with behavior problems: (4) the emotionally disturbed and (5) the socially maladjusted.

Pupils with (6) speech problems.

Pupils with impaired hearing: (7) the deaf and (8) the hard of hearing.

Pupils with impaired vision: (9) the blind and (10) the partially seeing.

Pupils with neurological and nonsensory physical impairments: (11) the crippled and (12) the chronic health cases.

Some educators ask: "Why are there so many areas of exceptionality? Could not the blind and partially seeing be combined in one group, called the visually limited?" Persons who specialize in these fields say not, for pupils in the two areas require somewhat different instructional competence, equipment, and materials, and some differences in curriculum content. In one instance, educationally blind pupils need to learn braille because they do not possess sufficient sight to read ink print. In another instance, partially seeing children have sufficient vision to read ink print, provided they have the use of either magnifiers or large-type print, and are working in an appropriate lighting environment.

The distinctive nature of each area of exceptionality notwithstanding, the sharp divisions among the various specialities have begun to undergo realignments in recent years. Because of improvements in low-vision optical aids, many children previously destined to use braille in reading can now utilize their sight to read ink print. Thus, the sharp line of demarcation between the areas of the blind and the partially seeing has shifted and faded. Similarly, improvements in hearing aids and other forms of sound amplification have decreased the number of children who formerly would have been considered deaf and shifted these over into the category, hard of hearing. Another factor merging the various areas is the increase in multiple exceptionalities, discussed earlier. All of these factors and others are reducing the sharp dividing lines among the various areas of exceptionality.

In the following paragraphs, the seven broad categories of exceptional children are discussed briefly to provide an overview for subsequent chapters. An attempt has been made to arrive at logical definitions which have meaning for education, and to translate these into operational terms which have as much clarity and utility as is possible with the present status of knowledge. To give *clarity*, the definition needs to employ objective measures—numerical scores, if possible. To give *utility*, the definition must be stated in terms useful for education purposes. Only a beginning has been made in developing operational definitions because the field of special education still lacks the precision of a science. To define exceptional children operationally, it will be necessary to utilize a multifactor rather than a single factor approach. However, until logical definitions are translated into quantifiable terms—usually test scores—they have little use either in research or in school practice. Conversely, a definition which is purely operational without any logical basis behind it, is little more than an empty shell. One is dependent on the other for any meaningful practical application. The years ahead should see marked improvements in the development of a taxonomy for special education (Jordan, 1961).

## PUPILS WITH INTELLECTUAL LIMITATIONS

Mental retardation has received more attention in recent years than any other area of exceptionality. While this development has been sparked by the parents' movement, other groups such as legislators, educators, the general public, and the press have also made excellent contributions.

Chapters 2 and 3 stress that special educators have assumed some responsibility for boys and girls with IQ's in approximately the 30–75 range. Schools have not been called upon, generally, to serve children whose IQ's fall below this range because no effective methods of teaching even self-care to them have yet been devised. *Educable* mentally retarded pupils have been defined as possessing IQ's between approximately 50 and 75 and either destined to have, or having difficulty in learning school materials. The IQ limits for this group are being redefined to range from 60 to 80. Inasmuch as their intellectual development reaches approximately eight to twelve years at maturity, they generally possess the capacity to become literate. Most of them become socially and economically self-sufficient in adulthood. *Trainable* mentally retarded children have been defined as possessing IQ scores between 30 and 50, but this range, too, is being redefined as 40–60. Because their mental ages approximate four to eight years by adulthood, they can be expected to develop rudimentary skills in self-care, socialization, and oral communication, but not to become literate. This group will need some social support or protection for all of their lives. However, many of them are able to perform useful tasks at home or in a sheltered environment, and a few obtain competitive employment. Seldom if ever do they marry.

## PUPILS WITH SUPERIOR INTELLECT

Gifted students are much discussed, yet have probably been more neglected in terms of special provisions, particularly in the elementary school, than have children of any other area of exceptionality. Some have declared it undemocratic to single them out for extra educational opportunities. Yet, there is evidence that much of the regular classroom teacher's time may be spent in gearing her efforts to the needs of the slow and the average, at the expense of the able student (Peabody College, Division of Surveys and Field Services, 1961). It is not enough merely to set normal grade standards for them or to leave them to their own devices on the assumption that they are well qualified to care for themselves. Such negligence and lack of appropriate instruction encourages some gifted students to operate on a "get-by" policy, while others become so bored they resort to asocial if not antisocial behavior.

In chapter 4, Lucito points out the great difficulties and debates which still arise in defining this group. For school purposes, he limits the gifted to those who possess superior potential for both critical and creative thinking—to the exclusion of those possessing unusual talents along only social or physical lines. He states that from such youngsters will come the evaluators and innovators of our society. While rapid strides have been made in developing psychological instruments for measuring the attributes of critical and creative thinking, it is still necessary in identifying the gifted to rely also on such evidence as consistently high scholastic performances, high ability in problem solving, sound ingenuity and originality, and repeated individual intelligence test scores of IQ 120–130 and above.

There is yet another need for developing our most able human resource—gifted children—namely to enhance our opportunities for survival in the great world-wide ideological and economic struggle. Gifted children of today—through the contributions they can make as our statesmen, economists, industrialists, engineers, and scientists —should become our mainstay of tomorrow in the defense of our way of life. If one accepts Lucito's premise that gifted persons will play different roles, namely, become the evaluators and innovators of our society, then it follows that they need a different school curriculum to prepare for these roles. We even need to ask ouselves if so-called enrichment programs, core curriculums, and ability groupings alone provide gifted pupils with adequate preparation for their adult roles and responsibilities. How much and what background will they eventually need in the humanities? To what extent must many of them become capable as linguists for the purposes of easy communication with and better understanding of other peoples of the world? What early foundation do they need on which to bu'
future insights involving the interplay and impacts of various international forces—social, economic, and political? What standards of personal, national, and international morality are particularly needed for such leadership roles, and by what curriculum content and precepts can the schools help to attain them?

## PUPILS WITH BEHAVIOR PROBLEMS

Educators have moved slowly in assuming responsibility for either emotionally disturbed or socially maladjusted children. This may have been caused in part by the fact that in neither of these areas are the responsibilities of educators and mental health workers well delineated. In his chapter, Pate has defined the *emotionally disturbed* as either being extremely withdrawn or acting out to the point where mental health specialists would classify them as mentally ill. They are neurotic, if not psychotic. They are so disturbed that regular class attendance (1) would be disrupting to the rest of the class, (2) would place undue pressure on the teacher, or (3) would increase the disturbance of the pupil himself. Therefore, any such child should be enrolled in an appropriate facility, such as in a special day school or class, in a residential school, or in a psychiatric facility.

Pate classifies as *socially maladjusted* young people who are chronic social offenders. Because of their norm-violating behavior, these delinquent youth are enrolled in such special facilities as the 600 schools in New York City. Others are provided a school program under legal confinement in a residential facility such as in a reform or training school or in a special camp. While these children and youth range across the spectrum of intellectual ability, many are both slow learners (IQ's 75–90) and educationally retarded (achieving two or more years below mental age capacity). Thus, a large number of them are in need of remedial instruction. While most of these delinquent youngsters have some problems of personal adjustment, emotional disturbance, or both, relatively few of them would be classified as mentally ill.

## PUPILS WITH SPEECH PROBLEMS

There are more speech-handicapped pupils than any other type of exceptional children. Hull, in his chapter, has used Van Riper's familiar definition to describe this group: "Speech is defective when it deviates so far from the speech of other people that it calls attention to itself, interferes with communication, or causes its possessor to be maladjusted." Much can and should be done by the regular grade teacher in correcting infantile and other minor speech problems, but the more difficult cases require the direct services of a speech therapist. However, even here, the properly prepared, regular teacher can be of assistance when guided by the therapist.

More pupils with speech disorders have articulation problems than any other type of malfunction. Some pupils stutter. Others have voice disorders involving pitch, loudness, quality, or duration. Still others possess organic disorders of speech including for example cleft-palate speech, delayed speech, and language problems caused by central nervous system damage, such as cerebral-palsied speech. Inasmuch as people communicate much more orally than by any other means, it is important that we help pupils with speech problems improve their oral communication.

## PUPILS WITH IMPAIRED HEARING

Because a hearing loss reduces or cuts off normal acquisition of language, pupils with such losses encounter more difficulty scholastically than children with other sensory disabilities. In addition, language development must be carefully taught. As a result, more competencies are needed by teachers who work with such children than are required by specialists in any other single area of exceptionality. Besides teaching subject matter, a teacher of the hearing impaired must offer instruction in speech development, speech reading, language, and auditory training, in most instances.

In chapter 7, Wooden defines the *hard of hearing* as those pupils in whom the loss of hearing is educationally significant but whose residual hearing is functional for acquiring language, usually with a hearing aid but sometimes without one. Under the *deaf*, he groups those whose sense of hearing is insufficient for understanding speech. Furthermore, he implies that speech and language are not synonymous. Speech is but one medium by which a person can convey language. He could, if he preferred and had the skills, use the printed or written word, tap out the Morse Code, finger spell, or use the wigwag system—to name some of the better known media.

Children who were either born deaf, or who lost their hearing before they learned to talk, must acquire their language concepts and their skills in speech and speech reading through special instruction. They can learn to make speech sounds unless there is some other defect to interfere. In fact, most deaf pupils today can say words, and a fair number can speak with sufficient clarity to be understood by a person with whom they have never before orally communicated. To attain this goal, formal training should begin at as early an age as practicable, preferably by the age of three.

As a rule, a deaf pupil will be found enrolled either in a special school for the deaf—day or residential—or in a special class for such children. However, the able ones who lost their hearing after having acquired language often make good progress if enrolled with the hard of hearing, and a few make good progress with hearing students in the regular grades.

School services for the hard of hearing are somewhat different from those for the deaf. The type of school program needed depends on the age of onset of loss; amount of loss; present age; amount of special training already received; and amount of language, speech, and speech reading proficiency attained. The severely hard of hearing who acquired their loss very early possess sufficient problems to warrant full time special instruction for lengthy periods. The less severely impaired may make adequate school progress in the regular grades when special instruction is provided by the itinerant speech and hearing therapist. Some hard of hearing pupils may eventually be able to dispense entirely with specialized instruction. In such cases, favorable seating near the front of the room and adequate hearing aids may be extremely important.

## PUPILS WITH IMPAIRED VISION

In chapter 8, Ashcroft has described *blind* pupils as those who have so little remaining vision that they must use braille as their reading medium. This does not mean they have a complete loss of vision—in fact, relatively few do. Some have light perception or shadow vision. Many have travel vision which means they can distinguish large objects adequately enough for mobility and orientation. Others may even be able to read large letters slowly but do not have sufficient vision to read them effectively. Ashcroft has defined the *partially seeing* as ranging from those pupils who retain a low degree of vision—just sufficient to read enlarged print under optimum conditions—to those who are able to read limited amounts of regular print under very special conditions.

Boys and girls who are blind seldom need special instruction before they are ready to learn braille, provided they receive intelligent help in a number of areas. They need to acquire skills in travel and mobility, in adjusting to group situations and strange environments, in avoiding undesirable facial expressions and mannerisms peculiar to the person who has never been able to observe himself, and in learning to explore the world about them by tactual means. As a result, a well-conducted regular preschool program will serve the needs of many young blind children. However, blind pupils need extensive help from specialists during their elementary school years when they are learning braille techniques and the use of the various specialized devices required by them. Some blind students continue to need specialized instruction through high school and university. However, except for certain types of vocational training, blind students on those levels often need only to have materials read aloud to them (reader service), possess record transcribers (talking books), or have access to such other specialized materials as braille books and tape recordings.

Partially seeing pupils are usually enrolled in some type of public day school program though a few attend residential schools. In both settings they can have the resources of a specialized program available to them. When they attend regular classrooms for all or part of the school day they enjoy the added privilege of working with normally seeing children (Jones, 1961).

## PUPILS WITH NEUROLOGICAL AND NONSENSORY PHYSICAL IMPAIRMENTS

Medical advances have changed the general nature of this field more than any other. As reported earlier, ways are being found for preventing and treating most contagious diseases which formerly resulted in various types of physical impairments. At the same time, the life of many a child with a congenital dysfunction is now being saved. Thus, the educational picture is shifting from pupils with disabilities resulting from such postnatal infections as poliomyelitis, osteomyelitis, and tuberculosis; toward such usually congenital neurological conditions as cerebral palsy and epilepsy; and such chronic health conditions as cardiac disorders, asthma, and diabetes.

Wilson, in her chapter, has defined pupils with nonsensory physical impairments as those having such severe crippling or chronic health problems that specialized instruction is needed—in a special school or class, in a hospital, or a home. *Crippling conditions* with few exceptions include malformations and malfunctions of bones, joints, or muscles. Before the increase in central nervous system sequela, such impairments were often called orthopedic conditions. *Chronic health problems* include a miscellaneous group of conditions other than those resulting in skeletal disorders—many times of a permanent nature—such as rheumatic fever and other cardiac disorders, nephritis, mononucleosis, hepatitis, epilepsy, and many others. Many neurological disorders may be found among both the crippling and special health conditions. Cerebral palsy is the most common such condition among the crippling conditions and epilepsy among the special health problems. Some neurological disorders are not typically classified as either a crippling or chronic health condition. As an example is aphasia which is a language disorder due to brain damage.

## Numbers of Exceptional Children

When educators are considering the development of special education services for handicapped and gifted pupils, they face the problem of determining what kind of program would be practicable for the number of children to be served. Unfortunately, few if any adequate school enumerations of exceptional children have been made. Those that have been done are fraught with definition and identification problems (Wilkins, 1959). There are many prevalence estimates in the professional literature in which some figures are too large for educational purposes. These over-estimates are often based upon noneducational frames of reference rather than from an educational one. For example, all children with postpolio crippling conditions would need to be counted for medical purposes, yet the majority of children who have a good recovery do not have unusual education needs and thus can and should be in the regular grades. Among pupils with chronic health problems, most of those with epilepsy, diabetes, rheumatic fever, and other illnesses that have adequate medical treatment can function without special education. Similarly, the number of medically exceptional among the children possessing many other given types of handicap exceeds the number within the group who are educationally exceptional.

At the same time, prevalence figures cannot be estimated from the number of exceptional children enrolled in special education services. For one reason, few school systems serve all their exceptional children. For another, multiple exceptionalities often exist which means that a child who has two educationally significant exceptionalities must frequently be counted more than once, though no hard and fast rule can be applied as a formula. However, if a school compiles a census and classifies each of its exceptional children only in terms of his major education needs, its figures for such children will underestimate the true index of the special services needed. More appropriate figures for calculating needed special education services will be somewhere between the total exceptional children classified by major area of exceptionality and the total number of exceptionalities of educational significance possessed by the pupils. This is so because different schools provide services in different ways. For example, a speech-impaired child who is gifted might receive two separately operated services, whereas a mentally retarded cerebral-palsied child would be aided by a single-operated service. Or a crippled blind child might be enrolled in a school for the blind and be also furnished the necessary ancillary services for his crippled condition in the same setting, whereas the same type child in another community would be enrolled in a school for crippled children that supplies special services for the blind.

The prevalence estimates given in this section include the figures which will serve to estimate the number of exceptional-pupil services needed. These figures do not include noneducational services taken from medical, psychological, or private health agency frames of reference. However, they do take into account the fact mentioned above that the special services load of educationally significant exceptionalities exceeds the number of exceptional children which would be identified by a census where an exceptional child is only counted once under his major special education need.

The total number of exceptional pupils cannot be found by summating the percentages in Table 1.1. This would approximate 12 percent for the U.S. Office of Education (USOE) figures and 9 percent for the Canadian ones. Yet it is our estimation that *approximately 8 percent of the school-age population are now so exceptional in one or more areas as to need one or more special education services.* This discrepancy has already been explained in terms of pupils with multiple exceptionalities. Thus, in Table 1.1, a number of pupils have been counted more than once.

The following illustration will indicate one use which may be made of these figures. In a community of 120,000 we may estimate that approximately one fourth (or 30,000) will be of school age.

TABLE 1.1 *Prevalence estimates of the school-age population classified as exceptional for special education purposes.*

| AREAS OF EXCEPTIONALITY[a] | PERCENTAGE ESTIMATED | |
| | *U.S.O.E.*[b] | *D.C.B.S.*[c] |
| --- | --- | --- |
| Intellectually limited | 2.3 | 2.0 |
| Educable mentally retarded | (2.0) | |
| Trainable mentally retarded | (0.3) | |
| Intellectually superior (gifted) | 2.0 | 2.0 |
| Disturbed and maladjusted | 2.0 | 2.0 |
| Emotionally disturbed | | |
| Socially maladjusted | | |
| Speech impaired | 3.5 | 2.10 |
| Hearing impaired | 0.6 | 0.54 |
| Hard of hearing | (0.5) | |
| Deaf | (0.1) | |
| Visually impaired | 0.09 | 0.13 |
| Partially seeing | (0.06) | |
| Blind | (0.03) | |
| Nonsensory physically impaired | 2.0 | 0.47 |
| Crippled | (1.0) | (0.1) |
| Chronic health problems | (1.0) | (0.37) |

[a] Pupils with multiple special education needs counted more than once.
[b] From Mackie, Romaine P. Personal communication, 1962.
[c] From the Dominion of Canada Bureau of Statistics, *Statistics of special education for exceptional children,* 1953–1954. Ottawa: Queen's Printers, 1959.

Thus, according to the USOE figures, the number of speech-impaired children in need of the services of speech correctionists will be 3.5 percent of 30,000 (or 1050 pupils). In this way, educators may estimate the prevalence of pupils in the various areas of exceptionality needing special education services.

A glance over the figures will show that speech impairments which are estimated at 3.5 percent are the most prevalent exceptional condition among school children, based on the USOE figures. The next largest group are the mentally retarded with 2.3 percent. Closely following are the gifted, disturbed and maladjusted and nonsensory physically impaired, each estimated at 2 percent. Well below these are the hearing impaired with 0.6 percent. The lowest prevalence figure is 0.09 percent for the visually limited. When these figures are broken down further, the lowest figure is 0.03 percent for the blind.

A number of words of caution are needed concerning these estimates. First of all, they cannot be very well documented. Hopefully the years ahead will make possible the cumulation of more nearly accurate census data. Second, these figures might be labeled national estimates. While they should hold up fairly well when applied to a state, province, or very large school district, they will be found lacking in specific instances, especially when applied to certain local communities. For example, the number of educable mentally retarded children will be much greater in the slums than in the wealthy suburbs of a city, while the reverse would hold true for the gifted. Certain states, and parts of states, such as Florida and southern California, attract families with children who are chronically ill, thereby distorting the figures. Communities around large day and residential schools for the blind or for the deaf will possess a greater number of the type children concerned because families move to be near such special services. All these factors caution against overdependency on the prevalence figures.

The prevalence estimates cited in Table 1.1 are below those given in other publications, especially those written some years ago. There are two primary reasons for this downward revision of certain estimates. First, other estimates have often used a noneducational frame of reference which resulted—as mentioned earlier—in figures too inflated for use as a basis for planning special education programs. Second, medical advances, improved general educational facilities, and technological improvements in aids that help over-come handicaps have reduced the prevalence of certain exceptional conditions or of their educational significance. A typical example is in the area of the visually limited where the prevalence of partially seeing used to be estimated at 0.2 percent (or 1 in 500) and where the USOE figure is now 0.06 percent. Improved lighting conditions in the regular classroom, the greater readability of the ink print used, and improved optical aids have made special educa-tion services no longer necessary for certain pupils with moderate vision problems. Thus, the prevalence of children classified as educationally partially seeing is being reduced by a greater per-centage than is the reduction for any other type of exceptionality (Jones, 1961).

The reader will find that various authors in their chapters later in the book will discuss in considerable detail prevalence estimates and show how these would vary from those in Table 1.1 according to the definition and type of service to be provided.

## Services for Exceptional Pupils

Information on the number of exceptional children receiving special-ized instruction is fragmentary and out-of-date by the time it is available. The United Nations Educational, Scientific, and Cultural Organization (1960) has published statistics on the extent of spe-cial education in 95 countries. It shows that Europe has generally the most comprehensive services. The bulletin reports that the number of children in special education, internationally is only 6 per 1000 children enrolled in the primary schools. If we assume that 8 percent of the children were exceptional, this would mean that 6:80 or about 7.5 percent were receiving special education. The UNESCO data show that more boys than girls are in special education programs, and also that most of the services are available at the elementary school level. It is interesting to note that no international prevalence estimates were made because of lack of uniformity in the criteria on which the various countries based their definitions.

For a more detailed look at special education statistics in the United States and Canada there are the U.S. Office of Education

TABLE 1.2 *Estimated enrollment of pupils in special education for the United States public schools, 1957–1958, and for Canadian schools, 1953–1954.*

| AREAS OF EXCEPTIONALITY | UNITED STATES 1957–1958 | | | CANADA 1953–1954 |
|---|---|---|---|---|
| | Totals | In local schoola districts | In state residential schools | Totalsb |
| Total school-age population | 40,000,000 | | | 2,500,000 |
| Total enrolled for all areas | | 882,066c | 114,800 | 38,395 |
| Intellectually limited | 246,185 | 218,185 | 28,000d | 15,792 |
| Educable mentally retarded | (212,406) | (201,406) | (11,000) | |
| Trainable mentally retarded | (33,779) | (16,779) | (17,000) | |
| Intellectually superior (gifted) | 52,269 | 52,269 | | 1591 |
| Disturbed and maladjusted | 93,260 | 28,260 | 65,000e | 2330 |
| Emotionally disturbed | | | (13,000) | |
| Socially maladjusted | | | (52,000) | |
| Speech impaired | 486,944 | 486,944 | | 10,393 |
| Hearing impaired | 33,943 | 19,537 | 14,406f | 1925 |
| Hard of hearing | (14,818) | (13,113) | (1705) | |
| Deaf | (19,125) | (6424) | (12,701) | |
| Visually limited | 18,242 | 11,442 | 6800g | 970 |
| Partially seeing | (9898) | (8598) | (1300) | |
| Blind | (8344) | (2844) | (5500) | |
| Nonsensory physically impaired | 52,388 | 52,388 | | 5394 |
| Crippled | (29,311) | (29,311) | | |
| Chronic health problems | (23,077) | (23,077) | | |

a Actual figures from Mackie, Romaine P., & Robbins, Patricia P. Exceptional children and youth: A chart book of special education enrollments in public day schools of the United States. *U.S. Office of Educ. Bull.,* OE–35019, Washington, D.C.: Government Printing Office, 1961.

b From the Dominion of Canada Bureau of Statistics. *Statistics of special education for exceptional children,* 1953–1954. Ottawa: Queen's Printers, 1959.

c The U.S. Office of Education lists an additional 13,041 exceptional pupils served by various combined services not given in the second column.

d Estimated from data provided by the Biometrics Branch, National Institute of Mental Health.

e From Pate's chapter 5.

f From American Annals of the Deaf, January 1958.

g From the registry of the American Printing House for the Blind.

figures published by Mackie and Robbins (1961) for 1957-1958, and Canadian data for 1953–1954 published by the Dominion Bureau of Statistics (1959). These are summarized in Table 1.2, supplemented by residential school statistics in the United States gathered from various sources.

By estimating the prevalence of exceptional children at 8 percent, we are able to compare the percentage of such pupils being served in the two countries. For the United States, about 30 percent of those needing special education were receiving it in the public schools in 1957–1958. Probably private agencies and schools provided services for not more than an additional 5 percent. Thus, it seems safe to estimate that, at the most, only about 35 percent of the exceptional children in the United States were receiving some special education services in 1957–1958. In 1953–1954, about 20 percent of Canadian exceptional children were in special education —divided among public and private, day and residential facilities. In considering the discrepancy between the figures for the United States and Canada, it must be borne in mind that the Canadian statistics were for four years earlier; if 1957–1958 data were available for Canada this differential would be reduced considerably since growth of special education in Canada in recent years has been rapid.

In Fig. 1.1, the percentage of children in each area of exceptionality receiving special education in day and residential schools of the United States has been contrasted. Again it must be pointed out that these calculations are only approximations. Of the 31 percent of all types of exceptional children receiving service in the public schools, 28 percent were enrolled in day schools, compared to 3 percent in residential schools. Day school services predominated in the areas of the gifted, the educable mentally retarded, the speech impaired, the hard of hearing, the partially seeing, the crippled, and the children with chronic health problems. Residential school services predominated in the areas of the deaf, the blind, and the combined total of the emotionally disturbed and socially maladjusted, with no breakdown to indicate the ratio between disturbed and maladjusted children. In the case of the trainable mentally retarded, the present percentages are about even between the two types of school settings, but in view of the rapidly accelerated growth of the day school program for this type of child that balance may no longer exist, since it must be pointed out again that these were 1957–1958 figures.

Of the two types of public schools, residential facilities are by far the older and have for years served a higher percentage of the children for whom they were intended than have the day

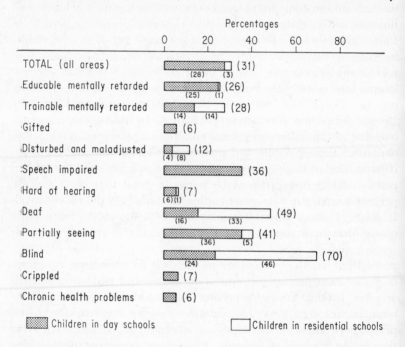

FIG. 1.1 Estimates of percentages of exceptional children receiving special services in the public schools of the United States 1957–1958 (calculated from Tables 1.1 and 1.2).

schools. They were originally established in preference to day schools largely because of the sparsity of the population, and they still continue to supply the principal services for the rural deaf and the rural blind. The day school which originated as an optional service had its beginning in the urban centers. As a result, it has much the greater potential for growth in three ways: first, in catching up on its backlog; second, in providing for the population shift from rural areas to urban centers; and third, in covering the growing number of interdistrict and county programs of special education in rural areas.

Measures of the increase in special education enrollments in public day schools have been charted by the U.S. Office of Education through its biennial surveys of education since 1870 (Mackie and Robbins, 1961; Mackie, et al., 1961; Martens, 1950; Rice and Hill, 1954; and others). Reproduced in Fig. 1.2 are the percentage increases in enrollments for the decade 1948–1958. This gives a good short-term picture of the day school movement. For a more longitudinal view the student is referred to the earlier biennial surveys. The over-all rise in special education enrollments for the 10-year period was 133 percent. Mackie and Robbins (1961) point out that sharp differences occurred in the rate of growth from one area of exceptionality to another. Four programs—the hard of hearing, the partially seeing, the crippled and the chronic health cases—did not even grow fast enough to keep pace with the 40 percent increase in *total* public school enrollments for *all* children. It may be that insufficient emphasis was given to expanding special education services in these areas. However, extension of services usually reflect demands. Thus, a more probable explanation is that many pupils who formerly would have been classified in these areas because of their need for special education service are now making adequate progress in an alternate school setting, often in the regular grades. Thus, in a sense, the prevalence has probably dropped. An alternate explanation seems more tenable in the area of the hard of hearing. A larger proportion of pupils with mild hearing losses were receiving instruction from itinerent speech and hearing therapists in 1958 than in 1948. The figures in Fig. 1.1 were collected in such a manner that these students were reported as speech impaired rather than as hard of hearing. Therefore the number of hard of hearing served has probably not decreased as much as the figures indicate.

For the 10-year period, the increase of over 400 percent in day school enrollments of the blind was the most striking expansion. The 260 percent increase in public day school services for the trainable mentally retarded in only five years, 1953–1958, is almost as impressive (no data were available in this area for 1948). Increases in special services in the areas of the deaf, speech-impaired, disturbed and maladjusted, educable mentally retarded, and gifted were substantially greater than increase in total public school enrollments and therefore heartening. While the over-all, quantitative growth in special education may not have been as

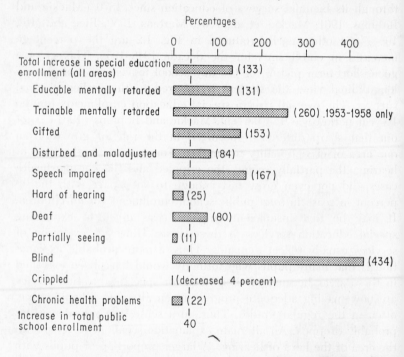

FIG. 1.2 Percentage increase in total public school enrollment and in special education enrollments in local day schools in the United States for the 10-year period 1948–1958. (From Mackie, Romaine P., and Robbins, Patricia P., Exceptional children and youth: A chart book of special education enrollments in public day schools of the United States. *U.S. Office of Educ., Bull.*, OE-35019, Washington, D.C.: Government Printing Office, 1961. Also from Rice, Mabel C., and Hill, Arthur S., Statistics of special education for exceptional children, 1952–1953. *Biennial survey of education in the U.S.*, 1952–1954. Washington, D.C.: Government Printing Office, 1954.)

spectacular as many would like, nevertheless it has been substantial. Equally important is qualitative progress and this is not reflected in increases in enrollment figures.

## Types of Special Education Programs

The overemphasis which special educators have placed on the relative merits of the various types of school organizations for exceptional children has probably been a retarding factor to proper attention on special methodology and curricula in the different areas of exceptionality. To avoid repetition later, the various administrative plans, their problems and solutions, are discussed here.

The most common types of special education service today are provided through:

1. The residential school
2. Hospital instruction
3. Homebound instruction
4. Day school plans
   a. Special schools
   b. Special classes
   c. The cooperative programs
   d. The resource room plan
   e. The itinerant specialist or contact plan
   f. Specialized consultants
   g. Boarding homes for day pupils
   h. Combined regular and special schools
   i. Interdistrict plans.

Each plan has its special usefulness and limitations. Little scientific evidence exists which establishes one plan as advantageous to another. Of greater importance than the general type of school organization is the competence by which instruction programs are operated. It is no doubt true that any arrangement may be good or bad for a particular pupil, depending on the quality of teaching and the type of curriculum offered.

## RESIDENTIAL SCHOOL

Residential units were designed to provide exceptional children with a 24-hour day, comprehensive instructional program or care. In some cases, such as for the gifted, blind, deaf, and some of the slightly mentally retarded, the prime purpose for enrolling a pupil in the residence is for his education. In other cases, such as for the delinquent or socially maladjusted, the emotionally disturbed, the severely mentally retarded, and the cerebral palsied, the residence may be provided primarily for the protection of society or the exceptional child, for corrective treatment of a noneducational nature, or for the care of the child. In such cases education is an adjunct to the total program. Probably in these latter cases, the institution should be called a residential facility rather than a residential school. Many residential schools enroll both day and resident pupils. Certainly, residence accommodation should be furnished only to those children living too far from the school either to walk or to be transported daily. In like manner, residence should be furnished only during the school week to the children residing close enough to return to their homes for the week end. In other words, the residential school has every obligation to keep each of its children in intimate contact with his home —first, through his residing there as much as possible; second, through fostering campus visits by his parents; and third, through assuring frequent correspondence or telephone conversations with members of his family or both. The school should not be used as an orphan asylum; a haven for children from undesirable homes; a boarding school for the convenience of parents, or a place to which day schools may transfer children who present special problems.

Most residential schools are large enough to provide well-developed guidance services, good grouping of children for instruction, and a variety of special-subject teachers in the upper grades, both academic and vocational. At the same time, such schools possess their special problems and challenges. Children and parents may be separated for much of the school year. Placement in a residential setting may deprive an exceptional child of living with and learning from so-called normal children. Residential schools have traditionally not been available to preschool children and those without self-care skills. Nevertheless, improvements are being made in all these regards. A special challenge is that of providing full value of services for the extra costs involved.

## HOSPITAL INSTRUCTION

Provision for instruction of children confined to hospitals, sanatoria, and convalescent homes is a traditional service of special education. The most frequent needs for prolonged hospitalization include treatment for emotional disturbances, rheumatic heart ailments, tuberculosis, postpolio disabilities, and other chronic ailments. The special teacher, in addition to serving these children who are more or less permanently on the register, works also with those who are hospitalized for shorter periods of time. The latter include the postoperative and the child who has recovered sufficiently from an illness or accident to be in need of some engrossing mental activity. The effects of hospital instruction are usually psychologically therapeutic as well as educationally useful. Both bedside tutoring and group instruction are provided whenever possible. A satisfactory over-all regimen for the child requires a team approach involving the physician, the nurse, the teacher, and other specialists in the hospital.

## HOMEBOUND INSTRUCTION

Homebound instruction is another traditional service of special education. It enrolls primarily two types of children: those so chronically ill—usually the bedridden—that they will never be able to attend school, and those ordinarily in school attendance but who are convalescing from an operation, accident, or temporary illness. Sometimes emotionally disturbed, retarded, and mentally handicapped pupils are also placed on homebound programs.

Services are provided by two techniques: (1) a full-time, itinerant teacher of the homebound who usually instructs each pupil in his home for one or two hour periods about three times a week; or (2) the regular classroom teacher who instructs, after school, one of her regular pupils who is temporarily homebound. The services are based on the belief that children, even when confined to their homes, are entitled both to an education and to the mental health values that such learning activities provide them.

A program for the homebound must accept the educational challenge produced by the confinement of the child to his home and the resulting isolation. Some schools do this through promoting a mimeographed news sheet edited by the students concerned. Some provide a plan for supplying the homebound with the companionship of normal children of like age. (The Junior Red Cross will, in certain communities, accept this responsibility.) Some assist a child to participate in community activities, such as making a Christmas toy for an underprivileged child. And some make it possible for an older child to participate in the classroom discussions of his grade at school, through the use of the home-to-school telephone. This teaching-by-telephone technique is being used increasingly as an adjunct, both to homebound and hospital-school instruction. The telephone companies are equipped to install a two-way communication system between the school and either the home or the hospital, thus allowing the student to gain the feeling that he is less isolated by having become a participant in a school group. This service works best for junior and senior high school youth, but is also used by some schools for one or two of the upper elementary grades. In mentioning this technique, the comment should be made that it is not intended to replace home teaching, but only to supplement it. Educational television is another means of supplementing homebound instruction which is becoming increasingly available.

A special challenge to home instruction is making sure that it never becomes a device for excluding from school those children who possess unfortunate physical or social problems. It should be used only for children whose problems are so serious that school attendance is impossible. An excellent measure of the comprehensiveness and quality of a school's special education program is the degree to which its homebound instruction is kept at a minimum consistent with the needs. This can be accomplished when the community provides a reasonably full range of special education programs, augmented by the necessary transportation.

**DAY SCHOOL PLANS**

*Special schools*—a special school is usually one that serves only one type of exceptional children. These schools are operated in nearly all areas of exceptionality, and are located in the larger cities for the most part. In general, they had their inception prior to 1920. Relatively few local school districts have opened new schools of this type in recent years except for trainable mentally retarded children. Examples of special schools include the Spaulding School for Crippled Children in Chicago, the Bronx High School of Science in New York for the gifted, and the Alexander Graham Bell School for the Deaf in Cleveland. Occasionally there is a special school operated as a separate unit but housed in a school building with regular grades.

In addition to the above, there is the special school which caters to the needs of two or more types of exceptionalities. These are most often found in smaller cities. Typical of the type is the David W. Smouse Opportunity School of Des Moines. Its chief asset is its use of various specialists to serve the multiple needs that fall within the scope of the major exceptionalities of the children enrolled.

Special schools have in many instances exercised leadership by pioneering in methods and facilities for the education and care of its pupils. They have provided research of value to the profession, and they have led in providing services for the significant secondary exceptionalities possessed by pupils. Two major problems of this type of school are the isolation from average children while at school, and the long period of time which many pupils must spend on the bus each morning and afternoon.

*Special classes*—these usually take the form of enrolling homogeneous groups of children with one type of exceptionality under the direction of an especially trained teacher in a classroom located in a regular public school. There may be only one or two such classes in a given school or as many as five or six. One or two special classes may serve one type of exceptional children while others may serve other types. Usually these special classes which are especially prevalent in the areas of mental retardation operate in a self-contained fashion. Because of this, they are often described as the *segregated plan,* meaning the pupils are physically separate for academic instruction from so-called normal children. Under the special class plan, pupils often receive their academic instruction in the special class but share with the children of the regular grades of the school such out-of-classroom activities as assembly, sports, school clubs, and dining. They may take industrial arts and home economics from the teachers who specialize in these fields at the school. In addition they may also receive instruction from such system-wide, itinerant specialists as the music, and art teachers, and the speech or hearing therapist. One advantage of such an organization structure is to reduce transportation to a minimum. The major challenge to the special teachers is to integrate the program into the school.

In a few states, especially in more rural communities, special classes have been established to serve children with a number of exceptionalities. While these classes may be better than no special education at all, it is difficult to see how one teacher could have all the competencies needed to work, for example, with crippled, hearing and visually impaired, as well as mentally retarded children. However, it is possible that a well-trained teacher could serve a less heterogenous group of children such as a combination of the intellectually and educationally retarded.

*The cooperative plan*—this is an innovation popularized by the field of the visually limited but not restricted solely to that area. The blind or partially seeing children are enrolled in special classes but take at least some, if not a great deal, of their academic instruction in the regular grades. Thus more physical integration of the exceptional child into the regular school program is possible than under the special class (or segregated) plan described above. However, there are dangers in this plan. The exceptional child may take an undue amount of the regular teacher's time and energy to the neglect of the rest of the class, or to be neglected himself. Children who are physically integrated into the regular grades may not be socially integrated. The special teacher may not be productive in carrying his fair share of teaching. He is responsible for both direct service to pupils and indirect services through advising and assisting the regular classroom teachers, and it is difficult to arrive at a good balance. However, all of these dangers can be avoided.

*The resource room teacher plan*—this is highly popular with educators who stress the importance of the usual and unusual child being together during school hours. The exceptional student is enrolled in the regular grade which is his homeroom. He receives much of his instruction there. He goes to the resource room only to use specialized equipment and to receive specialized instruction, either in a tutored situation or in a small group, all of the members of which have the same need for special instruction. The special teacher in charge of the resource room is both a teacher and a consultant. Besides being popular in the areas of the blind and partially seeing, this plan is used to a lesser degree for older and abler hearing impaired and crippled children. Under this plan, as in the special class approach, the resource room and its teacher may serve a single area of exceptionality, or a more heterogeneous group such as the blind and the partially seeing. Occasionally the number of exceptionalities served is even greater. The major difference between the cooperative and the resource room plans is the home room placement of the exceptional children enrolled.

The plan is suitable for any type of child who can succeed in the regular grades when provided with a small amount of extra assistance. One of the problems of the plan develops in the case of a child who, when he is in the regular classroom, needs equipment for his own welfare that is in the resource room. The second problem develops in the case of a child who needs a maximum of assistance to function satisfactorily, either under a limited part-time program in the regular grades or in a full program in the special room. A third problem is to assure that basic responsibility for any child who needs more than a minimum of special help is not shifted from the special to the regular teacher.

The usual pattern of a resource room plan is for each such room to be staffed by a person fully trained to offer all necessary assistance to any child assigned her. Another plan, sometimes used in a small village setting, is to staff the room with a person responsible either for giving or for obtaining services for several types of exceptionality. The teacher in charge may be specially trained in only one area such as mental retardation, remedial instruction for the educationally retarded, or instruction of the gifted children. At the same time he attempts to develop a working acquaintance with the other fields of exceptionality, but not to assume responsibility for the severe cases in those fields. In the community there may be no blind, deaf, or severely hard of hearing child. If there is one, the resource teacher makes arrangements for enrollment of the pupil either in the state residential school or in a nearby city day school—at least until he is able, if ever, to succeed in the local school with such special help as the resource room teacher could give. If there is a crippled child in need of examination, he sees that the pupil gets to the clinic and that any pertinent report is shared with other teachers. If the child needs physical therapy, the resource teacher arranges with the parents or others for his transportation to a center where such services are available. It probably is not necessary to review the manner in which the resource teacher handles each type of child. It should be sufficient to say that he depends upon clinical findings for all cases and that he only handles personally those for which he is either competently trained, or for which he can follow specific directions from a specialist who has made a thorough diagnosis and prognosis. Where possible, he attends all clinic sessions both for his own information and the working rapport he can establish with the specialists.

A resource room serving a number of exceptionalities cannot be said to constitute a complete program of special education, but to the extent that it brings to each exceptional child a school environment to which he can adjust and make progress, it can be termed successful. One of the challenges of such a program is that of staffing the room with a teacher who knows how to organize his work, who possesses a broad range of competencies, and who fully understands where his competencies begin and terminate. Another challenge is that of keeping the assigned load within bounds so that the resource teacher does not become solely a consultant, with too little time available for resource teaching. Others include: developing an adequate communication system with other teachers of the school, gaining and maintaining community acceptance, and providing more comprehensive special education services when it is practicable.

*The itinerant specialist or contact plan*—under this plan, an exceptional child receives assistance from an itinerant teacher, but is enrolled for all his class work under a regular teacher in the neighborhood public school. The plan is used both in urban and rural areas. Such a traveling teacher or therapist visits the child's school on a regular schedule to provide special instruction. From time to time, he performs such other duties as are required, including consultation with the child's regular teacher and providing special materials and equipment. Some of the challenges are to keep the itinerant teacher's load within the limits which permit the doing of a good professional job, to avoid the assignment of pupils to the service who are in need of more help than it can provide, and to avoid schedules which place an excessive demand on travel time. The plan is most commonly used in the case of speech-impaired children. It is used to a lesser degree for visually limited and hearing impaired.

*Specialized consultants*—consultants are central office staff members who do not instruct directly exceptional children but serve them by working with the special and regular classroom teachers where the pupils are enrolled. They also serve in a liaison between special and general education. They operate by two basic patterns. One type of consultant is a specialist in a particular area of exceptionality who works only in that field. This person will have had a background of teaching experience and college preparation in the area. His major responsibility is working in a supervisory capacity with teachers who have that particular type of exceptional child assigned to them. However, he also may occasionally instruct the pupil as a demonstration, and counsel with both pupils and parents. The plan is adaptable for either urban or rural areas. Probably the greatest problem it presents is that of making sure the teacher being assisted has the time, insights, materials, and skills to perform a creditable job with only consultation from a specialist.

The second type of consultant is one who has a broad working knowledge in a number of areas of exceptionality, but actual teaching experience in only one or two of them. He consults in the various areas, giving great assistance in his speciality and a reasonable amount of assistance in the others. The problem of this pattern is doing an adequate job in the areas in which the consultant has never taught and has little specialized preparation.

*Boarding homes for day pupils*—pupils in some day school plans are enrolled from a distance and reside with local residents during the school week. The challenge this plan presents is that of making sure that such school-week "house-parents" are not only desirable individuals personally, but that they understand the type of child they board and lodge, that they accept him into the family group, and that they take time to furnish him with the social, recreational, and cultural activities needed for his out-of-school development. Careful selection of homes, the use of good in-service training programs for these house-parents, and ample supervision are needed.

*Combined regular and special schools*—this type of facility serves all the normal children of the immediate neighborhood within the given grade limits for the school, plus the exceptional children of a larger geographical area. One example is the Ann J. Kellogg School in Battle Creek, Michigan. Usually the school serves a number of different types of exceptional children with a broad range of general and special education programs provided. Special classes and other facilities may be scattered throughout the school or constitute a specific position or wing of it.

A large number of the plans already described may be employed in this setting of a combined regular and special school. Thus the resource room approach may be found plus the itinerant specialist plan. Also, specialized consultants may serve both the special and regular teachers of the school.

The first challenge of this type school is whether it can provide the necessary clinical procedures and evaluations necessary for proper placement and follow up. Another challenge is that of developing a staff of regular teachers with the interest and qualifications for proper fulfillments of their functions in serving both average and exceptional pupils. Administrative leadership, inspiring professional meetings, in-service training, and a system of channeling all essential information to each such teacher as rapidly as it is acquired, are essential. A third and major challenge is that of producing psychological, as well as physical integration when the exceptional children do not come from the immediate neighborhood where the average children reside.

*Interdistrict plans*—all of the organization plans cited for the instruction of exceptional children have been presented with a single school district in mind. However, there are a variety of inter-district plans in operation. Any of the organization plans mentioned above could be applied to an interdistrict operation with few, if any, modifications.

Perhaps the three principal interdistrict operations can be best described as follows. Plan I is based on a locally initiated, voluntary arrangement in which two or more districts decide to cooperate in providing special education for one or more types of exceptional children. One aspect of the special education program is placed in one district but children from the cooperating districts also attend. The difficulties involved include those of providing proper coordination in organization, operation, administration, and in transportation.

Plan II is based upon state financial support for a number of school districts cooperating in offering a shared special education service. Often the program is supervised from the office of the county superintendent of schools. Under this plan each district maintains its sovereignty over the destinies of its own pupils, but the state financial aid and the quality of program that can be developed under a professional staff are adequate inducements for participation. The challenges of this are not too different from those of Plan I so far as what happens in the classroom. However, the problems presented the county director of special education in finding the children and establishing centers in the right locations are considerable.

Plan III is based on the organization of a separate special education school district with its own board of education, professional staff, and budget. This special education school district is superimposed upon a number of regular public school districts. An example is the Special School District for the Education and Training of Handicapped Children in St. Louis County, Missouri. This system has to solve the problems of a separate tax structure, the complicated transportation, and other such mechanics of the undertaking.

The excellent chart book in which the United States Office of Education reported on its 1958 survey of special education in public day schools contrasts the proportion of enrollments in a number of the types of special education programs which have just been described (Mackie and Robbins, 1961). Fig. 1.3 is reproduced from that book.

Many considerations need to be taken into account by a school placement committee in determining the best assignment for any individual exceptional child. The more choices at the disposal of a committee, the greater discretion it can exercise, with a resulting narrowing of the range of problems any single teacher must be asked to assume. Influencing factors in decision making for a particular pupil include: (1) type and degree of exceptionality; (2) number of exceptionalities; (3) age at onset of condition; (4) present age of pupil; (5) scholastic aptitudes, interests, and achievements; (6) behavioral characteristics; (7) social maturity; (8) vocational goals; (9) alternate education programs available; (10) relationship of added costs to possible gains; (11) special competencies of different teachers available; (12) types of related services available to the school system; (13) locations of the different special education services; (14) distances of the services from the child's home; (15) parent attitudes and interests; (16) home conditions; (17) neighborhood conditions; (18) pressures on the child himself, his family, and his teachers; (19) any unusual factors peculiar to a given case.

## Axioms on Special Education

It is impossible to formulate a set of universal axioms that hold for all exceptional children in all communities. Nevertheless, an attempt has been made to outline those which seem to come closest to accomplishing it.

1. Each exceptional child is primarily a child with the same rights to acceptance, understanding, and education as other children.

2. Wide individual differences exist among children in each area of exceptionality.

3. Early screening, identification, and placement in a special education program are generally necessary if exceptional children are to make optimal progress in school.

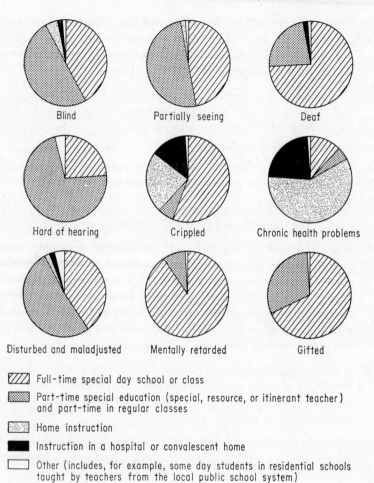

Blind      Partially seeing      Deaf

Hard of hearing      Crippled      Chronic health problems

Disturbed and maladjusted      Mentally retarded      Gifted

◪ Full-time special day school or class

▨ Part-time special education (special, resource, or itinerant teacher) and part-time in regular classes

▨ Home instruction

■ Instruction in a hospital or convalescent home

☐ Other (includes, for example, some day students in residential schools taught by teachers from the local public school system)

FIG. 1.3 Proportion of enrollments in the various types of special education services in public day schools, 1957–1958. (Reproduced from Mackie, Romaine P., and Robbins, Patricia P., *Exceptional children and youth: A chart book of special education enrollments in public day schools of the United States. U.S. Office of Educ. Bull.,* OE-35019, Washington, D.C.: Government Printing Office, 1961.)

4. The team approach to comprehensive case study involves medical, social, and psychological, as well as educational specialists, but educational diagnosis and placement are central responsibilities of the education authority in charge.

5. The success of a particular type of special education service will depend on well developed criteria for placement so that pupils with other types of problems and needs are not inappropriately enrolled in it.

6. Programs should not be initiated or continued unless well-trained, competent personnel are available.

7. Specialized curriculum, materials and equipment are needed, though the quantity and type will vary from area to area.

8. Since the general objective of "developing personal, social and economic effectiveness" is too broad to permit careful curriculum development or appraisal of teaching and learning effectiveness, specific goals need to be developed for all special education programs with an emphasis on both scholastic and social learning, on the national purposes of education, and on the aptitudes and potentials of the pupils concerned.

9. A mental health approach in terms of accepting each pupil and providing a warm classroom climate is a profitable entree for assisting a student to self acceptance, self evaluation, and the development of realistic goals.

10. Clinical-education instruction is needed for exceptional children which involves individualized teaching procedures based upon careful appraisal of each pupil's abilities and disabilities.

11. Education for exceptional children should be an integral part of a total education program when possible and practical.

12. Continuous re-assessment of exceptional children and re-evaluation of school programs are essential to progress.

13. Follow-up of each student after he leaves school, and placement assistance where needed, are responsibilities of the school.

14. Community-wide cooperation among educational and nonedu-

cational services for exceptional children will broaden the comprehensiveness and avoid gaps and duplications.

15. Special education programs are strengthened by frequent interpretation of them to educators, parents, legislators, and the public.

16. The promotion of educational research, teacher preparation, and instructional services in education for exceptional children are the joint responsibilities of national, state, and local agencies.

## Recent Trends in Special Education

Trends in the education of exceptional children are difficult to discern due to the many ramifications of the field including its rapid growth.

1. *A sharp increase in research is apparent in education for exceptional children.* It has long been known that most educational practices are based on tradition and philosophy, and not on scientific evidence. In special education particularly, progress toward correcting this deficiency has been recently accelerated. The years ahead could constitute a bright era for the exceptional child if the rate of change from practice based on tradition to practice based on sound experimentation continues to pick up speed. Summaries of the present status of knowledge are found in the *Encyclopedia of Educational Research* (Harris, 1960), in the *Review of Educational Research* (Hunt, 1963), and in Kirk and Weiner (1963).

2. *There has been a decrease in the proportion of children with single disabilities, and an increase in the proportion of those with multiple disabilities.* The implications of this trend are still unclear. On the one hand, it is possible that educators will be trained more comprehensively so as to work with the increased number of children who possess several serious disabling conditions. On the other hand, we may organize our schools so as to bring together a number of specialists to work with one particular pupil who has multiple exceptionalities. Either could provide the necessary program of instruction.

3. *We are extending more and better services to our exceptional children.* In 1930, it was claimed at the White House Conference that the United States was serving only 10 percent of its exceptional children. By 1957–1958, as already reported, the number was estimated to have increased to about 35 percent. But the quantitative aspects do not tell the complete story. Quality of instruction has been given increased attention and should get more. The competence of the teachers has increased and will continue to increase; teacher preparation programs are becoming more substantial since our body of knowledge is increasing. In the past, services were usually available only at the elementary school level. Recently there has been a shift toward providing more services at the junior and senior high school levels. Another promising development has been the effort to shift as many pupils as possible from homebound instruction to regular or special school attendance, particularly in those areas where the latter has constituted the principal educational opportunity for the severely nonsensory handicapped. And finally, an attempt is being made to provide more and better consultative services to the regular classroom teachers, especially in rural areas.

4. *More teacher-preparation in the field of specialization is being done through an undergraduate, or five-year integrated university program.* Persons through career planning are selecting special education earlier in their collegiate preparation. Fewer regular classroom teachers are being recruited to special education after many, many years of regular classroom teaching experience with normal children.

5. *There has been a continuous shift over the years in the financing of special education programs.* Traditionally, private agencies and parent groups have assumed a pump-priming role. They have felt that it was their responsibility to demonstrate the effectiveness and need for a particular special education service. In other words, they have provided the risk capital. The most recent program so initiated was that for the trainable mentally retarded. However, after a need has been demonstrated, the parents and the private agencies look to society to accept the responsibility. As public support is realized, these private agencies then proceed to other

services which are needed and for which public funds are not yet available.

6. *There has been a dramatic extension of education services to the trainable mentally retarded.* Even 10 years ago most school administrators took the position that the public schools were not the agency to serve the trainable mentally retarded. Today their stand is rapidly being altered, primarily as a result of the parent movement —one of the significant special education events of recent years. Similarly, severely handicapped cerebral-palsied children have been excluded from school attendance in the past. A public movement in their behalf, originating a number of years ago, has gradually opened school doors to them in many more communities.

7. *There has been a reappraisal of our definitions of the words integration and segregation.* We appear to have passed through the era of extreme pressure for physical integration of exceptional children into the regular grades. It now seems clear that we cannot assume that handicapped children will be accepted by their non-handicapped peers simply by placing them in the regular classroom (Force, 1956; Johnson and Kirk, 1950). In other words, physical integration does not assure social integration. In fact pupils may be more cruelly segregated socially in a program when they are not accepted by their classmates than in one where they are physically separated from average pupils during school hours for academic instruction. Whenever a child is rejected by his peers, it is the responsibility of the school to work at gaining social acceptance for him. When he cannot find success and social recognition in the regular grades (or even in some modification of the regular school plan), he should be provided the opportunity of finding acceptance in another program. Social segregation with physical integration is always a possibility with the unusual child in the regular classroom. The attitudes fostered by the administration among faculty, pupils, and parents and the ingenuity exhibited in solving the problems involved, constitute approaches that can produce both social acceptance and psychological integration.

8. *There has been an improvement in attitudes toward special education programs, both by persons within the field and those*

*outside it.* Recent years have witnessed a growing tolerance toward the philosophical differences within special education ranks, including those differences existing between day and residential school personnel. The causes of these changes are not entirely clear. However, it may be said for the residential schools that more of them have become an integral part of the public school system in their respective states; many, if not all of them, have raised their standards; those engaged in teacher education programs are now doing so under college or university auspices; and modern transportation has made for less isolation of resident pupils from their homes. At the same time, some day schools are entering the residential area by providing programs requiring boarding home facilities. This has increased their understanding of the problems inherent in a residential service. Any or all of the above circumstances may be contributing factors to better understanding and mutual respect between day and residential school educators.

At the same time, the growing demand by parents for separate public day school facilities for such severely impaired groups as the trainable mentally retarded and the cerebral palsied may have helped to reduce the disfavor in which special schools and classes were formerly held by those favoring integrated programs within the regular public day schools. In addition, the strong insistence by special educators themselves that their programs be operated as much as possible within the main stream of education has perhaps also contributed to the new attitudes of acceptance. In any event, special education, in spite of all its problems, seems to be enjoying the best relations of its existence—both interprofessional and public.

9. *One of the growing developments in special education is the increase in day school services for exceptional children.* A little before the turn of the century, almost 100 percent of the blind and the deaf children who received special services were in residential schools, whereas the trainable mentally retarded were located in residential facilities for the mentally retarded. Today half of the trainables and approximately one third each of the deaf and the blind are in day schools (Fig. 1.1). This evidence for the day school movement is particularly significant because it involves three groups of children who have severe disabilities. In addition, the growing urbanization of the United States and the increased number

of cooperative, rural special education programs portends the development of more day programs for all areas of exceptionality. This does not imply there has been a reduction in the number of pupils enrolled in residential schools. In fact, generally, the enrollment in both day and residential facilities has increased, but the increment has been greater in the day schools.

10. *We are taking a new look at the effectiveness of our services to gifted youth.* This has become a critical problem: first, because our limited efforts of the past have left us with a long distance to go; second, because of the population explosion; and, third, because of our ideological world struggle for survival. However, the social and political trends (some good, some bad) seem to be stimulating continued development of better opportunities for the gifted. Increased public interest as expressed in the criticisms of "soft" textbooks and courses, and in the elections of school officials is accompanied by a demand for more sophisticated education programs for practically all children and youth. Foreign languages and more advanced science and mathematics are receiving greater emphasis in the elementary schools. Certain former college-level programs are now appearing in the high schools. In addition the high schools are finding many ways of upgrading their work. The National Defense Act has helped in the areas of technology. New text books are being developed. After-school and Saturday classes for the gifted have been initiated in some communities as well as increased numbers of the more conventional-type special programs in others. And a long-term campaign in behalf of the colleges and universities has brought forth funds from various industries and funding agencies, which has helped many toward better facilities and faculties. All these factors, combined with the urgency felt for the democracies to keep ahead of nations seeking world supremacy, are bringing new benefits to the gifted.

11. *A movement to provide special educational services for emotionally disturbed children is beginning.* Mental health personnel such as psychiatrists and clinical psychologists are not available in sufficient numbers to serve emotionally disturbed pupils in need of help. Experimentation is under way to test the effectiveness of specially trained teachers in dealing with childrens' emotional prob-

lems, while at the same time providing them with appropriate educational instruction (Hobbs, 1961). If it is found that these educators are effective in both instruction and alleviating emotional disturbances, the door will have been opened to a sharp increase in the manpower pool available to serve this type of school child.

## Summary ✓

The trend in modern education to provide for individual differences among pupils is well illustrated by efforts to afford education opportunities for exceptional children equal to those available to average pupils. Equality is not achieved by providing identical school programs for all children, but rather by making available, through special teaching procedures and curriculum content, the needed adjustments that will enable any child with an unusual problem to work toward his potentialities at his own pace.

Exceptional children are defined as those who differ sufficiently from the average to make the regular school program unsuited to their needs, thereby necessitating specialized services for them. The twelve types of exceptional children are the (1) educable mentally retarded, (2) trainable mentally retarded, (3) gifted, (4) emotionally disturbed, (5) socially maladjusted, (6) speech impaired, (7) hard of hearing, (8) deaf, (9) partially seeing, (10) blind, (11) crippled, and (12) those with chronic health problems.

Of the estimated 8 percent of pupils who can be classified as exceptional, about 35 percent of that number in the United States were estimated by 1957–1958 to be receiving some special education services in the combination of public and private facilities of all sorts. The media through which these services were being received included (1) residential school programs; (2) hospital instruction; (3) homebound teaching; and (4) such day school plans as special schools and classes, resource room instruction, itinerant teacher services, consultative services, and others. Included among the basic principles essential to an adequate school program for exceptional children are early screening, identification, and placement. Well-developed criteria for teacher selection and pupil placement are needed to keep the programs functioning on a sufficiently professional level to bring important values to the pupils concerned.

A clinical-educational approach to teaching which includes tutoring, and small and large group instruction based upon a careful appraisal of each pupil's abilities and disabilities is the key to successful instruction of those children who possess unusual needs.

Trends in special education include increased numbers of children with severe multiple disabilities; a sharp increase in provision of education services; better teacher preparation; larger increments in the growth of day programs than in residential programs; increased interest in the gifted, the cerebral palsied, the emotionally disturbed, and the socially maladjusted; improved professional relations; and greater acceptance of exceptional children. If such children are to be accepted into the general stream of education, it becomes imperative that the professional personnel of the schools become familiar with the characteristics and educational needs of each of the various types enrolled.

In a very real sense, either group of children—our gifted or our handicapped—present a far-reaching challenge and great responsibility to a profession dedicated to the principle of equal education opportunities for all.

## CHAPTER REFERENCES

Dominion Bureau of Statistics. *Statistics of special education for exceptional children,* 1953–1954. Ottawa: Queen's Printers, 1959.

Force, D. G. Social status of physically handicapped children. *Except. Child.,* 1956, **23**, 104–107.

Harris C. (Ed.) *Encyclopedia of education research.* Washington, D.C.: NEA, American Educational Research Ass., 1960.

Hobbs, N. *Reeducation of disturbed children: a demonstration project.* Nashville, Tenn.: Peabody College, 1961.

Hunt, J. T. The education of exceptional children. *Rev. Educ. Res.,* 1963, **33,** (Feb. issue).

Johnson, G. O., & Kirk, S. A. Are mentally-handicapped children segregated in the regular grades? *Except. Child.,* 1950, **17**, 65–68, 87–88.

Jones. J. W. Blind children: Degree of vision, mode of reading. *U.S.*

*Office of Educ. Bull.*, 1961, No. 24, Washington, D.C.: Government Printing Office, 1961.

Jordan, T. E. Conceptual issues in the development of a taxonomy for special education. *Except. Child.*, 1961, **28**, 7–12.

Kirk, S. A., & Weiner, Bluma B. (Eds.) *Behavioral research on exceptional children.* Washington, D.C.: The Council for Exceptional Children, 1963.

Mackie, Romaine P., Dunn, L. M., & Cain, L. F. Professional preparation for teachers of exceptional children: An overview. *U.S. Office of Educ. Bull.*, 1959, No. 6, Washington, D.C.: Government Printing Office, 1960.

————, & Robbins, Patricia P. Exceptional children and youth: A chart book of special education enrollments in public day schools of the United States. *U.S. Office of Educ. Bull.*, OE-35019, Washington, D.C.: Government Printing Office, 1961.

————, Williams, H. M., & Robbins, Patricia P. Special education enrollments in local school systems: A directory. *U.S. Office of Educ. Bull.*, OE-35027, Washington, D.C.: Government Printing Office, 1961.

Martens, Elise H. Statistics of special schools and classes for exceptional children, 1947–1948. *Biennial survey of education in the U.S.*, 1946–1948. Washington, D.C.: Government Printing Office, 1950.

Peabody College, Division of Surveys and Field Services. *Scholastic achievement in Robertson County, Tennessee: A summary report.* Nashville, Tenn.: Peabody College, 1961.

Rice, Mabel C., & Hill, A. S. Statistics of special education for exceptional children, 1952–1953. *Biennial survey of education in the U.S.*, 1952–1954. Washington, D.C.: Government Printing Office, 1954.

UNESCO. *Statistics on special education.* New York: United Nations Educational, Scientific, & Cultural Organization Publishing Center, 1960.

Wilkins, G. T. (issued by) *The prevalence of exceptional children in Illinois in 1958.* Springfield, Ill.: State Department of Public Instruction, 1959.

Wishik, S. M. Handicapped children in Georgia: A study of prevalence, disability, needs and resources. *Amer. J. Public Health*, 1956, **46**, 195–203.

Zedler, Empress Y. Public opinion and public education of the exceptional child—court decisions 1873–1950. *Except. Child.*, 1953, **19**, 187–198.

## ADDITIONAL REFERENCES

Baker, H. J. *Introduction to exceptional children.* (3rd ed.) New York: Macmillan, 1959.

Barker, R. G., Wright, Beatrice, Myerson, L., & Gonick, M. *Adjustment to physical handicap and illness: A survey of the social psychology of physique and disability.* New York: Social Science Research Council, 1953.

Bowers, Joan E., Clement, J., Francis, M. I., & Johnston, M. C. *Exceptional children in home, school, and community.* Toronto: J. M. Dent, 1960.

Cruickshank, W. M. (Ed.) *Psychology of exceptional children and youth* (2nd ed.) Englewood Cliffs, N.J.: Prentice-Hall, 963.

————, & Johnson, G. O. (Eds.) *Education of exceptional children and youth.* Englewood Cliffs, N.J.: Prentice-Hall, 1958.

Dunn, L. M. The education of handicapped and gifted pupils in the secondary school. *Bull. Nat. Ass. Sec. Sch. Princ.,* Washington, D.C.: The Association, January, 1955.

Frampton, M. E., & Rowell, H. G. (Eds.) *Education of the handicapped.* 2 vols. New York: Harcourt, Brace & World, 1938.

————, & Gall, Elena D. (Eds.) *Special education for the exceptional.* 3 vols. Boston: Porter Sargent, 1955.

Garrett, J. F., & Levine, Edna S. (Eds.) *Psychological practices with the physically disabled.* New York: Columbia Univer. Press, 1962.

Garrison, K. C., & Force, D. G. *The psychology of exceptional children.* (3rd ed.) New York: Ronald Press, 1959.

Goodenough, Florence L. *Exceptional children.* New York: Appleton-Century-Crofts, 1956.

Heck, A. O. *The education of exceptional children.* (2nd ed.) New York: McGraw-Hill, 1953.

Jordan, T. E. *The exceptional child.* Columbus, Ohio: Charles E. Merrill, 1962.

Kirk, S. A. (Chair.) The education of exceptional children. *49th Yearbook, Part II, National Society for the Study of Education, Chicago:* University of Chicago Press, 1950.

————, *Educating exceptional children.* Boston: Houghton Mifflin, 1962.

Louttit, C. M. *Clinical psychology of exceptional children.* (3rd ed.) New York: Harper & Row, 1957.

Magary, J. F., & Eichorn, J. R. *The exceptional child: A book of readings.* New York: Holt, Rinehart and Winston, 1960.

Magnifico, L. X. *Education for the exceptional child.* New York: Longmans Green, 1958.

Pintner, R., Eisenson, J., & Stanton, Mildred. *The psychology of the physically handicapped.* New York: Appleton-Century-Crofts, 1941.

Roucek, J. S. (Ed.) *The unusual child.* New York: Philosophical Library, 1962.

Rusalem, H. *Guiding the physically handicapped student.* New York, Bureau of Publications, Columbia Univer., Teacher's College, 1962.

Taylor, W. W., & Taylor, Isabelle W. *Special education of physically handicapped children in Western Europe.* New York: International Society for the Rehabilitation of the Disabled, 1960.

Trapp, E. P., & Himelstein, P. (Eds.) *Readings on the exceptional children: Research and theory.* New York: Appleton-Century-Crofts, 1962.

Wright, Beatrice. *Physical disability: A psychological approach.* New York: Harper & Row, 1960.

## RESOURCES

The information below covers exceptional children generally. At the end of each chapter in this book, a short section similar to this one has been included. In each are outlined the agencies, organizations, literature, and other resources that the reader will find most helpful for the particular areas of exceptionality under consideration.

The Council for Exceptional Children (CEC), formerly known as the International Council for the Education of Exceptional Children, had its inception in 1922. Its unique function as a professional organization is to bring together special educators of the United States and Canada in all areas of exceptionality. In 1941, CEC became a department of the National Education Association and in 1950 established its office at NEA headquarters, 1201 16th Street, NW., Washington 6, D.C. By 1962, its membership had grown to over 15,000. It subsumes state and provincial federations and local chapters, as well as the international organization. A number of divisions have already formed within CEC, including the Association for the Gifted, the Association of Educators of Homebound and Hospitalized Children, the Council for the Education of the Partially Seeing, the Council of Administrators of Special

Education, and the Division on Teacher Education. Publishing constitutes a major activity of CEC. The journal *Exceptional Children* includes professional articles on all areas of exceptionality. The organization also publishes the *CEC Research Monographs* and a *CEC Special Publication Series.*

The U.S. Department of Health, Education, and Welfare (HEW) includes many public agencies concerned with exceptional children. Among these are the U.S. Office of Education (USOE), Children's Bureau (CB), the Office of Vocational Rehabilitation (OVR), and the U.S. Public Health Service (USPHS). All offer professional services upon request. The U.S. Office of Education maintains a professional staff in the education of exceptional children, including specialists in mental retardation, in the visually limited, in the deaf, in speech and hearing, in crippling conditions, and in the gifted. The office publishes various directories, statistics, reports, and special bulletins on education for exceptional children. The mailing address for the Department of Health, Education, and Welfare is Washington 25, D.C.

Special mention in this section is given to *Rehabilitation Literature,* published by the National Society for Crippled Children and Adults, 2023 West Ogden Avenue, Chicago, Illinois. Next to the Journal *Exceptional Children,* this is the most valuable single reference for a student interested in the field. It contains annotated reviews and abstracts on current literature in all areas of disability and major review articles in selected topics. Readers are encouraged to use *Rehabilitation Literature* as a major secondary source for current articles and books of interest to all disciplines concerned with rehabilitation of the handicapped in its broadest sense.

Persons with a problem about the education of an exceptional child may also communicate with the directors of special education in their state or provincial departments of education. A few of these departments have consultants in a number of areas of exceptionalities whose services are available upon request. These departments provide a wide range of other services, such as furnishing large print books on request. Of course, increasing numbers of local school systems are also employing consultants in special education who can render invaluable assistance.

## SELECTED 16 MM SOUND FILMS

*For those who are exceptional.* 43 min, color. Illinois State Department of Public Instruction, Springfield, Illinois. Special education programs are shown for the retarded, crippled, hearing impaired, speech handicapped, and emotionally disturbed.

*Education of exceptional children.* 30 min, black & white. Visual Aids Service, University of Illinois Extension, Urbana, Illinois. Illustrates teaching methods with various types of handicapped children.

*Individual differences: introduction.* 30 min, color. National Educational Television Film Service, Indiana University, Bloomington, Indiana. First of a series of 15 films on exceptional children prepared by Syracuse University.

*Special education services in the school district of Erie.* 40 min, black & white. Special Education Department, Erie, (Pa.) School District, 224 French Street, Erie, Pensylvania. Introduces public school programs for each of the areas of exceptionality with emphasis on the need for complete diagnosis, correct placement, and proper curriculum.

*Medical genetics.* 34 min, color. National Foundation, 800 Second Avenue, New York City 17, New York. Gives the physical basis of inheritance and some chromosomal abnormalities in man.

*Sensory processes and perception.* 30 min, black & white. National Educational Television and Radio Center, 10 Columbus Circle, New York 19, New York. Discusses the processing of information received by the organism from the environment.

*America's untapped asset.* 14 min, black & white. President's Committee on Employment of the Handicapped, Washington 25, D.C. Shows the successful employment of the physically handicapped.

*The undefeated.* 35 min, black & white. International Rehabilitation Film Library, 701 First Avenue, New York City 17, New York. English film showing a young pilot who lost legs and speech but determined to be an active community member.

*Comeback.* 26½ min, color. U.S. Office of Rehabilitation, Washington 25, D.C. Shows services for the disabled provided by the state-federal system of vocational rehabilitation.

*Return to life.* 25 min, color. University of Illinois, Division of Services for Crippled Children, Urbana, Illinois. Through the story of one disabled boy, this film traces the various services needed by handicapped children.

*To live again.* 29 min, color. Modern Talking Picture Service, 3 East 54 Street, New York 22, New York. A story of a romance between a paraplegic young woman and a rehabilitation counsellor, including her return to a full life.

*Discovering individual differences.* 25 min, black & white. New York University Film Library, 26 Washington Place, New York 3, New York. By a case history approach, shows how teachers can identify and meet the individual needs of their pupils.

*Search.* 20 min, black & white. National Society for Crippled Children and Adults, 11 S. LaSalle Street, Chicago, Illinois. Danny, an 11 year old cerebral palsied boy, portrays the problems the handicapped face in being accepted by society.

*Handicapped go camping.* 11 min, color. Bailey Films Inc., 6509 De Longpre Avenue, Hollywood 28, California. An experiment in camp life for both normal and handicapped children.

## CHAPTER 2

# Educable
# Mentally Retarded
# Children

LLOYD M. DUNN

As schools have opened their doors wider to children with intellectual limitations, mentally retarded pupils have presented an increasing challenge to educators. Most teachers place high value on intellectual endeavors. Yet the retarded are usually poor in the acquisition and retention of academic knowledge. As a result, such questions as the following are frequently asked by teachers: Why can't he achieve like other children his age? What should he be taught? Should he remain in school? Why is he such a behavior problem? What's wrong with my teaching? The central purpose of this chapter and the next is to provide teachers with a framework for dealing with such questions as these. The mentally retarded are discussed separately, the *educable* mentally retarded in this chapter and the *trainable* mentally retarded in the next. However, first, brief presentations are made of the meaning of mental retardation, intelligence testing, and causes of mental retardation since these topics cut across both groups of retarded children.

## The Meaning of Mental Retardation

Over the years, the term *mental retardation* has defied a definition which is satisfactory to all of the professional and lay groups who are concerned with the field. In fact, even the term itself has been altered many times. For example, terminology has shifted among idiocy, amentia, oligophrenia, feeblemindedness, mental deficiency, mental subnormality and slow learner, though most educators use the term "slow learner" when referring to the dull normal whose IQ's are usually in the 75–90 range. This confusion is probably due to three main reasons. First, western civilization prizes intellect so highly that negative values are soon attached to any term used to describe persons with intellectual limitations. Thus there has been a continuous search for a new term which is usually more socially acceptable at the outset. However, before too long it too becomes stigmatized, and the search continues. Second, mental retardation is such a complicated area, with so many different causes and levels of functioning that it approaches the impossible to include such diversity under one rubric. Yet we continue to search for a term that will do the job. Third, many disciplines including education, psychology, sociology, medicine, and the social service fields have some responsibility for different aspects of the field. Thus each is inclined to coin a term or develop a definition suited to its area. But usually a good definition for one discipline makes a very poor one for another. In spite of the confusion over terminology and the great heterogeneity of the field, there is one characteristic which is common to all persons who are mentally retarded and that is their intellectual subnormality. This is reflected in nearly all definitions of the term (Rothstein, 1961).

Heber in his manual for the American Association on Mental Deficiency (Heber, 1961a; Heber, 1961b), recognizing that only a broad description would encompass the diversity of the field, the many disciplines involved, and all ages of retardates, arrived at the following definition: "Mental retardation refers to (1) subaverage general intellectual functioning, (2) which originates during the developmental period, and (3) is associated with impairments in adaptive behavior" (Heber, 1961b, p. 499). Under this definition, *all three conditions must ensue before a person should be labelled mentally retarded.* Heber points out that *subaverage general intellectual functioning* is measured by an individual intelligence test. It is represented by IQ scores at least more than one standard deviation below the mean (see Fig. 2.1). (Since such better-known individual intelligence tests as the Stanford-Binet (S-B), the Wechsler Intelligence Scale for Children (WISC), and the Wechsler Adult Intelligence Scale (WAIS) have a mean IQ score of 100 and a standard deviation of 15 or 16 IQ points, the mentally retarded—according to this definition—obtain IQ scores below 85.) The developmental period mentioned in the definition approximates the first 16 years of life. Persons who had normal intelligence in childhood but obtain low IQ scores in adulthood due to neurological damage or mental illness should not be

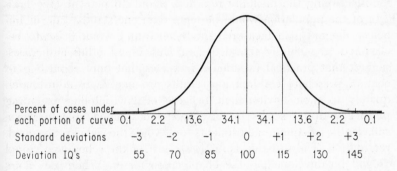

| Percent of cases under each portion of curve | 0.1 | 2.2 | 13.6 | 34.1 | 34.1 | 13.6 | 2.2 | 0.1 |
|---|---|---|---|---|---|---|---|---|
| Standard deviations | | -3 | -2 | -1 | 0 | +1 | +2 | +3 |
| Deviation IQ's | | 55 | 70 | 85 | 100 | 115 | 130 | 145 |

FIG. 2.1 Distribution of deviation IQ scores based upon the normal probability curve of intelligence. (From the Wechsler Intelligence Scale for Children with mean = 100, and standard deviation = 15.)

classified as mentally retarded. In early years, the impairment in *adaptive behavior* is recognized by a slow rate of development in such developmental skills as walking, talking, and other sensory-motor accomplishments. During school years, impaired learning ability is the maladaptive behavior which qualifies a pupil for classification as mentally retarded. Among adults, poor social adjustment in terms of an inability to maintain oneself a home and a family independently, or to earn a living in competitive employment is the prime criterion of maladaptive behavior for mental retardation. There are many causes other than mental retardation for children being slow in learning to talk, for pupils having difficulty in school, and for adults having difficulties in getting and holding a job. Persons cannot be labeled mentally retarded just because they have an impairment in adaptive behavior, any more than a low, valid IQ score alone justifies attaching the label mentally retarded to an individual. This low IQ score must always be accompanied by an impairment in at least one of the three types of adaptive behavior, and must have originated before the person was 16 years of age. Thus, as far as the schools are concerned, a pupil is identified as mentally retarded only when he is both low in measured intelligence and impaired in learning ability. It must be pointed out that, if IQ scores were used as the sole criterion for identifying the mentally retarded, about 16 percent (see Fig. 2.1) of the population would be more than one standard deviation below the mean in measured intelligence and would have to be classified as mentally retarded. But Heber and other authorities suggest that practical experience indicates that only about 3 percent of preschool children and adults are unable to adjust adequately to their environment because of low intelligence, most persons with IQ scores in the 70s and 80s being able to make sufficiently adequate adjustments to avoid the label of mental retardation. The situation is far less clear for the school-age group as will be developed as the chapter progresses. While only 2 to 3 percent have been considered educable mentally retarded for school purposes to date, this number may need to include nearly all of the 16 percent in the future.

Levels of impairment in intellectual functioning under the American Association Mental Deficiency classification are described in Table 2.1. Educators in the United States have not used AAMD demarcation lines that divide the retarded group into four categories. Instead, as yet, educators continue to classify the mentally retarded for educational purposes into three subgroups: the *educable* mentally retarded (EMR) who are found among pupils approximately in the IQ range 50–75, the *trainable* or severely mentally retarded, (TMR or SMR) who obtain IQ scores of approximately 30–50, and the *custodial,* or dependent mentally retarded, (CMR or DMR) who score below IQ 30. In the grossest terms, education has assumed some responsibility for mentally retarded boys and girls with IQ's in the 30–75 range. As yet they have not been called upon to serve children whose IQ's fall below this range since no effective methods of teaching them even self-

TABLE 2.1 *Levels of impairment in measured intelligence under the American Association on Mental Deficiency Classification.*[a]

| LEVELS OF IMPAIRMENT | IMPAIRMENT IN DEGREE OF MEASURED INTELLIGENCE | STANDARD DEVIATION RANGES | IQ SCORES FOR TESTS WITH SD'S OF 15 |
|---|---|---|---|
| − 1 | Borderline | − 1.01 − − 2.00 | 70–84 |
| − 2 | Mild | − 2.01 − − 3.00 | 55–69 |
| − 3 | Moderate | − 3.01 − − 4.00 | 40–54 |
| − 4 | Severe | − 4.01 − − 5.00 | 25–39 |
| − 5 | Profound | Below − 5.00 | Below 25 |

[a] Not all persons who obtained IQ scores of − 1.00 standard deviation and below are classified as mentally retarded; only those who also demonstrate impaired adaptative behavior before the age of 16 years are so considered.
*Source:* Heber, R. F. Modification in the manual on terminology and classification in mental retardation. *Amer. J. ment. Defic.*, 1961, **65**, 499–500.

care have yet been devised. Generally, the educable subgroup *EMR* have been so classified because they have the capacity to acquire sufficient academic skills to become literate. The trainable subgroup have been so designated because they are able to acquire rudimentary skills in self-care, socialization, and oral communication, but are not able to become literate. There are indications that this tricotomy is shifting as a result of more refined treatment procedures in education. This is good. Almost a century ago the retarded were classified into three categories; simpletons, fools, and idiots. Later, the labels were changed to morons, imbeciles, and idiots. Replacing these terms with educable, trainable and custodial as we do today is hardly a sufficient advance of which to be proud.

The AAMD categories—mild, moderate, severe, and profound—carry less stigma and have significance for differential educational treatments which are emerging.

## Intelligence Testing

Educators, more than any other group, have found scores on individual intelligence tests useful (Hunt, 1961). While these tests have been much maligned—often with justification since we have thought IQ scores more infallible and permanent than they are—a test score still provides the best single predictor of school success available, especially for the educable mentally retarded. Therefore, it is not surprising that, to a large measure, the mentally retarded around the world have been classified for educational purposes on the basis of measured intelligence, although IQ must not be the only determining factor (UNESCO, 1960).

It is impossible here to provide even an introduction to the nature and measurement of intelligence. For additional information, the reader is directed to textbooks in this area (Anastasi, 1961; Cronbach, 1960; Thorndike and Hagen, 1961). Individual intelligence tests such as the Stanford-Binet and Wechsler scales are composed of a number of items or subtests which measure different aspects of intellectual functioning. For example, the six verbal subtests of the WISC are information, comprehension, arithmetic reasoning, similarities, vocabulary, and digit span. The six performance subtests include picture completion, picture arrangement, block design, object assembly, coding, and mazes. The raw scores on these subtests are summated and converted to derived scores which enables one to compare the pupil being tested with the hundreds of other subjects of a similar age who were examined when the test was standardized. The verbal subtests yield a verbal intelligence quotient (VIQ), the performance subtests a performance intelligence quotient (PIQ), and the total subtests a full scale intelligence quotient (FSIQ).

The most popular derived score today is the *deviation IQ* based on a mean (average) IQ of 100 and a standard deviation of 15 for any one age group. This spreads the IQ scores along the normal probability curve as was shown in Fig. 2.1. If an eight-year-old obtained a deviation IQ of 85 we would know that his score falls one standard deviation below the mean for his age group and, therefore, that for every 100 eight-year-olds who were given the test when it was standardized, 16 scored below and 84 above him. Similarly, if a 12-year-old obtained a deviation IQ score of 70, we know his score fell exactly two standard deviations below the mean for his age group and, therefore, that 97.7 percent of the 12-year-old subjects on whom the test was standardized scored above him and 2.3 percent below. Thus, deviation IQ's tell the examiner the relative position of a pupil with respect to his age mates on whom the test was standardized. This is a useful general measure of scholastic aptitude. It can best be utilized by the teacher when he has a group of pupils of the same age. It gives a measure of the relative brightness of a particular pupil compared with his age peers. However, it does not tell the level at which that pupil should be achieving in school. Deviation IQ scores seldom go below 55 and therefore cannot be used with the trainable and custodial mentally retarded.

The best single derived score from an intelligence test for giving a measure of the level at which a child has the capacity to achieve in school is the *mental age* (MA). This was the original derived score for individual intelligence tests. It was introduced by Binet and Simon of Paris, France, into their 1911 revision of the original Binet-Simon scale. After an examiner finds the total raw score for a subject, he converts it to a mental age score by means of a conversion table or by some other technique. The table gives the mean (average) raw score obtained by each age group of subjects on whom the test was standardized. Thus a person with an MA = 9–0 (nine years zero months) obtains a score equivalent to the mean score made by all nine year olds upon whom the test was standardized. Therefore, we assume he has the capacity to achieve at the *level* of the average nine-year-old pupil. The mental age score is an extremely useful measure for a teacher of the educable mentally retarded. More credence can usually be placed on it when it is obtained from individual intelligence tests which are administered by qualified psychologists, rather than group intelligence tests administered by teachers. The Peabody Picture Vocabulary Test (Dunn, 1959) is an individual intelligence test designed so teachers can effectively administer and score it in less than 20 minutes. This test measures across the full range of intellect but is especially useful in ascertaining the mental ages of the educable mentally retarded (Dunn and Brooks, 1960). The number one law for the teacher, when dealing with the academic subjects, is to keep the mental ages of his pupils in mind. Perhaps the most common error made in teaching the educable mentally retarded is expecting them to work up to their chronological age (CA) rather than their mental age (MA). When a teacher knows the mental age of a pupil he can easily convert this to his corresponding grade capacity (GC) by applying the *Rule of Five*. Five subtracted from the mental age equals the grade level at which a pupil has the intellectual capacity to function:

$$GC = MA - 5$$

Thus, a retarded pupil with the MA = 9–0 should be working at the grade four level. However, it must be kept in mind that many factors other than intelligence should be taken into consideration in making a prognosis for a particular pupil in terms of school success. Important among these are physical conditions, home background, personal adjustment, and interests.

A teacher needs to be able to calculate the estimated MA's of his pupils when he knows their CA's and IQ's. Especially does this need to be done at the beginning of the school year. The cumulative folders should give the IQ scores obtained by each of the pupils when last given an intelligence test. The CA's are calculated from birthdates. The MA's can be estimated by using a transposed version of the familiar *ratio* IQ formula (IQ = MA/CA × 100), which was devised by Stern of Germany about 1912. The formula in calculating the estimated MA's is as follows:

$$\text{Estimated MA} = \frac{IQ \times CA}{100}$$

For example, a nine-year-old pupil with an IQ of 75 will have an estimated MA of six years.

$$\text{Estimated MA} = \frac{75 \times 9}{100} = 6 \text{ years}$$

By using the estimated MA and the *Rule of Five*, we find he has the intellectual capacity to achieve at the beginning grade one level. This relatively crude approach for estimating MA's from previous IQ scores has two major weaknesses. First, the assumption is made that the IQ score remains constant; this is becoming more and more indefensible (Hunt, 1961). In fact, scholars now speak of the "training of intellect" and the "educability of intelligence." The constancy of the IQ concept has also been challenged by studies in child development which suggest that measured intelligence is influenced by personality and motivational characteristics, cultural opportunities, as well as other factors. In fact, Sontag and his associates (1958) point out that "62 percent of the children change more than 15 IQ points sometime during the course of mental development from age three to age ten." These changes would be due, in varying amounts, to the interaction of the training and experiences of the children, their changes in personality and interests, and errors of measurements of the intelligence tests. Second, the ratio IQ implies a linear growth in mental development (mental age) with chronological age. This too is indefensible since it is a curvilinear function, but holds best for ages three through thirteen. For pupils over 13 years of age, one is well-advised to follow the Terman-Merrill rule in the 1937 Revised Stanford-Binet of dropping one out of every three additional months of chronological age from 13 to 16 years for purposes of arriving at a corrected CA divisor for the formula. For anyone 16 years of age and older the corrected CA divisor would remain at 15–0. For example, a 21-year-old person with an IQ score of 60 would have an estimated MA of 9–0.

$$\text{Estimated MA} = \frac{60 \times 15}{100} = 9 \text{ years}$$

In working out more accurately the estimated MA, the CA's and MA's must be converted to months, and later the MA's converted back to years and months. Applying these rules, we arrive at the data in Table 2.2 which show estimated mental ages for increasing chronological ages and intelligence quotients, but do not correct for curvilinearity from 13 to 16 years.

It can be easily demonstrated that the range of individual differences in mental age among all pupils, including the educable mentally retarded, increases with age. When mental age growth is plotted against chronological age growth for different IQ scores we arrive at Fig. 2.2, which presents this important principle. Thus, if a grade one teacher has pupils ranging in IQ's from 50 to 150, the mental age range will approximate three through nine years,

TABLE 2.2 *Estimated mental ages for increasing chronological ages and intelligence quotient scores.*

| IQ | CHRONOLOGICAL AGES | | | | | | | | | | |
|---|---|---|---|---|---|---|---|---|---|---|---|
| | 6 | 7 | 8 | 9 | 10 | 11 | 12 | 13 | 14 | 15 | 16 & ON |
| 30 | 1-10 | 2-1 | 2-5 | 2-8 | 3-0 | 3-3 | 3-7 | 3-11 | 4-2 | 4-5 | 4-10 |
| 40 | 2-5 | 2-10 | 3-2 | 3-7 | 4-0 | 4-5 | 4-10 | 5-2 | 5-7 | 6-0 | 6-5 |
| 50 | 3-0 | 3-6 | 4-0 | 4-6 | 5-0 | 5-6 | 6-0 | 6-6 | 7-0 | 7-6 | 8-0 |
| 55 | 3-4 | 3-10 | 4-5 | 4-11 | 5-6 | 6-1 | 6-6 | 7-2 | 7-8 | 8-3 | 8-9 |
| 60 | 3-7 | 4-2 | 4-10 | 5-4 | 6-0 | 6-7 | 7-2 | 7-9 | 8-4 | 8-11 | 9-7 |
| 65 | 3-11 | 4-7 | 5-2 | 5-10 | 6-6 | 7-2 | 7-9 | 8-5 | 9-1 | 9-8 | 10-4 |
| 70 | 4-3 | 4-11 | 5-7 | 6-4 | 7-0 | 7-8 | 8-5 | 9-1 | 9-9 | 10-5 | 11-2 |
| 75 | 4-6 | 5-3 | 6-0 | 6-9 | 7-6 | 8-3 | 9-0 | 9-9 | 10-6 | 11-3 | 12-0 |
| 85 | 5-1 | 5-11 | 6-10 | 7-8 | 8-6 | 9-4 | 10-2 | 11-0 | 11-11 | 12-9 | 13-7 |

*Rule of Five:* To derive grade capacity subtract 5 from the mental age, so for a pupil with a mental age of 8-0, subtract 5, to find his capacity for school work is at the beginning grade three level.

or a range of six years. If these same children remain together until they are 12 years of age, the mental age range for the same pupils will have increased to 6 through 18 years for a difference of 12 years, or *double*. One is immediately impressed with the fact that the teacher of older pupils has to deal with a much greater diversity of levels of mental development among his pupils than the teacher of younger pupils. We see that intellectually the mentally retarded keep falling further and further behind brighter children as they move into junior and senior high school. Said in another way, high school teachers face an even greater challenge in instructing at the appropriate level of the mentally retarded than do elementary school teachers, yet they have been the least effective.

Finally, as we learn more about the nature of intelligence and the measurement of specific intellectual aptitudes, we will probably

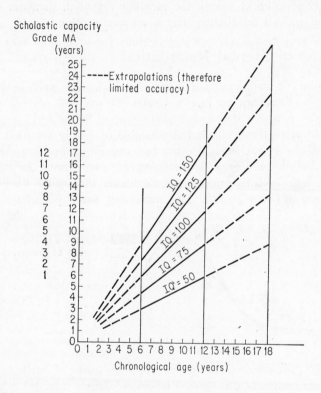

FIG. 2.2 Increase with age of individual differences in scholastic aptitude among pupils.

lean less heavily on the global IQ score. By global IQ is meant a single score which represents the over-all intellectual ability of the individual. Examples are the IQ score obtained on the SB, and the FSIQ obtained on the WISC and WAIS. We found the Wechsler scales yield more specific information through the VIQ's and PIQ's. Some new tests such as the Differential Aptitude Test (DAT) do not give a global IQ at all but a series of measures of specific aptitudes among high school students such as verbal reasoning, numerical reasoning, abstract reasoning, and spatial relations. When and if we have sufficiently sensitive tools to measure these different aspects of intellect among the mentally retarded, then our definition of mental retardation may need modification.

## Causes of Mental Retardation

In spite of rapid advances in the biological and behavioral sciences, there are no known causes for over 90 percent of the mentally retarded individuals in the United States and Canada today. Most of these fall in the educable or mildly retarded group with a few in each of the other two categories, and are classified as *unknown etiologies, nonpathological, endogenous,* or *cultural-familial.* In such cases there is no evidence discernible to the neurologist of brain lesions. The remaining small percentage have

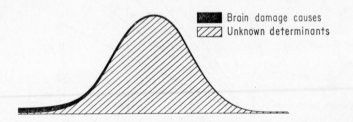

FIG. 2.3 Skewness of the normal probability curve of intelligence due to brain damage. (This figure is schematic and not intended to present actual proportions.)

organic brain pathologies. They spread across the full range of intelligence but are concentrated into the trainable and custodial categories. These have been variously classified as *known etiologies, pathological, exogenous, organic, brain-injured,* or *neurologically impaired.*

For years we have recognized that the theoretical normal probability (Gaussian) curve of intelligence shown in Fig. 2.1 is a hypothetical one. There is strong evidence that intelligence is not normally distributed but skewed to the lower end. This is due to an overlay of the pathologically or neurologically impaired which pile up in the trainable and custodial categories, as shown in Fig. 2.3. Dingman and Tarjan (1960) have calculated the proportions under the normal probability curve and in the overlay or excess. Their figures are given in Table 2.3. It will be seen that only 6 percent over-all of those below IQ 70 fall outside the regular curve and 94 percent under it. This represents only 1 percent of the IQ 50–70 group, 55 percent of the 20–50 group, and over 99 percent of the 0–20 group. Said another way, there are no discernible neuro-

TABLE 2.3 *Population with IQ's 70 and below in the United States.*

| IQ | CALCULATED FROM NORMAL PROBABILITY CURVE | ESTIMATED PREVALENCE | EXCESSES[a] | PERCENT OF PREVALENCE |
|---|---|---|---|---|
| 0–20 | 50 | 87,500 | 87,450 | Over 99 |
| 20–50 | 155,529 | 350,000 | 194,471 | 55 |
| 50–70 | 5,224,255 | 5,276,755 | 52,500 | 1 |
| Totals | 5,379,834 (94 percent) | 5,714,255 | 334,421 | 6 |

[a] Known pathological etiologies (organic brain damage group).
*Source:* Dingman, H. F. & Tarjan, G. Mental retardation and the normal distribution curve. *Amer. J. ment. Defic.,* 1960, **64**, 991–994.

logical impairments for 99 percent of the IQ 50–70 group, for 45 percent of the IQ 20–50 group, and for less than 1 percent of the IQ below 20 group, according to these data.

## UNKNOWN ETIOLOGIES

There is much debate about the cause of mental retardation among the 94 percent who fall under the Gaussian curve, who are concentrated at the higher IQ end of the retarded category, and who have been labeled nonpathological because no evidence of organic brain damage can yet be detected. On the one hand, many in the biological sciences hold to the *biological hypothesis,* contending that research of the future will reveal subtle physiological abnormalities among this group due to genetic, biochemical, and other defects. On the other hand, most persons in the behavioral sciences hold the *stimulus deprivation hypothesis,* contending that mental retardation is due in large measure to early cultural inadequacies, inadequate social environments, and such psychopathological problems as early maternal deprivation. Both hypotheses need to be thoroughly researched. In the meantime, educators usually choose to call this large group of the mentally retarded *cultural-familial,* suggesting that causation is due to a complex interaction of both environmental and hereditary factors. The retardates come from families in severely underprivileged city slums or rural areas in which deficiencies in intellectual, social, and emotional stimulation abound. These conditions are brought on by a vicious cycle. First, scientists tell us that a number of members of society appear at the tag end of the continuum on most human traits including intelligence due probably to complex hereditary characteristics. Since these persons are less well-endowed intellectually, they have difficulty in competing for well-paying jobs. As a result, they find their way into underprivileged areas because they cannot afford anything better. Here their offspring are born into an inadequate environment with some inherited predisposition to intellectual subnormality. Thus we see that causation appears to be due to both familial and cultural factors. Even though many researchers have concerned themselves with the cultural effects on intelligence (Hunt, 1961; Kirk, 1958; Sarason and Gladwin, 1959), it cannot be inferred that mental retardation is due to cultural factors alone. While these studies have given enough data to show that environment plays an important part, a fairer statement would be that heredity sets the limits on intellectual functioning while environment facilitates or hinders the fulfillment of one's inherited potentialities. The cultural-familial group which we have been describing tend to be more average in appearance, coordination, and adjustment than the pathological group. However, they have great difficulty in school. In addition to inadequate home and community conditions, these children have to attend the poorest schools in the slums where teachers, curriculum, library facilities, and physical plants are often inadequate (Conant, 1961). With this combination, one cannot expect such children to be intellectually curious, stimulated, or interested in conventional schoolwork.

## PATHOLOGICAL ETIOLOGIES

There are innumerable causes of mental retardation for the 6 percent of the below IQ 70 group who have recognizable *pathological* conditions. Some of these include chromosomal anomalies, abnormalities of gestation, maternal dietary deficiencies, metabolic disorders, virus infections of the mother and newborn, blood-type incompatability, and poisoning of the fetus due to lead poisoning, carbon monoxide, and other poisonous fumes inhaled by the mother. In past years it had been thought that most cases of damage to the brain resulted primarily from birth injuries. Masland (1958), after a careful review of the literature, concluded that the predisposing problem is more likely to have arisen early in the gestation period, primarily by the end of the third month of pregnancy. The resulting fetus, being abnormal, will produce an abnormal pregnancy which results in birth difficulties. No longer are anoxia at birth, prematurity and instrument births assumed to be the major cause of mental retardation. Both the birth difficulties and the intellectual deficiency are often results of factors present at conception or by the end of the first trimester of pregnancy. Thus, in recent years, there has been a renewed interest in genetic determinants, embryological problems, and maternal infections. Nevertheless, birth trauma, and children's diseases which result in severe infections of brain tissue (meningo-encephalitis), as well as accidents, occasionally can and do cause mental retardation. However, the relative occurrence of these is rare today.

The biochemical disorders which result in brain damage are just beginning to be researched and include such conditions as galactosemia (a genetic defect resulting in an inability of the body to metabolize galactose, a sugar found in milk) and phenylketonuria (also a genetic defect resulting in a lack of an enzyme needed to digest phenylalanine which is an amino acid in proteins). In these two cases, a special diet is prescribed and when given early enough reduces markedly the damage to the brain which would result from an accumulation of the poison (such as phenylpyruvic acid) in the body. There appears to be a rather consistent link between metabolic disorder and genetic determinants. The future will likely find a number of the other causes of mental retardation similiar to galacto-semia and phenylketonuria.

Wilson, in chapter 9, has pointed out that cerebral palsy is motor incoordination due to brain injury. It is not surprising that brain damage severe enough to result in motor dysfunction can also result in intellectual dysfunction. In fact, as Wilson indicates, research shows that about 50 percent of cerebral palsied children have IQ scores below 70. (She has outlined some of the educational tech-niques for serving children with neurological damage which results, among other things, in severe dysfunction of the limbs.)

Not only can brain injury result from a large number of factors, but very different types of central nervous system damage may occur. In most cases, the injury will be diffused and general. In other cases, a specific area of the brain may be much more damaged than others. Therefore, the behavioral characteristics of children with brain damage will vary greatly or extremely. Depending on the area and extent of the brain which has been damaged, these children may be hypoactive (lethargic), normal in activity level, or hyperactive (hyperkinetic). Some may be skinny and bony; others flabby and fat; and still others may have average bodies. Some may be grossly incoordinated, while others will have normal body movements. Some may be susceptible to epilepsy while others will not be. Therefore, it is impossible to talk about brain injured children as a homogeneous group. However, this group is generally more retarded in intellect and more multiply disabled than the cultural-familial group. They do come from homes which extend from the very poorest to the very best with most of them coming from average or above socio-economic settings.

## THE STRAUSS SYNDROME

At this point, it is important to introduce a controversial term, namely, the "Strauss syndrome" or "Strauss-type child." Concern for these children has been high among educators and psychologists since the publication of Volume 1 of *Psychopathology and Education of the Brain-injured Child* by Strauss and Lehtinen (1947). Later, a second volume was published by Strauss and Kephart (1955) but it has not received the attention given Volume 1. Strauss (now deceased) was a medical doctor who emigrated from Europe in World War II, worked for a time at the Wayne County Training School and finally established the Cove Schools for brain-injured children at Racine, Wisconsin, and Evanston, Illinois. His co-author, Laura E. Lehtinen, is an educator who worked closely with him in identifying the Strauss-type syndrome and especially in developing the teaching procedures based on the characteristics of such youth. The Strauss-Lehtinen text has made the biggest contribution of its decade to the field. It has also stirred up much confusion, misunderstanding, and professional concern.

How do you identify children with the Strauss syndrome? There are seven criteria, the first four being behavioral and the last three being biological in nature: (1) *perceptual disorders*—such children when viewing pictures see parts instead of wholes and make figure-ground distortions; (2) *perseveration*—they continue at an activity once started and have great difficulty in changing sets; (3) *thinking or conceptual disorders*—they organize materials and thoughts differently from most average individuals; (4) *behavioral disorders*—included are such characteristics as hyperactive, explosive, erratic, and uninhibited behavior; (5) *slight neurological signs;* (6) *a history of a neurological impairment;* and (7) *no history of mental retardation in the family.* The last three biological signs may be negative and still the child may be diagnosed as having the Strauss-type syndrome on the behavioral characteristics.

It is most unfortunate that Strauss and Lehtinen named their pupils brain injured or exogenous. People in the field have not read the fine print in the Strauss-Lehtinen book and have equated a Strauss-type child with a neurologically impaired child. The Strauss-type child is recognized by his *behavior* pattern of hyperactivity, uninhibited actions, perseveration, and perceptual disorders, not by his brain injury. In fact, it is not at all necessary to assume an etiology of neurological impairment. Future research may demonstrate the syndrome is due to metabolic disorders or genetic factors. Thus, the author of this chapter has chosen to accept the recommendation of Stevens and Birch (1957) dropping the terms "brain injured" and "exogenous" in favor of the "Strauss Syndrome."

It could be argued that Strauss-type children should not be included in this chapter. One reason for excluding them would be the valid argument that mental retardation is not a criterion for their identification. While most children with the Strauss-syndrome are mentally retarded, Strauss contended they fell across the full range of intellect up through, in rare cases, the gifted. An alternative would have been to include this discussion in Wilson's chapter on the neurologically impaired and nonsensory physically impaired. However, signs of neurological and physical impairments may be negative. Another approach could have been to include a separate chapter on this topic. However, the status of knowledge about such children does not yet warrant such attention in a survey text. Thus, these children have been described here. Later in the chapter is a brief description of the Lehtinen methods for teaching the pupil with the Strauss-syndrome.

## OTHER TERMS

Finally, the word "exogenous" has been introduced into the text, and this should be discussed in the context of "exogenous-endogenous." These terms have been used differently by different authorities in the field. Some use endogenous to include all genetic causes of mental retardation, and exogenous to include all known and unknown causes from conception and on. Others have equated endogenous with cultural-familial (or nonpathological) cases, and exogenous with all pathological conditions even when hereditarily predetermined. Strauss restricted exogenous to his own Strauss-syndrome and appeared to classify all other cases as endogenous. Thus, when confronted by the terms exogenous-endogenous one needs to ascertain the particular writer's meaning.

There is similar confusion between the terms "mentally retarded" and "mentally deficient." To some authorities these terms are synonymous. To others mental deficiency refers to the subgroup with severe pathological conditions (IQ's below 50 mostly), and mental retardation to the subgroup with milder conditions (IQ's above 50). The author uses the term "mental retardation" as AAMD does, ascribing to it a broad and generic meaning, including all levels of mental subnormality severe enough to result in any type of mal-adaptive behavior. However, the term "mentally deficient" is re-served for *adults* who are both (1) low in intelligence, and (2) socially incompetent (Dunn, 1960). In other words, the Heber adult type of mental retardation is the same as Dunn's mental deficiency. By social incompetence we mean an inability to look after oneself at a time when this is customary. In other words, many persons classified as mentally retarded in childhood will not be classified as mentally deficient in adulthood since the large ma-jority will be able to look after themselves. Thus, among *educable, trainable,* and *dependent* mentally retarded pupils, very few of the educable mentally retarded will be called mentally deficient in adulthood since most will become socially competent; nearly all of the trainable mentally retarded will be marginally dependent all of their lives and therefore in adulthood under this definition would be classified as mentally deficient; all of the dependent children with IQ's below 30 would be classified as mentally defi-cient in adulthood since they will be totally dependent all of their lives. This meaning of mental deficiency has significance for adult retardates but not for children. Furthermore, it is a sociological, rather than an educational or biological definition. When confronted by the term "mental deficiency," it is necessary to ascertain the particular writer's meaning.

## The Educable Mentally Retarded Defined

The "educable" mentally retarded pupils have been defined as hav-ing IQ scores between 50–75 and as having, or a prognosis that they will have, learning difficulties in the regular grades. In other words, the educable mentally retarded have difficulty in school because their intellectual development is only about one half to three fourths of that of the average child.

Utilizing Table 2.2 and the *Rule of Five*, we see that a pupil whose IQ score is 75 will have a mental age of only 4–6 when he reaches a chronological age of 6–0; he will not reach a mental age of 6–0 until he is 8–0; even when he is 12–0 years old he will only have the capacity to do beginning grade four work (MA = 9–0). At 16 he will have accumulated only the capacity to perform at the beginning grade seven level (MA = 12–0). A pupil whose IQ is 50 will have acquired a mental age of only 3 years when he reaches the chronological age of 6 years; he will not have reached a mental age of 6–0 until he is 12 years of age; at 16 he will have accumulated only the mental age capacity of 8 years, giving him the ability to perform at the beginning grade three level in academic work.

Thus, we see that educable mentally retarded children, when they enter school, will range in mental age from 3–0 to 4–6. It will take six years of readiness experience and maturation for a pupil with an IQ of 50 to acquire a mental age of six years at which time he can begin to succeed at the basic school subjects. A pupil with an IQ of 75 will have a mental age of six years when he reaches a chronological age of 8–0. At school-leaving age and through adulthood, the educable mentally retarded will range in mental ages from 8–0 to 12–0 (when the IQ range 50–75 is used as the frame of reference), which means scholastically they will only have the capacity to achieve between the grade three and seven level. A rough rule of thumb is to say that most "educable" pupils will, in late adolescence, have the capacity, on the average, to achieve somewhere around the grade four to five level. Since this is the recognized point of literacy, it may be said that the educable mentally retarded, *as a group,* have the ability to be literate. While this generally holds true, most authorities recognize that few pupils with IQ's in the 50 range will acquire this goal. They will not learn sufficiently in the three R's to read and write for information or to handle their finances without assistance. It is not surprising then that the lower IQ limit is shifting upward from 50 to about 60 or 65. The upper limit is shifting from IQ 75 to about 80 or 85 due to the increased complexity of our society, to the competition for employment, and other factors. Some recent research presented later in this chapter bears on this shift. In fact, there are already more children in special classes with IQ's above 75 than those in the 50–60 range. Thus, the AAMD definition by Heber agrees with practical experience which indicates that a number of pupils with IQ's above the traditional cutoff point of 75 need special educational services.

In this context it is interesting to note the great variability from country to country of IQ limits for special education of the educable mentally retarded (UNESCO, 1960). Argentina, Australia, and Peru use 50–80 as their limits. The German Federal Republic place children with IQ's 65–85 in special schools. Switzerland uses IQ 70–90 as its limits for placement in special classes. In Norway children with IQ's between 50–70 attend special schools, and those between 70 and 85 have special classes. Generally, the higher the culture's emphasis on academic excellence in the regular grades, the higher the IQ limits for special school and class placement. The Soviet Union is the one country which does not use IQ scores, believing these discriminate against the working class (Dunn and Kirk, 1963).

Finally, it must be pointed out that mentally retarded children may or may not be educationally retarded. By *educationally* retarded we generally mean that a child is achieving academically below his mental age capacity, not his chronological age or grade placement. After the age of nine years, a pupil is classified as educationally retarded when he is achieving academically two or more years below his mental age. Before that he is classified as educationally retarded when he is achieving only one grade below mental age. Using this classification, mentally retarded children would not be classified as educationally retarded when their traditional school work is at or near mental age capacity. Thus, a 12-year-old boy in grade seven with an IQ of 75 who was working at or near the grade four level in school would not be educationally retarded. However, if his achievement was only at the grade one or two level, then he would be educationally as well as mentally retarded. This is a useful distinction in planning school programs.

## Prevalence

It was estimated in Table 1.1 in chapter 1 that the prevalence of the educable mentally retarded children has been set at about 2 percent of the school population. Yet, according to the normal probability curve of intelligence, about 5 percent of the school population obtain IQ scores between 50–75. This discrepancy between the 2 and 5 percent figures could be explained as follows. While 5 percent of the school population obtain IQ scores of between 50–75, about one half of this number work up to or near capacity in the regular grades and seem to be reasonably well-adjusted. Therefore, they have not been labeled mentally retarded. Special education has been designed to serve only those youngsters who are not making reasonably good progress in the regular grades. In fact, the general practice in most school districts in past years has been to place all children including the educable mentally retarded in the regular grades at the outset of their school careers. After two or three years of failure in such a school placement, the educable mentally retarded have then been identified and referred for special class or school placement. Just under one half of the 5 percent (or 2 percent) of those with IQ's between 50 and 75 have been referred for special class placement in school districts with extensive programs for the retarded. Therefore, they may be designated as educable mentally retarded in keeping with the AAMD definition described earlier in the chapter, since they have low measured intelligence, are under 16 years of age, and have an inability to adapt to the regular school program. It needs repeating, labeling a child as mentally retarded is a serious step and should not be done on the basis of an IQ score alone. It should be done only when a special school placement or treatment is planned. Therefore, it is only justifiable to identify the educable mentally retarded as a separate group when differentiated educational procedures are available for them which should be more beneficial than a regular school program.

Our prevalence figure may shift sharply upward as we find a greater proportion of the educable mentally retarded having difficulties in social and emotional adjustment and academic success in regular grades. Conceivably in the future, special services may be provided children with IQ scores as high as 80 or 85 *at the outset of their school careers.* This may provide a much better opportunity for educable mentally retarded pupils to achieve social and vocational competence. Should this become a practice, then our prevalence of educable mentally retarded children would increase to as much as 15 or 16 percent of the school population, as discussed earlier (see Fig. 2.1).

## Identification

Unless intelligence tests are routinely administered to all pupils before they enter school, prime responsibility for initial detection and referral of the educable mentally retarded child rests with the regular classroom teacher. In fact, it has often been said that the educable mentally retarded child who is not so very far below average is not recognized as such before entering school and loses his identity upon graduation. Group tests of intelligence are helpful as a screening technique (see Appendix III of Thorndike and Hagen, 1961, for an up-to-date annotated list of such tests). Pupils who obtain IQ scores between 50 and 75 form a pool from which most of the educable mentally retarded may later be identified. However, the pool of pupils who get scores of 50 to 75 on group tests will not only contain the educable mentally retarded but other boys and girls with higher IQ's whose capacities have not been optimally tapped by the group test. When these pupils are administered appropriate individual intelligence tests under optimal conditions, a higher and more accurate picture of their intelligence is likely to be obtained. When a teacher refers to a pupil as potentially mentally retarded, beside group IQ scores, he should consider such other factors as group achievement test scores, school achievement two or more years below grade placement, plus such basic characteristics of the mentally retarded as lack of abstract reasoning ability, and an inability to generalize.

Following screening, a comprehensive examination administered by a competent school psychologist or educational diagnostician is necessary to identify the educable mentally retarded. The most essential instrument to be administered is an appropriate individual intelligence test such as the 1960 Stanford Binet, or the Wechsler Intelligence Scale for Children. It is also important to have a picture of the school achievement and learning difficulties of the child. Of course, he is very likely to have educational problems when he has been referred by the teacher as having trouble in school. The good examiner will employ a wide battery of instruments so as to make as accurate a diagnosis as possible. Besides intelligence and achievement tests, there may be tests of personality, interest inventories, and the like. The diagnostician will want to rule out where emotional maladjustment, physical impairment in vision or hearing, or educational retardation are the primary disabilities. This examination plus other diagnostic information gathered from the school files, home visits, medical reports, and other records are crucial to the effective selection of the educable mentally retarded. It is as incongruous for educators to devise procedures for the limited learner without diagnostic data as for physicians to prescribe treatment without having made a careful and thorough diagnosis. Final responsibility for the selection of an educable mentally retarded pupil for special services should rest with the educators. Psychologists, social workers, and sometimes medical personnel may contribute valuable information upon which educators may base their decisions. However, educators are in the best position to decide which types of educational provisions are most likely to serve the best interests of the pupil. In most cases the decision is between leaving a child in the regular grade or placing him in a special school or class. It cannot be stressed too strongly that labeling a child "educable mentally retarded" is no badge of distinction and must be done only after a judicious consideration of all the evidence and a firm conviction that identifying the child as such will result in his receiving a more beneficial program of instruction.

Of course, if in the future educable mentally retarded are placed in a special program at the outset of their school careers, which may begin as early as at three years of age, then much of the procedure described above for identifying the retarded will change radically. Identification will be based largely on a valid individual intelligence test score obtained before the pupil enters school, supported where possible by a physical examination and home visit data obtained by a multidisciplinary team working in diagnostic clinics on referred cases. (It is to be hoped that schools of the future will require individual tests of scholastic aptitude on all pupils prior to school entrance.)

## Characteristics

As mentioned earlier, in only two characteristics are all educable mentally retarded pupils alike. They have IQ scores between approximately 50 and 75, and are having, or have a prognosis that they will have, learning difficulties in a regular school curriculum. Otherwise, they vary greatly in most human traits. However, research enables us to make some generalizations about retarded pupils, *as a group,* though there will be many exceptions. Thus, the reader is cautioned that the characteristics presented below resulted from comparisons of groups of educable mentally retarded children with groups of children who possess average or above intelligence. *These characteristics do not apply to all individuals classified as retarded.* Many exceptions will exist for each generality.

Generally, it can be stated the educable mentally retarded compare unfavorably on most traits with pupils of average and above intellect. The retarded tend to be inferior while the gifted tend to be superior. As mentioned earlier, the largest subgroup (over 90 percent) of the educable mentally retarded are classified as unknown, cultural-familial, or nonpathological while the remainder are classified as pathological, or neurologically impaired in terms of etiology. Where research is available which distinguishes the characteristics of the pathological from the others, this is pointed out under the subheadings which follow.

## PHYSICAL AND MOTOR DEVELOPMENT

As a group, even when the cultural-familial and neurologically impaired are combined, the educable mentally retarded are more nearly like children with normal and above intellect in physical and motor characteristics than in any other trait (Cantor and Stacey, 1951; Dayton, 1928; Francis and Rarick, 1960; Howe, 1959; Sloan, 1951). Nevertheless, they tend to be slightly lighter in weight and slightly shorter in stature than the average, though if socioeconomic levels were controlled this might not occur, especially among the cultural-familial group. They are somewhat more handicapped in motor skills. For example, Francis and Rarick (1960) found that, at age 14, the mentally retarded could not make squat thrusts and standard broad jumps as well as eight year olds of the same sex. The 14-year-old's performance in running speed was only up to the standard of normal 10-year-olds. They lagged one to three years behind the average child in tests of strength and were as much as four years behind published norms for average children in the vertical jump. The research by Sloan (1951) suggests the retarded are even more below par in the finer and more intricate motor coordination skills. This finding is extremely important for educational practices. Early in the century, a philosophy of "a weak mind and a strong back" operated. Many educators believed the mentally retarded who were unsuccessful in academic areas should have a curriculum which emphasized arts and crafts. The mentally retarded were not particularly successful under such a teaching emphasis since they lacked the necessary fine motor skills. In terms of the studies just mentioned, it is not surprising that there has been a shifting away from such an approach.

Children who are classified as cultural-familial are usually superior in physical characteristics to those who are neurologically impaired. Many of the brain injured have great problems of motor coordination. Finally, it should be pointed out that, among the retarded generally, there is often a preschool history of lateness in reaching various levels of physical development. The group is usually slower in walking and learning other motor tasks. This, of course, is part of the AAMD definition of retardation, especially for the preschool child.

## FAMILY BACKGROUND

Teachers have special difficulty in accepting the cultural-familial group because the mores and values in such families are so different from their own. These families live in conditions where cultural deprivation and other forms of stimulus deprivation may be extreme (Conant, 1961). Since teachers come primarily from the middle classes they are frankly shocked when they first enter the homes of many of the cultural-familial group. It is beyond their comprehension that Americans and Canadians live in such conditions in an age which is characterized by affluency, in that we have the highest standard of living in the history of man. Teachers who make home visits as a part of their teaching responsibilities repeatedly report a high prevalence of broken homes, malnutrition, neglect of children, flagrantly bad housekeeping conditions, sparse furnishings, and no reading materials in these homes. Usually the parents, as may be expected, are somewhat retarded intellectually and have not progressed far themselves in school.

Neurologically impaired children are found in homes of every socioeconomic level. The large proportion of cultural-familial children overshadows the relatively few pathological cases in the educable group. In the wealthy areas, where little or no cultural-familial mental retardation exists, the relatively few educable mentally retarded to be found have obvious neurological impairments. Very often a selective factor operates in pupil placement. Special classes located in schools which serve the lower socioeconomic levels of the community enroll mostly children classified as cultural-familial, while the few special classes in the well-to-do section of the town serve primarily neurologically impaired children.

Teacher statements obtained by Dunn of home conditions and parent-child relations of a random sample of twenty boys in special classes in a mid-western town follow (in Dunn and Capobianco, 1956). Only a glance at these statements will inform the reader of the location of these classes in the community since all but a few of the pupils would probably be classified as nonpathological or cultural-familial.

1. Rejected by father; strong sibling rivalry. *NO FATHER*
2. Mother bore child by boarder; then divorced husband and married boarder. *male friends*
3. Father alcoholic; often on penal farm; mother poor organizer.
4. Live in shack made of paper and orange crates; father gathers junk. *slum + low income area*
5. Mother is apparently mentally retarded. *slow -*
6. Boy rejected by his parents.
7. Father died recently; mother rejects boy, has numerous boy friends.
8. Harmonious relations in home; entire family delivers daily newspapers.
9. Harmonious relations in home; entire family delivers daily newspapers (8 and 9 were identical twins).
10. Parents elderly; boy is over-protected.
11. Boy has stepmother; father takes the money boy earns to get drunk.

12. Boy has stepfather who rejects him.

13. Family is deeply religious; foreign language spoken in home.

14. Parents puzzled and disappointed with boy; clean home.

15. Father away from home much of time driving truck.

16. Poor parent-child relations.

17. Much strife between parents and among siblings.

18. Boy lives with mother only, but never speaks of her.

19. Boy adopted by foster parents, who are disappointed with him.

20. Boy lives with mother only; she is a poor provider.

## SOCIAL AND EMOTIONAL ADJUSTMENT

A number of sociometric studies (Baldwin, 1958; Johnson, 1950; Johnson and Kirk, 1950; Miller, 1956) indicate that the educable mentally retarded placed in regular classrooms obtained lower social status positions than their intellectually superior peers. In other words, the retarded are socially segregated even when they are physically integrated into the regular classes. The retarded pupils are not rejected by their classmates because they are slow in learning school subjects but generally due to lack of cleanliness and unacceptable behavior patterns of aggressiveness—probably as a reaction to failure.

Miller's study (1956) included a comparison of the abilities of retarded, gifted, and average pupils to predict the sociometric choices of their classmates. The gifted were significantly better than the other two groups; the retarded had the greatest difficulty in comprehending social situations. When rejection and inability to understand social situations are combined, it is no wonder that, as a group, the retarded are reported to be socially maladjusted. The fact that retarded pupils are rejected by their peers in the regular grades has been a strong argument for providing such youngsters with special classes.

What is the evidence on the acceptance of the retarded by one another in special classes? Jordan (1960) researched the social acceptance of the educable mentally retarded in special classes. Using an unlimited choice sociometric questionnaire, she found the sociometric picture of the retarded child in the special class was much the same as that in the regular class. Children with the lowest intellectual abilities remained in the lower social positions even in the special class structure. A weakness of Jordan's study was that there were no comparative data on retarded pupils remaining in the regular grades. While they may have trouble getting accepted in the special class, they may have even greater difficulty in the regular grades.

Jordan and de Charms (1959) and Johnson (1961) compared retarded children in the special classes and in the regular grades. They found the retarded in the regular grades to be more rejected and to have more fear of failure than retarded children in special classes. It would appear that pressure for academic achievement in the regular grades is producing fear of failure.

These findings suggest some justification for special classes in terms of the adjustment of the pupils. However, the Jordan study (1960), which did not paint a bright picture, suggests that even in the special class there develops a hierarchy of acceptance with the most retarded at the bottom. Special class teachers must work hard at developing in the retarded behavioral patterns which will make them more acceptable to others. Children with the lowest intelligence in the special classes need the most help.

Further understandings of the characteristics of retarded children can be gleaned from the research of Cromwell and his associates which was based on Rotter's social learning theory (Cromwell, 1961). They found that retarded pupils as a group have a higher expectancy for failure than the intellectually normal. Thus, in a novel task, it is exceedingly important to give initial success experiences to counter this generalized expectancy for failure and to establish a higher level of aspiration than would ordinarily be set. However, here again one cannot generalize to all retardates. These same investigators have found that a few retarded children have personality characteristics which enable them to profit from failure and to be stimulated to perform at a higher level by it, the performance of most of the retarded deteriorates with failure experiences.

Another index of social adjustment is available from studies of delinquency. Almost invariably the mean IQ score for delinquent populations is below 100. For different studies, the means range from 72 to 92, suggesting that the high educable mentally retarded and slow learners are more involved with the law than the average or above (Wallin, 1956). Here, it should be indicated that it is generally the cultural-familial group which finds itself in trouble with the law. Well-to-do parents of the neurologically impaired are more influential with law enforcement officials and also are more likely to exert greater social control over their children. In reviewing the field Blatt (1960) has pointed out that low IQ in itself does not play an important role in causing delinquency and criminality unless combined with such other factors as a broken home, alcoholism, and underprivileged conditions.

Mentally subnormal children do not have to become delinquent; nor can we explain delinquency as a manifestation of the subnormality. It is not surprising that some of these children become delinquents; it is amazing that more do not. Society must recognize the need for psychiatric and social services, realistic education, and vocational counseling for all its citizens. More important, we must cease looking with derision at those in a different cultural milieu. (p. 59)

Pate, in chapter 5, has more information on the characteristics of delinquent children. No studies have yet been found which compare the social acceptance and emotional adjustment of pathological and nonpathological subjects.

## LEARNING CHARACTERISTICS

Nothing is more central to teaching than the learning process. Yet up to 1958, only 28 studies were found in the literature on the topic (McPherson, 1958). Recent research activity reveals increased productivity, though the emphasis has been on basic learning theory rather than on studies with direct application to the classroom (Dunn and Capobianco, 1959; Ellis, 1963). The vast majority of studies support commonly held beliefs that the retarded neither learn as quickly nor achieve as much academically as children of normal intellect. They forget even more rapidly. In fact, a "leaky bucket" theory of the rapid forgetting of the mentally retarded has recently been in vogue. In addition, the retarded have been considered extremely inept in the transfer of learning.

Some recent investigations, including studies by Johnson and Blake (1960), raise some doubts about these generalizations. In a comparison of the learning, retention, and transfer of learning skills of older educable retardates and younger normal subjects of equivalent mental ages, these investigators found over-all that IQ did not appreciably affect performance on laboratory tasks. In fact, as anticipated, older retardates, as a group, performed better than younger normals on simple sensory motor tasks involving puzzle assembly and card sorting since less high mental processes were involved. The results were equivocal on rote learning tasks involving serial and paired associates nonsense syllables. There were no significant differences on retention as measured by recognition, recall, and saving scores on relearning. On transfer of learning, as measured by similar paired associates and reasoning tasks, the two groups performed equally well. Even though the results of this series of studies are not directly applicable to classroom learning since laboratory tasks were used rather than the three R's, two implications seem indicated. First and foremost, it should be pointed out to teachers that educable retardates are able to learn, retain and transfer quite complex motor and verbal skills, according to their mental ages. Some educators have rationalized that, since the learning abilities of educable retardates are so limited, it is not in the best interests of either the teachers or the pupils to expect them to acquire appreciable knowledge. Such an escape is not tenable. It may be that pupil attitudes and motivation may be greater detriments to school learning than intellectual incapability.

Most of the learning studies have compared much older retardates with much younger normal subjects, so that the mental ages of the two groups were equated. But when left in the regular grades, the retarded are forced to compete with brighter peers who are only a year or two younger than they are, even when they are retained in the same grade once or twice. Studies would probably demonstrate that compared with average pupils of approximately the same age, the retarded would have much greater difficulty in learning, retaining, and transferring. Ellis (1963) postulates a "stimulus trace theory" for the retarded in which he contends that, on learning trials, this trace decays faster for the retarded than for the normal of the same age since they have central nervous system dysfunctions possibly of a biochemical nature. Thus, they have poorer short-term memory than the average. However, once they have thoroughly learned, they may retain as well as the average even on a long-term basis. Thus, the problem may not be one of rapid forgetting as suggested by the "leaky bucket" theory but one of difficulty in original learning and in not providing for over-learning. Some empirical studies have supported the Ellis Theory, especially one by Vergason (1962) who demonstrated that even after 30 days the retarded retained verbal materials as well as normals when there was extensive, original overlearning. The implication for teachers of the retarded is clear. They must select tasks which are brief enough and easy enough for the retarded to learn, for instance to repeat from memory as in a sight vocabulary list. Then there must be much overlearning (successfully repeated trials) immediately. Under such carefully controlled conditions, the retarded may retain as much simple, rote learning material which does not involve intellectual manipulation as normals of the same age.

## SPEECH AND LANGUAGE DEVELOPMENT

Language sets mankind above all other forms of life. It is the key to human communication and a major tool to human thought. Language involves reception (decoding), association (integration), and expression (encoding). Receptive language includes listening and reading abilities, while expressive language includes speaking and writing abilities. Thus, we speak of oral and written language. The integrator for the individual is the brain where the association and generation of ideas take place. It is not surprising that a close relationship exists between language and intellectual development. In fact, since the original Binet scale was published, size and complexity of vocabulary has been recognized as one of the best single measures of verbal intelligence. Another way of expressing this is to point out that research has demonstrated that the greater the extent of mental retardation, the greater the degree of language disability. Thus, the dependent retarded seldom develops sufficient speech and language to communicate orally in even simple sentences; some never attach meaning to even one word they hear, while others understand a few simple commands and still others have a minimal speaking vocabulary usually of a few simple words. By adulthood, the trainable retarded have reasonably good skills in simple oral communication, but do not become literate. The educable retarded develop quite adequate skills in oral communication for ordinary conversation, and develop reading and writing skills at maturity in the grade three to five range. Language age closely parallels mental age.

In recent years, oral communication of the educable mentally retarded has received increased attention (Smith, 1962a). Estimates of the prevalence of articulation and other speech problems among the educable range from 8 to 37 percent. The extent of delayed language among the retarded is even greater. Lack of a rich vocabulary, lack of ability to associate ideas, and lack of skill in verbal expression are more serious problems than difficulty in making the various speech sounds.

There have been a number of studies of the effectiveness of speech therapy programs for the retarded provided by speech therapists. The results have been generally positive. For example, Lassers and Low (1960) compared a conventional speech therapy approach where the emphasis was on the production of sounds with a communication-centered approach where the emphasis was on the socially meaningful production of responses containing the troublesome sounds. The latter approach was found more effective in correcting misarticulated speech sounds, but neither program improved the general language ability significantly. There is little evidence to support those speech correctionists who say educable retardates cannot profit from speech therapy in terms of improving articulation.

While the speech therapist has an important role to play in helping the retarded correct their speech, the teacher has an even more important one. He must provide a pervasive language development program as a major part of his curriculum. This must go far beyond the development and correction of speech sounds. A new test, the Illinois Test of Psycholinguistic Abilities (Kirk and McCarthy, 1961), provides a profile of nine aspects of decoding, association, and encoding abilities upon which the teacher can build a comprehensive language program. Such a program should be built on a three-pronged approach. First, there should be a highly stimulating and enriching set of experiences for these pupils who have been so often underprivileged. Both auditory and visual stimulation is needed. They must be taught to attend (pay attention) for increasing periods of time and to differentiate appropriate cues. In particular, their hearing vocabulary needs to be extended. Second, systematic attention must be given to the association processes. Exercises include responding to commands, solving verbal problems, organizing thoughts so as to be able to tell a story, and experiences in critical and creative thinking, elemental as this may be. They need special help in analyzing information and questioning it wisely. Third, and very important, are exercises in verbal expression and productivity. A common fault of teachers of older pupils especially is not giving them sufficient opportunity and instruction in talking coherently, logically and clearly.

Smith (1962b) performed an experimental study in which he provided a group language instruction program to small groups of educable retardates. With just 45 minutes of instruction, three times weekly, for three months, he was able to produce a significant increase in language age (LA) over control groups. His detailed lesson plans in the Peabody Research Monograph (Smith, 1962c) should be of major help to teachers who need to give more emphasis to psycholinguistics in their teaching.

The reader will get other suggestions on language development from the additional references in Hull's chapter on the speech impaired, these include Cypreansen, Wiley and Laase (1959), Scott and Thompson (1951), and Van Riper and Butler (1955). Further guidance will be gleaned from the section on language development in Wooden's chapter on the hearing impaired.

## Postschool Adjustment

### FOLLOW-UP STUDIES

What happens to adults who were labeled educable mentally retarded while in school? Numerous follow-up studies have been done on such persons to measure their social and vocational adjustment. Only a few of these can be discussed here. Those wishing a more thorough review of the literature should consult Carriker (1957),

Clarke and Clarke (1958), Goldstein in Heber and Stevens (1963), and Reynolds and Stunkard (1960).

Most studies of graduates from special classes for the educable mentally retarded show that the majority of both males and females make successful social adjustments in the community. They tend to marry mates who have higher ability than themselves and to have offspring which are more average in intelligence. For example, Charles (1953) found that 80 percent of his retarded group were married. They had an average of 2.03 children whose average IQ was 95. Charles also found that 40 percent of his group had a record of some kind of law violation, while Kennedy (1948) found that 66.3 percent of her retarded group as compared with 44.8 percent of her normal controls of comparable socioeconomic status had court records. It will be seen that studies indicate a rather higher rate of arrests of the retarded than of normals but that most of the crimes are of a minor or misdemeanor nature. Thus, the alarm of the early 1900s concerning the high criminality rate of the retardate has not been supported.

In terms of vocational adjustment, most studies show that approximately 75–85 percent of the educable mentally retarded who attended special classes have been finding competitive employment in unskilled, semi-skilled, and service fields, during eras of prosperity. Only in rare instances could employment be classified as skilled labor. Among the most important traits for holding jobs were: courtesy, trustworthiness, punctuality, personal appearance, good health, physical fitness, good naturedness, ability to take advice, deftness in handling materials, work of acceptable quality, and willingness to do a full day's work. These good interpersonal relations and work habits appear to be more important than degree of intelligence when the spread of intelligence is not large. Krishef and Hall (1955) found no difference in the amount of income earned by individuals of IQ 50–59 and of individuals of IQ 60–79. However, Collmann and Newlyn (1957) found that as the IQ level increased, so did the proportion of workers in skilled positions, but this investigation was conducted on subjects who ranged from educable mentally retarded, to slow learners, to the average in intellect. Much more research is needed relating IQ and educational preparation, to job level.

Porter and Milazzo (1958) compared educable mentally retarded graduates from regular and special classes. Over-all, the special class group were better adjusted. A greater percentage were gainfully employed, fewer had gotten into trouble with the law, and employer interviews revealed they were doing well. Carriker (1957) conducted a similar study with the special class graduates being less well, or no better adjusted than the regular class group.

Two recent studies are not as encouraging as the earlier research. Lee, Hegge, Voelker (1959) followed up graduates from Detroit special classes and from the Wayne County Training School. Only 61 percent of the special class and 28 percent of the residential training school graduates had achieved even minimal social and economic adequacy in young adulthood. A considerable percentage failed to abide by the laws; a large proportion of the girls were sexually delinquent. Peterson and Smith (1960) compared 45 retardates who had graduated from special classes in Iowa City with 45 subjects of normal intelligence coming from similar socioeconomic backgrounds. They found that the retarded had substantially more problems with social and economic adjustment in adulthood than their more normal peers. The differential between these recent studies and earlier ones may be due to a number of factors, not the least being the increasingly complex society in which we live, technological advances in industry including automation, and the population explosion, which make it more difficult for the retarded to find competitive employment. However, the rather dismal picture may also be explained by the fact that these studies were conducted during a period of "mild depression." Over the years it has been recognized that the educable retardate is hard hit during poor economic times but tends to find a job again under improved economic conditions.

The following points should be made: (1) research bears out the fact that approximately 80 percent of the educable mentally retarded are able to become self-supporting, contributing members of society; (2) they tend to marry higher IQ spouses and give birth to almost normal children; (3) retardates do particularly well during times of high employment and national emergencies and have difficulties during times of depression; (4) crime records are slightly higher than for persons of higher IQ, but offenses are of a minor nature; (5) most commonly held jobs include food preparation and service, laundry and cleaning, janitorial service, factory production, housekeeping and other forms of personal service; and (6) the increasingly complex society has made it more difficult for the unskilled, less intelligent youth to find employment.

## THE FUTURE

What about the future? Fraenkel (1961) has reasoned that the retarded will be helped by automation. He points out that retarded persons have found their greatest employment opportunities in the service occupations. Automation actually brings about a growth of these since it brings more leisure for all by reducing the work week. Persons with leisure demand more services since they take more vacations, eat more meals in restaurants, and so on. To satisfy these demands, more and more people will be needed in the service occupations, including, Fraenkel anticipates, more and more of the retarded. Others argue that the job future for unskilled youth and adults, including the retarded, will worsen. Jobs generally will be harder to find because of the rapid increase in the labor force. In fact, it is easier for youth of average or better intelligence to get into college than find employment. There has been a gradual upward trend to the more highly skilled occupations. Thus, there has been a steady increase in the degree of intelligence and education required for successive generations of American workers. All of this, combined with the restrictions placed on workers by trade unions, and the increased competition for unskilled and service jobs created by semiretired persons and by normally intelligent adolescents who drop out of school, suggests that the job future for the retarded is not good.

A major question is what the schools can do to provide an impressive record for the future. Will a heavy emphasis on academic subjects in the special classes provide the best preparation for adult living? Should retarded pupils be given specific training for a specific job? In the past, schools have attempted to provide general training in good work habits and interpersonal relations rather than to teach the retarded a trade, since they have found that the retarded rarely work at the specific skills in which they have been trained. The role of the school in vocational preparation of the retarded is discussed later in the chapter.

## School Goals

Educational authorities in mental retardation agree that the broad goal for the educable retarded is to develop independent living skills. Thus, in terms of this broad objective, the aim of education for the retarded is the same as for average children. Most individuals in both groups will marry, raise families, and become independent through gainful, competitive employment in society. By contrast, the goals for trainable retarded are very different since most persons in this category will not live independently as adults. Therefore, teaching objectives for the trainable stress the development of minimal skills for living and working in sheltered environments.

The objective for the educable mentally retarded as developing independent living skills is too broad for curriculum planning. Textbooks in the field (Hudson, 1958; Ingram, 1960; Kirk and Johnson, 1951) and curriculum guides (Goldstein and Seigle, 1958; Thiel, 1960) have broken this down. Typical ingredients include: (1) oral and written communication, (2) interpersonal relations, (3) managing money, (4) measuring, (5) understanding nature, (6) understanding society, (7) earning a living, (8) housekeeping, (9) traveling, (10) using leisure time, (11) living safely, (12) healthful living, (13) developing personal adequacy, and (14) enjoying and appreciating beauty. Orr (1962) has identified seven major curriculum ingredients: (1) communicative arts, (2) practical arts, (3) domestic arts, (4) leisure arts, (5) natural sciences, (6) social sciences, and (7) computational sciences. Some have argued that even if we do profess a concern for the whole child, it does not make sense for the schools to be responsible for developing all of a child's needed skills. Such an argument would be true to a greater degree for average and above children who have a greater likelihood of having an adequate home and community. In the case of the educable retardate, so many of whom come from nonstimulating and non-wholesome environments, the schools must assume some responsibility for areas often left largely to the home, such as personal grooming. Otherwise the chances of the pupils' becoming independent adults are minimized. Some of the specific objectives listed above should be considered in this light.

Additional insight into these more specific teaching objectives may result from grouping and discussing them under four headings: family, social and civic skills; good work habits and skills; essential academic skills; and personal adjustment.

## FAMILY, SOCIAL, AND CIVIC SKILLS

A very important objective of the school program is the development of family, social and civic skills. A considerable proportion, though less than one half of the pupils in the special classes are girls. Most of these will become housewives, and will bear and raise children. For them especially, but also for the males in the class, some of whom will remain bachelors, it is important that they learn in school the domestic arts of family living. Cooking, cleaning, mending, and purchasing should be highlighted. Since most of the retarded lose their identity as adults and since they are less likely than children of average intellect to gain knowledge in this area at home, it is important that they learn as much as they can about government and voting while in school. They should be taught both their rights and responsibilities as citizens and as much about the social order as is possible. Generally, the emphasis should be on the local scene followed by state and national responsibilities. It is doubtful if many educable pupils will have interests or abilities in understanding world-wide international problems.

## GOOD WORK HABITS AND SKILLS

Above all, it is important that pupils develop good work habits and skills so they may be competitively employed in adulthood. The teacher of the retarded can do much to foster good work habits. First, the teacher's classroom management for many of the school activities should emphasize independent work. The teacher should set his standards for the pupils especially high in this regard. This probably deserves greater attention than the teaching of the 3 R's which traditionally has occupied a large proportion of the curriculum. Second, the practical arts can be important in developing good work habits and skills. However, arts and crafts should not be an end in themselves but a means of developing vocational, social, and personal adjustment. It is too late to wait until pupils enter vocational training or study-work programs in their youth before concentrating on the development of good, independent work habits.

## ESSENTIAL ACADEMIC SKILLS

The educable mentally retarded need to develop optimal skills in the essential academic areas. As mentioned before, the educable retardate has the capacity to achieve between the grade three to seven levels. Most of those with IQ's of 60 and above have the potential to be literate adults since grade four achievement is a realistic, ultimate goal for such pupils. The communicative arts are a major curriculum ingredient. The preacademic period (CA = 6, 7, and often 8) should concentrate on the development of skills needed in informal social intercourse (listening, speaking, understanding others, and being understood by others) and essential readiness skills which must be established before moving to the more formal communicative arts. Special attention needs to be given to providing an enriched experiential background for children from nonstimulating environments. After pupils develop adequate mental ability (thought by many to be a minimum mental age of 6½ years), the emphasis should shift to systematic instruction in reading, spelling, and writing. The computational sciences should stress practical arithmetic needed for everyday living. The central focus should be on the concrete problems of handling money, telling time, and common measurements. The natural sciences should emphasize everyday phenomenon in the physical and biological world about them. Special attention should be given to understanding useful facts such as those about plant and animal life, weather, and electricity. The use and repair of labor-saving devices around the home should be emphasized. The teacher must concentrate on the essentials which the retardate will require for community living in youth and adulthood. Studying people in other lands, foreign language, more complex mathematics of even the upper elementary grades, and other academic skills so essential for students going on to college are beyond the interests, capabilities, and needs of the retarded. In general, the practical academic learning should be concentrated into the late preadolescent and adolescent years of the pupils.

## PERSONAL ADJUSTMENT

Basic to effective living is personal adjustment. Since society places such high value on intellectual prowess, and since the retarded are teased more than their fellows and lack in social sophistication, it is understandable that they need special help from the schools in accepting and understanding themselves, in winning the approval and acceptance of others, and in building their personal securities and competencies. Above all, since the retarded are easily swayed into antisocial acts by others, emphasis should be placed on developing character. The retarded have special difficulty in abstractions, and certainly right and wrong is a most complex abstraction. Thus, rules and patterns of daily living must be stressed by the teacher. Closely tied together then is the need to develop in the retarded a feeling of human worth and dignity, a set of socially accepted behavior patterns, and a plan for leading a full and worthwhile life commensurate with their limited abilities. Both because it will help them develop a feeling of worth and because of the increased time free from work which they are likely to have in the future, it is important that the retarded be taught the leisure arts as an integral part of the curriculum. The retarded need to develop hobbies and the habit of participating in community esthetic functions. Too, they need to learn the joy of serving on community projects for the welfare of others. These leisure arts are not likely to develop unless they are specifically and systematically taught.

## Administrative Provisions

The large majority of educable mentally retarded receiving special services are enrolled in special day classes in the regular public schools. These classes are usually organized by levels according to a combination of the chronological and mental ages of the pupils (see Table 2.4). Pupils are not usually grouped by IQ, sex, etiology, or environmental background. These classes may be scattered around the school district with the majority in schools located in the lower socioeconomic areas of the community. In other cases, a group of special classes of various levels will be housed in centrally located, or regionally positioned schools. The primary and intermediate special classes are housed in regular elementary schools, and the secondary ones in regular junior and senior high schools. At the elementary school level these operate largely as self-contained

TABLE 2.4 *Scholastic characteristics and needs of educable mentally retarded pupils.*

| ADMINISTRATIVE GROUPINGS | CA'S (YEARS) | MA'S (YEARS) | GRADE CAPACITY | CURRICULUM EMPHASIS |
|---|---|---|---|---|
| Preschool | 4–6 | 2–3 | Nursery | Perceptual, conceptual, language and social development |
| Primary | 6–10 | 3–6½ | Kindergarten | (as above) |
| Intermediate | 10–13 | 6–9 | 1–4 | Basic skill subjects and work habits |
| Secondary | 13–18 | 8–12 | 2–7 | Life adjustment and study-work programs |
| Postschool | 16 and on | 8–12 | 3–7 | Social and vocational adjustment |

special classes. At the high school levels the pupils often participate in the departmental programs offered by home economics and shop. Special teachers of music, art and physical education are often available to the pupils.

## PRESCHOOL SPECIAL CLASS PROGRAMS

In the past there have been few preschool programs for the educable mentally retarded. In a large measure such pupils have not been recognized as such until the grade one teacher begins to work with them. However, recent research by Kirk (1958) suggests that certain educable children need to be placed in a special preschool program at as early an age as possible. In a longitudinal study, Kirk provided enriching preschool programs for community and residential school groups of educable mentally retarded children. At the same time, he identified contrast groups that remained at home and on the wards of the residential units. Some children were even placed in foster homes to determine the effects of this variable. After one to three years of this very enriching preschool program for the experimental subjects, the various groups were followed up into the regular grades and special classes. The general conclusion reached was that preschool education is desirable for retardates who live in conditions of extreme cultural deprivation, whereas the age of six is not too late to begin formal schooling for pupils who dwell in more adequate environments. The implications and challenges of this study are obvious. So many of the educable group come from low socioeconomic environments. Yet these pupils with the greatest need for preschool education live in areas in large cities where kindergartens are lacking in quality and quantity. So often new schools for children under six with vast playgrounds and modern equipment are located in the wealthier suburbs where they are needed least. This pattern needs to be rectified (Conant, 1961). Furthermore, foster homes should be considered for those children who come from extremely disintegrated homes. It is our responsibility as educators to find ways of overcoming the deprivation of so many retarded children before it is too late.

Much of the curriculum of the regular nursery and kindergarten is applicable to the educable mentally retarded. Activities in the following areas are important: social living, oral communication, and self-help skills. These need to be supplemented by the readiness activities outlined by Kephart (1960). Sensory-motor training should stress work in the areas of gross motor movements, eye-hand coordination, posture, laterality, and directionality. Training in the perceptual processes should focus on visual and auditory memory, scanning, binocular and monocular training, copying figures, and training in form perception and discrimination. Much of this can be done through games and other activities which are highly interesting to young children.

## PRIMARY SPECIAL CLASS PROGRAMS

Children in primary special classes have chronological ages of 6 to 10 years, and develop mentally to the ages from 3 to 6½ years. Generally the chief criterion for moving a child from the primary to the intermediate group is not his chronological age but the fact that he has developed a mental age of 6 or 6½. Of course, other factors such as personality development and physical growth must also be considered. At that time, he has a reasonable chance of profiting from formal instruction in the skill subjects. Prior to that time the curriculum should be a continuation of that just outlined for the preschool level, emphasizing self-care, social skills, and sensory-motor readiness experiences. In social adjustment, heavy emphasis needs to be placed on oral language especially on enlarging the speaking vocabulary of the retarded. There is a need to stress not only clarity in enunciation and correctness in pronunciation but also ability in structuring one's ideas clearly and in listening attentively so as to understand the spoken word.

Stress needs to be placed on self-care and habit training, particularly personal cleanliness, neatness, care of personal property, and safety. Sharing, playing together and conforming to accepted social standards of behavior are important. In terms of readiness, the teacher should emphasize broadening of the experiential backgrounds of the pupils, lengthening their attention span, and developing good independent work habits. Too, improvement in motor coordination should be stressed. There is also a place for sense training which should center on such activities as matching colors, recognizing objects, and discriminating with the various senses. Rhythm exercises, arm movements, coloring, hammering, caring for household articles, cutting paper, and looking after pets are other types of activities which often make up the primary curriculum. A beginning at learning to count and recognizing a few letters and words may have a place, though this should not be a major focus in the primary group. The biggest single error made by teachers at this level is in pushing the academics before the retarded are ready for them.

## INTERMEDIATE SPECIAL CLASS PROGRAMS

Children in the intermediate special classes usually range in age from about 10 to 13 years chronologically and have mental ages from about 6 to 9 years. They are now ready for more formal instruction in the basic skill subjects. These should be taught only as growth in intellectual capacity permits and not to the neglect of social development. The intermediate curriculum is much more structured than the primary one. Learning tool subjects essential to everyday living requires systematic individualized instruction. The biggest single error made by teachers at this level is in stressing total and small group instruction to the neglect of individual tutoring and self-study under close supervision. A balanced program should make possible individual instruction without neglecting group instruction. It is usually possible for most retarded children to acquire academic skills at about the grade three to four level before leaving the intermediate group, though some will be fortunate to be working at the upper grade one or beginning grade two level when they reach adolescence. The chief criterion for moving a pupil from the intermediate group to the secondary group is the reaching of adolescence rather than in terms of academics.

## SECONDARY SPECIAL CLASS PROGRAMS

Adolescents in secondary special classes range in age from 13 to 18 years and have mental ages ranging from about 8 to 12 years. The central focus here is on life adjustment and occupational education. The curriculum is by now broadened to include practical reading and arithmetic, science, social studies, household arts, and even a little of the fine arts. Adolescents, since their mental ages keep on increasing, should continue to be taught additional basic skill subjects. Arithmetic should stress handling money; figuring out wages; opening bank accounts; borrowing and paying back money; paying rent, taxes, and debts; and other practical tasks with which the retarded will be confronted in later life. These would include problems involving time, timetables, and road maps. By now, reading and writing skills should be sufficient for the retarded to begin reading a newspaper and other simple materials for information and pleasure. He should gain practice in filling out application forms for employment, reading instructions, studying want ads, and applying in writing for jobs. Oral communication in business and social settings must continue to be stressed. Special emphasis needs to be placed on social development. The boys and girls need help in feeling comfortable with the opposite sex.

Preparation for work is a major aspect of the secondary school's curriculum for mentally retarded youth. At the junior high school level, while the pupils are 13–15 years of age, the general pattern is to provide in-school work experiences. A pupil may be assigned for one or more periods a day to janitorial, cafeteria, shop, office, or other duties. He should be shifted every two or three months to a different work situation to evaluate his interest in, and competence at, the various work experiences. Both the person in charge of the program and the special class teacher need to observe and evaluate the trainee. Personal guidance and support are important ingredients in a successful in-school work program.

At the senior high school level, part-time placement in community work experiences are becoming standard practice (Syden, 1962). The Federal Wage and Hour Division of the U.S. Department of Labor has been most cooperative in many communities in allowing many schools to offer study-work programs for the retardate who is under 16 years of age. In some systems, the employer is paid by the school district to serve as a trainer. These *study-work programs,* which involve pupils working part-time and attending school part-time, take a number of forms. Pupils may attend school in the morning and engage in out-of-school work experiences in the afternoon. Another variation is for a trainee to alternate with another one in two or three weeks of full-time community work, alternated with the same amount of full-time school attendance. In some programs the special class teacher functions as a teacher, a placement officer, and a counselor. In fact, he may be known as a teacher-counselor. In other school systems, special counselors as well as special teachers are employed. As soon as the retarded youth reaches 16 years of age he is eligible for on-the-job training and other services from the State Vocational Rehabilitation Agency, which is improving its services for the retarded. The vocational counselor usually desires to begin preplanning when the educable retarded reach 14 years of age. In many school districts, when the educable mentally retarded pupil is able to hold a full-time job, he is encouraged to do so and excused from school—if he has reached the legal school-leaving age.

In the past, educators have stressed the development of good work habits and attitudes rather than the teaching of specific trades. This approach is understandable if one takes the position that the retarded will move from casual job to casual job where few specific skills are needed. However, there is some evidence that this approach is not necessarily the best one. In certain communities there are specific jobs for which the retarded can be trained for proficiency. These may be on assembly lines, in the hotel trades, or in the food industry—to mention only three. With changes in the labor field and with more vocational counselors available to assist the retarded in the transition from school to work, preparation for specific employment may become the pattern. The future for the retarded will probably rest with his being especially prepared for one specific job. Some, if not much, of this could be done by study-work and full-time, on-the-job training.

Another procedure would be to provide specific job preparation in school. Conceivably, secondary special class programs of the future may be in-school employment centered. Here the core would take the form of producing materials for sale such as the Junior Achievement Clubs now do on an out-of-school club basis. The other social and academic learnings would grow out of this central focus. This is not a new concept. Duncan (1943) initiated such a program in England years ago for retarded pupils whose practical intelligence was higher than their verbal intelligence.

Finally, even with improved vocational preparation, it may be necessary in the future for the schools or some other agency to provide *terminal* sheltered workshops similar to those now available to the trainable. An intermediate step would be *transitional* sheltered workshops for job training. It may even be necessary by Federal government action to reserve certain jobs for the retarded or give them preferential treatment if they are to be afforded the right and dignity of gainful employment in the age of automation and population explosion.

## POSTSCHOOL PROGRAM

Even after retarded young people obtain full-time jobs in the community, their need for school services does not completely cease. A new frontier in the education of the mentally retarded is the provision of such postschool services (DiMichael, 1949; Dinger, 1961, Mackie et al., 1959). In a large measure these take the form of night school in which the graduates participate once or twice a week. Major emphasis is placed on personal and vocational counseling. However, individual tutoring also has a place. Thus, if the schools continue to keep their doors open to him, the retarded adolescent or adult has a haven, a pillar of strength, and a source of information in his time of need and stress. Such follow-up school programs would seem to be professionally, economically, and ethically sound. The Lansing (Michigan) Public Schools (Mackie et al., 1959) require graduates of special classes to be employed full-time for three years in the community and to attend night school two hours a week during this period of time before they are granted a high school diploma. Beekman, who is in charge of the Lansing High and Post School program, in a personal communication, has reported that none of the graduates of that program have become delinquent. In light of the Lansing finding, it is important to recall the high prevalence of delinquency in the Detroit study (Lee et al., 1959). This differential may be attributed to the well-executed, postschool program provided by the Lansing Public Schools.

## OTHER ADMINISTRATIVE PLANS

As already pointed out, nearly all educable retarded children who receive special services do so in special day classes which are divided into primary, intermediate, and secondary levels. However, in some smaller school systems, especially in rural areas, only one special class is operated. In such cases, pupils over the full age range of six through sixteen or more years may attend.

In a few large cities, special day schools are operated for educable pupils. In both special schools and special classes the trend has been to have the groups co-educational in nature. However, there are a few special schools whose main emphasis is on learning a trade, where the sexes are served separately. Under this plan, special attention needs to be given to the social adjustment of the adolescent as he relates to the opposite sex.

Some other types of organization are available. For example, while our residential facilities for the retarded primarily serve the dependent and trainable persons, some educable children and youth are enrolled in special education programs in such facilities. Table 1.2 and Fig. 1.3 in chapter 1 showed the distribution. For each educable child enrolled in a residential school there were 20 enrolled in special schools and classes operated by local school districts.

In one state, Georgia, an experiment with itinerant teacher service for the educable mentally retarded was conducted by Ainsworth and others (1959). Under this plan retarded pupils remained in the regular grades. An especially trained itinerant teacher of the retarded was available to tutor him individually two or three times a week and to serve as a consultant to the regular classroom teacher. The investigators found that children in this itinerant plan made no more, and no less, progress academically than a group of special class pupils or a control group of retarded children who received only regular classroom instruction. Thus, the efficacy of this itinerant plan for the retarded has yet to be demonstrated.

Wrightstone and others (1959) studied the values of dividing educable pupils in New York City into two subgroups called the adaptive and the nonadaptive. This has become known as the two-track plan. The adaptive had a better prognosis for independent adult living and usually had IQ's in the 65–80 range. The nonadaptive pupils were less likely to be completely independent in adulthood, and had IQ's generally in the 50–65 range. Much greater emphasis was placed on community adjustment skills for the adaptive group, while a heavy emphasis on social adjustment in a more sheltered environment was given the nonadaptive group. The study did not demonstrate that this plan is superior to the traditional special class approach. However, this project is still continuing and its merits may well be shown as improved instrumentation becomes available and after the pupils have had a longer period of time to profit from the arrangement.

Thiel, of Florida State University, is experimenting with still another plan. Retarded pupils and those with other disabilities are enrolled in the regular grades. A resource room is available in the school under the direction of a teacher prepared to instruct children with varying exceptionalities. The children with problems then come to the resource room singly and in groups for special instruction. The efficacy of this plan has not yet been demonstrated. However, its virtues in a nonurban community are obvious.

The Soviet Union and some other European countries do not believe that either regular or special *day* schools or classes can provide the intensive instruction needed by the educable retardate. They provide special-purpose boarding schools for 100–200 pupils on a 5½ day week. Here the children receive an around-the-clock regimen with day teachers stressing academic and vocational learnings, and another set of teachers working on social learnings after school hours. Residential camps are provided these educable children during summer months. It seems desirable that the United States and Canada experiment with such *boarding schools* and *summer camps* for educable mentally retarded pupils who come from inadequate homes and communities. (Dunn and Kirk, 1963).

## Curricular Approaches

Three approaches to curriculum have dominated special education services for the educable mentally retarded. These have been oriented to (1) arts and crafts, (2) subject matter, and (3) the unit method.

Only vestiges remain of the extreme emphasis which used to be placed on arts and crafts. Frequently in the past, and occasionally today, retarded pupils were found spending nearly all of their time at weaving looms, doing lathe work, modeling with clay, or engaged at carpentry. This approach was especially popular at the turn of the century when special classes were first begun. However, educators soon found that the retarded were below average not only scholastically but in motor skills as well. Furthermore, recognition grew that the educable needed to learn much besides how to weave a rug or build a night table so as to be effective citizens in adulthood. Today, when arts and crafts are found in the well-rounded curriculum, they are designed to foster good work habits and leisure-time interests. The shift has been toward the domestic and practical arts which are so necessary for effective daily living.

Today, the subject-matter oriented curriculum frequently dominates many special class programs. This extreme preoccupation with the three R's is a result of the background of the special class teachers. They began as regular classroom teachers where high value was placed on scholarship, and brought to the special classes this same set of values. It is not uncommon to find such teachers of the retarded emphasizing intricate fractions and long division to the neglect of other more practical arithmetic skills involved in the handling of money. They may teach their retarded pupils world geography when they have not learned the procedure for voting. An extreme academic approach usually neglects the development of personal and social skills necessary for adult adjustment.

In contrast to the traditional subject matter curriculum, some teachers use a unit or core approach almost exclusively. Martens (1950) has devised a popular curriculum guide for the mentally retarded which stresses the unit of experience. She has recommended half of the school day for teaching academic and manual skills, and the other half for the unit. Ingram (1960, p. 202), a leading advocate of the unit method, but not its exclusive use, has listed the following values for this approach:

... (1) it brings real purpose into much of the child's work and play; (2) it enables him to experience things first-hand—to have sensory experiences; contacts with realities; (3) it gives meaning and interest to the commonplace in his environment; (4) it enables him to plan, execute, and judge in a simple way at the level of his stage of maturity; (5) it teaches him how to do things and how to conduct himself in actual situations so that behavior is integrated.

There are many variations to this activity method approach. Included are the short-term project, the long-term center-of-interest units, and the core curriculum which integrates most, if not all, of the course of study. The occupational education approach developed by the New York group (Hungerford et al., 1950), which emphasizes cores of interest, may be viewed as a special example of the latter. This curriculum is programmed into eight cores, one for each year level from eight through sixteen and extending outward from the home, to the neighborhood, to the city, to job areas, and finally to life as a good citizen and worker. The unit-type curriculum has the central advantage of stimulating interest in school work. It can provide for a more realistic and meaningful school program, and, it places an emphasis on learning social skills.

The unit approach does have certain potential disadvantages. Much time may be wasted on unnecessary activities. It is difficult to provide for individual differences. The emphasis may be on social skills and social studies to the neglect of tool subjects and individual work habits. Balance is difficult to attain. However, one of the strongest arguments supporting the core approach is based on the follow-up studies of the retarded reported earlier in the chapter.

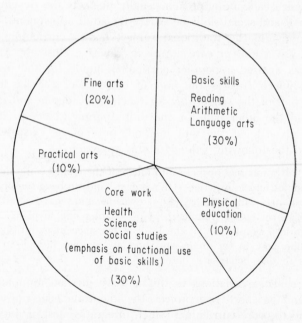

FIG. 2.4  Distribution of time in an intermediate special class program for the educable mentally retarded. (From Erdman, R. L., *Educable retarded children in elementary schools*. Washington, D.C.: Council for Except. Child., 1961.)

They showed the prime reasons for failure on the job were due to poor interpersonal relations and work habits, and not to poor academic achievement. The implications for curriculum are obvious. Emphasis should be placed on person-social development and good work habits. The core or unit approach is one of the most effective means for developing such skills in the social milieu of the school and classroom.

In actual fact, a well-balanced curriculum is built upon a varied approach, with the unit receiving about 30–50 percent of the time. There is a place for arts and crafts, academic instruction, as well as units of work. Erdman (1961) has suggested a time distribution for the intermediate level which allows for these three approaches and ingredients as well as others. He has assigned 30 percent of the time to both basic skills and core work. He suggests 20 percent of the time for fine arts, and 10 percent each for practical arts and physical education. This is shown in Fig. 2.4

# Teaching
## the Strauss-type Child

Lehtinen has outlined the teaching procedures recommended by her and Strauss for pupils with the Strauss-syndrome described earlier in the chapter (Strauss and Lehtinen, 1947). These include the following guidelines: (1) A nondistracting school environment should be provided. Translucent rather than transparent window panes should be used. The dress of the teacher should be plain and free from ornaments. The class should be located on the top floor and made free from distracting stimuli. Cubicles and screens should be utilized to reduce distractions. (2) Instruction should be individualized. The class group should be small with twelve children as a maximum. For individual work, pupils should be removed to the periphery of the group, faced toward a wall, or screened off from the rest by the cubicles. (3) An elemental rather than a global approach to teaching should be utilized. The teaching of reading should begin with the learning of individual letters. Later, these should be assembled into words. Finally, the words should be used in sentences, paragraphs, and stories. The basic textbook and workbooks in common use in the grades today have no place in the program. (4) Emphasis should be placed on the use of colored letters, words and numbers, as well as other concrete cues. (5) Motor activities should be involved in academic learning. Thus, heavy emphasis is on concrete manipulative materials reduced to their essentials. (6) Strong emphasis is placed on the basic tool subjects. Instruction in social studies, geography, and science is incidental. (7) No use is made of the project or unit method in the classroom, such as the post office, store or bank. (8) Social activities, group learning, oral language are de-emphasized. (9) Cursive rather than manuscript writing should be used. (10) Concepts are taught with concrete objects. This is but a brief glimpse at the Lehtinen methods. While most educators will find part one of Strauss and Lehtinen's text heavy going, they should enjoy reading part two which deals solely with educational methodology.

What has research shown us about the effectiveness of the Lehtinen techniques? First, it must be pointed out that their utility with the Strauss-type child has been investigated very little to date. In fact, most researchers have become preoccupied with the term "brain injury" and have selected their experimental groups because they were neurologically impaired rather than because they had behavior characteristics of children with the Strauss-syndrome. One of the first studies was done by Capobianco (Dunn and Capobianco, 1956) in which he compared the arithmetic processes of cultural-familial and neurologically impaired subjects, some of which may have displayed the Strauss-syndrome. He found no differences in computation, reasoning, achievement, reversals, and understandings of the concept of zero. Capobianco and Miller (1958) analyzed the reading process of cultural-familial and neurologically impaired subjects, finding little or no difference between the two groups in their reading achievement or in their patterns of reading errors.

Gallagher (1960) conducted a three-year experiment on tutoring children of seven to nine years of age with neurological impairments in a residential school setting using a non-Strauss type approach. Each pupil was given one hour a day of individualized tutoring based upon that individual's own pattern of intellectual strengths and weaknesses focused on a crash program of perceptual, conceptual, and language development. As compared to a control group, his experimental subjects improved in intellectual development, increased in attention span, and achieved more in verbal than in nonverbal skills. He concluded:

It is quite likely that history will also record that we have been entirely too pessimistic about the possible training potential of the brain injured, and that this pessimism has prevented us from giving them the intellectual and educational stimulation that we would wish for all of our children (p. 168).

Yet he found it was not necessary to use the Strauss-Lehtinen techniques to achieve moderately good results with the neurologically impaired. In a follow-up of his subjects to determine the effects of removal of the special tutoring for one to two years, Gallagher (1962) argued that early training can modify verbal development permanently, unless the gains are suppressed by the unstimulating environment of a residential facility, as was the case with his subjects. He pleaded for an intensive, individualized approach to build conceptualization among young neurologically impaired pupils rather than almost exclusive devotion or attention to the development of social skills, as has often been the case.

Cruickshank and others (1961) conducted a two-year demonstration study project with 40 subjects, half of whom were diagnosed as brain injured and half as emotionally disturbed. The brain injured were not only identified by neurological tests but were hyperactive-aggressive as well. A nonstimulating classroom environment was used with at least the experimental groups. The investigators concluded that "while still further evidence needs to be obtained, it is the opinion of the authors that hyperactive children in a nonstimulating environment and structured program demonstrated sufficient progress to warrant continuation of this approach with such children" (p. 421). Here is the first study presented so far which provides some evidence to support the use of the Lehtinen procedures with the Strauss-type child, though it is difficult to see how their statistical results justify their conclusion. Perhaps the authors were relying on clinical judgment.

Vance (1956) provided similar daily, highly structured, educational programs in reading readiness over an eight-month period with matched groups of non–brain-injured and neurologically impaired children in a residential school. She found no significant difference between the groups at any time on reading and reading readiness tests, indicating both groups learn equally well under the treatment she provided.

Frey (1960) conducted a study which tested the Lehtinen teaching techniques with Strauss-type children. He selected a group of 20 neurologically impaired children who, on psychological tests, also exhibited perceptual disorders, and who had been under a special instructional program utilizing Lehtinen techniques. These were compared with twenty non–brain-injured retarded children of similar ages and intellect who had been attending conventional programs in regular and special classes. In his survey of the reading behavior of these two groups, Frey found the Strauss-type group to be superior in silent reading tests and in sound-blending ability. Too, he found the Strauss-type children to have a normal profile of reading errors while the non–brain-injured group showed excessive errors in faulty vowels, faulty consonants, omissions of sounds and substitution of words. The Frey study is extremely important because it demonstrates that the Lehtinen techniques appear to work—at least in reading—for Strauss-type children. Whether these techniques will work equally well in other areas of instruction and with the cultural-familial retarded—and even with the intellectually normal—has yet to be demonstrated. However, until evidence is accumulated to the contrary, teachers will apparently be on safe grounds in experimenting with the use of Lehtinen techniques in teaching children who have the Strauss-syndrome. Too, school systems cannot be discouraged from experimenting with special classes for the Strauss-type pupil.

## Regular versus Special Class

## Placement

In the last twenty years a good deal of research has accumulated on this topic. A general conclusion would be that neither type of school placement has been universally satisfactory for the educable retardate. Changes in educational practices are indicated for the future. Let us examine this conclusion.

First of all, it is recognized that the vast preponderance of educable mentally retarded boys and girls still obtain all of their education in the regular grades and will continue to do so in the years ahead. Since they are lowest in intellectual capacity, they have the greatest difficulty in achieving academically. Yet academics, very understandably, are usually a central focus in the regular school program. While the retarded may be working up to or apparently even above their limited theoretical capacity in the academic subjects, they are still far behind their more intellectually endowed classmates. As they get older they get even further behind and the pressures increase even more. Finally, their choices are to withdraw from class discussion, to get attention and recognition through nonacademic channels, or to drop out of school at the earliest possible moment. The usual route is to resort to aggressive and other antisocial behavior until drop-out time. Here there is a sex differential, though there is much overlapping. Girls are generally more inclined to resign themselves to school failure while boys tend to resist it. Thus, more boys than girls get referred for special class placement. If they do remain in the regular grades, very few educable pupils stay in school beyond the compulsory school attendance years. Instead, they drop out at the earliest opportunity, usually ill-equipped for community living.

Two studies are significant in demonstrating what happens to the retarded when they remain in the regular grades where scholastic endeavor is highly stressed. The Peabody College Division of Surveys and Field Services (1961), in studying large numbers of pupils in a large local school system, compared pupil achievement with pupil capacity. It was discovered that the large middle section of children with IQ's of roughly 85–115 were working nearly up to mental age capacity. Brighter children with IQ's above 115 were generally achieving far below capacity. Children with IQ's of 85 and below were, as a group, achieving *above* theoretical capacity as measured by a Horne formula which involves both mental and chronological ages. Here is strong evidence that regular classroom teachers are inclined to devote a major portion of their time in attempting to bring the slow learner and the mentally retarded up to grade and age standards academically. In so doing, they probably neglect brighter children, put too much academic pressure on pupils of limited ability, and ignore the development of their social and vocational skills which will be so important for them in terms of succeeding in the work-a-day world. Thurstone's study (1959) in which she compared the relative effectiveness of special and regular class placement for the educable mentally retarded, provided tabular data which are useful in understanding what happens academically to the retarded when they remain in the regular grades. For the special class group, the ratio of actual achievement gains to expected gains based on mental age remained relatively low but constant over the full age range from 6 through 16 years. For the regular class group, the age group 6 through 10 gained 0.49 of a grade per year; the 11 through 13 year group slipped to 0.38 of a grade per year; and the 14 through 16 year old group dropped still further to 0.33 of a grade per year. These data suggest that retarded pupils who remain in the regular grades slip further and further behind until finally their gains in achievement are only about one third of expectancy. In the meantime, the brighter pupils have been neglected and the mental health of the teacher and the retarded pupils badly strained.

Special class placement for the educable mentally retarded child may be justified on four major counts: (1) to provide a more adequate curriculum which stresses the development of social and vocational skills as well as the acquisition of skills in the basic tool subjects, (2) to enable more individual instruction since the special class enrollments are usually only about one-half of that in the regular grades, (3) to remove the pressure on the retarded through reducing failure and providing a sound mental health approach, and (4) to enable the regular teacher to give more attention to average and bright students when the range of individual differences is reduced.

Let us now take a look at what has been happening to the educable mentally retarded when they are placed in special classes. For over forty years we have been comparing the school achievement of the retarded, especially in reading, with his mental capacity. By 1953, eleven studies had found the mentally retarded in special classes to be achieving below mental age expectancy, while only three investigations had found this group to work at or above expectancy (Dunn and Capobianco, 1956). In each of these latter cases increased attention had been given to the teaching of reading. Thus, it would appear that the retarded can be taught to achieve at least in reading up to mental age capacity when enrolled in special classes.

More recently, there has been a series of comparisons of mentally retarded pupils in regular and special classes. In these it has been found that retarded children in special classes compared unfavorably with the retarded in regular grades in school achievement (Blatt, 1958; Cassidy and Stanton, 1959; Elenbogen, 1957; Mullen and Itkin, 1961; Thurstone, 1959). The early investigations of the 1930s had the methodological weakness of selecting both special and regular class retardates from the same school system where most of those out of rapport with the school were placed in special classes. However, in studies of the 1950s and 1960s even with this factor partially controlled, the general findings remain the same. Retarded children who stayed in the regular grades did as well, or better, academically, than those in the special class. *Neither group worked up to mental age expectancy.* A brighter side to these studies was the indication that retarded pupils in the protective environment of special classes had better social and personal adjustment scores than those of comparable intellect who were competing in the regular grades (Blatt, 1958; Cassidy and Stanton, 1959; Elenbogen, 1957; Thurstone, 1959). The sociometric studies, with the exception of that done by Jordan (1960) reported earlier in the chapter, tend to support this finding.

Why is the picture not brighter on the academic effectiveness of the special classes? First, it must be pointed out that most school systems do not place the educable mentally retarded in special classes immediately upon enrolling in school. Instead, they wait until the retarded child has been in the regular grades two or three years, has experienced repeated failure in that setting, and is out of rapport with the school. This is an exceedingly important factor to consider. It is likely that two or three years of failure in the regular grades predisposes lack of success after special class placement. An important study by Goldstein, Jordon, and Moss (1962) is under way in which the effectiveness of special class programs is being studied. Pupils were identified as retarded at the outset of their school careers. The experimental group were placed immediately in special classes, while the control group remained in the regular grades. As was predicted, the control retardates in the regular grades made significantly greater gains during the first years in school achievement as contrasted with the experimental subjects in the special classes. The special class subjects were given a curriculum sequence which emphasized readiness for both social and academic learning during the first year, while the regular class subjects were given the typical grade one program which emphasized learning to read, count, and print. However, the special class group were expected to catch up and by-pass academically the retarded who were left in the regular grades as well as have a more rounded and appropriate total curriculum. It is interesting to note that both groups increased an average of seven IQ points during the first two years, again suggesting the educability of intellect, and refuting the constancy of the IQ concept. Finally, Tisdall (1962), in studying the productive thinking of these same Illinois children, showed an advantage for the experimental over the control portion of the sample. He concluded that the curriculum and environment of the special class enabled the experimental children to be more fluent in their speech, more original in their concepts, and more flexible in their thinking.

We have accumulated evidence which suggests that special class programs where pupils are not placed in them until they have failed in the regular grades for two or three years have not paid off. As a result the following six major changes in practices are suggested for day schools: (1) Educable retardates should be placed in special classes not later than their first year in school. (2) Retarded children from conditions of extreme cultural deprivation should be provided an enriching preschool program. (3) The IQ limits for special class placement of the educable pupils probably should be shifted upward from 50 to 75, to 60 to 80. (4) Increased individual instruction and self-teaching should be provided. (5) A balanced curriculum should be developed which stresses personal-social development, the acquisition of good work habits, as well as the learning of needed skills in the three R's for independent living. (6) Work-study programs should be extended for the adolescent and young adult.

# Guidelines for Teaching

Because of the need for brevity, it is necessary to over-generalize in these guidelines for low IQ pupils. Certainly it must be recognized that there are exceptions to every rule. These suggestions do not run counter to research. For some there is supportive evidence. For others the best that can be said is that there does not appear to be sufficient evidence to date to refute them.

1. Pre-academic experiences for the retarded should emphasize a program of perceptual, conceptual, and language development. The development of social skills should not occupy more than half of the time schedule.

2. After the child has developed a mental age of at least 6½ years, it is important to begin a balanced program for basic tool subjects, but not to the neglect of good work habits and social skills. It is not an either/or proposition. There is time in the school day to instruct each retarded pupil in the academics up to his scholastic capacity and yet find large blocks of time for developing good social, vocational, and personal adjustment skills.

3. Retarded pupils have usually experienced so much defeat and rejection in the regular grades that they have acquired negative attitudes toward themselves, teachers, school and society. Because of this, it is important to find ways to motivate such children to learn. Success on a particular task, by starting at such a low level that this is assured, is a particularly effective device. Praise and external rewards will also be effective with most pupils. Care must be taken to choose materials and activities of interest to the pupils.

4. Do not use traditional textbooks and workbooks. These are generally unsuitable for the retarded child. The illustrations are often too childish, and too middle and upper-class oriented. The interest levels are below these older boys and girls. There is not enough repetition and drill. The exercises are not broken down into small enough steps. Instead use teacher-made materials, and choose from the growing number of books of low-vocabulary–high-interest which can be read by, identified with, and understood by the re-

tarded (Sullivan and Tolman, 1956). In addition, Stanwix House and Science Research Associates publish materials especially designed for the educable retardate.

5. Use an elemental rather than a global approach in teaching academics to the retarded. It is unfortunate that educators have reasoned by analogies in applying the Gestalt perceptual phenomenon to the teaching of the skill subjects. It is not efficient to begin by teaching the retarded whole stories, followed by whole sentences, then whole words and finally word-attack skills. Instead, they seem to learn better in this order: listening comprehension for instructions and stories, auditory discrimination of familiar sounds and then speech sounds, sound blending ability, visual discrimination for individual letters, association of sounds with individual letters, word-attack skills, and so on. Later on we can be concerned about applying these basic reading skills to the reading of sentences, stories and eventually books. Reading mechanics must be taught and learned before moving on to reading comprehension.

6. Special emphasis needs to be placed on comprehension after the needed background skills are acquired. Often teachers are too preoccupied for too long with the mechanics, failing to provide experiences in applying them to meaningful problems. This is particularly true in arithmetic. Children may be able to add, subtract (and even multiply, divide and handle fractions) yet be unable to use these skills in even the most elementary arithmetic reasoning procedures. Similarly, reading skills need to be applied to job applications, road signs, newspapers, and the reading and writing of friendly and business letters.

7. Stress systematic, sequential instruction rather than incidental teaching when instructing in the more academic subjects. The unit and project method alone will not get the job done of teaching the basic skills. However, the core will enable pupils to apply the academic skills which they have learned through receiving individual instruction and by self study. The teacher needs to divide her curriculum into individual learning and group learning. Acquiring academic skills is individual learning. Group learning can best be taught in settings that most closely resemble the kinds of social

situations in which the retarded will find themselves in daily life. Thus, if boys and girls are to develop table manners, this can be best done through eating together at the table under supervision. Similarly, if they are to develop the graces of social dancing, they should do so through supervised social dancing.

8. Teachers must learn to apply the basic principles of learning, since teaching presupposes learning. We need especially to apply Hull's basic principle which is *repeated, rewarded trials*. Correct responses need to be assured and then immediately rewarded. The golden rule for teaching the retarded is the same as for all children: take the child where he is, moving along only at as fast a rate and in as small steps as will insure learning.

9. The word "drill" is in good standing in the field of the retarded, but a better one would be overlearning. A pupil repeats activities at which he has succeeded and withdraws from those where he has failed. Remember, overlearning can be fostered in a variety of ways. It is important to get correct responses, and then provide practice in repeating these.

10. For the acquisition of skills in the tool subjects, much more emphasis should be placed on self-teaching. Recent research on programmed instruction utilizing teaching machines may well revolutionize the teaching of many skills to the retarded (Stolorow, 1960).

11. Results of recent research suggest that the training of intellect (Guilford, 1959; Kirk, 1958; and others) is possible especially among low IQ children who have lacked adequate stimulation. Thus, the educability of intelligence (raising the IQ) through educational treatment has an important place in the curriculum, especially for the non–brain-injured mentally retarded.

12. It is especially important to employ a clinical diagnostic approach in teaching the mentally retarded (Dunn, 1961). Each individual child should be studied *by the teacher* and others to determine his strengths, weaknesses, attitudes, interests, and capabilities. After finding out where his interests and abilities lie, teaching procedures should be planned in keeping with the special problems of the individual child to be instructed. Some diagnostic information is usually available through the cumulative school

record, including medical and psychological reports. However, the teacher himself must gather much of the information through interviews with the pupil, his parents, and his former teachers. He will also need to give sociometric and educational tests. The teacher's own observations are also important. There are many causes for learning inability besides intellectual subnormality. Included are: lack of interest; home, school, and community conditions; hearing and vision problems; mixed lateral dominance and other neurological impairments; and other multiple disabilities. It is important for a teacher to study continuously each of his pupils to find an optimal educational program. The key is test, teach, retest, reteach, and continue the process.

13. Some teachers may wish to experiment with having the abler and older retarded pupils proctor their peers, though many authorities would violently disagree with such a proposal. The word proctoring is used advisedly since the teacher must remain the teacher. There will be need on his part for systematic planning, careful supervision, and good evaluation. The negative arguments of exploitation and teaching false concepts in peer-proctoring are recognized. However, there are good arguments for this approach. For example, it is probable that the pupil who does the proctoring may gain the most in terms of new insights into the content being taught, as well as into his skills in interpersonal relations.

14. We should not expect all children with even valid IQ scores of 50–75 to develop sufficient functional skills in the basic school subjects to label them literate. Few children with IQ's below 60–65 will, upon reaching adulthood, read appreciable amounts for enjoyment or information. When a letter is to be written or read, persons with IQ's in the 50s will call upon their brighter relatives or friends to do it for them.

## Summary

Educable mentally retarded pupils have a moderate intellectual endowment which enables them to acquire limited skills in the academics and to become self-supporting adults in casual service and unskilled employment. They are primarily identified by means of in

dividual intelligence tests. In the past, pupils having IQ scores between 50 and 75, and having difficulty with the skill subjects in the
regular grades, have been recommended for special class placement.
There is a trend to shift the IQ limits upward to 60–80, and not to
wait until these children have school problems before providing special education services. This could increase the prevalence estimates
from the present-day 2 percent to as much as 15 or 16 percent. The
majority of educable retardates come from low socioeconomic
backgrounds and are classified as nonpathological (or cultural-
familial). The remaining group come from all levels of society (but
make up the preponderance of mental retardation in average and
above average homes) and often have pathological impairments.

Most educable mentally retarded pupils are only slightly below
average in physical development. Their greatest difficulty is with
abstract concepts, including academic subjects and moral issues.
It has been said that they are not identified until they enter school
and lose their identity as such upon graduation. If left in the regular
grades they are pressured to achieve academically above their
theoretical mental-age capacity and are socially ostracized by their
more intellectually endowed peers. When placed in a special class
there is a reduced, but adequate, emphasis on academic content.
More stress is placed on developing good work habits, and on
getting along with others.

Study-work programs are becoming increasingly popular for adolescent retardates. This plan involves part-time work experience in
the community and part-time school attendance, leading to full-time
community employment. Upon reaching their teens, the retarded
often have available to them rehabilitation counselors to guide
them toward gainful employment, though direct assistance is not
available until they reach their sixteenth birthday. As adults, most
former educable pupils marry, raise families, and find competitive
employment. Many of those who graduate from school become reasonably well-accepted members of society. The challenge of the
immediate future for the schools is to give sufficient preparation
to a larger percentage of pupils with retarded intellectual development so they can make satisfactory occupational, community, and
family adjustments in an age of automation and population explosion. To date our record has been only reasonably good.

## CHAPTER REFERENCES

Ainsworth, S. H., et al. *An exploratory study of educational, social and emotional factors in the education of mentally retarded children in Georgia public schools.* Athens, Ga.: Univer. of Georgia, 1959.

Anastasi, Anne. *Psyschological testing.* (2nd ed.) New York: Macmillan, 1961.

Baldwin, Willie K. The educable mentally retarded child in the regular grades. *Except. Child.,* 1958, **25**, 106–108, 112.

Blatt, B. The physical, personality, and academic status of children who are mentally retarded attending special classes as compared with children who are mentally retarded attending regular classes. *Amer. J. ment. Defic.,* 1958, **62**, 810–818.

———. Some persistently recurring assumptions concerning the mentally subnormal. *Train. sch. Bull.,* 1960, **57**, 48–59.

Cantor, G. N., & Stacey, C. L. Manipulative dexterity of mental defectives. *Amer. J. ment. Defic.,* 1951, **56**, 401–410.

Capobianco, R. J., & Miller, D. Y. *Quantitative and qualitative analysis of exogenous and endogenous children in some reading processes.* Syracuse, N.Y.: Syracuse Univer. Research Institute, 1958.

Carriker, W. R. A. A comparison of postschool adjustments of regular and special class retarded individuals served in Lincoln and Omaha, Nebraska public schools. *Dissertation Abstr.* Ann Arbor, Mich.: Univer. of Michigan, 1957, **17**, 2206–2207.

Cassidy, Viola M., & Stanton, Jeannette E. *An investigation of factors involved in the educational placement of mentally retarded children: A study of differences between children in special and regular classes in Ohio.* Columbus, Ohio: Ohio State Univer., 1959.

Charles, D. C. Ability and accomplishment of persons earlier judged mentally deficient. *Genet. Psychol. Monogr.,* 1953, **47**, 3–71.

Clarke, Ann M., & Clarke, A. D. B. *Mental deficiency: The changing outlook.* London: Methuen, 1958.

Collmann, R. D., & Newlyn, D. Employment success of mentally dull and intellectually normal ex-pupils in England. *Amer. J. ment. Defic.* 1957, **61**, 484–490.

Conant, J. B. *Slums and suburbs.* New York: McGraw-Hill, 1961.

Cromwell, R. L. (Ed.) *Abstracts of psychological studies in mental deficiency.* Vols. I & II, Nashville, Tenn.: Peabody College, 1960 & 1962.

————. Selected aspects of personality development in mentally retarded children. *Except. Child.,* 1961, **28**, 44–51.

Cronbach, L. J. *Essentials of psychological testing.* (2nd ed.) New York: Harper & Row, 1960.

Cruickshank, W. M., Bentzen, Frances A., Ratzeburg, F. H., & Tannhauser, Mirian T. *A teaching method for brain-injured and hyperactive children.* Syracuse, N.Y.: Syracuse Univer. Press, 1961.

Dayton, N. A. The relationship between physical defect and intelligence. *J. Psycho-aesthetics,* 1928, **34**, 112–139.

DiMichael, S. G. Employment of the mentally retarded. *J. Rehab.,* 1949, **15**, 3–7.

Dinger, J. C. Post-school adjustment of former educable retarded pupils. *Except. Child.,* 1961, **27**, 353–360.

Dingman, H. F., & Tarjan, G. Mental retardation and the normal distribution curve. *Amer. J. ment. Defic.,* 1960, **64**, 991–994.

Duncan, J. *The education of the ordinary child.* New York: Ronald Press, 1943.

Dunn, L. M., & Capobianco, R. J. Studies in reading and arithmetic in mentally retarded boys. *Monogr. soc. res. Child Develpm.* 1954, **19**, No. 1. Lafayette, Ind.: Child Develpm. Publ., 1956.

————. *Peabody picture vocabulary test.* Minneapolis, Minn.: American Guidance Service, 1959.

————. Mentally retarded children. *Encyclo. educ. Res.* (3rd ed.), 1960, 835–848.

————. The role of educators in evaluating mentally retarded children. *Amer. J. ment. Defic.,* 1961, **65**, 796–800.

————, & Brooks, Sadye. Peabody picture vocabulary test performance of educable mentally retarded children. *Train. Sch. Bull.,* 1960, **57**, 35–40.

————, & Kirk, S. A. Impressions of Soviet psycho-educational service and research in mental retardation. *Except. Child.,* 1963, **29**, 299–311.

Elenbogen, M. L. A comparative study of some aspects of academic and social adjustment of two groups of mentally retarded children in special classes and in regular grades. *Dissert. Abstr.,* 1957, **17**, 2496.

Ellis, N. R. *Handbook in mental deficiency: Psychological theory and research*. New York: McGraw-Hill, 1963.

Erdman, R. L. *Educable retarded children in elementary schools*. Washington, D.C.: Council for Except. Child., 1961.

Fraenkel, W. A. *The mentally retarded and their vocational rehabilitation: A resource handbook*. New York: National Ass. for Retarded Child., 1961.

Francis, R. J., & Rarick, G. L. *Motor characteristics of the mentally retarded*. Cooperative Research Bull. No. 1, USOE 35005. Washington, D.C.: Government Printing Office, 1960.

Frey, R. M. Reading behavior of brain-injured and non-brain-injured children of average and retarded mental development. Unpublished doctoral dissertation, Univer. of Illinois, 1960.

Gallagher, J. J. Changes in verbal and non-verbal ability of brain-injured mentally retarded children following removal of special stimulation, *Amer. J. ment. Defic.*, 1962, **66**, 774–781.

————. *Tutoring of brain-injured mentally retarded children*. Springfield, Ill.: Charles C. Thomas, 1960.

Gardner, W. I., & Nisonger, H. W. A manual on program development in mental retardation. *Monogr. Suppl. Amer. J. ment. Defic.*, 1962, **66**, 1–186.

Goldstein, H., & Seigle, Dorothy M. (Eds.) *A curriculum guide for teachers of the educable mentally handicapped*. Springfield, Ill.: Illinois State Department of Public Instruction, 1958.

————, Jordon, Laura, & Moss, J. W. *Early school development of low IQ children: A study of special class placement: Interim report*. Urbana, Ill.: Univer. of Illinois Institute for Research on Except. Child., 1962.

Guilford, J. P. Three faces of intellect. *Amer. Psychol.*, 1959, **14**, 469–479.

Heber, R. F. A manual on terminology and classification in mental retardation. *Monogr. Supp. Amer. J. ment. Defic.*, (2nd ed.) 1961a, 1–109.

————. Modification in the manual on terminology and classification in mental retardation. *Amer. J. Ment. Defic.*, 1961b, **65**, 499–500.

————, & Stevens, H. A. *Research in mental retardation*. Chicago: Univer. of Chicago Press, 1963.

Howe, C. E. A comparison of motor skills of mentally retarded and normal children. *Except. Child.*, 1959, **25**, 352–354.

Hudson, Margaret. *Methods of teaching mentally retarded children.* Nashville, Tenn.: Peabody College, 1958.

Hungerford, R. H., DeProspo, C. J., & Rosenzweig, L. E. Education of the mentally handicapped in childhood and adolescence. In DiMichael, S. G. (Ed.) *Vocational rehabilitation of the mentally retarded.* Rehabilitation Services Series No. 1231. Washington, D.C.: Government Printing Office, 1950.

Hunt, J. M. *Intelligence and experience.* New York: Ronald Press, 1961.

Ingram, Christine P. *Education of the slow learning child.* (3rd ed.) New York: Ronald Press, 1960.

Johnson, G. O. A study of social position of mentally handicapped children in the regular grades. *Amer. J. ment. Defic.,* 1950, **55**, 60–89.

————. *A comparative study of the personal and social adjustment of mentally handicapped children placed in special classes with mentally handicapped children who remain in regular classes.* Syracuse, N.Y.: Syracuse Univer. Research Institute, 1961.

————, & Blake, Katherine A. Learning performance of retarded and normal children. *Syracuse univer. spec. educ. and rehab. Monogr.,* Series No. 5. Syracuse, N.Y.: Syracuse Univer. Press, 1960.

————, & Kirk, S. A. Are mentally handicapped children segregated in the regular grades? *Except. Child.,* 1950, **17**, 65–68, 87–88.

Jordan, June B. Intelligence as a factor in social position—a sociometric study in special classes for the mentally handicappd. Unpublished doctoral dissertation. Univer. of Illinois, 1960.

Jordan, T. E., & de Charms, R. The achievement motive in normal and mentally retarded children. *Amer. J. ment. Defic.,* 1959, **64**, 457–466.

Kennedy, Ruby J. *The social adjustment of morons in a Connecticut city.* Hartford, Conn.: Mansfield-Southbury Social Service, 1948.

Kephart, N. C. *The slow learner in the classroom.* Columbus, Ohio: Charles E. Merrill, 1960.

Kirk, S. A. *Early education of the mentally retarded: An experimental study.* Urbana, Ill.: Univer. of Illinois Press, 1958.

————, & Johnson, G. O. *Educating the retarded child.* Boston: Houghton Mifflin, 1951.

————, & McCarthy, J. J. The Illinois test of psycholinguistics abilities—an approach to differential diagnosis. *Amer. J. ment. Defic.,* 1961, **66**, 399–412.

Krishef, C. H. & Hall, M. A. Employment of the mentally retarded in Hennepin County, Minn. *Amer. J. ment. Defic.,* 1955, **60**, 182–189.

Lassers, L. R., & Low, G. Symposium on assessing and developing communicative effectiveness in mentally retarded children. *Asha*, 1960, **2**, 377.

Lee, J. J., Hegge, T. G., & Voelker, P. H. *A study of social adequacy and social failure of mentally retarded youth in Wayne County, Mich.* Detroit, Mich.: Wayne State Univer., 1959.

Mackie, Romaine P., Dabelstein, D. H., & Heber, R. F. *Preparation of mentally handicapped youth for gainful employment.* Washington, D.C.: Government Printing Office, 1959.

Martens, Elise H. Curriculum adjustments for the mentally retarded. *U.S. Office of Educ. Bull., 1950, No. 2.* Washington, D.C.: Government Printing Office, 1950.

Masland, R. L. *Mental subnormality.* New York: Basic Books, 1958.

McPherson, Marion W. Learning and mental deficiency. *Amer. J. ment. Defic.*, 1958, **62**, 870–877.

Miller, R. V. Social status and socioemphatic differences among mentally superior, mentally typical, and mentally retarded children. *Except. Child.*, 1956, **23**, 114–119.

Mullen, Frances A., & Itkin, W. The value of special classes for the mentally handicapped. *Chicago Sch. J.*, 1961, **42**, 353–363.

Orr, K. N. *Cardinal objectives in teaching the educable mentally retarded.* Terre Haute, Ind.: Indiana State Teachers College, 1962.

Peabody College, Division of Surveys & Field Services. *Scholastic achievement in Robertson County, Tennessee.* Nashville, Tenn.: Peabody College, 1961.

Peterson, L., & Smith, L. L. The postschool adjustment of educable mentally retarded adults with that of adults of normal intelligence. *Except. Child.*, 1960, **26**, 404–408.

Porter, R. B., & Milazzo, T. C. A comparison of mentally retarded adults. *Except. Child.*, 1958, **24**, 410–412.

Reynolds, M. C., & Stunkard, C. L. A comparative study of day class *vs.* institutionalized educable retardates. Coop. Res. Project No. 192. Minneapolis, Minn.: Univer. of Minnesota, 1960.

Rothstein, J. H. (Ed.) *Mental retardation: Readings and resources.* New York: Holt, Rinehart and Winston, 1961.

Sarason, S. B., & Gladwin, T. *Psychological problems in mental deficiency.* (3rd ed.) New York: Harper & Row, 1959.

Sloan, W. Motor proficiency and intelligence. *Amer. J. ment. Defic.*, 1951, **55**, 394–405.

Sontag, L. W., Baker, C. T., & Nelson, Virginia. Mental growth and personality development: A longitudinal study. *Child Develpm. Monogr.*, 1958, **23**, 1–123.

Smith, J. O. Speech and language of the retarded. *Train. Sch. Bull.*, 1962a, **58**, 111–123.

————. Group language development for educable mental retardates. *Except. Child.*, 1962b, **29**, 95–101.

————. Effects of a group language development program upon the psycholinguistic abilities of educable mental retardates. *Peabody College Special Education Research Monograph Series 1*, Nashville, Tenn.: George Peabody College for Teachers, 1962(c).

Stevens, G. D., & Birch, J. W. A proposal of clarification of the terminology and to describe brain-injured children. *Except. Child.*, 1957, **23**, 346–349.

Stolurow, L. Automation in special education. *Except. Child.*, 1960, **27**, 78–83.

Strauss, A. A., & Kephart, N. C. *Psychopathology and education of the brain-injured child.* Vol. II. New York: Grune & Stratton, 1955.

————, & Lehtinen, Laura E. *Psychopathology and education of the brain-injured child.* Vol. I. New York: Grune & Stratton, 1947.

Sullivan, Helen B., & Tolman, Lorraine E. High-interest—low-vocabulary reading materials: A selected booklist. *J. Educ.*, 1956, **139**, 2, 1–132.

Syden, M. Preparation for work: An aspect of the secondary school's curriculum for mentally retarded youth. *Except. Child.*, 1962, **28**, 325–331.

Thiel, Ellen. *Design for daily living: A framework for curriculum development for children and youth with intellectual handicaps.* Tallahassee, Fla.: Florida State Univer., 1960.

Thorndike, R. L., & Hagen, Elizabeth. *Measurement and evaluation in psychology and education.* (2nd ed.) New York: Wiley, 1961.

Thurstone, Thelma. *An evaluation of educating mentally handicapped children in special classes and in regular grades.* Chapel Hill, N.C.: Univer. of North Carolina, 1959.

Tisdall, W. The efficacy of a special class program on the productive thinking abilities of educable mentally retarded children. Unpublished doctoral dissertation, Univer. of Illinois, 1962.

UNESCO. *Organization of special education for mentally deficient children.* Geneva: International Bureau of Education, 1960.

Vance, Helen S. Psychological and educational study of brain-injured and non-brain damaged mentally retarded children. *Dissert. Abstr.*, 1956, **17**, 1033.

Vergason, G. Retention in educable retarded and normal adolescent boys as a function of amount of original training. Unpublished doctoral dissertation. George Peabody College for Teachers, 1962.

Wallin, J. E. W. *Mental deficiency.* Brandon, Vt.: Journal of Clinical Psychology, 1956.

Wrightstone, J. W., Forlano, G., Lepkowski, J. R., & Sontag, M. *A comparison of educational outcomes under single-track and two-track plans for educable mentally retarded children.* New York: Board of Education, 1959.

## ADDITIONAL REFERENCES

Allen, Amy A., & Baker, Virginia. *Slow learning children in Ohio schools.* Columbus, Ohio: State Department of Education, 1962.

Cleugh, M. F. (Ed.) *Teaching the slow learner in the primary school.* London: Methuen, 1961.

————. *Teaching the slow learner in the special school.* London: Methuen, 1961.

Detroit Board of Education. *Curriculum guide for teachers of mentally retarded pupils.* 3 vols. Detroit: Board of Education, 1953.

Dunn, L. M., & Capobianco, R. J. Mental retardation. *Rev. educ. Res.*, 1959, **29**, 451–470.

Goldstein, H. *The educable mentally retarded child in the elementary school.* Washington, D.C.: NEA, Department of Classroom Teachers, 1962.

Hegge, T. G., Kirk, S. A., & Kirk, Winifred D. *Remedial reading drills.* Ann Arbor, Mich.: George Wahr, 1936.

Johnson, G. O. *Education for the slow learners.* Englewood Cliffs, N.J.: Prentice-Hall, 1963.

Jordon, T. E. *The mentally retarded.* Columbus, Ohio: Charles E. Merrill, 1961.

Kirk, S. A. *Teaching of reading to slow learning children.* Boston: Houghton Mifflin, 1940.

Mayo, L. W. (Chair.) *Report to the President: A proposed program for national action to combat mental retardation.* Washington, D.C.: The President's Panel on Mental Retardation, 1962.

Montessori, Maria. *The Montessori elementary material: The advanced Montessori method*. Philadelphia: F. A. Stokes, 1917.

Riessman, F. *The culturally deprived child*. New York, Harper & Row, 1962.

Tansley, A. E., & Gulliford, R. *The education of slow-learning children*. London: Routledge & Kegan Paul, 1960.

## RESOURCES

The agencies and other resources that the reader will find useful in serving children who are mentally retarded are described briefly. For additional information see Rothstein (1961), and Gardner and Nisonger (1962).

The best-known professional association centrally concerned with the field of mental retardation is the American Association on Mental Deficiency (AAMD), which had its inception in 1876. It is a multi-disciplinary organization that has membership from the fields of medicine, psychology, education, and social work. By 1960, its membership had grown to over 5000 persons, and it had established its first permanent headquarters with a full-time executive secretary at 1601 West Broad Street, Columbus 16, Ohio. The association holds conventions and special conferences and publishes the *American Journal of Mental Deficiency* (bimonthly) and a new journal *Mental Retardation* (bimonthly). These publications carry professional articles written by persons in each of the disciplines listed. The association also publishes a directory of state and private schools and hospitals for the retarded, as well as special monographs. Too, it provides an excellent abstracting service.

Another American journal, the *Training School Bulletin*, is published by The Training School at Vineland, New Jersey. It is issued quarterly and is devoted exclusively to articles on mental retardation. There are three British journals in the field. These are the *Journal of Mental Deficiency Research*, the *Journal of Mental Subnormality*, and *Forward Trends*. The latter is published by the Guild of Teachers of Backward Children. Another journal written in English is the *Australian Journal on the Education of Backward Children*. While intended primarily for parents, two other publications deserve special mention. These are *Children Limited*, published bimonthly by the National Association for Retarded Children, 386 Park Avenue South, New York City, and *The Bulletin*, published quarterly by the Canadian Association for Retarded

Children, 317 Avenue Road, Toronto 7, Ontario. Both carry abstracts of professional articles and book reviews, which are especially useful for current events.

Many public agencies provide services for the mentally retarded and their families. At the national level, many of these are housed in the U.S. Department of Health, Education and Welfare. They are the U.S. Office of Education, the Vocational Rehabilitation Administration, the National Institute of Mental Health, the National Institute of Neurological Diseases and Blindness, the Children's Bureau, and the Social Security Administration. The U.S. Office of Education (USOE) and other branches of HEW maintain a professional staff, which includes specialists in mental retardation. In addition to providing consultative services, these specialists publish bulletins and other guidelines that will assist teachers in planning the best possible school program for the retarded child. The USOE supports a fellowship program for graduate training in mental retardation and many research projects. As in other areas of exceptionality, some state departments of education have special education sections that employ specialists in mental retardation. These persons are available upon request for consultative services to local school systems. Often these specialists make available curriculum guides and other materials that are of help to the teacher.

The Vocational Rehabilitation Administration supports studies and demonstrations related to the gainful employment of retarded adolescents and adults. Most of its direct services are available through a system of state vocational rehabilitation agencies. These employ rehabilitation counselors and have funds available for the habilitation and job placement of the retarded. While the vocational rehabilitation agencies cannot legally assume responsibility for the retarded until they reach the age of 16, rehabilitation counselors are usually anxious to begin studying the retarded adolescent at an earlier age (about 14 years) so as to make plans for his occupational training. Therefore, it is essential that teachers of retarded teenagers contact the state vocational rehabilitation agency.

## SELECTED 16 MM SOUND FILMS

*Individual differences and psychological tests.* 30 min, black & white. National Educational Television and Radio Center, 10 Columbus Circle, New York 19, New York. Explains the measurement of human abilities, and individual differences of living organisms.

*Testing intelligence with the Stanford-Binet.* 18 min, black & white. Psychological Register, Pennsylvania State University, University Park, Pennsylvania. Excerpts from test administrations to four children plus discussion of MA and IQ scores.

*The brain and the nervous system.* 30 min, black & white. National Educational Television and Radio Center, 10 Columbus Circle, New York 19, New York. Presents research on the brain and the nervous system with a discussion of brain functions by areas.

*How the nervous system works.* 30 min, black & white. National Educational Television Film Service, Indiana University, Bloomington, Indiana. Explains the structure and function of the nervous system using diagrams.

*What the brain does.* 30 min, black & white. National Educational Television Film Service, Indiana University, Bloomington, Indiana. Uses models of the brain to point out the various functions of different parts of the nervous system.

*Class for Tommy.* 21 min, black & white. Bailey Films, 20-44 North Berendo Street, Hollywood 27, California. Primary special class program for a six year old educable mentally retarded child.

*Arts and crafts for the slow learner.* 27 min, black & white. Free loan from SWS Films, 744 North Fuller Avenue, Hollywood 46, California. Shows craft activities in special day classes for educable retardates utilizing free and inexpensive materials.

*Educable mentally handicapped.* 29 min, black & white. National Educational Television Service, Indiana University, Bloomington, Indiana. Explains characteristics and special class school programs for such children.

*There was a door.* 38 min, black & white. Contemporary Films, 13 East 37 Street, New York 16, New York. Shows community services for the retarded in Great Britain in contrast to large residential facilities.

*Tuesday's child.* 14 min, color, black & white. National Association for Retarded Children, 386 Park Avenue South, New York 16, New York. General film on retardation.

*Children limited.* 30 min, color. Washington Association for Retarded Children, 4008 Arcade Building, Seattle 1, Washington. General presentation of mental retardation with emphasis on residential services.

*What is Anna.* 25 min, color. Billings Mental Hygiene Clinic, 1500 North 30 Street, Billings, Montana. Shows diagnostic services for a young pseudo-retarded girl.

## CHAPTER 3

# Trainable Mentally Retarded Children

LLOYD M. DUNN

Since 1950, the growth of special day classes for trainable mentally retarded children has been remarkable. Even in the short five-year period from 1953 to 1958 the percentage increase in enrollments was 260 percent, an amount larger than for any other area of exceptionality (see Fig. 1.2). This growth resulted mainly from the demands of parents of these children, rather than from the desire of educators to assume responsibility for this group. In fact, prior to the day school movement for trainable children, such boys and girls were usually excluded from school by school laws or regulations because they were not of educable mind. Parents of such children were expected to care for them at home or place them in a residential facility. However, about 1950, the parents of the mentally retarded established their own organization, now known as the *National Association for Retarded Children* (NARC). One of the chief aims of this organization and its state and local affiliates was to foster public day school services for the trainable. As never before, parents wished to keep their children at home and in the community; yet they hesitated to do so unless every opportunity were given them to develop intellectually. This implied formal training by qualified teachers. Parents contended they were taxpayers, and their children could learn. Therefore the schools had as great a responsibility to trainable children as toward other children. Parents carried their demands to state legislators. As a result, legislation was passed in the vast majority of states authorizing local public school systems to establish special day class programs for this group. With legal authority and the promise of state reimbursement for a considerable portion of the costs of the program, parents petitioned local school boards and school administrators for the establishment of such special classes. The rapid growth of these classes attests to the strength of their demands.

Nevertheless the issue of whether trainable children are, or are not, the responsibility of the public schools and the teaching profession continues. However, the question is rapidly becoming an academic one, since programs are becoming more widespread yearly.

## Definition

Children who are classified as trainable have already been defined as having IQ's from about 30 or 35, to 50 or 55. This means they develop intellectually at about one third to one half the rate of the average child. As seen in Table 2.2 at six years of age they are mentally like children of two to three years of age. In adulthood their mental development approaches five to eight years.

Trainable children are so intellectually subnormal they are not likely to acquire sufficient skills in the three R's to operate at the grade four level and beyond, which is the standard for literacy. Thus they are noneducable in the academic sense and are unable to profit academically from participation in either the regular public school program, or in special classes designed for the educable mentally retarded. In adulthood, with a possible rare exception, they will neither read a newspaper nor other written materials for pleasure or information. Furthermore, they will not be able to care judicially for their earnings, or for other monies which they acquire.

The trainable mentally retarded do have sufficient ability: (1) to develop self-care skills in dressing, toileting, and eating; (2) to learn to talk and carry on a simple conversation though they will have little verbal communicative skills during preschool years; (3) to guard themselves against common dangers in a protective environment or in familiar community settings; and (4) to perform simple chores in a sheltered environment in the home or community. As adults they will seldom be independent, socially or economically. Instead, they will need some care and supervision all of their lives. Thus, they seldom if ever marry, raise families, or set up independent living in their own homes. They usually continue to live with parents, relatives, or friends, or are cared for by some social agency which usually takes the form of a residential facility for the mentally retarded, but may be a halfway house or an independent living unit.

## Prevalence

As in the other areas of exceptionality, attempts to find the prevalence of trainable mentally retarded children are beset by problems of lack of precision in definition. Nevertheless, the task of determining the numbers of trainable children is much less difficult than in the educable category. Two studies, one in Illinois and the other in Michigan have been reported by Wirtz and Guenther (1957). The Illinois study took place in two urban and three rural communities. Referrals were made by educators, nurses, physicians, welfare workers, and parents. Thus, the figures can be considered minimal estimates. Over the school age range from six through eighteen the prevalence of trainable mentally retarded children residing in the communities was found to be 1.49 per 1000; in addition 0.85 children per 1000 were in residential facilities. Thus the over-all prevalence estimate was 2.34 per 1000 for trainable children in both community and institutional settings. The Michigan results were slightly above this figure at 3.4 per 1000, due probably to the fact that a private residential facility was in operation in a city near one of the three communities included in the survey. A recent survey in the United Kingdom (Goodman and Tizard, 1962) found a prevalence figure of 2.53 per 1000 for trainable plus untrainable (below IQ 30) children. An interesting finding of this study was that there had been an over-all decline of about one-quarter in the prevalence of such children in the past 30 or 35 years, with the number of mongoloids increasing fourfold, relatively, while the total of all other forms of mental defect declined one third.

It can be seen that prevalence estimates range from one fifth to three tenths of 1 percent. For a typical community, it seems safe to expect that, for every 1000 school-age children, one or two will be of trainable intellect and living at home, while another one will be in a residential facility. Certainly the 0.2 percent used in Table 1.1 is a conservative one. Utilizing this minimal estimate, in a community with 50,000 school aged children we would anticipate that 100 children ($1/500 \times 50,000$) would fall within that group of children we have called trainable.

## Identification

The vast majority of trainable children are identified either at birth or during their preschool years. In the case of mongoloid children who are typically no more than trainable in intellectual development, the attending obstetrician will usually identify them because of their physical stigmata. Other children in the trainable population, although they may later have a miscellaneous collection of syndromes, usually will not be so quickly discovered. In most cases, the symptoms are incoordination, and a slowness in learning to walk, talk, and look after themselves. Thus, by late in the child's first year or shortly thereafter, the suspicions and concerns of the mother are aroused. She in turn looks to the family physician to identify the difficulty. In some cases this physician, in cooperation with a child psychologist, soon makes the diagnosis. However, seldom is the family physician an authority in mental retardation. Therefore, he often refers the family of a child who is not developing normally to an interprofessional clinic for diagnosis and evaluation. These are becoming increasingly available, sponsored by various state and local agencies. In some cases they are not designed solely for the mentally retarded. In other cases they are. The latter are often supported in part by the Children's Bureau of the U.S. Department of Health, Education, and Welfare.

Here the physician, psychologist, social worker and others who have special competence in mental retardation cooperate in the identification process. However, it may take many years before the diagnosis of trainable mentally retarded is accepted by the parents. In the meantime, they shift from one professional person to another hoping against hope that some label other than this will be placed on their child. In their eyes, almost anything else would be more desirable, probably because it would seem more ameliorable by treatment.

In a recent unpublished survey by the author three questions were asked a group of parents. The following responses were typical replies to each question:

1. *When did you first suspect your child was retarded in intellectual development and why?*

   At birth when the physician told us we had a mongoloid child.
   At four months, when he didn't smile, sit alone, or notice things.
   At about 2½ years because he squealed a lot, had odd mannerisms, didn't talk, was slow in walking, and lacked coordination.

2. *What were you told by the family physician when you first went to him with your problem?*

   That my child was brain injured, evidently from birth.
   That my child was nervous and would probably outgrow it.
   That my child was retarded and should be placed in a residential school.

3. *How old was your child when you were told he was retarded, and who told you?*

   My obstetrician told me in the hospital that my baby did not respond as he should; my probing revealed that the doctor was thinking of mental retardation.
   When our boy was six months old, the brain surgeon told us he would always be retarded.
   The psychologist at 2½ years told me that my child could live a fairly normal life and be taught a trade in later years, but would not learn academically.

## Classification and Characteristics

With the exception that all trainable children obtain IQ scores on global individual tests of intelligence in approximately the 30–50 range, trainable children are extremely heterogeneous in physical and psychological characteristics. Hottel (1956), in studying 257 trainable children in 23 special classes classified them as shown in Table 3.1. Cain and Levine (1961), on the basis of information provided by family physicians or clinics, obtained about the same compostion in their study of 182 trainable children, classifying 27

TABLE 3.1 *Classification of trainable mentally retarded children.*

| CATEGORIES | PERCENTAGES |
| --- | --- |
| Organic brain injury | 37.15 |
| Mongolism (Down's syndrome) | 33.05 |
| Undifferentiated and unknown | 26.94 |
| Cretinism | 1.22 |
| Cultural-familial | 0.82 |
| Microcephaly | 0.41 |
| Other | 0.41 |
| Total | 100.00 |

*Source:* Hottel, J. V. *The Tennessee experimental program of day classes for severely mentally retarded (trainable) children: Interim report of the study.* Nashville, Tenn.: Peabody College, 1956.

percent as organically brain injured, 40 percent as mongoloid, and 32 percent as undifferentiated. Connor and Goldberg (1960) and Wirtz and Guenther (1957) obtained about the same divisions. Thus it seems safe to conclude that about one third of the group are mongoloid, another one third have known organic (or pathological) etiologies and the remaining one third include a miscellaneous group including undifferentiated, unknown, and possibly even some familial cases.

## MONGOLISM (DOWN'S SYNDROME)

Mongolism is by far the most common clinical type of mental deficiency. Tredgold and Soddy (1956) have estimated that "of all children diagnosed as mentally deficient during the first year of life, between 40 and 50 percent are mongols. Of all children under five years of age who are diagnosed as mentally deficient, about 25 percent are mongols." It has just been pointed out they make up 30 to 40 percent of the pupils in public school classes for trainable pupils.

Mongolism occurs in all races including Caucasian, Negro, Oriental, and others. In 1866, J. Langdon Down, a British physician, labeled children with this syndrome as mongol because of their resemblance in physical characteristics to the Mongolian race of Asia. While any ethnic relationship has long ago been refuted, the term mongolism is still applied to the syndrome. Other names such as peristatic amentia and fetalism have been suggested but none of them have become popular. However, Down's Syndrome has been used widely in Europe for some time, and is growing in popularity in North America.

Educators have been preoccupied with the physical signs of mongolism although these have little meaning for educational treatment. Nevertheless, they are reviewed here briefly. First of all, it must be pointed out that few mongoloid children have all of the typical external characteristics, and some have very few. When most of the physical stigmata are present a layman can readily recognize most mongoloid children. The danger is that some persons with many of the physical features are not mongoloid. A tentative diagnosis of mongolism can usually be made in early infancy and frequently at birth. The grave danger of making a final diagnosis on physical signs alone cannot be overstressed. It should be based on a combination of physical stigmata, measures of intelligence, and, perhaps before too long, measures of chromosomal anomalies which will be discussed later. Valid measures of intelligence are difficult to obtain before a child is at least two or three years of age. Prior to recent chromosomal research in mongolism, the most essential characteristic to measure was very low intellect. In fact, without this the diagnosis was not appropriate.

At birth, mongoloid children are called "unfinished." Throughout their lives they remain short in stature with protruding abdomen. They tend to be light and florid in complexion with coarse, dry skin and hair. Characteristics of the head are especially indicative. They include a small skull; a moon-shaped face with almond-shaped, slanting eyes; a short, thick neck; protruding ears; and thick, often-fissured tongue. Other typical physical stigmata include a deep cleft between the big and second toes, a flabby hand with a transverse crease, and a short, inward-curving little finger resulting from mal-development of bones in that digit. Other signs include under-developed genitalia, congenital heart problems, eye incoordination, susceptibility to respiratory ailments, and lack of muscle tone. In their teens, mongoloid youth are often labeled old men and women because of their early aging and because their life span tends to be shorter than average. In recent years, life expectancy has shifted upward sharply. In the past, many died of respiratory infections. These deaths have now been reduced so much by antibiotic treatment that the prevalence of mongolism among 10-year old children quadrupled from 1 in 4000 in 1929 to 1 in 1000 by 1958 (Carter reported in Goodman and Tizard, 1962). Until recently, it was unusual to find a mongoloid person as old as 30 years and many died at a much earlier age. However, it is not unusual today to find persons who are mongoloid living up into the forties, fifties, and even sixties.

In terms of psychological characteristics many of the old beliefs about mongolism are being dispelled. For years such boys and girls were known as mongoloid idiots, implying they were completely dependent, unable to develop even minimal skills in self-care and socialization. Medical treatment and training have made such a term untenable. McNeill (1954), in his extensive study, found a mean IQ of 33 for mongoloids who remained at home, and a mean IQ of 22 for those living in residential schools. The highest IQ score in each group was 56. Another commonly held belief was that mongoloids had unusual ability in mimicry and rhythm. Studies by Cantor and Girardeau (1958) indicate that mongoloids are not significantly different in these traits from normal boys and girls of the same mental age. In learning characteristics, Cantor and Girardeau found they did not differ significantly from other trainable children. Another belief was that all mongoloids had cheerful and affectionate dispositions. Most of them do have this trait during their earlier years. A few do not, especially those who have reached adolescence and adulthood. Nevertheless, as a group, they fit in better at home and in the community than do those trainable children with organic brain injury who display explosive behavior and high excitability.

Since the syndrome of mongolism was first identified and described in the literature there has been an unusual interest in the cause (or etiology) of this condition. Many etiological theories have been postulated. These included: (1) reversion to a primitive ancestral type; (2) embryo damage due to an abnormal uterine mucous membrane resulting from such factors as conception too rapidly after a miscarriage, long interval between pregnancies, immature mucous membrane in very young mothers, and damage due to induced abortions (Engler, 1952); (3) damage to the embryo and fetus because the body chemistry of the aging or run-down mother was not adequate to sustain the new life; (4) malforming and malfunctioning of the embryo and fetus due to the fertilization of an aging ovum; (5) embryo damage due to maternal infections in the first trimester such as rubella or another virus, anoxia in the mother, and poisoning (Ingalls, 1957); (6) damage to the embryo and fetus due to hormone imbalance during pregnancy especially of the pituitary glands (Benda, 1949); (7) damage to the brain of the child after birth due to an endocrine dysfunction.

All of these theories now appear to be outdated due to research by a group of French investigators (Lejeune et al., 1959). They found that three of the mongoloids they studied had 47 instead of the 46 chromosomes, the normal number for human beings. Later that year British scientists reported the same extra chromosome for a larger number of subjects and this fact has been substantiated many times since then (Rowley, 1962).

The implications of this extra chromosome are still not clear. Is it associated with cause or is it just another characteristic of the syndrome? Part of the problem is the still inadequate method of examining and counting these minute thread-like rods within each cell. The counts are done on such bits of tissue as bone marrow, blood, skin, and muscle. The tissue is allowed to grow and divide in a test tube. Cell division is then arrested by a chemical. A drop of the culture is flattened out on a piece of glass and mounted in a microscope where it is then photographed. The photographs are then greatly enlarged and the slow, tedious job of counting chromosomes begins. There are still many reasons for inaccuracies and inconsistencies in counts, just one of these being the ease with which cells and chromosomes rupture. However, technical difficulties are likely to be overcome rapidly. At that time, we will more clearly see the implications of this new technique and knowledge. Certainly, it appears that it will revolutionize the study of human genetics. As yet, prospective parents cannot routinely have their chromosome structure studied to determine if they are carriers of mongolism by having an extra chromosome. In fact, the evidence to date on the significance of heredity in the matter is very confusing. Some parents and other relatives of mongoloid children have abnormal chromosome counts and some do not. In fact the extra chromosome in the offspring may not be inherited from parents. The anomaly may come about when the egg is fertilized, or when it first divides. Thus it cannot yet be stated that mongolism is inherited, or that it is due to the extra chromosome.

In the meantime a multiple causation of mongolism is a recognized possibility. It may be that one factor produces mongolism in one case, and another in others. There is still the mystery of why the probability of giving birth to mongoloid children increases with the age of the mother, yet some very young mothers of under twenty years of age have a first child which is a mongoloid and then subsequently have normal children. Nevertheless, as Warkany (1960) has pointed out "although it is recognized that the 39 theories of the past will now be replaced by 40 new theories on mongolism, there can be no doubt that the discovery of an extra chromosome in the cells of the mongols will completely change the direction of etiological research." [1]

---

[1] Most recent research suggests that well over 90 percent of mongolism is not familial (inherited) but results from abnormal cell division soon after the egg is fertilized; however, there is a rare type of familial mongolism, usually inherited from the mother. The chromosomal count and abnormality for different types vary. Three have been identified: (1) the common, nonfamilial type where the chromosomal count is 47 (an extra chromosome 21–three instead of the usual pair); (2) the very rare nonfamilial type where some body cells have 46 and others 47 chromosomes; and (3) the rare familial type where the actual count is 46 with the extra chromosome 21 attached to some other chromosome.

With no effective medical treatment yet devised, and with genetic counseling only a prospect for the future, the weight of treatment rests on instruction and training for the mongoloid child. The goal is to guide the mongoloid child to optimal use of his limited potential. As will be seen later in this chapter we have as yet had only minimal success.

## OTHER CLASSIFICATIONS

We have seen that nearly all the remaining two thirds of trainable children (in addition to the one third or so which are mongoloid) have organic brain injury, or other miscellaneous etiologies including undifferentiated, unknown and possibly familial conditions. Pathological conditions were discussed in chapter 2. This is such a "catch all" term that some authorities have said that all trainable retardates could be so classified—including the mongoloids —since, with the exception of the rare case designated as cultural familial, there is probably a physiological base to all occurrences of mental retardation. Heber (1961), in his manual for the American Association on Mental Deficiency, has a detailed discussion of the various types of mental retardation. Even a glance at this volume will impress the reader with the complexity of the field and the vast number of clinical types (groups of individuals with similar biological and/or behavioral characteristics). In spite of their number, *the clinical types,* aside from mongolism, make up such a small proportion of the trainable group that only three of the slightly more common ones (though rare) are briefly described here.

*Hydrocephalus* is "water on the brain", or more correctly, pressure on the brain and skull from cerebral-spinal fluid. This pressure results from blockages in the brain passages, defective absorption of the fluid, or oversecretion of it. Hydrocephalus can now frequently be arrested when it is detected early and a surgical shunt inserted (a tube from the cerebral cavity to the jugular vein or some other part of the body). Uncorrected hydrocephalus results in progressive brain deterioration, a greatly enlarged skull, loss of ambulation, severe mental defect, bedboundness, and early death. Arrested hydrocephalus may result in only a slight loss in intellectual functioning and even average school progress in the regular grades.

In other cases where considerable brain damage has resulted, attendance in special classes for the trainable may be indicated.

*Microcephaly* is characterized by a small head with the skull being especially reduced in size. The forehead is often receded and the occiput (back of head) flattened. The scalp is often wrinkled. This condition is usually inherited, but may result from unusual environmental factors such as X-ray radiation of the pregnant mother. This rare condition usually results in the child's being born severely retarded. Thus occasionally children with this condition are found in classes for trainable pupils. More often they are found at home or in a residential facility.

*Cretinism* was a fairly common clinical type in the past. Now it is seldom that one sees a person with all the clinical signs of this condition. Improved prevention, diagnosis and medical treatment has greatly ameliorated the problem. Cretinism results from a severe thyroid deficiency which reduces the body metabolism to such a degree that the child becomes dwarfish and bloated. Dry, scaly, sallow skin and severe mental retardation are other clinical signs. (Superficially, cretins and mongoloids resemble one another in their short stature and sallow skin.) Iodized salt now prevents many cases, while thyroxine dosages given at an early age and throughout life to the child destined to be a cretin will greatly reduce the physical characteristics, and appreciably reduce the amount of mental retardation.

A number of trainable children may be classified as *cerebral palsied*. In fact, Goodman and Tizard (1962) in their group of retardates found that 9 percent showed some degree of cerebral palsy. In her chapter 9, Wilson has discussed the cerebral palsied, also pointing out that many fall in the trainable category.

Most of the trainable group are generally characterized by both physical and intellectual limitations; physical defects are numerous. In fact, with the occasional exception, multiple handicaps are the rule. Motor incoordination is almost universal. While there are few clinical types among the educable group there are many among the trainable. Cerebral palsy and epilepsy are not uncommon. Thus, in terms of designing effective training programs, the trainable group present many problems.

## BEHAVIORAL CHARACTERISTICS

It is difficult if not impossible to describe the behavior of trainable children in special schools and classes. They vary in age from six through the late teens, and are a heterogeneous group in physical and psychological characteristics. A laıge number of the pupils will be happy, friendly young people. However, one can expect more behavior problems among this group than among those of higher intellectual endowment. Though some may be average in activity or even lethargic, others are almost in constant motion—swaying, running, and talking—and are therefore labeled hyperactive. A number are easily excited, blowing up or having some other catastrophic reaction under even the slightest pressure or upset in routine. In fact, one sees the Strauss Syndrome more in special classes for the trainable then those for the educable.

Also evident in special classes are cases of extreme withdrawal behavior, dazed conditions, odd body and facial mannerisms, excessive fondling of others, distractability, attacks on others, and unusual emotional states. These characteristics are most common among children within the organic brain injury category. Too, these unusual mannerisms are more numerous among children with IQ scores in the 30s. Even when properly classified and placed, trainable pupils need constant supervision. Because of the many problems they present special class enrollments are usually limited to about 12 pupils, and frequently an attendant is hired to assist the teacher.

After at least one year of special class instruction, 24 teachers in Illinois rated their 198 pupils who were six through eighteen years of age on self-care tasks (Goldstein, 1956). Exceptions existed in all categories. A quite adequate average rating was given the group on toileting. A fairly adequate average rating was given the group on eating, drinking, dressing and undressing, washing, putting away toys, crossing streets, self-play, listening and responding to others. Fair average ratings were assigned to skills in talking, group play, serving food, housekeeping tasks, use of clothes, toothbrushing, use of handkerchief, and resting. Ratings were low in the skills involved in riding a bus and reading signs. These data provide a picture of the skills which teachers report the trainable are able to develop.

# School Programs for Trainable Pupils

## OBJECTIVES

The broad goal for educable retardates is to develop their independent living skills. By contrast, the goals for the trainable are very different since they will be dependent or semi-dependent all of their lives. Therefore program objectives emphasize the development of the minimal skills needed in living and working in sheltered environments. In broad terms, (1) self-help, (2) socialization, and (3) oral communication are stressed. Textbooks in the field (Baumgarner, 1960; Perry, 1960; Rosenzweigh and Long, 1960) elaborate on these broad objectives. Typical ingredients of courses include: (1) intellectual development, (2) self-help skills, (3) oral language development, (4) social development and adjustment, (5) mental health, (6) motor and sense training, (7) occupational skills, and (8) leisure-time activities.

## EARLY CURRICULAR APPROACHES

Three European physicians—first Itard, later Seguin, and more recently Montessori—provided the major early contributions to the field. The work of these pioneers and their disciples during the nineteenth century may well be viewed as the first golden age for trainable children.

*Jean Marc Itard* (1774–1838) is recognized as the first person to use methods of experimental psychology in attempting to teach or enculturate a retarded child. For five years, he worked with a 12 year old, so-called wild boy, Victor, captured in the forest of Aveyron in Southern France about 1800. Itard, a sensationalist, environmentalist, and physician, considered the boy's animal-like behavior to be due only to lack of socialization and education, resulting from years alone in the forest, and therefore remedial. While he had some success in teaching Victor, most authorities have since come to believe that the boy was severely mentally retarded and abandoned by his parents just shortly before he was captured. Nevertheless, Itard's teaching methodology is still modern today.

Itard was successful in getting the boy to control his actions and read a few words. To do so, he employed the basic rule of learning since posited by such learning theorists as Thorndike and Hull, "repeated rewarding trials." Systematic instruction by Itard and his helper resulted in Victor making appreciable gains judging from what we believe now to have been his very limited intellectual endowment. While Itard felt his experiment was a failure, teachers of trainable children need to look today to his teaching procedures. His goals were to develop in Victor language, self-help, and socialization skills. The same three are today recognized as major goals in classes for trainable children. The following account from the *Wild Boy of Aveyon* (Itard, 1962 p. 47) illustrates his technique.

One morning when he was waiting impatiently for the milk which he always had for breakfast, I carried to him his board which I had specially arranged the evening before with the four letters L A I T. Madame Guerin, whom I had warned, approached, looked at the letters and immediately gave me a cup of milk which I pretended to drink myself. A moment after I approached Victor, gave him the four letters that I had lifted from the board, and pointed to it with one hand while in the other I held the jug full of milk. The letters were immediately replaced but in inverted order, so that they showed T I A L instead of L A I T. I indicated the corrections to be made by designating with my fingers the letters to transpose and the proper place of each. When these changes had reproduced the sign, he was allowed to have his milk.

In conclusion, Itard's work shows the effectiveness (1) of individualized instruction, (2) of systematic programming of learning experiences, and (3) of motivation and rewards.

*Edward Seguin* (1812–1880), a student of Itard and also a physician, picked up where Itard left off on the development of instructional procedures for the severely retarded. Instead of working with a single boy like Victor, he established the first public residential facility in France for mentally retarded children and devised a curriculum for them. His was a neurophysiological technique based upon the belief that the impaired nervous systems of the retarded could be re-educated by motor and sensory training. He developed extensive didactic materials, asking his teachers to follow his systematic training procedures in a systematic fashion. Nevertheless, he used colors, music and other devices to motivate the child.

Samuel Gridley Howe (Richards, 1909) was instrumental in getting Seguin to move to the United States so that he could introduce his particular method of teaching into the first state residential facility for the retarded in the United States. This was created in 1848 under the guidance of the versatile Dr. Howe. At that time Howe wrote, "I have luckily secured Dr. Seguin, formerly the life and soul of the French school for idiots." In his second book written after he emigrated from France to the United States, Seguin (1907) outlined a residential school program which could be utilized today. Excerpts follow:

Near at hand must be the large-sized room, in which involuntary exercises of the feet are taught; the self-acting swing, opposed to a springboard, from which the feet borrow strength and elasticity; the ladder lying on the floor forcing the child, who must walk between its rounds, to raise his feet; the treadmill whose floor moves, and makes the child walk "in situ"; the blocks rising from the floor at regular walking distances; and parallel to them, the painted footprints on the floor; the former to make the regular walk compulsive, the latter to make it obligatory. . . .

. . . The room in which are performed the exercises of personal imitation, must be exempt from noise, ornament, or attraction of any sort. Its floor must be marked here and there with straight and curved lines, and with series of footprints upon which each child is expected to stand, or fall back to in due time. . . . The development of the human voice being favored by the voice of instruments, there is a piano in the room devoted to purely vocal exercises. There, one child at a time, or many together, are trained to emit tones, short or long, high or low, single or by pairs, or in series. . . . The education of the touch demands separate accommodations. The room in which it is done must be easily deprived of light, well supplied with closets containing a selection of substances, productions of art or of nature, whose characteristic properties fall under the control of the tact. . . . Though auditory exercises are not all confined to a single room, we may describe only the principal one devoted to it. In it the child is spoken to, close by, and at various distances; directly from the mouth to ear, or through the medium of hollow tubes, speaking-trumpets, etc.; or he is submitted to the direct agency of watches, bells, pianos; that room must be supplied for such emergencies. . . . Drawing, writing, reading, are taught in one room. . . . The objects gathered with the express view of giving object-lessons, do not need to be always in sight; but need careful arrangement and storage. . . . When room is scarce, we may put together, but never confusedly: (1) On the higher shelves, the patterns of simple things that the children may occasionally have to execute in wax, clay, wood, etc. (2) Somewhat lower, and easily seen but not touched, the standard toys, expansive, delicate, conveying more ideas by the sight than they would pleasure by handling. (3) Still lower, within reach of prehension, the playthings proper, bright, cheap, and easily broken contrivances, which are so necessary to the happiness of children, and from which they learn so much, even when destroying them. A room sufficiently large to contain all the children and visitors, is used daily for the common singing, and occasionally for musical and other festivities. . . .

. . . But happy the time when the gymnasium and most of the rooms can be vacated, and training and teaching may be transferred to the open air. There another and more natural school is prepared for them, and by their own efforts. . . . The intellectual institution is the living counterpart of the method. We discover in it the same flexibility of adaptation to all the physiological deficiencies, to bodily and mental weakness. In it the rotatory system is substantiated; we see the child moving from one mode of training to another, as in the method we could realize, his feeble mind led from one perception to another, and elevated, not by direct ascension, but by side-lifting and propagation of forces, as levers act on apparently immovable masses (pp. 175, 176, 177, 178, 179, 180, 181, 182, 183).[2]

It is interesting to read Howe's evaluation of Seguin (Richards, 1909).

Seguin has been here two months, and proves to be a man of great vigour of intellect, and full of resources; he has done wonders—but we can hardly keep him; he is full of self-esteem and *exigeant* to the uttermost; one of his conditions is that the Trustees shall not be allowed to hold any meetings without his being present. Another that neither the matron nor any teachers shall hold any communication with the parents of the pupils, &c., &c. Besides, he is choleric, not benevolent, and not very high in his motives. *C'est la gloire—la gloire.* (pp. 367–368)

Seguin was not successful in restoring severely retarded children to normal functioning. Society's early high hope for the residential school soon faded. At the end of the nineteenth century, a wave

---

[2] Seguin, E. *Idiocy and its treatment by the physiological method.* New York. Columbia Univer. Press, 1907.

of pessimism swept the country. No longer were residential schools viewed as training institutions for the habilitation of the mentally retarded. Instead, they were viewed as custodial facilities for children and adults who were hopelessly dependent. Only in the last decade or so has there been a strong resurgence in training.

*Maria Montessori* (1870–1956), an Italian physician, elaborated still further upon the Itard and Seguin procedures in developing a training program for retarded children in the residential facilities of Rome. Her productive work took place in this century. Her techniques for the retarded were given less of a trial in the United States than in some countries of Europe and Asia because of the pessimism which was sweeping the country following Seguin's efforts. Her greatest impact in this country was in regular kindergarten education. Her methods and materials are still distributed throughout the world today through the *International Montessori Association* with headquarters in Holland, and have made a slight re-entry into the Americas. Another evidence of the resurgence of interest in the Montessori Method is a recent book by Standing (1957) on her life and work. Montessori (1912) stressed "auto-education" or self-teaching through the use of such didactic materials as blocks, cut-outs, dressing frames, colored objects, and embossed letters. Her ten rules of education, which she appeared to consider equally appropriate for preschool normal and school-age trainable children, may well have been written in the 1960s. (1) Children are different from adults and need to be approached differently. (2) Learning comes from within and is spontaneous; the child must be interested in an activity to be motivated. (3) Children need a childhood environment which stresses free play, games and colorful materials. (4) Children love order. (5) Children must have freedom of choice; therefore they need sufficient materials so they may move from activity to activity as interest and attention span dictate. (6) Children love silence. (7) Children prefer work to play. (8) Children love repetition. (9) Children have a sense of personal dignity; thus we cannot expect them to do exactly as we command them to do. (10) Children utilize their environment to improve themselves whereas adults use themselves to perfect their environment.

## PRESENT-DAY CURRICULAR APPROACHES

Present-day curriculum for trainable children in the United States and Canada has been influenced by progressive education and informal teaching in regular kindergartens. Thus, in theory at least, and in contrast to Itard, Seguin, and Montessori who used an individual approach, American and Canadian educators have emphasized group activities, including group play, as the chief method for developing self-care and socialization.

Until recently, textbooks on school programs for the trainable child have been nonexistent. Instead teachers have had to rely on curriculum guides developed by state and local school districts. Recently this condition has been ameliorated by three good texts (Baumgartner, 1960; Perry, 1960; Rosenzweig and Long, 1960). To a considerable degree these parallel one another in outlining in considerable detail procedures for developing self-help, social, motor, occupational, and other skills. Among self-help skills are: feeding, dressing, toileting, washing, grooming, brushing teeth, using handkerchiefs, completing tasks, and following directions. Under social skills are: considering others, obeying rules, being courteous to others, and the like. Motor skills include walking, running, climbing, skipping, marching, dancing, throwing, catching, manipulating, eating, using finger muscles, using arm muscles, and playing alone and in groups. Other skills recommended for development are visual and auditory discrimination; speaking; using simple arithmetic terms as all, up, and down; rote counting, reading one's own name, and music participation. Occupational skills include running errands, dusting, sweeping, setting the table, washing and drying dishes, washing and ironing, sewing, homemaking, using tools, using the telephone, and traveling in the familiar parts of the community. As one would surmise, these skills are to be largely developed through social and group activities.

Hudson (1960a, 1960b) conducted the most comprehensive study to date in an attempt to identify techniques for instructing trainable mentally retarded children. She observed instructional procedures in 29 classrooms for trainable children for two 100 minute periods. Descriptions of techniques and lesson areas were dictated directly into tape recorders in the classroom and a detailed analysis, including a factor analytical study, was made later of the protocols.

In her analysis, she arrived at the 15 major lesson categories shown in Table 3.2. Detailed descriptions of what she found in each area may be found in her monograph (Hudson, 1960a).

TABLE 3.2 *Rank order and amount of emphasis placed on major lesson areas.*

| RANKS | LESSON AREAS | WEIGHTS OF EMPHASIS | | |
|---|---|---|---|---|
| | | Total | Fall | Spring |
| 1. | Language development | 1623 | 834 | 789 |
| 2. | Motor development | 899 | 434 | 395 |
| 3. | Mental development | 782 | 331 | 451 |
| 4. | Sensory training | 748 | 377 | 371 |
| 5. | Music | 677 | 305 | 372 |
| 6. | Health and safety | 668 | 298 | 370 |
| 7. | Social studies | 606 | 327 | 279 |
| 8. | Arithmetic concepts | 580 | 305 | 275 |
| 9. | Self-help | 463 | 241 | 222 |
| 10. | Occupational education | 425 | 211 | 214 |
| 11. | Socialization | 415 | 214 | 201 |
| 12. | Arts and crafts | 342 | 187 | 155 |
| 13. | Dramatization | 263 | 137 | 126 |
| 14. | Science concepts | 192 | 87 | 105 |
| 15. | Practical arts | 155 | 59 | 96 |

*Source:* Hudson, Margaret. An exploration of classroom procedures for teaching trainable mentally retarded children. *CEC Res. Monogr.*, Series A, No. 2, Washington, D.C.: Council for Except. Child., 1960.

Language development appeared to be getting major attention in special classes for the trainable, the next highest ranking activity, motor development, getting only about one half as much emphasis. As Hudson (1960b) has pointed out, because teachers place high status on verbal activities, perhaps too much time is spent on language development to the neglect of other areas. For example, practical arts in terms of cooking, sewing, dishwashing, cleaning, gardening, setting the table, doing chores, preparing food, and serving and clearing the table obtained the least attention. No doubt this is partially due to the backgrounds and values of the teachers who largely came from the regular classrooms. It may also have been due to the fact that all of the special classes were located in regular public schools and were equipped with chalkboards, desks, and other academic materials. One cannot help but wonder how much more emphasis would have been placed on the practical arts had the program been housed in a cottage which as nearly as possible replicated a typical home in the community.

Perhaps the most valuable outcome of the Hudson study was a teacher competency check list. This was arrived at by a cluster analysis (a correlational technique) which identified seven major instructional techniques. Then an analysis was made of the items under each which discriminated between more-effective and less-effective teachers in terms of rankings by the investigator and supervisors. The complete check list gives nine or ten items under each of the seven areas. Only two of them are included here by way of illustration.

1. Individual and Group Control: (emphasis on preventive aspects, helping the children develop self-control).

   a. Does not depend entirely on verbal approach; leads the child by touch to do what he is supposed to do.

   b. Helps prevent problems by structuring any period of movement about the room so confusion and undesirable behavior are at a minimum.

2. Getting the Children Started on Work; Keeping Them at Work and Interested.

   a. Uses sincere praise, to bring a real feeling of achievement and success (more than a perfunctory "good").

   b. Calls on the children so they will participate in the lesson; uses little of the "lecture" approach.

3. Building a Feeling of Personal Worth in the Children.

   a. Gives admiration, compliments, recognition for something personal, not connected with the lesson (i.e., appearance, clothes, something the child did).

    b. Gives different children errands or jobs in the room or out, so each can contribute something in the way of "service."

4. Structuring or Guiding the Learning.

    a. Uses physical guidance of the child's movements as needed until the child can gradually take over for himself as he gets the feel of it.

    b. Tells the children (gives a prior warning) before it is time to clean up, so they can finish what they are doing and not be upset by a sudden stop to an activity.

5. Encouraging Cooperative Interpersonal Interactions.

    a. Encourages the child to volunteer for jobs and activities.

    b. Children are encouraged to take turns, to give the other persons a chance to answer or to do something.

6. Providing for a Mind-set, or Attention.

    a. Gets the children's attention before starting a lesson.

    b. Makes sure a child is listening before trying to tell him something.

7. Drawing from the Children (as well as just "pouring-in").

    a. Uses guiding questions as clues to stimulate memory, thinking, association.

    b. Comments or questions a child as he is telling about something, to prompt him to tell more.[3]

The textbooks by Baumgartner, Perry, Rosenzweig, and Long and the Hudson report provide a consistent pattern of the present-day American curriculum employed in special day schools and classes for the trainable child. As has been repeatedly demonstrated, the major, avowed, purposes of special classes has been to develop the ability of the trainable pupil to look after himself and to perform helpful chores about the home or immediate neighborhood. The question arises as to how effective our techniques have been in developing such skills. Is this the best type of curriculum to offer the trainable child? Would we be better to return to the indi-

---

[3] Hudson, Margaret. Lesson areas for the trainable child. *Except. Child.*, 1960, 27, 224–229.

vidualized teaching of Itard, Seguin, and Montessori? Would we be still better off to move on to the training of the various aspects of intellect, which works such as Guilford (1959) are attempting to identify? What role has automated teaching and operant conditioning in this field (Stolurow, 1960; Ellis, 1960)? To ascertain the importance of such questions as these it is necessary to examine the research on the effectiveness of present-day programs.

## EFFECTIVENESS OF SPECIAL DAY CLASSES

In no other area of special education, or for that matter, of general education has there accumulated so much research evidence in such a short period of time. The series of comprehensive studies available to us resulted in large measure from the hesitancy of educators to establish such programs. When finally pressured by parent groups and state legislation to do so, they asked that these be set up on an experimental basis, so their effectiveness could be studied. As a result we have a good body of knowledge upon which to draw.

In the *Minnesota study,* Reynolds and Kiland (1953) evaluated four Minneapolis and St. Paul special classes with 49 trainable children enrolled in them. The pupils ranged in age from seven through 20 years and had been in the program from six months to six years. The chief instruments used were questionnaires and interviews. In terms of findings, the parents and teachers both reported the children had made progress in the special classes. The higher IQ youngsters benefited more from the special class than the lower IQ group. Parents lessened their expectations for academic learning as the program continued. The children did not learn appreciable skills in the three R's. The investigators concluded that the classes had provided a real service by giving the mothers relief in caring for their children for a few hours of the day, and that the children had made substantial progress in self-care and socialization. They went on to recommend a comprehensive state-wide long-term program since the needs of trainable children would not be fully met through public school special day classes, thus implying the need for residential facilities as well.

In the *Illinois study,* Goldstein (1956) reported on a two year investigation requested by the Illinois general assembly in 1953. Involved were 22 classes for 173 children. Only 125 remained in the program throughout the two year period, the rest dropping out for various reasons. Instruments used included individual intelligence tests, social maturity scales, behavior check-lists, and interviews with parents and school administrators. Some of the results of the study were as follows: (1) the average cost per child per year in special classes approximated $900; (2) there was a slight increase in IQ's though this increase was not significant, (3) both parents and teachers reported more progress during the first than second year, (4) mongoloids progressed as much as nonmongoloids, (5) children with IQ's of 25 and below and those with extreme behavior problems had to be excluded, (6) parents began to realize that their children could not become self-sufficient.

In the *Michigan study,* Guenther (1956) reported on a three-year investigation in which he compared the effectiveness of a special school in a rural community that served all levels of mental retardation with a special school for young trainable mentally retarded children (CA four to eight) in an urban area, and with a home training program for trainable youth over 16 years of age. Findings included the following: (1) the teacher who operated the rural school which enrolled 15 children of educable, trainable and untrainable levels reported the children in the trainable range made slight to considerable progress; (2) no attempt was made to evaluate the special class for younger children since there was rapid turnover and instruments for measuring growth were not available; (3) the itinerant teacher reported that home instruction for the 24 adolescent retardates did not seem to change the situation perceptibly since only two were able to get employment—one as a dishwasher and the other as an assistant janitor in a class for retarded children.

In the *New York study,* Johnson and Capobianco (1957) reported on a two-year investigation comparing the effectiveness of seven special day classes enrolling 41 children, with 10 half-day classes in residential facilities enrolling 96 children. Instruments included behavior check lists, the Vineland Social Maturity Scale, intelligence tests, an articulation test, a language test, and a Fels Child Behavior Rating Scale. They found the social quotient increased from three to five points on the average but not for children with IQ's below 25. In terms of self-care and socialization, children with IQ's above 30 made considerable progress while those below 30 made little or none. Both groups showed positive changes in terms of behavior, the group with the higher IQ being somewhat superior. The day school group made slightly larger gains on the articulation test. However, over-all, there were no statistically significant differences between the day and residential groups. The researchers concluded that improvements were no greater than that which could have been expected from mental age growth alone. They too pointed out that children with IQ's below 30 could not profit from a school program, and that special day classes are not the complete solution to the problem of providing for the trainable retardates.

In the *Tennessee study,* Hottel (1958) compared for a one-year period 21 matched pairs of trainable children, one group at school and the other at home. The pairs were matched at the outset on sex, etiology, chronological age, mental age, and social age. His was the first investigation in which, by inferential statistics, a school group was compared with a home group, and a higher IQ group (IQ's 40–50) with a lower IQ group (IQ's 30–40). Three hypotheses were tested: (1) that day class training would produce desirable changes in the behavior of the children, (2) that day class training would produce desirable changes in parent-child relation by taking pressure off the home, and (3) that children with IQ's 40–50 at school would make significantly greater progress than a similar group at home or the school group with IQ's of 30–40. Instruments included the Revised Stanford-Binet, the Vineland Social Maturity Scale, Fels Parent-Child Relationships Scale, and a Behavior Check List. His first two hypotheses were not supported but his third was. In other words, children with IQ's of 40–50 in school grew significantly more intellectually than the matched children at home. The high IQ group at school also improved more than the low IQ group at school. This led Hottel to recommend that the lower limit for special education classes be established at the IQ 40 level—though he did not research any other IQ division line such as 35.

In the *San Francisco study,* Cain and Levine (1961) developed two new instruments the San Francisco Social Competency Scale, and the San Francisco Parent Adaptability Scale. With the first, they measured self-care and socialization; with the second they assessed parent flexibility and empathy. Four groups of trainable children were studied for a two-year experimental period: 46 trainable children attending community day schools, 63 trainable children in the community but remaining at home, 33 trainable children attending school in residential facilities, and 40 trainable children in residential facilities not attending school. In terms of social competence, both groups of community children, those in school and those remaining at home, increased significantly, but there were no differences in growth between these two groups. Both the institutional school and nonschool groups showed significant decreases in their social competency scores. It was concluded that the public day and residential school program, as they are now conducted, do not foster social competency development of trainable children beyond that of children not attending such programs. Also indicated is that the environment within residential facilities, as they are now constituted, is not conducive to the social development of trainable children. These findings do not support the contention that special day classes are effective, but they do suggest the ineffectiveness of our present-day large, multipurpose residential facilities. In terms of the social development of these trainable children, parents would be well advised to keep their trainable children out of existing institutions. However, there may be very strong reasons for placing them there in terms of the adjustment of the rest of the family. In terms of the San Francisco Parent Adaptability Interview Schedule, parents of trainable children in both of the community groups decreased in flexibility and empathy. The day school program did not have the salutary effects on parents which had been predicted. The researchers suggest that this finding may have been reversed by more and better parent-teacher contacts. However, it may be that the results reflect the increasing pressure on parents who have a trainable child at home.

This series of studies has many weaknesses. Included among the limitations are the following: (1) few of them have control or contrast groups; (2) there continues to be a lack of adequate measuring devices; (3) what is measured is different from what is being stressed, and what is presently in the program often differs from avowed objectives for the classes; (4) training periods extended only over short periods of time (one or two years); (5) sample sizes have been small; and (6) teacher competency has been studied little (conceivably pooling many poor with a few good teachers resulted in the over-all, general negative results). Nevertheless, the results are so parallel that a few conclusions seem in order. (1) There is little evidence that special day classes, as presently constituted, which emphasize the development of self-care and socialization by informal group instruction are effective for homogeneous groups of trainable children with IQ's over the full range from 25–50. (2) Educators should give serious consideration to including in special day classes for the trainable only children with IQ's above 35 or 40. (3) There is a great need for long term studies which will follow the children through the schools and into adulthood to study their competence in community living. (4) We need to study the relative efficiency of different teachers and different instructional procedures. The ultimate effectiveness of special classes rests on many factors including the effect on the children themselves, on the parents, on the siblings, and on the community. Already we have some evidence from follow-up studies on what happens to trainable children after they leave special classes, and this is presented later in the chapter.

## ADMISSION AND EXCLUSION PRACTICES

Kirk (1957), Johnson and Capobianco (1957), Rosenzweig and Long (1960) and others have evolved somewhat similar sets of criteria for the trainable retardate on selection and dismissal from special day classes. The following are built largely upon standards found in this literature.

1. A committee should be appointed to advise on admission practices and placement standards. The committee should also be responsible for screening applicants and for advising on admission, exclusion, and termination of stay for each pupil.
2. Placement in special classes for the trainable should be made only where the basic defect is one of mental retardation. For

example, there must be no severe personality problems indicating the primary problem is emotional rather than intellectual subnormality. Vision and hearing problems need also be considered.

3. Children who are sufficiently intelligent to be eligible for placement in the regular grades or in special classes for the educable retardate, and those who are untrainable and best served in day or residential care programs or some similar service should be declared ineligible for placement.

4. The age of admission should not be less than that set for regular school attendance. It may be even later if the child has not developed the self-care skills recommended below as prerequisites. However, it is doubtful if teen-aged youth who have never attended should be placed in the special classes.

5. The prime criterion for placement, though not the sole one, should be an IQ score of approximately 35–55 obtained by a qualified psychological examiner using an individual intelligence test such as the 1960 Stanford Binet.

6. Applicants should be ambulatory, toilet trained to the point of being able to make at least his elimination needs known, and able to at least partially feed and dress himself.

7. Applicants should have the ability to remain away from their mother for a school day. Often a gradual introduction with the class is desirable and necessary.

8. Applicants should have at least sufficient skills in communication to express their needs and respond to simple direction.

9. Children who are a danger to themselves or others, who have frequent seizures, who require frequent restraint, and who are a very disruptive influence in the class should be excluded.

10. A psychological report should be available which goes beyond giving IQ scores, and includes information on perceptual disorders, personal and social adjustment, and specific aptitudes and limitations.

11. A medical report should be available on all applicants outlining visual, auditory, circulatory, respiratory, motor, and other physical limitations. In particular, information on neurological damage, seizures and drug therapy is needed.

12. Reports by a social worker, an educational diagnostician, and speech and hearing specialists are also desirable. These will provide data on home conditions, on achievement in self-help skills and social, learnings, and on language skills and disorders.

13. Teachers should have access to the psychological, medical and social work reports and participate in the screening and re-evaluation procedures.

14. All children screened for admission should be placed in the special classes on a trial basis of one to four months to see if they can function in a group setting. At the end of each year, all pupils should be re-examined to ascertain the extent to which they have adjusted and profited from special class placement. Children unable to profit should be excluded after a reasonable trial period. They may be given other trials after they get older.

15. Parents whose children are not admitted to the program or are later rejected, should be counseled personally by the person in charge of the special education program and an official letter sent by the superintendent of schools.

16. The age of discharge from the special class program should be dependent upon the ability to profit from the program and upon the availability of sheltered workshops and other community facilities for the graduates. Multispecial class programs with a curriculum adapted for adolescents are able to retain a pupil much longer than programs with only one or two special classes serving in each a wide age and ability range. School responsibility should generally terminate when pupils are 16–21 years of age.

## PHILOSOPHICAL ISSUES

Earlier in this chapter, the question was raised, "Are the trainable mentally retarded a public school responsibility?" Some educators such as Cruickshank have answered "no" (see the debate by Goldberg and Cruickshank, 1958). They have based their position on the following arguments. (1) The unique function of the schools is to educate children who can learn academically and the trainable mentally retarded can neither acquire appreciable skills in the three R's nor can they do abstract reasoning, make abstract judgments, or solve adult problems. (2) Trainable mentally retarded children cannot return to society what society has invested in their schooling. (3) Placing trainable children in public school classes sets up false hopes for their parents. (4) Teachers in their teacher preparation are taught to value academic knowledge and to teach academic subjects, thus they do not have the preparation to teach self-care, socialization, and economic usefulness. (5) After passing through the special classes, these youngsters will continue to be a charge for the family and community, thus a more permanent and comprehensive program of services is desirable. (6) Experimental studies have shown trainable children can learn as much at home as in special classes. Other arguments have included: (7) the teacher shortage, and (8) school housing shortages. But, the prime argument has centered around *educability* versus *trainability*. Most authorities averse to these special day classes have hinged their argument on the position that the school's responsibility, as a social institution, is to educate children first of all in the tool subjects and then in the conventional academic subjects. Thus, trainable children should be excluded since they cannot hope to accomplish these goals.

Other educators such as Goldberg (see Goldberg and Cruickshank, 1958) have argued that special classes for the trainable mentally retarded are the responsibility of the public schools. They base their position on the following arguments. (1) Parents of the trainable child are taxpayers and therefore have the right to expect the schools to find a place for their children. (2) the popular educational philosophy of our day says that the schools have a responsibility to provide an education for all the children of all the people, and that the goals of education must be broad enough to encompass self-care and socialization. (3) This is an academic question since parents and political leaders have the responsibility for determining the role of the schools in our society, having elected to place responsibility for the trainable on the school, it is therefore the responsibility of educators to provide the requested service. (4) They argue that studies on the effectiveness of day classes have many weaknesses and especially that the children have profited from the program even if the research workers have not been able to measure the growth. (5) Special classes can be justified in terms of taking pressure off the parents, even though appreciable gains are not measured in the children. (6) Special day classes are more economical than permanent care in a residential facility.

The question is now largely a theoretical one since the number of day classes has become so extensive. In fact, by 1961, the *National Association for Retarded Children* reported that 39 states had provided state-level support for special classes for the trainable in the public day schools. Since 1950, trainable children in the thousands have been removed from home care and parent-sponsored community schools into programs provided by the public schools.

It would seem that the trainable child is the responsibility of the public schools, as a *social institution*, but not necessarily the responsibility of the teaching profession. The public schools, as an institution of society, appear to be the most appropriate social agency to provide instructional programs for groups of children during daylight hours. Certainly the public schools employ personnel in addition to classroom teachers (psychologists, physicians, social workers, speech correctionists, attendants, and others). Likewise, they could employ some other professional groups more appropriately prepared to provide the needed training programs for trainable children. So far teachers have been quite unsuccessful in the training of these retarded children. This could be explained in terms of their inappropriate professional preparation for serving these children and their negative attitude toward those who cannot learn academically. It could be explained in various other ways. Perhaps the time has come to create a new profession to instruct trainable children.

If this course of action is not acceptable, and if the teaching profession is to continue to instruct the trainable, some marked changes are needed. It is suggested that teachers with regular teacher preparation and especially with a background of teaching experience in the regular grades above the primary level, are incorrectly prepared for work in the field. In fact, it is probably not in the best interests of trainable pupils for them to have a teacher who has ever taught in the regular grades. Those with nursery and kindergarten teaching experience would seem to have more appropriate backgrounds. Probably, it would be even better if instructors of the trainable had no teaching experience with average pupils. They need a radically changed teacher education curriculum to prepare them to instruct the pupils we have under consideration. Preparation in counseling, learning and conditioning, motor and sense training, homemaking, and other areas seem more appropriate.

It is difficult to say whether the future will dictate a new professional group outside of the teaching profession or a unique specialty within the teaching profession. In either event other changes are needed. Present-day special classes within regular public schools, with desks and chalkboards, seem completely inappropriate for preparing the trainable pupil to live dependently at home and in other sheltered settings. Haitema (1961) has initiated an approach utilizing a much more suitable facility. It is in the form of a cottage, purchased and operated by the public schools, and located out in the community away from a regular school. The building is furnished as nearly as possible to resemble a regular home. Children look after the lawns, shrubs, and garden. They care for the house, cook in the kitchen, eat in the dining room, and clear up afterwards. They learn how to wash a car, use a bathroom, clean the bedding, and get and store materials in cupboards. They have bedrooms for their use, linen closets, and a washer and dryer. They live in a living room, eat in a dining room, and play in back and front yards. Surely there is much greater carry-over from such a facility, than from a pseudo-practical program provided by modifying a classroom in a regular school building. Yet, few if any public schools aside from the Mount Clemens, Michigan School District where Haitema is director of special education provide such a facility.

There is little doubt that the public schools are going to continue to provide instruction for the trainable child. Even if changes are made in the preparation of persons who will guide and instruct these pupils, and in the types of facilities in which the instruction will take place, much more needs to be done.

Research should be conducted on what makes some instructors effective and some ineffective. Different curricular approaches need to be evolved and tested. There is good evidence that the informal group instructions stressing self-care and socialization may not be the complete answer. There is probably a need to re-examine the Seguin (1907) and Montessori (1912) approaches. We need to look at the possible application of the training of intellect research (Guilford, 1959) and teaching machines (Stolurow, 1960). Furthermore, experimental psychologists in the area of learning need to research new techniques in modifying the behavior of trainable children. The *shaping* technique in which behavior is modified through repeated, rewarded approximations, and other forms of *operant conditioning* may have applicability, not only to the trainable child, but to the ambulatory youngster who is even more retarded (Ellis, 1960). Through carefully modifying behavior, by shaping and motivation, it may be possible to train children to a far greater degree than has yet been envisioned.

## RESIDENTIAL SCHOOL PROGRAMS

It was pointed out in chapter 1 that in 1958 there were still slightly more trainable children going to school in residential facilities than in public day schools (see Table 1.2), 17,000 being enrolled in institutions in contrast to 16,779 in local school districts. While new statistical studies will show more in day than in residential settings, nevertheless, the number placed in institutions is likely to remain large if not increased in the years ahead. Therefore it is necessary to at least look briefly at the programs they receive and their effectiveness.

By 1960, all states with the exception of Alaska and Nevada reported the operation of State Training Schools (see 1960 directory of the AAMD). In practically all (if not all) cases, these took the form of large, multipurpose residential facilities, serving retardates of all ages and of all levels of intellect. These facilities are asked to provide all types of care, treatment, and habilitation, usually with inadequate buildings, and inadequate staffs. These large multipurpose residences have some advantages. They are less expensive to operate. They permit an interdisciplinary approach to treatment. They provide a large population of retardates for research purposes. They have high visibility for political purposes. They permit locating them regionally within the state so as to be closer to the residents' home communities and parents. However, they have many disadvantages. They often are unable to attract top-flight professional personnel. They are so large that a massed, impersonalized approach to treatment usually prevails. They are often custodial, rather than intensive treatment oriented. There is frequently interdisciplinary rivalry and buck-passing; much of the service is provided by untrained attendants, while the professionals engage in administrative tasks. Funds are often spent on the physical plant at the expense of adequate staff and services. Because of these grave disadvantages these large multipurpose residences can no longer be justified, *in their present form*. They need either to be vastly improved, or augmented or surplanted by small, single purpose, intensive-treatment, residential units. Dybwad (1959) in examining the different residential treatment needs of retarded persons reached the same conclusion: "It stands to reason that so many different types of needs call for a number of clearly differentiated types of residential facilities of different sizes, with different staffs, different buildings, different programs, even in our smaller states." In terms of trainable children, it was clear from the Cain and Levine (1961) study reported earlier in the chapter that such children did not make as much progress socially in large multiple purpose facilities as those either staying at home or attending special day classes.

A recent study by Tizard (1962) and his associates, suggests a different type of residential school is desirable for the trainable. This "Brooklands" experiment was conducted in the United Kingdom from 1958–1960.[4] A group of 32 subjects, half whom were mongoloids, with ages four through 10 years were divided into matched pairs on diagnosis, sex, age, and nonverbal IQ scores. One half served as controls, remaining in a very large, multipurpose residential facility in London where a school program was provided in addition to the usual ward care. The other half served as the experimental group, being placed in a small residential unit called "Brooklands" in the country on the outskirts of London which had formerly been a beautiful estate. Here they were provided an enriching program by teachers who had *nursery school* backgrounds. The program of instruction utilized nursery school techniques. The subjects were divided into two family groups of eight pupils, each family having its own living room and bedroom and with the

---

[4] A 16 mm sound film on their experiment called "Mentally Retarded Children Growing Up" is available for loan. See the list of films at the end of this chapter.

former nursery teachers serving as mother surrogates. An informal approach was employed based on play, games, and family living. The results showed that the Brooklands group made significantly greater gains in verbal intelligence than the control group. Their speech also significantly improved. There were also striking changes in their motor coordination, and especially in their social and personal adjustment. Children who banged their head, stood alone for hours in a corner, or resorted to temper tantrums and screaming outbursts at the outset dropped these unacceptable behavior patterns. There were no claims that even the Brookland's group would become self-sufficient in adulthood. The per capita costs for the smaller unit was higher than for the larger unit. However, in the long view, there may have been some economic advantages since self-care skills were learned which could be called upon throughout the lives of the pupils. But surely economic factors should not replace humanitarian ones in our democratic society. Nonetheless, the implications are clear. First, the small special purpose residential facility proved superior to the large multipurpose institution. Second, nursery school teachers utilizing nursery school techniques were very successful. It would appear that the United Kingdom experiment can teach us in the United States and Canada much about improving our residential facilities.

# Community, Occupational and Family Adjustment

## POSTSCHOOL ADJUSTMENT

While the day school movement for trainable retardates is largely a phenomenon of the 1950s, a few programs have been in operation for many years. Classes were opened in St. Louis, Missouri as early as 1914, in New York City by 1929, and in St. Paul, Minn., by 1934. Some evidence is available on what has happened to the graduates of the St. Paul and New York City programs.

Delp and Lorenz (1953) followed up 84 special class pupils with IQ's below 50 who were at one time enrolled in the St. Paul classes. When the study was conducted in 1952, the median age of the group was 22 years with a range from 9 to 32 years. Of the former students, 41 were still residing at home, 25 were in residential facilities, 9 were deceased, and 9 had moved out of the state. None had established their own homes. Medical diagnoses classified 15 as mongols, 9 as cerebral palsied, 5 as cretins, 5 as epileptics, while 44 were listed as "diagnosis unavailable"; the remaining 6 included the less common types. It was found that only two graduates had ever held full-time jobs, while a total of only ten (all males) had ever been gainfully employed. The two in full-time jobs were a hospital janitor and a worker in a department store commissary. Most of the group who were living at home were socially accepted in the neighborhood and were useful about the house. The majority were able to get about the neighborhood, eat in restaurants, go for groceries, attend movies, and enjoy popular entertainment. As a result, Delp and Lorenz concluded the special classes had been important in training children better than could have been done in the home alone, though this conclusion is not justified since no control was utilized. The final statement is worth quoting:

Without an appreciation of the value and limitations of the public school, many parents are already insisting that their children be admitted to special classes and be taught the usual academic subjects—"with modification, of course." This fetish of the three R's is still with us. Merely because the child is 10 years old (but with a mental age of perhaps four years), parents insist that he learn to read. Such is beyond possibility, beyond the intent of the classes such as the Betas, and more particularly beyond the best interests of the children whom we hope to help (p. 182).

Saenger (1957) followed up some 2640 adults, formerly enrolled in special classes for the trainable child in New York City during the period 1929–1955. The main body of his report was based on interviews with 520 parents. Saenger found two thirds of the graduates living at home, compared with one half noted by Delp and Lorenz. Of the remaining one third, Saenger found 26 percent were institutionalized and 8 percent had died since leaving school. He found that one quarter of his follow-up subjects had worked or were working for pay within the community, with older retardates (over 30 years) making better social and economic adjustments than the younger ones. IQ data were not available on all the subjects, but in general most of those who were gainfully employed had IQ's above 40, and many had IQ's in the 50s, which probably explains why the Saenger study paints a generally brighter picture than the Delp and Lorenz study. Employed men outnumbered employed women four to one. Many of the jobs were found with (or through) relatives, Saenger went on to say that one in five of his subjects assumed major responsibility for such household chores as cleaning the apartment, helping with the dishes, and running errands. One half took responsibility for taking care of their own things and cleaning their rooms.

Tisdall (1960) followed up 126 children who were enrolled in special day classes for the trainable mentally retarded in Illinois during the previous five years. A vast majority of these subjects ranged in IQ from 30 to 40 with a mean of 33. Thus, they were appreciably below the sample reported on by Delp and Lorenz and even more below the Saenger sample. One fourth of the follow-up subjects were found to be at home where they were receiving no formal training. One fourth were still in special classes. One fifth were located in parent-sponsored classes for school-age trainable mentally retarded children. The remainder were in institutions, were working in sheltered workshops, were attending classes for the educable mentally retarded, had moved out of the community, or were deceased. It would appear that the age range of the children extended from 10 through 23 years, with only three of the graduates gainfully employed in the community. Only one of the three received a regular salary. The subjects were self-sufficient in eating, washing, and dressing. Interviews with the parents indicated that the school curriculum which had stressed self-care, social adjustment, and economic usefulness had been effective since the children were not disturbing influences upon the family.

Such a conclusion is heartening, but needs to be evaluated in the light of a study conducted by Jewell (1941) on 190 children from the District of Columbia who, in the 1930s had been *excluded* from school because of low intelligence, their IQ's ranging from 30 to 50. The majority of these subjects were reported to be getting along well at home, but only a few were employed for pay. These young people, without special class training, appeared to have become as effective in later life as those who graduated from the Minnesota, New York, and Illinois special classes. Thus, the follow-up studies must be viewed as inconclusive in terms of supporting special classes.

## SHELTERED WORKSHOPS

In 1920, the Office of Vocational Rehabilitation (OVR), which is now part of the U.S. Department of Health, Education, and Welfare, was established by Congress. For 23 years its services were restricted to the physically handicapped. In 1943 the services of OVR were broaden to include the mentally ill and mentally retarded. However, only those with the potential for gainful, competitive employment were eligible for assistance. Thus most of the educable mentally retarded could be served but not trainable youth. In 1954, a new law made possible special project grants for such activities as sheltered workshops which could serve trainable persons. Since then the number of such employment centers has increased rapidly. However, even previous to 1954, sheltered workshops were being established by such agencies as civic groups, school systems, Goodwill Industries, the Salvation Army, and parent groups.

Sheltered workshops usually serve trainable retardates as well as other disabled adolescents and adults. Work programs include filling subcontracts for industry, producing items for sale, and restoring damaged articles. The success of these centers demonstrates that the mentally retarded can be productively employed in a wide variety of jobs when a sheltered setting is provided. They are likely to increase many fold in the years ahead. Not only do they provide employment, but also recreation, counseling for both the retarded youth and his parents, and occasionally even housing. Fraenkel (1961) has provided an excellent resource handbook for establishing such facilities. In the meantime some exciting research is coming out of Britain on the employment of the trainable retardates. O'Connor and Tizard (1956) found that trainable youth were able to fold more boxes in the factory after training than a control group of educable retardates. The hint of the effectiveness of on-the-job systematic training along with adequate programming and motivation bears study and repetition in the United States and Canada. In devising a comprehensive program for the trainable retardate, one must plan for sheltered employment.

## FAMILY ADJUSTMENT

Farber and his associates (1960) have studied the effects of a trainable mentally retarded child on family integration. They found great variability in their impact. For example, as a group, Catholic homes were better able to tolerate and integrate a trainable child than Protestant or Jewish homes. A trainable child has a more disintegrating effect upon an older sister than an older brother. (This is explained by the observation that the older sisters are asked to care for the trainable child, while older brothers are given freedom since the parents are devoting so much attention to the retarded member of the family.) Families which stressed home and family life were better able to integrate a trainable child than those who were involved in many community activities.

Saenger (1960) found institutionalization highly related to the degree of retardation. One out of every nine retardates in New York City with IQ's 20–49 were committed. Secondary disabilities, unless severe, played no apparent role in commitment. No correlation was found between institutionalization and parental income or family size. Children of Puerto Rican and Negro families were more frequently institutionalized than others. Aside from the degree of retardation, behavior problems of the retarded person was the next most important factor in institutionalization. Broken homes, parental inadequacy, and family deprivation were contributing factors to institutionalization.

Tizard and Grad (1961) in a social survey of the mentally handicapped and their families conducted in London, England, studied 150 families where the retarded offspring lived at home, and 150 families where the child was institutionalized. Over-all, they found that many parents of the home group wanted to continue to keep their retarded child at home, even though they were having greater difficulties than families who had placed their child in a residential setting. As Farber found, and as common sense dictates, keeping a retarded child at home puts pressure on the family, but usually the child does not make home life hell on earth. One third of the group who lived at home were severe management problems; one third were moderate management problems; and one third were slight or no management problems. Tizard and Grad, as did Saenger, found that the most severely retarded children were more likely to be institutionalized. Homes where institutionalization had taken place were poorer, had more over-crowding, and had larger families. When the retarded child lived at home, there were much fewer social contracts, and the siblings had many more problems in their social relations.

All of these studies add to our understanding of the effects of retarded children on families. Obviously no simple answer exists to the question: What is it like to have a retarded child, and should he be placed in a residential facility? Perhaps the only safe generalization is that each family will need to evaluate its own situation, and plan its own course of action. But, families often do need professional help in exploring their problems and possible solutions. Data of the sort presented should be helpful in assisting the family in determining whether their trainable child should remain at home or be placed in a residential facility. Certainly one justification for both day and residential schools is the reduction of pressure on the family. In such cases, this might improve mental health of the parents and siblings. There are a few homes where the trainable child is an integrating factor. Therefore thorough understanding of the family setting is needed to counsel with parents on the proper placement for their child. There are no pat answers.

A growing number of guidelines are available to help parents of retarded children. These are especially useful while the children are in their preschool years. Levinson (1952) in advising parents set down ten commandments:

1. Get medical advice early and follow the program outlines
2. Don't adopt a defeatist attitude
3. Don't develop a complex of shame or guilt
4. Don't neglect your normal children because of your retarded child
5. Don't pauperize yourself to give your child the best
6. Don't push your child beyond his capabilities
7. Try to meet your child's emotional problems

8. Don't be afraid to have other children
9. Do not covet the child of your neighbor
10. Help further the cause of the mentally retarded

Kirk, Karnes and Kirk (1955) have an especially valuable behavior patterns schedule. A careful listing is made of what the average child is able to do at various ages from three to four months up through the six year level. Practical suggestions are outlined for helping the retarded child in learning the various self-help and social skills. Dittmann (1959), in a Children's Bureau manual, also gives suggestions for toilet training, dressing, cleanliness and manners, discipline, speech, play, and group experiences. Other manuals are listed in the references at the end of the chapter. Carlson and Ginglend (1961), have published a useful book of play activities for the retarded child. This growing body of literature has become a major source of information to assist more able and better adjusted parents to understand and help their retarded children. Cianci (1947) has outlined a home counseling service where professional persons—usually teachers or public health nurses—make regular calls on mothers of retarded children advising and demonstrating on home care and training. This should be an especially helpful approach. The future should see additional services provided to families who elect to keep their retarded children at home. For example, already day care centers are becoming available for pre-school trainable children, and for children in the IQ 20 to 35 range.

## Summary

Individuals with IQ's in the 35–55 range, as yet, cannot be expected to become self-sufficient. Thus a comprehensive, long-term program of care and training must be developed by society if they are to be adequately served. Custom has dictated that parents keep at home, and provide most of the care for, their preschool children of all intellectual levels except the most severely defective, though it is recognized that nursery and kindergarten programs are becoming more available. Since parents have an expectancy for this responsibility, it is not unfair to look to them to provide for their trainable children in the home for at least the first six years. However, some professional help must be provided. It must be pointed out that additional tension is placed on the home when the trainable youngster does not learn to walk and talk at the same time as other children, and in addition is a behavior problem. Furthermore, these children demand much more care and protection than their intellectually normal peers. In addition, parents are likely to have more medical problems with these children. Thus, while there is need for more public nurseries and kindergartens for average children, there is a still greater need for day care centers for preschool trainable children, as well as for special home counseling.

Throughout the traditional school years of ages six through eighteen, parents expect society, usually the schools, to provide for their children for five hours a day, 180 days a year. Thus, at this point if not before, it is reasonable for the parents to demand that society assume some responsibility for trainable children. Here residential and special day class facilities have found their place.

Trainable youth and adults are very different from their more intellectually endowed peers in that they do not attain social and economic independence as they reach adulthood. Here again, society has responsibilities to both the retarded and the parents. We have traditionally provided service through residential facilities. It seems improbable that we will be able to build and staff sufficient of these to meet the need. Ways must be found of keeping more of this group of persons in the community. So far the terminal sheltered workshop seems to be the major solution on the scene to employment. As yet, these sheltered workshops have only been moderately effective. We need to improve training procedures by borrowing methods from the psychological laboratories so that more productivity will be obtained. Residential facilities will still be needed where parents and relatives are no longer available to provide homes for retarded persons, or where other factors make commitment necessary. Half-way houses and other boarding facilities, counseling, and other services for the adult need to be broadened.

Trainable children are no longer hidden from the public, and parents are placing increased demands on society. Good progress has been made but much remains to be done. Services for trainable children are becoming more systematic and comprehensive; services for adult trainable retardates are still sporadic and inconsistent.

Therefore, if we are to develop a comprehensive total program we must undergo a metamorphosis in terms of community understanding and responsibility. Our salvation is to keep many of these persons in the community; our challenge is to find ways of doing this which are socially desirable and economically feasible. People are concerned with the total problem of mental retardation as never before, as evidenced by the report of President Kennedy's Panel on Mental Retardation (1962). In a solution of this problem, education must of necessity play an important part. A special challenge for educators is to develop imaginative procedures through insightful research so that noteworthy contributions in the development of trainable children and youth will be achieved.

## CHAPTER REFERENCES

Baumgartner, Bernice B. *Helping the trainable mentally retarded child.* New York: Bureau of Publications, Columbia Univer., Teachers College, 1960.

Benda, C. E. *Mongolism and cretinism.* (2nd ed.) New York: Grune & Stratton, 1949.

Cain, L. F., & Levine, S. *A study of the effects of community and institutional school classes for trainable mentally retarded children.* San Francisco, Calif.: San Francisco State College, 1961.

Cantor, G. N., & Girardeau, F. L. *An investigation of discrimination learning ability in mongoloid and normal children of comparable mental age.* Nashville, Tenn.: Peabody College, 1958.

Carlson, Bernice W., & Ginglend, D. R. *Play activities for the retarded child.* Nashville, Tenn.: Abingdon Press, 1961.

Cianci, V. Home supervision of mental deficients in New Jersey. *Amer. J. ment. Defic.,* 1947, **51**, 519–524.

Connor, Frances P., & Goldberg, I. I. Opinions of some teachers regarding their work with trainable children: Implications for teacher education. *Amer J. ment. Defic.,* 1960, **64**, 658–670.

Delp, H. A., & Lorenz, Marcella. Follow-up of 84 public school special class pupils with IQ's below 50. *Amer. J. ment. Defic.,* 1953, **58**, 175–182.

Dittmann, Laura L. The mentally retarded child at home. *Children's Bureau, Publ.* No. 374, Washington, D.C.: Government Printing Office, 1959.

Dybwad, G. New directions in residential care of the mentally retarded. Unpublished manuscript. New York: National Association for Retarded Children, 1959.

Ellis, N. R. Clinical and training implications of operant conditioning methods with mental defectives. Paper presented at APA, Chicago, 1960.

Engler, M. A comparative study of the causation of mongolism, peristatic amentia, and other types of mental defect. *J. ment. Sci.,* 1952, **98**, 316–325.

Farber, B., Jenne, W. C., & Toigo, R. Family crisis and the decision to institutionalize the retarded child. *CEC Res. Monogr.,* Series A, No. 1. Washington D.C.: Council for Exceptional Children, 1960.

Fraenkel, W. A. *The mentally retarded and their vocational rehabilitation: A resource handbook.* New York: National Association for Retarded Children, 1961.

Goldberg, I. I. Current status of education and training for trainable mentally retarded children. *Except. Child.,* 1957, **24**, 146–154.

————, & Cruickshank, W. M. The trainable but non-educable: Whose responsibility. *NEA J.,* 1958, **47**, 622–623.

Goldstein, H. *Report number two on study projects for trainable mentally handicapped children.* Springfield, Ill.: Superintendent of Public Instruction, 1956.

Goodman, N., & Tizard, J. Prevalence of imbecility and idiocy among children. *Brit. Med. J.,* 1962, **5273**, 216–219.

Guenther, R. J. *Final report of the Michigan demonstration research project for the severely retarded.* Lansing, Mich.: State Department of Public Instruction, 1956.

Guilford, J. P. Three faces of intellect. *Amer. Psychologist,* 1959, **14**, 469–479.

Haitema, J. S. A public school program and facility for severely mentally retarded children. Unpublished paper. Mount Clemens, Mich.: Macomb County Board of Education, 1961.

Heber, R. F. A manual on terminology and classification in mental retardation. *Monogr. Suppl. Amer. J. ment. Defic.,* (2nd ed.) 1961.

Hottel, J. V. *The Tennessee experimental program of day classes for severely mentally retarded (trainable) children: Interim report of the study.* Nashville, Tenn.: Peabody College, 1956.

————. *An evaluation of Tennessee's day class program for severely mentally retarded children: Final report.* Nashville, Tenn.: Peabody College, 1958.

Hudson, Margaret. An exploration of classroom procedures for teaching trainable mentally retarded children. *CEC Res. Monogr.*, Series A, No. 2. Washington, D.C.: Council for Except. Child., 1960a.

————. Lesson areas for the trainable child. *Except. Child.*, 1960b, **27**, 224–229.

Ingalls, T. H., Babbott, J., & Philbrook, R. The mothers of mongoloid babies: a retrospective appraisal of their health during pregnancy. *Amer. J. Obs. & Gyn.*, 1957, **74**, 572–581.

Itard, J. M. G. *The wild boy of Aveyron.* New York: Appleton-Century-Crofts, 1962.

Jewell, A. M. A follow-up study of 190 mentally deficient children excluded because of low mentality from the public schools of the District of Columbia. *Amer. J. ment. Defic.*, 1941, **45**, 413–420.

Johnson, G. O., & Capobianco, R. J. *Research project on severely retarded children.* Albany, N.Y.: New York State Interdepartmental Health Resources Board, 1957.

Kirk, S. A. *Public school provisions for severely retarded children.* Albany, N.Y.: New York State Interdepartmental Health Resources Board, 1957.

————, Karnes, Merle B., & Kirk, Winifred D. *You and your retarded child.* New York: Macmillan, 1955.

Lejeune, J., Gautier, M., & Turpin, R. Les chromosomes humains en culture de tissus. *C. R. Acad. Sci. Paris,* 1959, **248**, 602.

Levinson, A. *The mentally retarded child: A guide for parents.* New York: John Day, 1952.

McNeill, W. D. D. Developmental patterns of mongoloid children: A study of certain aspects of their growth and development. Unpublished doctoral dissertation. Urbana, Ill.: Univer. of Illinois, 1954.

Montessori, Maria. *The Montessori method.* Philadelphia: F. A. Stokes, 1912.

O'Connor, N., & Tizard, J. *The social problem of mental deficiency.* New York: Pergamon Press, 1956.

Perry, Natalie. *Teaching the mentally retarded child.* New York: Columbia Univer. Press, 1960.

Reynolds, M. C., & Kiland, J. R. *A study of public school children with severe mental retardation.* St. Paul, Minn.: State Department of Education, 1953.

Richards, Laura E. *Letters and journals of Samuel Gridley Howe.* Boston: Dana Estes, 1909.

Rosenzweig, L. E., & Long, Julia. *Understanding and teaching the dependent retarded child.* Darien, Conn.: Educational Publishing Corp., 1960.

Rowley, Janet D. A review of recent studies of chromosomes in mongolism. *Amer. J. ment. Defic.*, 1962, **66**, 529–532.

Saenger, G. *The adjustment of severely retarded adults in the community.* Albany, N.Y.: New York State Interdepartmental Health Resources Board, 1957.

———. *Factors influencing the institutionalization of mentally retarded individuals in New York City.* Albany, N.Y.: New York State Interdepartmental Health Resources Board, 1960.

Seguin, E. *Idiocy and its treatment by the physiological method.* New York: Columbia Univer. Press, 1907.

Standing, E. M. *Maria Montessori: Her life and work.* London: Hollis and Carter, 1957.

Stolurow, L. M. Teaching machine and special education. *Educ. psychol. Measmt.*, 1960, **20**, 429–440.

Tisdall, W. J. A follow-up study of trainable mentally handicapped children in Illinois. *Amer. J. ment. Defic.*, 1960, **65**, 11–16.

———. The residential care of mentally handicapped children. *Proceedings of the London Conference on the Scientific Study of Mental Deficiency*, 1962, **2**, 659–666.

Tizard, J., & Grad, Jacqueline C. *The mentally handicapped and their families: A social survey.* (Maudsley Monogr. #7) London: Oxford Univer. Press, 1961.

Tredgold, R. F., & Soddy, K. *A textbook of mental deficiency.* (9th ed.) Baltimore: William & Wilkens, 1956.

Warkany, J. Etiology of mongolism. *J. Pediat.*, 1960, **56**, 412.

Wirtz, M. D., & Guenther, R. J. The incidence of trainable mentally handicapped children. *Except. Child.*, 1957, **23**, 171–172, 175.

## ADDITIONAL REFERENCES

Abraham, W. *Barbara: A prologue.* New York: Holt, Rinehart and Winston, 1958.

Amoss, H., *et al. Suggested classroom activities for trainable retarded children.* Toronto: Ryerson Press, 1954.

Baumgartner, Bernice B. *A curriculum guide for teachers of trainable mentally handicapped children.* Springfield, Ill.: Illinois Department of Public Instruction, 1955.

Buck, Pearl S. *The child who never grew.* New York: John Day, 1950.

Daly, Flora M. *A report on the public school programs for severely mentally retarded children.* Sacramento, Calif.: California State Department of Education, 1958.

Davis, S. P., & Ecob, Katherine G. *The mentally retarded in society.* New York: Columbia Univer. Press, 1959.

Department of National Health and Welfare. *The backward child.* Ottawa: Queen's Printer, 1957.

Earl, C. J. C. *Subnormal personalities.* Baltimore: Williams & Wilkens, 1961.

Gunzberg, H. C. *Social rehabilitation of the subnormal.* Baltimore: Williams & Wilkens, 1960.

Luria, A. R. *Problems of the higher nervous activity of normal and abnormal children.* Moscow: Academy of Pedagogical Sciences of the RSFSR, 1956—1958. 2 vols.

Masland, R. L., Sarason, S. B., & Gladwin, T. *Mental subnormality.* New York: Basic Books, 1958.

Montgomery County, Maryland, Public Schools. *Guide for teachers of trainable children.* Bull. No. 140. Montgomery Public Schools, 1955.

St. Paul Department of Education. *A study of school children with severe mental retardation: Research project No. 6.* St. Paul, Minn.: Department of Education, Statistical Division, 1953.

San Diego County Board of Education. *Suggested activities for special training classes.* San Diego, Calif.: Superintendent of Public Instruction, San Diego County, 1958.

San Francisco Unified School District, Atypical Department. *Curriculum materials for severely mentally retarded.* San Francisco: San Francisco Unified School District, 1956.

Schonell, F. J., Richardson, J. A., & McConnel, Thelma S. *The sub-normal child at home.* London: Macmillan, 1958.

Stacey, C. L., & DeMartino, M. F. *Counseling and psychotherapy with the mentally retarded: A book of readings.* New York: Free Press, 1957.

Williams, H. M. The retarded child goes to school. *U.S. Office of Educ. Pamphlet No. 123.* Washington, D.C.: Government Printing Office, 1960.

————. Education of the severely retarded child: Classroom programs. *U.S. Office of Educ. Bull., 1961, No. 20.* Washington, D.C.: Government Printing Office, 1961.

## RESOURCES

There has been a gratifying increase in references and resources in the field of mental retardation in the last ten years. Most of these were outlined at the end of the last chapter. A few additional ones are included in the list of additional references for this chapter.

The parent organizations deserve special mention here. The present National Association for Retarded Children in the United States was founded in 1950 with a membership of 40 individuals. By 1960, the membership had grown to more than 50,000 persons. State federations had been formed in 46 states, and over 700 local parent groups were organized. Its periodical *Children Limited* is widely circulated. The Canadian Association for Retarded Children was incorporated in 1958. It, too, is a parent organization dedicated to helping mentally handicapped persons regardless of race, color, creed, or age. It is a federation of the ten provincial associations. By 1960, it had over 200 local affiliates. Its quarterly publication, *The Bulletin,* has a circulation of about 10,000. These parent organizations have had a great impact on the field of mental retardation. Their strength in fostering more adequate legislation, funds, research, and services have made the second half of the twentieth century the second golden age for the severely retarded.

## SELECTED 16 MM SOUND FILMS

*Eternal children.* 30 min, black & white. Canadian Film Institute, 1762 Carling Avenue, Ottawa 3, Ontario, Canada. Appraises the problem of severely retarded children and shows the training methods used in special schools and institutions across Canada.

*Trainable mentally handicapped.* 29 min, black & white. National Educational Television Film Service, Indiana University, Bloomington, Indiana. Uses classroom scenes to show the characteristics and training methods for such children.

*The least of these.* 20 min, color. Bureau of Community Services, New Jersey Department of Institutions, 222 West State Street, Trenton, New Jersey. A residential facility program for severely retarded children.

*Forget not these children.* 27 min, color. Bureau of Community Services, New Jersey Department of Institutions, 222 West State Street, Trenton, New Jersey. Depicts services for more capable retarded girls in a residential facility.

*Mentally handicapped children growing up.* 30 min, black & white. National Association for Retarded Children, 386 Park Avenue South, New York 16, New York. Presents the Brooklands experiment utilizing nursery school techniques in a small residential facility in Great Britain for trainable children.

*One small candle.* 22 min, color. Orchard School, 8600 Grosse Point Road, Skokie, Illinois. Shows services in a private clinic and school for the severely retarded.

*Wanted: special teachers.* 30 min, color. New Haven State College, New Haven, Connecticut. Shows special day classes and residential facilities for both the educable and trainable mentally retarded.

*And crown thy good.* 35 min, color. Orchard School, 8600 Grosse Point Road, Skokie, Illinois. Shows a community program for trainable children over a six year period.

*A light to my path.* 15 min, color. Junior League, 935 Franklin Road, Tampa, Florida. Shows community services for the trainable from the nursery school through sheltered workshop.

*No less precious.* 14 min, black & white. Associated Films, 561 Hillgrove Avenue, La Grange, Illinois. A fast moving newsreel on programs for the retarded throughout the United States.

*The darkest side.* 60 min, black & white. Minnesota Association for Retarded Children, 2742 Hennapin Avenue, Minneapolis 8, Minnesota. A report of the Governor's Advisory Committee on Mental Retardation which examines the consequences of inadequate support for residential care and treatment of the retarded, and outlines needed community and residential services for a complete program.

*A wind is rising.* 30 min, black & white. Michigan Association for Retarded Children, 510 Michigan National Towers, Lansing 8, Michigan. A TV documentary prepared in cooperation with WJRT-TV, Detroit, which examines the inadequacy of residential services for the retarded at an overcrowded, understaffed, and underfinanced large multipurpose state residential facility.

*There was a door.* 38 min, black & white. Contemporary Films, 13 East 37 Street, New York 16, New York. By focusing on one family, it shows the trend in Great Britain away from large multipurpose residential facilities toward community services.

## CHAPTER 4

# Gifted Children

LEONARD J. LUCITO

Within the last ten years there has been a tremendous increase of lay and professional literature on the education of the gifted. This mass of publications reflects a growing interest in educational programs for pupils with superior intellect. Although there are undoubtedly many reasons motivating this expression of interest, only four of the more important ones will be mentioned here. They represent some of the dynamic forces influencing the development of programs for these students.

The people of the United States are committed to a humanistic value system which incorporates the notion that everyone should be given equal opportunity to develop to the limit of his potential. Experiences of educators and psychologists have repeatedly demonstrated the advisability of differential educational treatment for students with varying intellectual abilities if each student is to reach the limit of his ability. Thus, this humanistic value system coupled with experiences in individual differences has led to the conclusion that some special provisions are needed for the gifted.

The international conflict between the ideologies of communism and western democracy has mobilized the public's interest in educating the gifted. It is also widely accepted that the cold war between these conflicting ideologies will probably exist for a long time. To survive in the struggle there is an urgent need for highly educated, intelligent leaders in science and politics. This is being forcefully demonstrated daily in the news media. Consequently, there is considerable pressure to initiate changes in the educational treatment of the gifted.

Even if the threat of cold or hot wars were to terminate, the recent elaborations and extensions of knowledge have caused a rapid acceleration in the complexity of roles some citizens must assume. There is also an increasing demand for larger numbers of individuals to play these extremely complex roles. This state of affairs implies that either the innate intellectual potential of the populace must in some way be raised, or more effective educational treatments must be devised to train superior students if the demand for highly trained personnel is to be met. The first alternative is not possible at this time. There is no way of manipulating the genetic structure of humans to increase their *innate* intellectual potential. Yet, a considerable body of evidence suggests that the general level of intellectual *functioning* of most groups has risen significantly during the past 30 or 40 years (Hunt, 1961). Since it is unlikely that a general improvement of innate ability has occurred through natural selection in so short a period of time, it seems reasonable to assume that a majority of the rise is due to more and better educational opportunities and life experiences. It is natural then for responsible people to become concerned with the development of effective educational treatments for the gifted to prepare them for the extremely complex roles of society.

Further reinforcement of the motivation to improve educational provisions for the gifted has resulted from evidence demonstrating there actually is a waste of high intellectual potential. Cole (1955) emphasized the loss of intellectual resources by noting the large number of superior high school students who did not enroll in college. Figures obtained by Wolfle (1960) while a member of the Commission on Human Resources and Advanced Training showed that of the top 30 percent of high school students only 60 percent entered college. Of these, only 40 percent earned a bachelor's degree. Many authorities have agreed with Wolfle's conclusion: compared to the past this is an improvement, but examined in light of the growing need for people with high intellectual ability and advanced training better ways should be found to tap this national resource.

As pressures to initiate new and better educational programs for the gifted have increased, three modes of responding to these demands can be identified. Many professional and lay people have proposed and adopted hasty, poorly conceptualized, and piece-meal school programs in an atmosphere of panic. A relatively smaller group has instituted well conceived programs as early as 40 or 50 years ago. They have responded by periodically improving and expanding their educational provisions as new research results became available and community acceptance for change increased. Others have been overly cautious. They contend not enough is known about the gifted to begin programs; therefore, they have used their energy "studying the problem" with little resultant action. Newland (1957, p. 3) has responded with the following statement:

... the results of the largest single study of any type of exceptional children have been available for use in the identification of the gifted, in delineating quite objectively their needs, and in suggesting kinds of educational adjustment for them (Terman et al., 1925; Terman et al., 1947). The largest single follow up study of any kind of exceptional children was done on bright children admitted prior to the conventional school-entering age, restudied in high school, and further studied at college entrance (Hobson, 1948). Major studies of the Cleveland major work class program have been made (Sumption, 1941), and a ten-year follow up study has been made of a single special school program for the gifted (Hildreth, 1952). Major objective evaluations of educational and social outcomes of college acceleration programs have been studied for seven years (Pressey, 1949). Three systematic statewide studies of educational mortality among high school potential college material were nearly 20 years ago .... Surely the extent and the nature of the need for some special provisions for the gifted, and information on the various possible provisions for the gifted are "on the record" for him who would but read.

Without a doubt, more research findings are in the literature than are reflected in educational practices.

Each of the sections in this chapter will briefly consider a major topic in the area of the gifted. It is hoped the treatment of the topics will give some perspective so that the reader will be better prepared to understand intelligently the mass of available literature.

## Definitions

There is considerable confusion as to the meaning of the term gifted.[1] Even the authorities in the field disagree. Abraham (1958) notes that one of his students identified 113 definitions of the gifted while preparing a term paper. The student reported he had examined most of the books on the gifted, but had just begun to explore the many articles when he despaired of making "head or tail of them." Additional definitions have appeared in the literature by now, and the disagreements have not decreased.

Definitions may overlap in some respects but not in others. That is, if two definitions were applied to the same population some students would be identified by both whereas others would not. The extent of overlap depends on which two definitions are being compared. Obviously, all of the definitions cannot be presented here; therefore, several important classes of definitions will be described and typical examples of each important class will be given. In addition, a new definition will be proposed by the author.

In the early literature the gifted were defined as those who had achieved outstanding stature in one of the professions. For the educator, this class of *ex post facto definitions* has the unfortunate disadvantage of allowing identification only after the student has completed school.

By the end of the nineteenth and the beginning of the twentieth century relatively objective and standardized measures were developed from which one might reasonably infer the potential intellectual power of a student at an early age. The big event in the field was the publishing of the first Binet-Simon Intelligence Scale in 1905. With such an instrument it was possible to group individuals along a continuum of intellect from superior to defective. Thus began a class of definitions which might be designated as the *IQ definitions* (see the section on intelligence testing in Chapter 2 for a discussion of IQ). Terman's famous studies (1925–1959) have used this type of definition. He referred to gifted children as

---

[1] Unless otherwise indicated in the text the term gifted will be considered synonymous to many other labels used in the literature, such as academically talented, rapid learner, high ability or superior students. Some distinctions can be made, but in a book of this nature there is no room to elaborate.

those having an IQ of 140 or above as measured by the Stanford-Binet Intelligence Scale. Two major modifications have been employed by other people using this class of definitions. Different IQ tests have been adopted, and the minimum IQ cutoff scores have been either raised or lowered—more frequently the latter.

As the field of the gifted developed, some of the workers became dissatisfied with the IQ score as a single criterion for defining giftedness. There were two major concerns. First, it was evident some individuals were in fact achieving at a level definitely indicating gifted ability, but were not scoring high enough on IQ tests to be classified as gifted. Second, these workers were concerned with the broader manpower needs of society for outstanding achievement. The IQ did not identify many students who were later able to excel in areas such as music and art. The latter type of individual became known as the "talented." Thus the term IQ was dropped from their definitions of giftedness, and the concept of giftedness was broadened to include the talented. Definitions by Cutts and Moseley (1957), DeHaan and Havighurst (1957), and Witty (1958) are examples of this third class of definitions—*social definitions*. Witty's definition is quoted since it was adopted by the American Association for Gifted Children and has had great influence in the field. He defined the gifted as children whose "performance, in a potentially valuable line of human activity, is consistently remarkable."

Other writers have used a fourth class—*percentage definitions*. An example of this class of definitions can be found in the National Education Association's bulletin "The Identification and Education of the Academically Talented Student in the American Secondary School" (National Education Association 1958). There Conant considers the academically talented to be those students within the upper 15–20 percent of the secondary school population.

Factor analytical studies on the nature of intellect by Guilford (1959, 1960) and his associates at the University of Southern California have stimulated great interest in aspects of intelligence not adequately measured by the IQ test. One such aspect is creativity. More and more leaders have begun to consider creativity an important dimension of giftedness. Getzels and Jackson (1958), Fliegler and Bish (1959), and Sumption and Luecking (1960) have included this new aspect in their conception, thus developing a fifth class—*creativity definitions.*

The author would like to encourage consideration of an additional definition which uses more of Guilford's model of intellect than the creativity definitions referred to above.

*The gifted are those students whose potential intellectual powers are at such a high ideational level in both productive and evaluative thinking that it can be reasonably assumed they could be the future problem solvers, innovators, and evaluators of the culture if adequate educational experiences are provided.*

*This productive-evaluative-thinking definition* attempts to define the gifted by drawing on one of the most extensive and latest conceptions of the nature of intellect. Guilford and Merrifield (1960) summarized the four basic operations (processes) in their model of intellect—cognition, memory, production, and evaluation. The following are their definitions of the four operations:

1. Cognition—"Discovery, awareness, rediscovery, or recognition of information in various forms; comprehension or understanding."

2. Memory—"Retention of information in any form."

3. Production
   a. Divergent production—"Generation of information from given information, where the emphasis is upon variety of output from the same source."
   b. Convergent production—"Generation of information from given information, where the emphasis is upon achieving unique or conventionally accepted or best outcomes."

4. Evaluation—"Reaching decisions or making judgments concerning the goodness (correctness, suitability, adequacy, desirability) of information in terms of criteria of identity, consistency, and goal satisfaction."

Emphasis is placed on two of these four intellectual functions in the author's definition. Since cognition and memory are *necessary* conditions for production and evaluation to occur, these operations are implied in the definition. This definition also focuses attention on students who have the potential to play the roles of problem solvers, innovators, and evaluators of the culture.

Production and evaluation include creative and critical thinking plus problem solving abilities. According to Guilford and Merrifield creativity cuts across the operations of divergent, convergent, and evaluative thinking. Nine of the thirteen factors they have identified in creative production are divergent; three are convergent; and one is evaluative. The divergent factors involve: (1) fluency —the number of different responses produced; (2) flexibility—the tendency to change approach or strategy; (3) uniqueness—the originality of responses; and (4) elaboration—adding detail to reach a meaningful goal. The three factors in convergent production cluster around the ability of redefinition—the transformation of the conception of an object or idea in order to use it, or part of it, in satisfying given conditions. The one evaluative process associated with creativity is sensitivity to problems—perceiving defects or needs in situations and ideas. Problem solving seems to shift from one combination of productive and evaluative factors to others depending on the type of problem. Critical thinking refers primarily to the evaluative operation of Guilford's model of intellect.

Recent research by Getzels and Jackson (1960, 1962) and Torrance (1962a) suggests that some students may have high IQ scores but relatively low creativity scores. Traditional IQ tests are strong in measuring cognition, memory, and convergent production but weak in assessing divergent production and evaluation. High IQ scores alone then do not insure inclusion of students into the gifted category under the proposed definition. These students certainly can make important contributions to society, but do not require major modifications in educational provisions (curriculum and methods). By presenting the content of the curriculum at an accelerated rate and allowing them to eventually learn higher level concepts, their major educational needs can be met. This is not true for the students included in the proposed definition. Major changes are needed which will be described in a later section. Justification for educators to construct a special category for giftedness can be made when: (1) gifted students require different objectives, curriculum, or methods to develop to the limit of their potential; and (2) the school is able through differential treatment of the gifted to supply the people society needs for its complex roles.

Another restriction is placed on the concept of giftedness in the proposed definition. Potential for *both* productive and evaluative thinking must be found in a student. This is to avoid considering bizarre behaving individuals in the category of gifted.

The social, creativity, and productive-evaluative-thinking definitions are logical definitions. These logical definitions are primarily concerned with denoting the types of persons who *ought* to be included in the category of gifted. They serve as a referent for validating the identification procedures. Whereas, the ex post facto, IQ, and percentage definitions are primarily sets of procedures (operational definitions) for identifying the gifted. Everyone must simultaneously entertain consistent logical and operational definitions to function most effectively in research or practical situations. Until the logical definition is translated into operational procedures, it is of little use. Conversely, an operational definition without reasonable logical constructs has little meaning!

## Identification Procedures

In adequately developed identification programs the usual approach is to partition the identification process into two parts—screening and final selection. During the screening process relatively untrained examiners use crude devices on the total pool of students to identify candidates for the final selection procedures. Including a screening program has the advantage of saving the time of more highly skilled personnel for the complex task of final selection.

Traditionally most writers in the field have recommended the use of standardized group IQ and achievement tests for screening. From the IQ tests we infer intellectual potential of the cognition, memory, convergent thinking variety. They are particularly useful in identifying students who do not achieve on the standardized achievement measures but have potential to do so. On the other hand, the achievement tests sometimes uncover pupils who have not shown up favorably on group IQ tests. Group IQ tests have a tendency to be inaccurate with some individuals under certain conditions, such as poor reading skills, low motivation to take tests, and the large measurement error found in group tests. Either an IQ score above 115–120, or achievement one to two years above grade level, usually allows the student to become a candidate for the final selection process.

If high IQ test scores alone were used what percentage of high creative students would be missed? The empirical data from the studies of Getzels and Jackson (1959, 1962) and Torrance and his associates (1960, 1962a) referred to in the previous section are suggestive. There is some overlap between IQ and creativity scores. To estimate the degree of overlap in the above studies, groups of students were given both IQ and a creativity tests. They were then ranked on each test separately from highest to lowest scores. The students scoring among the top 20 percent on a test were labeled high performers. Ranking below the 20 percent cutoff labeled a student as low on that test. Thus three groups were formed: (1) high on the IQ meaure but low on creativity—$H_{IQ}L_C$; (2) high on both IQ and creativity measures—$H_{IQ}H_C$; and (3) low on the IQ measure but high on creativity—$L_{IQ}H_C$. The range of overlap ($H_{IQ}H_C$) was from 23 to 53 percent and averaged 33 percent. "In other words, we would miss about 67 percent of the upper 20 percent on creative thinking, if we were to rely upon the traditional measures of intellectual promise (Torrance et al., 1960, p. 14)." These data can be viewed in another way. *On the average approximately one third of the students can be expected to be in each of the three groups—$H_{IQ}L_C$, $H_{IQ}H_C$, and $L_{IQ}H_C$.*

Further information about these studies can be helpful in the identification process. From Table 4.1 it can be seen that the mean (average) level of IQ scores for the $L_{IQ}H_C$ samples is not low in the usual sense of the term. Of the seven samples in the table five have mean IQ scores above average. Only Samples 3 and 4 from Torrance's study are in the average IQ range. It is significant that the $L_{IQ}H_C$ groups achieve as well academically as the $H_{IQ}L_C$ groups except for Samples 3 and 4—the two samples where the mean IQ scores are in the average range. Torrance (1962a) concludes that a minimum of approximately 115–120 on an IQ test must be reached before high creativity can be expected to occur. This is consistent with the position of the writer taken earlier in the chapter when he discussed the necessity of minimum levels of cognition, memory, and aspects of convergent thinking before productive-evaluative thinking can occur.

What percentage of highly creative thinkers could be identified if high scores on *either* IQ *or* achievement tests qualified a student to candidacy for final selection procedures? No percentage figures are available from the data in the literature. However, the data in Table 4.1 suggest the possibility of identifying a large number of highly creative students in the screening stage if high achievers with IQ scores as low as 115 or 120 were considered candidates for the final selection procedures.

TABLE 4.1 *Comparison of mean IQ scores of $H_{IQ}L_C$ and $L_{IQ}H_C$ groups.*

| STUDY | TEST | MEAN IQ SCORES | | ACADEMIC ACHIEVEMENT |
|---|---|---|---|---|
| | | $H_{IQ}L_C$ | $L_{IQ}H_C$ | |
| Getzels and Jackson | Stanford-Binet | 150.0 | 127.0 | Same |
| Torrance | | | | |
| Sample 1 | Stanford-Binet | 152.1 | 126.5 | Same |
| Sample 2 | Stanford-Binet | 143.5 | 121.9 | Same |
| Sample 3 | Otis Quick-Scoring | 113.5 | 97.9 | Different |
| Sample 4 | Kuhlmann-Anderson | 118.6 | 106.9 | Different |
| Sample 5 | California Mental Maturity | 139.8 | 112.3 | Same |
| Sample 6 | Lorge-Thorndike | 141.7 | 122.0 | Same |

*Sources:* Getzels, J. W., & Jackson, P. W. *Creativity and intelligence.* New York: Wiley, 1962. Torrance, E. P. *Guiding creative talent.* Englewood Cliffs, N.J.: Prentice-Hall, 1962, p. 58.

Operational procedures for identifying the gifted consistent with the logical definition proposed by the author can be borrowed from Guilford and Merrifield (1960). They describe several tests for each aspects of the definition. These tests have been used successfully by them with students as early as junior high school. Getzels and Jackson (1962) have published descriptions of creativity items and scoring procedures for the high school level. Meanwhile, Torrance and his associates (1960, 1962a) have published tentative norms and scoring techniques for students from kindergarten through elementary school. These experimental tests are more difficult to score than the standardized IQ and achievement tests; also they are less readily available. Fortunately, considerable effort is being devoted to the development of these instruments. It should not be too long before tests of productive and evaluative thinking will become as routinely used as IQ tests.

Observations by teachers and others have been used as one supplemental device to group IQ and achievement testing. Teachers have been asked to name the students in their classrooms that are gifted. Usually no definition has been given; each teacher has been free to interpret giftedness in his own way. As might be expected the batting average of teachers under these conditions has been poor. In the study by Pegnato and Birch (1959) teachers missed approximately 55 percent of the gifted and referred 31 percent who were not gifted as defined by the investigators. A better procedure has been to provide the teacher with a check list of behaviors to observe. Elaborate lists of behaviors for identifying the gifted have been published. Lists by Abraham (1958) and Kough and DeHaan (1955) are typical. The following are samples of items found in such lists:

1. Learns to walk and talk before the average child
2. Above average for his chronological age in height, weight, and physical endurance
3. Learns rapidly
4. Retains without much rote drill
5. Has a large and complex vocabulary for his age
6. Reasons and sees relationships well
7. Is interested in a wide range of things
8. Does some academic work one to two years in advance of class
9. Interested in hobbies of collecting and classifying birds, stamps, pictures of famous people.

These lists should be used with care. Many of them were constructed from the results of a large number of studies on the characteristics of gifted students. Because different operational definitions were used across studies these lists usually give a composite portrait and blur over subgroup differences. In other instances the lists were designed to match a particular logical conception of the gifted. The user may then find himself in disagreement with the notion of giftedness implied in the list. To illustrate, sample items one and two above are irrelevant if giftedness is restricted to intellectual superiority. Item seven is irrelevant if educators assume responsibility for stimulating interests and emphasize identification of potential ability in their definition. In that case, the specification of these interests only becomes relevant as motivating devices during the educational treatment stage.

Another common supplemental screening procedure is the examination of school grades made by students. Usually, a large proportion of A's and B's is considered suggestive of giftedness. The major difficulty with this procedure is that grading is often based on criteria other than intellectual achievement or potential. A's and B's are sometimes given to motivate. At other times students are disciplined by lowering their grades.

In the final selection procedure, a highly trained examiner selects and applies those techniques by which he may infer the best estimate of the student's potential ability as defined by some logical constructs. More reliable and valid measurement instruments are available to the trained examiner than to the untrained. He has been trained to select and interpret psychological assessment devices which are appropriate to the type of youngster. For example, the selection and interpretation of individual intelligence tests are different for minority groups such as the physically handicapped, the emotionally disturbed, or the culturally deprived. Furthermore, he has the sophistication to use advisedly experimental instruments such as the ones on productive and evaluative thinking. Educators without the necessary training and experience should depend on these trained examiners to complete the identification process.

The lack of trained examiners often forces the schools to use screening techniques as final selection procedures. Martinson and Lessinger (1960) and Pegnato and Birch (1959) give evidence to indicate the dangers of this practice. Of 332 pupils scoring 130 or above on the Stanford-Binet, Martinson and Lessinger found less than 50 percent of the group scores as high as 130 on a group IQ test. Pegnato and Birch obtained similar results. When group tests were used all students scoring above 115 needed to be considered candidates for final selection in order to identify 92 percent of those above 135 on an individual IQ test.

More importantly, Pegnato and Birch devised two criteria (effectiveness and efficiency) for evaluating screening techniques no matter what type of screening and final selection procedures are used. Their measure of effectiveness is computed by dividing the number of students identified as gifted by final selection procedures into the number of students identified as gifted by *both* screening and final selection procedures. To illustrate, if 100 gifted students in a population were identified as gifted by final selection procedures and only 20 were identified both by the screening and final selection procedures, then the method would be 20 percent effective. Efficiency is the proportion of gifted students found by the final selection procedures to the number of pupils referred by the screening procedures. For example, if 30 students were judged gifted in the final selection and 100 had been referred by the screening, the efficiency would be 30 percent. When effectiveness and efficiency are maximized the best screening procedure has been obtained.

## Prevalence

Various estimates have been given of the number or percentage of gifted individuals in the total school population. They have ranged from one half of 1 percent to 20 percent. What is the state of affairs concerning prevalence estimates? There is no one prevalence figure for the gifted. In fact many of the figures are not comparable. It is meaningless to ask if one estimate is better than another unless the same logical definition is being entertained. Some embrace a broader conception of giftedness than others. Quite naturally different prevalence figures have been reported by investigators. In the social definitions described earlier giftedness is conceived of more broadly than the creativity definitions which restrict giftedness to intellectual superiority in specific mental abilities. This implies that the social definitions will tend to include a larger number of students than the creativity ones. DeHaan and Havighurst, using a social definition which included the talented[2], found approximately 15 percent of the Quincy, Illinois group met his criteria of giftedness (French, 1959). However, Sumption and Luecking (1960) estimate that between 5 and 10 percent of the student population would meet their creativity definition. The task of estimating prevalence under any logical definition is hazardous unless the operational procedures are specified.

Some operational procedures have been more thoroughly investigated than others; therefore, more confidence can be placed in the former than the latter. Operational definitions based on IQ scores have had a tremendous amount of data collected about them. Anyone using IQ score definitions can obtain an estimate by looking at the standardization manual of the specific test. The size of the estimate will increase as the cutoff score is lowered. In Fig. 2.1 Dunn presents the percentage of students that can be expected to be above different IQ cutoff scores on the Wechsler Intelligence Scale for Children. A cutoff score of approximately 130 will yield about the 2 percent estimate cited for giftedness in the first chapter. Reference to the standardization data of a test however will not give the prevalence of the gifted if additional restrictions are placed on the IQ definition. To illustrate, the 2 percent estimate above will be reduced if the further condition of high scores on an achievement test is imposed.

The prevalence figure is automatically determined when the gifted are defined as being the upper 1, 3, 5, or any other percent. Estimates have been as high as 15–20 percent (Conant, 1959).

An additional problem is encountered in estimating prevalence for logical definitions which depend on the newer concepts of productive, creative, and/or evaluative thinking. There are a number of ways to measure each of these concepts. For the present, one measurement procedure may be considered as reasonable as another due to the lack of adequate information about competing tests. As a result estimates will tend to vary since differences between operational definitions exist even when they purport to measure the same logical definition. Risk in estimating prevalence

---

[2] The term talented used in this context is meant to refer to those students who display unusual skill in one area such as music, art, or motor skills, but are not necessarily intellectually superior.

also increases with the newer concepts because the results from large testing programs are not in the literature. Only tentative norms are available now. Nevertheless, these concepts have captured the imaginations of investigators, and some data should be available soon. For example, the University of Pittsburgh, in the spring of 1960, cooperated with the U.S. Office of Education, the National Institute of Mental Health, and the Office of Naval Research in a venture known as Project Talent. They collected test scores on one half million high school students for a national inventory of aptitudes and abilities. The results from the section on creativity (Dailey and Shaycoft, 1961) will provide some definitive data to

TABLE 4.2 *Approximate proportions of school populations at various intellectual levels.*

| STANFORD-BINET INTELLECTUAL LEVELS | PERCENT OF SCHOOL POPULATIONS | |
|---|---|---|
| | *Average community* | *Superior socioeconomic community* |
| IQ above 140 | 0.5–1 | 2–3 |
| IQ above 130 | 2–4 | 6–12 |
| IQ above 125 | 5–7 | 15–20 |
| IQ above 120 | 10–12 | 30–40 |
| IQ above 115 | 16–20 | 45–60 |

*Source:* Gallagher, J. J. *The gifted child in the elementary school.* Washington, D.C.: NEA, Department of Classroom Teachers, 1959, p. 5.

estimate prevalence for Project Talent's operational definition. The same amount of interest has not been shown by researchers in evaluative thinking. Consequently, it is not possible at this time to make a very accurate estimate of prevalence for the definition proposed earlier by the author who includes a combination of productive and evaluative thinking.

Up to this point, the estimates have been for the country as a whole. It is a well accepted fact that differences do exist from community to community in the prevalence of gifted persons. Gallagher (1959), presented a table, which is partially reproduced here as Table 4.2, illustrating the variability between average and superior socioeconomic communities when using an IQ definition. Note there are about three times as many high IQ pupils in the superior communities as in the average ones. Presumably differences in prevalence estimates between communities could be demonstrated for any of the definitions.

## Characteristics

There is not enough space in this section or even chapter to sort the research on the basis of the operational definitions used in each study so that different sets of characteristics might be presented; therefore, a composite picture of the gifted will be presented. The great majority of studies have used IQ definitions, and in a crude way there is some comparability across studies. This oversimplification will not do too great violence to a general sketch of the gifted for the purpose of introducing the reader to the field. Nevertheless, the reader should be sensitive to this deficiency in the following presentation. An additional subsection will be added to acquaint the reader with the findings of a growing body of literature which contrasts the characteristics of high creative low IQ and high IQ low creative groups of pupils.

One caution should be remembered throughout this section. The characteristics attributed to the gifted are based on the comparison of *groups* as opposed to individuals. *As a group* the gifted compare favorably with other groups on most traits. Still there is often in a study a small subgroup within the gifted whose performances on specific traits are below the top performers of the nongifted group. Occasionally a gifted person is found who has a large collection of unfavorable traits—small for his age, socially and emotionally maladjusted, educationally retarded, and intellectually unmotivated.

### PHYSICAL CHARACTERISTICS

The gifted, as a group, are slightly better than their average peers in most measures of physical traits (Terman et al., 1925; Hildreth, 1938; Miles, 1954). They tend to be taller, heavier, and better looking. Furthermore, they tend to be superior in measures of strength of grip, leg strength, push and pull, pumping, running, and other motor activities involving either the whole body or parts of it. Although differences can be found between the physical aspects of the gifted and the average as groups, these are the least reliable and quantitatively the smallest of all the differences.

## CULTURAL AND FAMILIAL BACKGROUND

More gifted children come from homes where the social and economic level is above average (Terman et al., 1925; Gallagher and Crowder, 1957). They tend to come more from homes with professional and managerial parents (Barbe, 1956; Cole, 1956). Parents of the gifted are in general better educated than those of the nongifted. The home environment is more intellectually stimulating. Indices which have been used to demonstrate a more stimulating home environment are: more magazines of high quality, varied hobbies and interests, less autocratic relationships between child and parents, more family travel, and greater number of books in the child's personal library.

Undoubtedly, cultural patterns of the family are important also. Kahl (1953) reported the influence of the father's attitude on considering a college career when socioeconomic class is held constant. Students of the lower middle class families whose fathers were interested in higher education were more prone to desire college attendance. Stouffer and Shea (1959) obtained similar results. Three fourths of the students whose fathers thought college was important planned to attend even though they could not readily afford the expense; whereas, only one fourth planned to attend college if their fathers thought it unimportant. Bond's data (1957) further emphasize the influence of family environment. A librarian's son is one thousand times more likely to win a National Merit Scholarship than a laborer's son.

Investigations of the frequency with which gifted pupils are found in the different racial and ethnic groups of the United States usually report English, German, French, Scandinavian, and Jewish groups as contributing more in proportion to their number than other groups (Terman et al., 1947; Sheldon, 1954; Barbe, 1956). Nevertheless, no racial or ethnic group has a monopoly on giftedness. There is no conclusive evidence to support or refute the genetic superiority of any of the groups. We know that there are differences in opportunity to develop one's potential among various subgroups in the United States. The latter seems to be the more plausible reason for differences between racial or cultural groups.

## SOCIAL AND EMOTIONAL ADJUSTMENT

Many studies have helped to challenge the once widely held notion that intellectual superiority is positively related to social and emotional maladjustment. There is considerable evidence to assert that gifted students are more socially accepted than pupils from other intellectual levels. The gifted in regular classrooms are chosen more often than the average by his peers in sociometric studies (Gallagher, 1958; Johnson, 1950; Miller, 1956). Kerstetter (1952) studied the social adjustment of students in special classes, and concluded the gifted as a group were well adjusted socially. Miller (1957) investigated the question of whether students who had been accelerated (young for grade placement) suffered social maladjustment. She found them to be socially well adjusted. Results from studies by Lucito (1959) and Hottel (1960) suggest that the gifted have less need to conform to peer group pressures than average or retarded students.

The Rorschach ink blot test has been used by some investigators to study the emotional adjustment of gifted pupils. Even though some emotional problems were identified among them, the problems were less frequent than might be expected in the total population (Gair, 1944; Gallagher and Crowder, 1957; Mensch, 1950). This finding is consistent with the results of studies using rating scales (Gallagher & Crowder, 1957; Hildreth, 1938; Terman et al., 1925). Furthermore, there is evidence that, as a group, the superior emotional stability and social adjustment of the gifted continue into adulthood (Barbe, 1957; Terman et al., 1959). Less mental illness, greater civic responsibility, and greater marital accord were found. Studies using standardized personality inventories have indicated less neurotic tendencies, more self-sufficiency, and less submissiveness among the gifted.

From a sample of high school boys Bonsall and Stefflre (1955) found some of the usual results on social and emotional adjustment variables. The gifted were superior to nongifted on thoughtfulness, restraint, ascendance, emotional stability, objectivity, and masculinity. However when the data were reanalyzed so that only gifted and nongifted students from the *same* socioeconomic levels were compared, little or no differences were found between the two groups. This suggests the possibility of socioeconomic class accounting for some of the differences generally attributed to intellectual differences.

## EDUCATIONAL ACHIEVEMENT

Examination of the many research studies related to educational achievement indicates that the gifted, as a group, achieve well in most areas, so that versatility rather than one-sidedness is the rule. They also tend to have higher achievement than the average in all school subjects regardless of the type of measures used. This is contrary to the often cited generalization that if someone is outstanding in one area of performance, he will be weak in others.

On standardized tests of achievement the gifted, as a group, exceed the performance of the average. In fact when Learned and Wood (1938) compared the scores of high school and college seniors on the General Culture Battery, 10 percent of the high school seniors were above the college senior median (middle score). At the elementary school level, reading has consistently been demonstrated to be the highest of the achievement scores. Arithmetic computation, on the other hand, seems to be the lower one; but even the arithmetic computation scores of the group are higher than the scores of the average population.

If school grades are used as a measure of achievement, again the gifted excel. They receive a larger proportion of "A's" and "B's" than the average group. Even youngsters who have been accelerated receive better grades than their older average classmates (Barnette, 1957; Justman, 1956; Shannon, 1957; Worcester, 1956).

Another way of indicating academic achievement is to examine the honors and scholarships they earn. In elementary schools they are more often the winners of contests such as essay or poster construction. At high school they continue to be the winners. In addition, they obtain more scholarships to college than the average.

Once in college, the group contributes more members proportion-
ally to the honor rolls and honorary organizations. The superior
achievement is maintained throughout the age levels. Even though
Cole (1955), Wolfle (1960), and many other writers have deplored
the number of gifted not attending college, or not completing a
program after having entered it, a college student with an IQ of
140 or above has 100 times as many chances of graduating with
honors as the average IQ student.

It is not surprising that the gifted are achieving above grade
level for their choronological age, but are they achieving up to
their potential? That is, are gifted students as a group underachievers? This is a difficult question to answer since estimating
potential for achievement of the gifted is a very complex task. A
number of attempts have been made; none have been particularly
satisfactory. By using the MA as a criterion for estimating potential
achievement[3], some educators and psychologists have concluded
that most gifted are underachievers. To justify this position, these
people usually point to the discrepancy generally found between
potential achievement as estimated by the MA and realized achievement as estimated by standarized achievement tests. To illustrate,
if an eight year old child has an IQ of 150 on the Binet, he would
have a MA of 12 years. Since the average youngster has a MA
of 12 years when he is 12 years of age and can be expected to
achieve at the beginning seventh grade level, it is reasoned that
the eight-year-old with a MA of 12 years should have the potential
to achieve at the beginning seventh grade level. Examination of
data from the cumulative record folders of elementary schools will
demonstrate that children who are only eight years of age with
MA's of 12 years do not achieve at the beginning seventh grade
level. Thus the conclusion is drawn that most gifted are underachievers. To accept this assertion is to assume that for the gifted
the MA is a reasonably valid estimate of potential for achievement.

Other educators and psychologists are not willing to make this
assumption. Although they agree the MA is adequate for students
with IQ's close to 100, the MA criterion progressively over-
estimates the potential of students as IQ increases. This is thought

---

[3] See chapter 2 for a method of computing MA from IQ and CA, and translating
the MA into potential for grade level achievement.

to be due to the lack of opportunity of the high IQ student to receive formal educational and life experiences necessary to perform up to his MA. One group at Los Angeles, using formulas derived by Horn (1941), has constructed a set of tables (Los Angeles City School Districts, 1955) which makes a correction for experience. Table 4.3 compares the grade level achievement ex-

TABLE 4.3 *Comparison of two methods of estimating potential for achievement at different IQ levels and chronological ages.*

| BINET IQ | APPROXIMATE CORRECTION OF MA ESTIMATES FOR EXPERIENCE[a] | 6 | 7 | 8 | 9 | 10 | 11 | 12 | 13 |
|---|---|---|---|---|---|---|---|---|---|
| 100 | 0.0 | 1.0[b] | 2.0 | 3.0 | 4.0 | 5.0 | 6.0 | 7.0 | 8.0 |
|  |  | 1.0 | 2.0 | 3.0 | 4.0 | 5.0 | 6.0 | 7.0 | 8.0 |
| 110 | − 0.3 | 1.6 | 2.7 | 3.8 | 4.9 | 6.0 | 7.1 | 8.2 | 9.3 |
|  |  | 1.3 | 2.4 | 3.5 | 4.6 | 5.7 | 6.8 | 7.9 | 9.0 |
| 120 | − 0.6 | 2.2 | 3.4 | 4.6 | 5.8 | 7.0 | 8.2 | 9.4 | 10.6 |
|  |  | 1.6 | 2.8 | 4.0 | 5.2 | 6.4 | 7.6 | 8.8 | 10.0 |
| 130 | − 0.9 | 2.8 | 4.1 | 5.4 | 6.7 | 8.0 | 9.3 | 10.6 | 11.9 |
|  |  | 1.9 | 3.2 | 4.5 | 5.8 | 7.1 | 8.4 | 9.7 | 11.0 |
| 140 | − 1.2 | 3.4 | 4.8 | 6.2 | 7.6 | 9.0 | 10.4 | 11.8 | 13.2 |
|  |  | 2.2 | 3.6 | 5.0 | 6.4 | 7.8 | 9.2 | 10.6 | 12.0 |
| 150[c] | − 1.5 | 4.0 | 5.5 | 7.0 | 8.5 | 10.0 | 11.5 | 13.0 | 14.5 |
|  |  | 2.5 | 4.0 | 5.5 | 7.0 | 8.5 | 10.0 | 11.5 | 13.0 |
| 160 | − 1.8 | 4.6 | 6.2 | 7.8 | 9.4 | 11.0 | 12.6 | 14.2 | 15.8 |
|  |  | 2.8 | 4.4 | 6.0 | 7.6 | 9.2 | 10.8 | 12.4 | 14.0 |

[a] *Rule of* − 0.3: An examination of the Los Angeles Expected Achievement Grade Placement Tables indicates that the subtraction of 0.3 of a year of achievement for each 10 points of IQ above 100 gives a reasonable approximation of the entries in the tables. Estimates for intermediate IQ's can be obtained by linear interpolation.

[b] The top number in each cell of the table is the MA estimate of potential for achievement in terms of grade level; the bottom number is an approximation of the Los Angeles tables using the rule of − 0.3. In no instance is the approximation more than 0.1 of a year in error.

[c] Since the Los Angeles tables only included IQ's through 140, extrapolation for IQ's above 140 were computed by the *Rule of* − 0.3.

pected by using the MA procedure and the approach of the Los Angeles group. Note the Los Angeles estimates are consistently below the MA estimates. From column two of the table, it can be seen that the Los Angeles estimates can be obtained by subtracting three tenths of a grade level from the MA estimate of grade level expectancy for each 10 IQ points above 100. On the strength of empirical evidence and logic the Los Angeles estimates are probably more realistic than MA alone. However, they are not completely satisfactory. The tables ignore differences in the size of correlations between IQ and achievement tests from subject to subject; for example, expected reading achievement should be higher than arithmetic (see Gallagher, 1959, for a discussion of the original Horn formulas). It is probably accurate to state that the gifted are not underachieving as much as some people believe, yet are in need of different educational treatments before they will even achieve up to the potential identified by the Los Angeles tables.

In spite of the difficulty in deciding if the gifted as a group are under achieving with respect to their potential, there are individuals who are functioning at such a low level they are obviously underachieving. Much research effort has been invested in trying to understand gifted underachievers. Gowan (1957, p. 100) evaluated many research studies and summarized the most likely dynamics involved in underachievement.

The common elements from these research reports indicate that achievement in gifted students versus underachievement seems related to the following factors:

1. Clearness and definiteness of academic and occupational choices versus the opposite.

2. Strong ego controls and strength versus weak ones.

3. Socialization and social interaction versus withdrawal and self-sufficiency.

4. Good use of time and money versus lack of such habits.

5. Reading and arithmetic ability versus lack of such competency.

6. Positive character integration versus psychotic or neurotic tendency.

7. Permissiveness, intraception, and creativity versus authoritarianism in the parental home environment or in the gifted individual himself.

8. Parents who motivated and took pains or interest, versus dominant, autocratic, or laissez-faire parents.

9. Some tension in task demands in childhood (the imposition of goals which are clear and possible to attain by parents) versus either no goal or impossible ones.

10. Maturity, responsibility, and seriousness of interests versus opposites.

11. Awareness of and concern for others versus disinterest.

12. Dominance, persuasiveness, and self-confidence versus their opposites.

13. Enthusiastic, socialized, activity-oriented view of life, versus apathetic withdrawal.

More recently, Hobbs (1960) points out the need for a new national character which would more highly value intellectual pursuits. It is assumed that the need to achieve is to some extent dependent on the adult models with whom the gifted might identify themselves.

## INTELLECTUAL CHARACTERISTICS

Obviously, there are quantitative differences in intellect between gifted students and other pupils, but are there qualitative differences? Much research has established that even the mentally retarded can perform to some degree on complex intellectual tasks such as transfer of training, reasoning, and creativity, if the tasks are simple enough. This has led many authorities to conclude that only quantitative differences exist. More recent research indicates there are qualitative differences in the organization of intellectual functions for the gifted. Gallagher and Lucito (1961) compared the patterns of intellectual strengths and weaknesses on Wechsler subtests for seven samples—three gifted, three retarded, and one of average ability. The subtest patterns of the gifted group were almost a mirror image of the patterns of the retarded groups. The gifted were strongest on the factor of verbal comprehension while they were poorest on tests relating to a perceptual organization factor. The average group had a pattern different from either the gifted or retarded groups. Since there was internal consistency in the patterns within both the gifted and retarded groups, there is some evidence to support the notion that different intellectual levels do have their specific patterns of intellect. Thompson and Finley (1962) essentially replicated the Gallagher-Lucito study with larger samples of people. The results confirm the earlier study.

## RANGE OF INTERESTS

The gifted usually exhibit a greater range of interests than the average. One of the most consistently reported leisure time activities is reading. They read a greater quantity of material and the list of topics is broader. Hobbies involving the collection of stamps, insects, rocks, and so on, are particular favorites for the gifted. Their collections usually are more extensive and show better organization than those of the average. Even though they are prone to occupy themselves with interests that require intellectual prowess, they also participate in the games usually played by their peers.

The occupational aspirations of the gifted usually involve the professions such as law, medicine, psychology. Furthermore, they do fill positions in the professions later on in life (Terman et al., 1959).

## HIGH CREATIVE VERSUS HIGH IQ

One of the most extensive reports of comparisons across the two groups ($H_CL_{IQ}$ and $L_{IQ}H_C$) defined earlier is given by Getzels and Jackson (1962).

Despite a 23-point difference in IQ scores the two groups achieved equally well. When the teachers were asked to rate these students on the degree to which they "enjoyed" having the pupils in class the high IQ group was more desired than the high creative one. This difference in desirability was further investigated by asking both groups of students to rate the personal traits of moral character, creativity, goal directedness, intelligence, superior school performance, wide range of interests, emotional stability, and sense of humor. They ranked these traits with a number of different sets: (1) the extent to which they wanted to be high on the trait—self-ideal score; (2) the degree to which high performance on these traits would lead to success in adult life—success image; and (3) the extent to which they thought teachers would prefer these traits—teacher perception. Of the eight personal traits the most important difference between the two groups was that sense of humor in the self-ideal set was ranked high by the creative group and last by the IQ group. Both groups had the same perception of the qualities needed for success as an adult and those preferred by teachers. Yet the high creative students did not want for themselves the traits which they perceived would lead to success or would be favored by teachers. In contrast, the high IQ students wanted for themselves the traits they perceived would lead to success and would be preferred by teachers. In light of this contrast it is not surprising that the high IQ students are more "enjoyable" to teachers than the high creative ones.

In analyzing verbal and nonverbal (drawings) imaginative productions it was found that the creative group was less stimulus bound by instruction, was more open to expressing and receiving experiences and feelings, and enjoyed the risk of relating elements in unconventional ways more than did the IQ group. Also, the creative group was better able to tolerate incongruous associations, ambiguity, aggression, and violence. They seemed to want to please themselves with the productions rather than others.

The two groups can also be differentiated by the quantity and quality of occupational goals. The creative group gave a greater variety of occupations. An analysis of the occupational goals chosen revealed that the creatives selected fewer conventional (lawyer, doctor, professor) and more unconventional (adventurer, inventor, writer) categories.

Reviews of other empirical studies (Carnegie Corporation, 1961; MacKinnon, 1962; Stein and Heinze, 1960; Torrance, 1962a) on the characteristics of highly creative people are essentially consistent with the findings of Getzels and Jackson (1962). Their results are even more convincing since differences in measures of the variables and age yielded similar outcomes.

## Educational Provisions

To understand or develop an educational program for gifted students, it is necessary to examine at least three major areas of decision making: (1) objectives—skills, knowledge, and attitudes; (2) educational procedures—curriculum and methods; and (3) administrative provisions—grouping of students, scheduling, physical facilities, and personnel responsibilities. Obviously these three areas are interrelated. The objectives give direction to program planning by defining the type of educational product desired. Both educational procedures and administrative provisions are means for attaining the objectives. A decision to change objectives could imply important changes in the other two areas. Should alterations in the objectives be made without reexamination of decisions in the other areas, it would be possible to produce an educational product which was not intended. Likewise, changes in educational procedures could influence the selection of administrative provisions. Particular administrative provisions may facilitate or hamper educational procedures depending on the degree of compatibility between them since both serve as means to the end of achieving the objectives.

The above discussion not only indicates the interrelatedness of the three areas, but also implies that a logical sequence of decision making exists among these areas. Without first stating the objectives, it is impossible to evaluate the effectiveness or efficiency of decisions made in the other two areas. Furthermore, since the educational procedures (treatments and experiences) are primarily instrumental in making the behavioral changes in students, decisions about administrative provisions should follow those of the educational procedures. To illustrate, special classes might be administratively organized for some gifted students, but these classes would not be instrumental in achieving the objectives for the gifted if the curriculum and methods appropriate for the mentally retarded were employed.

After only a superficial examination of the literature, it becomes apparent that more pages of educational provisions are devoted to administrative techniques than to educational treatments and experiences. One possible reason for this situation is that curriculum and methods for the gifted are difficult to distinguish from those recommended as the best procedures for average students. Much of the progressive or modern approaches for the average seem to have been based on research conducted with subjects from college laboratory schools or from outstanding schools of the suburbs and cities. The populations of these schools tend to more closely approximate gifted populations than average ones. If it should happen that general educators have been generalizing the results of studies from high ability students to the average, a series of studies may be necessary to compare the effectiveness of these methods with students of different levels of intellectual ability.

In some instances preoccupation with administrative provisions has resulted in the practice of deciding on administrative provisions before deciding which treatments are appropriate for the gifted. This is putting the cart before the horse. As discussed earlier, administrative provisions should only be considered as means for facilitating the treatment, not as the treatment itself. Thus, a three stage approach is needed. First, decide on the type of product the program should turn out in light of the unique role expectations of the gifted. Second, select treatments (experiences) which will achieve these objectives. And third, choose the administrative procedures most compatible with the treatments.

The remainder of this section will be devoted to discussing these three areas of decision making—objectives, educational procedures, and administrative provisions. Emphasis will be placed on elaborating the differences between gifted and nongifted programs not on considering the overlap in objectives, educational procedures, and administrative provisions. Also, very little attention will be paid to program adaptations for students with high IQ's but low creativity, problem solving, and evaluative thinking potential. Even though the high IQ pupils legitimately may be considered a subgroup of the gifted, fewer educational modifications are necessary as compared to the future innovators, complex problem solvers, and evaluators. As mentioned earlier, the high IQ group can be served primarily through increasing the scope and level of content for comprehension and the rate of presentation. With this type of education they will be able to play the important high level maintenance roles of society.

## OBJECTIVES

Are the objectives for gifted and nongifted the same? Certainly at the abstract level used by the Educational Policies Commission of the National Education Association (1946) there is no difference.

Who would deny that achievements of self-realization, adequate human relationships, economic efficiency, and civic responsibility are worthy objectives for all pupils? This level of thinking, however, is too general for engineering a differential program for gifted students. A more detailed level must be sought, one which is specific enough to differentiate the gifted from nongifted. Assistance can be obtained by borrowing the concept of roles from sociology and applying it to the problem of defining relatively unique objectives for the gifted. Everyone plays numerous roles in society. Many of these roles are not significantly different for the gifted and nongifted; for example, parent, sports spectator, purchaser of consumer goods. However, there are some categories of roles which are so complex that only people with superior intellectual ability can play them successfuly. What are these categories of unique roles? First, the gifted can be expected to be the major contributors to knowledge by offering innovations, evaluating them, and solving complex problems. Second, they can be expected to be the major participants in complex, practical decision making.[4] The first role category can be illustrated by a research psychologist who contributes to the scientific body of knowledge by formulating an original theory of motivation and by evaluating it through empirical studies. The second role category (complex, practical decision making) can be exemplified by another psychologist, or even the same one, who perceives the importance of this formulation of motivation, and applies it successfully for the *first* time to a client in psychotherapy. These two categories of unique roles plus the skills, knowledge, and attitudes necessary to play them successfully are the bases for differentiating and justifying the objectives of the gifted from the average.

If innovating, evaluating, and problem solving are assumed to be partially dependent on competency in productive and evaluative thinking, then the teaching of these types of thinking plus the supporting skills and attitudes become the primary core of the unique curriculum objectives for gifted programs. With an analysis

---

[4] See the later section on Problems in Developing Educational Programs for the Gifted for a discussion of the distinction and relation between practical and scientific decisions.

of these components, one can generate more specific objectives. Fortunately, many scholars (Guilford and Merrifield, 1960; Myers, 1961; Taylor, 1955, 1957, 1959; Torrance, 1961, 1962a; Wilson, 1958) are engaged in exploring the multifacets of productive and evaluative thinking. Since the primary core of the unique curriculum objectives is too complex and lengthy for an introductory text and it has not been extensively mapped anyway, only some of the more important objectives will be listed under educational procedures. The listing of these more specific objectives is postponed to avoid duplication and to afford the reader a better opportunity to see the relationships of illustrative methods and curriculum to specific objectives.

**EDUCATIONAL PROCEDURES**

A recent trend in the literature is the appearance of more attempts to deal with curriculum and methods. Two examples of this trend are the books of Ward (1961) and Fliegler (1961). Ward has made the most comprehensive statement of principles for distinguishing the educational procedures of the gifted from the average. Fliegler has approached the problem differently. He, in association with recognized curriculum and methods specialists, has presented education procedures for specific content fields such as social studies, reading, and mathematics. Even though these have been worthy efforts, there is a pressing need for research in the area. The complete story is yet to be written. Nevertheless, certain basic dimensions of method and curriculum modification for gifted students become discernable when research findings, theorizing by authorities, and the primary objectives are combined.

## Developing Thinking

The operations of productive and evaluative thinking can be performed on all types of content. Some authorities are experimenting with the notion of designing exercises for teaching these skills. It is assumed there will be transfer of the skills to subject matter areas.

Myers (1961) has constructed 20 such exercises. Some sample items and their purposes (objectives) are reproduced:

1. Combining Ideas and Elements . . . This is an exercise in which you are asked to use your imagination. Try to invent an animal "that never was"—or, perhaps, an animal that might exist on another planet. . . . Draw a picture of the animal . . . Name your creature. . . . Explain its actions and its habits—how it moves, eats, and communicates.

2. Exploring Possibilities . . . Write down as many different possible uses for each of the following objects as you can think of: Needle . . . Pencil . . . Match . . .

3. Exploring Possibilities . . . What do you suppose would happen if someone discovered that there is an important deposit of oil beneath home base on our baseball diamond? List all of the consequences which would result from such a discovery . . .

4. Analyzing Ideas . . . Some people think that we shouldn't be given a permanent first name (such as Gary, Shirley, or Lawrence) until we are old enough to decide for ourselves upon a name by which we would like to be known. What would be the advantages and the disadvantages of being able to select your own first name? . . . Can you think of any other customs which might be changed? . . .

5. Seeing Relationships . . . What possible relationships can you see between the following pairs of things? Explain the connection as clearly as you can. . . . puddle—rusty knife, Coca-Cola—forest fire, broken glasses—faded sweater . . .

6. Seeing Relationships . . . If you look closely at the numbers given below, you can see that the numbers in each row are related to each other in a *regular* way. When you think that you have discovered how the numbers in a series are related, write the missing number in the blank space. . . .
   1 3 2 4 3__4 6 5 . . .

7. Seeing Relationships . . . This is an exercise which will test your ability to think of many different items in a short period of time. You are to list all of the things you can think of which are both *flat* and *round*. Write down anything which combines the properties of flatness and roundness. . . .

8. Sensitivity and Awareness . . . Sit quietly in your seat for several minutes. Try to be aware of what is going on around you and also of what is going on inside you. Are there things around you which

you have never noticed before? . . . Do not share your observations with others. . . . Write down what you see, what you hear, what you smell, and what you feel. . . . When you feel that you have accurately described all that you are aware of, turn in your paper.[5]

Wilson (1958) suggests some similar and overlapping types of activities which may be used as models for devising additional exercises.

1. Sensitivity to problems—What would happen if . . . pills were developed which would substitute for food . . . everyone always told the truth about everything? . . . the ocean dried up? . . .

2. Ideational fluency—List on a piece of paper all the uses you can think of for a brick . . . Write as many things as you can think of that are square in shape . . . List all the nouns you can think of that might bring you comfort if you were hot. . . .

3. Originality—A poem may be read to the class and the pupils asked to brainstorm appropriate or clever titles for the poem. Then putting themselves in the position of an editor they may proceed to select the best title. . . .

4. Redefinition—List all the things you can think of that might serve as a hammer for pounding a nail into the wall to hang a picture. . . .

Further examples can be gotten from an article by Guilford (1960) entitled "Frontiers in Thinking That Teachers Should Know About."

These samples of exercises and their purposes (objectives), in a sense, define aspects of productive and evaluating thinking. It is possible to extend these models to subject matter areas. The ability to see relationships can be taught in many ways. One approach has been to cut across traditional lines of subject matter to enhance perceptions of relationships between content areas. In mathematics, a number of groups are reorganizing the content. The University of Illinois' committee on school mathematics is an example. Algebra, geometry, and trigonometry are taught as integrated, logical parts. A similar approach would be to reorganize the arithmetic program of the first grade with respect to addition and subtraction. These processes would not be taught separately; rather, they would be introduced at the same time by using the more general concept

---

[5] R. E. Myers' *An experimental training program in creative thinking.* Minneapolis, Minn.: Univer. of Minnesota: Bureau of Educational Research, 1961.

of addition of positive and negative numbers. Some teachers have been successful in teaching this more general concept in the primary grades by using the number line. Instead of confusing the gifted, as it would undoubtedly do the average, the more abstract approach should be more efficient because of the greater applicability of the larger generalization. This emphasis on teaching for relationships is not restricted to any subject. Physical education programs of the gifted can be reorganized to develop the ability to see relationships by having the students create new and modify old games instead of just learning the rules. They can then explore the effects of rule changes on amount of enjoyment.

Occasionally the gifted student's ability to see relationships may hamper the accomplishment of certain skills. It is a common occurrence to find fifth and sixth grade gifted students who can not accurately compute simple arithmetic problems. Usually they do not know the arithmetic combinations. Because they understand the relationships between the numbers they have learned some of the combinations and interpolate to the ones they have not memorized. Perhaps a change in the sequence of meaning and memorization of combinations would remedy the situation. Students could be taught the combinations by rote before the meaning of numbers was explained.

A large variety of examples could be given where the reorganization of content and the presentation of material at a more abstract level makes sense with the gifted, but is questionable for the average.

Gallagher (1960), Maltzman (1960), Osborn (1953), and Torrance (1962b) are a few of the people who have reported on ways of creating a climate for enhancing productive thinking. Torrance (1962b) has summarized some of the major features:

a. Free the student from the threat of evaluation during the creative phase of thinking.
b. Structure the situation as if it were just for fun.
c. Increase motivation by inducing a little competition—
   "... children in the elementary grades produce about twice as many ideas and a larger number of original ideas than they do when we use other types of motivation ..."

   **d.** Increase expectations for more original responses gradually so that the warm-up is progressive.

   **e.** Tolerate and encourage seemingly wild ideas during the productive phase.

## Wide Scope of Information

The probability of productive and evaluative thinking increases when students possess a wide background of information. They cannot think in a vacuum; there must be information on which to perform the operations of productive and evaluative thinking. As noted earlier these operations are not restricted to a few subject areas such as writing or art. Productive and evaluative thinking can be performed on all types of content.

Increasing the store of information is one of the easiest objectives to achieve with gifted students because they retain great quantities of material after few exposures. Providing an extensive library of books across a wide spectrum of topics and time to read them is an obvious method. Sharing of information during periods for reporting to the class is another method. More formally, extra subjects or topics, such as a foreign language, can be added to the curriculum. Teaching machines also can be used to increase the store of information, thus allowing more classroom hours for the time consuming tasks of permitting each student opportunities to crystalize his ideas and test them on his intellectual peers through discussions.

## Higher Level of Concepts

Quality contributions to the body of knowledge depends on high level ideational thinking. The sooner gifted students are exposed to difficult concepts at their level the more opportunities teachers will have to instruct pupils in productive and evaluative thinking. A general trend in providing for the gifted is to allow them to progress to higher levels of subject matter as rapidly as they can. This means no restrictions should be placed on the use of textbooks or other instructional materials just because they traditionally belong to a higher grade level. The gifted can be expected to reach higher levels of conceptualization at a younger age, and eventually be able to deal adequately with levels average students will never reach.

## Attitudes

There are certain attitudes which support productive and evaluative thinking, and assist students to interject their innovations and evaluations into the cultural stream.

1. Independent work skills and habits—The frontiers of knowledge are lonely; therefore, the gifted should be taught to plan and work independently. Through teacher enthusiasm and respect for the solution of difficult problems, students should become emotionally committed to solving difficult problems and enjoy the mental stimulation of intellectual exercise.

2. Independence from peer group pressures on judgments—Evidence from social psychology suggests that success experiences lead to more independence. The writer has developed a theory based on the frequency of successful verification of one's predictions (Lucito, 1959).

3. Tolerance for different opinions and a predisposition to examine many sides of an issue—Teaching by the discussion method should increase students' tolerance if the teacher sets an appropriate model by tolerating many different positions.

4. Ability to delay gratification of rewards—Hobbs (1960) suggests gifted students should be weaned from excessive, immediate rewards.

5. Predisposition to critically evaluate accepted ways of doing things—As students mature, fewer areas should be exempt from critical examination. Even such ideas as the scientific method are fair game. At times students tend to become overly critical. One device is to insist that they either offer a way of improving the situation or publicly admit their inability to do better.

6. Assume responsibility for the betterment of society—Knowing that society is in fact depending on them because of the scarcity of people with their intellectual ability will persuade some to

assume this responsibility. Others may be persuaded by a critical examination of their dependency on their fellow man in a complex society. A good example to cite is the garbage collector's importance to their own health and comfort.

## Leadership Skills

Group leadership skills offer students many opportunities to play the leadership role. They further teach them techniques of changing the leader through orderly processes. Students should not be encouraged to tolerate poor leadership.

## Enrichment

Before turning to a consideration of administrative provisions, consideration of the term "enrichment" is appropriate. Enrichment is the most reported approach to the treatment of gifted students. An examination of suggested enrichment practices in the literature will uncover everything from busy-work activities to changes in curriculum content and methods. Generally, the method and the content to be included is left up to the individual teacher. This is probably why enrichment has meant so many different things. It certainly has become an ambiguous term which must be specifically defined if understanding is not to suffer.

## ADMINISTRATIVE PROVISIONS

Three continua have been constructed in Table 4.4 to summarize the major administrative reorganizational provisions for the gifted at the elementary school, high school, and college levels. Note that the degree of administrative reorganization required for the plans increases as the continua are followed from left to right. Actually in practice some of the major reorganizational plans have been modified by combining parts of the various administrative provisions along the continua. Almost every variety that one can imagine has been tried in one school or another.

TABLE 4.4 Major administrative provisions for the gifted.

ELEMENTARY SCHOOLS:

| No administrative provisions | Extra curricular activities | Acceleration | Consultants | Itinerant teachers | Partial segregation | Special classes | Special schools |
|---|---|---|---|---|---|---|---|

HIGH SCHOOLS:

| No administrative provisions | Extra curricular activities | Summers sessions | Comprehensive high school with ability grouping | Honors schools within comprehensive high school | | | Special schools |
|---|---|---|---|---|---|---|---|

COLLEGES AND UNIVERSITIES:

| No administrative provisions | Extra curricular activities | Acceleration | Honors programs | Graduate colleges | Postdoctoral studies |
|---|---|---|---|---|---|

## Elementary Schools

There are many elementary schools which still have made *no administrative provisions* for the gifted. Some of these schools have a sincere interest in various types of reorganizations, but they have not been able to select one for action. Other groups delay action because they believe that equal educational opportunities should be interpreted to mean the same provisions for all students. Therefore, they studiously avoid making any provisions for the gifted.

The next point along the continuum toward more elaborate administrative organization is that of *extra curricular activities*. This type of arrangement in a school is not unusual. Nor is it necessarily a provision for the gifted. If schools encourage all pupils to participate in the same activities there is a tendency for the level and scope of the work to become too restrictive for the gifted. When students are allowed to voluntarily join these extra activities the gifted tend to gain control; then this organization may function as a provision for the gifted. In other instances, separate activities are planned for different ability students.

A more direct attempt to organize for the gifted has been termed *acceleration*. Three types of acceleration are found in the elementary schools. One form, which was popular prior to the progressive movement in education in the 1930s, has been called grade skipping. Students are double promoted at the end of a school term; for example, the students who finish third grade are placed in fifth grade the following school term.

Another type of acceleration, rapid progress, requires the co-operation of teachers in two adjacent grades. Students are allowed to finish the work of one grade in two-thirds of the school term, and begin working on the material for the next grade during the remainder of that school year. The next teacher receiving these students continues the school program where the pupils left off instead of at the beginning of the second grade involved. Thus, during the first third of the second year, students complete the second year of work begun with the first teacher. The remainder of the time spent with the second teacher is used to complete another year of work. In this manner three years of work are accomplished in two. Most educators believe rapid progress acceleration has an advantage over grade skipping. The former does not leave gaps in the educational background of students.

Another approach which attempts to offer acceleration and avoid gaps in the student's background is called early admission. This procedure allows children to enter kindergarten or first grade at a younger chronological age than is usual. Early admission is predicated on two considerations. Some students are emotionally, socially, and mentally mature enough to profit from school experiences before the usually accepted chronological age. In addition, reducing the number of school years allows the gifted to contribute to society at an earlier age.

The provision of *consultants* to work with regular classroom teachers is next on the continuum. These consultants are knowledgeable about the gifted and help the regular classroom teacher to meet curriculum and methodology problems she encounters. Consultants are usually found in large school districts where the administration believes that the social adjustment of the gifted may be negatively affected by separating them from their chronological peers. In smaller communities where it is not economical to have more elaborate organizational plans because of the small number of gifted children consultants are also found.

Other school systems have adopted the *itinerant teacher* approach. Here a consultant on the gifted has as his primary responsibility the teaching of the gifted children themselves and only secondarily consulting with teachers. Several times a week a group of gifted children are taken out of the regular classroom and given instructions in areas which are usually not a part of the elementary program. These programs have been criticized because a few hours a week do not seem to be sufficient modification for the gifted.

Moving up the continuum is the plan of *partial segregation*. Gifted students are grouped into separate sections for academic type studies and remain in the regular classroom for nonacademic studies. A good example of this is the Colfax Plan which has been in operation in Pittsburgh for a number of years. There one half of the day is spent in the segregated academic setting and the other half day with the regular class. Through this point on the continuum one of the most influential reasons for choosing one of these administrative organizations has been fear of ill effects from segregating gifted students from their less well-endowed peers. Some of the commonly expressed fears are the inability to communicate with less endowed citizens of a democracy, snobbishness, social and emotional maladjustment, and unhappiness. Studies by Barbe (1957), Kerstetter (1952), and Shannon (1957) are examples of the many investigations which demonstrate that the feared outcomes of segregation plans do not necessarily occur.

*Special classes* within the elementary school are composed of only gifted children. These students are placed under the supervision of a teacher for the entire day, in the same sense that any elementary school classroom is self-contained. An outstanding example of this arrangement has been operating in the Cleveland Elementary Schools since the early 1900s. Cleveland calls them the Major Work Class (Norris, 1958). Other large cities such as Chicago, Los Angeles, New York also have special classes. These classes offer opportunities for changing the curriculum content and reducing the range of mental abilities within a classroom. Some authorities believe the task of teaching is made more feasible when the range of intellectual abilities is restricted.

The most elaborate provision is the development of *special schools* for the gifted. They are usually private rather than public; or they are associated with some college for demonstration and research purposes. Hunter College in New York is an example of the latter (Brumbaugh, 1944).

## High Schools

The administrative provisions at the secondary level parallel in some respects those at the elementary. There are high schools which make no distinction between the offerings for gifted and nongifted students. The same kinds of reasoning described for *no administrative provisions* at the elementary level have probably been operative here.

*Extra curricular activities* at the high school level take the form of biology, chemistry, physics, mathematics, art, and photography clubs, to name a few. They are more elaborate, formalized, and specific to areas of knowledge than those in the elementary schools. Again the same mechanism seems to be operating here at the secondary level as at the elementary. To the extent that participation is voluntary there is a tendency for these groups to be dominated by the gifted and to become provisions for them. Since the launching of Sputnik in 1957 much interest has been stimulated in the science areas with a resultant increase in extra curricular activities for science. The Polytechnic High School in San Francisco, for example, has an electronics lab which industry helps to support. There youngsters work on science after school, on Saturdays, and in the summer.

Recently *summer sessions* have also become very popular as a method of providing for the gifted. Due to the cold war struggle with Russia these programs tend to offer courses in the physical sciences more often than the arts or social sciences. Some educators have been disturbed by this pressure to emphasize the physical sciences to the neglect of other areas of knowledge. Some summer session programs have been viewed as a form of acceleration. In some instances students are able to acquire the required number of credits to graduate in a faster period of time. Other programs have been developed as an attempt to elaborate the usual subject areas to an extent which is in keeping with the outstanding ability of the gifted student to learn. In the latter type of summer session programs no credit is given for attending. Many times the no-credit courses have been labeled enrichment. The National Science Foundation has encouraged summer programs by giving financial aid to schools throughout the country.

Some of the *comprehensive high schools* have instituted *ability groupings* for individual courses or followed the usual multitract approach. Courses developed solely for gifted membership are sometimes called honors courses. A more recent reorganization for the gifted has included an *honors school within the comprehensive high school.* Here the curriculum is modified to prepare the student for the type of role he will be playing in the future. This usually means careful preparation for college. The school-within-a-school plan has a separate and distinct administrative organization from the remainder of the school, and generally has an administrator directly under the principal who is responsible for the program. New York City has examples of the honor schools.

The most elaborate provisions are those made at the *special schools*. These high schools are not only different in that they are mainly for the gifted who are achieving outstandingly, but they also emphasize a specific area of knowledge. New York City has the High School of Music and Art, the High School of Performing Arts, the High School of Science, and others. Because one area of knowledge is emphasized, it does not mean that the other areas are neglected. To illustrate, the first year at the High School of Science offers English, social studies, science, and mathematics. The Sophomore and Junior years develop general educational aims in order to prepare students for meeting the admission requirements of first-rate colleges and technical schools. During the last year, students are allowed to pursue any special interest within mathematics and science they have acquired during their more general education years (Michael, 1958).

Occasionally, a rural high school will buy a correspondence course for a gifted youth due to the lack of qualified faculty to teach particularly technical courses such as physics or chemistry.

## Colleges and Universities

The college-university continuum in Table 4.4 begins in the same way as the other two continua—*no administrative provisions*. But traditionally the high schools and more so the colleges were primarily organized to educate the more able. Even though America has broadened the function of these two levels to include less able students some of the character of their original function still remains. To this extent many high school and most college programs can be considered gifted programs.

Again the next point on the college continuum duplicates the other two continua. *Extra curricular activities* are generally increased at the college level. Honorary fraternities and sororities become a part of the picture. In addition, the students are more highly selected with respect to intelligence at the college level than at either of the other two levels. Hence most of the extra curricular organizations are designed for the training of the gifted.

*Acceleration* also has its place on the college continuum. The Ford Foundation Fund for the Advancement of Education has a project entitled Early Admissions to College. The project focuses on the acceleration of gifted students, following in general outline the pattern established at the University of Chicago. These programs are essentially the same as the early admissions into kindergarten and first grade. Depending on the college or university, criteria are established to decide whether a high school student can enter its program before completing the usual four year high school program. Another form of acceleration, also supported by the Ford Fund, is called Admission with Advanced Standing. Either the student is given credit for college courses taken while enrolled in high school, or he is allowed to go on to more advanced courses in the college curriculum, if he can pass achievement proficiency exams.

*Honors programs* have included everything from a single seminar during the senior year all the way to completely different curriculum for the gifted, a different faculty, and separate housing facilities.

*Graduate colleges* are quite common throughout the United States. They are purposely set up for advanced training. The implication is that the schools have been designed primarily for the intellectual heavyweights.

Agencies of the federal government, various foundations, and private industries are awarding postdoctoral fellowships to promising young adults who have recently completed the most advanced degree offered at American universities. It is generally agreed that spending four years at the undergraduate level, one year at the Master's, and three years at the doctoral level still does not make a finished product in the more complex fields. Too, there are programs of advanced study which allow established leaders of various disciplines time away from their routine duties to study and create new ideas. The advanced *postdoctoral study* programs at Princeton and Stanford are outstanding examples of this approach.

# Problems in Developing Educational Programs for the Gifted

Even though most lay and professional people agree educational provisions should be made for the gifted, only a small percentage of the gifted in the public schools are receiving special services.

As it was indicated by Dunn in chapter 1, 6 percent of the gifted population were receiving these services during the 1957–1958 school year, using a 2 percent prevalence figure. More recent data would probably show an increase of services, but they would be far short of the mark if both quantity and quality of services are considered. Why should this condition of relatively little services for the gifted continue to exist when there is strong lay and professional verbal commitment to providing educational services for these students?

## DISAGREEMENT AMONG EXPERTS

Quite naturally in a relatively new field such as the gifted, many people consider themselves expert, and are considered to be expert by others, without adequate training and experience. To illustrate, one of these "experts" has recently published a pamphlet on the gifted. The text is filled with inaccurate statements and asks questions for which there are reasonably adequate answers in the literature. Investigation into this individual's background revealed that he had not even read *one* of the standard textbooks in the area of the gifted. He has attended a five-day workshop on the gifted, and consequently considers himself an authority. Obviously this is an extreme example; nevertheless too often uninformed persons speak with authority concerning the gifted.

Anyone familiar with the literature on the gifted, particularly in the area of curriculum and methods, becomes acutely aware of the sharp disagreements between experts. Conscientious school administrators, teachers, and related personnel who peruse the literature to obtain information for making decisions in a school setting have been confused. This has led to indecision on the part of school personnel who are responsible for initiating programs. It is not uncommon to find school systems with elaborate study committees devoting energy toward investigating what their particular school should do for the gifted. In many localities these committees have been studying the problem for five or more years without initiating any action. Many of these committees may continue in the future to study the problem without generating any significant action.

Disagreement among the experts on defining the gifted also contributes to the lack of action by both lay and school people. Without a definitive population in mind it is difficult to devise identification procedures and educational treatments efficiently and effectively. The inability of many people to realize that the gifted are not a homogeneous group has heated up many discussions which have been a waste of time. Eventually we may move toward subgroups within the gifted analogous to the subgroups of educable, trainable, and dependent mentally retarded children, even though the dimensions may be different. This does not lead to the conclusion that one definition is as good as another, but suggests that for the purpose of educational treatment some subcategories of gifted may need to be treated quite differently (unachievers versus achievers, high creatives versus high IQ's). Perhaps one of the organizations devoted to the interests of gifted students might sponsor a manual on terminology and classification as did the American Association of Mental Deficiency (Heber, 1961) for the mentally retarded. Such a project would have a number of benefits. It should facilitate the search for information in the literature about the particular subcategory of gifted in which one might be interested. It may help to clarify some of the reasons for seemingly contradictory results in research. Also, it could stimulate a number of comparative studies within the category of gifted to supplement those comparative studies between the gifted and nongifted. More importantly, it could aid in clarifying the subclass of gifted students being discussed by offering a frame of reference within which interested persons might communicate.

Anyone expecting competent, serious professionals in any academic area to completely agree would be dooming that field to a very static existence. The possibility of further development in the area would be reduced. Therefore it is contended that some confusion can be expected to exist at the scientific level as long as the field is alive and progressing. Anyone who waits until the confusion is cleared up before initiating programs for the gifted will probably have a very long wait. If this is an accurate description of the state of affairs, does it mean that we are to ignore the experts or can they be used in some particular sense? The latter approach seems the more fruitful. Before this can become understandable, it is necessary to discuss the nature of practical and scientific decisions.

The distinction between scientific and practical decision making can be demonstrated by considering a hypothetical situation. Let the reader assume he is on the second floor of a building when a fire breaks out in the hall. He is faced with a practical decision now. Three alternatives are available: (1) he can jump out the window to escape from the fire; (2) he can try to run to safety through the fire in the hallway; or (3) he can remain in the room and hope that the fire will be put out before it reaches him. Once the person makes a decision and acts upon it, it is not practical to test the other alternatives. This is an essential feature of practical decision making; whereas, for scientific purposes it is necessary to test the relative effects of the three alternatives. If someone were to approach the problem in a scientific manner he would probably obtain some animals. One group could be forced to run through the fire, another dropped from the window, and the third staked in the room. At the end of the experiment the animals would be recovered and the damage to each group would then be compared. If this distinction is a reasonable one, then teachers, administrators, and other persons involved in initiating programs for the gifted cannot expect to use the scientific approach. Although the scientific method cannot be used directly in practical decision making, it does play an important part. It is from the scientific body of knowledge that practical decision maker chooses those generalizations which seem to fit his present situation. Then, if the choice proves to be successful, the person verifies that the correct generalization was chosen from the body of knowledge. The scientific validity of the generalizations usually cannot be tested in a practical situation.

In spite of disagreement among the experts at the scientific level, sufficient data from a California study (Martinson, 1961) is available to demonstrate that *any systematic educational program adequately considered by professionals familiar with the gifted elicits better results than no program at all.* The California study used a variety of approaches at both the administrative and educational treatment levels, including cluster grouping, special classes, and independent study. The results indicate that in all the dimensions measured, such as academic achievement and social adjustment, the children who are given any of the special services exceeded those without special services. This should allay the fears of many people who are hesitant to institute programs for the gifted because it may not be the *best* approach for the gifted.

## STATUS OF KNOWLEDGE ABOUT THE GIFTED

The bulk of knowledge about the gifted has been generated by psychologists. Consequently the quantity and quality of research on identification, motivation, and other psychological variables compare favorably with that of any other area of exceptional children. Until recently individuals with the needed sophistication in research skills plus the experimental background and interest in educational procedures for the classroom have not been available. Personnel of this nature are becoming available and the literature has begun to reflect this new emphasis. Because the literature is largely psychological or administrative in nature, it is not surprising that many people who have explored the literature are somewhat apprehensive about the status of our educational knowledge on the gifted. Though it is incomplete, educational programs for other areas of exceptionality and for the average have been initiated and continue with comparable amounts of scientific research to draw upon.

The status of our knowledge about the gifted is sometimes judged by the number of differences that can be enumerated. People are more impressed by long lists of differences which might be overbalanced by one or two very important ones. The single fact that the gifted have qualitative differences in the organization of intellectual functions (Gallagher and Lucito, 1961) combined with the expectations of differential roles during adulthood is enough to justify differential educational procedures for these children.

## VALUE STRUCTURE OF SOCIETY AND PEOPLE
## ASSOCIATED WITH EDUCATION

Even though most educators and psychologists would like to believe that people no longer equate democratic education with identical treatment, there are still a substantial number of lay and professional people who subscribe to identical treatment and justify it with the concept of democracy. Since anything labeled democratic is held in high esteem there is a tendency for these people to avoid differentiating treatment for the gifted.

Another value high in most societies is that a person is not supposed to publicize his own virtues—society insists upon modesty from its members. This makes its difficult for parents of the gifted child to acknowledge publicly that their child is gifted. A typical statement from parents of a gifted child is: "Something should be done for the gifted, but my child is not gifted. He is just a *good, average* student." One of the common mechanisms used by other areas of exceptionality and regular education is to organize support from the parents of the students. As long as modesty hinders a large number of parents from admitting their child is gifted, they are not able to identify with any parent group working toward a betterment of educational practices for the gifted. Parents of gifted children are probably the most unorganized of all parent groups.

Furthermore, there is a generalized fear of deviant behavior. Illustrative of this feeling is the coining of such phrases as "egghead," "the brain," and "bookworm." The gifted are different, and can be expected to behave differently.

In the past, people have been unwilling to allocate enough money to education in general. Education is an expensive business. Until people are willing to support the necessities for quality educational programs, not only on the verbal level but on the hard cash level, the initiation and continuation of programs for the gifted will suffer.

## COSTS

Additional costs for operating a gifted educational program are not as high as many people believe. A study of six programs in the State of Illinois (Gallagher and Nelson, 1958) indicates that in no case did cost exceed one half of 1 percent of the total school budget. There was a wide range of costs which depended on (1) the number of children served, (2) the size of classes, (3) the design of a program, and (4) how much free help was available. The number of children involved in the program will depend to some extent on the definition used. This is obvious when one uses the operational definition of the percentage type. No matter how minimal the cost, if the percentage of students is increased, the costs go up. Too by decreasing the size of classes, the need for teacher personnel increases and the costs rise. To the extent the program is experimentally oriented costs will increase. This is due to the extra cost for expensive personnel to design and carry out the research. The experimental programs also tend to be more radical in the degree of differences between average and gifted programs. This usually means an increase in relatively unique equipment, supplies, and services. Fairly often costs are substantially reduced by obtaining free help from universities who assist the development of programs for the gifted by supplying trained personnel. At other times members of the community with professional skills can be used to supplement the instructional staff. Foundations such as Berg, Carnegie, and Ford have subsidized a number of programs. Some states, such as California, Illinois, and Ohio, are studying the question of whether it would be wise to assist financially the school districts which initiate and sustain programs.

## POWER STRUGGLE OF THE PROFESSIONALS

There seems to be just below the surface and at times openly, a power struggle between the regular educators and special educators for jurisdiction of gifted programs. This is a very unfortunate situation. Both groups can work together in deciding what curriculum and methods are needed by each subgroup of gifted students. Then the question of whether this a part of regular education or special education should be decided at the local level depending upon which group is in the best position to give support to experiences consistent with the planned program. Whether the gifted belong in regular or special education is more of an administrative matter that should be decided only after the more crucial aspects of the program have been planned.

## NOT A DISTURBING PROBLEM

The gifted student usually is not an irritating problem to the schools or his parents. The most frequent types of problems are the lack of motivation to achieve up to his potential and extra amounts of curiosity which may get in the way of routine. More often than not people associated with the gifted do not recognize the problem of underachievement especially if he is achieving above grade level. When emotional and social difficulties appear, they tend to be moderate rather than extreme. Thus, the gifted usually do not have the emotional appeal nor the urgency of the mentally retarded, blind, or crippled students. Some teachers are afraid programs for the gifted will siphon off the better students from their classes, and cause them to appear less effective teachers.

## ROLE CONFUSION

One of the most difficult problems in initiating or sustaining a program is defining and coordinating the roles of various groups—lay community members including parents, local school personnel, and state and federal offices of education. Most school districts require permission of the parents to place a student in a gifted program. This can thwart the best of educational plans if the parents are not sold on differential treatment for the gifted. Therefore, most local educators operate on the principle that having parents and important lay community members on school study committees and other similar activities will sell the program the local school people have already developed. This is a very dangerous approach. Once these lay groups invest time and energy to draw conclusions which conflict with the plan the school prefers, a bitter battle can result. Furthermore once the door is opened to consider the study of programs there is a tendency for the groups to spread their work into technical areas for which they have few skills, no preparation, and little time to acquire them. Such areas as identification procedures, placement, and curriculum are examples. Thus, the lay members of the community can infringe on the roles of the professional educators and disrupt program development. Local educators are then forced to make continual attempts to reclaim their appropriate roles in order to function in line with their best judgments. This robs the educator of time which could be better spent on program development. Frank discussions between lay groups, local educators, and representatives of state and federal offices of education are needed to clarify the roles each can play most effectively. Some "guts" to speak straight from the shoulder would be helpful to the educators in this situation. Then the lay groups probably would realize they must delegate some of their authority to the educators to make necessary decisions for improving the education of students. For example, an overwhelming majority of parents do not have the sophistication in educational matters to decide whether or not their youngster would be better off educationally if placed in a differential program for the gifted. The decision of placing or retaining a sudent in first, second, or third grade is of the same technical order as placing students in other educational groupings. Parents could better spend their time: (1) supporting parent organization for raising funds and influencing state and federal legislation, and (2) learning techniques to aid their own youngsters toward high achievement.

Additional evidence of the lack of clarity of role definitions can be seen in that few states offer financial assistance or have special certification requirements for the teachers of the gifted such as that accorded to other specialists in education. On the federal level, it was not until the middle of 1961 that the U.S. Office of Education created a specialist post for the area of the gifted.

## TRAINED PERSONNEL

Availability of trained personnel is always a problem in new and growing fields. But the problem is even more acute for this field because the nature of developing and servicing educational programs for gifted students requires personnel with superior intellect. There is great competition from other fields. Not many persons with the necessary intellect to implement the type of curriculum and methods described earlier in this chapter can be attracted into the teaching profession. The pay has been relatively low, and the position has had little status in the community. In addition, such working conditions as large class size, and harassment from vocal critics are not conducive to recruiting intellectually superior teachers.

An even bigger bottleneck is the scarcity of course offerings at the colleges and universities for training not only teachers but also support personnel, such as administrators, supervisors, psychologists, college professors, and research workers. Most institutions of higher education only teach about the gifted as part of various courses, typicaly through a unit on individual differences. A number of institutions now offer a survey course entirely devoted to the gifted, but few offer complete sequences of courses. This is partly due to the shortage of professors with adequate doctoral training in the area of the gifted or appropriate experiences to compensate for the lack of advanced training. Of those qualified, only a handful spend the major portion of their time teaching or researching the gifted area. Consequently, the necessary manpower to do the training is either occupied with other duties or not available. Another condition which works against obtaining leadership personnel is that scholarships and fellowships are readily available in other areas of special and regular education at the doctoral level, but are relatively scarce for one interested in training for the gifted.

## Summary

After reviewing a wide variety of definitions of giftedness, the author proposed one based on the student's potential for both productive and evaluative thinking. It was noted that identification, prevalence, characteristics, and educational provisions are dependent on the definition selected. Using any of the definitions discussed, the gifted as a group compare favorably with the average on most physical and psychological characteristics. Obviously, the largest discrepancies exist for those characteristics which depend on intellect. Educational provisions were then developed from three points of view—objectives, curriculum and methods, and administrative provisions. The interrelationships between these three aspects were emphasized. Finally, some of the problems associated with initiating and continuing educational programs for the gifted were discussed.

### CHAPTER REFERENCES

Abraham, W. *Common sense about gifted children.* New York: Harper & Row, 1958.

Barbe, W. B. A study of the family background of the gifted. *J. Psychol.,* 1956, **47**, 302–309.

————. What happens to graduates of special classes for the gifted. *Educ. Res. Bull.,* 1957, **36**, 13–16.

Barnette, W. L. Advance credit for the superior high-school student. *J. Higher Educ.,* 1957, **28**, 15–20.

Bond, H. M. The productivity of National Merit Scholars by occupational class. *Sch. & Soc.*, 1957, **85**, 267–268.

Bonsall, Marcella, & Stefflre, B. The temperament of gifted children. *Calif. J. Educ. Res.*, 1955, **6**, 195–199.

Brumbaugh, Florence Newell. A school for gifted children. *Child. Educ.*, 1944, **20**, 325–327.

Carnegie Corporation of New York. Creativity. *Quarterly*, 1961, **9** (3), 1–8.

Cole, C. C., Jr. Current loss of talent from high school. *Higher Educ.*, 1955, **12**, 35–38.

———. *Encouraging scientific talent: A report to the National Science Foundation.* New York: College Entrance Examination Board, 1956.

Conant, J. B. *The American high school today.* New York: McGraw-Hill, 1959.

Cutts, N. E., & Moseley, N. *Teaching the bright and gifted.* Englewood Cliffs, N.J.: Prentice-Hall, 1957.

Dailey, J. T., & Shaycoft, M. F. Types of tests in project talent. *Cooperative Res. Monogr.*, 1961, No. 9 (Whole No. OE-25014).

DeHaan, F., & Havighurst, R. J. *Educating gifted children.* Chicago: Univer. of Chicago Press, 1957.

Fliegler, L. A., & Bish, C. E. The gifted and talented. *Rev. Educ. Res.*, 1959, **29**, 408–450.

———. (Ed.) *Curriculum planning for the gifted.* Englewood Cliffs, N.J.: Prentice-Hall, 1961.

French, J. L. (Ed.) *Educating the gifted: A book of readings.* New York: Holt, Rinehart and Winston, 1959.

Gair, Mollie. Rorschach characteristics of a group of very superior seven year old children. *Rorschach Res. Exch.*, 1944, **8**, 31–37.

Gallagher, J. J., & Crowder, Thora H. Adjustment of gifted children in the regular classroom. *Except. Child.*, 1957, **23**, 306–312, 317–319.

———. Social status of children related to intelligence, propinquity, and social perception. *Elem. Sch. J.*, 1958, **58**, 225–231.

———, & Nelson, W. H. Report on programs for gifted children in state of Illinois. *Educ. Press Bull.*, 1958, **49** (3), 9–33.

———. *The gifted child in the elementary school.* Washington, D.C.: NEA, Department of Classroom Teachers, 1959.

———. *Analysis of research on the education of gifted children.* Springfield, Ill.: Office of the Illinois Superintendent of Public Instruction, 1960.

Gallagher, J. J., & Lucito, L. J. Intellectual patterns of gifted compared with average and retarded. *Except. Child.*, 1961, **27**, 479–482.

Getzels, J. W., & Jackson, P. W. The meaning of giftedness: An examination of an expanding concept. *Phi Delta Kappan*, 1958, **40**, 75–77.

————, & ————. The highly intelligent and the highly creative adolescent: A summary of some research findings. In C. W. Taylor (Ed.) *The third University of Utah research conference on the identification of creative scientific talent.* Salt Lake City, Utah: Univer. of Utah Press, 1959.

————, & ————. The gifted student. *Cooperative Res. Monogr.*, 1960, No. 2 (Whole No. OE-35016).

————, & ————. *Creativity and intelligence.* New York: Wiley, 1962.

Gowan, J. C. Dynamics of the underachievement of gifted students. *Except. Child.*, 1957, **24**, 98–107.

Guilford, J. P. Three faces of intellect. *Amer. Psychologist*, 1959, **14**, 469–479.

————. Frontiers in thinking that teachers should know about. *Reading Teacher*, Feb. 1960.

————, & Merrifield, P. R. The structure of intellect model: Its uses and implications. *Rep. psychol. Lab.*, No. 24, Los Angeles: Univer. of Southern California, 1960.

Heber, R. F. A manual on terminology and classification in mental retardation. *Monogr. suppl. Amer. J. ment. Defic.*, (2nd ed.) 1961.

Hildreth, Gertrude. *Educating gifted children.* New York: Harper & Row, 1952.

————. Characteristics of young gifted children. *J. genet. Psychol.*, 1938, **53**, 287–311.

Hobbs, N. Motivation to high achievement. In B. Shertzer (Ed.), *Working with superior students: Theories and practices.* Chicago: Science Research Associates, 1960, 247–264.

Hobson, J. R. Mental age as a workable criterion for school admission. *Elem. sch. J.*, 1948, **48**, 312–321.

Horn, Alice. Uneven distribution of the effects of specific factors. *Southern Calif. Educ. Monog.*, Univer. of Southern California, **12**, 1941.

Hottel, J. V. The influence of age and intelligence on independence-conformity behavior of children. Unpublished doctoral dissertation, Peabody College, 1960.

Hunt, J. M. *Intelligence and experience.* New York: Ronald Press, 1961.

Johnson, G. O. A study of the social position of mentally handicapped children in the regular grades. *Amer. J. ment. Defic.*, 1950, **55**, 60–89.

Justman, J. Acceleration in the junior high school. *High School J.*, 1956, **40**, 121–126.

Kahl, J. A. Educational aspirations of "common man" boys. *Harvard Educ. Rev.*, 1953, **23**, 186–203.

Kerstetter, Leona. A sociometric study of the classroom roles of a group of highly gifted children. Unpublished doctoral dissertation, New York Univer., 1952.

Kough, J., & DeHaan, R. F. *Teacher's guidance handbook.* (Part 1) Chicago: Science Research Associates, 1955.

Learned, W. S., & Wood, B. D. *The student and his knowledge.* New York: The Carnegie Foundation for the Advancement of Teaching, 1938.

Los Angeles City School Districts, Evaluation and Research Section. *Expected achievement grade placement tables.* Los Angeles, Calif.: Division of Instructional Services, Publication No. GC-6, 1955.

Lucito, L. J. A comparison of the independence-conformity behavior of intellectually bright and dull children. Unpublished doctoral dissertation, Univer. of Illinois, 1959.

MacKinnon, D. W. What makes a person creative? *Sat. Rev.*, Feb. 1962.

Maltzman, I. On the training of originality. *Psychol. Rev.*, 1960, **67**, 229–242.

Martinson, Ruth A., & Lessinger, L. M. Problems in the identification of intellectually gifted pupils. *Except. Child.*, 1960, **26**, 227–231, 242.
———. *Educational programs for gifted pupils.* Sacramento, Calif.: California State Department of Education, 1961.

Mensch, I. Rorschach study of the gifted child. *J. exper. Child,* 1950, **17**, 8–14.

Michael, L. S. Secondary-school programs. In N. B. Henry (Ed.), Education for the gifted. *Yearb. nat. Soc. Stud. Educ.*, 1958, **57**, Part 2.

Miles, Catherine C. Gifted children. In L. Carmichael (Ed.), *Manual of child psychology.* New York: Wiley, 1954, 984–1063.

Miller, R. V. Social status and socioempathic differences among mentally superior, mentally typical, and mentally retarded children. *Except. Child.*, 1956, **23**, 114–119.

Miller, Vera. Academic achievement and social adjustment of children young for their grade placement. *Elem. School J.*, 1957, **57**, 257–263.

Myers, R. E. *An experimental training program in creative thinking.* Minneapolis, Minn.: Univer. of Minnesota, Bureau of Educational Research, 1961.

National Education Association, Educational Policies Commission. *Policies for education in American democracy.* Washington, D.C.: NEA, 1946.

————. *The identification and education of the academically talented student in the American secondary school.* Washington, D.C.: NEA, 1958.

Newland, T. E. Something *can* be done for the gifted. *Cook County Educ. Dig.,* 1957, **20**, 3–4, 8.

Norris, Dorothy E. Programs in the elementary schools. In N. B. Henry (Ed.) , Education for the gifted. *Yearb. nat. Soc. Stud. Educ.,* 1958, **57**, Part II.

Osborn, A. *Applied imagination.* New York: Scribner's, 1953.

Pegnato, C. V., & Birch, J. W. Locating gifted children in junior high schools. *Except. Child.,* 1959, **25**, 300–304.

Pressey, S. L. Educational acceleration: Appraisal and basic problems, *Ohio State Univer., Bur. educ. Res. Monogr.,* 1949, No. 31.

Shannon, D. C. What research says about acceleration. *Phi Delta Kappan,* 1957, **39**, 70–73.

Sheldon, P. M. The families of highly gifted children. *Marriage and Family Living,* 1954, **16**, 59–81.

Stein, M. I., & Heinze, Shirley J. *Creativity and the individual.* New York: Free Press, 1960.

Stouffer, S. A., & Shea, P. D. *Your educational plans.* Chicago: Science Research Associates, 1959.

Sumption, M. R. *Three hundred gifted children.* New York: Harcourt, Brace & World, 1941.

————, & Luecking, Evelyn M. *Education of the gifted.* New York: Ronald Press, 1960.

Taylor, C. W. (Ed.) *Research conference on identification of creative scientific talent.* Salt Lake City, Utah: Univer. of Utah Press, 1955.

————. (Ed.) *Second research conference on identification of creative scientific talent.* Salt Lake City, Utah: Univer. of Utah Press, 1957.

————. (Ed.) *Third research conference on identification of creative scientific talent.* Salt Lake City, Utah: Univer. of Utah Press, 1959.

Terman, L. M., et al. *Genetic studies of genius*. Stanford, Calif.: Stanford Univer. Press, 1925–1959. 5 vols.

Thompson, J. M., & Finley, Carmen J. A further comparison of the intellectual patterns of gifted and mentally retarded children. *Except. Child.*, 1962, **28**, 379–381.

Torrance, E. P. Curriculum frontiers for the elementary gifted pupil: Flying monkeys and silent lions. *Except. Child.*, 1961, **28**, 119–127.

————, Yamamoto, K., Schenetzki, D., Palamutlu, N., & Luther, B. *Assessing the creative thinking abilities of children*. Minneapolis, Minn.: Univer. of Minnesota, Bureau of Educational Research, 1960.

————. *Guiding creative talent*. Englewood Cliffs, N.J.: Prentice-Hall, 1962a.

————. Freeing the creative thinking abilities through teaching. Paper presented to Classroom Teacher Work Conference, Athens, Ga., Jan. 1962b.

Ward, V. S. *Educating the gifted: An axiomatic approach*. Columbus, Ohio: Charles E. Merrill, 1961.

Wilson, R. C. Creativity. In N. B. Henry (Ed.), Education for the gifted. *Yearb. nat. Soc. Stud. Educ.*, 1958, **57**, Part II.

Witty, P. Who are the gifted? In N. B. Henry (Ed.), Education for the gifted. *Yearb. nat. Soc. Stud. Educ.*, 1958, **57**, Part II.

Wolfle, D. Diversity of talent. *Amer. Psychologist*, 1960, **15**, 535–545.

Worcester, D. A. *The education of children of above average mentality*. Lincoln, Neb.: Univer. of Nebraska Press, 1956.

## ADDITIONAL REFERENCES

Anderson, K. E. (Ed.) *Research on the academically talented student*. Washington, D.C.: NEA, 1961.

Freehill, M. F. *Gifted children*. New York: Macmillan, 1961.

Gibbony, Hazel M. *Enrichment: Classroom challenge*. Columbus, Ohio: Ohio Department of Education, 1962.

Gowan, J. C. *An annotated bibliography on the academically talented student*. Washington, D.C.: NEA, 1961.

Henry, N. B. (Ed.) Education for the gifted. *Yearb. nat. Soc. Stud. Educ.*, 1958, **57**, Part 2.

Lewis, Gertrude M. *Educating the more able children in grades four, five, and six.* Washington, D.C.: U. S. Office of Education Bulletin, No. 1, 1961.

National Education Association. *Publications of the NEA project on the academically talented student* (12 titles). Washington, D.C.: Nat. Educ. Ass., 1958–1961.

Miller, L. M. *Guidance for the underachiever with superior ability.* Washington, D.C.: U. S. Office of Education Bulletin, No. 25, 1961.

Ohio Department of Education, Superintendent of Public Instruction. *A selected and annotated bibliography on the gifted.* Columbus, Ohio: Ohio Department of Education, 1960.

Southern Regional Education Board. *The gifted student: A manual for program improvement.* Atlanta, Ga.: South. Reg. Educ. Bd., 1962.

Taylor, C. W. & Barron, F. (Eds) *Scientific creativity: Its recognition and development.* New York: Wiley 1963.

## RESOURCES

### ORGANIZATIONS AND THEIR SERVICES

A number of organizations offer a variety of services to the field of the gifted. Below are listed some of the important ones with a brief description of their services.

The American Association for Gifted Children, 15 Gramercy Park, New York 3, New York, has a membership consisting of lay and professional individuals and groups. Its major purpose is to promote the interests of gifted children. Services of the association include sponsoring writing of books and distributing reprints of articles by members (publication list available).

The Association for the Gifted is a division of the Council for Exceptional Children, 1201 16th Street, NW., Washington 6, D.C. Its membership includes predominantly professional individuals. Plans are being made to form community, district, state, and/or regional affiliates to the national body. The association is devoted to the sensitization of society to the needs of the gifted, the stimulation of research, and the facilitation of information exchange. A newsletter is issued three times a year.

The Joe Berg Foundation, 1713 South Michigan Avenue, Chicago 16, Illinois, is a nonprofit foundation organized to promote seminars for the gifted at elementary and high school levels, using professionals from the community as teachers, to develop materials for seminars, and to offer assistance in establishing seminars at no charge to the community.

The Educational Testing Service, Nassau Street, Princeton, New Jersey, maintains the Creativity Research Exchange as a clearing house. Researchers send outlines of major phases of studies as completed and ETS reproduces and distributes them to professionals within a few weeks.

The Inter-University Committee on the Superior Student, 229 McKenna, University of Colorado, Boulder, Colorado, has no formal membership, only mailing list of approximately 9000. Its purposes are to encourage the development of special programs for the superior student in American higher education (particularly in four-year public institutions). The committee serves as a clearing house for information on special programs, holds national and regional conferences, arranges personal visits by its staff to assist schools seeking to establish or revise special programs, and publishes during the academic year the *Superior Student*, a monthly newsletter.

The National Association for Gifted Children, 409 Clinton Avenue, Cincinnati 17, Ohio, incorporated as a nonprofit educational organization, has a membership of approximately 1000 persons, chiefly professional, but the association is also open to lay persons. Its purposes are to maximize the potentialities of the gifted by providing better understanding of their problems and needs and how these may be satisfactorily met. It sponsors annual national and state meetings, charters local affiliated chapters, and publishes the *Gifted Child Quarterly*.

The National Education Association Project on the Academically Talented Student, 1201 16th Street, NW., Washington 6, D.C., sponsors conferences and produces inexpensive paperback publications on the gifted (publication lists available).

The purposes of Project Talent, American Institute of Research, 410 Amberson Avenue, Pittsburgh 32, Pennsylvania, are to describe and measure the social variables, aptitudes, and abilities of a half million high school students and follow their careers for 20 plus years to promote better understanding of talents. The organization's primary financial support is from the U.S. Office of Education, supplemented by the Office of Naval Research, the National Science Foundation, and the National Institute of Mental Health.

The Special Study Project for Gifted Children, 105 University High School, University of Illinois, Urbana, Illinois, was established to assist the Illinois legislature to plan permanent legislation to assist districts in providing for gifted. A publication list is available.

Superior and Talented Student Project, 5454 South Shore Drive, Chicago 15, Illinois, Room 718, is a voluntary association of secondary schools committed to programs designed to serve youth with above average abilities. Its membership of approximately 200 schools is open to secondary schools by application through the following regional accrediting agencies: New England Association of Colleges and Secondary Schools; North Central Association of Colleges and Secondary Schools; Northwest Association of Secondary and Higher Schools; Southern Association of Colleges and Secondary Schools; Western Colleges Association; and California Association of Secondary School Administrators. The purpose of the project is to involve secondary schools in cooperative action programs which identify, guide, motivate, and provide for capable youth; some consultative services are available to groups of schools. A list of publications is sent on request.

Talented Youth Project, Horace Mann-Lincoln Institute, Teachers College, Columbia University, New York 27, New York, is a research project providing services to school systems and individuals as an outgrowth of research activities. Publication lists and a selected bibliography are available.

The Gifted Child Society, Inc., 75 Andover Avenue, Dumont, New Jersey, has a membership consisting primarily of parents, with some professionals. The society's purpose is to offer activities (lectures, field trips, workshops) for gifted students and members of the organization. A bimonthly newsletter is published.

### PERIODICALS

Other than the few periodicals published by the organizations listed above, there are no journals devoted solely to the gifted. Articles can be found scattered in educational and psychological literature. Frequently articles on the gifted are found in *Exceptional Children,* the *Instructor,* the *Journal of Genetic Psychology,* the *National Education Association Research Bulletin, School Life, School Review,* and *Science Teacher.* The location of articles in other periodicals can be facilitated by referring to the two bibliographies listed under Additional References in this chapter (Gowan, 1961; Ohio Department of Education, 1960). The following publications are also helpful: *Educational Index, Encyclopedia of Educational Research, Psychological Abstracts,* and *Review of Educational Research.*

## SELECTED 16 MM SOUND FILMS

*A time for talent.* 29 min, black & white, color. National Education Association Press and Radio Relations, 1201–16 Street, NW., Washington 6, D.C. Shows how bright pupils are identified and explores three programs for gifted students.

*Gifted child.* 29 min, black & white. National Educational Television Film Service, Indiana University, Bloomington, Indiana. Shows negative influences of home and school in the gifted, and follows a day in the life of a well-adjusted gifted child.

*Gifted ones.* 22 min, black & white. Contemporary Films, 267 West 25 Street, New York 1, New York. Two Canadian educators discuss the gifted while gifted children are observed in their regular school activities.

*Meeting the challenge of the gifted.* 20 min, black & white. McGraw-Hill Text-Film Department, 330 West 42 Street, New York 36, New York. Shows what one school in California is doing for the gifted.

*Ted Mack camp.* 10 min, color. Ball Productions, 507 Fifth Avenue, New York 17, New York. Presents Ted Mack's summer haven for children aged seven through 18 who show unusual talents in the creative arts, including modern dance, music, acting, and outdoor crafts.

## CHAPTER 5

# Emotionally Disturbed and Socially Maladjusted Children

JOHN E. PATE

Educators are well aware of the profound effects of emotional and social factors on school success. As a result, school curricula throughout the country reflect their concern for emotional and social influences in the lives of children. It is commonplace to find the academic curriculum augmented by such supportive services as:

Selective placement of pupils with teachers skilled in dealing with personality problems

Remedial instruction

Guidance and counseling services

Specially trained teachers serving as mental health consultants in a school unit

School psychological services

School social workers or visiting teachers

Individual and group therapy by mental health specialists.

Through support of such services, many children are able to remain in school where they can receive the type of education and guidance they need. Thus many unhappy children are enabled to work through minor problems and effect a satisfactory adjustment to life. But emotional and social problems are exceedingly complex and painfully delicate. Supportive services are not effective with all children. Some children present such severe problems to themselves and to the community that they require more intensive and specialized assistance.

This chapter is concerned with extreme behavior problems—pupils who cannot remain in a regular classroom even with the benefit of supportive services. The concern here will be with children whose behavior is persistently so disturbed or maladjusted that they need special education.

For purposes of educational planning, these children fall into two categories, the emotionally disturbed and the socially maladjusted. *Emotionally disturbed* children suffer from mental illness. Their personal problems prevent them from adjusting to regular classroom situations. Their overt behavior may cover the gamut of extremes, ranging from aggressive destruction to morbid withdrawal. Disturbed pupils are handicapped by psychological stress —they are unable to do what is expected of their more normal peers. They are found in any school district, in any social class, and in any family. *Socially maladjusted* children are chronic juvenile offenders who regularly disregard broader social values and rules as a matter of course, substituting in their stead the values and rules of their peer group. They make up delinquent gangs who are constantly in trouble with the law. Their accepted code of conduct is truancy, fighting, and defiance against constituted authority. Socially maladjusted children are handicapped by their provincial pattern of social values; they do not share the respect for standards expected of normal children. Most often, maladjusted children are the offspring of multiproblem families nurtured in urban slums.

Typically, the distinction between the two categories is quite clear, but there may be some overlapping in individual cases. Some members of socially maladjusted gangs are also emotionally disturbed, but this is not to say that emotional disturbance and social maladjustment are identities. Gang membership requires a high degree of sociability, conformity, and purposefulness which can rarely be achieved by emotionally disturbed youngsters. Some emotionally disturbed children do violate laws and are classified as delinquent in the legal sense. But isolated illegal actions are hardly equivalent to being an accepted member of a delinquent gang, organized and directed toward violence and disregard for law. Some authorities (Kvaraceus and Miller, 1959) feel that no more than 25 percent of delinquent acts are attributable to emotionally disturbed children.

From the outset, the reader must accept two ground rules. First, emotionally disturbed and socially maladjusted are concepts which have defied precise definiton and objective delimitation. The inherent problems are apparent—the terms are sometimes grouped, sometimes interchanged. Reporting and research findings are often shrouded and meaningless due to cloudy terminology. Second, an introductory survey text imposes very real limits. Popular concepts and usages must be employed and many important topics must bow to the pressures of priority. These are disconcerting conditions the reader must live with.

Since emotional disturbance and social maladajustment have different implications for educational planning, they will be discussed in separate sections within this chapter. Each section will be viewed from the educator's chair, emphasizng the problems of teaching and adminstration. A concluding section deals with the teacher of pupils with behavior problems as an emerging professional specialization.

## Emotionally Disturbed Children

Education is only one of many professions engaged in identifying and planning for emotionally disturbed children. Disturbed children are exceptional because of their emotional problems, or more pointedly, their mental illness. Special education programming in their interest rests upon close cooperation with mental health specialists. Thus it provides a common ground where educators and mental hygienists augment one another, each discipline approaching the common ground from different frames of reference.

## DEFINITION

A child is emotionally disturbed when his reactions to life situations are so personally unrewarding and so inappropriate as to be unacceptable to his peers and adults. Thus, disturbed children are viewed as having limited patterns of behavior and lacking flexibility to govern and modify their behavior. Their behavior differs considerably from others in their circumstances, not by kind but by degree. They are too excitable or too withdrawn, too brave or too fearful. They are the extremes of any variable of behavior.

Though this definiton affords a common ground for educator and mental health specialist alike, they cannot pause there for long. Educators must be concerned with school programming for disturbed children. Mental health specialists must be concerned with the psychiatric illness of children.

For the *educator,* a child is disturbed when his behavior is so inappropriate that regular class attendance (1) would be disrupting for the rest of the class, (2) would place undue pressure on the teacher, or (3) further the disturbance of the pupil. In his frame of reference, the educator must consider the entire school program and must reserve the right to assign all pupils, including the emotionally disturbed. He must also consider the unreasonable demands which some children place upon their teachers. Regular school teachers are not play therapists and should not be expected to work with children who are severely mentally ill. Though educators bear ultimate responsiblty for school placement of the child, their decisions should reflect the professional consultation of mental health specialists who know most about children's emotional conditions.

For *mental health specialists,* emotional disturbance is a blanket term covering a number of diagnostic categories formulated for the American Psychiatric Association (1952). It includes:

Psychiatric disturbances *without clearly defined physical cause* or without structural damage to the brain; that is to psychoses, psychophysiologic disturbances, psychoneuroses, personality disorders (with the exception of sociopathy) and transient situational disturbances (Eisenburg, 1960, p. 275).

To gain some appreciation for the wide range of personality types included in the term "emotional disturbance," a brief introduction to each category will be presented under identification and characteristics.

## PREVALENCE

Mental health—or the lack of it—is widely recognized as a most pressing social problem of the last few decades. The National Committee Against Mental Illness (1959) cautions that one out of every twelve school children will spend some part of his life as a patient in a mental hospital if current rates continue. Today more than half of our hospital beds are occupied by mental patients. Some authorities (Abrahamson, 1955; Bower, 1961) submit that at least 10 percent of our school age population need psychiatric help. In the schools, a large majority of the 10 percent need supportive services only but some few will need a more intensive special education. These few probably represent 0.5 percent of the school age population. Some are the half mililon severely disturbed youngsters who are excluded from school by expulsion or refusal of admission, according to estimates by the League for Emotionally Disturbed Children (Southern Regional Education Board, 1961). Among them will be the one child in 2000 who needs full-time intensive treatment, according to estimates from the states of Connecticut and Wisconsin; a few will be from the 13,000 young people in state mental hospitals at any one day (Southern Regional Education Board, 1961). Most are in the regular classrooms now, retreating further and further from normal social relationships or disrupting the school program.

For harassed classroom teachers who see "streams of unhappy children" move through the schools, an estimate of 0.5 percent for special education may seem entirely too conservative. But the following considerations must not be overlooked. (1) Special education for the disturbed means temporary assignment in most cases. Disturbed children can recover; they can master their handicap; they can be returned to regular classrooms. (2) Special education for the disturbed is based upon a complex of educational and psychological services which would ultimately reduce the numbers of children requiring special placement. Thorough programs of supportive services with special education for the few severe cases would foster preventive measures, early identification, and well planned transition to and from the regular class. (3) There seems to be a tendency to over-estimate the actual numbers of disturbed children. In the face of the estimates of Abrahamson (1955) and Bower (1961) that 10 percent need psychiatric help, only 0.34 percent of the school-age population served are seen as new admissions at community mental health clinics (Bahn and Norman, 1959). In view of these three considerations, it seems advisable to plan special education provisions for one out of every 200 in the school population.

Applying the 0.5 percent estimate to a city of 100,000 would mean that special education would be provided for at least 125 emotionally disturbed children. Quite naturally, school districts in which residential centers are located will be called upon to meet special demands. They may be requested to supply teachers to the center or provide classes for patients in regular school units. But unfortunately, such special demands will not be made to many school districts because there are only 40 recognized residential treatment centers for disturbed children in the United States (Southern Regional Education Board, 1961).

Emotional disturbance is *not distributed evenly* through all populations of children and youth. In the general population, there appear to be age and sex differences related to emotional disturbance. MacFarlane and others (1954) pointed out that school children tend to have the largest number of behavior problems during early puberty which occurs several years earlier among girls than among boys. In new admissions to mental health clinics, boys outnumber girls four to one (Bahn and Norman, 1959). Among the specific psychiatric disorders (terms to be explained more fully under "characteristics"), psychotic and personality disorders seem to be most prevalent among the 14–16-year old group. Psychoneurosis is found most often in 10–13-year olds; situational disorders among the 5–9-year group; but psychophysiological disorders seem to appear in all age groups at about the same rate (Bahn and Norman, 1959).

Although disturbed children can be found in all social classes, lower sociocultural classes produce far more than their share. In the California study, Bower (1961) reported that certain occupational groups seemed to produce more disturbed children percentage-wise. Families in which the father's occupations were classified as "service" and those classified as "semi-skilled," produced more than twice as many emotionally disturbed children as would be expected by their proportion of the state's population. Families in occupational categories of "professional and managerial," "clerical and sales," "skilled," and "unskilled" produced fewer than expected. In an analysis of community patterns, Myers and Robertson (1959) reported that certain types of disorders appeared more frequently among particular patterns of cultural values. In general, conditions in lower sociocultural classes are more conducive to emotional disturbance, since stability and security are often lacking (Hollingshead and Redlich, 1958). In view of Lucito's discussion of "cultural and familial background" and "social and emotional adjustment" of the gifted in chapter 4, higher sociocultural families produce fewer emotionally disturbed children. The notion that "madness is one step beyond genius" is simply a popular fallacy.

## IDENTIFICATION AND CHARACTERISTICS

School is the one institution where specially trained adults are in prolonged, close contact with all children and youth. Thus, it can perform a unique function in the total mental health effort, and classroom teachers occupy the strategic position. By applying their skills in observing and guiding behavior, teachers prove to be extremely accurate in recognizing children who need psychiatric help with emotional problems (Fitzsimmons, 1958). Schools are the most active source of referrals to mental health clinics.

*Screening* disturbed children is second nature for teachers. Their experience with large numbers of children tells them what to expect and what is unusual in children. The writer recalls one instance in which a kindergarten teacher noticed the first symptom of a youngster's impending emotional disturbance. The teacher observed that the child's art work had deteriorated suddenly; the use of form had regressed and choices of color became somber. Although she told the parents of her concern about the little girl, the warnings were ignored. In several months the youngster had lost her speech and appetite and required hospitalization due to severe emotional illness.

Educators have developed excellent guides to systematize and refine their observations of children in school situations. Careful use of these guides, such as the sample which follows, is very effective in screening for disturbed children.

1. Needs an unusual amount of prodding to get work completed.
2. Is inattentive, indifferent, or apparently lazy.
3. Exhibits nervous reactions such as nail-biting, sucking thumb or fingers, stuttering, extreme restlessness, muscle twitching, hair twisting, picking and scratching, deep and frequent sighing.
4. Is actively excluded by most of the children whenever they get a chance.
5. Failure in school for no apparent reason.
6. Is absent from school frequently or dislikes school intensely.
7. Seems to be more unhappy than most of the children.
8. Achieves much less in school than his ability indicates he should.
9. Jealous or over competitive (Kough and DeHaan, 1955, p. 62).

Screening procedure can be made more intricate and perhaps more accurate by addition of other devices. California's statewide study (Bower, 1961) employed teacher ratings, peer ratings, and self ratings to screen for children whom the researchers felt were best described as "emotionally handicapped." A host of standardized personality tests and inventories have been developed for use in screening disturbed children. Buros (1959) catalogues and describes these instruments in his compendium of psychological tests. It must be noted that most personality tests are complex psychological instruments and should be administered and interpreted by a qualified psychologist. Only a few group personality tests are designed for use in the elementary school level where early screening should begin. Most are restricted to secondary school and college uses. However, three of the most widely used group tests of personality are: California Psychological Inventory, Edwards Personal Preference Schedule, Minnesota Multiphasic Personality Inventory.

*Identification,* or more properly, diagnosis of emotionally disturbed children is the province of mental health specialists. Acting as a mental health team, three disciplines are involved in evaluating children who have been screened and referred by schools. Social workers are skilled interviewers who gather the psychosocial history—an historical account of important people and events affecting the child's life. Psychologists specialize in administering projective tests (such as Rorschach, Thematic Apperception Test, and Children's Apperception Test), intelligence tests (such as WISC and Stanford-Binet), and tests of organic brain damage (such as the Bender Gestalt). Psychiatrists are medical specialists on the team who employ a number of interviewing and testing skills, together with physical (medical and neurological) examination. Findings of the three specialists are shared and a diagnosis is made.

Under the previous section on "definitions" it was pointed out that mental health specialists view emotional disturbance as a blanket term covering five psychiatric disorders. Each of these disorders are discussed briefly in the following paragraphs to suggest the variety of *characteristics* presented by emotionally disturbed children.

1. *Psychosis* is the most severe and debilitating of the psychiatric disturbances. Psychotic children lose contact with reality; they may hear unreal sounds, see imaginary objects, or create a dream world to live in. They may be oblivious to the world of real people and things about them and only react to their own private imaginary scheme of life. Of the many types of psychosis, childhood schizophrenia has received the greatest attention in professional literature. The term has lost much of its original meaning and is now used loosely to describe at least eight separate conditions (King, 1960). But the following is a description of one of the writer's former students who was diagnosed as suffering from childhood schizophrenia:

Carl was obsessed by bizarre and strange impulses, such as operating door locks over and over again, gazing transfixed at holes and studying the phenomenon of changing angles and perspectives as doors were opened or shut. He would ask "why" of his parents again and again, while his arms flailed wildly and he stood in deep absorbed study of some insignificant object or event. Answers never satisfied him. He struggled intellectually to understand his world to the point of abstract absurdity. Frustrated, lonely, fearful of living, obsessed with dying and terrified by his inability to grasp the real world of other children, Carl watched helplessly as the other neighborhood children joyously went to school (Help, 1960, p 2).

The autistic type of childhood schizophrenia has held a special fascination for students of emotional disturbances. The term "early infantile autism" was introduced in 1943 by Kanner to describe children with extreme withdrawal tendencies. They have peculiarities in communication and do not use language to convey meaning to others. Words are parrotted and personal pronouns are used just as heard. Change is very unpleasant to them, and they relate much better to objects than to people.

The common denominator in all these patients is a disability to relate themselves in an ordinary way to people and situations from the beginning of life. Their parents refer to them as always having been "self-sufficient," "like in a shell," "happiest when left alone," "acting as if people weren't there," "giving the impression of silent wisdom." The case histories indicate invariably the presence from the start of extreme autistic aloneness which, when possible, shuts out anything that comes to the child from the outside (Kanner, 1960, p. 739).

2. *Psychophysiologic disorders* are emotional disturbances resulting in physical malfunctioning but without apparent anxiety on the part of the person effected. Children with psychophysiologic disorders may have severe eczema or asthma but be unaware of the emotional overlay. They may suffer from excruciatingly painful migraine or from anorexia nervosa, a persistent loss of appetite. The anorexic child may not only lose a desire for food but also may not be able to tolerate food if force-fed. One such 15-year-old youngster was 64 inches tall, but weighed only 70 pounds. She would compulsively gorge on pies, pastries, and sweets and then induce vomiting by sticking her finger down her throat. She would not voluntarily take any other nourishment and became nauseated at the prospect. Unfortunately many children undergo extensive medical treatment before their condition is diagnosed as a psychophysiologic complaint.

3. *Psychoneurosis* is a condition in which a child has a distorted view of some aspects of the real world but is able to function fairly well in other aspects. As someone once remarked, psychoneurotic children build air castles, and psychotic children live in them. Psychoneurotic children may have inordinate fears (phobias) or inordinate desires (manias). Certainly, no child is completely free from some neurotic problems (MacFarlane et al., 1954), but when neurotic processes control the child or call attention to his strange behavior and prevent adjustment to life situations, the condition can be considered psychoneurotic. For example, many children are cautious, even a bit frightened by furry animals. But some psychoneurotic children might be terrified into panic reactions or uncontrollable crying when excited by conscious or unconscious reminders of whatever the fur symbolizes to them.

4. *Personality disorders* include long term chronic behavior patterns which present serious problems to the people they characterize and to society. These are children who best can be described as having an inadequate personality or who are extremely shy or who are too outgoing or who feel the world is set against them. Children with personality disorders have very consistent patterns of reacting to situations. They act in rigid habit sets, lacking the resiliency to develop better ways of meeting emotional problems. Personality disorders become part of the makeup of a person and that person feels no tension or anxiety about the way he is behaving. His behavior does not serve as a release or as an attempted solution to a pressing emotional stress.

5. *Transient situational personality disorders* are acute reactions to catastrophic psychological pressures. Every classroom teacher has seen some child shattered and completely confused over the loss of a loved one from death or divorce. Unexpected menarche or witnessing a terrifying accident may have a devastating effect upon youngsters who formerly met and solved their emotional problems adequately. Situational disorders are usually abrupt changes in emotional behavior, often attributable to traumatic or distressing circumstances, and without apparent chronic underlying personality disturbance.

The *etiology* or cause of emotional disturbance is a hotly contested but unresolved field of research. Research findings flow in from geneticists, physiologists, neurologists, biochemists, psychologists, sociologists, and a host of other disciplines, but they do not lend themselves to discussion here. Rather, the reader should consult a reputable review of pertinent literature, such as Jackson (1960) or Spiegel (1960). However, it is safe to venture that theory and practice with disturbed children is dominated by developmental psychology with a heavy Freudian bias.

*Treatment* has changed radically during the last two decades. Even though the incidence has increased, the population of hospitalized mental patients has decreased markedly (National Committee Against Mental Illness, 1959). With the advent of effective tranquilling and antidepressant drugs (Cole et al., 1960), many disturbed persons demonstrate astonishing improvement and respond much more quickly to psychotherapy. Severely regressed patients under drug therapy often become more self-sufficient, thereby releasing professional time for intensive work with more promising patients. Mental hospitals have taken on new proportions as the "open hospital" concept spreads. In the open hospital, patients are free to move about the premises. Some may live in private homes and spend their day under hospital supervision; or some may need a hospital setting at night but hold regular jobs off the grounds during the day. Disturbed children, then, might live in their own homes, or foster homes but need the close attention provided in school within a psychiatric setting. Or in some cases, a youngster might live in a residential institution but attend a nearby public school.

## EDUCATIONAL PROGRAMS

Emotionally disturbed children need a strong special education program for three reasons. First, going to school is the occupation of children in this culture. That is what everyone expects them to do and that is what they want to do. Special education must somehow make the disturbed child's "occupation" as near like other children's "occupations" as can be tolerated. Second, if disturbed children are to make a successful return to the regular classroom, they must be able to meet the academic and social requirements of regular classrooms. If they are educationally retarded or socially "different" they may once again begin to run in the same psychological treadmill. Third, the educative process gives disturbed children new strengths and abilities to deal with problems.

Educators should enlist psychiatric consultation before undertaking any type of special planning for emotionally disturbed children. The medical specialty of psychiatry has legal sanction in the mental health field and should be represented on planning committees. Generally the professions of psychiatry, psychology, and social work are favorably disposed and eager to cooperate in providing special education for disturbed children. It is interesting to observe that many children's psychiatric units have for some time offered school programs. Consequently, they offer a valuable background of experience to share with educators.

Common sense dictates that programs should be organized cautiously and modified to meet existing circumstances. Joint committees of educators and mental health personnel must first appraise the need, survey resources, and formulate some comprehensive plans. Through such processes educators can find the best situation to try out some experimental classes.

Ideally, special education should provide a complex of facilities through which disturbed children move as their progress indicates. At least four different settings are advisable:[1]

1. Privately sponsored day schools, usually provided for children who are too young or too regressed to be considered educable (Abbate et al., 1957).

2. Special classes in residential psychiatric centers (Rabinow, 1955).

3. Special classes in out-patient mental health centers (LaVietes et al., 1960).

4. Special classes in conventional school unit (Rubin and Simion, 1960).

Pupils assigned to any of the classes cited above could be drawn from residential centers or from their homes. Cooperative planning

---

[1] Space does not permit a detailed examination of these types of settings but the reader is referred to a descriptive source for each at the end of this chapter.

must determine whether a particular disturbed youngster seems capable of living at home and attending school in situation two, or whether he could tolerate large numbers of children around the school ground in situation four.

Flexibility in planning is necessary because disturbance is a dynamic condition. Dramatic changes in personality and behavior will demand changes in placement and planning. A disturbed youngster may not always need special education. If his condition can be screened and identified early, and if the youngster can be given appropriate treatment and special education, it is very likely that he can be returned to regular home and school activities quickly. Even among children who are so severely disturbed as to be placed in residential treatment centers, almost half are discharged in less than one year (Reid and Hagan, 1952).

Throughout North America, educators are testing a variety of special education provisions for use with disturbed children. The California project (Bower, 1961) is an ambitious long range study involving large populations to compare the effectiveness of various types of provisions. Approximately 45,000 pupils in fifty California school districts were screened by teacher ratings, peer ratings, and self-ratings. Mental health specialists examined children selected through screening. Of the 1200 "emotionally handicapped" children used in the study, half were randomly selected for experimental programs and the other 600 were left in regular classrooms. Experimental programs were compared on the bases of pupils' improvement on teacher-, peer-, and self-ratings and on administrative feasibility. The project is much too comprehensive for a fair summarization here. However, results of experimental provisions are presented in Table 5.1 to stimulate study on the project report.

Through a National Institute of Mental Health grant, the states of Tennessee and North Carolina in cooperation with George Peabody College for Teachers have embarked on an eight year cooperative project to establish and staff "re-education" residential schools for emotionally disturbed children (Hobbs, 1961). Each state operates a residential school to accommodate forty emotionally disturbed youngsters between the ages of six and twelve years. Peabody College is training the teaching staff. Project Re-Ed, as it is appropriately named, envisions a new professional specialization

TABLE 5.1 *Comparison of the results of special provisions for experimental groups with those of regular provisions for control groups,[a] and with the ratings of administrative feasibility of each type of provision.*

| PROVISION | IQ | ACHIEVEMENT | PEER RATING | TEACHER RATING | ADMINISTRATIVE RATING[b] | TOTAL RATING |
|---|---|---|---|---|---|---|
| Special class—elementary | + | + | ❋ | + | A | + |
| Special class—secondary | 0 | + | 0 | 0 | A | + |
| Special placement | 0 | 0 | − | 0 | C | 0 |
| Mental health consultation | + | 0 | 0 | 0 | A | 0 |
| Child study | ❋ | 0 | 0 | 0 | A | 0 |
| Adolescent group counseling | 0 | + | 0 | + | A | + |
| Special activity groups | − | 0 | + | 0 | B | 0 |
| Learning disability grouping | + | ❋ | ❋ | + | B | + |
| Parent group counseling | − | − | − | − | C | − |
| Home economics | 0 | 0 | 0 | 0 | B | 0 |
| Identification | 0 | 0 | + | 0 | B | 0 |

[a] ❋ difference significant at <.10; + difference significant at <.30> .10; 0 not significant; − difference significant at <.30> .10 in favor of control groups;

[b] A administrative assets heavily outweigh liabilities; B administrative assets and liabilities about equal; C administrative liabilities outweigh assets.

*Source:* Bower, E. M. *The education of emotionally handicapped children.* Sacramento, Calif.: Calif. State Dept. of Education, 1961, p. 47.

the teacher-counselor. Modeled after the French educateur, teacher-counselors are to be experienced classroom teachers with an additional graduate year of specific training for the new profession. Each teacher-counselor will be assigned to a group of eight children in residence at the Re-Ed School and then alternate between living in as a parent surrogate during evenings and nights and acting as a teacher-group worker during the day. Responsibility for planning the full 24-hour daily program rests exclusively with teacher-counselors, constituting a marked departure from conventional planning for emotionally disturbed children. Mental health personnel are available as consultants but not primarily to provide psychotherapy for the children.

*Pupil-teacher* ratio is determined by the type of child served and the nature of the educational program. Disturbed children vary markedly—some can tolerate groups; others exhaust teachers' energies in a one to one relationship. Programs vary as well. A school day for disturbed children should be as similar to a regular school day as can be tolerated. Normally, teachers direct children's activities during much of the day. However, in some residential programs, teachers are responsible for academic subjects only. Music, recreation, crafts, and the like may be under the direction of other specialists. So administrators must consider the type of child and schedule of teaching responsibility. In making recommendations for treatment of in-patient disturbed children, the American Psychiatric Association (1957) recommends one teacher for each four children in residence. The Child Guidance Clinic in St. Louis, Missouri has six pupils for one teacher in an out-patient day school. Special classes in regular school units could enroll eight disturbed children in a class but an attendent or helper should be readily available. The six-to-one ratio is the best rule of thumb.

*Teaching disturbed children* is neither regular teaching nor is it psychotherapy. Rather, it is a melding of elements of each. The demands are so unique and the concept so young that a new term, "therapeutic education," has been developed to describe the process. As Fig. 5.1 indicates,[2] the teaching role is maximal with most children, and the therapeutic role is minimal. With severely

2 Suggested by Dr. Ray Balester, Training and Research Branch, NIMH.

disturbed children, the teaching role is minimal and the therapeutic role is maximal. Therapeutic educators find their most fertile field among children who need psychotherapeutic experiences in an educational framework.

Therapeutic educators function as *members of a mental health team*. As such they must understand psychological measures, family influences, and personality dynamics; they must administer and interpret educational tests; they must plan educational experiences toward therapeutic goals and share their observations in team conference. Teaching procedures must reflect the therapeutic plan:

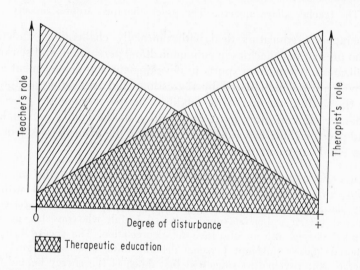

FIG. 5.1 The role of teaching and therapy in relation to degree of pupil disturbance.

some behavior can be tolerated, some must be anticipated and redirected, some should be elicited and mobilized for purposeful activity—depending upon the therapeutic process. Although equally concerned with disturbed behavior, therapeutic educators have a unique identity, as teachers. Distinctions between teacher and therapist are readily observable, as Hirschberg (1953, p. 688) pointed out:

> The teacher-child relationship is seldom interpreted. The psychotherapist-child relationship is almost always interpreted.
>
> The teacher needs to know a child's healthy defense patterns and support them. The psychotherapist tries to give insight into them.
>
> The teacher helps the child with reality pressures. The psychotherapist frees the child from internal drives.
>
> The teacher is concerned with the "situational" present. The psychotherapist is concerned with the "historical" past.
>
> The teacher allays anxiety. The psychotherapist arouses anxiety.

Therapeutic educators deal with unusually challenging students who present peculiarities in communication, perception, and sensory utilization. Astonishing spurts in development and achievement are almost always punctuated by regressions and frustrating attitudes as the child's personality is modified in the therapeutic process. Therapeutic educators must be sensitive to the child's personality and pace teaching experiences according to the team's assessment of the child's movement in psychotherapy.

Maria was a strikingly attractive ten year old, so pathetically shy and withdrawn that she was placed in a day school connected with a psychiatric clinic. An excellent student of superior intellect, Maria considered herself a horrible ogre, despised by all who saw her as she slipped deeper into an obsessive self-depreciation. The special teacher ignored Maria's unkempt personal disarray until, after some weeks of therapy, the psychiatrist suggested that much of the energy behind the symptoms had been mitigated and that Maria might be responsive to planned "incidental" experiences in grooming and personal care. Sporadic gains and losses marked Maria's acceptance of blossoming womanhood, her growth in self-esteem, and her return to the regular classroom (adapted from writer's professional files).

*Structuring limits* in the classroom is first priority. Disturbed children are struggling to bring order out of emotional chaos; they strive for predictability. With the aid of psychiatric consultation, teachers design limits which are more than negative restrictions. They structure limits which give support and direction to activities. For example, as one youngster begins to increase his tension level and flaunts authority, he may desperately need and want a firm, reliable hand to help him curb his aggressive behavior which he, himself, fears. Another youngster may want and need to flaunt authority so that he can break through his magical thoughts and come to grips with reality.

Some experimental attempts have been made to study classroom atmospheres which seem especially valuable in working with disturbed children. Groups of aggressive acting-out youngsters have been brought together into special classes for experimental purposes. Under the hypothesis that these children lacked order and structure in their environment and emotional life, two experimental classes, each with eight disturbed children, were given a highly structured school day in a school environment designed for minimal distraction. Another 15 disturbed children, serving as controls, were left in the regular classes without designed manipulation of teachers or school environment. Still another class of 15 older problem children were considered as a "secondary" control. The investigators reported that experimental classes under rigidly structured conditions made twice as much gain as the controls and thirty-five times as much gain as the secondary controls on measures of academic achievement (Phillips and Haring, 1959). Other experiments in the reduction of stimuli, akin to the Strauss and Lehtinen (1947) techniques discussed in chapter 2, are being conducted in several psychiatric facilities. The writer observed a situation in the Children's Neuropsychiatric Hospital of the University of Michigan in which excitable children had carrels fashioned from boxes. Youngsters could be seated, place the shield on their desk, and lean their head and upper trunk into the box, shutting out the room and distracting influences from view.

*Subject matter* itself has different significance for teachers of disturbed children. There is little value in concluding disturbed children are simply educationally retarded. As Devereux points out (1956, p. 116), there may be many reasons why children have deficits or distorted views of information which may be essential to social or academic learning:

1. The child did not have the opportunity to learn certain things

which it should know at its age (words, concepts, attitudes, facts).

2. Information was deliberately withheld from the child by neurotically rigid adults (e.g., the facts of procreation).

3. The child was systematically misinformed (e.g., babies are brought by storks).

4. There is a definite contradiction between socially sanctioned beliefs and simple common sense (e.g., society often pretends something is true because it wants it to be true. Race superiority, for example.)

5. Society offers only taboos, instead of positive guidance.

In addition to the reasons cited by Devereux, children often have neurotic involvements with specific topics. For them a particular area may be emotionally loaded. Children who abhor food (anarexia) might do poorly while studying the basic seven food groupings. Exaggerated fears of animals might cause a youngster to avoid reading Uncle Remus Tales. Traumatic experiences with parents might cause more than mild discomfort for the beginning reader struggling with his primer. Consider that much commercially prepared school material is based around content which possibly has pathological significance for disturbed children. Screening and reducing emotionally loaded material in the teaching environment demands minute analysis of educational planning in view of its psychiatric implications. The process is sometimes referred to as "neutralization" (Jacobson and Faegre, 1959). Careful analysis of subject matter can also be directed positively. *Bibliotherapy* (Cohoe, 1960), the use of selected readings, has long been established as a valuable therapeutic and educational tool.

*Group dynamics* techniques are particularly vital for teachers of disturbed children. Group dynamics take place when children are together, whether or not they are guided. Many teachers use group techniques intuitively but planned therapeutic use is an exacting art. Routine teaching decisions can have therapeutic significance. Seating arrangements and relative physical positions of teacher and pupils can be designed to encourage desired interaction or internalization of limits. Thus teachers of disturbed children find innumerable possibilities to use *proximity control*. Directed group activity allows participants to break inhibitions and to perform differently as a group member. Most of us behave differently when alone than we do at a football game. This sociological phenomenon, called *de-individuation* (Festinger et al., 1955), offers interesting opportunities for teachers of disturbed children. *Psychodrama* and *role playing* are familiar classroom techniques with special significance for the disturbed since they tend to deal with the preconscious level of thought process (Berkowitz and Rothman, 1960).

After studying 68 classroom programs, Hollister and Goldston (1962) developed an outline of considerations for planning classes for disturbed children. Considerations are presented as brief topic headings orgnized within four sections: administration, pupil selection and study, classroom operations, and supportive operations. The outline guide has special significance in attempting to organize and clarify what is involved in teaching disturbed children. It is quite likely that any teacher will find it interesting and useful.

## EFFECTIVENESS OF SCHOOL PROGRAMS

Very few controlled experiments have tested the effectiveness of special education for disturbed children. As cited earlier, Philips and Haring (1959) found special classes with a highly structured approach to be superior to regular class placement. Two limitations of the study, small sampling and brief duration of the experimental treatment, are not present in the California study (Bower, 1961). Although the latter project is in its infancy, every indication points to the success of special education for "emotionally handicapped" children. Brief, cross-sectional studies can not be considered conclusive. Short-term modification of behavior is not the same as pervasive change in personality structure. Only long range follow up studies provide information needed to evaluate the effectiveness of educational programs. But educators should not be discouraged. It has always been extremely difficult to evaluate any mental health program. In fact, debate continues to rage over the idea that psychotherapy of any sort is effective with children (Levitt, 1960), or whether it is not (Hood-Williams, 1960).

## Socially Maladjusted Children

Aroused by the clamor about problem children, twentieth century Americans can take some consolation in knowing it didn't begin here. Delinquent and socially maladjusted children appeared in the great American dream no later than the establishment of Plymouth Colony. William Bradford and Richard Winslow recorded the shameful deeds of Francis Billington in their *Chronicles*:

The fifth day (of December 1620), we through Gods mercy escaped a great danger by the foolishness of a boy, one Francis of Billingtons sonnes, who in his fathers absence had got gunpowder and shot off a piece or two and made squibs, and there being a fowling piece charged in his fathers cabbin shot her off in the cabbin.

There being a little barrell of powder halfe full scattered in and about the cabbin, the fire being within four foote of the bed betweene deckes and many flints and iron things about and so many people about the fire. And yet by Gods mercy no harm was done.

Apparently young Francis was a victim of the seventeenth century counterpart of a "multiproblem" family, being described as "one of ye profanest families amongst them." Mother Billington spent time in the stocks for "slandering Deacon Doane," and Mr. Billington was the first colonist to be hanged for murder.

Society has always had some socially maladjusted children and probably always will. But two recent developments make the problem particularly appropriate for a book about educating exceptional children. First, the total number and the rate of juvenile crimes are soaring alarmingly—to the proportion of a major social problem. Second, schools are being called upon to assume more responsibility in the prevention and correction of youthful offenders. Educators must act with imagination if they are to fulfill the new responsibility.

### DEFINITION

Socially maladjusted children are chronic juvenile offenders who persistently refuse to meet minimum standards of conduct required in regular schools and classrooms. They defy teachers and disrupt the school program. They intimidate and harass other students. Their behavior is so antagonistic to the purpose and program of schools that they must be excluded from regular class attendance.

As was stated at the outset of the chapter, social maladjustment and emotional disturbance are not equivalent terms. It bears repeating here that the two conditions are substantially different. At the risk of oversimplification, social maladjustment can be considered a sociological problem and emotional disturbance can be considered psychological. Maladjusted youngsters follow a pattern of repeated law violations and defiance in school to gain acceptance from their peers, and to maintain status in the delinquent gang. But disturbed children are seldom capable of winning peer approval. They are too disorganized to function effectively in the complex social structure of the delinquent gang. Occasional overlapping of conditions are exceptions to the rule. When discussing the psychiatric definition of disturbance earlier in this chapter, sociopathy —a near equivalent of social maladjustment—was excluded from the list of relevant psychiatric disorders.

Social maladjustment and juvenile delinquency are not equivalent terms. Maladjustment reflects a chronic pattern of repeated violence and disregard for constituted authority. It implies a characteristic way of behaving, of accepting standards of the delinquent gang and defying adult standards. Juvenile delinquency is a legal concept meaning that a youth has violated a law and has been apprehended. It does not suggest what laws were violated or how frequently. Smoking cigarettes and auto theft are two of 34 different statutory definitions of delinquency in the law of the United States (Sussman, 1950). Anyone apprehended for violating either law would be equally delinquent—at least as far as reporting is concerned. Model students may commit one infraction of the law and be considered delinquent. But schools are concerned with youngsters who refuse to respect the rights of others, who characteristically cause trouble and rebel against the purpose and intent of school programs. Their illegal acts, their delinquency is an established repetitive pattern— a way of life.

## PREVALENCE

Educators must face the prospect of providing special education for children too maladjusted to participate in regular school programs. Although the need will vary widely from one school district to the next, urban school districts will find about 1.5 percent of all 10–16-year old children so socially maladjusted as to need special education. This estimate is offered with strong qualifications. Some school districts have more serious social problems than others, while the stable, economically sound residential areas have few juvenile problems, relatively speaking. Services for maladjusted children may be administered by education in one district and by juvenile welfare in another.

Socially maladjusted children are not distributed randomly through the hamlets, cities, and metropolitan areas of North America. Over 60 percent of the population of the United States live in metropolitan statistical areas. Within these metropolitan areas, crime rates are about twice as high as rates for cities outside the metropolitan areas and three times as high as rural crime rates (U.S. Justice Department, 1960). Thus, the majority of school children live in metropolitan areas where children become involved in proportionately more crime. However, it must be remembered that delinquency rates are only indices to juvenile crime—the actual tally is several time higher. But in contradistinction, high delinquency rates are only indices to maladjustment—the actual tally is much lower.

Not all neighborhoods are likely to *produce maladjusted children.* Sociologists have carefully studied relationships between urban zones and crime; law enforcement agencies know it too well through experience. Shaw and McKay (1942) conducted the classic study in this field, pointing out that crime rates declined steadily with movement from inner urban zones to outer zones. They found juvenile problems correlated positively with high percentages of families on relief, low medium rentals, high percentages of foreign born or Negro heads of households, and low percentage of home ownership. Such conditions of social degradation and disorganization foster maladjustment in children. Transitional slums were once the "Hell's Kitchen" for foreign immigrants—now they are ghettos for Negro and Puerto Rican minorities. Educators must realize that the same conditions which produced Italian and Irish gangs a generation ago are now operating against urbanized Negroes. Crime rates for this racial minority are much higher than for whites or for other nonwhites (U.S. Justice Department, 1960). For example, in a four year period according to Lander (1954, p. 20).

Approximately forty per cent of the Negro boys aged fourteen and fifteen and twenty-six per cent of the boys aged ten to thirteen were registered in the Baltimore Juvenile Court on delinquency petitions during the four year period covered by the study. Of the white male population, approximately twelve per cent of the fourteen to fifteen age category and seven per cent of the ten to thirteen were in courts as alleged delinquents.

Urban areas which produce high delinquency rates produce many maladjusted children. Unhappily, educators are well acquainted with that fact.

Age is also a factor in the prevalence of social maladjustment. The Lander quotation suggests that children may become maladjusted while quite young. Juvenile offenses increase steadily until the sixteenth year when the rate begins to decline gradually (U.S. Justice Department, 1960). It is interesting to observe that the peak is reached during the customary final year for compulsory attendance.

Many more boys than girls are socially maladjusted and need special education. Boys get into trouble more often and for different types of offenses than girls. During 1955, girls accounted for only one fifth of juvenile arrests in the United States but only one out of eight in Canada (United Nations, 1958). Interestingly enough, the proportion of Canadian girls-to-boys arrested is about the same proportion of girls-to-boys in correctional institutions of the United States in 1950 (United Nations, 1958). This ratio, eight boys to one girl, can be expected among special education programs for socially maladjusted children.

There are more than 325 governmental and private *correctional institutions* in the United States. Canada has 27 provincial institutions but makes wide use of an undisclosed number of private institutions on a per-child fee basis (United Nations, 1958). Approximately 105,000 juveniles were in institutions in the States and nearly 2000 in Canadian institutions in 1950 (United Nations, 1958). School programs for these large numbers will place extra demands on school districts in which institutions are located. If these numbers do not stagger the average educator then he may also look forward to dealing with another 150,000 youngsters who are placed on court probation each year because they need close supervision from the courts (Perlman, 1960, p. 6).

## IDENTIFICATION AND CHARACTERISTICS

Socially maladjusted children are as obvious as a nose on the teacher's face. They want to be noticed. They purposely cause trouble to gain approval from their peers. Maladjusted youths climb the status ladder by tearing down the very principles for which schools stand. By persistent truancy, rebellion, and crime, maladjusted children are well-known to police, attendance personnel, teachers, and principals.

It profits society nothing to piously point fingers at youngsters who have already demonstrated their contempt for the values of broader society. There is no problem in picking out surly, defiant, maladjusted youth after problem behavior is full-blown. Emphasis must be placed upon *prediction*. Valid predictors could identify potentially maladjusted children while they are still quite young and responsive to corrective measures. Current research activity is seeking to develop standardized measures for predicting delinquency, the precursor of maladjustment. Perhaps as Kvaraceus quipped, "so far, these are useful only to research persons interested in further development of them" (Moore, 1958, p. 22). However, three of the most publicized devices merit attention: Glueck Social Prediction Table, KD Proneness Scale and Checklist, and Minnesota Multiphasis Personality Inventory.

It has been difficult to predict maladjustment because it is difficult to isolate *characteristics* peculiar to maladjusted youth— other than a tragic series of legal infractions. The Gluecks attempted to ferret out unique characteristics by comparing 500 delinquent and 500 nondelinquent boys (Glueck and Glueck, 1950). The two groups were matched in terms of age, general intelligence, ethnoracial origin, and residence in underpriviledged neighborhood. Data included extensive interviews to explore family and personal background, and the results of physical, intellectual, and projective measurements. Delinquent youth were found to come from families characterized by instability, erratic discipline, rejection of off-spring, and disregard for legitimate authority. Concluding statements, however, reported no unique attributes peculiar to the delinquent. Indeed, differences between the two groups were neither unexpected nor spectacular. Delinquents are distinguished from the non-delinquents:

1. Physically, in being essentially mesomorphic in constitution (solid, closely knit, muscular)
2. Temperamentally, in being restlessly energetic, impulsive, extroverted, aggressive, destructive (often sadistic)—traits which may be related more or less to the erratic growth pattern and its physiologic correlates or consequences
3. In attitude, by being hostile, defiant, resentful, suspicious, stubborn, socially assertive, adventurous, unconventional, nonsubmissive to authority
4. Psychologically, in tending to direct and concrete, rather than symbolic and intellectual expression, and being less methodical in approach to problems
5. Socioculturally, in having been reared to a far greater extent than the control group in the homes of little understanding, affection, stability, or moral fibre by parents usually unfit to be effective guides and protectors or, according to psychoanalytic theory, desirable sources for emulation and the construction of a consistent, well-behaved, and socially normal superego during the early stages of character development (Glueck and Glueck, 1950, pp. 281–282).

There can be little doubt that *socioeconomic factors contribute to, but do not determine maladjustment.* Social injustice, economic deprivation, and personal hopelessness are components, but only that. Maladjustment is much more complex. From the same poor socioeconomic area come chronic offenders and model citizens—

they may live in the same building, the same family. Landor (1954) attacked the problem of relationships between certain socioeconomic indices and delinquency through factor analysis. He found one factor, which he called "anomie," with heavy loadings on delinquency rates, many Negroes, many rentors, and few foreign born. A second factor had heavy loadings on low education, low rent, overcrowding, substandard housing, and many foreign born, but a low loading on delinquency rate. He then suggested that social disorganization, rather than economic conditions alone, contributed to delinquency. In this vein, Strodtbeck (1958) pointed out how various ethnic groups impose different value systems upon their children. Family patterns and religious practices are factors in shaping children's lives. Some ethnic groups produce few maladjusted children while other groups in the same neighborhood produce many.

Typically socially maladjusted children live in culturally deprived areas in which the *extended family* is the basic social unit. Extended families have many children and many parents—grandparents and aunts, cousins and nieces, all living together in one household for support in their unstable world. (Riessman, 1962). Homes are crowded and noisy. Intense parent-child relationships are rare and there is little sibling rivalry. Discipline is enforced by swift physical punishment—not by withholding love and affection. Love is not the central note in child rearing practices among the deprived as it is among middle class families. In extended families, children do not have to win love nor do they lose it by disobeying, reported Riessman. They are not expected to do household chores but they are expected to feed and clothe themselves earlier. Adolescents in an extended family are much less dependent on parents since they are either part-time wage earners or anticipate working shortly. The extended family unit teaches children a unique pattern of relationships with adults and peers.

*Delinquent gangs* are midwives to social maladjustment. Gang membership offers the principal avenue to security and status among peers in most social classes. But in the slums, the gang's business is more sinister and violent. It becomes the main theme in the youngster's unhappy life. Members are attracted for thrill-seeking, status-seeking; some join voluntarily for protection while others are coerced. It is through the gang and for the gang that much offensive behavior is carried out. Paradoxically, it is through and with the gang that the most effective prevention and correction can be carried out.

Society itself—the system—contributes to social maladjustment by default. Many of our juvenile legal codes are designed to punish rather than rehabilitate. Somehow, these codes are tenaciously resistant to change (Rubin, 1962). Enforcement and adjudication machinery may even obstruct proper handling of juveniles and prevent their transfer to an appropriate court (Advisory Council of Judges, 1962). Much more about helping juvenile offenders is known than practiced.

## EDUCATIONAL PROGRAMS
## FOR SOCIALLY MALADJUSTED CHILDREN

Schools have a critically important role to play in prevention, detection, and correction of socially maladjusted children. Often school is the only stable influence in some youngsters' lives. Often it offers the only opportunity to develop social and economic skills needed to climb out of slum life. A small but noisy group of children will not cooperate with the regular instructional program. They can not be tolerated in the regular class and yet school offers them the most certain route to social adjustment. What can be done with them; what can be done for them?

Educators are testing a number of *administrative procedures*. One approach has been to extend the school day and offer a variety of closely supervised afternoon activities in schools located in high delinquency areas. This is part of the regular program in many schools. But it becomes special education when it approaches the proportions of the All Day Neighborhood Schools of New York. Six group teachers and one administrator are assigned to each of the ADN Schools (Ginzberg, 1960). The special program continues from eleven in the morning until five in the afternoon. A teacher is a combination of academic teacher, remedial instructor, social group worker, and parent surrogate. He guides academic and remedial studies, recreation, arts, hobbies, and clubwork—but in a very special way. Children participate through fluid groupings directed by, in some instances, one teacher, or at other times, by teams of teachers. Groups are also under close observation of psychiatric social workers who guide and assist teachers in utilizing group dynamics techniques. Thus neglected and underprivileged children are given an opportunity for wholesome recreation and meaningful education over and above the regular school program. Special education helps them to learn to live together constructively.

*Special schools* and *classes* are a popular special education provision for socially maladjusted youth. Such classes make up the third largest area of special education in Chicago and Philadelphia (Kvaraceus and Ulrich, 1959), exceeded only by programs for the mentally retarded and speech impaired. Birch (1956) found that 15 of the 50 largest cities in the United States had special classes for the maladjusted and that there is a definite trend toward expansion.

Unfortunately some special classes are little more than holding operations. They have even been referred to as "troublemakers' classes." But in contrast the 600 schools of New York have designed programs to rehabilitate these youngsters and move them to useful citizenship. Students are given a rich school experience and, most important, they are accepted and understood for what they are. Acceptance of middle class standards is a goal—not a requirement of the 600 schools. The Gertrude M. Godwin School of Boston has worked with more than 6000 boys in the last 20 years who have demonstrated their inability to adjust to standards of society and schools (Handy, 1955). Remedial instruction is emphasized at the school and a remarkably wide variety of vocational subjects are offered. Tailoring, mechanics, baking, and a host of other trades are taught in a functional setting. Teachers at Godwin need to know the utility of subject matter, as well as the content. They must be able to channel the impulsiveness of maladjusted children into socially acceptable activity. Firm, but not harsh, discipline is directed toward a re-education of social learnings and abilities.

Special education must be provided for at least 120,000 juveniles in correctional institutions of the United States (U.S. Census of Population, Report of Institutional Populations, 1952, Tables 4 and 11). Already there are over 200 public and 130 private correctional institutions in the States and the number is rapidly increasing with the popularity of forestry camps (United Nations, 1958). In Canada, governmental correctional institutions number about 30 (United Nations, 1958). Few institutions are operated by state, provincial, or local departments of education. In most instances, they are operated by other agencies and supplied with independent school staffing. Whatever arrangements may be in effect, a school program is of primary import. Over 98 percent of residential correctional institutions have teachers on their staff and offer some type of educational programs for the juvenile inmates (United Nations, 1958). The Children's Bureau recommends that schools in correctional institutions be separate administrative units with specialized supervision. Other recommendations were as follows:

1. Pupil-teacher ratio should not exceed 15 pupils per teacher.
2. Teaching schedules should be comparable with other teachers'.
3. Classroom teaching assignments should not exceed 30 hours per week.
4. Teachers should not be assigned to non-school duties.
5. Club sponsorship, hobby hours, and the like should merit adjustment in teaching schedule.
6. Teachers should not be required to live on campus.
7. Salaries should be in line with other specialized teachers.
8. An equitable salary schedule should be provided.
9. Teachers should have specialized training for teaching delinquents and in particular areas, such as vocational and remedial teaching.
10. Teachers should have access to teacher training courses and institutes designed to improve their effectiveness (adapted from Children's Bureau, 1957, p. 66).

*Teaching socially maladjusted youth* has its special demands and its special rewards. Maladjusted children destroy school property, abuse privileges, mock responsibility, and ridicule their teachers. They thrive on conflict with authority and gain status by defying adults. They are educationally retarded and appear as though they could not care less whether school kept open. Teachers must be prepared to work with the values these youngsters bring with them to school. Their world is so different that their school must be different. Shireman (1960) discussed the particular emphases of correctional schools under the following topics:

1. A healthy experience with authority
2. Use of limits
3. Socially acceptable achievement
4. Peer relationships
5. Relationships with older adults
6. Moral values
7. The role of counseling

These points may be taken for granted in regular school curricula by virtue of pupils being able to tolerate the regular classroom. But obviously, maladjusted children need help in these areas.

Teaching in a residential institution differs from day school primarily in the efforts made to coordinate and blend school into a concerted rehabilitation plan. Teachers share their observations and programming with other specialists and design experiences for individual children through planning conferences. For example, Jackie and Sam may be on the same level in arithmetic and, with the same general intelligence and behavior characteristics, would appear to profit by grouping for instruction. Within the closely supervised structure of the classroom, they both appear to be adapting and responding equally well to the teacher. Conferences with cottage parents, however, reveal that Jackie is easily frustrated and confused in completing assignments at the cottage—he needs personal support, and an emphasis of successes and minimizing of error patterns. Sam, it is reported, works impetuously and overlooks the obvious while completing his work at the cottage in order to watch television on free time—he needs guidance in organizing his efforts through recognition of errors and facing the consequences of half-hearted effort. Planning conferences may suggest that the teacher should separate the two lads for instructional purposes since their work patterns outside the classroom are so different.

Teachers must help maladjusted students come to terms with societal limits and find their individuality enhanced through productive group membership. To illustrate, remedial education will demand that teachers understand and utilize values and perspective of students. The savoir-faire of the street fosters a special type of maturity. Idiomatically speaking, socially maladjusted youngsters may be new models but they have a lot of mileage. Required for such assignments are "educators who see themselves not merely as 'teaching school' but as contributing cooperatively to a total living situation for helping children readjust their behavior to conform to the demands society makes upon them" (Children's Bureau, 1957).

Educators have found that maladjusted children have a characteristic set for learning. Regular textbooks and teachers' manuals do not provide the information, activities, and guidance necessary. These youngsters learn well with instructional materials reflecting their style of learning. Maladjusted children, like the deprived children described by Riessman (1962, p. 72) need learning opportunities capitalizing on their facility with the: (1) physical and visual rather than the aural, (2) content-centered rather than form-centered, (3) externally oriented rather than introspective, (4) problem-centered rather than abstract-centered, (5) inductive rather than deductive, (6) spatial rather than temporal, (7) slow, careful, patient, persevering (in areas of importance, rather than quick, clever, facile, and flexible.

New curricular concepts for maladjusted youth incorporate elements of work, study, recreation, and social responsibility into special techniques. Los Angeles County Reception Center for Boys undertakes to supplant negative, asocial learning with a new set of "habits, understandings, purposes, goals, ideals, feelings, and attitudes" (Kvaraceus and Ulrich, 1959). Relearning is instrumented by teachers skilled in directing behavior toward the "habits society demands as a condition of freedom." Students are expected to live by 27 positive behaviors and to avoid 21 negative behaviors. All activities emphasize vocational, prevocational, and job-connected skills. Academic matter is divided into "jobs" and "tools" which are scaled for varying difficulty levels and assigned by teachers according to the student's ability. The "jobs and tools" concept applies in academic subjects as well as vocational. For example, certain tools must be mastered for the job of filing applications. Students are rigidly supervised and examined by fellow students and teachers before moving to another job. Dependability, neatness, courteous conduct, and the host of other salable work habits are developed through social relationships, guided and instructed by the teacher.

Controlled longitudinal studies are needed to adequately *evaluate* the effectiveness of special education to curb and rehabilitate maladjusted youth. Some studies have examined follow-up records of maladjusted children and others have attributed decline in delinquency rate to special school programs. Although such may not be scientifically neat research, they at least afford interesting information. One New York principal of a 600 School believed that at least 90 percent of these chronic juvenile offenders became useful citizens (Moore, 1958). Of the 6000 boys remanded to Godwin School during the last 20 years, 84 percent have taken their place as responsible citizens (Handy, 1955). In both instances, these youngsters had deeply grained patterns of criminal and antisocial behavior.

Bowman (1959) reported a controlled study of the effect of a revised school program for below average eighth graders. Most of the subjects were educationally retarded, discipline problems and 41 percent had police records. Two experimental groups received special education and a third control group remained in regular classes. Delinquency rates for the control group tripled while those for the two experimental groups declined by one third.

More important than the empirical findings have been the procedural developments uncovered through experience with maladjusted youth. Intensive re-education of value systems is increasingly seen as the goal of special education for maladjusted youth. Successes at Highfield (McCorkle et al., 1958), though informal discussions led by sociologists, encourage the quest for bold measures to close the hiatus between mass punishment on the one hand and individual psychotherapy on the other. Implications from research conducted by psychologists who have studied perceptual processes hold particular promise. Their research activity in assumptions, social perception, and learning of values should be closely followed by educators of maladjusted children. Of immediate importance to teachers is Toch and Cantril's (1961) study on the learning of values through experimentation with the "hitch" threshold—that point where routine is interrupted by the individual's active inquiry into his own values and goals. By presenting subjects with experimental crisis situations and analyzing their responses, the investigators suggested "modest hunches as to possible first steps to active inquiry and possible revaluation." Their analysis yielded a tentative list of possible factors involved in re-evaluation:

1. Making implications for action explicit
2. Reformation in more concrete terms
3. The discovery of connections with relevant experience
4. Expressions of appeal
5. Creative synthesis
6. Self-examination
7. Recognition of own weakness (Toch and Cantril, 1961, p. 330).

Their results were not offered as solutions to a problem, but rather as stimuli to additional research and accelerated action. Their challenge has a special appeal in this field where the need is so great and the answers are so few.

## Teachers for Disturbed and Maladjusted Youth

The U.S. Office of Education attempted to decide what skills are useful in teaching "socially and emotionally maladjusted children" (Mackie et al., 1957). Seventy-five teachers of socially and emotionally maladjusted children were presented with a list of competencies to rank in order of importance. Among the first 10 competencies ranked "very important" were concerns for instructional techniques, such as relieving classroom tensions, providing success experiences, individualizing the curriculum, and fostering self-discipline. Among the first 10 also were found elements of child study, such as understanding basic human physical and psychological needs and the ability to differentiate between maladjustment and mental retardation. The 10 competencies ranked lowest included the abilities required to administer aptitude tests, individual intelligence tests, personality and projective tests, and maturity scales. This sample of teachers also considered methods of teaching at the secondary level and knowledge of patterns of other societies as being of little importance.

It must be pointed out that no distinction was made between

teachers of emotionally disturbed and socially maladjusted children. It is significant, in the writer's view, that most of the respondents lacked special preparation for such teaching assignments. The writer's experience would indicate that psychological measures and anthropological considerations are indispensible for programming and teaching these youngsters.

Many professional disciplines should be involved in preparing teachers of disturbed and maladjusted youth. Rabinow (1960) pointed to eight general areas which should contribute to preparing teachers for the specializations:

The psychiatric profession

The psychological field

The sociological sciences

The structure and function of community organization

The nature and coordination of the interdisciplinary team

The dynamics of group work

The practical arts and use of concrete media

A one year practicum with children manifesting various behavior problems.

Perhaps teachers of both types of exceptionality would draw from the same general areas, but each would need a different combination of the eight. The writer recently completely a study of college programs to prepare teachers of disturbed children (Pate, 1960). Although experienced elementary teachers were favored for both specialities, 30 experts thought they needed different training. Seventy-five teachers of disturbed children (maladjusted children were specifically excluded) strongly endorsed practicum and observation, specialized methods and remedial instruction as the heart of training programs.

Shortages of competent teachers for disturbed children have prompted many governmental agencies to assist in recruiting and training. California offers internships in which student-teachers take collegiate courses and practicum in an on-the-job situation. Interns have civil service classifications and are compensated during their period of preparation. LaRue Carter Memorial Hospital of Indianapolis selects superior teachers from adjacent schools and assigns them to assist in the summer school programs. Close observation and supervision help identify the most interested and promising who then receive a gradual induction into full responsibility as a teacher of emotionally disturbed children.

However ambitious any special program for disturbed and maladjusted children may be, teacher selection will determine its ultimate success. For the present, selection must be based on subjective considerations. Prolonged exposure under close supervision offers the best screening device. Decisions for selection should be weighed very carefully—especially in this field. Teaching disturbed and maladjusted children is "singularly attractive to crackpots" (Rabinow, 1960).

## Summary

Some children with pronounced emotional or social handicaps have behavior problems which cannot be handled in regular classrooms. For special education programming, some are considered emotionally disturbed while others are considered socially maladjusted.

Emotionally disturbed children are mentally ill and unable to function appropriately in school situations. Numerically they are distributed fairly evenly through school populations although boys outnumber girls five to one. About one half of 1 percent of any school age population are so withdrawn or so overtly aggressive as to be considered emotionally disturbed and in need of special education in either residential or day psychiatric school or special class in regular school. Thus, educators and mental health specialists cooperate in identification, diagnosis, and school planning. Special education for disturbed children entails mental health consultation for the teacher and psychotherapy for pupils, well equipped classrooms with no more than six students per teacher, and individually designed therapeutic education to return these children to regular home and school adjustment.

Socially maladjusted children are unable to attend regular classes because they repeatedly disregard constituted law and school rules. They are members of delinquent gangs found almost exclusively in urban slums and comprise about 1.5 percent of the school population above 10 years of age. Boys outnumber girls about eight to one. Educational and legal-correctional agencies develop corrective programs for maladjusted children in residential and day remand schools and in special programs in regular schools. Remand schools emphasize vocational and remedial subjects, instill respect for authority, and foster social awareness and responsibility. In regular schools, special classes serve socially maladjusted children who are otherwise unmanageable. Some programs provide specially trained teachers to supervise afternoon social, recreational, and remedial activities designed to redirect and supplant antisocial patterns of behavior.

Increasing numbers of teacher education institutions offer training for teachers of children with behavior problems. State and federal interest is evidenced by expanded recruitment inducements for teachers and by special education programs for disturbed and maladjusted children. State-wide experimental studies and region-wide demonstration projects are currently searching for more effective means of selecting and training teachers and for developing special education for children with problem behavior.

## CHAPTER REFERENCES

Abbate, Grace M., Dunaeff, Dorothy, & Fenichel, C. A pilot study of schizophrenic children in a non-residential school. *Amer. J. Orthopsychiat.*, 1957, **27**, 107–116.

Abrahamsen, D. Status of mental hygiene and child guidance facilities in the public school in the United States. *J. Pediat.*, 1955, **46**, 107–118.

Advisory Council of Judges, National Council on Crime and Delinquency. Transfer of cases between juvenile and criminal courts. *Crime and Delinqu.*, 1962, **8**, 3–11.

American Psychiatric Association. *Mental disorders: Diagnostic and statistical manual.* Washington, D.C.: Amer. Psychiat. Ass., 1952.

————. *Psychiatric inpatient treatment of children.* Washington, D.C.: Amer. Psychiat. Ass., 1957.

Bahn, Anita, & Norman, Vivian B. First national report on patients of mental health clinics. *Publ. Hlth. Rep.*, 1959, **74**, 943–956.

Berkowitz, Pearl W., & Rothman, Ester P. *The disturbed child.* New York: New York Univer. Press, 1960.

Birch, J. M. Special classes and schools for maladjusted children. *Except. Child.*, 1956, **22**, 332–337.

Bower, E. M. *The education of emotionally handicapped children.* Sacramento, Calif.: Calif. State Dept. of Education, 1961.

Bowman, P. H. Effects of a revised school program on potential delinquents. *Ann. Amer. Acad. Pol. Sci.*, 1959, **322**, 53–61.

Buros, O. K. (Ed.) *The fifth mental measurements yearbook.* Highland Park, N.J.: The Gryphon Press, 1959.

Children's Bureau. *Institutions serving delinquent children: guides and goals.* Washington, D.C.: Government Printing Office, 1957.

Cohoe, Edith. Bibliotherapy for handicapped children. *NEA. J.*, 1960, **49**, 34–36.

Cole, J. O., Klerman, G. L., & Jones, R. I. Drug therapy. In E. A. Spiegel (Ed.) *Progress in neurology and psychiatry.* New York: Grune & Stratton, 1960.

Devereux, G. *Therapeutic education: Its theoretical bases and practice.* New York: Harper & Row, 1956.

Eisenberg, L. Emotionally disturbed children and youth. In *Children and Youth in the 1960's.* Washington, D.C.: White House Conference on Children and Youth, 1960.

Festinger, L., Pepitone, A., & Newcomb, T. M. Some consequences of de-individuation in a group. In A. P. Hare, E. F. Borgotta, & R. F. Bales, *Small Groups.* New York: Knopf, 1955.

FitzSimmons, M. J. The predictive value of teachers' referrals. In M. Krugman (Ed.) *Orthopsychiatry and the school.* New York: Amer. Orthopsychiat. Ass., 1958.

Ginzberg, E. (Ed.) *The nation's children: no. 2, development and education.* New York: Columbia Univer. Press, 1960.

Glueck, S., & Glueck, Eleanor. *Unraveling juvenile delinquency.* New York: The Commonwealth Fund, 1950.

Handy, Mary. Willingly to school. *NEA. J.*, 1955, **44**, 544–545.

HELP Emotionally handicapped children. *Newsletter*, 1960, **1**, No. 4.

Hirschberg, J. C. The role of education in the treatment of emotionally disturbed children through planned ego development. *Amer. J. Orthopsychiat.*, 1953, **23**, 684–690.

Hobbs. N. *Reeducation of disturbed children: a demonstration project.* Nashville, Tenn.: Peabody College, 1961.

Hollingshead, A. B., & Redlich, F. C. *Social class and mental illness* New York: Wiley, 1958.

Hollister, W. G., & Goldston, S. E. *Considerations for planning classes for the emotionally handicapped.* Washington, D.C.: The Council for Except. Child., 1962.

Hood-William, J. The results of psychotherapy with children: An evaluation. *J. consult. Psychol.,* 1960, **24**, 84–88.

Jackson, D. D. (Ed.) *The etiology of schizophrenia.* New York: Basic Books, 1960.

Jacobson, S., & Faegre, C. Neutralization: A tool for the teacher of disturbed children. *Except. Child.,* 1959, **25**, 243–246.

Kanner, L. *Child psychiatry.* Springfield, Ill.: Charles C Thomas, 1960.

King, G. *The mentally ill child in America.* New York: National Organization for Mentally Ill Children, 1960.

Kough, J., & DeHaan, R. F. *Identifying children with special needs.* Vol. I. Chicago, Ill.: Science Research Associates, 1955.

Kvaraceus, W. C., & Miller, W. B. *Delinquent behavior: culture and the individual.* Washington, D.C.: NEA Juvenile Delinquency Project, 1959

————, & Ulrich, W. C. *Delinquent behavior: principles and practices.* Washington, D.C.: NEA Juvenile Delinquency Project, 1959.

Lander, B. *Towards an understanding of juvenile delinquency.* New York: Columbia Univer. Press, 1954.

LaVietes, Ruth L., Hulse, W. C., & Elau, A. A psychiatric day treatment center and school for young children and their parents. *Amer. J. Orthopsychiat.,* 1960, **30**, 468–483.

Levitt, E. E. Reply to Hood Williams. *J. consult. Psychol.,* 1960, **24**, 89–91.

MacFarlane, Jean W., Allen, Lucille, & Honsik, Marjorie P. *A developmental study of the behavior problems of normal children between twenty-one months and fourteen years.* Berkeley, Calif.: Univer. of California Press, 1954.

Mackie, Romaine P., Kvaraceus, W. C., & Williams, H. C. *Teachers of children who are socially and emotionally maladjusted.* Washington, D.C.: U.S. Office of Education, 1957.

McCorkle, L. W., Elias, A., & Bixby, F. L. *The highfields story.* New York: Holt, Rinehart and Winston, 1958.

Moore, Bernice M. *Juvenile delinquency: research, theory, and comment.* Washington, D.C.: Association for the Supervision of Curriculum Development, 1958.

Myers, J. K., & Robertson, B. H. *Family and class dynamics in mental illness.* New York: Wiley, 1959.

National Committee Against Mental Illness: *What are the facts about mental illness?* Washington, D.C.: National Committee Against Mental Illness, 1959.

Pate, J. E. Practices and opinions regarding pre-service preparation for teachers of emotionally disturbed chlidren. Unpublished doctoral dissertation, Peabody College, 1960.

Perlman, I. R. *Delinquency prevention: the size of the problem.* Washington, D.C.: Children's Bureau, 1960, No. 4.

Phillips, E. L., & Haring, N. G. Results from special techniques for teaching emotionally disturbed children. *Except. Child.,* 1959, **26**, 64–67.

*Re-Education of disturbed children: a demonstration project.* Nashville, Tenn.: Peabody College, 1961.

Rabinow, B. A training program for teachers of the emotionally disturbed and the socially maladjusted. *Except. Child.,* 1960, **26**, 287–293.

————. The role of the school in residential treatment. *Amer. J. Orthopsychiat.,* 1955, **25**, 685–691.

Reid, J. H., & Hagan, Helen R. *Residential treatment of emotionally disturbed children.* New York: Child Welfare League of America, 1952.

Riessman, F. *The culturally deprived child.* New York: Harper & Row, 1962.

Rubin, E. Z., & Simion, C. B. A special class program for the emotionally disturbed child in school: A proposal. *Amer. J. Orthopsychiat.,* 1960, **30**, 144–145.

Rubin, S. Developments in correctional law. *Crime and Delinqu.,* 1962, **8**, 65–73.

Shaw, C. R., & McKay, H. D. *Juvenile delinquency and urban areas.* Chicago: Univer. of Chicago Press, 1942.

Shireman, C. R. How can the correctional school correct? *Crime and Delinqu.,* 1960, **4**, 267–274.

Southern Regional Education Board. The emotionally disturbed child. *Mental Health Forum, Vol. 4, No. 2,* Atlanta, Ga.: South. Reg. Educ. Bd., 1961.

Spiegel, E. A. (Ed.) *Progress in neurology and psychiatry.* Vol. XV, New York: Grune & Stratton, 1960.

Strauss, A. A., & Lehtinen, Laura E. *Psychopathology and education of the brain-injured child.* New York: Grune & Stratton, 1947.

Strodtbeck, F. L. Family interaction, values, and achievement. In D.C. McClelland, A. L. Baldwin, U. Bronfenbrenner, & F. L. Strodtbeck, *Talent and society.* Princeton, N.J.: Van Nostrand, 1958.

Sussman, F. B. *Law of juvenile delinquency.* New York: Oceana, 1950.

Toch, H. H., & Cantril, H. The learning of values: An experimental inquiry. In F. P. Kilpatrick, (Ed.) *Exploration in transactional psychology.* New York: New York Univer. Press, 1961.

U.S. Census of Population. *Report of increased population.* Washington, D.C.: Government Printing Office, 1952.

U.S. Justice Dept., Fed. Bur. Invest., *Uniform Crime Reports,* 1959 (1960).

United Nations. *Comparative survey of juvenile delinquency, Part 1 North America.* New York: Department of Economics & Social Affairs, United Nations, 1958.

## ADDITIONAL REFERENCES

Aichhorn, A. *Wayward youth.* London: Imago Publishing Co., 1951.

Bettelheim, B. *Truants from life.* New York: Free Press, 1955.

Block, H. A., & Flynn, F. T. *Delinquency: The juvenile offender in America today.* New York: Random House, 1958.

Cohen, A. K. *Delinquent boys: The culture of the gang.* New York: Free Press, 1955.

Glueck, S., & Glueck, E. *Delinquency in the making: Paths to prevention.* New York: Harper & Row, 1952.

Haring, N. G., & Phillips, E. L. *Educating emotionally disturbed children.* New York: McGraw-Hill, 1962.

Kornberg, L. *A class for disturbed children.* New York: Bureau of Publications, Columbia Univer., Teachers College, 1955.

Lenhoff, F. G. *Exceptional children.* New York: Taplinger, 1962.

Pearson, G. H. J. *Psychotherapy and the education of the child.* New York: Norton, 1954.

Redl, F., & Wineman, D. *The aggressive child.* New York: Free Press, 1957.

Rubin, T. I. *Jordi.* New York: Macmillan, 1960.

# RESOURCES

Treatment and rehabilitation of disturbed and maladjusted children are essentially remedial measures; the real promise lies in prevention. Toward this end, professional and lay organizations are chaneling much of their activity into community mobilization and education. Educators can tap a flourishing reservoir of materials and experience by seeking the counsel of the following organizations.

American Academy of Pediatrics, 1801 Henman Avenue, Evanston, Illinois

American Association of Psychiatric Clinics for Children, 1300 Columbus Circle, New York 19, New York

American Foundation for Mental Hygiene, 1790 Broadway, New York 19, New York

American Group Psychotherapy Association, 345 East 46th Street, New York 19, New York

American Orthopsychiatric Association, 1790 Broadway, New York 19, New York

American Psychiatric Association, 1785 Massachusetts Avenue, NW., Washington 8, D.C.

American Psychological Association, 1333 16th Street, NW., Washington, D.C.

American Public Welfare Association, 1313 East 16th Street, Chicago 37, Illinois

Child Study Association of America, 132 East 74th Street, New York 31, New York

Child Welfare League of America, 345 East 45th Street, New York 17, New York

Conference of Superintendents of Correctional Institutions for Girls and Women, 10 Greenwich Avenue, New York 11, N.Y.

Family Service Association of America, 192 Lexington Avenue, New York 16, New York

Hogg Foundation, University of Texas, Austin, Texas

League for Emotionally Disturbed Children, 171 Madison Avenue, New York 17, New York

National Association for Mental Health, 10 Columbus Circle, New York 19, New York

National Association of Training Schools and Juvenile Agencies, The Glenn Mills School, Glen Mills, Pennsylvania

National Committee against Mental Illness, Inc., 1028 Connecticut Avenue, NW., Washington 6, D.C.

National Council on Crime and Delinquency, 1790 Broadway, New York 19, New York

National Conference of Superintendents of Training Schools and Reformatories, P.O. Box 8, Otisville State Training School for Boys, Otisville, New York

National Federation of Settlements and Neighborhood Centers, 228 West 47th Street, New York 36, New York

## SELECTED 16 MM SOUND FILMS

*Children in search of a self.* 30 min, black & white. Memorial Guidance Clinic, 3001 Fifth Avenue, Richmond, Virginia. Theories of etiology, symptoms, and methods of therapy for autistic children.

*The quiet one.* 75 min, black & white. Athena Films, 16 West 46 Street, New York 19, New York. Shows the effect of environment in shaping delinquent patterns and how one school attempts to meet the problem.

*Diagnosis of childhood schizophrenic.* 40 min, black & white. New York University Film Library, 25 Washington Place, New York 3, New York. Focuses on the mental health disciplines and their roles in identifying schizophrenia as a distinct psychopathology.

*Angry boy.* 32 min, black & white. National Association for Mental Health, Film Library, 267 West 25 Street, New York 1, New York. A pre-adolescent boy is caught stealing and seeks help in a child guidance clinic.

*Who's delinquent.* 16 min, black & white. Canadian Film Institute, 1762 Carling Avenue, Ottawa 3, Ontario, Canada. A newspaper editor looks at the educational, housing, and recreational facilities in a high delinquency area and asks, "Who's delinquent—our children, or us?"

*Hard brought up.* 40 min, black & white. International Film Bureau, 57 East Jackson Boulevard, Chicago 4, Illinois. Examines various aspects of juvenile delinquency, focusing on environmental factors, child welfare agencies, and efforts to cope with the conditions.

*Problem children.* 20 min, black & white. Psychological Cinema Register, Audio-Visual Aids Library, The Pennsylvania State University, University Park, Pennsylvania. Points out clearly that most children have some personality problems associated with every day living.

*Boy with a knife.* 19 min, black & white. National Association for Mental Health, 267 West 25 Street, New York 1, New York. Follows one case from the files of a youth service agency and dramatizes how the group worker handled it.

*Delinquent child.* 32 min, color. Wyeth Film Library, P.O. Box 8299, Philadelphia 1, Pennsylvania. Dramatizes the experiences of a delinquent disturbed girl while in an institution which provides a multifaceted program of medical management and adjunctive therapy.

## CHAPTER 6

# Speech-Impaired Children

FORREST M. HULL

Since man's early history, society has been concerned with the efficiency of human communication. Such concern is warranted because the ability to exchange ideas is one of the unique characteristics of man which distinguishes him from all lower forms of animals. Probably the most universally used form of communication among all societies is oral speech. Although some societies may not have a written form of language, all use vocalizations in communicating.

It is not strange that concern for the individual who has a speech defect predates, by many centuries, interest in normal speech. As early as 340 B.C. Grecian philosophers and physicians prescribed "cures" for stuttering, a common disorder which continues to plague mankind. The concern for speech deviations evoked so long ago has reached down through the years to present day research and development of successful therapeutic techniques. Many parents, feeling inadequate in alleviating a speech defect themselves, look desperately about for help if their child's speech has failed to develop according to their expectations. Teachers have long recognized the need for trained persons to work with children who have speech disorders. In recent years, many large and an increasing number of small school systems have attempted to meet this need by employing trained speech therapists.

Only within the past 50 years or so have studies of normal function of the human speech mechanism become available. Obviously if deviations are to be coped with, it is essential to have a thorough understanding of the acquisition and production of speech and of factors which affect its development.

# Oral Communication

### SPEECH AND LANGUAGE

Although the terms speech and language have been applied interchangeably in reference to human communication, most authorities agree that there are real differences when a careful analysis of the phenomenon of communications is considered. For example, Myklebust (1954) describes language as "an intricate form of symbolization which is essentially unique with human beings." Man uses spoken words as symbols to express thoughts, ideas, and concepts which are meaningful to the listener as well as to the speaker; therefore, language may be viewed as a basic ability of which speech is a utilitarian facet. When speech is meaningful it can be assumed that language ability is intact, although the lack of meaningful speech does not necessarily indicate a language disturbance. Unfortunately, it is extremely difficult to evaluate language ability when verbalization is not present. The quality and extent of any existing verbalization may provide some indication as to the integrity of the language ability. The discussion of normal speech development and speech disorders in this chapter will be limited to deviations of speech rather than language. Because of the close interrelationship of these two processes, however, a discussion follows in which language and speech are considered collectively as an oral communication system involving a speaker and listener.

### ORAL COMMUNICATION CYCLE

Oral communication is the process by which one person transmits an idea to another person by means of spoken words. In such a process a speaker (who expresses the idea) and a listener (who receives the idea) provide the basic human elements in a complete cycle of communication. An extremely simplified model of a communication system based on diagrams presented by Fairbanks (1954) is shown in Fig. 6.1.

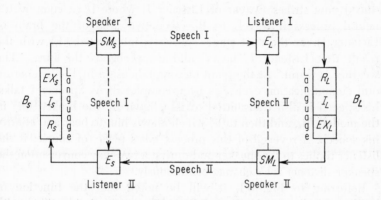

FIG. 6.1

Model of an oral communication cycle involving two persons, Speaker I and Listener I. With speaking and listening roles reversed, Listener I becomes Speaker II and Speaker I is Listener II.

$B_s$ — brain of Speaker I; $R_s$ — receptive area of $B_s$; $I_s$ — integrative area of $B_s$; $EX_s$ — expressive area of $B_s$; $SM_s$ — speech mechanism of Speaker I; $E_s$ — ear of Speaker I.

$B_L$ — brain of Listener I; $R_L$ — receptive area of $B_L$; $I_L$ — integrative area of $B_L$; $EX_L$ — expressive area of $B_L$; $SM_L$ — speech mechanism of Listener I; $E_L$ — ear of Listener I.

In the model, Speaker I and Listener I both possess the intact anatomic structures required for production as well as reception of speech. Naturally, a person may function either as speaker or listener. At the beginning of a cycle of oral communication the *idea* to be expressed originates in the integrative area, $I_s$ of the brain, $B_s$ of Speaker I. For purposes of illustration, let us say the idea to be expressed in words eventually is the statement, "The weather is warm." The idea (in the form of neural impulses) is transmitted through $EX_s$ (expressive area of the brain) to $SM_s$ (speech mechanism). At $SM_s$ the idea is converted to coordinated movements of the speech mechanism which produces speech in the form of sound waves (Speech I) representing the original idea. The speech produced now strikes $E_l$ (ear of Listener I) where by a complicated neural process it travels to $R_l$ (receptive area of the brain of Listener I). At the next stage, speech is interpreted ($I_l$) with the result that Listener I "hears" and comprehends the idea, "The weather is warm." At the point of comprehension by the listener an oral communication cycle has been completed. As Speaker I talks, his speech is also transmitted to $E_s$ (shown by the broken line in the model), $R_s$, and then to $I_s$, which allows him to hear and control his speech. A reversal of this process takes place, of course, if the listener replies to the speaker and during a two-way conversation the speaker–listener roles change continuously.

Referring to Fig. 6.1, it will be noted that the function of language is located in $B_s$ and $B_1$, while speech is identified with the function of $SM_s$ and $SM_1$.

## COMPONENTS OF SPEECH

In its simplest form speech is made up of combinations of vowels and consonants which are so arranged as to form words and groups of words which have meaning for the listener. When all dialects spoken in the United States are considered, approximately 22 vowels and diphthongs and 25 consonants and consonant combinations are found.

A vowel is a voiced speech sound and has a "tonal" or "musical" quality. Typical vowels, familiar to everyone, are the "a" in cat and "oo" in boot. Consonants, considerably more important to the intelligibility of speech than vowels, are speech sounds which may be voiced or unvoiced. Note, for instance, the consonants "c" and "t" in "cat" are unvoiced and the "b" in boot is voiced. If one says "cat" or "boot" while observing himself in a mirror he will also notice that different anatomic structures (tongue, lips, and jaw) move in various patterns to form the words. These structures and their movements are a part of the speech mechanism which is in turn responsible for the final stage of speech production.

## SPEECH MECHANISM

Fundamentally speech is a biological activity which at times involves all systems of the body for proper functioning. This will be more readily understood by a consideration of the three most important biological systems which are directly involved in speech. The first of these is a source of energy (breath stream), which is created by the lungs, diaphragm, and the primary muscles of respiration. The second is the vibrator, which creates phonation and includes the larynx, vocal folds, and laryngeal muscles. The third system is composed of a resonator and articulators, which form speech, and includes lips, tongue, teeth, palate, and the throat, mouth, and nasal cavities. These structures comprise $SM_s$ and $SM_1$ in Fig. 6.1.

These three biological systems must be coordinated precisely in a very short span of time if normal speech is to be produced. For example it requires less than a second to say "cat", yet it would require several minutes to describe all of the detailed activity involved in the production of that one simple word. A careful analysis of these highly refined muscular movements impels one to marvel at the efficiency of the speech mechanism.

# Normal Development of Speech

The birth cry is considered to be the first speech uttered by the infant although there is some evidence of prenatal vocalizations. Observations and numerous studies of speech development which have been reported over a period of years have yielded much valuable information concerning characteristic patterns of change in speech as the child matures. Many aspects of both speech and language have been studied on a development basis, including articulation, vocabulary, sentence structure, speech discrimination, mean length of response, as well as the variables that influence speech maturation. The studies of Davis (1937 and 1938), on mean sentence length and development of parts of speech distribution,

Metraux's (1950) speech profiles of preschool children, Poole's (1934) analysis of genetic development of articulation, and Templin's (1957) recent complete and well controlled study of articulation, vocabulary, sentence structure, and speech discrimination of children have contributed significantly to our knowledge of speech development.

Speech is an acquired function requiring the modification of specific vital biological activities for normal development since all of the body systems involved in speech initially play a more vital role in survival. For example, the breathing mechanism fundamentally provides oxygen for the body; the larynx serves as a protective valve for the lungs and is part of the air-passage tube; and the lips, tongue, teeth, and jaws help to prepare food for use by the body. All of the above vital functions must be modified in order that speech may be produced. It is a process of gradational modification of these basic functions, beginning at birth, which comprise the development of speech. In this sense one may say that speech is an acquired secondary ability. The total process is not simple, however, since many factors such as intelligence, personality traits, emotional status, and environment continuously influence the speech development.

There are many ways to measure speech development but the three profiles which are most frequently used are *general characteristics, vocabulary level,* and *articulatory ability.* A compilation of these indicators of speech development based on chronological age is shown in Table 6.1. The original sources from which the assembled information was primarily derived include McCarthy (1954), Gesell and Ilg (1949), Davis (1937), Poole (1934), Travis (1957), Metraux (1950), Van Riper (1954, chapter 5), and Templin (1957).

Although differences in the rate and nature of developmental patterns from child to child have been observed, the sequential pattern is reliable enough to establish rather broad norms related to chronological age levels, as indicated in Table 6.1. One observes that vocalizations for the first four months are more or less undifferentiated except in specific situations which are related to basic feelings and needs. At about 4 months babbling (specific articulatory movements) begins and may become quite intense at about 6 months. A change gradually occurs bringing the speech into a pattern of

TABLE 6.1 *Chronological development of speech from birth to eight years of age.*

| AGE | GENERAL CHARACTERISTICS | VOCABULARY WORDS | ARTICULATION |
|---|---|---|---|
| **Months** | | | |
| 1 | Crying: related to causes and circumstances | | |
| 2 | Some differential vocalization—cooing & babbling | | |
| 3 | Coos and smiles when looked at | | |
| 4 | Babbling; uses sound to get attention; laughs, chuckles | | |
| 5 | Specific vocalization (displeasure when object removed) | | |
| 6 | Babbling increasing; vocalizes to mirror image | | |
| 7 | Lalling begins (movements of tongue with vocalization) | | |
| 8 | Vocalizes recognition | | |
| 9 | Combines syllables; copies sounds heard; echolalia | 1 | |
| 12 | Echolalia continues; first words | 1–3 | Vowels |
| 18 | Fluent jargon; one-word sentences | 18–22 | |
| **Years** | | | |
| 2 | Two word sentences; naming; begins to use personal pronouns | 300 | |
| 2½ | Three word sentences; repeats syllables | 450 | h, w, hw |
| 3 | Uses language to tell stories; speech understood | 900 | p, b, m |
| 3½ | Speech disfluencies, concepts expressed with words; complete sentences, sentence length 4–5 words | 1200 | t, d, n |
| 4 | Imaginary speech; very verbal; motor development | 1500 | k, g, ng |
| 5 | Language complete in structure and form; can tell stories; less concrete; complex sentences | 2200 | f, v |
| 6 | Learns to read; intelligibility of speech is excellent | | l, r, y s, z, sh |
| 7 | Increases in complexity of sentence structure | Increasing | ch, zh, j |
| 8 | Speech should be "perfectly" articulated | Increasing | th (voiced and unvoiced) |

syllables used in an imitative fashion, by 9 months. By this time the child will have produced in babbling all of the speech sounds he will ever use in completely articulated speech and the early developer may even have a meaningful vocabulary of one word. Since emergence of the first word traditionally has been considered an important landmark in child development there have been many attempts to define "the first word." Darley and Winitz (1961) evaluated several studies concerned with the age of occurrence of the first word but were unable to present a clear-cut definition which could be conveniently applied. Their review of 10 independent investigations showed that appearance of the first word ranged from an age of 4 months, according to one investigator, to 60 months for another, with an average age of about 1 year.

By 12 months the child has mastered all the vowels and may have as many as three words in a meaningful vocabulary. Vowels develop prior to consonants primarily because they are all voiced and do not require the precise placement of several articulators as do the consonants. From 18 months through the fourth year the increase of vocabulary and acquisition of consonants is rapid. Poole (1934) found that about 50 percent of the children studied had mastered all consonants by four years of age although all children would not be expected to reach this level until between seven and eight years. *Nevertheless intelligible speech can be expected by the time the child is four years of age.*

The sketched profiles illustrated in Table 6.1 point up two characteristics of speech development which are worthy of special mention. In the first place, development progresses from gross vocalizations related to biological needs, to precise articulation necessary for the child to communicate ideas. Secondly, since speech can be "normal" at any age, only by knowing what can be expected at a given age can one properly evaluate the status of a child's speech development.

## FACTORS RELATED TO SPEECH DEVELOPMENT

In the previous discussion it was seen that speech develops with the growth of the child. As there are many factors, both intrinsic and extrinsic, which affect over-all maturation it follows logically that many of these same factors will influence the speech developmental pattern. Probably the most important factor related to the development of normal speech is the integrity of the total biological system.

## Speech Disorders Defined

A variety of approaches to a definition for speech disorders has been reported in the literature. In arriving at a definition, most authorities (including those discussed in this section), make allowances for the speech developmental process which occurs in the early years of a child's life. West et al., (1957) stressed the problems involved in a specific definition, because of the varying "standards" of correct speech. Speech considered acceptable in one environment, social or occupation group, may be considered below "standard" or even defective in another. In his discussion, West has listed six detailed conditions for defective speech. Briefly, the points concern: (1) weak voice, (2) lowered intelligibility of speech due to misarticulations, (3) lowered intelligibility of speech due to lapses in grammar and syntax, (4) speech unpleasant to listener, (5) quality of speech and voice distracting to listener due to strong differences from average speech for age and sex, and (6) speech accompanied by distracting sounds, gestures and grimaces.

Berry and Eisenson (1956) consider defective speech from two points of view: subjective and objective. Subjectively, speech may be considered defective if the speaker's manner of speaking attracts more attention than the content of his communication. Another subjective consideration is the speaker's self-conscious reaction to his own speech. Objectively, they consider speech defective if characterized by conditions similar to those suggested by West.

Although numerous other authorities have described and defined speech disorders, the familiar, concise definition by Van Riper (1954) is widely accepted and quite adequate for the purpose of the discussion to follow: "Speech is defective when it deviates so far from the speech of other people that it calls attention to itself, interferes with communication, or causes its possessor to be maladjusted."

In consideration of the first point of this definition the sentence "The rabbit ran after the red hen" would certainly attract attention if spoken by a 10-year-old child in the following manner: "Duh wabbit wan aftuh duh wed hen." Referring to the developmental scale for speech sounds (Table 6.1), one can readily see that such articulation produced by a preschool child would not elicit particular concern. It is extremely important to note that a child may have a speech disorder at any specified age. Admittedly the disorder is easier to observe in a five-year-old than at 18 months since at five the total process is more firmly established. This means, of course, that speech disorders exist among preschool children and that the disturbed patterns are not typical of school-age children alone. Unfortunately, parents tend to be much less concerned about the unintelligible speech of the kindergarten child than that of the first grader. In the early summer months it is a common occurrence for community speech clinics to receive an increased number of requests for speech correction services for a child who will begin the first grade in September. The urgency, of course, for immediate speech correction services revolves around the problems which the parents fear will develop if the child begins school with a speech disorder. It is evident that age is one important aspect to consider in deciding when misarticulated speech can actually be called defective.

In addition to age, one must also consider the sex of the child. According to Poole (1934) there is a general tendency for the speech of girls to develop somewhat earlier than that of boys. The geographical area will also influence the decision as to whether or not certain speech patterns are to be viewed as defective. Certainly the omission of the medial and final "r" in the midwest would be a deviation from the speech of the region and therefore call attention to itself. A question often raised is "Does a person with a pronounced southern dialect have a speech defect, if he moves to the midwest?" It can be seen that such a dialect could certainly meet all three parts of Van Riper's definition. If the dialect "calls attention to itself" only and does not interfere with communication nor cause maladjustment, then it should not be considered defective. In such cases the person may or may not desire to change the dialect. However, if the individual finds that he is frequently misunderstood, and becomes unhappy and sensitive about his speech, then his dialect would be detrimental to him and could be considered defective speech.

In the second part of his definition, Van Riper states that speech is defective when it "interferes with communication." This requirement is certainly met when speech is misarticulated to the point of unintelligibility. In the case of a severe stutterer, the facial contortions and muscular spasms may completely break down communication with his listener. This could also be true in the case of the child with cleft-palate speech, who may be unable to effectively communicate because of his distorted speech sounds as well as the accompanying nasality.

Van Riper's third point "causes its possessor to be maladjusted" can be observed in the withdrawal or overt hostility which sometimes occurs in children with severe speech disorders. One can easily imagine the emotional distress and embarrassment suffered by a child whose repeated attempts at speech result in a collection of garbled sounds, totally incomprehensible to the listener. Whether the speech disorder was the result of, or the cause of the emotional upheaval, such disturbances are frequently reduced by successful speech therapy.

Although all of Van Riper's three conditions for a speech defect can be fulfilled by all of the speech disorder types, the fact that a school-age child manifests a speech deviation which attracts attention only is reason enough for a thorough investigation and should not be dismissed lightly.

In conclusion of these remarks on definition, the terms *organic* and *functional* should be mentioned in relation to speech disorders. A *functional* speech disorder is one which has no observable deviation of structure underlying the problem. Disorders of articulation and stuttering exemplify this classification. Such disorders as cleft palate and cerebral-palsy speech are considered *organic* as there exists a definite structural involvement.

## Prevalence of Speech Disorders

The number of speech disorders one can expect to find in a given population is a factor of considerable importance in planning corrective or rehabilitative services for children of school age. The inherent dynamic characteristics of the speech process itself creates a variance in prevalence figures since the speech disorder must be defined before it can be included in an over-all prevalence figure. Survey estimates are not particularly reliable as they tend to vary considerably depending upon the original purpose of obtaining the survey. Where high standards of acceptable speech are held one can naturally expect a high prevalence figure; however, if the purpose of the survey is to determine how many children are in serious need of immediate professional help many slight and even moderate deviations of speech will be excluded and the prevalence figure will be lower.

The following prevalence figures were obtained from material presented by Johnson (1959) in a publication of the U.S. Office of Education, and were purposely based on a rather narrow concept. He urges that these figures be taken as minimal and states: "They represent only children whose speech and hearing handicaps are of such severe grade that they are certain to go through life

TABLE 6.2 *Prevalence estimates of school-age children with severe speech disorders.*

| TYPE OF SPEECH DISORDER | NUMBER PER 1000 | PERCENT |
|---|---|---|
| Articulation | 25 | 2.5 |
| Voice | 1 | 0.1 |
| Stuttering | 7 | 0.7 |
| Cleft palate and lip | 0.5 | 0.05 |
| Delayed speech development | 0.5 | 0.05 |
| Cerebral palsy and other types of neuromuscular impairment | 0.5 | 0.05 |
| Miscellaneous fluency and rate problems | 0.5 | 0.05 |
| Total | 35.0 | 3.50 |

*Source:* Johnson, W. *Children with speech and hearing impairment.* Washington, D.C.: Office of Education Bulletin, No. 5, 1959.

at a serious disadvantage vocationally, socially and in intimately personal ways if not given appropriate corrective attention."

Johnson further stresses that it is important to realize that if all the children who would benefit from both speech and hearing services were included, the number shown would be approximately doubled. In Table 6.2 a modification of Johnson's table presents data showing that an estimated 3.5 percent of school-age children in the United States were in need of speech therapy. Even when applying such conservative estimates, it can be seen that the presence of 3 to 4 percent of the school population in need of professional speech therapy services presents a serious problem indeed.

Although the prevalence figure for speech disorders represents the highest single figure for all areas of exceptionality treated in this book, it should not be inferred that the speech disorder is the most serious category. Still, probably more has been done for this group of children than any of the others. Fortunately, most speech problems do lend themselves to significant improvement and even complete correction.

# Types of Speech Disorders

Classification of the various types of speech disorders which prevail among school children may be done in several ways and each has its merits. One of the most useful methods and the one used in this chapter is classification by description of the symptoms exhibited. The types of disorders to be considered, arranged for the most part according to prevalence, are disorders of articulation, stuttering, voice disorders, cleft-palate speech, delayed speech, language disturbances due to brain injury, and cerebral palsy speech.

## ARTICULATION DISORDERS

This is probably the most frequently diagnosed type of speech disorder. In table 6.2 the prevalence figure for this group is 2.5 percent of school-age children. The number of children with an articulation disorder is greater, however, at the preschool level, and becomes smaller in the upper intermediate and high school levels. One important factor responsible for the decrease in number, of course, is the relative ease in recognition of this defect and its excellent response to therapy. Maturation, too, may exert some influence on the decrease in prevalence, but the teacher or parent who complacently relies on this process is risking the danger of compounding a problem which could have been easily dealt with in the child's early years.

A number of apt descriptions have been given to the articulation disorder: "infantile speech," "lalling," and "lazy tongue." These tend to emphasize a particular part of the vocal mechanism as the culprit, which is not necessarily true. In a general way the articulation disorder presents a pattern which can be described as a form of mispronunciation involving a part or all of the word or words. The outstanding characteristics of the articulation disorder are omissions, substitutions, distortions and additions of consonants or vowels or both. These are commonly called articulation errors and any degree of severity of any of the four types of errors can exist within a given child's speech pattern.

1. *Omissions*—In this type of error certain speech sounds are omitted and the child may say "at" for "cat," "lay" for "lady," "do" for "dog" and so forth. To illustrate this point further, repeat the following sentence but eliminate each "s" and "t" noticing how the omission affects the overall speech pattern: "Sam sat on the sidewalk to spin his top."

2. *Substitutions*—This error involves such utterances as "tat" for "cat," "wabbit" for "rabbit," and "gog" for "dog." Repeat the following sentence, substituting "t" for each "k" or "c" and "f" for each "th": "Katy thought she hurt her thumb when Clara threw the ball." One can readily understand how incomprehensible a child's speech would be if a substitution were used for each consonant sound. Some of the most common sound substitutions found among children in the early grades are "t" for "k" or "k" for "t," "b" for "v," "f" for "th," "th" for "s," and "w" for "l" or "r." The "th" for "s" substitution is frequently referred to as a "lisp," although there are other disorders of "s" and "z" often included in this category. Other sound substitutions are less usual but perhaps even more destructive to the total articulation pattern. A second grade child has been found who substituted "h" for every consonant sound.

3. *Distortions*—This error is a much debated form of articulation deviation. Van Riper and Irwin (1958) argue that there is no justification for including the distortion error as a separate class. Their

rationale is that all distortions are forms of sound substitutions which the speaker does not ordinarily use, although this same sound may be quite acceptable in another language. Be that as it may the classification of some erred sounds as "distortions" is a distinct aid in describing the severity of a disorder. An interesting example of this type of error involves an "s" sound produced when the child sucked in air over the teeth, which resulted in a slushy hiss. Such a sound, used in speech, is certainly distorted yet not clearly identified as any other kind of speech sound normally used by the speaker.

4. *Additions*—These errors which occur infrequently can be found in the use of "furog" for "frog" and "forgest" for "forget."

In children with functional disorders of articulation there is no apparent or obvious structural deviation, whereas in an organic articulation disorder an obvious structural deviation does exist which can account for the speech errors. A child with a paralyzed tongue, for instance, has a definite structural anomaly which results in misarticulation that is related to the structural deviation itself. Usually such conditions as cleft palate and cerebral palsy are described as organic disorders because of the known etiological factors related to the defective speech patterns. In these conditions, as well as in other organic conditions, articulation defects may be present and implications for corrective procedures are dependent on an understanding of the functional–organic dichotomy.

For years speech pathologists have been investigating the etiology of articulation disorders with little success in so far as conclusive evidence is concerned. For example, it is frequently thought that there is a direct relationship between missing front teeth and some types of articulation disorders among young children. Recently however, Bankson and Byrne (1962), after comparing the speech and dentition of over 300 children, concluded that a condition of missing teeth alone does not always affect the speech patterns. In order to draw the accumulated information together and present a total picture, Powers (1957) compiled an excellent and comprehensive review of the literature on factors related to articulation disorders. The principal items included in the studies were motor ability, intelligence, hearing, vision, personality, environmental influence, and emotional problems. The conclusions drawn from this survey revealed that only environmental and emotional factors have been found to be positively related to these disorders. Even so, the evidence was not overwhelming.

One outstanding environmental factor is the influence of the parent's speech pattern on the child's speech development. Every public school speech therapist has had the experience of endeavoring diligently to correct the lisp of a child only to confer with the parent who proves to have an even more severe lisp. One fourth grade boy who had nearly corrected his lisp in therapy sessions, informed his therapist that he was teaching his mother, who also lisped, how to say her "s" correctly. He reported that his mother was very happy over her improvement and she used his word lists for her daily practice.

Another environmental factor is sibling order. An older child may notice the attention a younger sibling receives with his infantile speech and may imitate this speech pattern until it becomes automatic. Lack of adequate speech stimulation in the home can also deprive the child of an opportunity to develop satisfactory articulation. Speech patterns seem to vary, too, with the socioeconomic level. These factors tend to overlap and it is impossible to determine that any single factor is the cause. As the child is a living organism endowed with certain potentials, the realization of these potentials, whether speech or academic achievement, will be dependent to a certain extent upon the circumstances which surround him. Children with intact ability, who have been stimulated by well adjusted parents with good speech and, who live in an average or upper socioeconomic level, tend to develop speech patterns which are superior to those of children who have not had these advantages. This is not to say that the converse is true, however. Since the etiology can rarely be traced, it is important to know the severity of the disorder and the corrective procedures which can be followed.

The age when the child is said to have an articulation disorder requiring professional attention is of utmost importance. On what basis does the school or the therapist in the school make a decision as to the time that therapy should be initiated for the child? Is it true that some articulation disorders will disappear or at least improve significantly with maturation? How long should one wait before therapy is started? As a rule of thumb based on clinical evidence, any child who does not have intelligible speech by the time he enters the first grade should have the immediate attention of the speech therapist. If the child were to outgrow the speech disorder, very little time will be required to correct it. If he would not have outgrown the disorder, then it will be evident that he needs therapy as the program progresses. In this way, an error in prediction will not be harmful to the child.

The expectation that a child with an articulatory defect will eventually have satisfactory speech is very good. This is especially true if there are no factors such as intellectual involvement or severe emotional disturbances which could complicate the disorder. Most school age children with speech disorders do respond to therapy. This response combined with assistance from the classroom teacher enhances progress immensely.

Any deficiencies in the ability to communicate will most certainly interfere with the child's ability to perform adequately in the classroom. Extensive research by several investigators has indicated possible relationships between reading achievement and defective speech. A recent study by Weaver, Furbee and Everhart (1960) using the Gates Reading Readiness Test and articulation tests as measures of performance confirmed a relationship between reading readiness and the acquisition of adequate speech, though they were unable to determine a common underlying causal factor. Another study (Sommers et al., 1961) explored the effects of speech improvement and speech therapy upon articulation and reading. Among other findings a gain in reading comprehension as well as in articulation was reported, in a group of first grade children with articulation problems who had received a combination of speech improvement and speech therapy. A matched group which received only speech improvement failed to show this gain.

In addition to school achievement, the interaction of the child with the speech disorder, with the school environment may have more serious consequences than the disorder itself. In the school setting children are brought together, asked to recite and realize that they are being evaluated not only by their classmates but also by the teacher. This places a great deal more pressure on their oral communicative ability than do many other situations and may cause a speech-defective child to become far more aware of his own deficiency which in turn may cause him to react in an unacceptable manner. Early recognition, diagnosis and therapy could prevent such developments in many instances.

An important phase of the therapy program is the automatic and consistent use of the newly learned speech patterns by the child at all times. "Carry-over," as this is called, is one of the most difficult aspects of the total therapy program because the newly learned speech sounds are not as well established as the old error patterns and there is always the tendency for this child to slip back. At this stage the classroom teacher's role is very important. She can augment the program by helping the pupil to practice and use the newly learned speech patterns in the classroom and on the playground. This will assist in bridging the gap between the closely supervised therapy sessions and the unsupervised conditions outside. This kind of program can be worked out cooperatively between the classroom teacher and the speech therapist.

Van Riper (1954) offers an excellent and systematic approach to carry-over valuable to therapists, teachers, and parents. He suggests a program which includes (1) definite school and home practice periods in which talking is done mainly for speech practice; (2) speech assignments designed for specific situations (i.e. the teacher may ask the child to report the number of absences for that day to the principal's office, with the child carefully using his newly learned sounds); (3) the child may check his own errors by marking a point for each mistake or penalizing himself a point for each error; (4) negative practice (the child purposely substitutes the error sound for the correct one thus raising it to the level of his consciousness); (5) a certain place specifically used for correct speech (for example, a certain room in which the child always uses very careful speech).

It must be remembered that such techniques are particularly valuable *after* the child has learned to produce the sound correctly in isolation, can correctly repeat it and can consistently use it in words and sentences. In addition, the child must be highly motivated for good speech if effective carry-over is to occur.

## STUTTERING

Of all the speech disorders, stuttering has received the largest amount of clinical and research attention. In spite of this, the unique characteristics of stuttering behavior are such that most therapy remains based on many unproved hypotheses which continue to be subjected to test. According to the estimate in Table 6.2, approximately 0.7 percent of the school age population are stutterers. Valid prevalence figures are arrived at with some difficulty as there is considerable disagreement among authorities concerning the nature of stuttering.

It is easier to describe stuttering behavior than to attempt a definition. *In its simplest form stuttering can be described as speech which is not fluent.* The descriptive term "nonfluency" is often found in the literature on stuttering. In a recent publication Johnson et al., (1961) used the term "disfluency." Lack of fluency or disfluency varies among individuals both in terms of manifested characteristics and degree of severity, but there are some predominant classic speech symptoms. These consist of prolongations, blocks, repetitions, and hesitations during speaking which interfere with the normal flow of speech.

Frequently the speaker is unable to begin talking because of a "block" or the flow of speech is prolonged or blocked abnormally during the speaking process. Blocks and prolongations may occur on the first word to be spoken, or at any time during speech on any part of a word in the sequence. In the sentence, "I am going to the store," the tongue may not move from one position to another thus the speaker would be "stuck" and could not go ahead. The sentence would sound like this: "I__a__m / go__ing to / the s__tore."

Repetitions of syllables, words, and sometimes phrases, accompanied by hesitations and pauses between words and other parts of the connected speech pattern also occur as a part of stuttering behavior. Therefore, "I am going to the store," becomes: "I_I_ am_ am_____gg_g_oing _ oing__ t_t_t_to the s_st_ore." Most of the time children who stutter tend to exhibit a combination of all the symptoms described, although one symptom may well predominate.

The typical stuttering errors are frequently accompanied by secondary symptoms such as facial grimacing, stamping of the feet, panting, eye-blinking, and other extraneous activities which have nothing to do with speech production. These symptoms appear as the severity of the condition increases. According to Van Riper (1954) the development of these secondary manifestations is a reaction to the fear of stuttering. Thus, stuttering behavior is self-perpetuating and at this stage the condition is referred to as secondary stuttering. In primary stuttering, on the other hand, the stuttering errors are less severe and are not accompanied by secondary symptoms. The school-age child may be a primary or secondary stutterer. Life can be miserable for the child who stutters, especially in the classroom where a great deal of attention is brought to bear on oral speech performance.

To date, no cause or group of causes for stuttering have been unearthed in spite of the tremendous amount of research that has been carried on for well over a century. Johnson (1959) has hypothesized that stuttering develops as a problem which involves an interaction between the speaking child, who exhibits "disfluent" speech patterns while talking, and an authority figure (generally a parent) who listens to the speech. The listener evaluates the disfluent speech as unacceptable and the child, in turn, perceives the listener's negative evaluation of his speech as threatening to him, thus prompting him to evaluate his own disfluent speech as unacceptable. The child then develops unsuccessful behavioral patterns in an effort to avoid the disfluent speech which caused the chain reaction in the first place. According to Johnson's theory, such a series of interactions may result in the onset of stuttering. Thus, in a broad sense, a society's acceptance or nonacceptance of disfluent speech will determine whether the disfluent speech pattern of the child will disappear or develop into a problem of stuttering. Stewart's (1960) extensive study of stuttering in some North American Indian societies, lends support to Johnson's "general interaction hypothesis." In his study, Stewart reported that the problem of stuttering does not exist in the Ute Indian society, furthermore, their language does not include a word for it. These people were found to have a warm and tolerant attitude toward all phases of the physical as well as the speech maturation of their children. However, in the Cowichan society, although somewhat permissive, stricter standards were imposed on the child's speech development and maturation. In this group a word for stuttering does exist and they do consider certain speech hesitations as undesirable.

Similar findings among other groups have been reported. Lemert (1962), a sociologist, compared groups of Polynesians and Japanese. Although stuttering appears in both groups, he concluded that the incidence of stuttering appeared to be low in Polynesian society and high in Japanese. The stricter social structures and greater conformity required of Japanese children appeared to reinforce and maintain the stuttering symptoms, while the more accepting attitude among the Polynesians seemed to provide an environment in which stuttering symptoms could more easily disappear. Thus, in societies where the expectation for speech fluency is higher and negative reactions are exhibited toward hesitations, stuttering is more likely to be present.

Hahn (1956) has discussed a great number of theories of stuttering. Some of these theories have been tested and others have been developed from them but as yet none have provided a basis for consistently successful therapeutic approaches. For instance, stuttering is found to occur more often among males than among females. One of the most complete studies on this factor was done by Schuell (1946) who found a range of two to ten males for every one female who stutters. The average is usually said to be around three or four to one. This rather consistent finding throughout most of the studies would lead one to believe a study of sex differences related to the disorder would prove highly significant in establishing the etiology. Such has not been the case. Due to the rather unique and sometimes bizarre symptoms associated with stuttering and the rigidity with which stuttering resists therapeutic procedures, it seems reasonable to expect that certain individual differences involving the speech initiating mechanism within the central nervous system are involved in a very similar manner from person to person who stutters.

The age of onset of stuttering is debatable. Normally between the ages of two and one-half to four years of age, children will pass through a period of disfluency. Since this happens in such a large number of children and disappears in most of them eventually, it is considered to be normal and therefore merely a phase in the acquisition of speech. The age of onset of stuttering is variable although the child usually develops symptoms of stuttering before or within the first three years of school and only infrequently after about the sixth grade. Just as the cause of stuttering has not been found, an assurance that the stuttering patterns can be alleviated completely is not yet possible. However, with careful handling of the child by speech clinics, parents, speech therapists and classroom teachers, a fairly large number of these children will show definite improvement and may overcome the problem before they reach adulthood.

The educational implications for a child who stutters may be more serious than for those with articulation disorders if one were to view the problem as a communication disorder rather than a speech disorder. These children are frequently more aware of the inadequacy of their speaking ability and tend to exhibit more emotional disturbances, anxiety, fear, and hostile behavior than do children with articulation disorders. Some stuttering children are silent during classroom recitation periods and indicate to the teacher that they do not know the answer to a question because of a fear of stuttering. Others react in a hostile manner with overt behavior that may lead to disciplinary action. Inconsistency in academic performance is frequently observed in the stutterer with poor quality of oral recitation but superior written work.

The child in school who stutters may need more specialized attention for this problem than do children with articulation disorders. The individual attention given them by someone who is trained to deal with such problems is of utmost importance if the stuttering behavior is to be brought under control. The full responsibility cannot be left to the classroom teacher as she does not have the time to devote individual attention to the child who is a severe stutterer. But the combined efforts of the speech therapist and the classroom teacher can be very effective. In the final analysis, the classroom teacher may prove extremely important because, in the eyes of the child, the teacher represents authority and is the one who will accept or reject him and his behavior.

The following are suggestions which could serve as guides for the teacher who has a stutterer in the classroom.

1. Accept the stutterer; do not merely tolerate him. The stutterer has been rejected too often, at least as far as he is concerned, and needs extra support for confidence. It must be remembered that in every other way he is very much like other children in school.

2. When he attempts to speak and stutters, *do not look away from him,* even though you may feel embarrassed by the situation.

3. Encourage the stutterer to talk but do not force him.

4. When he is speaking do not help him by "saying it for him" even if you are aware of what he will eventually say.

5. Build up his self-confidence by emphasizing his assets. If Jimmy, who stutters, excels in building model airplanes, he should be praised, not only privately but before his classmates.

6. Encourage the stutterer to participate in group activities. He need not have "speaking roles," but can participate in many activities in other ways.

7. The general reaction of other children in school to the child who stutters will depend to a great degree on the teacher's attitude. Therefore, the teacher is the key person and should not underestimate her role in this type of situation.

8. In some way let the stutterer know you are aware of his speech problem but that this makes no difference with respect to friendship, academic status or any other relationship in school.

9. Assign the stutterer some responsibility such as emptying wastebaskets or caring for the bulletin board. This will give him a feeling of importance and thus enhance his self-confidence.

In summary, the teacher must handle the stuttering child discreetly and with tact. It is essential that he be made to feel that he is an integral part of the group and that he does not stand alone because of his difficulty with speech.

The onset of stuttering appears to be associated with the development of speech during the preschool years and thus related to the dynamics of the home environment. Since the child continues to be strongly identified with the home after he has begun to attend school, the parents do play an important role in stuttering therapy. The ultimate goal is to have acceptable speech in the classroom, on the playground, at home and in any speaking situation. Through group parent meetings held jointly with the speech therapist and classroom teachers, the many aspects of the therapy program can be discussed with mutual benefit for all concerned. Individual parent counseling allows opportunity to discuss specific problems which are related to the home program.

## VOICE DISORDERS

The prevalence figure of 0.1 percent for voice disorders is the lowest of all categories of speech disturbance as indicated in Table 6.2. Earlier in the chapter it was pointed out that some speech sounds are voiced while others are voiceless. Voicing, or phonation, resulting from the vibration of the vocal folds located in the larynx is similar to singing because it has a musical quality. When the vocal folds do not vibrate no voicing takes place and the air coming from the lungs merely passes out of the mouth cavity as a voiceless stream of exhaled air.

There are four basic characteristics of any voice, namely, *pitch, loudness, quality,* and *duration.* Pitch is defined as the highness or lowness of the voice as related to the musical scale. Loudness is the strength or weakness of voice and is related to the amount of energy. Quality is the characteristic of voice, independent of pitch and loudness, that provides a basis for differentiating two voices. Duration is the total length of time that phonation exists.

A voice disorder is an abnormal deviation of any of the four characteristics described above and etiologically may be classified as either functional or organic. The discussion in this section will emphasize functional disorders, although it will be noted that many of the etiological factors are of an organic nature.

In the broad category of voice disorders a great amount of variability is allowed in determining whether the observed characteristics of a particular voice deviate enough from a normal voice to be classified as a disorder. For example, age and sex factors must be taken into consideration. Children have normally higher pitched and weaker voices than adults. Boys and girls at seven years of age differ only slightly with respect to pitch but by 13 years the differences are significant. Thus the deviation must be significant for the individual before it can be called a voice disorder.

Some children use a pitch level which is too low for their ages and this sometimes leads to the development of hoarse, unpleasant voices. The use of an abnormally high pitch level by some children is observed frequently. Many teachers and parents will readily admit that school-age children's voices are always too loud; however, such a state of affairs must be viewed as normal because of the overwhelming amount of evidence. Of more concern is the child with a weak voice. Children with abnormally weak voices tend to manifest less precision in articulation which frequently can be improved by increasing the loudness of the speech.

Quality disorders are found in school children more often than any other type of voice disorder. Fairbanks (1959) describes four types of voice quality disorders: breathiness, harshness, hoarseness, and nasality.

The breathy voice appears to be similar to a whispered voice. More air than is needed flows through the larynx, without being used to produce phonation. This type of voice is generally weak. The harsh voice is discordant, raspy, low pitched, and louder than normal. Hoarseness is typical of laryngeal irritation which follows excessive yelling or possibly certain acute infections in the throat area. It is extremely difficult to differentiate harshness from hoarseness. The hoarse quality has important health implications as it is an indicator of laryngeal pathology and, if persistent, should receive medical attention. In the nasal quality disorder (hypernasality) too much of the sound passes through the nasal cavities and out through the nose. When most of the speech sounds pass through the nasal cavity the typical impression of "talking through the nose" results.

The term "de-nasality" is applied to a voice disorder in which the speech has a muffled quality giving the impression that the person has a head cold. In children the condition is frequently due to enlarged adenoids which can prevent easy passage of the "m," "n," and "ng" sounds through the nasal cavity. When such a condition occurs, "mop" sounds like "bop" and "name" sounds like "dabe" and so on. Removal of the excess tissue will improve the condition considerably; however, in some cases the muscles and structures involved fail to resume their proper function and it may be necessary for the speech therapist to teach the child how to produce the sound correctly.

A voice disorder involving significant deviations of duration occurs when the phonation periods of speech are either abnormally long or short. In either instance speech sounds, especially vowels, may be distorted. When a vowel, or any other voiced speech sound is too long the natural characteristics of the sound may be altered in such a way that intelligibility is affected. If the voiced speech sounds are too short, there is a tendency for them to blend with one another and with other speech sounds to the extent that words, and thus the entire speech pattern is blurred. Either condition reduces the intelligibility of speech and is distracting to the listener. Although voice disorders of a durational nature occur as isolated problems, they may also exist in disorders of articulation, cleft-palate speech and stuttering. Three major causes of functional voice disorders are: imitation of another voice unnatural to the individual, psychological factors, and voice changes.

The development of speech through the early years is accomplished through imitation more than any other voluntary activity. Therefore, the speech patterns which fall on the child's ears are those which he will attempt to duplicate. He is thus inclined to experiment with many modes of talking and occasionally an unacceptable pattern is adopted. Occasionally children will attempt to imitate the speech of others with whom they are closely identified and in so doing, they may acquire a pattern, such as abnormally low pitch, which is not natural. For example, a child who at a very early age greatly admired his father who possessed a very low pitched voice, began talking on inhalation thus causing his voice to be low pitched for his age. The resultant poor voice quality and the low pitch eventually disappeared without any specific treatment but it was suspected that he had temporarily attempted to imitate his father's voice.

There is a reasonable amount of evidence in the literature that voice quality characteristics indicate certain personality traits. The research of Moses (1954) in the area of personality disorders and voice provides a great deal of evidence which indicates a relation-ship between the two. It is not uncommon for people to correlate a manner of speaking with some subjective evaluation of personality. For instance, a weak, indistinct voice is often associated with shyness or timidity. In extreme cases a child may refuse to speak at all because of his unwillingess to relate with others in strange situations. However, there is very little research reported which would permit any gross generalizations concerning the rela-tionship between personality and voice. If any such relationship does exist, it would be apparent only in older children and adults.

As has been noted, the pitch level of the male voice begins to descend at about eight years of age. The lowering of the pitch accel-erates during adolescence until the adult level is stabilized at about 18 years of age. During this period abrupt shifts of pitch occur which cause the voice to "break." These normal voice breaks are related to the accelerated growth of the larynx at this time which appears to cause the vocal fold function to be unstable resulting in uncontrolled pitch changes. Practically everyone has heard voice breaks and can remember the fun that is poked at boys when it happens. It is important for the classroom teacher and also the unfortunate boy to understand that this is a normal phenomenon which will disappear by the eighteenth birthday. Occasionally, though, the new low-pitched voice does not develop as expected and the boy will retain a preadolescent high pitch, or he may con-tinue to suffer the voice breaks. This can be devastating for the young adult male but can be helped. If, in fact, psychological dis-turbances underly these conditions, it will be necessary that these be treated by someone other than a speech therapist. In all instances referral should be made to the properly trained professional people who can be of service. In chronic cases of voice disorders of any kind, especially those of hoarseness and harshness, medical atten-tion should be sought as a first step in therapy for the individual. If the organic conditions are not too severe or if the problems are not symptoms of deep-seated psychological disturbances, many of the voice disorders can be improved and corrected through speech therapy.

The implications of voice disorders for the school-age child with respect to his performance in school are somewhat indirect. There is no evidence of a relationship between voice disorders and intelligence for example, and therefore, the problems created by the voice disorder will revolve around the personality disturbances which might accompany the defect. Intelligibility of speech is not as profoundly affected by the voice disorder as by the articulation disorder. In most instances it will be easy enough for the child to be understood in the classroom.

Functional voice disorders among school-age children are one of the most difficult groups of speech problems to correct. During the elementary years the voice producing mechanism is changing constantly and it is not easy to obtain consistency in its function. After medical clearance has been obtained, the speech therapist's primary responsibility will be to initiate the type of therapy program indicated by the nature of the voice disorder. The classroom teacher should have some knowledge of the functional principles of the breathing, phonatory and articulatory mechanism in order to appreciate the problems involved in corrective programs. It is emphasized here that voice quality problems can be improved by concentrating on a coexisting articulation disorder, as Williamson (1944) and others have reported. The reason for this is that many of the quality characteristics of the voice are determined by the same anatomical structures that are responsible for the articulation of the speech sounds.

### CLEFT-PALATE SPEECH

The speech problem associated with cleft palate is considered as a separate disorder of speech because of the underlying factors involved. This particular problem is classified as an *organic* disorder of speech because there is a specific structural deviation which has caused the characteristic speech patterns. The prevalence of speech problems associated with cleft palate and lip as estimated in Table 6.2 is about 1 in 2000 or about 0.05 percent of school-age children. This estimate is somewhat lower than the usual incidence figures given for the number of cleft-palate births which is about 1 in 800. The latter figure includes all children with cleft palates regardless of severity. In some cases the involvement would not be severe enough to result in a speech disorder.

The terms cleft palate and cleft lip describe specific types of anomalies which are congenital in origin. The condition is caused by a failure of the bones forming the hard palate and upper jaw, and the tissues of the lips and soft palate to develop normally in the embryo. At birth the cleft (opening) may involve only a part of the palate or it may extend the entire length of the roof of the mouth including the gum ridge. A cleft of the palate creates an abnormal opening between the mouth and nasal cavities which allows air, and therefore speech sounds, to be emitted through the nose without control. From birth the child is a medical and health problem. The earliest difficulties are those of chewing, sucking, and swallowing which interfere with nutrition as well as the normal development of speech. Surgery is generally required for a great number of these children in order to correct the structural defect. Occasionally surgery is not feasible and false palates and other types of prosthodontic aids are created to compensate for the lack of adequate structures in the speech mechanism. Even with successful surgery, speech therapy is usually necessary before the child can be expected to have acceptable speech.

McDonald and Baker (1951) have suggested that three characteristics of the speech of the child with cleft palate are outstanding: *hypernasality, nasal emission,* and *faulty articulation.* From this, one would infer that cleft-palate speech includes some of the same types of speech errors that have been described under articulation and voice disorders. This is true to a certain extent, but with some additions which have not been discussed previously.

In normal speech the muscles of the soft palate and the back of the throat must function in such a manner that a "closure" is effected, directing the breath through the mouth and preventing its escape through the nasal passages. With the exception of three nasalized consonants, "m," "n," and "ng," all speech sounds are so emitted. When the child lacks the ability to control the flow of air through the nasal passages, much of his speech has a strongly nasal quality. In addition, it is extremely difficult for the child to build up adequate pressure to produce such explosive sounds as "p," "b," "t," and "d." The result is that the air stream is released through the nose in the form of a nasal emission or "nasal snort." Finally, the articulatory patterns are usually distorted which can be related back to the child's attempts to compensate for the lack of control. As adequate compensatory movements are seldom achieved, the resultant speech patterns remain distorted. Frequently, the child with a cleft palate will attempt to use the back of his tongue to keep the air from passing through the nasal cavity, but in doing so the tongue is out of position to articulate certain speech sounds. Because the tongue is not flexible enough, both the articulatory patterns and voice quality are distorted.

It must be borne in mind, however, that it is not always possible for the child with a repaired cleft palate to produce all speech sounds to the satisfaction of the speech therapist. In such cases, compensatory movements of the tongue and lips are desirable. The aim in speech therapy for the child with cleft palate speech must be consistent use of the best possible speech within his limitations.

The incidence of hearing loss in the cleft-palate population is somewhat higher than among children who do not have the cleft palate. Because of the nature of the structural anomaly, the child is subject to more than the usual number of nasopharyngeal infections which lead to secondary middle ear infection via the eustachian tube. Therefore a cleft-palate speech problem can be complicated further by the additional deficiencies in communication created by a hearing loss.

The cause of cleft palate is not known at the present time. Schwartz (1954) has reported most recently on investigations concerning etiology, and his research has indicated that hereditary factors comprise the largest group of factors which are related to the cause. Other possibilities include poor nutrition of the mother during pregnancy, disease with high fever during early pregnancy, and the Rh factor.

The prognosis for acquisition of normal or significantly improved speech is dependent upon many conditions, some of which are beyond control of speech therapists alone. One of the primary factors is the results obtained from surgical or prosthodontic treatment which is generally done before speech therapy is attempted. Much of the success of these procedures is dependent upon the initial severity of the condition and of growth factors related to specific structures involved; however, most cleft-palate speech responds to therapy when other factors can be controlled adequately.

This type of problem requires the assistance of the professionally trained speech therapist. In a therapy program two factors must be considered, the success of the restorative procedures and the amount of compensation of which the individual is capable.

In the classroom, the child with a cleft palate faces many problems. When the condition is severe enough to involve the lip and other peripheral structures the cosmetic factors may create an adjustment problem which in itself can affect over-all school performance adversely. The child with a severe nasal emission condition during speech may be ridiculed by classmates and his articulatory errors are frequently severe enough to affect intelligibility.

In addition to cosmetic factors and speech problems there is some evidence, which should be mentioned, of intellectual impairment among children with cleft palates. Goodstein (1961) compared the intelligence scores of carefully matched groups of non-cleft-palate children and children with cleft lips and palates. His results indicated that a significantly larger group of children with cleft lips and palates had intelligence in the range of dull-normal (80–89) or lower, than was found among the noncleft-palate children tested. A significantly smaller group of children with cleft palate and lip had intelligence in the range of bright normal (110–119) than was found among the noncleft-palate group. Obviously, one must by no means assume that intellectual impairment will invariably be found among children with cleft palates and lips but in order to insure successful academic handling, the classroom teacher must be aware of this possibility.

As in other types of disorders, the speech therapist will have to play the major role in initiating and carrying out a program of speech training for the child. In this kind of problem it is even more important that the classroom teacher have knowledge of the nature of the anatomical involvement and how the abnormalities affect the total function. Too often it has been assumed that surgical treatment will correct the speech disorder. Even with successful surgery, it must be remembered that new structures have been created which are not completely functional and therefore need to be "trained." The child must learn how to use them and the task is exceedingly difficult because the structures are only substitutes, at best.

The classroom teacher who has a knowledge of the complexity of this problem can cooperate with the parents and with the speech therapist in reinforcing the progress made in speech training and in supporting the child psychologically. It will be possible for her to give the child invaluable aid in developing an adequate personality by assuming an objective attitude toward the child and helping him to understand why his "face looks that way." If the parents are counseled early in the child's life, and later, aided by an understanding attitude on the part of each classroom teacher, this child can develop into a happy well-adjusted adult.

## DELAYED SPEECH

Occasionally a child is found whose verbal communication is notably slow in development or has failed to develop at all. This delay in speech development is often recognized by parents and aid is sought by the time he is three or four years of age; therefore, the more obvious symptoms of speech delay are seldom found in the regular classroom. Sometimes, of course, the underlying cause of the speech delay is so serious that the child may never reach the regular classroom at all. In less severe cases, even though the child is talking by the time he is in school, he may exhibit an articulatory defect and indications of delayed development in other abilities. According to Brown (1956), a child who has had delayed speech development may be slow in learning to read and later have difficulty expressing himself in written language. Van Riper (1954) and Brown (1956) have described three principal characteristics of delayed speech: (1) vocabulary deficiency, (2) retarded development of sentence structure, and (3) deficiency in the ability to formulate ideas. From these characteristics it is evident that such a child would present many problems.

One illustration of the problem under consideration concerns a boy who, at the age of three years, was speechless. Development in areas other than speech seemed to be within normal limits, but his principal means of communication was through gestures. At one time members of the family seriously considered institutionalizing him because it was thought that he was mentally retarded. The mother refused to heed the relatives' advice, and upon recommendation of the pediatrician, brought the child to the speech clinic. After assessing hearing and intelligence, which seemed to be normal, speech therapy was initiated with an emphasis on eliciting verbal responses and building a basic vocabulary. The program followed the normal development scheme beginning with random vocalization and continuing on through the development of vocabulary, parts of speech, phrases, and conversation.

One of the most important phases of the program was the work with the mother who had to be taught the value and necessity of reading interesting stories on his level to the child, and the importance of giving her attention to his attempted conversation. As speech developed, from time to time it was necessary for the speech therapist to give direct aid in the articulation of some consonants. The child progressed and although he experienced a period of disfluency between five and seven years, language continued to develop. At the age of six he entered school with an adequate vocabulary and good articulation and his general performance was satisfactory. The disfluency eventually disappeared leaving him with normal speech. Contrary to the family's early diagnosis, this child had no hearing loss, no perceptual deficiencies, and no intellectual impairment. Without speech and language therapy this child's chances for normal speech development and acceptable school performance would have been greatly minimized.

The prevalence figure for delayed speech shown in Table 6.2 is about 0.05 percent of school-age children. From this it will be noted that very few teachers will find a child with delayed speech in her classes. In rare instances, a child may appear in kindergarten or first grade who shows symptoms of speech delay which for one reason or another have not been recognized by the parent and for which no help has been given the child. In such cases, the classroom teacher should recommend the child to the school speech therapist or if none is available to the school nurse who can seek help for the child through the proper channels.

The etiological factors related to delayed speech include low intelligence, emotional disturbances, central nervous system damage, hearing loss, early severe illnesses, and adverse environmental conditions. Obviously any of these factors could be more of a handicap to the child in school than the speech problem alone.

The prognosis in this condition varies according to the severity of the etiological factors involved. Even if the lack of speech appears to be due to low intelligence, a child can sometimes be taught a few verbal responses which would aid the parents in caring for him. Emotional factors in some cases can be alleviated by psychological guidance and speech allowed to develop. With special handling, speech can be developed in varying degrees in cases of central nervous system damage, hearing loss, and early severe illnesses. Probably the best chances for successful therapy for children with delayed speech lies with those whose delay is due principally to poor motivation and an unstimulating speech environment, and these are the children who will more often be seen in the regular classroom.

When the child with delayed speech symptoms is handled in the school speech-therapy program, both group and individual therapy may be used. Direct training techniques are useful in building vocabulary, correcting articulatory errors, and developing syntax. In dealing with these children the therapist and classroom teacher must work very closely since there tends to be more of a language problem than in those with articulation disorders. When there is no speech therapist in the school system, the teacher might need to assume the responsibility of working with the parents and the physician to obtain an assessment of hearing, intelligence, and physical conditions. If these factors are not involved, the teacher would then need to avail herself of all possible information on language development and utilize her skills in helping the child. The classroom teacher's opportunity for direct management of the problem is greater than in many other types of speech disorders because of the unlimited linguistic situations presented in reading, arithmetic, spelling, and other classroom activities.

## LANGUAGE DISORDERS

As stated previously, language is referred to as a form of symbolic behavior composed of the appreciation and expression of thoughts, ideas, and concepts. Since basically, language is a function of the central nervous system, it is possible that damage to the brain will result in a language disorder. In such a condition, there may or may not be an easily observable muscular incoordination depending upon the location and extent of the brain damage. Children who, in addition to other symptoms, manifest language disorders are often referred to by such terms as "childhood aphasia," "aphasoid," "autistic," and "emotionally disturbed." The fact that the above terms may represent distinct constellations of symptoms is not denied; however, it is assumed here that *any language disorder is related specifically to a malfunctioning central nervous system whether or not demonstrable.* In support of this point, Kastein (1961) has recently reported the final data on a longitudinal study of children with communication disorders. The results support previous findings that "lack of, or deviation in, the development of language and speech in children often is the first and only manifestation of central nervous system deficit."

It must be emphasized that there is no clear cut etiology for this type of disorder. A child who does not talk may be brought to the speech and hearing clinic for diagnosis, even though there does not seem to be any reason for his communication problem. He does not fit the picture for the child previously described under "delayed speech" (although there may be some overlapping of symptoms) because of certain manifested behavioral patterns. Diagnosis and separation of these children into a distinct classification of speech disorders is relatively new and it is suggested that until more knowledge of them is accumulated, they be described by symptoms exhibited, rather than labeled. For this reason, the prevalence of children's language disorders is not known, and at best the estimates are vague. In Table 6.2 this group is included with the "cerebral palsy and other types" group which has a prevalence of 1 in every 2000 school-age children.

Most children with a definite language disorder are not found in the regular classes of the public schools because the disturbance is severe enough that special educational facilities must be provided. However, a teacher may find a child in school who, in a mild form, manifests some of the classic symptoms of damage to the brain. They have reading problems, lack skill in language, and are not progressing satisfactorily academically. These children present a problem to the classroom teacher because there is no distinct group of symptoms that indicates what the problem may be or how an adequate educational program can be established for them. Under such circumstances the child should be referred to a speech and hearing center, remedial reading clinic, mental health center or similar agency which has facilities for making a complete evaluation and recommendations.

The following are some of the symptoms associated with language disorders which will aid the teacher in recognizing and understanding the problem.

1. Hearing loss—the child is not able to hear well enough to acquire language
2. Auditory perceptual disturbance—child does not seem to comprehend speech
3. May comprehend spoken and written speech but unable to use expressive language
4. Does not talk and may not attempt speech
5. Gestures used for communication
6. Low vocabulary level
7. Visual perceptual disturbance
8. Reading disturbances
9. Withdrawn and fearful in social situations
10. Inconsistent behavior—seems alert one day and dull the next
11. Distractible—not able to concentrate on a single task as attention shifts to something else
12. Perseverates—has difficulty shifting from one activity to another

Any of the above symptoms are found in varying degrees of severity and prominence in the total behavioral pattern. Thus, there is no particular group of symptoms which determines the extent of the problem. A complete diagnosis must be made.

## CEREBRAL PALSY SPEECH

Damage to the central nervous system can cause a condition known as cerebral palsy and usually occurs before, during, or shortly after birth. The predominant characteristic is in the lack of control in coordinating the movements of the body (see chapter 9). The severity of the condition varies in relation to the extent of the muscular system it involves. Three terms (spasticity, athetosis, and ataxia) are used to describe the major classes of cerebral palsy. Spasticity is characterized by a greatly increased muscular tone which results in exaggerated muscle contraction. In athetosis there are uncontrolled, twisting movements primarily of the extremities, but other muscle components may be involved. In ataxia there is a disturbance of balance and coordination, and visual defects are often present. In this condition, the muscles are generally of a low muscular tone and the symptoms are most prominent when voluntary movements are attempted.

About 90 percent of the children with cerebral palsy exhibit significant speech disorders simply because speech is basically a neurophysiological activity and will be affected by any disturbance in the neuromuscular system. The disturbed speech patterns are not caused by the brain damage, since they do not exist when the brain damage occurs. The speech disorder is the result of the child's attempts to develop speech in spite of a defective fundamental mechanism. In addition to speech disorders, many children with cerebral palsy have language disturbances which increase the severity of the total problem. Palmer (1952) discusses several basic deficiencies associated with cerebral palsy. His findings clearly illustrate the pervasiveness of the damage to the brain, which may result in an extreme disturbance of the oral communication process. In a group of 100 cerebral-palsied cases he found that a significant number exhibited abnormal chewing, sucking and swallowing patterns, abnormal breathing and tongue movements and visual and hearing disorders. Because of the fundamental character of these processes, their disturbance may create disorders of both speech and language which are extremely difficult to modify.

The prevalence figure for cerebral palsy is an approximation only. It must be remembered too, that there are some children with cerebral palsy who do not have speech defects. Table 6.2 lists cerebral palsy with other types of neuromuscular impairments and gives the prevalence figure as about 1 in every 2000 school children, so that the estimate for cerebral palsy alone would be somewhat less than this.

Speech and language training for the child with cerebral palsy should be started at least by the time he is a year old and will necessarily be continued for many years in most instances. With this group of children, the responsibilities of the speech therapist are most challenging because of the irreparable nature of the damage to the central nervous system and the grave lack of compensatory ability in the severe cases.

Whether or not the cerebral-palsied child will be found in the regular classroom depends, of course, largely on the severity of the condition. Wilson's (chapter 9) later discussion of children with neurological and nonsensory physical impairments points up in detail, the relationship of the speech disorder to the complex problems of the cerebral-palsied child in an educational program. The monograph, "Speech Therapy for the Cerebral Palsied," by Westlake and Rutherford (1961), is recommended for specific information about speech and language training procedures.

## The School Program

### RESPONSIBILITY OF THE SCHOOL

Because children in need of speech therapy services spend a major portion of their day in the school environment it seems practical that such speech therapy services be made available through the school system. It is also an economical approach for reaching speech-impaired children who otherwise might not have an opportunity for therapy.

Since the prevalence figures in Table 6.2 are minimal, it is suggested here that a school system of 2000 or more students can utilize the services of a speech therapist. If the school is to assume the responsibility for providing professional services, how can this be accomplished? As a basic requirement there must be, first of all, trained personnel to carry on the speech therapy program. A person with a survey course in speech correction is not trained, no matter how interested he is in speech disorders. It is difficult for the uninitiated to comprehend the high degree of technical knowledge and skill necessary to an adequate performance as a speech therapist. Equally important is the therapist as an individual, his personality, his effectiveness in dealing with other personalities and his professional attitude.

In addition to a trained speech therapist, adequate facilities should be provided for the therapy program. In the ideal situation, the therapist would be provided a room of moderate dimensions, relatively quiet and located in the vicinity of the lower elementary rooms with a table, chairs and a shelf for materials. Few schools have been able to provide such a room for speech therapy purposes in the construction of a school. As a result the therapist is usually put into whatever space is not in immediate use at the time the therapist is in the building. In some instances the room provided is excellent; in others the space may vary from a spacious unused classroom large enough to seat 40 children to a small closet shared with mops and buckets. The nurse's office, though not in constant use, is not satisfactory for the therapist, as an ill child may need to use the room at any time. Many therapists are able to use a room on alternate days with an itinerant music teacher; however, these days and hours may not easily fit in with the remainder of the therapist's schedule. A nationwide survey of public school speech and hearing services in the United States was recently conducted by Steer et al., (1961). In the report, which includes responses from over 700 public school speech and hearing therapists, about 50 percent indicated that therapy space was inadequate. Such studies as this are very helpful in pointing up areas which need attention. With increased recognition of the problem by school administrators, facilities for school programs have been improved and will continue to improve. Since the provision of adequate space is a difficult problem in all areas of education, the therapist tries to make as few demands as possible, but as a minimum provision he should have space which both he and the children can count upon for regular use in the therapy sessions.

Once a speech-therapy program is initiated, the school system also has a responsibility in supporting the therapist and aiding him in seeking cooperation from principals and teachers. This is dependent to a large extent upon the attitude of the therapist toward the school system, which will be discussed later under the responsibility of the therapist; however, the administration's belief in the therapy program will go far in establishing rapport.

## THE SPEECH THERAPIST

A qualified speech therapist must have at least a Bachelor's degree. Many therapists hold more advanced degress. The specific requirements vary from one training institution to another but in general, accredited colleges and universities with a speech therapy curriculum attempt to meet or exceed the standards set by the American Speech and Hearing Association. Course content may include all or part of the following: anatomy and physiology of the ear and vocal mechanism, semantics, phonetics, speech science, psychology of speech, courses dealing with pathology and therapy for each of the various types of speech disorders, course work in normal development and mental hygiene; study of hearing problems including testing of hearing, and speech and language training techniques for the hard of hearing. The minimum supervised clinical practicum required of the student is 200 clock hours. Most of the practicum is done in the college or university clinic, but it is frequently possible for arrangements to be made which allow part of the practicum to be done in the public schools under supervision.

A recent statement "Services and Functions of Speech and Hearing Specialists in Public Schools" (1962) published by the American Speech and Hearing Association, clearly delineates the role of the public school therapist. The statement clarifies some misunderstandings which have led to inappropriate requirements in the education, certification and responsibilities of the speech and hearing therapist in the public schools. In essence, the function of the therapist is neither as a regular classroom teacher nor as a special classroom teacher. His program does not involve the teaching of curricular materials. He is trained to provide a therapeutic service which will enable children with speech disorders to participate more fully in the regular classroom. If the therapist attempts to manage children in too large numbers or spread his services too thinly he cannot accomplish his purpose. The goal of the therapist is to administer therapy of the highest quality to the speech defective child, while working "in harmony with his surroundings," whether in a hospital, rehabilitation center, community clinic, college or university clinic or in the public schools.

In most urban school systems, the therapist is "itinerant" and works at more than one school each day. Valuable time is lost when it is necessary to travel from one school to another. In some rural school systems the itinerant speech therapist's record is long on travel and short on therapy. Ideally the therapy program should be conducted in no more than one school each day. In one school system a very successful plan has been effected. The therapist goes to one school on Mondays, Wednesday, and Fridays, and to another school on Tuesdays and Thursdays—the following week the three-day school is attended two days and the two-day school attended three days so that in a month's time both schools have received an equal amount of therapy. This schedule could conceivably be alternated by months or semester, if preferred. In some schools the case load may not be great enough to justify a therapist for a full day. In such cases, a change from one school to another may be done during the lunch period; however, the number of changes should be minimal in order for the therapist to conduct a program of quality.

## THE RESPONSIBILITY OF THE THERAPIST

When the speech therapy program is initiated in the school, it is essential that the principals and teachers be oriented to the program. The therapist should have an opportunity to explain in a teacher's meeting, the various types of speech disorders and the goals in therapy. There should be questions and answers concerning the teacher's role in carry-over and an explanation of the total set-up of the program. In addition, the therapist must learn as much as he can about the school's daily schedule, general philosophy, methods used in the teaching of reading, and show a genuine interest in the work the classroom teachers are doing with their children. The therapist will also find the school nurse an invaluable ally in serving as the intermediary for medical services when necessary, and in providing helpful material regarding the child's background. The therapist may be "specially trained" in this field, but he is no more of a "special person" than any other individual on the staff. A good, warm, effective relationship between therapist and school personnel can go far toward creating success in a child's therapy and in the total program.

The therapist must establish an organized method for finding the speech defective children. One method is for the therapist to screen all children in one grade each year, for instance the second grade, and to accept teacher referrals from any other grade. In an established program this may work fairly well, but in the formation of a new program all grades would have to be screened. Teacher referrals provide the therapist with an excellent opportunity to inform the classroom teacher further about the characteristics of the various types of speech defects, if he is careful to discuss the results of screening and testing of the referrals. Referrals are also important in that new children frequently move in during the school year and thus are missed in the grade screening which is usually done only in the fall. In many schools the speech therapist functions as both speech and hearing therapist and is frequently responsible for screening for hearing defects as well as speech defects. When a hearing problem is found, the child should be referred to a physician for medical diagnosis, and for a complete hearing evaluation if indicated. In some cases, medical attention may alleviate the hearing problem. In others, audiological assessment may indicate a need for some type of therapy, such as speech-reading or auditory training or some articulation work may be necessary, any of which would be administered by the public school therapist.

Following the screening program, speech-defective children are selected for further testing and scheduling. The selection is made on the basis of maturation, severity and prognosis. If group work is to be done, many factors must be taken into consideration in grouping the children. Items to be considered are personality, type of speech defect, a favorable time for the child to leave the regular classroom for therapy and so on. One may casually assume that it is easy to group all lispers together. This is not always practicable, as not all lispers lisp alike. Another problem is involved since the children in a group of lispers may come from several different rooms which operate on different time schedules. Some therapists group children from one room together regardless of the speech defect; however, many public school therapists seem to prefer to group by type of disorder or by sounds missed, when possible. One disadvantage in heterogeneous grouping is that it often means that some children in the group are working on sounds they know, while the ones who need intensive work are hampered by not getting the individual attention they need. Heterogeneous grouping is sometimes done for specific reasons. Backus and Beasley (1951) have described a group therapy procedure in which children with various types of speech defects are purposely grouped together. The goal in this situation is to achieve correct speech through interpersonal relationships involving conversational speech. The attitude is that the particular kind of defect is not as important as the common desire shared by all members of the group; that of achieving adequate speech.

In individual therapy, children are scheduled one at a time for therapy sessions. The program for each child is planned and conducted entirely in light of his specific needs. Working individually allows the therapist great flexibility in adjusting the program at any time, solely on the basis of the best procedures for the child. During the 30-minute therapy session, he receives the undivided attention of the therapist and is allowed to progress according to his own ability to learn. A child who may have emotional problems associated with his speech disorder will not be inhibited due to group pressures. As the child progresses, the therapist may find it desirable to place the child in a group as a carry-over procedure, combining both the individual and group approaches. Public school therapy programs utilizing individual therapy with group activities used as an ancillary procedure for special purposes are very effective. The speed with which the child can learn in an individual setting appears in many cases to outweigh the value to be gained from working only in a group. There are innumerable occasions for the child to perform speechwise in a group, which should be used as a part of carry-over, but the individual therapy session can provide maximum participation on the part of the child and optimum conditions for his gain.

Unfortunately, far too frequently, grouping of children for speech therapy has been done in the public schools in order to see large numbers of children in accordance with an administrative requirement, rather than for reasons of greatest benefit to the children. The usual case load limit set by the State Board of Education in many states is around 75–100 children. Some states require many more, some less. Ainsworth (1955) stresses that it is extremely important that the therapist have the freedom to reduce the number well below these figures if a large number of severe cases are found. Although the therapist may find more cases than this, only the number which can be worked with effectively should be scheduled and the remainder placed on a waiting list. If this is not done the value of the program will be greatly decreased.

In a well organized program, the therapist could work out a schedule, which provides individual therapy each thirty minutes on the Monday-Wednesday-Friday and Tuesday-Thursday basis suggested earlier. The waiting list would be kept up-to-date in order to add another child when one moves away or is corrected. It is conceivable that one or two smoothly working groups could be scheduled, appropriate after the child has had enough individual therapy to benefit from a group situation. It seems highly probable that such a program could show a much greater percentage correction than is currently being shown.

The cooperation of therapist, teacher, and parents is an essential part of a good program. Some of the carry-over techniques were discussed earlier in relation to specific disorders. The therapist should inform the teacher of each new sound learned in the case of a child with an articulation disorder. Specific suggestions should be given for the use of the sounds. The teacher can also be of great help in acquainting the therapist with the child's home background and parent relationships.

Whenever possible the parents, especially the mother, should be helped to realize the importance of their role in the speech-therapy process. A study by Tufts and Holliday (1959) indicated that mothers trained by speech therapists, can be effective in the improvement of a child's speech even at preschool age, which disputes the age-old theory that parents cannot teach their own children.

The amount of time the classroom teacher can contribute to the program is limited although there are many ways in which she can help. A few suggestions follow:

1. A teacher's manifested attitude toward the speech defective child is important. Complete acceptance of the child with a speech disorder will be noted by the child's classmates.

2. Assets of the child should be emphasized. Most children want to be included in group activities, even if only minimally. It is not necessary that he have a speaking role in plays, he might prefer being stage manager.

3. Teachers can facilitate the therapy program by reinforcing newly learned speech patterns in all speaking activities, plays, recitations and occasionally in reading aloud. How much and how often this is done may be arranged between the teacher and therapist. The idea is to keep the child aware of speech in situations beyond the speech therapy program. The carry-over phase of speech therapy is by no means easy.

Another important part of the program is the extensive reporting which is required. It is advisable to secure some sort of a case history of the child before therapy is begun. During therapy an individual daily case record must be kept for each child. These can be brief but must show the work attempted, successes or failures of each therapy session and any note which might be helpful toward planning future therapy for the child. In addition to these, there are usually quarterly and annual reports as to the numbers of children in therapy, number dismissed with maximum improvement, number retained or other disposition, numbers by type of speech defect and numbers by grade.

In communities where there is a well-staffed community speech and hearing clinic, the therapist will frequently refer cases who need more help than public school therapy can provide. The therapist must also know what agencies are available to provide financial aid for clinic speech therapy in case of need.

In addition to the other duties the therapist is often asked to speak before PTA meetings, or other community meetings and to serve on in-service teacher-training panels. Any of these opportunities should be welcomed by the therapist as additional situations for the provision of more information for better handling of speech defective children.

This section has presented suggestions for the speech-therapy program in the school. The aspects which are covered included the means for establishing the need, the importance of trained personnel, case load of the therapist, physical facilities and philosophy of the procedure. All of these can be provided through the combined efforts of the speech therapist and the educator. School systems must assume direct responsibility for some aspects of the program. If the total program appears to be too ambitious, it is suggested that the only real difference between this program and one which is less expensive is *quality*. There is a good chance that superficial speech therapy programs accomplish no more than the effect of maturation alone. If this is true, the ideal program would be less expensive ultimately.

## PROGRAM WITHOUT A SPEECH THERAPIST

Some schools do not have the services of a speech therapist. In such cases, the following suggestions may be helpful to the classroom teacher who finds a child whom she suspects may have a speech or language problem:

1. If there is a community speech and hearing clinic, all speech problems should be referred for complete evaluation. Inquiries can also be made to the nearest college or university, regarding the availability of speech clinical services. Such clinics can provide parents with expert counseling and recommendations.

2. Children learn to talk by listening and watching. This is also the way they learn to read. Much can be done toward diminishing the articulation errors through phonic methods used in reading. Use of teacher's handbooks accompanying workbooks for a phonic approach to reading are of value, since therapy programs for articulation disorders are frequently begun by introducing "ear training" techniques, including speech sound identification and discrimination, which are outlined to some extent in these books.

3. As children learn primarily through visual and auditory channels, they should be able to see and hear the speaker simultaneously. Some speech sounds have more visual cues than do others. Loudness increases preciseness of articulation thus affording clear cues for sound recognition. The more cues made available to the child the better his chances will be for improved speech.

## Summary

A discussion of speech considered under six major topics has been presented: speech as a part of an oral communication cycle, the normal development of speech and language, a definition of speech disorders, the prevalence of speech disorders, the types and etiologies of speech disorders more commonly found in the public schools, and the public school speech-therapy program.

Normal speech develops in an orderly fashion beginning at birth and continues to develop over a period of at least seven or eight years. Its development is influenced by such factors as the rate of maturation, the sex of the child, intelligence, and environment. The integrity of the total biological system is highly essential to the normal development of speech.

A recent estimate indicates that about 3.5 percent of the children in public schools have speech defects which need formal corrective work. *Articulation disorders* are the most prevalent among school children, comprising about 70 percent of all disorders diagnosed. Expectation for normal or acceptable speech is good for this group when early corrective procedures are introduced. Classroom teachers and parents can be very helpful in assisting the school therapy program for these children. *Stuttering* is considered a more complex disorder than that of articulation. Problems in the educational handling of the stuttering child may occur because of the pervasiveness of the stuttering symptoms, their resistance to corrective procedures, and in relation to the child's interaction with his environment. There is a low prevalence of *functional voice disorders* and these are infrequently found in the schools. It is important to remember that a harsh or hoarse voice may indicate a pathological condition and the child should be referred for medical attention. Speech defects due to *cleft palate, cleft lip,* or both require either surgical repair or the fitting of an artificial palate before the necessary speech-therapy program can be begun. When the teacher has more than casual knowledge of the nature of the structural deviation involved in cleft-palate speech, her effectiveness is furthered in handling the child psychologically as well as assisting in the speech-therapy program. In problems of *delayed speech* the symptoms are frequently associated with poor classroom performance as evidenced by a deficient vocabulary, sentence structure level, and abstracting ability although the child may possess normal intelligence. Even though some symptoms of a *language disorder* frequently overlap those of the delayed speech group, a difference exists because of the predominance of language disturbances which are closely related to a malfunctioning central nervous system. Disorders in language constitute a more serious problem than delayed speech. Speech disorders associated with *cerebral palsy* can include any of those previously described although of a more serious nature since damage to the central nervous system is irreparable. Improvement of speech, although slow, is highly encouraging and worthwhile to the child, parents and teachers.

A speech-therapy program in the schools requires the cooperation of the speech therapist, school personnel, and parents. Some presently existing speech programs in the schools tend to fall short of the goals they are intended to meet. Therapists themselves are aware of the shortcomings of their programs which in some cases may include: inadequate facilities for carrying out a speech therapy program, a required caseload which may be too high for effective professional management, and too little professional supervision. Planning, organization and administration of realistic and effective school-therapy programs in some cases have not kept pace with the development of techniques and knowledge in the field of speech therapy.

In spite of the problems, tremendous progress in public school speech therapy has been made over the years. Therapists are in demand in large and small school systems. Funds are appropriated for the development of programs. Teachers, parents, school nurses, and other members of the school team recognize the importance of speech therapy in the public schools and have demonstrated their willingness to cooperate. Teachers, parents, and the aspirant to a career in the field of speech therapy may be assured that with the aid of research, and a realistic view of handling speech problems in the schools, new and better programs are being and will continue to be evolved.

## CHAPTER REFERENCES

Ainsworth, S. H. The education of children with speech handicaps. In W. M. Cruickshank & G. O. Johnson (Eds), *Education of exceptional children and youth*. Englewood Cliffs, N.J.: Prentice-Hall, 1955.

Backus, Ollie L., & Beasley, Jane. *Speech therapy with children*. Boston: Houghton Mifflin, 1951.

Bankson, N. W., & Byrne, Margaret C. The relationship between missing teeth and selected consonant sounds. *J. Speech Hearing Disord.*, 1962, **27**, 341–348.

Berry, Mildred E., & Eisenson, J. *Speech disorders*. New York: Appleton-Century-Crofts, 1956.

Brown, S. F. Retarded speech development. In W. Johnson (Ed.), *Speech handicapped school children*. New York: Harper & Row, 1956.

Darley, F. L., & Winitz, H. Age of first word: Review of research. *J. Speech Hearing Disord.*, 1961, **26**, 272–290.

Davis, Edith A. Developmental changes in the distribution of parts of speech. *Child Develpm.*, 1938, **9**, 309–317.

———. Mean sentence length compared with long and short sentences as a reliable measure of language development. *Child Develpm.*, 1937, **8**, 69–79.

Fairbanks, G. *Voice and articulation drillbook*. (2nd ed.) New York: Harper & Row, 1959.

———. Systematic research in experimental phonetics: 1. A theory of the speech mechanism as a servosystem. *J. Speech Hearing Disord.*, 1954, **19**, 133–139.

Gesell, A., & Ilg, Frances L. *Child Development*. New York: Harper & Row, 1949.

Goodstein, L. D. Intellectual impairment in children with cleft palates. *J. Speech Hearing Res.*, 1961, **4**, 287–294.

Hahn, E. F. *Stuttering: Significant theories and therapies.* (2nd ed.) Stanford, Calif.: Stanford Univ. Press, 1956.

Johnson, W. *Children with speech and hearing impairment.* Washington, D.C.: U.S. Office of Education Bulletin, No. 5, 1959.

————, *et al.* Studies of speech disfluency and rate of stutterers and nonstutterers. *J. Speech Hearing Disord.,* Monogr. Suppl. 7, 1961, 1–82.

————., *et al. The onset of stuttering.* Minneapolis, Minn.: Univer. of Minnesota Press, 1959.

Kastein, Shulamith. Observations, implications and findings of a collaborative study of twenty-eight children with communication disorders. *Asha,* 1961, **3**, 367–368.

Lemert, E. M. Stuttering and social structure in two pacific societies. *J. Speech Hearing Disord.,* 1962, **27**, 3–10.

McCarthy, Dorothea. Language development in children. In L. Carmichael (Ed.) *Manual of child psychology.* New York: Wiley, 1954.

McDonald, E. T., & Baker, H. K. Cleft palate speech: An integration of research and clinical observation. *J. Speech Hearing Disord.,* 1951, **16**, 9–20.

Metraux, Ruth W. Speech profiles of the preschool child 18–54 months. *J. Speech Hearing Disord.,* 1950, **15**, 37–53.

Moses, P. J. *The voice of neurosis.* New York: Grune & Stratton, 1954.

Myklebust, H. R. *Auditory disorders in children.* New York: Grune & Stratton, 1954.

Palmer, M. F. Speech therapy in cerebral palsy. *J. Pediatrics,* 1952, **40**, 514–524.

Poole, Irene. Genetic development of articulation of consonant sounds in speech. *Elem. Eng. Rev.,* 1934, **11**, 159–161.

Powers, Margaret H. Functional disorders of articulation—symptomatology and etiology. In L. E. Travis (Ed.), *Handbook of speech pathology.* New York: Appleton-Century-Crofts, 1957.

Schuell, Hildred. Sex differences in relation to stuttering: Part I. *J. Speech Hearing Disord.,* 1946, **11**, 277–295.

Schwartz, R. Familial incidence of cleft palate. *J. Speech Hearing Disord.,* 1954, **19**, 228–238.

Services and functions of speech and hearing specialists in public schools. *Asha,* 1962, **4**, 99–100. (A statement by the American Speech and Hearing Association).

Sommers, R. K., *et al.* Effects of speech therapy and speech improvement upon articulation and reading. *J. Speech Hearing Disord.*, 1961, **26**, 27–37.

Steer, M. D., *et al.* Public school speech and hearing services. *J. Speech Hearing Disord.*, Monogr. Suppl. 8, U.S. Office of Education, Coop. Research Project No. 649 (8191), July, 1961.

Stewart, J. L. The problem of stuttering in certain North American Indian societies. *J. Speech Hearing Disord.*, Monogr. Suppl. 6, 1960, **6**, 1–87.

Templin, Mildred C. *Certain language skills in children.* Minneapolis, Minn.: Univer. of Minnesota Press, 1957.

Travis, L. E. (Ed.) *Handbook of speech pathology.* New York: Appleton-Century-Crofts, 1957.

Tufts, La Rene C., & Holliday, Audrey R. Effectiveness of trained parents as speech therapists. *J. Speech Hearing Disord.*, 1959, **24**, 395–401.

Van Riper, C. *Speech correction: Principles and methods.* (4th ed.) Englewood Cliffs, N.J.: Prentice-Hall, 1954.

————, & Irwin, J. V. *Voice and articulation.* Englewood Cliffs, N.J.: Prentice-Hall, 1958.

Weaver, C. H., Furbee, Catherine, & Everhart, R. W. Articulatory competency and reading readiness. *J. Speech Hearing Res.*, 1960, **3**, 174–180.

Westlake, H., & Rutherford, D. *Speech therapy for the cerebral palsied.* Chicago: National Society for Crippled Children and Adults, 1961.

West, R., Ansberry, M., & Carr, Anna. *The rehabilitation of speech.* (3rd ed.) New York: Harper & Row, 1957.

Williamson, A. B. Diagnosis and treatment of eighty-four cases of nasality. *Quart. J. Speech.*, 1944, **30**, 471–479.

## ADDITIONAL REFERENCES

Ainsworth, S. *Galloping sounds.* Boston: Expression, 1946.

Cypreansen, Lucille, Wiley, J., & Laase, L. T. *Speech development, improvement and correction.* New York: Ronald Press, 1959.

Dupuis, R. M. The therapist and public school personnel. *West. Speech*, 1961, **25**, 10–13.

Eisenson, J. & Ogilvie, Mardel. *Speech correction in the schools.* (2nd ed.) New York: Macmillan, 1963.

Irwin, Ruth B. *Speech and hearing therapy.* Englewood Cliffs, N.J.: Prentice-Hall, 1953.

Johnson, W. An open letter to the mother of a "stuttering" child, in *Speech handicapped school children*. New York: Harper & Row, 1956. Pp. 558–567.

———. (Ed.) *Speech problems of children*. New York: Grune & Stratton, 1950.

Mecham, M. J., Berko, M. J., & Berko, Frances G. *Speech therapy in cerebral palsy*. Springfield, Ill.: Charles C Thomas, 1960.

Palmer, M. F. Speech disorders in cerebral palsy. *Nervous Child*, 1949, **8**, 193–202.

Powers, Margaret H. What makes an effective public school therapist? *J. Speech Hearing Disord.*, 1956, **21**, 461–467.

Rutherford, Bernice. *Give them a chance to talk*. Minneapolis, Minn.: Burgess Publishing, 1950.

Schoolfield, L. D. *Better speech and better reading*. Boston: Expression, 1951.

Schreiber, Flora R. *Your child's speech*. New York: Putnam's, 1956.

Scott, Louise B., & Thompson, J. J. *Talking time*. St. Louis: Webster Publishing Company, 1951.

———, & ———. *Speech ways*. St. Louis: Webster Publishing Company, 1955.

Van Riper, C., & Butler, Katherine G. *Speech in the elementary classroom*. New York: Harper & Row, 1955.

———. *Teaching your child to talk*. New York: Harper & Row, 1950.

## RESOURCES

Additional information concerning speech and hearing disorders can be obtained by writing: Executive Secretary, The American Speech and Hearing Association, 1001 Connecticut Avenue, NW., Washington 6, D.C.

The American Speech and Hearing Association by 1963 had a membership of over 9000 professionally trained and other interested persons. The association publishes two professional journals, the *Journal of Speech and Hearing Disorders* and the *Journal of Speech and Hearing Research*, plus a nontechnical journal, *Asha*, as well as numerous monographs and special bulletins for its members and others.

The association has within its structure a professional certification committee that certifies professionally trained persons in speech and hearing disorders. Members who have completed a specified amount of academic and practicum training may apply for clinical certification. For many years the American Speech and Hearing Association has actively supported the continuous elevation of professional standards throughout the United States and other countries. The association publishes an annual directory that lists all members, noting the level of professional certification held by each.

In addition to the national organization, there are many state speech and hearing associations that serve as sources of information at the local level. Most state organizations publish a periodic bulletin containing information of a professional nature. Information about state speech and hearing organizations can generally be obtained from state departments of education or the American Speech and Hearing Association.

The monograph, *Public School Speech and Hearing Services*, is a special report prepared by the Research Committee of the American Speech and Hearing Association, and comprises a comprehensive accumulation of data concerning many aspects of public school speech and hearing services in the United States today. Dr. Mack D. Steer was chairman of the Research Committee and Project Director for this survey.

## SELECTED 16 MM SOUND FILMS

*Introduction to speech disorders.* 25 min, color. Audio-Visual Center, Wayne State University, Detroit 2, Michigan. Presents several patients with various types of organic and functional speech disorders.

*A survey of children's speech disorders.* 29 min, color. Bureau of Audio Visual Institution, State University of Iowa, Iowa City, Iowa. Produced by State University of Iowa.

*Speech disorders: physical handicaps.* 29 min, black & white. National Educational Television Film Service, Indiana University, Bloomington, Indiana. Points out the various kinds of speech handicaps, their causes, diagnosis, and treatment.

*Voice production: the vibrating larynx.* 45 min, black & white. SFW-UNFI. Catherine Sengel 59, Utrecht, Netherlands. Shows how the human larynx functions to produce voice.

*Great clinicians series.* 30 min, black & white. Bureau of Audio-Visual, University of Wisconsin, 1312 West Johnson Street, Madison 6, Wisconsin. A series of 11 films—four on aphasia, three on audiometry, one on hearing aids, and the rest on stuttering.

*Good speech for Gary.* 30 min, color, (2 reels). New York University, 26 Washington Place, New York 3, New York. Second grader is provided a well organized speech program with help provided by both the speech correctionist and the classroom teacher.

*For better speech.* Division of Special Education, Baltimore City Schools, 3 East 25 Street, Baltimore 18, Maryland. TV series in speech improvement which shows speech improvement materials for the primary grades.

*Report on Donald.* 19 min, black & white. Audio-Visual Department, University of Minnesota, Minneapolis, Minnesota. Donald overcomes his stuttering and makes a satisfactory readjustment through the services of the University of Minnesota Speech Clinic.

*Speech disorders: stuttering.* 29 min, black & white. National Educational Television Film Service, Indiana University, Bloomington, Indiana. Interviews several children who overcame stuttering and shows the therapy they received.

*Stuttering from the horse's mouth.* 33 min, black & white. Bureau of Audio Visual Institution, State University of Iowa, Iowa City, Iowa. Discusses the nature of stuttering.

*Principles of respiratory mechanics.* Parts 1 & 2, 20 min each, color. The National Foundation, 800 Second Avenue, New York 17, New York. Film used normal subjects and patients with respiratory disturbances to illustrate changes in the mechanics of breathing. Models and animated drawings are also used.

*The Bobath approach in cerebral palsy habilitation.* 30 min, color. Newington Hospital for Crippled Children, Newington, Connecticut. Film covers human reflexive maturation, suppression of tonic reflexes, facilitation of righting and equilibrium reactions, and techniques devoted to speech habilitation with techniques for the facilitation of vocalization.

*Examining the oral mechanism.* 25 min, color. Bureau of Audio-Visual Instruction, State University of Iowa, Iowa City, Iowa. The film demonstrates how an oral mechanism examination might be administered most effectively when the objective is to seek out physical problems which may affect speech.

*Tongue thrust: an orthodontic and speech syndrome.* 41 min, color. M. D. Foundation, 6252 Primrose Avenue, Hollywood 28, California. This film presents essential factors for the diagnosis of the "Tongue thrust syndrome".

## CHAPTER 7

# Deaf and Hard of Hearing Children

HARLEY Z WOODEN

*author*

Possibly no disability exerts an impact on so many aspects of a child's development as does an early, severe hearing impairment. Intelligence, language, oral communication, school achievement, general adjustment, and ability to relate tend to be adversely affected. But such tendencies are no *real* measure of a child's potentials or human worth. Therefore, it is to society's as well as his advantage that he be provided with the most skilled instruction education can devise.

## The Deaf and the Hard of Hearing Defined

Losses in hearing vary along a continuum which extends from the insignificant to total. Any loss great enough to require the services of a special teacher for at least part time over a period of months or years is classified as *educationally significant*. Children with such losses are divided into two groups—the deaf and the hard of hearing. However the profession possesses the dubious distinction of owning two conflicting sets of definitions by which to designate these groups. One set developed in 1937 by the Conference of Executives of American Schools for the Deaf (1938) is based on the ability to interpret speech through hearing.[1] According to the Executives persons that have an impairment, but who still possess "functional" hearing with, if not without, a hearing aid are hard of hearing. Those with an impairment that is not sufficiently functional to interpret speech, even with a hearing aid, are deaf. The other set developed by the White House Conference on Child Health and Protection (1931), is based on the presence of speech and language[2] acquired through hearing—not on the ability to understand speech. Thus the hard of hearing include both those who can interpret speech through hearing and some who cannot. The deaf are those who lost their hearing before acquiring speech and language, and therefore constitute only part of the people who lack sufficient auditory acuity for interpreting speech. Such a conflict with conventional connotations is confusing to the reader, and traps many an author into saying things he does not mean. A second major source of confusion arises in attempting to develop operational or quantitative definitions. Not until the profession establishes uniformly acceptable definitions for performance levels will there be anything to which it can assign scientifically established quantitative values. And a third source of confusion resides in the fact that a scientific measurement of a loss of hearing is not necessarily a statistically reliable measure of ability to understand speech with the residual hearing that is left.

## THE DECIBEL

A person's *hearing level* (his own threshold or lowest point at which he begins to detect sound) is stated in decibels, which is a measure of change in intensity. Thus a decibel is not a fixed unit. A change in the intensity of sound means a change in the amount of energy

---

[1] The ability to interpret speech through hearing is called *auding* by some authorities.

[2] Language and speech are not to be interpreted as synonymous. As pointed out in chapters 1 and 6, speech is only one of the mediums through which language may be expressed.

transmitted per second, thus a change in power. Zero db (decibel) is very near the *mean* point for each important speech frequency at which young people with normal ears, and using both of them, can detect the faintest sound of which they are capable. As practical examples of intensities, the average whisper according to Streng

TABLE 7.1 *Comparison of decibels of sound intensity on the tympanic membrane with the corresponding power in watts per square centimeter.*

| SOUND INTENSITY IN DECIBELS | DESCRIPTION OF POINT ON THE SCALE | POWER IN WATTS[a] FOR THE CORRESPONDING SOUND INTENSITY IN DECIBELS | NUMBER OF TIMES BY WHICH THE WATTS OF POWER CONCERNED ARE GREATER THAN THE $10^{-16}$ WATTS AT ZERO DECIBELS[b] |
|---|---|---|---|
| 0 | Threshold of normal audibility | $10^{-16}$ | $10^0$ or 1 |
| 20 | Average whisper | $10^{-14}$ | $10^2$ or 100 |
| 50 | Moderate conversation | $10^{-11}$ | $10^5$ or 100,000 |
| 120 | Threshold of discomfort | $10^{-4}$ | $10^{12}$ or one trillion |
| 140 | Threshold of pain | $10^{-2}$ | $10^{14}$ or 100 trillion |

[a] The watt is a unit of power. One ampere of current flowing under one volt pressure equals one watt. Small electric alarm clocks are usually stamped as either two- or three-watt instruments.

[b] Zero db of sound intensity also has an acoustic *pressure* value of 0.0002 dynes per cm², which increases $\sqrt{10}$ fold for each increase of 10 db of intensity. And finally the sensation of *loudness* increases two fold for each such intensity increase. From Davis in *Hearing and deafness* by Davis, H., and Silverman, S. R. Copyright © 1960, Holt, Rinehart and Winston, Inc., publishers. Pp. 29–60. The dyne is a force equivalent to the weight of approximately one milligram.

(1960) is measured at about 20 db, and ordinary conversation at 50 to 60 db. The threshold of discomfort, the point at which sound becomes uncomfortable to the ear, is attained at about 120 db. And the threshold of pain is reached at the upper limits of hearing acuity, namely at about 140 db. The decibel scale is an arithmetic progression or linear scale in steps of 10, from 0 to 120. (See the *audiogram*, a chart for plotting a loss of hearing, shown later in this chapter.) But the intensity of the sound measured by the decibel is expressed in a geometric progression or logarithmic scale. Table 7.1 illustrates this relationship for five selected points on the scale. According to the medically oriented definitions of Davis and Fowler (1960), normal hearing levels vary from − 10 db to + 15 db.[3] The "handicap" for interpreting speech (the level at and above which a person is deaf) falls at the 82 db level, therefore the hard of hearing are those whose hearing level for speech falls within the 16–81 db range. Silverman (1960) estimates a hearing threshold of 30 db as the minimum level at which children begin to encounter problems in school. He lists 60–80 db as a borderline hearing-level range in which many of the children are *educationally deaf* (those in need of special instruction to acquire speech and language). This leaves the educationally hard of hearing as possessing hearing levels of 30 to 59 db or slightly higher. Children with hearing levels above 80 db he classifies as unquestionably educationally deaf. Silverman determines a child's hearing level by averaging his test-result levels for 500, 1000, and 4000 cps (cycles or vibrations per second)—frequencies significantly representative of those found in speech.

## VARIABLE FACTORS AFFECTING PERFORMANCE

Meyerson (1955) is convinced that labels devoid of operational definitions are meaningless. As a researcher, he despairs of the numerous existing concepts concerning those who constitute either the hard of hearing or the deaf. He disagrees that either the age at onset or the hearing level in decibels is an adequate criterion for predicting performance. Thus be concludes that the terms "deaf" and "hard of hearing" are of no practical value in research investigations and

---

[3] Inasmuch as normal hearing varies from −10 to +15 db it would not be correct to label a 25 db threshold of audibility as a 25 db loss. Therefore, the term *hearing level* is recommended by Davis and Fowler (1960) when hearing status is expressed in decibels. Thus the greater the hearing impairment the more decibels of sound intensity are required to reach the subject's threshold of audibility, and therefore the higher the numerical value of the hearing level.

recommends that investigators describe the types of children under study rather than label them.

The problems of a researcher are in contrast to those of the pupil-placement official and teacher. The researcher needs to isolate or control all variables except the one under measurement. The educator needs to be fully aware of all the variables and use to advantage those that enhance performance, while helping children circumvent, overcome, or compensate for those that handicap performance.

## OBSERVATIONS AND RECOMMENDATIONS

The following concepts seem logical:

1. The educational differences between the deaf and the hard of hearing are dramatic and significant, except for the borderline cases.

2. Nonquantitative definitions based on performance levels are useful for making gross distinctions among the hearing impaired.

3. Quantitative definitions of the hearing impaired based on hearing levels in decibels possess too much overlapping in performance either for research or classification of individual pupils, but are useful for understanding approximate group performance.

4. Quantitative definitions of the hearing impaired based on some new multifactor unit, scientifically derived from the significant variables that affect performance, would be useful to the extent such a unit became a reliable measure of performance. It is impossible though to predict whether or not a unit of this kind will ever be available.

Some unified action on definitions by those in the field of the hearing impaired is highly desirable. One of the hallmarks of any profession is the possession of a common language with which to communicate. Either of our present sets of definitions could be amended and used, but it would be more satisfactory to borrow the educationally oriented features from the White House Conference definitions and the conventional connotations from the Executives' definitions, and consolidate them into a new set. The following are suggested.

The *deaf* are those in whom the sense of hearing, either with or without a hearing aid, is insufficient for interpreting speech. The *prelanguage deaf* are those in whom deafness *preceded* a firm establishment of language and speech. The *postlanguage deaf* are those in whom deafness occurred *after* good language and speech had been acquired.

The *hard of hearing* are those in whom the loss of hearing is educationally significant, but whose residual hearing is sufficient for interpreting speech with—if not without—a hearing aid.

A *natural-language group* is one composed of the hard of hearing and those postlanguage deaf who have retained their normally acquired speech and language.

# Sound and How it is Measured

### CHARACTERISTICS OF SOUND

Sound as we ordinarily experience it is the result of creating vibrations in the air, which upon striking the tympanic membrane vibrate it, thereby transmitting the sound wave to the inner ear through movements of the *ossicles* (bones of the middle ear). In the inner ear the sound waves are analyzed and converted into nerve impulses which are transmitted by the *eighth cranial* (acoustic or auditory) nerve to the hearing center in the brain where they produce the sensation of sound.

The vibrations emanating from a tuning fork create a continuous chain of condensations and rarefactions, which move back and forth in the air at the same rate as the prongs. As soon as either prong of the fork starts to move in the opposite direction, the molecules of the first condensation rush back to fill the new partial vacuum, only to be struck by the prong and sent bouncing out again (Fig. 7.1). Sound waves though do not travel solely in a straight line, but rather three dimensionally in spherical fashion. However they are of greatest intensity in the vibrating body's plane of vibration, unless otherwise affected.

Sound travels at about 1100 feet per second near sea level and increases as air density decreases. Thus the higher the elevation or the higher the temperature, the greater the sound's speed (Boylan,

1959). The distance between any two like parts in the chain of sound waves, such as from the beginning of one condensation to the beginning of the next one, is a wave length. Therefore, the shorter the wave length in any given density of air the greater is the number of waves that reach the tympanic membrane per second, and the higher is the frequency and pitch. Of all the sound waves produced, only certain frequencies are audible to the human ear, namely those between about 16 and 20,000 cps. This gives a hearing range of about 10 octaves. The frequencies to which the ear is most sensitive are in the 500–4000 cps range. Those considered most important for understanding the spoken word vary between 300 or 400 cps and 3000 cps—a frequency spread known as the *speech range*. Frequency and intensity are the two characteristics of sound employed in measuring hearing.

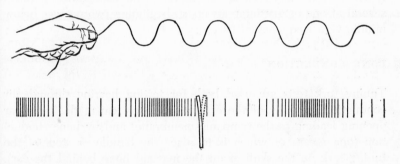

FIG. 7.1 Transverse and longitudinal waves. *Above,* transverse wave may be produced by flipping a rope in steady rhythmic fashion. The movements within the rope are at right angles to the horizontal left-to-right direction in which the wave is traveling. *Below,* longitudinal sound wave may be produced in the air by vibrating a highly elastic metal prong. The particles of air are thereby set in short-distance oscillations in the wave's radii of travel.

## EARLY MEANS OF TESTING HEARING

Most modern tests of hearing level employ pure tones (tones of one frequency each). The subject's threshold of audibility is checked for each tone included in the test. Early tests were made by such means as the human voice in ordinary conversational tone, the whisper test, watch tick, coin clicking, or vibrating tuning fork. For rough checks such tests still have value. In fact the Encyclopedia Americana recommends the voice and whisper tests as being the most desirable. The thinking is probably based on the fact that ability to understand speech is the ear's most important function. The old watch and coin tests emit sounds of higher frequency than those in the speech range. Thus it is sometimes possible for a person to hear them better than he can hear speech, in which case the test results are misleading. However it is more probable that such tests will detect an approaching loss of hearing, which can generally be discovered first in the high frequencies. The tuning fork tests have the advantage of revealing the exact frequencies in which there is involvement. The *otologist* (an MD ear specialist, sometimes called an aurist) who uses forks, requires several at one octave intervals apart, beginning two octaves below middle C, a frequency of 64 cps.

## BONE CONDUCTION

Tuning fork tests are used both for testing hearing through air conduction (by way of the external auditory canal, the outer-ear opening leading to the tympanic membrane) and by bone conduction (one means of which is to place the handle or stem of the tuning fork on the skull or on the mastoid bone behind the ear). Bone conduction is useful for bypassing a *conductive loss* (a loss in the transmission of the sound waves to the inner ear). Conduction by bone transmits the sound waves directly to the inner ear by way of the bones of the head. It is not successful for bypassing either a damaged inner ear or acoustic nerve. A normally hearing person can detect very little sound by bone conduction except when the air conduction of the sound is either nonexistent or is masked by plugging the ears. Sound by bone conduction can be obtained from a spinning phonograph record without creating any appreciable air conduction. The subject should grip firmly between his teeth the large end of a long slender darning needle, lean over and engage the point in a groove of the record, on the edge that is moving away from him. He will thus hear the recording distinctly, though somewhat softly.

## THE AUDIOMETER

The audiometer is an electronic device for measuring hearing levels in decibels. The two types that have been most used for testing school children are the pure-tone oscillator and the electrically transcribed recording. The latter machine is for screening up to 40 children at one time. It is operated in the manner of an ordinary record player except that the sound is usually transmitted to each child through a single individual head phone. In this manner right ears are tested at one time and left ears at another. The recordings often contain different tests using the human voice in descending intensities to which the children respond with paper and pencil. The advantage of this instrument is in the fact that it tests the children's abilities to understand the spoken word, using both a man's and a woman's voice. Two disadvantages lie: (1) in the necessity for the children to respond in writing and (2) in the problem of allowing just the proper amount of time for response so that the children are neither rushed nor given time for diversionary activities. The pure-tone oscillator can be used either for group or individual screening and for followup. It is now transistorized and smaller than formerly. The ordinary ones have frequencies at octave-step intervals of 125 cps to 8000 cps. They are equipped to test either by air or bone conduction in hearing level steps of 5 db up to 110 db or 120 db. The more sophisticated machines contain additional intermediary frequencies, such as 750, 1500, 3000, and 6000 cps, plus certain other features for better determination of the type of hearing loss involved. The pure-tone audiometer can be fitted with head phones for testing a large group of children simultaneously, either in sweepcheck (using a limited number of selected frequencies) or in a full-screen test (using all frequencies). The more comprehensive sweep-check tests include 250, 500, 1000, 2000, and 8000 cps. Others include less frequencies, such as either 500 or 1000 cps and 4000 cps. The theory for the reduced number of checks is that 4000 cps will catch evi-

dence of possible losses in the higher frequencies and that either
500 or 1000 cps will catch evidence of losses in the lower ones.

## THE AUDIOGRAM

Individually administered pure-tone audiometer tests are recorded
on an audiogram chart using either a red mark for the right ear

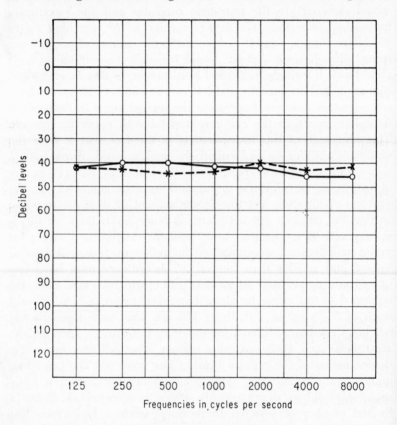

FIG. 7.2 Audiogram chart. This chart is intended to show a rather flat
loss, typical for those caused by middle-ear infection. Such a loss is known
as conductive, and will respond better to a bone-conduction hearing aid
than to air conduction.

and another color for the left or a circle for the right and an "X" for the left. Each mark indicates the subject's threshold of hearing for a given frequency. The threshold checkmarks on the successive frequencies tested for each ear are then connected by either a dotted or solid line, thereby resulting in an audiogram chart. (Fig. 7.2). However, any test made for diagnostic purposes is of necessity concerned with much more than loss of hearing. In fact such tests constitute only one aspect of a careful medical examination.

# Identification and Prevalence

# of Hearing Impairments

Various means are used by schools to find the hearing impaired child. Certain schools possess a good working relationship with public health personnel, pediatricians, otologists, visiting nurses, and others, which brings forth referrals both of suspected and confirmed losses. In addition, teachers of regular classrooms can be taught to be observant of loss of hearing evidence. However, such symptoms as inattentiveness, apparent dullness, tendency to fatigue or tendency to become confused sometimes exhibited by the hearing impaired are not exclusive with them. Symptoms of greater significance include pain in a child's ear or mastoid bone, a tendency to turn his head more to one side than to the other when listening, ability to understand only when the speaker is close, tendency to omit sounds from his speech, and the ability to hear considerably more speech than he seems to understand. The referrals made by teachers will include names of some children who have no loss and will omit others who have one. However, the better trained the teachers are for such a task the better judgments they will exercise.

## SCREENING TESTS

The best procedure for identifying children with losses of hearing is a systematic periodic testing program. The first step involves a screening test. The person in charge must be well trained in administering such tests and all other personnel should understand their respective responsibilities. The parents need to be notified in a manner that will carry no unintentional implications of suspected impairment. The audiometer needs to be in proper calibration. The room selected for the tests should be relatively free from extraneous noises and distractions, and the children must be properly prepared for the occasion—free of fears and in a spirit of readiness and cooperation. All of these are pass-or-fail type tests which are made without determining the exact hearing level. A test at 15 db intensity identifies all children who may possess any degree of loss; one at 20 db intensity identifies all children who may possess a loss of medical significance. Failure is usually set at about two errors on a group test and one on an individual test. Those who fail a screening test are referred for a more comprehensive individual test.

## COMPREHENSIVE INDIVIDUAL TEST

The purpose of this type test is to determine the extent of loss within the speech range at each octave and intermediary frequency selected. Sometimes the test includes frequencies beyond the speech range. The examiner in charge should be an audiologist (a Ph. D., specialist in hearing testing, capable of interpreting the nonmedical aspects of the results). Children who show a 20 db *monaural* loss (in one ear) in two frequencies are usually recommended for a complete medical diagnostic test by either an otologist or an *otolaryngologist* (an MD specialist in diseases of the ear, nose, and throat). A psychogalvanic skin response test (PGSR, sometimes referred to as electrodermal audiometry, EDA) is used with children too young to respond to the usual testing techniques. It is based on a Pavlovian conditioned-type response. A tiny electric shock to the child's hand is coordinated with an amplified sound transmitted through the headphones. An automatic recording of the child's involuntary reactions is synchronized with a recording of the stimulus given. Once the association between the shock and the sound is established, the sound alone is used. Thus a record is automatically made of each sound a child hears. For a quick check on evidence of loss, without the necessity of the child's active cooperation, different types of noise makers are used, one at a time, at either side of the child, slightly back of his view. During this process, the child is observed to determine under what conditions of distance, intensity, and type of sound his attention is attracted.

## OTOLOGICAL DIAGNOSIS

It is the function of the otologist to make a complete hearing and medical diagnosis, prognosis, and recommendations—based on his examinations and the information supplied by the audiologist and parents. He will be concerned about many things: the extent of loss, whether it is congenital or adventitious, the history of any hearing loss in the family, and the response of the child to air versus bone conduction. If the loss is adventitious he will wish to know how it was acquired, what part of the hearing mechanism has been affected, the existence of any aggravating factors, the probable course of the condition, and whether medication or surgery is indicated. However, all of this is preliminary to the real purpose at hand. Plans and procedures must be established for whatever action is required whether it be medication, surgery, a hearing aid, special education services, or mere watching to assure a prompt medical referral in case the course of the impairment has not been arrested.

## PREVALENCE OF EDUCATIONALLY SIGNIFICANT LOSSES

Early prevalence reports often included children with "some degree" of loss and quoted decibel levels we no longer consider educationally significant. Baker (1959) points out that in recent years more careful methods of testing and improvements in diagnosis have lowered the estimates. Furthermore, better medical treatments, and their greater availability, plus improved convalescent care have meant an actual decrease in the percentage of acquired losses of hearing. The prevalence figure for educationally significant losses of hearing was estimated in 1953 by the U. S. Office of Education as 1.5 percent (Mackie and Dunn, 1954). However, the most recent figures from that Office provide an estimate of 0.6 percent and the latest estimate released by the

Dominion of Canada Bureau of Statistics sets the figure for that country at 0.54 percent (Table 1.1). Both of these new estimates seem to be in keeping with what has been happening in this area of exceptionality.

## The Human Ear

The human ear, functioning as a total unit in concert with the neural centers with which it is connected, constitutes a psychobiological marvel. Hearing begins with the stimulus of a sound wave of minute pressure vibrating against the tympanic membrane and culminates in a mental concept which is recognized and understood by the speech center of the brain.

### BINAURAL HEARING

The person possessing two normally functioning ears enjoys advantages in excess of the mere ability either to identify sounds or to understand speech. The location of the ears aids him in sensing the direction from which a sound is emanating and its speed and direction if moving—provided too much of it has not been reflected. He finds it quite easy in a crowd to ignore those conversations in which he is disinterested, or he can engage in one conversation while scanning others that are taking place nearby. This is in marked contrast to listening to the mixed sounds that may come forth from a radio broadcast originating in a gathering of people. The loud speaker does not relate the listener to the source, thereby making it difficult to sort the desired sounds from the undesired.

### THE OUTER EAR

The total ear is known for possessing three main divisions the first of which is the outer ear. The *auricle or pinna* (external portion of the outer ear) is a rather inefficient device for intercepting sound waves and directing them into the external auditory canal. The canal passes through cartilage and bone of the head, and contains hair growth, oil glands, and wax glands, which perform a protective function against dust and insects. The outer ear is not subject to many ailments or diseases that terminate in a loss of hearing. It is of course subject to malformation, injury, hardening of the wax in it, or to becoming clogged by the intrusion of some foreign object. However, only a physician should be permitted to remove anything from the canal lest damage be done either to its walls or to the tympanic membrane.

## THE MIDDLE EAR

The tympanic membrane often improperly called the eardrum is the beginning of the middle ear. In a healthy condition it is pearl gray in color, slightly cone-shaped and set at an angle in the canal.

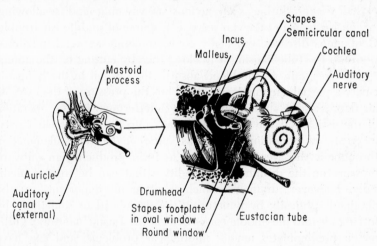

FIG. 7.3  The human ear. The middle and inner ears of the larger scale drawing are turned farther to the left, except for the cochlea, than in the smaller drawing. The cochlea remains in about the same position to show its coils more clearly. From Davis in *Hearing and deafness* by Davis, H., and Silverman, S. R. Copyright © 1960, Holt, Rinehart and Winston, Inc., publishers.

The middle ear is located in the temporal bone in what is known as the tympanic cavity, which as a whole constitutes the eardrum. Thus the tympanic membrane is the drumhead of the tympanic cavity. This membrane is sufficiently flexible to respond to sound waves, but the amplitude of its movements is almost imperceptible. The mechanical operation of the middle ear is supplied through the ossicles—the *malleus, incus,* and *stapes* (hammer, anvil, and stirrup) (Fig. 7.3). They reduce the amplitude through which the tympanic membrane would otherwise vibrate and in some respects increase the force of vibration, thereby improving the transmission of the sound waves. The Eustachian tube which connects the middle ear with the pharynx acts as a means of maintaining equal air pressure on either side of the tympanic membrane and provides drainage and ventilation for the tympanic cavity. The upper portion of the tube is always open whereas the lower portion remains closed except during such actions as yawning and swallowing.

The Eustachian tube can serve as a source of middle ear trouble. Contagious diseases, especially colds, sometimes spread inflammation into the tube causing it to close, thereby cutting off the admission of fresh air. As the blood absorbs the oxygen in the tympanic cavity a partial vacuum is created. Thus the pressure of the external air depresses the drumhead, thereby interfering with the operation of the ossicles. If the infection spreads into the middle ear cavity, it creates a condition known as *otitis media* (an inflammation throughout the area). Pus begins to form producing an outward pressure on the drumhead, a condition that can be treated medically. However, drainage, which is often all important, can be obtained surgically by puncturing the drumhead or sometimes by forcing air into the middle ear cavity via the Eustachian tube. Otitis media predominates among middle ear problems, and can have devastating effects on the ossicles, the drumhead, and the mastoid process. However, the miracle drugs have made mastoiditis and other such after-effects little-known conditions today. Causes of a few other problems of the middle ear include congenital malformations, various types of injuries, and the development of cysts.

Another important cause of middle ear trouble is *otosclerosis.* This hereditary disease is much more common in the white race than in others. Many persons possess it in mild enough form to cause no noticeable loss of hearing. It starts in young people, occurring twice as often in the female, and is characterized by a bony growth particularly below and in front of the oval window

(Scheer, 1960). As the growth proceeds, the action of the stapes is progressively impeded, developing a moderate to severe loss. Even though the loss is a conductive one, an air-conduction hearing aid is of value for some time, but its usefulness decreases as the immobilization of the stapes increases (Davis and Fowler, 1960). The correction of this problem is by surgery.

## THE INNER EAR

The inner ear is by far the most complicated part of the total ear structure. It is located in the temporal bone of the head. Its name, the labyrinth, is derived from its unusual shape consisting of various chambers. At one end are the semicircular canals, at the other end is the cochlea and between them is the vestibule. Within this bony labyrinth are membranous tubes and sacs constituting a membranous labyrinth containing all operating mechanisms, sensory cells, and neural connections. The endolymph, a slightly viscous fluid, fills the remaining spaces in the membranous labyrinth, whereas a somewhat similar fluid, the perilymph, fills the spaces surrounding it. The sensory cells within the *ampula* (enlarged end of each semicircular canal) possesses hairlike extensions the distal ends of which are swayed by the drag or inertia of the endolymph when the head moves. This bending of the hairs seems to stimulate the sensory properties of the cells thereby not only giving us our sense of balance, but automatically contracting the muscles of the eyes, limbs, and trunk in a protective manner against losing it (Brown, 1956). The relative positions of these canals, with each located at approximately right angles to the other two, is an essential feature for covering all directions of movement. The utricle, a membranous sac located in the vestibule near the base of the semicircular canals, contains sensory cells that are stimulated in a slightly modified manner by the pull of gravity and the acceleration or deceleration with which one moves. The bony cochlea contains two large canals, the vestibular and the tympanic, that extend the length of it to join at the apex. Between them is the cochlea canal, separated from the others by Reissner's and the basilar membranes (Fig. 7.4). On the basilar membrane rests the *organ of Corti* (the end organ of the auditory nerve), which extends nearly the full length of the spiral. A sound impulse entering the oval window at the end of the vestibular canal is fluid borne to the round window in the tympanic canal, thereby rocking the organ of Corti located between them. According to Davis (1960, pp. 61–79) this action

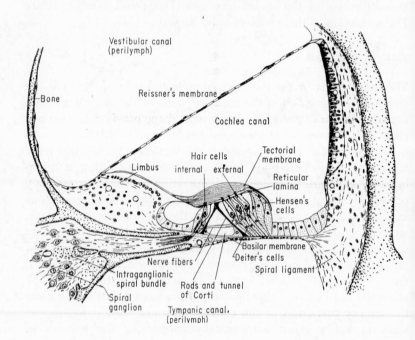

FIG. 7.4 The membranous cochlea canal. Cross-sectional drawing of the cochlea canal (a part of the membranous labyrinth, which is filled with endolymph) in the second turn of a guinea pig's cochlea. The human cochlea is very similar to this. The rods and Deiter's and Hensen's cells are shown as supporting the organ of Corti. The connections made by the nerve fibers leading from the nerve center of the spiral ganglion are shown passing through one of the many tiny holes in the spiral shelf and connecting with the sensory cells somewhat above the basilar membrane. The hairlike extensions of the sensory cells project above the reticular lamina and are imbedded in the tectorial membrane. From Davis in *Hearing And Deafness* by Davis, H., and Silverman, S. R., Copyright © 1960, Holt, Rinehart and Winston, Inc., publishers.

bends the hairlike extensions of the sensory cells, as demonstrated in Fig. 7.5, thus setting up appropriate nerve impulses for transmission to the brain. The tones one hears are determined to some extent by that section of the basilar membrane most activated and

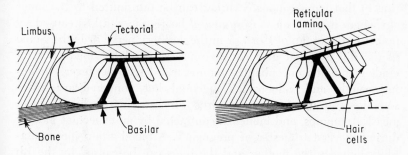

FIG. 7.5 Interaction between tectorial membrane and reticular lamina. At the left the organ of Corti and the tectorial membrane are in the position of rest. Their respective "hinge points" where they attach to the limbus (a tough solid covering of the upper side of the bony shelf) and the bony lamina (plate) are shown by heavy arrows. The more flexible part of the partition (between the organ of Corti and the spiral ligament) at the right has moved "upward." (See Fig. 7.4 for area concerned). Because of its different hinge point the tectorial membrane must slide past the recticular lamina and bend the hairs. From Davis in *Hearing And Deafness* by Davis, H., and Silverman, S. R., Copyright © 1960, Holt, Rinehart and Winston, Inc., publishers.

thus by the particular sensory cells most stimulated. However, there are additional factors that also contribute to our sense of pitch which need not be discussed here. In the process of fluid-borne transmission the membrane that covers the round window bulges into the middle ear cavity, but the normal air pressure there tends to restore it to its usual position as the stapes pressure is released. Sound waves may enter the inner ear by such ways also as the round window or a fenestration (window produced surgically in an ampulla of the semicircular canals) but space will not permit discussion of the necessary conditions involved (Hanckel, 1960).

The inner ear is vulnerable to impairment. The damaging effects of otosclerosis may spread to it. Or complications resulting from otitis media may reach it via the skull from which the cerebrospinal fluid surrounding the brain is in direct contact with the perilymph of the inner ear. As a result any infection or toxic condition occurring in that membranous covering can be transmitted to the inner ear where it creates a *sensory-neural* hearing loss (a loss caused by defect in the organ of Corti or in the auditory nerve or both). Some of the diseases that give rise to sensory-neural hearing losses include meningitis, encephalitis, mumps, measles, scarlet fever, whooping cough, and influenza. Congenital but nonhereditary losses sometimes result from such virus diseases as rubella (German measles), mumps, and influenza contracted by an expectant mother during the first trimester of pregnancy. A blood-group incompatability between the mother and the fetus can be caused by the Rh factor (a blood component). The situation is especially serious if the mother's blood is negative and the child's is positive. Sensory-neural losses result also on occasion from a hereditary trait. In such cases the child may be born with a loss or may lose part or all of his hearing later. In congenital losses, it is sometimes difficult to distinguish the hereditary from the nonhereditary. Newby (1958) states that in event both parents are congenitally deaf the children are also likely to be deaf. Best (1943) states that incidence is not so dependent on whether one or both parents are deaf as upon whether both of them have deaf relatives. Either or both might possess an acquired loss—a loss that could not be transmitted to their children. Or, both parents might have normal hearing, yet possess family histories of hearing impairments, either in direct ascendents or in collateral branches, that would provide a good chance for their children to inherit the tendency. However, according to Best (1943) one of the surest cues on heredity is whether any of the hearing impaired child's siblings also possesses a loss.

Another hearing impairment of several varieties is known as *dysacusis*. Davis and Fowler (1960) point out that it involves a malfunction or injury to the sense organ of the inner ear, the auditory nerve, or the central nervous system, that is not characterized by a loss of auditory sensitivity. A few types include: (1) discrimination failure for words, syllables, or *phonemes* (smallest distinctive group of speech sound, which contrast with one another, such as "bit," "bin," and "pit."); (2) receptive aphasia, known as word deafness, involves difficulties understanding either speech or the printed word although some type of hearing is present; (3) binaural diplacusis involves a sensation of difference in pitch when the same pure tone is presented first to one ear and then to the other; and (4) hysterical deafness that possesses an emotional rather than auditory basis.

Sensory-neural losses of hearing are most likely to originate in the high frequencies, and there is a tendency for conductive losses to be greater in the low frequencies. This difference facilitates the diagnosis of the type of loss. Diagnosis is also facilitated by checking bone conduction against air conduction. A *mixed loss* (both conductive and sensory-neural) shows a less satisfactory bone conduction than a good inner ear would provide. However, further precaution is necessary because a partial immobilization of the stapes could sufficiently dampen the vibration of the fluids of the inner ear to simulate symptoms of a slight sensory-neural loss.

## PERCENTAGES BY CAUSE OF LOSS

Myklebust (1960) indicates that according to reports gathered from schools for the deaf, losses were distributed as follows: 11.3 percent from meningitis, 27.8 percent from other exogenous causes, 22.6 percent from endogenous causes, and 38.3 percent from undetermined origin. These statistics are an example of the inadequacy of our medical histories. Not only is a 38 percent gap too great, but we have no census of the children who possess the less severe and the postlanguage impairments. A significant number of them will have returned to regular classes after a period of special instruction, and certain others may have never attended a special program.

## SUPPLEMENTARY COMMENTS

The prevalence of educationally significant hearing impairments is among the lowest for the exceptionalities. However, the causes of ear diseases and the losses resulting therefrom are varied and complicated. More extensive preventative measures and treatment are indicated. The fact that hazards to the middle ear have been reduced is encouraging. But the fact that unattended problems are a serious threat even to the inner ear gives cause for concern. Any deterioration of either the sensory cells or the nerve fibers constitutes a condition that is beyond either medical intervention or bypassing with a hearing aid.

# Characteristics of the Hearing Impaired

Reference to a few of the effects that a loss of hearing exerts on a child's personal characteristics were enumerated in the opening statement to this chapter. This section will constitute an elaboration and extension of that subject.

## INTELLIGENCE

Pintner, Eisenson, and Stanton (1945) believed that the Binet Scale was unsuited for testing the deaf because of the deaf's language deficiencies. Therefore the results of *nonlanguage* and *performance* tests were investigated. In doing so, they gave greater weight to the nonlanguage test results because that type test had been administered to the widest range of samplings. Some of the tests involved in the survey included the Porteus Maze, the Grace Arthur Performance Test, the Goodenough Draw-a-Man Test, the Ontario School Ability Test, and the Pintner-Patterson NonLanguage Group Test. The *means* and *medians* reported varied from about 86 to 95. The investigators also considered studies that had been made with the Symbol-Digit test (a learning test), the results of which seemed to confirm the conclusions that they had already reached, namely that the deaf possess an *average* IQ of a little less than 90. However it was the opinion of these investigators that there are three kinds of intelligence, *abstract*, *concrete*, and *social*, and that the test results studied were largely measures of concrete intelligence. Their findings included (1) no difference in intelligence on the basis of age at onset, (2) no difference on the average between the congenitally and the adventitiously deaf, (3) a higher average intelligence among day than among residential pupils, (4) very little difference in intelligence between those taught *orally* (by spoken word) and those taught by the *combined method* (spoken word and finger spelling), and (5) a lower average intelligence for those taught by the *manual method* (finger spelling or signing or both). This was considered attributable to the selection of pupils.

Myklebust (1960) bases his discussions concerning the characteristics of the hearing impaired on 20 years of studies. He concurs with Guilford (1959) that there are five types of mental operation namely "*cognition*: ability to recognize and see relationships; *memory*: ability to retain and recall; *convergent thinking*: ability to see the best and logical order in a given sequence; to see relationships of given information; *divergent thinking*: ability to elaborate from given information; trial and error thinking, originality and variety in associations; *evaluation*: judgment of goodness, adequacy, suitability and adaptation of the given and familiar to new and unusual purposes." Myklebust concludes as did Pintner, Eisenson, and Stanton (1945) that deafness affects intelligence more in the verbal and abstract areas than in others. At the same time, Myklebust points out that verbal functions *can be involved* in *any* of the five mental operations but that divergent thinking and evaluation are *particularly affected* because "These functions entail use of experience more broadly, with fluidity, flexibility and generalizing ability playing a significant role."

One purpose in intelligence testing is to obtain a picture of the existing mental capacities of the population as a whole. There is reason to collect the same kind of information about the deaf and the hard of hearing populations. *However, the measure of difference in intelligence between the deaf and the normally hearing and the measure by which deafness adversely affects intelligence are not necessarily one and the same.* If it is accurate to say that the average IQ of the deaf is 90, it does not automatically follow that deafness is the causative factor for the full 10-point difference. A loss of hearing and a reduction in mental capacity may possess a common etiology, such as prenatal diseases of the mother and postnatal diseases of the type and severity that do damage to the central nervous system. In addition, deaf children who incur their losses early show weakness in the verbal aspects of mental operations—an educational rather than an intellectual characteristic. Therefore deafness probably causes less actual reduction in mental capacity than is generally attributed to it

Consideration of most characteristics of the hard of hearing will be presented somewhat more briefly than for the deaf. Their problems are generally less acute, whereas their ability to interpret speech through hearing is a great asset to them. The limited number of studies on their intelligence seem to agree fairly well that on verbal tests they earn a slightly but significantly lower score than is obtained by the normally hearing, whereas on nonlanguage tests they come close to normal. Pintner and Lev (1939) reported that some 1400 hard of hearing children scored a mean IQ of 94.7 on the verbal Pintner Intelligence Test while a control group of normally hearing children scored a mean IQ of 100.6.

## ACHIEVEMENT

Pintner, Eisenson, and Stanton (1945) called attention to the positive correlation between later ages at onset and the development of language, but found no difference between the achievement of children who lost their hearing before two and those who lost it between two and five. Myklebust (1960) indicates that children who lost their hearing at six possibly have more subtle concepts of language than those who lost theirs at two or three years of age. Pintner, Eisenson, and Stanton (1945) judged the deaf as three or four years academically retarded, with the older children being the greatest number of years in arrears. Kirk (1962) estimated the deaf to be two to five years academically retarded, and Meyerson (1955) gave an estimate of three to five years. At the same time Schick (1936) reported two years of academic retardation found in a five-year study of 237 pupils in attendance at the Central Institute for the Deaf of St. Louis, Missouri. To whatever extent there was selectivity in admission procedures, the scores would have been affected accordingly. However if no selectivity was at play, the results were extraordinary.

Achievement has many facets. Johnson (1948) conducted a study to determine the ability of children in a residential school for the deaf to understand various methods of communication. She used pupils from three departments of the Illinois school—manual, oral, and *acoustic* (a department for children who can understand amplified speech). One significant finding was that children in the acoustic department achieved better in school than the other children possessing the same amount of residual hearing and intelligence, and possessing the same age at onset of loss. Additional conclusions were: (1) finger spelling would probably improve the language of the manual group if it replaced signs entirely; (2) *auditory training* (training to use residual hearing as an aid to understanding speech) would improve the scholarship and communication of oral pupils possessing residual hearing; and (3) some finger spelling for certain oral pupils (namely a combined method of instruction) would improve the progress of those whose oral communication aptitudes were weak. The conclusions of this study emphasized the need to keep all communications in English and to develop fully every remnant of residual hearing.

The scholastic problems deaf students encounter limit the number who reach college level. However, a few each year are successful in regular higher education programs, especially if they possess good speech and speechreading skills or are granted concessions in note-taking at class lectures. Most deaf students wishing to attend college, but who need a special education program, enroll in an accredited institution of higher education for the deaf, Gallaudet College of Washington, D.C. A study of the records of applicants (not enrollees) of this college made on the Stanford Achievement Test was conducted by Fusfeld (1954). Most of the applicants were state residential school graduates, many of whose schools had offered no work beyond the tenth grade. However, the average number of years they had spent in school was nearly 13. A close study of Table 7.2 reveals several interesting things, including the fact these students did better in punctuation, capitalization and grammar (labelled as the "language" section of the test) than they did in word and paragraph meaning. In more recent years such applicants have done better, a situation that is probably typical of a general improvement in instruction in all types of schools and classes for the deaf. Better research, teacher education, certification requirements, clinical facilities, and auditory training are some of the reasons why higher achievements should be expected. Studies made at Gallaudet confirm our expectations. Fusfeld (1940) found that the median norm for students accepted by the Gallaudet College preparatory department in 1939 fell within the eleventh

TABLE 7.2  *School grade achievement of applicants to the twelfth grade preparatory class of Gallaudet College as measured on the Stanford Achievement Test.*

| SECTION | $Q_1$ | MEDIAN | $Q_3$ |
|---|---|---|---|
| Language | 9.6 | 11.6 | 12.8 |
| Arithmetic computation | 9.4 | 10.5 | 11.5 |
| Spelling | 9.2 | 10.5 | 11.5 |
| Social studies | 8.3 | 9.9 | 10.7 |
| Arithmetic reasoning | 8.1 | 9.4 | 10.8 |
| Study skills | 6.9 | 8.4 | 10.3 |
| Paragraph meaning | 6.8 | 8.2 | 10.0 |
| Science | 6.4 | 7.7 | 9.4 |
| Word meaning | 5.3 | 6.7 | 9.1 |
| Grade Equivalent for entire test | 8.2 | 9.2 | 10.2 |
| Range of grade equivalents | 4.5+ | to | 12+ |

*Source:* Fusfeld, I. S. A cross-section evaluation of the academic program of schools for the deaf. *Gallaudet College Bull.*, 1954, **3**, No. 1.

grade, compared to a ninth grade level in 1929. Today the level is still within the eleventh grade in spite of a change in the student body. The reduction in acquired deafness through better medication has resulted in a higher percentage of prelanguage deaf students. Yet they enter with as high academic records as former students possessed which, if there have been no special selectivity factors at play, is a tribute to better instruction in their schools.

The achievement of the hard of hearing more nearly approximates that of the normally hearing. However, the hard of hearing fail grades and courses more often and their achievement on verbal tests is slightly lower than standard norms. A report on the vocabulary levels of such children was made by Young and McConnell (1957). They tested 20 hard of hearing children who were enrolled in the regular grades, and who varied between eight and fourteen years of age. Each had developed basic oral language, "however inadequate," without special instruction and possessed a speech-range hearing level of more than 30 db in the better ear, with a mean for the group of 51 db. All had sufficient hearing during their preschool years to learn speech in the normal manner. They were matched with 20 normally hearing children after which both groups were tested with the Ammons Full-Range Picture Vocabulary Test. The results not only indicated a significant difference between the two groups, but no hard of hearing child measured up verbally to his intellectual potential. If the hard of hearing children's school program was as well suited to their needs as the control group's program was suited to theirs, then even marginal and moderate losses of hearing have considerable impact on verbal achievement. It would be interesting though to repeat this piece of research by adding a matched group of children receiving the usual special instruction services.

## ADJUSTMENT

In general the impact of an impairment varies with its severity and the age at onset. A child who incurs a severe loss of hearing after having reached some 12 years of age may suffer real shock from it. He will find it more difficult to make new friends than formerly. His ambitions and concepts of his own role in life may appear destroyed. However, he will possess his speech, which with training can be well preserved. He will possess good functional language —the most essential tool in acquiring an education. He may be able to acquire good speechreading skills and he may possess residual hearing of more or less value for interpreting amplified speech. Thus if he can be taught to assess properly his assets in life and to develop a reasonable degree of tolerance for his disability, his past experience in identifying with his peers should stand him in good stead. However the situation for the prelanguage deaf child is much more difficult. It is true he will have undergone no shock, but neither will he possess language or normal experiences for helping to solve his problems. During his preschool and early school years his most meaningful communication is frequently limited to pointing and pantomime. As a result he lives in psychological isolation with little intellectual identification with others. The long delay entailed in his language development is one of the most serious problems he faces—not only educationally, but in terms of personality, emotional adjustment, and other characteristics.

However Pintner and Brunschwig (1936) found an exception. The deaf children in families possessing no other deaf members showed lower adjustment scores on the Brunschwig Adjustment Inventory than such children from families containing other deaf members. One interpretation of this finding credits the deaf adults with better understanding of the deaf child thereby facilitating his ability to adjust. Another credits the communication outlet of signs as giving the child more opportunity to understand and to relate to his environment—thereby enhancing his adjustment. Myklebust (1960) reports results from the Human Figure Test administered to 830 children in schools for the deaf—511 from residential schools and 319 from day schools. The test consists of drawing a man, father, mother, and self. Awareness of details, perspective, and other features are interpreted as indicative of the child's concepts concerning the subject being drawn. Myklebust's general conclusions are: (1) a hearing loss cannot be considered as a single isolated or unitary factor; its effect is not limited to the function of the ears, but is organismic in nature involving the total person, (2) the deaf as a result of their loss of hearing integrate their experiences in a different manner than the normally hearing, (3) deafness has a negative effect on a person's ability to identify, (4) deaf children are affected by their school environments even though the psychology of deafness may not be reversible, (5) emotional disturbance is not the primary involvement in the deaf, (6) the primary factor resulting from a study of the deaf is the difference in the psychological organization and structure existing between the prelanguage and the postlanguage groups. A few of the specific results from the Human Figure Test were: (1) identification was more disturbed in day pupils than in residential and more in boys than in girls; (2) day pupils showed more emotional stress, conflict, and frustration; (3) residential pupils possessed a more adequately altered psychological structure and organization, but at a lower level; (4) day pupils evidenced more effort to behave normally and demonstrated better concepts of the body image and self perception; and (5) the residential pupils showed less feelings of isolation.

These reports by Pintner and Brunschwig, and Myklebust indicate results that are contrary to the assumptions many of us have long held. However, if the test results were reliable, then we must conclude that insufficient recognition for individual differences has been made in some of our oral-language programs. This is asking children to compensate the hard way for the limits of human competence. When, for any reason, demands on children markedly exceed their capacity, the experience can lead to disturbing problems of self-concept. Many feel either ashamed or inferior for having failed to accomplish what they think was expected of them—a problem that has been forcefully brought to our attention by a number of authorities, including Meyerson (1955). This calls for new evaluations, concepts, and research regarding how better to instruct the deaf.

In the case of the hard of hearing, Pintner (1942) tested the personality traits of approximately 1200 such children against a control group of about 1200 normally hearing children. He used the Aspects of Personality Test to measure ascendance-submission, extroversion-introversion, and emotionality. Full information on hearing levels was not supplied, but no significant differences were found between the two groups in either the ascendance-submission or the extroversion-introversion phases of the test. In the emotionality phase there was a tendency for those with greater losses of hearing to score slightly lower. Levine (1949) made a study of the emotional and mental aspects of the personality of 31 "normal deaf adolescent girls" to determine whether certain specific traits characterized their personalities and if so what they were. She obtained her subjects from an oral residential school and her data through the Rorschach Test, supplemented by school records, interviews with the girls, frequent observation, and teacher reports. The deaf girls according to her findings were: (1) retarded in conceptual forms of mental activity, (2) possessed a lag in meaningful insight into the dynamics of the world about them, (3) evaluated their environment in terms of ego satisfactions, and (4) made withdrawal of affective responsiveness to a narrow or more secure area. It was her conclusion that the girls were not maladjusted or emotionally unstable. She judged that they possessed emotional and conceptual immaturity resulting from deafness-imposed environmental blocks, a condition that she thought possessed the possibility of correction. If her conclusions were sound they constitute as she indicated a challenge to educators of the deaf. A comprehensive report on personalities is made by Myklebust (1960) covering the results of the Minnesota Multiphasic Personality Test administered both to deaf and hard of hearing subjects. The test includes 10 scales—depression, hypochrondriasis, hypomania, hysteria, interest, paranoia, psychasthenia, psychopathic deviation, schizophrenia, and social introversion. The results showed that the hearing impaired possess more emotional problems than the normally hearing. When compared with the opposite sex, the males, among both the deaf and the hard of hearing, exhibit greater emotional problems than their female counterparts. Of the four groups, the hard of hearing females deviate the least from the normally hearing. The greatest maladjustment shown by either the deaf males or by the deaf females was of a psychotic rather than neurotic nature. Likewise the highest maladjustment shown by hard of hearing males was in the same direction, but this was not true of the hard of hearing females. The one scale in which the hard of hearing, both male and female, showed more maladjustment than the deaf was in depression.

## SOCIAL ACCEPTANCE

Elser (1959) conducted a study on the social position of hearing handicapped children in the regular grades. The 45 children concerned were divided into two groups according to selected hearing levels, one of which was 35–49 db and the other 50–80 db. He found that the hearing handicapped as a group were not as well accepted on the basis of personal friendships scores and did not receive as favorable reputation scores. When the data were divided into the several subgroups, the only significant cases were those that involved children having the milder losses and those not wearing hearing aids. Elser speculated that normally hearing peers may be better able to accept those with a noticeable loss of hearing, but fail to understand children with a minor loss who in response to social pressures try to "get by."

The teaching of acceptable social conduct and means of gaining the favor and acceptance of others is not an easy concept to convey to any child. For the prelanguage deaf, it involves abstract considerations for which he is totally unequipped in his younger years. However if he is to be one with whom others can live, certain modes of behavior must be obtained without benefit of appropriate verbal motivation or clear understanding of the reasons for such expectations. Young deaf children may respond without resentment, in fact they may be overly submissive. But the goals they embrace are likely to be goals adults have imposed, and for which they have few convictions. As a result they usually possess less inhibitions and taboos than normally hearing children. However, nearly any group of children can learn to extend "acceptance" beyond their immediate friends of the moment. This involves learning to like others of different intellectual and interest levels and to be tolerant and helpful toward those with special problems. The normally hearing are quick to show patience and empathy once they understand the problems involved. But the hearing impaired also have their responsibilities to exercise—just as rapidly as they can develop understanding of them. A school working toward such environmental goals has a much different impact on the hearing impaired child than one that leaves the development of children's group attitudes and behavior to chance.

## SOCIAL COMPETENCE

Bradway (1937) made a study of the social competence of 92 prelanguage deaf children at the New Jersey School for the Deaf through use of the Vineland Social Maturity Scale. "For all subjects the loss of hearing for the better ear was 65 percent or more." (Under the *point-eight rule* this would equal 65 ÷ 0.8 or a hearing level of 81 db in the speech range). The age varied from 5 to 21. No adequate psychometric data were available, but in the absence of indications to the contrary it was assumed that all had average intelligence. Skill in conventional communication was considered to be an element of social competence. Therefore no allowances were made for deficiencies in that area. The results indicated an average SQ for each age group of about 80. A supplementary study using children who incurred their loss of hearing after five years of age showed no significant difference in SQ. Thus the test indicated no inability of the deaf to acquire social competence—only a lag in its acquisition. Streng and Kirk (1938) reported a study of the social competence of the hearing impaired using children of the Paul Binner Day School of Milwaukee, aged 6 to 18. All were from homes where communication was by speech and only three were from homes in which the speech was non-English. The results indicated an average SQ of 96.2. A low positive correlation existed between SQ's and the IQ's derived from performance and nonverbal tests. There were no significant differences between either the IQ's or the SQ's of the deaf and the hard of hearing. And like the Bradway (1937) study the SQ was not altered by the age at onset of loss. If the children of the New Jersey and the Paul Binner schools can be considered as typical respectively of state residential and oral day schools, and if no other significant variables were operating, then the social maturity of oral day pupils as measured by the Vineland Scale must be considered as significantly higher than that of state residential pupils.

Avery (1948) also used the Vineland Scale to study the social competence of preschool hearing-impaired children. She wondered whether the maladjustments shown in previous studies had resulted from unwise home and school guidance. Data were gathered from mothers and dormitory matrons on 50 children who varied in age from 10 months to 6 years. Most of the children had been enrolled either in "a residential school or day school kindergarten for the deaf from a relatively early age." When the tests were scored according to instructions, these children were found to be normal in social maturity. When credit was allowed for any form of successful communication they scored above normal. Avery attributed the results to these assumptions: (1) the young deaf child is more on his own than the young normally hearing, (2) the nursery program offered opportunity for socialization and self independence, (3) the early medical and educational attention given to the losses, and (4) the possibility that speech and language play a lesser role in the social development of the very young child. However, she pointed out that her findings and conclusions were in conflict with those of Burchard and Myklebust (1942). They had speculated that acoustically handicapped infants are inferior to normally hearing infants in social maturity but gain as they grow older.

It is logical to grant that skills in the conventional means of communication constitute an important aspect of social competence, as judged by Bradway. However the Bradway studies showed no significant differences in the social competences of the prelanguage and postlanguage deaf and the Streng-Kirk studies showed none between the deaf and the hard of hearing. In view of these facts and in view of Avery's findings with children in preschool training, three questions must be asked. Were Avery's findings reliable? If so, to what extent did the other studies measure lack of training as well as a loss of hearing? If one were to establish for the deaf and the hard of hearing equally good training in the social competences, should not the hard of hearing make faster progress? Social competencies must be taught if a child is to possess his share of them. It matters not whether a child is deaf or hard of hearing or whether he lives at home, in a dormitory, or in a boarding home, such competences cannot be acquired in a sociocultural vacuum. Furthermore, the learning difficulties of a prelanguage deaf child are generally considered to require as much of a parent's or a teacher's time as five normally hearing children. Thus, a top-rate program in a residential school requires a well-trained competent residence staff of houseparents, recreation personnel, and others about equal in numbers to the teaching staff. It also requires that such persons not only possess an abundance of facilities both on campus and in the community, but also that they be free of all such time-consuming tasks as cooking, laundering, mending, and taking care of the ill. Their basic job must be to provide for the out-of-class educational, recreational, social, and cultural experiences of the children.

The same requirements are needed at the day-school boarding-home. The fact that the residence is a home for the people who live there makes it no "home" for the hearing-impaired child unless he receives opportunities for the experiences he needs for social growth. No boarding house mother can meet the needs of her own family and of the hearing-impaired child without adequate assistance from some source. The same holds true in the child's own home. Sacrifices must be made in some manner or the final results are likely to be much less than desired.

## COMMENTS

Some interesting and worthwhile research has been performed in the area of the hearing impaired. However, one must agree with Meyerson (1955) that our findings have too often been contaminated by uncontrolled variables. Findings in achievement may at times be more attributable to such variables as the qualifications of teachers, class sizes, clincial services, and instructional facilities than to some special factor under consideration. In the area of emotional stability the problem may be more dependent on the intelligence with which a proper environment is created for a hearing-impaired child than on the direct effects of his loss of hearing. And finally the frustrations and various deprivations that result from deficiencies in language may eventually prove to be even more significant in the development of personality and other characteristics than we have already recognized. However, the encouraging aspect is the fact that many of these adjustment problems seem to be preventable —an opinion shared by Levine (1949), Meyerson (1955), and Myklebust (1960). What we need most in addition to refining our research on the psychological status and behavioral characteristics of the hearing impaired is research designed for finding better psycho-educational approaches for their instruction and better mental health approaches to their school and home environments. If we can make marked improvements in the instruction of children with impaired hearing and establish home and school environments better suited to their needs, it is possible that many of their deviant characteristics which we now try to measure will be greatly reduced.

# Education

Educational methods for instructing the hearing impaired were transplanted to the United States and Canada from Europe. Thomas Hopkins Gallaudet was sent overseas by interested United States citizens to study the oral methods used in England. However operators of the English schools seem to have had trade secrets they were unwilling to share. As a result Gallaudet proceeded to France where he learned the manual method. The American School of West Hartford, Conn., established in 1817, was the first permanent public school for the deaf developed in the United States. The first permanent Canadian school, the Institution Catholique des Sourds-Muets for boys, was established in Montreal in 1848.

## TYPES OF SCHOOLS

All of the early regional and state schools that followed the American were residential. They were intended for the deaf, but inasmuch as no special programs existed for the hard of hearing, many such children were also enrolled. The manual program in use was ill suited to their needs, but it was the only education opportunity available to them. About 50 years later permanent private oral residential schools were established, some of which have since become state supported. In the latter part of the last century the day center movement under the leadership of Alexander Graham Bell gained momentum. Today a majority of the hard of hearing pupils are enrolled in the public day centers whereas a majority of the deaf are in the public residential centers. (see Fig. 1.1) Certain public residential schools assist the day centers by accepting transfers of deaf pupils who possess inadequate aptitudes for oral instruction. At the same time the residential schools have become more oral in nature and both types of schools now make wide use of the hearing aid for maximum instruction through hearing. As a result, one can find any type of public residential school, from the strictly oral to those that emphasized the use of the *simultaneous method* (signs, finger spelling, and speech). In addition modern transportation has brought the homes of residential children relatively "closer" to the school. This makes it possible for a larger percentage of such pupils to reside full time at home and for many others to return to their homes on weekends. At the same time, present-day transportation has made possible the establishment of day centers covering larger geographical areas, some of whose pupils reside in boarding homes from Monday to Friday each week.

Also in recent years the residential schools have become more an integral part of the public school system, legally and professionally. The trend has been conducive to the development of various cooperative arrangements between residential and the day centers. The State of Ohio operates a joint clinic to which any hearing-impaired child is referred for all essential examinations before placement. Placement is then made by a joint committee, whose decision is based on consideration of the child's needs and the parents' wishes.[4] Texas has a different cooperative plan. Its admission policies require deaf children, 6–13 years of age, residing in the five most populous counties to attend their respective county-wide special programs. The parents of a student 14–21 years of age may elect for him to remain in the county program or transfer to the Texas School for the Deaf.[5] Unique relationships exist also between the residential schools and the regular schools. The Michigan School for the Deaf sponsors six-week rehabilitation programs for the hard of hearing children of the state for whom no local facilities are available (Poulos, 1961). Children are selected whose hearing impairments are great enough to cause unsatisfactory regular school progress but not great enough to justify enrollment in a regular special-class program. Also each child must be able to profit from an individual hearing aid. Following the usual examinations, he is fitted with an aid, instructed in its use and care, and enrolled for the short-term special instruction. The program in operation since 1950 has averaged 38 such pupils annually. An opinion-questionnaire survey indicated that 75 percent of the efforts are successful.

## HIGHER EDUCATION

Gallaudet College, which offers B.A. and B.S. degrees and an M.S. in Ed., has for years provided the only special program in higher education for deaf youth. However, Riverside City College, California, is now offering deaf students a two-year terminal program with a vocational emphasis, but which includes classes in English, psychology, history, science, and health. Plans are well under way to establish a four-year St. Joseph College for the Deaf at Buffalo, N.Y., in about 1966, as the first such Catholic institution. Courses will be offered in art, business, homemaking, and physical education.

---

[4] The statement represents a digest of the Ohio State Board of Education's policies governing admissions to the Ohio School for the Deaf, released December 6, 1960 by E. E. Holt, superintendent of public instruction.

[5] Digest of a personal communication, June 6, 1962, from Chas. S. Eskridge, assistant commissioner for vocational rehabilitation and special education, Texas Education Agency.

## PARENT EDUCATION

The special learning problems that befall the hearing impaired call for as great a reduction in their early deprivation of opportunities as possible. The normally hearing child has the advantage of about five years of learning experiences under the guidance of his parents before he enters kindergarten. However, many parents confronted with the rearing of a child possessing a severe hearing impairment are overwhelmed for lack of understanding concerning what they can and should do. They know that a normally hearing child learns to communicate, play games, and participate on his level in family activities—physically, mentally, and socially. But they do not always understand the importance of this or how they can start their hearing-impaired child toward similar goals. However, to hold a child's social and educational development in near-total suspension pending special-school enrollment at five or six is a tragic waste of precious years. It is therefore important to make "education" of the hearing-impaired child's parents one of the first steps toward his education. The John Tracy Clinic offers two means of promoting parent education—one through a correspondence course and the other through films. The Alexander Graham Bell Association for the Deaf and the Conference of Executives of American Schools for the Deaf issue kits of literature dealing with the problems and needs of deaf children. The American Hearing Society through its local chapters offers services for parents of hard of hearing children. (See the Resources, at the end of this chapter for permanent offices of the JTC, AGBAD, and AHS, and for the editorial office of the CEASD.) Also a few residential and day centers conduct parent-education programs. A day center may hold one or two meetings with a group of parents per month, whereas the residential school is more likely to concentrate its program into a full-time project for one or two weeks. Under either program it is usually the mother who is able to attend. And as a rule her needs are better served if her child can be in a nursery-school program at the same time. While the children are occupied, the group of mothers listen to lectures by otologists, educators, rehabilitation workers, and others. They observe the progress of the children in nursery school, study the methods used by the teachers, observe older children in class, view special movies on the subject, study pertinent aspects of child growth and development as related to the hearing-impaired child, and hold open discussions. Such a limited number of sessions are of course inadequate for covering all that a mother needs to learn on the subject. However she does acquire some basic information about the education of the hearing impaired, learns where the sources of additional help are located, and gains a new and more realistic outlook regarding her child's future. As a result, some schools consider their parent education program to be one of their most fruitful endeavors.

## PRESCHOOL EDUCATION

In addition to short-term nursery schools more than 3300 United States hearing-impaired children under six years of age were enrolled full-time in day and residential centers in 1961–1962 (Conference of Executives of American Schools for the Deaf, 1962). The average enrollment age varies from 4.5 for public residential schools to 2.5 in denominational and private day centers. A number of day centers—demominational, private and public—accept children as young as one year of age. Many people might ask whether young children in preschool residence suffer by separation from home for five or more days at a time. The lack of research to indicate that the deaf child possesses the same emotional ties with his family that young normally hearing children possess and the evidence of nursery school benefits found by Avery (1948) would seem to indicate that a good preschool program is worth a trial whether residential or day.

The item of immediate priority in a nursery program is to evaluate the loss of hearing of each pupil. Children are admitted on the basis of audiometric and other minimum preenrollment examinations. The results are then used, both in education planning and in the medical study of those possessing correctable conditions. The program for these young children is conducted for relatively short segments of the day. It involves play and rest as well as sensory training, socialization, orientation to amplified sound, and beginning efforts in communication. All of this is very good because it represents decided progress over our efforts some years ago for such young children. However, our inability to fill the language gap adequately still leaves us with a major problem. For example, we know that the normally hearing child's readiness for reading depends in no small degree on the richness of his personal experiences. To the extent such experiences are missing, his conversations and reading tend to be verbalizations. But to provide the hearing-impaired child with a *rich* experience before he possesses sufficient receptive language through which to learn how to interpret that experience is a real problem.

Myklebust (1960) points out that the child must understand meaning before he can give expression. And he seems to say that educators of the deaf may place too much emphasis on speech before the child's receptive or inner language has been developed. He concedes that the deaf could do better using a visual symbol system, but rules out that possibility because he considers preschool deaf children too immature. He then concludes that "if speech-reading were taught as the basic language the deaf would learn to comprehend the spoken word through this means, and it would constitute his basic inner language symbol system." Such a suggestion if possible of accomplishment would go far toward removing the educational handicaps caused by deafness. Certainly the idea is worthy of our best research efforts to determine the potentials involved. However, there is a major problem associated with it. Many well-educated adults who lose their hearing cannot learn to recognize on the lips a language they have used all their lives. This fact is not a good recommendation for speech reading as the medium in which to limit language instruction to preschool children.

Signing is the easiest means of communication for the deaf. To a degree it is pantomime. Quite often a sign is suggestive of the word or idea it symbolizes (Higgins, 1959). According to Taylor (1937), a former head of an oral program, many deaf children of intelligent deaf parents entered his school "with a mental development far greater than that of other deaf children of approximately equal ability." He wondered whether such children would not have been even more ready for school had their parents taught them finger spelling instead of signs. Some deaf parents have done this, the most notable case probably being the teaching accomplishments by the parents of Hofsteater (1959). All of his instruction was received at home in finger spelling until he was nine. He then finished the twelfth grade of the Alabama School for the Deaf in five and one half years, entered Gallaudet College at less than 15 and has since done graduate work at the University of Illinois. His mastery of English would do credit to a normally hearing college graduate. Another unusual instance was that of an older deaf girl who was taught language through handwriting by her stepmother, apparently with equal success. The story of this case appears as an autobiography by Helen Heckman (1928). Either of these cases is an example of unusual success under tutorial conditions. A case of highly successful group instruction using the printed word will be discussed later in this chapter. The point to be made here is the fact that in each instance cited, including that of group instruction, *the one common denominator among the various media used was a comprehensive and simultaneous dramatization or illustration of the language presented or both—the same method whereby normally hearing children acquire language.* The normally hearing do not learn language by merely hearing it. One could listen to transcriptions of foreign-language records indefinitely without learning the meaning of a single word. Neither does one learn language by merely reading it. No one reads a language he does not understand.

The normally hearing child learns his language through seeing it dramatized by others either while they are playing with him or providing for his wants. We ask if he wishes his bottle when we give it to him; we show him various objects and tell him what they are; or we count his fingers and toes as we point to them one by one. By somewhat similar dramatization we teach him to understand abstract concepts through providing a multitude of concrete situations from which he can generalize. There are innumerable situations in which he or someone else is complimented as *being good,* in which a food is said to *taste good,* or in which a toy or some other product is said to be of *good material.* Thus he gains an understanding of the abstract concept of *good* and its many applications. Also he is fortunate enough to be immersed in a language environment that gives him the essential repetitions for fixing his understanding of auditory symbols of spoken language—both the concrete and the abstract. The deaf preschool child on the contrary lives in an environment of receptive-language deprivation. Unlike the normally hearing, he must always be in a favorable position to "receive" speech. In addition he must use the single sense of sight to receive both the language and its dramatization. And finally, the choice of the most effective visual-language medium with which to initiate the child's education must be made with some uncertainty as to what is best. Speech reading, the most desirable medium, is the weakest as previously pointed out. And there has long been a question regarding the age at which a child can begin to learn language in printed, written, or finger spelled symbols. Hofsteater's parents began to use finger spelling with him when he was still a baby in the crib. And according to the records he soon began to respond in abbreviated fashion by finger spelling one or two letters to represent a word. Thus our concepts as to the age children are able to use such visual symbols of English may be in need of revision. In addition we have been told for many years that a preschool child's eyes are not adequately developed for such fine discrimination and close work as reading the printed page. Yet it is known that many children do read early with ease, especially large type at a distance. Therefore some careful research performed in conjunction with the medical profession is desirable to determine at what age and under what conditions deaf children can be safely introduced to the printed word.

## LANGUAGE INSTRUCTION

The language background of a hearing-impaired child upon his entrance to school will depend largely on the severity and nature of his loss, the time at onset, his intellectual ability, and his preschool training. As a result he may possess any language level from a good foundation to one so devoid that he does not know he has a name. In contrast the normally hearing child at six years of age possesses a vocabulary according to Olson (1949) of several thousand words (see Table 6.1). The findings vary because researchers using quite different designs have attained equally different results. However, regardless of who is right, the language gulf between the normally hearing and the prelanguage deaf is huge, necessitating quite unlike types of early academic programs. For example when the normally hearing child is introduced to the printed word it is primarily for the purpose of teaching him to interpret visual language symbols in terms of the auditory language symbols he

TABLE 7.3 *Oral communication performance levels and needs in relation to a loss of hearing acquired before language.*

| LEVEL | SYMPTOMS | TREATMENT |
|---|---|---|
| | *Effect of a loss of hearing on language development, interpretation of speech, and speech development.* | *Special facilities, adjustments, and services needed.* |
| MILD, 20–30 DB | Will be unable to hear faint or distant speech clearly. Will probably adjust satisfactorily to school situations. Will have no defective speech resulting from loss of hearing. | Speech reading. Individual hearing aid—for selected primary children with hearing levels approaching 30 db. Help in vocabulary development. Preferential seating. |
| MARGINAL, 30–40 DB | Will be able to understand conversational speech at a distance of three to five feet without much difficulty. Will probably miss as much as 50 percent of class discussions if voices are faint or if face is not visible. May have defective speech if loss is of high-frequency type. May have limited vocabulary. | Speech reading. Individual hearing aid if prescribed. Training of hearing. Speech training if necessary. Help in vocabulary development. Preferential seating or, for selected children, special class placements. |
| MODERATE, 40–60 DB | Conversational speech must be loud to be understood. Will have considerable difficulty in following classroom discussions. May exhibit deviations in articulation and quality of voice. May misunderstand directions at times. May have limited language, with vocabulary and usage affected. | Speech reading. Individual hearing aid, if prescribed. Auditory training. Use of group hearing aid for those with hearing levels approaching 60 db. Speech training. Special help in language arts. Preferential seating and/or special class placement for elementary pupils with hearing levels approaching 60 db. |

TABLE 7.3 *Oral communication performance levels and needs in relation to a loss of hearing acquired before language. (continued)*

| LEVEL | SYMPTOMS | TREATMENT |
|-------|----------|-----------|
| | *Effect of a loss of hearing on language development, interpretation of speech, and speech development.* | *Special facilities, adjustments, and services needed.* |
| SEVERE, 60–80 DB | May hear loud voice at one foot from ear and moderate voice several inches from ear. Will be able to hear loud noises, such as sirens and airplanes. Speech and language are not learned normally without early amplification. May be able to distinguish vowels but not all consonants even at close range. | Speech reading. Individual hearing aid, if prescribed, and training on group aid. Integration of language and speech program by special teachers. Special class placement at elementary level except for few pupils selected for placement in regular classes. Regular classes for those high school students achieving exceptionally well in communication skills. Vocational guidance, and vocational education for most. |
| PROFOUND, 80 + DB | May be able to hear a loud shout about one inch from ear, or may be unable to hear anything. Not aware of loud noises. Speech and language do not develop. | Speech reading. Training on group aid, any remnant of hearing. Use of individual aid elective. Special techniques required to develop language and speech. Special class or school for elementary children. Regular class for those high school students achieving exceptionally well in communication skills. Vocational guidance and education. |

*Source:* Streng, Alice. *Children with impaired hearing.* Washington, D.C.: Council for Except. Child., 1960.

already understands. But when a child with a very severe pre-language hearing impairment is introduced to such symbols it is for the purpose of using them as a language teaching medium.

Streng (1960) presented a picture of the oral communication capabilities and needs of hearing impaired children based on hearing levels incurred prior to the acquisition of language. The accompanying Table 7.3 is a slightly reworded version of her presentation. A study of it reveals clearly the gradated continuum of hearing levels among those possessing such impairments—including the growing loss in their oral capabilities and the gradual increase in their special needs as the loss of hearing becomes greater. At the same time Streng calls attention to the fact that dividing children into specific groups is bound to be arbitrary. However, her classifications are nonetheless helpful: (1) they are indicative of the range of performance within which specific groups of hearing-impaired children are most likely to fall, (2) they show the relationship between needs and performance levels, and (3) they reveal the great range of special provisions that are essential in an oral program.

English is one of the more difficult languages to learn, because of its irregular construction, its nonphonetic spelling, its many words with multiple meanings, and the unique use we make of words regardless of their conventional meanings. Consequently before the deaf child gets a given connotation of a word fixed he encounters it in quite a different setting. This is especially confusing in the case of words with the more abstract or subtle meanings. As a result about 50 percent of a prelanguage deaf child's vocabulary is composed of nouns, with most of the balance divided between verbs and adjectives. Words which in certain uses are classified as structure words (Roberts, 1956, 1958) deserve special comment. Although limited to about 200 in number they constitute one third of our daily output. They include prepositions; conjunctions; auxiliary verbs—"are," "will be," "have been"; determiners—"my," "every," "a"; intensifiers—"pretty," "most," "somewhat"; and other structure groups. However, these highly important words are among those with which the deaf child encounters his most trouble, and for good reason. For example the word "for" possesses about 30 different meanings. The words "so" and "up" possess less meanings, but either can be used not only as an adverb and a noun, "so" can assume the role of a conjunction, a pronoun, and an interjection, and "up" can be used as a preposition, an adjective, and a verb. Thus, between these two words, we find them employed in all eight principal parts of speech.

Selected examples of unique uses that English makes of words include such expressions as (1) "the boy walks back and forth to school." It would be more logical to the child with a serious pre-language impairment to say that the boy walks "forth and back from school." (2) "How do you do?" is an idiomatic expression in which the greeter is not inquiring how anything is done. In addition the first "do" has no real meaning; it is a structure word that merely indicates a question is coming. (3) "There were a thousand people there" is a sentence in which the first "there" is another structure word that permits the verb and subject to be transposed without changing the meaning of the sentence. And (4) "The beautiful lady dropped her eyes to the floor" is a type of metaphor that can convey the concept of a weird and shocking tragedy.

As a means of overcoming these language problems Smith (1916) developed a list of idioms and unusual expressions for class use. Others developed grammatical approaches to language instruction, one of the more recent of which, known as the Fitzgerald Key, was first published in 1926 by Fitzgerald (1949). She developed several so-called plates or charts bearing her outline of guide words and symbols. In the early lessons the guide words *"whose," "who,"* and *"what"* help the child to identify and fill in the subject. A symbol then indicates where to place the verb, which is followed by the guide words *"what"* and *"whom"* to lead the child to identify and fill in the object if one exists. This and other plates provide also for more complicated sentences. The Fitzgerald system gained favor among some because of its flexibility and the fact that it is intended to supplement rather than replace the natural method of language instruction. One of the prominent exponents of the natural method has been Groht (1958) who somewhat deplores the introduction of the grammatical or analytical method. Her plan calls for very little teaching of language as such, but rather for the use of the children's interests and needs as focal points around which to utilize language.

However we have not solved the problem yet. So long as children with serious losses of hearing come to school with little or no language, the most promising classroom approach would seem to be through expansion and refinement of the method used by Thompson (1927). Her undertaking was part of a research project in which she employed two matched groups whose average age was 6 years 10 months and whose average schooling was nearly one and a half years in an oral school for the deaf. Both groups were continued under the conventional methods of instruction, except for one hour per day during which members of the experimental group were withdrawn for special instruction. They used some 40 profusely illustrated mimeographed booklets which: (1) illustrated the structure words in numerous abstract situations, as well as words representing objects and action; (2) involved the children in meaningful activity in connection with the lessons; and (3) provided abundant opportunities for individualized work and needed repetition.

TABLE 7.4 *Reading scores of experimental and control groups of young deaf compared with standard scores of normally hearing.*

| | READING TEST SCORES | | | |
|---|---|---|---|---|
| GROUP OF CHILDREN | Detroit Reading Test | Gates Word Recognition | Gates Phrase and Sentence | Gates Reading of Directions |
| Control | 6.5 | 13.7 | 11.1 | 0.3 |
| Experimental | 19.9 | 23.4 | 18.5 | 5.4 |
| Normally hearing end of grade one | 20.0 | 21.2 | 18.0 | 5.7 |

*Source:* Thompson, Helen. An experimental study of the beginning reading of deaf mutes. *Teach. Coll.* (Columbia Univer.) *Contr. Educ.*, 1927, No. 254.

At the end of eight months a series of tests was administered to the two groups. Omitting the subjective and less relevant, the results from the four most pertinent tests are shown in Table 7.4. These were not treated statistically because of the limited number of pupils. The experimental group exceeded the standard norm on two of these and fell slightly below on two, while dramatically exceeding the control group on all four. However, in studying the scores two important things should be remembered. First, the standard scores represented the normally hearing children's reading language skills, not their receptive auditory language skills, which perhaps were 10 times as great. Second the experimental group's scores represented their highest receptive language skills of any kind. These facts though do not diminish the spectacular nature of the group's achievement.

Expansion and refinement of the Thompson approach should involve research designed to explore the usefulness and development of a number of promising features. There is need: (1) to prepare a vocabulary that will employ no word in more than one connotation until after it becomes a part of the child's inner language, and that will place emphasis on the type of words most needed for understanding language; (2) to rewrite and develop subject-matter materials in the new vocabulary; (3) to develop special captioned sound films to dramatize language—thus helping the child to distinguish statements, questions, and requests from one another, to understand tense, and to accomplish other special purposes; (4) to develop sound projection equipment, with individual headphones, designed for a flexible multisensory approach to language—with a sound cutoff, a caption cutoff (for screening out captions) and a tactile plate (for providing a sense of the rhythm of speech)—all arranged to permit optional use in any combination desired with the pictured dramatization and visible speech; and (5) to prepare programmed-instruction materials for use at as early an age level as the children can successfully manage this type of approach.

Such a supply of equipment and materials would not necessarily create a major revision in any school's method of instruction. It would merely provide teachers with a large increase in the number of materials for the dramatization they have always improvised as well as their time and facilities would permit. Second, although all materials would be prepared in the special vocabulary for faster learning, these could be supplemented or modified at will. Third, the plan would provide much more repetition, drill, and independent study, thereby hastening the firm establishment of language concepts.

The number of media in which beginning language should be

simultaneously introduced is perhaps a matter for suspended judgment. Would learning be faster if the multisensory approach—visual, tactual (and auditory for those with residual hearing)—were delayed for any given word until it has become a part of the inner language chosen for the child? Or would he make faster progress and select his own inner language if his education is started with the multisensory approach? A normally hearing child's inner language is auditory. When he begins his first reading he therefore wants to read aloud because he understands better in that medium. This is quite in contrast to the diverse preferences shown by the hearing impaired for the different inner language media available to them. The author of this chapter once heard Helen Keller express a strong preference for reading finger spelling that was spelled into her hand rather than to read speech tactually from the face of the person with whom she was communicating—saying that finger spelling was her mother tongue. Such an inner language consists of the tactual images of finger spelling. Certain other types of inner language detected among deaf and severely hard of hearing children include: (1) vocally kinesthetic images (images derived from the sensation of throat muscle movements) in which a very young child showed no evidence of understanding speech-read instructions until he had vocalized them, (2) manually kinesthetic images in which a child would finger spell—without looking at his hand—any unfamiliar word encountered in reading, and (3) visual speech read images in which a child would use a mirror to speech read from his own lips as he tried to pronounce an unfamiliar word. The profession needs some answers from research regarding the implications of a mother tongue, the strongest medium in which to develop it, the sequence and timing for development of language in other media, and the useful differences in children's aptitudes for the different language media.

## HEARING AIDS

Through the years persons with a loss of hearing have used various devices for directing more sound into the ear. Streng et al. (1958) presents a digest of the evolution in aids. Cupping a hand behind the auricle or using a megaphonelike instrument or "horn" proved to be of some help. However, the introduction of the electric hearing aid provided a much more effective piece of equipment and one that brought speech to persons with a greater loss than it was previously possible to overcome. As the science of electronics grew, hearing aids amplified sound with greater fidelity and intensity and became lighter in weight. At the present time the small transistorized wearable aid can produce enough intensity to reach the threshold of discomfort. According to Silverman, Taylor, and Davis (1960), the gain obtainable for speech is about 45 db, at 1000 cps, when measured as the difference in an individual's theshold for speech with and without his hearing aid. Early efforts to amplify speech for the child in the classroom were made with such instruments as Goldstein's simplex hearing tube. It was a device that could be home made, fashioned of rubber tubing somewhat in the style of a physician's stethoscope with a funnel-shaped mouth piece into which to direct speech to the child. However most of today's schools for the hearing impaired are equipped with group hearing aids that will accommodate about 10 children. One modern group hearing aid uses concealed wiring and jack-equipped headphones which permits the child to make connections at his desk, study table, or blackboard. This provides freedom of movement with only limited interruption in sound reception. A second type permits the child to use his individual hearing aid also as a group aid. The room "broadcasting equipment" provides electromagnetic sound waves emanating from a loop of wire strung a few feet from the walls, parallel to ceiling and near enough to it to be clear of classroom activities. By switching his microphone from conventional to special pickup, he tunes into the group aid with a freedom of movement that at no time interrupts reception. Individual binaural aids are now available, but of course not for integration with a group aid facility. When worn with the microphones at the sides of the head each amplifying for the ear to which it is adjacent, indentification with the sound environment is more nearly normal. However, the limitations of these or any other hearing aid should not be overlooked. A pair of glasses can improve vision by refraction of light for many whose eyes produce a blurred or distorted image. However, a hearing aid cannot bring speech into "focus" that imperfect ears distort; it can only amplify what it receives. In addition there are the problems of becoming accustomed to an aid, particularly if the loss of hearing is great. The range between the threshold of audibility for the person with a severe loss and the threshold of discomfort may be very narrow. Thus the amplification of some frequencies can create discomfort before others are loud enough to be heard. To correct this may result in some distortion of the speech received. In addition high amplification of sound calls for a snugly fitting earpiece. Any leakage of sound around the earpiece is likely to be picked up as feedback by the microphone and amplified, resulting in a squeal. Another limitation of the hearing aid is related to the type of impairment. Losses involving a deterioration of the sensory cells or of the auditory nerve or any impairment not representing a loss of sensitivity cannot be reduced by use of a hearing aid. Thus the aid with all its assets has many limitations for its task of improving the hearing impaired's ability to interpret speech.

## AUDITORY TRAINING

Every hearing-impaired child should be taught to make as much use of his residual hearing as possible—and at an early date. Johnson (1948) found that the hard of hearing children with the least experience in the use of hearing and speech were the most retarded in reading. Large amounts of residual hearing appeared to be of no real value to them for interpreting speech unless they had been given the proper auditory experience backgrounds. Hudgins (1953) conducted an experiment with a small group of children averaging 11 years and 11 months of age. He gave them the advantage of a special powerful group hearing aid possessing *compression amplification* (amplification that automatically controls its own maximum intensity, a feature that also helps reduce distortion) and a filter that attenuated the frequencies below 500 cps. In addition he placed the group in an acoustically treated classroom. The control group was taught by similar methods in an untreated room and with the type hearing aid manufactured before 1948. After two years the experimental group showed significantly greater gains in the intelligibility of their own speech.

These results are encouraging and important as an indication of what can be accomplished if the auditory program is both a good one and timely. The problem of introducing a child to speech who has a serious prelanguage impairment is affected both by the degree of his loss and his present age. The longer he has lived without having used his hearing and the more he has learned to depend on other media of communication, whatever they may be, the more effort is required to initiate an auditory training program. Sound is a strange experience to some of these children with the result that they must be taught sound discrimination. For this reason teachers use a gradual procedure, beginning with an orientation to gross sounds and hopefully terminating eventually with an acquired discrimination between the similar sounds of speech. For example, in the nursery schools for very young children, different types of noise makers may be used to advantage in play with them. For older children, simple percussion instruments, including cymbals, triangles, drums and tambourines are often used in group activities. After the child has become oriented to sound and can distinguish between the different ones produced by these and other devices he is introduced to unlike sounds of speech. Teachers who use the natural method for language instruction are likely to start with whole words or short sentences rather than with the strong vowel sounds, syllables, or other unmeaningful speech. As soon as the child is able readily to distinguish the differences among the unlike sounds of speech, effort is made to teach him to distinguish like-sounding words from one another. This final step is the ultimate test of his ability to acquire adequate skill for an accurate understanding of speech.

According to Table 7.3 auditory training is a probable necessity for any child possessing a hearing level of 30 db or more. However, for a marginal hearing level of 40 db or less the amount of training is likely to be very limited, especially if the loss of hearing is rather uniform for all frequencies. Such a child will possess good residual hearing throughout the speech range on which to build any needed improvements. However, the child whose associates cannot comprehend why he does not "understand" in view of the fact that he "hears" when spoken to may present a more difficult teaching problem. He possibly has very inadequate hearing in the high frequencies but fairly good in the middle and low ones. As a result he will experience difficulty learning to identify the weak speech sounds from among the strong ones that he easily hears. If he is to understand oral communication, it probably will be necessary for him to depend on speech reading skills to help fill in the gaps in his auditory reception. Auditory training naturally becomes progressively more urgent and time-consuming as the hearing level becomes worse. However, a hearing aid greatly facilitates the solution for many children, although their introduction to more sounds than those to which they have been accustomed can be disturbing to them. Even the chirping of birds in a tree outside the classroom window may be distracting. Thus it is always desirable, particularly with a very young child, to limit his first use of an aid to brief periods filled with as meaningful experience as possible. For the child with a very severe loss where the range between the threshold of audibility and the threshold of discomfort is narrow, unusual care is needed lest he be frightened or hurt. Some will possess less tolerance for sound at first than others, and therefore be in special need of a gradual approach. In addition, the children's attitudes toward wearing an aid can be conditioned by the school's ability to establish good rapport with them and gain their confidence and interest. If their experiences with aids are relatively pleasant, if the vast majority receive benefits which in the course of time become very obvious to them, if they are taught how properly to take care of their aids, and if there are adequate checkups to assure that the aids are always functioning at maximum efficiency, then to wear a hearing aid in such a school can become the proper if not indeed the popular thing to do.

## SPEECH READING

Ability by the hearing impaired to speech read and speak are skills second in importance only to language and an education. However, as indicated by Pauls (1960) "only about a third of speech sounds are clearly visible." Speech is a very rapid and transitory medium of communication. Lip movements although important are only a part of the operations involved in speech production. The movements of the *velum* (soft palate) are never seen, and the significant positions of the tongue and teeth are only occasionally seen. Thus the speech reader is provided with limited cues for his task of understanding the spoken word. Nitchie (1950) cites some of the things a child must be taught to observe in speech reading. The shapes of the lips are different for different sounds. The space between them may be wide, medium or narrow. They may be extended, relaxed, or puckered. Or they may move to a closed position as in making the sound of "m" in "mama" and open for making "v" in "van." Certain sounds visibly involve the teeth and tongue as "t" in "tail." Some sounds are called *explosive* or *plosive* because of the suddenness with which the lips are parted at the moment a small burst of breath is emitted as for "b" in "ball." There are also the *diphthongs* (composed of two vowels blended), double and triple consonants, and homophonous words (those that look alike on the lips) such as "black," "blank," "plank," and "plaque." These are but a few of the problems in speech reading. Bunger (1952) points out that the speech reader has no control over the kinds of lips he must try to read. There are thin and thick ones; there are those that are only slightly mobile and those with exaggerated movements. And finally there are problems in the quality of the lighting, its orientation to the speaker, and the distance at which the speaker is located. She also emphasizes the necessity for the speech reader to be alert but relaxed and self confident. Speech reading can be a tension-producing experience, especially when no help is obtained through hearing. The person must fill the gaps between the sounds he recognizes, by doing some educated guessing based on the general context of the discussion. In fact, speech reading is more an art of getting the idea without necessarily deciphering each word. A relaxed attitude can help in this process. Pauls (1960) suggests that the speech reader associate his own kinesthetic images of the throat and mouth movements necessary to produce what he sees on the speaker's lips. It would be interesting to know whether any group possessing a hearing loss—the prelanguage deaf, the postlanguage deaf, the hard of hearing—would show a markedly greater aptitude for this skill than the others, and what association, if any, exists between such a skill and a person's inner language.

The hard of hearing person with a good hearing aid has the advantage of a two-sensory means for interpreting speech. Usually these media complement one another very well; what is missed in one is caught in the other. In addition the hard of hearing and the postlanguage deaf have a learning advantage for speech reading. They possess a better concept of what they are looking for and can compare with more assurance what they see on the lips of others with their visual images of what they have observed on their own. In contrast the prelanguage deaf must yet develop speech. Therefore they must begin their speech reading with the basic speech movements.

Important as speech reading is to any hearing-impaired child, it presents the profession with a dilemma, particularly in the case of certain prelanguage deaf. The well-known research of Heider and Heider (1940) using 86 children aged 7 to 17 of the Clarke School for the Deaf reveals some disturbing findings. Employing motion-picture tests over a five-year period, they found among other things that: (1) the rank order in speech-reading skills among the children changed very little with time, (2) progress from year to year was small, and (3) most important, the individual differences in speech reading skills could not be attributed to the length of training. If these findings are reliable, then they possess significant implications. In the cases of successful achievement in speech reading, the educator's task usually presents few serious problems. But in the unsuccessful cases particularly among the deaf, he has some important decisions to make. No child should be kept on a treadmill that is going nowhere. Every effort should be put forth to provide motivation of various kinds, including that in which he obtains for himself some immediate practical advantages by recognizing what he sees on the lips. At the same time, an analysis of the sounds the child recognizes and those he misses should be made. And all known means of instruction and practice should be used to correct shortcomings. However, if the above provides nothing but frustration and diminishing returns of little value, a minimum oral program should be established that will preserve what speech reading skills the child has, and his education should be pursued through the media of such language symbols as the printed and the handwritten word and finger spelling. At the same time the profession should conduct some new extensive research in a further analysis of the general problems involved in speech reading.

## SPEECH

The production of speech is a complicated process. (See chapter 6). The normally hearing infant derives pleasure in listening to himself babble and in experimenting with variations of pitch, intensity, and quality of vocal sounds. When he acquires an understanding of a word of importance to him he tries to reproduce it. However, the five- or six-year-old child with a serious prelanguage loss probably never had the opportunity to learn anything from his vocalizations. In event he did learn something he soon forgot it following the onset of his loss. This means that when he enters school it is usually necessary to go back to the foundations of speech for his instruction in that field. When the normally hearing child begins to reproduce speech he can monitor his own efforts with the same sensory organ through which he receives the speech of others. The hearing impaired child who tries to produce a speech sound that he cannot hear is unable to monitor his kinesthetic sensations of mouth and throat movements by viewing the lip movements of others.

Most teachers instruct the child in the use of two substitutes. The first is that of employing a large mirror to help him make visual comparisons. The teacher seats the child in front of the mirror and seats himself either beside or behind and above the child. Thus the child is enabled easily to observe both his own lip movements and those of the teacher. However this provides only a few moments from time to time for monitoring a few segments of speech production. The second monitoring substitute is that of teaching the child to use his tactual senses and to identify the location and rhythm of speech sounds. For example the child is lead to place his hand on the teacher's throat to obtain the feel for voiced speech. He then places his hand on his own throat to monitor his efforts in reproducing it. This process is repeated for other speech by placing the hand on the cheek for the vowel-like sounds, on the side of the nose for nasal sounds, and on top of the head to check resonance. Also he may place his hand before his lips to check breath sounds or he may use a light fluffy feather with which to check them visually. If the child possesses prelanguage deafness it will probably be necessary to teach him how to use his lungs as bellows to force air through the larynx and thus produce sound. After learning how to do that it becomes his task to learn where each useful speech sound is produced in the vocal apparatus and the positions and movements required to produce it. In addition he must try for as good quality, rhythm, and intonation as possible. And he must work for an acceptable degree of loudness with as much correct emphasis in the right places as he can learn to employ. The profession has made various approaches to the problem of phonics. In the earlier efforts charts were developed to show the vowels, consonants, and *digraphs* (combinations of letters possessing single sounds), sometimes with symbols to indicate the pronunciation. Probably the best known are the Northampton charts developed at the Clarke School for the Deaf. They help to eliminate the confusion created by the multiple sound values represented by various letters of our alphabet and by our nonphonetic spelling (Silverman, Lane, and Doehring, 1960).

The use of a chart, with its analytical approach to speech, is thought by some to call too much attention to details, thereby slowing the speech process and reducing fluency. The alternate extreme in approaches is the natural method, starting with whole words and sometimes with whole expressions. Unless carefully pursued this can result in much mispronunciation and lack of understanding about the use of certain sounds. It is probable that most teachers employ elements of both approaches.

Speech training for the postlanguage deaf if initiated immediately following the loss of hearing is a matter of speech conservation. The younger the child the greater is the urgency for prompt action. The process is principally to help the child associate the proper kinesthetic cues with the good speech pattern he already possesses. To whatever degree there are imperfections or deterioration of speech the task of course more nearly resembles instruction for the prelanguage deaf. The development of speech for the hard of hearing in most instances involves teaching the child the use of visual-kinesthetic-tactual cues along with whatever residual hearing he possesses.

The test of a child's speech is its intelligibility. Hudgins and Numbers (1942) performed an important piece of research involving

192 pupils, aged eight to twenty: (1) to determine the intelligibility of the speech of deaf children; (2) to analyze, classify, and determine the frequency of errors; and (3) to determine the relative effects of the respective types of errors on speech intelligibility. They found the errors to be in the most important speech elements—the *surd-consonants* (voiceless or nonoral), the compound or blended consonants, and the proper release of consonants in speaking. If conditions have changed but little since 1942, the findings are significant. First they show in what areas we are failing to do the job that needs to be done. Some prelanguage deaf master speech to a good degree considering the fact that they have never heard it, some master it well enough for use among family and close friends, and others acquire it to an insufficient degree for more than partial if any practical use. At the same time these findings demonstrate how close the profession is to accomplishing its purpose. If the children's greatest errors involve the most discriminating elements of speech, then each slight improvement could result in considerable increase in speech intelligibility.

Fruitful research in the area of speech improvement would no doubt be lengthy and expensive. Special equipment has been used to help a child visualize his speech pattern for a given sound against that of the teacher's pattern for the same sound. The oscilloscope is such an instrument used by a few schools. An electric current sets up a straight-horizontal-line luminescence on the screen of a cathode-ray tube (similar to a small version of the picture tube in a television set). Activation of the microphone circuit by a particular speech sound causes the straight line always to dance into the same peculiar pattern of jagged peaks and valleys. This equipment has never won wide adoption. A few years ago the Bell Telephone Laboratories developed an experimental piece of equipment that produced enough of the elements of speech in a fixed stabilized pattern on a rotating phosphorescent screen that held its brightness long enough to be read. The equipment is still being used for research purposes. It is possible that some type of helpful device will eventually be developed. The same general type of captioned sound-projection equipment suggested for language but designed to do the following might possess the most merit. It should: (1) present animated drawings of the positions and movements required of each organ of speech for certain speech sounds, words, and phrases, (2) show on the screen the printed speech sound and phonetic symbols involved, (3) amplify the appropriate accompanying speech simultaneously for whatever number of headphones are desired, (4) provide the rhythm of the speech on a tactile plate, and (5) equip the machine with whatever electronic speech-pattern producing devise is found to be desirable. There are several possible ways of presenting the correct speech pattern, namely—printed cards, film sound track, or magnetic-disc recordings. Thus a proper arrangement of circuits could enable the child to check his speech on a mono-sensory, bisensory, or multisensory basis.

## FINGER SPELLING

Finger spelling is a form of symbolized language, as is any handwriting or printing that uses an alphabet. This manual alphabet may be found in most large dictionaries under the heading *dactylology*. It is used with great rapidity, without capitalization, with little punctuation and with barely perceptible pauses between words and sentences. In fact the experts spell so rapidly that at times it is probably read more by the configuration of the words than by the individual letters of which the words are composed. Some schools utilize finger spelling in class, especially in conjunction with speech in the combined method of instruction for the deaf. The officials of these schools hold the theory that the child makes better progress in English and spelling under this method, and that in event the teacher holds his hand near his face while finger spelling, the child can recognize on the fingers anything he misses on the lips. Finger spelling is also used in certain schools for those children capable of learning English but who are seemingly incapable of mastering speech and speech reading. It is a clear and distinct medium in spite of its transitory nature and the speed with which it is used. In fact the relative ease with which it can be learned and used is the reason why some educators fear it for school purposes. It is their theory that such an easy medium destroys the incentive to use speech and speech reading and thereby denies the child the necessary practice and experience in oral skills. No doubt finger spelling possesses its advantages and disadvantages, but systematic comprehensive research is too inadequate on which to take a position. However, it is obvious that there is a minimum of practice below which oral skills will not develop. At the same time there seems to be a maximum limit according to Heider and Heider (1940) beyond which additional practice produces little or no returns. At the same time, Russian educators in at least one project claim an interesting experience with finger spelling and oral skills. According to Morkovin (1960) the Russians became dissatisfied with the vocabulary and educational development their preschool children were acquiring under a strictly oral program. They therefore added finger spelling, and report that the speech reading skills are greatly accelerated and that the children drop their finger spelling as rapidly as they acquire good speech and speech-reading. These statements seem like an oversimplification of the probable facts. It is doubtful whether finger spelling could contribute directly to the Russian children's speech development. However, it is an easier language medium than speech reading and therefore could hasten their language development, which in turn could give a foundation on which to build speech. That is the same sequence by which Helen Keller mastered her language, speech, and speech reading. At the same time it is logical to assume that the Russian children's shift from an easy to a more difficult medium of communication resulted from some strong motivation or exercised authority.

Criticism of the Russian program is based on possible improvements in their curriculum and on the fact that finger spelled nonphonetic English would not have the same values as finger spelled phonetic Russian. However the first question before us is whether children can acquire language more rapidly with the aid of finger spelling and along with it a background and readiness of value for acquiring skills in speech and speech reading. The second question is to what extent could learning to spell a phonetic language aid the deaf in speech development? If materially there are systems available in which characters and digraphs represent one phonetic value each. Three systems include: (1) the International Phonetic Alphabet, published under the introductory topics at the front of many dictionaries; (2) the Augmented Roman Alphabet, the extra characters of which lend considerable resemblance to the Roman alphabet. This system is under serious official study in selected English schools with a number of books already in print (Tune, 1961); and (3) World English sponsored by America's Simpler Spelling Association and using only the Roman Alphabet in single letters and combinations, as in this bit of witty sarcasm: "Just bekauz wee'v bin duuing it aul rong for senchuriz is noe reezun tuu chaenj nou." (Spelling Progress Bulletin). The adoption of any phonetic spelling would of course mean that during the language-learning period specially prepared books would be required and that after mastery of language the children would need to learn conventional spelling. However according to Bowyer (1961) there are missionary fields in Asia, Africa and the islands of the sea where phonetic spelling is used in the beginning teaching of English to the natives. She adds that the results they obtain put "to shame our traditional system with its traditional spelling." Interestingly enough she comments also on Russian spelling and indicates that normally hearing Russian children entering school at seven are reading within two or three months. It would seem premature to recommend that phonetic spelling be adopted in the early instruction of deaf children. However, if dramatized language can be taught the deaf with the speed demonstrated in the Thompson (1927) research, and if normally hearing children can learn within less than half a year to read phonetically spelled language to the limits of their auditory language, and if a phonetically spelled language constitutes a decided aid in teaching speech to the deaf, then the profession owes these possibilities some thorough research.

## SIGN LANGUAGE

The sign language is entirely different from finger spelling. It is based on gestures, each of which may represent a word or idea. Signs are not English, but rather another language with a limited vocabulary that necessitates reliance on finger spelling for proper nouns and technical terms. Signs constitute the easiest medium of communication for the deaf to learn, but they also constitute the most controversial problem in the education of such children. However for the deaf child too retarded to master English they serve as his only available communication medium. The question of whether signs are bad or good depends on the use made of them.

It is revealing to observe the frustration-free relationship that may exist between a deaf infant and his deaf parents who communicate with him in signs. The early school successes of such children indicate that signs must have given them more meaningful preschool experiences. However any competent deaf child seeking a good education needs to be equipped during his school years with more than a highly limited and literatureless inner language symbol system. Achievement can never exceed the sophistication, refinement, and discriminating qualities of the medium in which a person acquires his knowledge and does his thinking.

## The Hearing-Impaired Adult

There is much overlapping among the self-classified adult deaf and the hard of hearing in their individual ability to interpret speech through hearing. In many cities the hard of hearing are organized into local associations of the American Hearing Society, and the deaf are organized into locals of the National Association of the Deaf. These groups originated both for social purposes and to find better ways and means of advancing their own interests. Any person possessing difficulties in communication—whether because of a foreign language background or a loss of hearing—has his problems integrating with the general population. Therefore he usually tends to seek others like himself for at least part of his social outlets. This is obviously more often true of the deaf than of the hard of hearing. Early discriminations against the deaf in such areas as employment, insurance, recreation, and social activities pulled them together to find ways of solving their problems. As a result they have for years worked for good vocational training in the schools for the deaf, have operated their own insurance company through the National Fraternal Society of the Deaf, operated their own social clubs, published their own newspapers and conducted national athletic events and World Olympics among deaf contestants. At the same time they have won recognition in industry, science, art, education, business, and other fields as responsible employees and in some instances own and operate their own businesses and small factories. They have also won recognition from various safety councils in the United States for driving with greater safety than normally hearing persons. Finesilver (1961) reports the life-time records of 100 deaf drivers of Colorado. These records were compared with the records of two other groups A and B each containing 100 normally hearing drivers selected at random. The total life-time violations of the deaf were 79 compared to 133 for group A and 192 for group B. Of particular interest was the low rate of serious-offense violations among the deaf, a record in harmony with that of various previous studies.

Meyerson (1955) calls attention to the independence of the deaf by citing a well-known example in which their associations defeated a bill in Congress that would have granted them an additional $600 federal income tax exemption. This typifies their official attitude of wanting to be self sufficient with no favors asked—in spite of the fact that society does not always make it easy for them to participate as full partners. The hard of hearing though constitute a less distinct group that is somewhat more integrated with society. However Myklebust (1960) reports a study made of the members of a local society of such persons. Included were 44 men with a mean age of about 40 years and a hearing level of 68 db. Its 83 women had a mean age of about 50 and a hearing level of 68 db. The group contained a high incidence of unmarried persons, with 60 percent of the men living with their parents and 33 percent of the women living with theirs. Only 75 percent of the men and 62.5 percent of the women were independent. These figures may be typical of so-called local hard of hearing associations, but the groups with which the author of this chapter is acquainted are composed of both hard of hearing and normally hearing individuals operating a program to promote better public understanding of hearing impairments, conducting hearing clinics, providing consultation services, speech reading classes, and performing other rehabilitation services. Such service programs are generally financed by the community-chest fund. The local association of course provides for social occasions at its own expense, but such activities are operated in a manner secondary to the service program. Both the associations of the deaf and of the hard of hearing are interested in the education of the hearing impaired. Inasmuch as more of the deaf are alumni of the state residential schools and the hard of hearing are alumni of day centers, each tends to lend its greater support accordingly. However, the differences between the interests of the two groups are in some cases decreasing. In Michigan the state-wide United Fund supports the program of the Michigan Association for Better Hearing, an affiliate of the American Hearing Society. That organization provides rehabilitation and other services for the adult deaf as well as for the hard of hearing and plays an active role in advancing all education programs for the hearing-impaired children of the state.

The last two or three decades have seen the status of hearing-impaired adults materially advanced. Two wars have opened the doors of factories to them that were previously closed, thereby giving them an opportunity to prove they are as dependable and safe workers as any. The modern hearing aid has made it possible for some to function in situations that formerly would have been outside their abilities. The improved scholastic standards of our schools as reported earlier have no doubt increased their employability. And of course the activities of both public and private rehabilitation agencies have been important factors. Further improvement in opportunities for hearing-impaired adults is in part a responsibility of the normally hearing. Mutual acceptance and integration of these people into the normally hearing world is not solely within their choice. Such segregation as exists among them is probably as much the result of the normally hearing failing to make them feel comfortable in our social structure as it is a rejection by them of that structure. Meyerson is no doubt correct in asserting that ability to find their places among both the normally hearing and the hearing impaired adds much to their adjustment and progress.

## Summary

Great progress has been made in the education of the hearing impaired since the founding of the first school a century and a half ago. During recent years that progress has been accelerated with the aid of medicine, psychology, and electronics. As a result we better understand the types of impairment and their impact on the child; we are better able to measure a hearing loss and to bring the spoken word to children who were formerly without it; and we have upgraded the quality of our research, teacher education, classroom instruction, and pupil achievement.

The teaching of good quality speech or speech reading to any child who does not hear the frequencies involved is a remarkable accomplishment, and so is the teaching of our native tongue to the prelanguage deaf. But we have much left to do. The hearing impaired not only score less as a group on intelligence, personality, adjustment, and social competence tests than the normally hearing, but academically they are underachievers. As Myklebust indicates in his writings, hearing is a pervasive thing. Any impairment acquired before language has been mastered affects the entire child—not just his sense of hearing. He sees and senses his environment differently than the normally hearing, thereby altering his reactions and personality. Many authorities believe that a reduction in the language barrier would greatly improve the prelanguage deaf's performance levels and make marked improvement in his achievement and other characteristics. To determine the facts, we need some good psycho-educational research, including a study of the implications of inner language and the methods and facilities necessary to develop effective communication.

The achievements of hearing-impaired adults, in spite of a physical disability and the social and vocational discriminations they have suffered, has been much above what might rightfully be expected. Through intensive effort and a spirit of independence their accomplishments constitute a record in which all concerned may well be proud.

## CHAPTER REFERENCES

Avery, Charlotte B. Social competence of pre-school, acoustically handicapped children. *J. Except. Child.*, 1948, **15**, 71–73, 88.

Baker, H. J. *Introduction to exceptional children.* New York: Macmillan, 1959.

Best, H. *Deafness and the deaf in the United States.* New York: Macmillan, 1943.

Bowyer, Helen. Not back to phonics—forward to phonetics! *Phi Delta Kappan,* 1961, **42**, 207–210.

Boylan, P. J. *Elements of physics.* Boston: Allyn and Bacon, 1959.

Bradway, Katherine P. Social competence of exceptional children: iii., the deaf, the blind, and crippled. *J. Except. Child.*, 1937, **4**, 64–69.

Brown, R. B. *Biology*. Boston: Heath, 1956.

Bunger, Anna M. *Speech reading, Jena method*. Danville, Ill.: Interstate, 1952.

Burchard, E. M. L., & Myklebust, H. R. A comparison of congenital and adventitious deafness with respect to its effects on intelligence, personality, and social maturity: Part II Social maturity. *Amer. Ann. Deaf*, 1942, **87**, 241–251.

Conference of Executives of American Schools for the Deaf. Report of the conference committee on nomenclature. *Amer. Ann. Deaf*, 1938, **83**, 1–3.

———. Tabular statement of American schools for the deaf. *Amer. Ann. Deaf*, 1962, **107**, 124–160.

Davis, H. Anatomy and physiology of the ear. In Hallowell Davis and S. Richard Silverman (Eds.), *Hearing and deafness*. (2nd ed.) New York: Holt, Rinehart and Winston, 1960. Pp. 61–79.

———. Physics and physiology of hearing. In Hallowell Davis and S. Richard Silverman (Eds.), *Hearing and deafness*. (2nd ed.) New York: Holt, Rinehart and Winston, 1960. Pp. 29–60.

———, & Fowler, E. P., Jr. Hearing and deafness. In Hallowell Davis and S. Richard Silverman (Eds.), *Hearing and deafness*. (2nd ed.) New York: Holt, Rinehart and Winston, 1960. Pp. 80–124.

Elser, R. P. The social position of hearing handicapped children in the regular grades. *Except. Child.*, 1959, **25**, 305–309.

Finesilver, S. G. They can't hear, but they get the message. *Traffic safety*, 1961, **59**, 10–12, 52–53.

Fitzgerald, Edith. *Straight language for the deaf*. (4th ed.) Washington, D.C.: Volta Bureau, 1949.

Fusfeld, I. S. A cross-section evaluation of the academic program of schools for the deaf. *Gallaudet College Bull.*, 1954, **3**, No. 1.

———. Research and testing at Gallaudet College. *Amer. Ann. Deaf*, 1940, **85**, 170–183.

Groht, Mildred A. *Natural language for deaf children*. Washington, D.C.: Volta Bureau, 1958.

Guilford, J. P. Three faces of intellect. *Amer. Psychologist*, 1959, **14**, 469–479.

Hanckel, R. W. Recent advances in otology. *J. of S.C. Med. Ass.*, 1960, **56**, 83–86.

Heckman, Helen. *My life transformed*. New York: Macmillan, 1928.

Heider, F. K., & Heider, Grace M. An experimental investigation of lip reading, *Psychol. Monogr.* 1940, **52**, No. 1, 125–253.

Higgins, D. D. *How to talk to the deaf.* Newark, N.J.: Int. Catholic Deaf Ass., Archdiocesan Audio-Visual, Archdiocese of Newark, 1959.

Hofsteater, H. T. *An experiment in preschool education.* Gallaudet College Bull., 1959, **8**, No. 3.

Hudgins, C. V. The response of profoundly deaf children to auditory training. *J. Sp. Hrng. Disorders,* 1953, **18**, 273–288.

———, & Numbers, F. An investigation of the intelligibility of the speech of the deaf. *Genet. Psychol. Monogr.,* 1942, **25**, 289–392.

Johnson, Elizabeth H. The ability of pupils in a school for the deaf to understand various methods of communications—1 and 2. *Amer. Ann. Deaf,* 1948, **93**, 194–213, 258–314.

Kirk, S. A. *Educating exceptional children.* Boston: Houghton Mifflin, 1962.

Levine, Edna S. *An investigation into the personality of normal deaf adolescent girls.* Unpublished doctoral dissertation in microfilm, New York Univer., 1949.

Mackie, Romaine P., & Dunn, L. M. College and university programs for the preparation of exceptional children. *U.S. Office of Educ. Bull.,* 1954, No. 13, Washington, D.C.: Government Printing Office, 1954.

Meyerson, L. A psychology of impaired hearing. In William M. Cruickshank (Ed.), *Psychology of exceptional children and youth.* Englewood Cliffs, N.J.: Prentice-Hall, 1955. Pp. 120–183.

Morkovin, B. V. Experiment in teaching deaf preschool children in Soviet Union. *Volta Rev.,* 1960, **62**, 260–263, 266–268.

Myklebust, H. R. *The psychology of deafness.* New York: Grune and Stratton, 1960.

Newby, H. A. *Audiology: principles and practice.* New York: Appleton-Century-Crofts, 1958.

Nitchie, Elizabeth H. *New lessons in lip reading.* Philadelphia: Lippincott, 1950.

Olson, W. C. *Child development.* (2nd ed.) Boston: Heath, 1959.

Pauls, Miriam D. Speechreading. In Hallowell Davis and S. Richard Silverman (Eds.), *Hearing and deafness.* (2nd ed.) New York: Holt, Rinehart and Winston, 1960. Pp. 353–367.

Pintner, R. Some personality traits of hard of hearing children. *J. Genet. Psychol.,* 1942, **60**, 143–151.

Pintner, R., & Brunschwig, Lily. Some personality adjustments of deaf children in relation to two different factors. *J. Genet. Psychol.*, 1936, **49**, 377–388.

———, & Lev, J. The intelligence of the hard of hearing school child. *J. Genet. Psychol.*, 1939, **55**, 31–48.

———, Eisenson, J., & Stanton, Mildred. *The psychology of the physically handicapped.* New York: Appleton-Century-Crofts, 1945.

Poulos, T. H. Short-term rehabilitation program for hard of hearing children. *Hrng. News*, 1961, **29**, 4–7.

Roberts, P. *Patterns of English.* New York: Harcourt, Brace & World, 1956.

———. *Understanding English.* New York: Harper & Row, 1958.

Scheer, A. A. Otosclerotic deafness and its surgical management. *Gen. Pract.*, 1960, **23**, 16–18.

Schick, Helen F. A five-year testing program to measure the educational achievement of the deaf. *Oralism and Auralism*, 1936, (June), 5–16.

Silverman, S. R. Hard of hearing children. In Hallowell Davis and S. Richard Silverman (Eds.), *Hearing and deafness.* (2nd ed.) New York: Holt, Rinehart and Winston, 1960. Pp. 452–458.

———, Lane, Helen S., & Doehring, D. G. Deaf children. In Hallowell Davis and S. Richard Silverman (Eds.), *Hearing and deafness.* (2nd ed.) New York: Holt, Rinehart and Winston, 1960. Pp. 413–451.

———, Taylor, S. G., & Davis, H. Hearing aids. In Hallowell Davis and S. Richard Silverman (Eds.), *Hearing and deafness.* (2nd ed.) New York: Holt, Rinehart and Winston, 1960. Pp. 265–328.

Smith, J. L. *English phrases and idioms.* Faribault, Minn.: The School for the Deaf, 1916.

Streng, Alice. *Children with impaired hearing.* Washington, D.C.: Council for Except. Child., 1960.

———, Fitch, J., Hedgecock, L. D., Phillips, J. W., & Carrell, J. A. *Hearing therapy for children.* (2nd ed.) New York: Grune & Stratton, 1958.

———, & Kirk, S. A. The social competence of deaf and hard of hearing children in a public day school. *Amer. Ann. Deaf*, 1938, **83**, 244–254.

Taylor, H. The missing mind. *Amer. Ann. Deaf*, 1937, **82**, 207–222.

Thompson, Helen. An experimental study of the beginning reading of deaf mutes. *Teach. Coll. Contr. Educ.*, 1927, No. 254.

Tune, N. W. The augmented Roman alphabet reading research project. *Spelling Progress Bull.*, 1961, **1**, 5–9.

White House Conference on Child Health and Protection. *Special education, the handicapped and the gifted: report of the committee on special classes (section III, education and training). Vol. 3-F.* New York: Appleton-Century-Crofts, 1931.

Young, C., & McConnell, F. Retardation of vocabulary development in hard of hearing children. *Except. Child.*, 1957, **23**, 368–370.

## ADDITIONAL REFERENCES

Barker, R. G., Wright, Beatrice A., Meyerson L., & Gonick, Mollie R. *Adjustment to physical handicap and illness.* (2nd ed.) New York: Social Science Research Council, 1953. Pp. 189–268, 394–404.

Brunschwig, Lily. *A study of some personality aspects of deaf children.* New York: Bureau of Publications, Teachers College, Columbia Univer., 1936.

Ewing, Irene R., & Ewing, A. W. G. *New opportunities for deaf children.* London: Univer. of London Press, 1958.

Gardner, W. H. Report of committee on hard of hearing children. *Hrng News*, 1950, **18**, (2) 5–8, (3) 8–14, (4) 6–9, (5) 8–20.

Getz, S. *Environment and the deaf child.* (2nd ed.) Springfield, Ill.: Charles C. Thomas, 1956.

Gray, G. W., & Wise, C. M. *The bases of speech.* New York: Harper & Row, 1959.

Groht, Mildred A. *Conceptual language teaching.* Report proc. 38th mtg. Amer. Instr. Deaf. Government Printing Office Doc. 66, 1960. Pp. 19–25.

Hirsch, I. J. *The measurement of hearing.* New York: McGraw-Hill, 1952.

Larr, A. L. Perceptual and conceptual abilities of residential school deaf children. *Except. Child.*, 1956, **23**, 63–66, 88.

Lavos, G. Interrelationships among three tests of nonlanguage intelligence administered to the deaf. *Amer. Ann. Deaf*, 1954, **99**, 303–313.

Lassman, Grace H. *Language for the preschool deaf child.* New York: Grune & Stratton, 1950.

Levine, Edna S. *The psychology of deafness.* New York: Columbia Univer. Press, 1960.

Levine, Edna S. *Youth in a soundless world.* New York: New York Univer. Press, 1956.

Lowell, E. *Research on speechreading.* Report proc. 39th mtg. Amer. Instr. Deaf. Government Printing Office Doc. 62, 1960. Pp. 68–73.

Lunde, A. S., & Bigman, S. K. *Occupational conditions among the deaf.* Washington, D.C.: Gallaudet Coll., 1959.

Mackie, Romaine P. *Teachers of children who are deaf.* U.S. Office of Educ. Bull. 1955, No. 6, Government Printing Office, 1956.

Myklebust, H. R. *Auditory disorders in children.* New York: Grune & Stratton, 1954.

Quigley, S. P., & Frisina, D. R. Institutionalization and psychoeducational development of deaf children. *Council Except. Child. Res. Monogr.,* 1961, Ser. A, No. 3.

Silverman, S. R. Clinical and educational procedures for the deaf. In L. Travis (Ed.), *Handbook of speech pathology.* New York: Appleton-Century-Crofts, 1957.

Volta Bureau. Films on hearing and deafness. (A list.) *Volta Rev.,* 1962, **64**, 77–83.

**REFERENCES FOR PARENTS**

Bennett, Daphne N. Parents as teachers of the preschool deaf child. *Except. Child.,* 1955, **22**, 101–103, 122.

Canfield, N. *Hearing: a handbook for laymen.* New York: Doubleday, 1959.

Illinois annual institute for mothers of deaf children. *If you have a deaf child.* Urbana, Ill.: Univer. of Illinois, 1949.

Levine, Edna S., & Groht, Mildred A. Nursery school and the deaf child. *Volta Rev.,* 1955, **57**, 199–209.

Montague, Harriet A. An open letter to mothers of two year olds. *Volta Rev.,* 1951, **53**, 343–344.

Myklebust, H. R. *Your deaf child, a guide to parents.* Springfield, Ill.: Charles C Thomas, 1950.

*NOTE:* See programs of membership organizations and agencies under "Resources" for services to parents. Also see Finesilver, Heckman, and Hofsteater under "Chapter References," Lunde and Volta Bureau under "Additional References," and the "Selected Films" list.

## RESOURCES

### MEMBERSHIP ORGANIZATIONS

The Alexander Graham Bell Association for the Deaf, 1537 – 35th Street, NW., Washington 7, D.C., is a professional and lay organization with Canadian and United States memberships. The association has a parents section and serves as a clearing house for information on the deaf. It conducts sales of professional and parent literature, publishes *Volta Review* and professional books, and holds conventions. The main library is open to researchers, and the association also operates a lending library.

The American Hearing Society, 919 – 18th Street, NW., Washington 6, D.C., is an interdisciplinary organization with lay Canadian and United States membership. The society has local and two state affiliates, which provide services direct to individuals. A clearing house on problems of the hard of hearing and speech impaired, the society promotes *Better Hearing Month* and publishes pamphlets, *Hearing News* and *AHS Bulletin Board*, and conducts conventions.

The American Instructors of the Deaf (headquarters at president's address) has professional Canadian and United States membership. It is the copublisher of *American Annals of the Deaf* and holds conventions. (See CEASD for joint editorial address.)

American Speech and Hearing Association, 1001 Connecticut Avenue, NW., Washington 6, D.C., has a professional membership. It conducts programs of certification of individuals, organizations, and institutions in areas of speech and hearing. Founder of the American Speech and Hearing Foundation, the association publishes *Journal of Speech and Hearing Disorders, Journal of Speech and Hearing Research,* and *Asha* and also holds conventions.

The Conference of Executives of American Schools for the Deaf (headquarters at president's address) is a professional organization of executive heads of schools for deaf of Canada and the United States. It conducts sales of literature for parents, certifies individuals and teacher training institutions in field of the deaf, and is copublisher (with AID) of *American Annals of the Deaf* (editorial offices at Gallaudet College, Florida Avenue, at 7th Street, NE., Washington 2, D.C.).

The International Congress on the Education of the Deaf (headquarters at president's address) holds world conferences at frequent but irregular intervals.

The National Association of the Deaf, 2495 Shattuck Avenue, Berkeley 4, California, lay organization of deaf adults, that admits persons professionally engaged in the field, publishes the *Silent Worker* devoted to problems and interests of the adult deaf. It also holds conventions.

## AGENCIES

The John Tracy Clinic, 806 Adams Boulevard, Los Angeles 7, California, extends services to preschool hearing-impaired children including conducting clinical and nursery schools. For parents its services include consultation, classes, correspondence courses, and a film library. Teacher-training courses with university cooperation are open to educators. The clinic also carries on research in the field.

United States Department of HEW, Washington 25, D.C.

1. The Children's Bureau offers grants to states as aid in programs for hearing-impaired children. Inquiries relative to the availability of a program should be directed to the department of health of the appropriate state.

2. The Office of Education—Captioned Films for the Deaf—places captions on selected 16 mm. sound films of an entertaining, cultural, or educational nature for the use of schools and associations of the deaf. The films are distributed only through the Indiana School for the Deaf, 1200 East 42nd Street, Indianapolis 5, Indiana.

## OTHER PUBLISHERS

Deafness Speech and Hearing Publications, Inc., with editorial offices at Gallaudet College, Florida Avenue, at 7th Street, NE., Washington 2, D.C. (business office, American Speech and Hearing Association, 1001 Connecticut Avenue, Washington 6, D.C.), publishes *dsh abstracts* from 300 magazines of world-wide selection and known books of importance.

Gallaudet College, Florida Avenue, at 7th Street, NE., Washington 2, D.C., publishes *Gallaudet College Bulletin* on education of and research on the deaf, irregularly about four times per year for free distribution upon request.

The Laryngoscope, 640 South Kingshighway, St. Louis 10, Missouri, publishes *The Laryngoscope,* a monthly journal on diseases of the ear, nose, and throat.

## SELECTED 16 MM SOUND FILMS

*What you hear and how.* 30 min, black & white. National Educational Television Film Service, Indiana University, Bloomington, Indiana. Reviews the complexities of sound, the anatomy of the ear, and how sounds are conducted in the ear.

*Too young to say.* 13½ min, color. Harsche-Rotman and Druck, Incorporated, 108 North State Street, Chicago 2, Illinois. Procedures in testing the hearing of preschool-age children.

*Reach into silence.* 13½ min, color. Harsche-Rotman and Druck, Incorporated, 108 North State Street, Chicago 2, Illinois. Designed for recruiting teachers of the deaf through showing methods used in training them.

*Parent education series.* 10 min, black & white. John Tracy Clinic, 806 West Adams Boulevard, Los Angeles 7, California. Consists of two series of nine films each, plus a 20 minute introductory film for both series and a 20 minute recording (33 rpm) to accompany each film. One series covers psychological problems of parents and the other concerns techniques of building communication skills in preschool-age deaf children.

*Thursday's children.* 30 min, black & white. Contemporary Films, Incorporated, 267 West 25 Street, New York 1, New York. Teaching language, speech reading, and speech to children of four to seven years of age at Margate School for the Deaf in England.

*Growing up with deafness.* 37 min, color, black & white. Campus Film Productions, Incorporated, 20 East 46 Street, New York 17, New York. A 10-year documentary of the progress made by a group of deaf children first photographed when three to 12 years of age.

*Beyond silence.* 15 min, black & white. College Library, Gallaudet College, Florida Avenue at 7 Street, NE., Washington 2, D.C. Adjustment of the deaf student to college life. Includes both oral and simultaneous methods of communication.

*The glass wall.* 27½ min, color. American Hearing Society, 919 – 18 Street, NW., Washington 6, D.C. Rehabilitation problems of the hard of hearing. Suitable for public showings to develop community interest.

*They do not walk alone.* 28 min, color. Clarke School for the Deaf, Northampton, Massachusetts. Oral graduates of Clarke School for the Deaf happily adjusted to life in a normally hearing world.

*A sound life.* 30 min, black & white. Atlanta Speech School, Incorporated, 2020 Peachtree Road, NW., Atlanta, Georgia. Problems of hearing-impaired children and how they are taught to speak.

*Children of the silent night.* 27 min, color. Campbell Films, Saxton River, Vermont. The deaf-blind program at the Perkins School for the Blind, Watertown, Massachusetts, including history, methods, and potentials for employment.

*Captioned films for the deaf.* Indiana School for the Deaf, 1200 East 42 Street, Indianapolis 5, Indiana. Includes films of an entertaining, cultural, or educational nature, for use in schools for, or by associations of, the deaf.

## CHAPTER 8

# Blind and Partially Seeing Children

SAMUEL C. ASHCROFT

Blindness and lesser visual impairments such as those of the partially seeing may have dramatically varying effects on children. To many young people, extreme loss of vision, even total blindness, seems to be merely an incidental inconvenience. To others, lesser losses seem almost catastrophic in their effects on education, normal activity, and adjustment. Where such broad latitude in reaction to different degrees of physical impairment prevails, educators find fascinating challenges. How can the child with a visual impairment be helped to attain the greatest possible personal competence? How can the personal, educational, and social effects of the impairment be minimized? No more intriguing and exciting challenges exist anywhere in education. The challenges are embodied in each child who has a visual problem. However, sometimes attention to visual problems obscures the central concern which is the child himself. As a frame of reference for reading and studying this chapter, the reader should hold in his mind's eye a whole and valued child much like any other school-age child.

Pupils with impaired vision are usually divided into two groups

413

for purposes of special education. These are the blind and the partially seeing. These groups are treated together in this text because of many commonalities they share and because many of their educational needs are similar.

## Definition

For educational purposes, the visually limited are distinguished from the normally seeing and within this group the partially seeing are differentiated from the blind primarily in terms of the degree of useful vision they retain, or in terms of the media in which they read and do school work. Blind children include those who have so little remaining useful vision that they must use braille as their reading medium. The traditional definition (AFB, 1961a) of the blind which has been accepted for economic and legal purposes and is often used for educational purposes is 20/200 or less in the better eye with the best possible correction or a restriction in field of vision to an angle subtending an arc of 20 degrees or less. The partially seeing are those children who retain a relatively low degree of vision and can read only enlarged print or those who have remaining vision making it possible for them to read limited amounts of regular print under very special conditions. The partially seeing (Hathaway, 1959) are traditionally defined as those who have remaining visual acuity between 20/200 and 20/70 in the better eye with the best possible correction or who in the opinion of eye specialists can benefit from either temporary or permanent use of appropriate special educational facilities. It is important to understand these definitions, the factors which influence their usefulness to educators, and current educational trends with regard to them. A brief discussion of visual acuity measurement will contribute to this understanding and suggest why definitions other than these traditional ones are more satisfactory.

## Measurement of Visual Acuity

Vision is typically described in terms of visual acuity which denotes sharpness or clearness of vision. Visual acuity is measured frequently with a test chart of block letters with which everyone is somewhat familiar. Virtually all vision tests are based on the

FIG. 8.1 Snellen Symbol Chart. From the National Society for the Prevention of Blindness, Inc., New York, N.Y. by permission.

principles underlying the Snellen Chart in Fig. 8.1. The Snellen test is the invention of Dr. Hermann Snellen (Farrell, 1958) who set the test distance at 20 feet and made the basic unit of measurement the visual angle of one minute of arc, a visual distance clearly distinguishable by the normal eye at 200 feet. The test was designed so that the top large letter, actually about 3.5 inches square, appears to be of the same size when viewed from 200 feet as a standard sized letter appears when viewed from 20 feet. The working or test distance from the test chart is set at 20 feet for convenience and because rays of light reflected from objects at such a distance tend to be parallel. With the test chart at 20 feet, the normal eye can focus light reflected from it while the eye muscles (which provide for accommodation) are at rest. When objects are viewed from less than 20 feet, the lens of the eye must be stretched to focus reflected light on the retina of the normal eye.

In tests of visual acuity, the individual is placed at a distance of 20 feet from a chart and reads letters or symbols to the best of his visual ability. The 20-foot distance becomes the top number in the visual acuity index and the bottom number describes the size of the line of letters he can read successfully. If the individual can stand at 20 feet and read the line of letters a person with emmetropic (or normal) vision can read at that distance, he is said to have 20/20 vision. If, standing at 20 feet, he can read only what the normally seeing person can read from a distance of 70 feet, he is said to have 20/70 or twenty over seventy vision. It should be noted that this index does not represent a fraction, neither does it denote a percentage of remaining vision. An abbreviated representation of a continuum of such visual acuity indexes is illustrated in Fig. 8.2. Related percentages of remaining vision or "visual efficiency" are also shown.

The field or range of peripheral or "side" vision as well as central visual acuity is important. Limitations in peripheral vision may also constitute a visual handicap. Peripheral vision is evaluated in terms of degrees of visual arc and is measured by the extent to which a standard visual stimulus can be seen on a black background viewed from about 39 inches when the eye is fixed on a central point. When the widest angle in which such a stimulus can be seen subtends an arc of 20 degrees or less in the better eye with correction, the person is also considered blind for legal and economic purposes, and has traditionally been considered educationally blind.

Visual acuity indexes are "clinical" measurements. At best they are obtained by trained specialists and under carefully standardized and controlled conditions of distance, lighting, and cooperation. At worst they are obtained under rough approximations to these con-

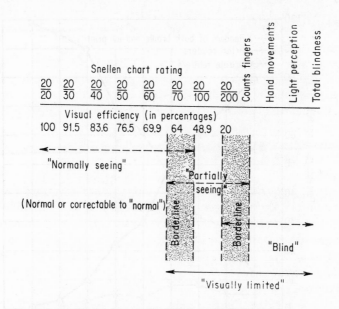

FIG. 8.2 Visual acuity continuum, with percentages of visual efficiency, and approximate ranges of vision in the visually limited groups.

ditions. In either case, they are usually only representative of a very small sampling of the visual behavior of individuals in very special circumstances. The complex physical and psychological characteristics of vision make ineffective for many purposes characterization of total visual efficiency solely in terms of such a short clinical test, no matter how carefully it might be obtained.

As pointed out in chapter 10, on adjustment to exceptionality, it is very difficult to equate measures of physical factors with psychological and behavioral characteristics. The point is well illustrated with regard to vision. While persons may be described as having the same vision characteristics in terms of clinical vision tests, their visual behavior may vary widely because of physical, psychological, social and environmental factors. There is consequent difficulty in determining whether a children with vision clinically described as

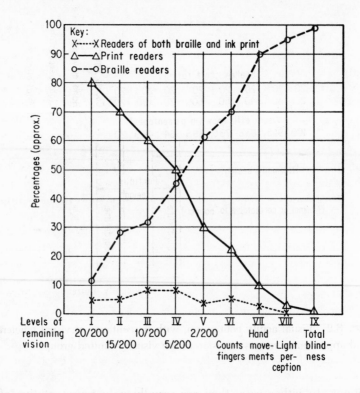

FIG. 8.3 Distribution of local and residential population combined by mode of reading. These figures represent the percent of children at each level of vision in terms of their mode of reading. The percentages are based on the total number of children registered at the American Printing House for the Blind as blind for legal purposes, namely 14, 125. From Jones, J. W. *Blind children: degree of vision, mode of reading.* Washington, D.C.: Government Printing Office, 1961.

20/200 should be classified as partially seeing and be educated in a program requiring the reading of print, or if such a child will need to use means, other than vision and reading print, to acquire his education. A recent outstanding study (Jones, 1961) of the registration data of 14,125 children described as blind for legal purposes indicates that about 80 percent of the children who were reported within the 20/200 vision category read print while about 12 percent of those in this same category read braille and 5 percent read both (Fig. 8.3). This is a startling fact. Among these children who are all described by this categorization as "legally" blind, many function as readers of print yet others read in braille. As educators have become increasingly aware of such problems, the trend in defining visually limited children *for educational purposes* has been toward utilizing criteria based on how the children *function* in school rather than how they perform and are measured on clinical tests. One important factor must be noted in this connection. In recent years, there has been a rather general "repeal of prohibition" on the use of residual vision. Medical eye specialists have increasingly emphasized the importance of *using* residual vision rather than limiting its use for "saving", or "conserving", it. In fact, use of vision is encouraged and we are told that to fail to use it is to lose it, rather than to save it. This fact is reflected in the change in name of facilities for educating partially seeing children from "sight-saving classes" to "programs for the partially seeing." Furthermore, education in its broad sense is not wholly based on reading. Many other types of activity and experience have great educational value. Not all of them are as crucially affected by good visual acuity as reading may be. To develop the total educational plan and determine placement in a program around the ability to read in one medium or another may be inappropriate for many individuals. Facts such as these have led to a revision in thinking about defining the child who is visually handicapped for educational purposes and suggest why definitions related primarily to visual acuities of 20/200 and 20/70 may be quite inappropriate for educational purposes.

The suggestion has been made (AFB, 1957) that psychovisual efficiency may better be used than visual acuity to differentiate educationally the blind, and the partially seeing. Definitions like the following are being found more useful and satisfactory for educational purposes for blind and partially seeing children than those traditional definitions which have been related more exclusively to visual acuity indexes.

The blind child is defined (AFB, 1957, p. 55) as one "whose vision loss indicates that he can and should function in his total educational program chiefly through the use of the braille system, audio-aids, and special equipment necessary for him to pursue his education effectively without the use of residual vision."

It has been proposed that the partially seeing child be defined as one who retains limited but useful vision for acquiring an education but whose visual impairment after needed treatment or correction or both reduces school progress to such an extent that special educational provisions are necessary.

While these definitions are not yet widely accepted or used, the writer recommends them and sees the aforementioned trend toward their increased use. Problems remain in their application and in determining with reasonable precision the incidence and prevalence of visually limited children in terms of such definitions. At this time, the most effective plan for educational use appears to be to utilize clinical measures for screening and identification purposes. Children meeting the criteria of the traditional definitions must then be observed by experienced educational personnel charged with making decisions and implementing them in educational programs. Decisions about educational programs will then be based on the type of program which will best enable the child to function in accordance with his scholastic aptitude. Such effective action can be taken only by educational personnel with adequate professional preparation and practical experience.

## Identification

The identification of school children who need special educational services because of limited vision is a very important teamwork task of educational, medical, and other personnel. Early recognition of potential eye defects and diseases provides the best means for preventing or ameliorating serious eye disorders and reducing the educational and social problems that may result. It would be fortunate, but it is not yet feasible, to have complete and regular eye examinations for everyone. In lieu of these, screening tests of vision accompanied by observations of physical and behavioral symptoms of eye trouble provide the best preventive and identification measures. A good program includes comprehensive screening for early discovery, referral for comprehensive eye-examinations for those who seem to have difficulties or symptoms indicating future problems, and follow-up to carry out recommendation of the complete eye examination. An adequate screening program will be of important concern to both general and special educators.

## VISION SCREENING

Vision screening and identification of visual problems should be programmatic in nature. Programmatic in this instance means carrying out a series of carefully planned steps from preparation for screening through identification, referral, follow-up and implementation of plans for education.

The preparation phase includes work with those who do the screening, related personnel, and those who are to be screened. Adequate screening for visual problems can be carried out effectively only by people who understand the proper use of the vision screening devices, the purposes of the program, and the nature of the group with which they will be working. The children themselves need to understand and appreciate the purposes of the screening program. As in any testing situation, adequate rapport is essential. Such rapport is best obtained when the subjects are well prepared for what is to take place.

There is a tendency to think of the screening and identification procedure as only the mechanical application of a clinical screening device. Research and experience show that the complete and adequate screening and identification program must include continuous observation for behavioral and physical signs and symptoms of potential difficulty. Such behavioral symptoms or signs of stress include holding reading material or other visual work abnormally near to or far from the eyes; walking overcautiously, faltering, stumbling, failing to see or running into objects not directly in the line of vision. Other signs include rubbing the eyes frequently, frowning, and distorting the face when using the eyes, shutting or covering one eye, tilting the head forward or to the side. Difficulty is suggested if individuals fail to see objects readily visible to others, are unduly sensitive to normal light levels, are unable to distinguish colors, or have difficulty estimating distance. Physical symptoms include red-rimmed, encrusted, or swollen eyelids or frequent styes. Watery, red, or bloodshot eyes may also signal problems. Children's complaints should be noticed when they are due to use of the eyes, as of dizziness, headache, or pain in the eyes, nausea, double vision or blurring, burning or itching eyelids.

Though observations are important it is always necessary to use a standard screening procedure, preferably including a battery of tests for appraising various aspects of vision. Many are available and are commonly used in community, preschool, school, and business, and industrial settings. Only well recognized and accepted ones should be used. Recommendations may be obtained from the National Society for the Prevention of Blindness, state or local health or educational agencies.

The Snellen tests already discussed may be used as an example of how vision screening can be conducted. Children who appear to have vision of 20/30 or less should be retested and referred if they continue to appear to fail the 20/30 line. Additional simple tests are available for hyperopia (farsightedness), for near vision (tests of printed paragraphs of graduated size or of Snellen type symbols at 14 to 16 inches), visual field, muscular imbalance, color vision, and depth perception.

Follow-up is an important aspect of the programmatic plan of screening and identification. In interpretation of findings of screening, it should be made clear that screening tests are not conclusive. If any difficulty is identified complete, professional eye examination should be recommended. It should also be understood by all concerned that when such referral for examination is made a problem is only suspected, not confirmed. After referrals have been made for complete examinations, follow up of eye examination and implementation of recommendations complete the screening and identification program.

Many kinds of personnel have responsibilities in a programmatic plan of screening such as that outlined briefly above. Roles in the program can be delineated for teachers, administrators, school and public health nurses, medical and nonmedical eye specialists, social workers, parents, and others. The National Society for the Prevention of Blindness, (NSPB, 1961) provides an excellent guide for a program. A useful film on this topic "Betty Sees a Bird" is also available from the same source. Other agencies provide similar information and many school systems have developed their own guides outlining programs for the purpose. The guide for vision screening of school children developed for the State of California by the State Department of Education in 1953 is an excellent example.

The educator will probably be familiar with most of the personnel which have been mentioned above, but many individuals do not understand the proper titles and roles for eye specialist personnel. Eye specialists include the ophthalmologist, the optometrist, the optician, and the orthoptist. The ophthalmologist (also called oculist) is the licensed physician who specializes in the treatment of eye diseases and optical defects and is qualified to practice all phases of medical activity related to vision. The optometrist is a nonmedical practitioner licensed to prescribe and fit glasses and to deal with optical defects of the eyes without the use of drugs or surgery. The optician grinds lenses and makes up glasses. The orthoptist provides eye exercise and orthoptic training on the prescription of the medical eye specialist. Each of these specialists has an important role to play. The educator should know when and how the services of each are most efficiently and effectively utilized.

## INCIDENCE AND PREVALENCE

Screening and identification procedures tend to reveal the number of vision problems requiring special educational provision. These incidence data result in prevalence information on which to base plans for special services for visually limited children. However, Hurlin (1962) noted, "Dependable statistics of blindness continue to be seriously lacking in this country." A commonly accepted figure of 1 in 500 children (0.2 percent) of school age being classified as partially seeing has long been quoted widely in the literature. This figure is based on the number of school-age children who are likely to be found to have visual acuity between 20/70 and 20/200 and related problems. Recently the National Society for Prevention of Blindness have used this prevalence figure to estimate that there were 85,000 partially seeing children of school age in this country. As suggested in the discussion on definition, prevalence data based solely on visual acuity information are likely to give inflated figures on the partially seeing who need comprehensive special educational services. Much more important as the criterion is the way in which the children are able to function in the everyday tasks (especially educational) of life. This 85,000 figure should be understood to describe the group of children that would be screened into a pool for further referral and for educational appraisal. The U.S. Office of Education now suggests that 0.06 percent of school children will actually need placement in special education facilities for the partially seeing.

With respect to blindness, a prevalence of 1 in 3000 (0.03 percent) is the widely accepted medico-legal estimate for children with corrected vision of 20/200 or less in the better eye. The number of pupils registered to participate in the Federal Act to Promote the Education of the Blind for 1963 is estimated at 17,700 with 55 percent expected to be in day and 45 percent in residential schools. An estimated 40 percent of these legally classified blind children use ink print as their primary mode of reading, and therefore could be classified as educationally partially seeing though legally blind. These facts help to resolve the apparent differences in the figures just cited and in Table 1.2.

Together then, the blind and partially seeing for whom special educational provisions are probably needed comprise about 0.09 percent of the school-age population according to the U.S. Office of Education. For convenience the reader may want to remember that the visually limited constitute the smallest area of exceptionality. This is not a sizeable group, but it is an important one to the educator.

## Characteristics

The most important characteristic of the visually limited child is that he is a valuable and important human individual much more like other children than different from them. This should not be forgotten in looking at discrete characteristics and attributes. The educator will be concerned about physical, mental, social, and emotional characteristics of visually limited children. Since the visually limited are grouped in terms of a physical impairment it is appropriate first to examine some of their physical characteristics. Usually, it would not be possible to differentiate a group of visually limited children from a group of normally seeing children in terms of their general physique. They do not tend to be taller, shorter, or leaner than their normally seeing peers. Not all of them have physical stigmata in or near their eyes. They do have in common some type of limitation in the use of vision for the ordinary tasks of life. In order to understand some of the common visual problems, a brief and simple review of some facts about the eye and vision will be useful.

### VISION

The sense of vision is complex. Good vision depends on the intactness and efficiency of an intricate physiological system (see Fig. 8.4). Difficulty in any part of the system may lead to visual impairment and potentially disturbing related problems.

The first portion of the system consists of surrounding protective structures. Among these are the bony eyesockets in the skull, the eyebrows, eyelids and eyelashes. The tear system provides protection through cleaning and lubricating. These structures and systems must be intact and functional to permit and preserve efficient vision.

The second part of the system provides for the refraction of light and for focusing it on the retina. In this portion the cornea, aqueous, lens, and vitreous are the main parts. Any malformation or opacity in these media interferes with the proper transmission, refraction, and focusing of light and results in faulty vision or blindness.

The third part of the system consists of muscles which function to coordinate and balance the movement of the eyes. These muscles turn, raise, and lower the eyes in response to cranial nerve impulses. When these muscles or the nerves which control them are impaired or fail to operate properly faulty vision results.

The fourth part of the system is centered in the brain where vision actually takes place. The optic nerve and its extension within the eye, the retina, are actually part of the brain. The retina is the end of the neural receptor system for vision. The most sensitive area of the retina is the macula and at the macular center is found the fovea, the area vital to discriminating exact details. Two types of receptor cells make up the retina, the familiar rods and cones. The cones are concentrated in the foveal area and seem to be responsible for detail and color vision. The rods provide "night vision" or vision under conditions of low illumination. This neural part of

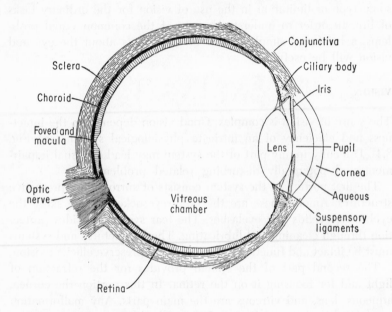

FIG. 8.4 Cross section of the human eye. From Marsland D., *Principles of modern biology*. Copyright (C) New York 1957, Holt, Rinehart and Winston, Inc., publishers.

the system conveys electro-chemical stimuli to the brain where sense and meaning are given to them.

In a system as complex and elaborate as that which produces vision, it is evident that many types of anomalies can occur. Among the common general problems are refractive errors, developmental anomalies, muscle defects, and diseases. Some of the more common defects (Fig. 8.5) indicate characteristic problems. The eyes of young children and abnormal eyes in some adults are too short from

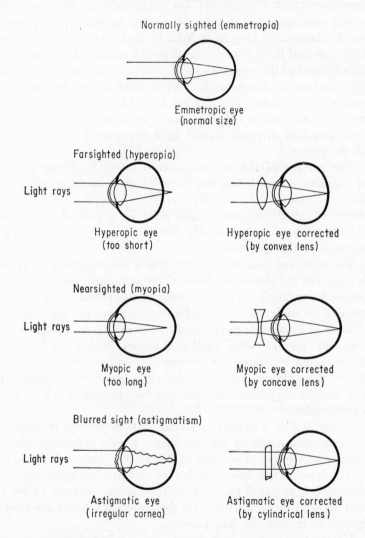

Normally sighted (emmetropia)

Emmetropic eye
(normal size)

Farsighted (hyperopia)

Light rays

Hyperopic eye
(too short)

Hyperopic eye corrected
(by convex lens)

Nearsighted (myopia)

Light rays

Myopic eye
(too long)

Myopic eye corrected
(by concave lens)

Blurred sight (astigmatism)

Light rays

Astigmatic eye
(irregular cornea)

Astigmatic eye corrected
(by cylindrical lens)

FIG. 8.5 Illustration of refraction in a normal eye, and common defects of refractions with their corrections.

front to back. In this case the lens, even when it is most relaxed, fails to focus light reflected from near objects on the retina. The point of focus of light would actually fall behind the retina. This condition is called "hyperopia" (or farsightedness). The convex lens, which converges rays of light, is required for correction. When the eye is abnormally long from front to back, the lens fails to focus light reflected from distant objects on the retina. The point of focus falls in front of the retina. The eye attempts to correct this condition by stretching or flattening the lens as much as possible. If the eye cannot accommodate or bring the light to focus on the retina the resulting condition is called "myopia" or nearsightedness. The concave lens that diverges rays of light is required to put the focus on the retina.

The surface of the eye, the cornea, normally forms a portion of a spherical lens. When this surface is deformed the transmission and refraction of light is faulty and blurred vision results. This condition is called astigmatism and must be corrected by use of a cylindrical lens, a lens which corrects in only one direction or meridan of the spherical cornea.

The two eyes must work together in a coordinated way. If there is muscular imbalance "strabismus" (or squinting) commonly called "crossed", or "wall" eyedness results. In this event, different images are cast on each retina. When these differences are great, they are difficult or impossible to be fused by the brain into a single impression and "double vision" (diplopia) occurs. Such a condition must be corrected by glasses, by exercise, by surgery, or by a combination of these efforts. If not corrected early in childhood vision in one eye may be suppressed and the eye may become weak or useless (amblyopia).

Congenital or adventitious (accidental) deformity, or opacity in the refractive media of the eye causes serious defects of vision or blindness. A frequent problem of this kind is "cataract", (an opacity of the lens or the lens capsule). In children an operation called discission is required to break up the opaque contents of the lens and allow it to be absorbed by the aqueous. Glasses are then required to replace the lens function.

Information on how such defects are distributed among the visually limited are provided in National Society for the Prevention of

Blindness studies by Kerby (1958). These data indicate the following information.

1. Causes of visual defects in a study of eye reports on the blind (given in percentages).

   a. Prenatal causes     56.1
   
       of undetermined origin     41.8
   
       of hereditary origin     14.3
   
   b. Poisonings     19.3
   
   c. Tumors     5.1
   
   d. Infectious diseases     7.4
   
   e. Undetermined or unspecified     6.5
   
   f. Injuries     4.9
   
   g. General diseases     .7

2. Causes of visual defects in a study of eye reports on the partially seeing (in percentages).

   a. Refractive errors     48.7
   
   b. Developmental anomalies of structure     21.5
   
   c. Defects of muscle function     18.2
   
   d. Diseases of defects     10.2
   
   e. Undetermined causes     1.4

Of special interest is a disease called retrolental fibroplasia (rlf). Its discovery, "rise," and prevention provide a dramatic historical incident. In the decade between 1942 when it was discovered (Terry, 1942) and 1953 when the problem was largely solved, rlf contributed many blind children to the school-age population. This condition was caused by an excess of oxygen administered to premature babies while they were in incubators. Characteristic of rlf children is very early, near-total blindness, which has special implications for educators. Prior to the appearance of rlf, there was a marked decline in the number of blind children. Retrolental fibroplasia reversed this trend. Now though largely prevented by appropriate control of oxygen therapy for the premature the population of blind children has continued to grow because of the general population explosion and because many children who formerly did not survive are now saved by advances in medical and surgical procedures. The "wave" of rlf caused an expansion of residential school facilities and an even more rapid development of day school programs stimulated by parents who wanted to keep their young blind children at home and in local school programs.

The age at onset of visual impairment is of interest and concern to educators because of the differential impact of this variable. Kerby's data (1958) indicate that 54.1 percent of the group for which information was available were blind at birth. Twenty-three percent became blind before the age of five. Those blind and blinded early have generally been considered by educators to be similar in their characteristics and needs since it is thought that visual imagery is not retained by those blinded by the middle of the first decade of life (Schlaegel, 1953). While precise information on this point should be of great value and should have significant educational implications, only limited scientific study is available. The problem should be more intensively studied so that educators would know to what extent visual memories may be capitalized upon in the development of concepts. This may be especially important for planning differential educational provisions for children blind from rlf, as contrasted with those pupils blinded some time after birth. Age at onset for partially seeing children, while important, is not so crucial to concept development as for blind children. However, its importance of impact on personal-social adjustment should not be underestimated.

The vision characteristics of visually limited children in special programs are suggested by the Jones data (1961) on degree of remaining vision among 14,125 "legally blind" children. Almost 31 percent had vision registered as 20/200. About 50 percent had visual acuities describable in numerical terms, that is about 2/200 or better. More than 60 percent had remaining vision above light perception. Less than 25 percent were totally blind. It is important for educators to be aware of the extent of remaining vision in so-called blind children and to enable children to utilize this vision to the optimum extent. These facts stress the importance of dealing with visually limited children in terms of what they have and how they function, and not in terms of what they lack.

The vision characteristics of partially seeing children in special programs are illustrated by data from Hathaway (1959) on degree of remaining vision among 7310 partially seeing children in 600 classes. Almost 20 percent had vision within the usual definition of blindness (20/200 or less); about 30 percent had vision between 20/70 and 20/200 (the commonly accepted visual acuity criteria limits for the partially seeing); and 40 percent had vision better than 20/70. Vision was not reported for almost 10 percent of the children. It appears that 40 percent are not eligible for these special educational provisions in terms of visual acuities alone and must therefore be so placed either because they have progressive eye conditions, because they have not learned to use the vision they have efficiently and effectively, or because of other factors. A recent study of partially seeing children by Bateman discovered close agreement to this on the number of children enrolled in programs for partially sighted, 28 percent had visual acuities of 20/200 or less; 34 percent were in the 20/70 to 20/200 category; 38 percent had vision better than 20/70. The subjects included about 90 percent of the partially seeing children in Illinois special programs for such pupils outside of the city of Chicago.

## INTELLECTUAL AND EDUCATIONAL CHARACTERISTICS

Opinions with respect to the intellectual characteristics of visually limited children vary widely. Villey (1930, p. 16) wrote, "no mental faculty of the blind is affected in any way, and all of them, under favorable circumstances, are susceptible of blossoming out to the highest degree of development to which a normal being can aspire." Conversely, Cutsforth (1951) wrote, "No single mental activity of the congenitally blind child is not distorted by the absence of sight." These two statements represent diametric extremes of opinion on the topic. The truth no doubt lies somewhere between these two positions. Unfortunately, the data available to resolve the issue leave much to be desired. However, some information is available which provides useful insight into the mental characteristics of visually limited children. Hayes (1950) has provided the most extensive study of intelligence of blind children over a period of more than 30 years. Hayes developed a "scissors and paste" adaptation of the 1937 Revision of the Stanford-Binet, named the Interim-Hayes Binet. It consisted of a combination of items from Forms L and M which do not require vision. He recognized its limitations for comparing the intelligence of the blind with that of the seeing and recommended its use only for comparisons among the blind. However, it has been widely used as a point of reference. The verbal scales of the Wechsler tests have also been used. Using these adapted tests, Hayes found that the the percentages of blind children at each intelligence level roughly followed comparable groups of seeing children. However, there were smaller percentages of children in the middle ranges of intelligence, slightly higher percentages at the superior level, and substantially higher percentages at the dull normal, borderline and mentally retarded levels. These data must be understood to represent mainly children in specialized school programs, and to be based on tests that have been adapted and may not adequately or validly represent the mental characteristics of blind children. Nevertheless, they provide the educator with the assurance that mental retardation is not a necessary concomitant of blindness or visual limitation and that most visually limited children do have aptitude for scholastic achievement fairly commensurate with that of their seeing peers.

Educational achievement tests (Ashcroft, 1959) while showing some academic retardation in the blind, show much less such retardation than is found among the deaf. In fact, achievement fairly equivalent to that of normative populations of seeing children on the Stanford Achievement Tests is found. It should be noted that adaptations of timing and administration developed and recommended by Hayes which are less stringent than those used with the normally seeing are also used in these tests and comparisons must be made with this in mind. Furthermore, the blind children are often found to be over age for their grade placements. This overageness for grade seems to result largely from several causes; (1) late entry to school, (2) years of failure in unspecialized programs before placement in appropriate programs, (3) loss of time in school due to surgery or treatment for eye conditions or illness, (4) lack of opportunity for schooling, and (5) the slower rate of acquiring information from reading in braille, large type or through auditory means.

Lowenfeld (1955) holds that two factors, cognitive functions and mobility, are intrinsic problems of blindness. These, he believes, lead to restrictions in the range and variety of concepts, in the ability to get about, in control of the environment and of the self in relationship to the environment. It has been noted that these observations have the force of logic and validity behind them. However, the research evidence from which they were derived has been largely done on adults. It is difficult to know the effect and extent of these restrictions on children and to what extent variables such as mental capacity, opportunities for learning, and social factors are influential as compared to blindness. Intensive research with children would be highly desirable. Much information is still needed for better understanding of the mental characteristics of blind children. Better instruments of evaluation are needed and additional, well prepared personnel, who will devote themselves to this special problem over a long period of time.

Much less intensive and extensive study of the mental characteristics of partially seeing children has been accomplished. Many reasons (Lowenfeld, 1955) have been given for this state of affairs, but little has yet been done to change the situation. Conventional instruments for appraisal of intelligence are typically used (Livingston, 1958). Some studies have indicated that the intelligence of the partially seeing tends to be lower than that of normally seeing children, but most such studies have been done primarily in children found in specialized programs. Such children may not be representative of the general population of partially seeing children since the brighter and better adjusted children may be succeeding well enough to avoid placement in the specialized programs. Kirk (1962) in his text which deals with exceptional children in terms of discrepancies in growth and development says, "The available evidence indicates that the development of partially sighted children does not deviate from that of seeing children nor does it show discrepancies in growth within the child." Bateman's study (1962) indicated a mean IQ of 100 for 131 children studied, with a mean IQ of 97.5 for 53 girls, and a mean IQ for the boys of 101.7. It should be remembered that these children represent those in school and in special programs rather than the total population. Much additional information is also needed on the intellectual and educational characteristics of the partially seeing.

## EMOTIONAL AND SOCIAL CHARACTERISTICS

The emotional and social characteristics of visually limited children have not been clearly described though many attempts have been made to do so. Meyerson (1953) has pointed up the confused state of affairs in research on the adjustment of the blind and the partially seeing. Chapter 10, on adjustment, provides an additional discussion of the topic.

In a recent study, Cowen et al., (1961) point out that their "Extensive review of relevant literature revealed a striking deficit in many prior investigations in this area." They point up inadequate design and methodological problems. Cowen and his colleagues studied the adjustment of three groups of children—the blind in day school programs, the blind in residential school programs, and a group of comparable seeing children. The investigators also studied the attitudes and understandings of the parents of these three groups. The findings are worth noting though the research is not entirely free of the problems typical of research in this area. No basic differences in adjustment were found among the three groups. Regarding the relationship between degree of disability and adjustment, better adjustment was associated with greater visual disability and it is suggested that the partially seeing have greater adjustment difficulties than do the blind. In conclusion the investigators say, "Any prior beliefs about inevitable contingencies between visual disability and maladjustment are severely challenged by the findings of the present investigation."

For purposes of this discussion, only three general statements are made and these should be understood to be opinions held by the author until more adequate research provides better answers.

1. Social and emotional maladjustment or both as typically defined and measured are not necessary consequences of limitations in vision.

2. Such maladjustment which does occur is not directly proportional in severity to, nor necessarily directly related to, visual limitation.

3. Negative attitudes (Murphy, 1960) toward visually limited individuals and negative self-regarding attitudes by the visually
   limited are found frequently and may produce a disproportionate
   amount of social and emotional maladjustment by comparison
   with that found among the normally seeing.

Much progress remains to be made on the physical, mental, social,
and emotional characteristics of the visually limited. Even in the
area of physical-medical characteristics where progress might be
expected to be most advanced, visual limitations from undetermined
causes still comprise a large proportion of the cases. The implementation of educational programs cannot await the more precise
and complete information that would be desirable. Education proceeds hopefully in the light of the best knowledge currently
available.

# Education

The education of the visually limited has had an interesting and
inspiring history in the United States. As early as 1828 (Frampton
and Kerney, 1953) plans were made for education in residential
schools and shortly thereafter (1866) founders' voices were heard
recommending limitations on such plans in the hope that local
programs could meet the needs of the visually limited. Day school
programs of the blind which had origins as early as 1834 in Scotland
(Farrell, 1956) began in 1900 in this country. In London in 1908
(Hathaway, 1959) was established the first program specifically for
the partially seeing. By 1913 the first class for the partially seeing
had been opened in Boston. In the same year the cooperative
system already functioning for blind children was extended to partially seeing children in Cleveland. Present trends indicate the
development of a continuum of educational planning for the visually limited (AFB, 1959) rather than dichotomous services among
day versus residential school programs. Every state (Jones, 1961b)
has some type of legislative provision enabling the development of
residential or local educational programs or both for visually limited
children. The writer strongly endorses a continuum of services, per-

haps best exemplified in the so called "Oregon Plan" (Lowenfeld, 1959), and the New Jersey Plan (Taylor, 1959) which are described later in the chapter. In both these plans, day and residential school provisions are available in terms of the needs of the *individual child* rather than in terms of administrative expediency. Essential to the effectiveness of such plans is the flexibility of individual placements and opportunity to change the plans for an individual child when the situation calls for it. Placement in one type of program or the other should not imply total or permanent commitment to it.

Visually limited children, like all children, are first of all the responsibility of general education. Only when it is clear that the regular educational provisions provided for all children are inadequate to meet the needs of the individual blind or partially seeing child, should special programming be sought. For additional understanding of educational planning of visually limited children some guidelines for the regular classrom teacher are presented followed by a brief review of some essential and unique features of various administrative plans as they relate to educational provisions for the visually limited.

## WHAT THE REGULAR CLASSROOM TEACHER CAN DO

Visually limited children will be found in regular classrooms under a number of conditions and arrangements. Some visually limited children will be found in regular classroom without any special program for them. Others will be found there who are enrolled in a residential school in the neighborhood and attend in a regular grades under a cooperative, liaison arrangement. Still other children will be in such regular classrooms with the resources of one of the specialized programs, such as the cooperative or resource room plans described in chapter 1. In any case, certain guidelines and suggestions will help the regular classroom teacher to maintain a comfortable, effective and productive relationship with the child and his program. Recent publications (Johnson, 1961; NSPB, 1961; AFB, 1954 and 1957) will be of additional help.

Of primary importance to the successful, comfortable functioning of the visually limited child in the regular classroom are the attitudes which he meets there, the self-regarding attitudes he takes there, and the attitudinal climate that develops. The positive attitudes that are essential are most likely to develop where accurate information is available. The following myths have often caused faulty attitudes to persist. The truths are presented to refute them.

| MYTHS | TRUTHS |
|---|---|
| Visually limited children are endowed with extrasensory powers or are compensated by nature for their defects. They have exceptional talents for music. They have supersensitive hearing, touch and taste. | The visually limited have no "ESP" and rather than being provided natural compensation are more likely to have additional limitations. Should they be found to have senses that are more keen or special musical talents they result from increased attention to the other senses, to diligent practice and opportunities for learning. |
| Residual vision is damaged by use. Reading in bed, in dim light or watching television "ruins" eyes. | Residual vision is lost or atrophied by disuse. We learn to see and the more we "look" the more we "see." |
| Vision problems are punishment for sin. | Vision problems result from disease, hereditary, and accidental causes. |
| Visually limited children have "facial vision" for obstacle perception. | Hearing and the use of auditory cues are known to be necessary and sufficient to explain obstacle perception. |
| Glasses will cure eye problems. | Eye glasses only change the characteristics of the visual stimulus. They do not cure pathological conditions. |

| MYTHS | TRUTHS |
|---|---|
| All visually limited children are mentally retarded or emotionally disturbed. | Mental retardation and emotional or social disturbance are not *necessary* correlates of lack of vision or the presence of vision problems. |

The following suggestions for the regular classroom teacher will be of help.

1. Be alert to the behavioral signs and physical symptoms of visual difficulties in all children. Be sure that proper referrals have been made and everything possible has been done to correct or ameliorate the problems.

2. Accept and provide for a wide range of individual differences on many dimensions, including vision.

3. View the visual limitation of the child as only one of his attributes, and not as if it was his most important characteristic. Many children have been "taught" to be handicapped and visual limitations have become the central focus in their lives because they were responded to as if the loss was paramount.

4. Make the visually limited child one of *your* pupils as much as you would any other. Do not consider him the residential school's, the resource teacher's, or the itinerant teacher's responsibility.

5. Provide a setting for, and expect achievement of, the pupil in terms of his scholastic aptitude and other attributes not in terms of visual disability. Differentiate the effects of limitations in vision from effects that have their source in other causes such as emotions, intellect, hearing, attitudes, background. Do not let the child exploit his visual limitation for special treatment.

6. Provide lesson presentations which appeal to, and utilize other senses as well as, vision. Teachers are usually gratified at the results of such efforts for all their children.

7. Arrange preferential seating for the visually limited child, as you would for the needs of any other child, but especially in terms of his range of vision and his needs for differential illumination.

8. Provide a visual environment conducive to comfortable eye work conditions for all children. A good visual environment is characterized in part by fifty foot candles of light on working surfaces, minimized glare, reduction in work-background contrast and provision of controlled lighting for different work and eye condition needs.

9. Obtain assistance in the form of constructive consultation and specialized materials and equipment from those who assume special responsibilities for visually limited children.

10. Help the child to develop concepts meaningful to him and in line with his own reality. Do not impose upon him artificial concepts he cannot understand or appreciate because of his visual limitations.

11. Develop a genuine respect for the child's media for learning (braille, large type; audio and tangible aids; his specialized tools for learning). Many of these can also enrich the education of all the children.

12. Remember that the visually limited child, perhaps only somewhat more than all children, needs first-hand experiences in preference to vicarious ones.

13. If the regular classroom teacher and the child have access to services from a resource or itinerant teacher, their roles should be clearly delineated. Do not expect the special teacher to re-teach what is supposed to have been taught in the regular classroom. The special teacher's role is to facilitate learning (more than to teach directly) through assistance to the regular teacher and to the child. Do not let the child "pit" or "play" one teacher "against" the other.

14. It is easy to exploit the visually limited child by showing him off to other children, teachers or to visitors. Treat him as you would any other pupil.

15. When in doubt, the regular teacher should do what she would consider best for any child.

16. Respect for and acceptance of individual differences are learned. These take time and effort. The regular classroom teacher should "give them a try."

## ADMINISTRATIVE PLANS

Six general types of administrative educational plans have been implemented for visually limited children. Although all of these have been discussed briefly in chapter 1, some repetition is desirable in this context to illustrate several points. Among specialized programs for the visually limited there are unique relationships that are essential to effective functioning therein by visually limited children. The plans are discussed in an order which is roughly in terms of the extensiveness of the provision.

Many visually limited have in the past been and continue to be educated with seeing children in settings where little if any formal special provisions are available. Such arrangements can only be evaluated positively if the visually limited children are making optimum progress toward the goals we hold for all children. It is apparent that acceptance and understanding on the part of school personnel is necessary to make it possible for visually limited pupils to succeed in such settings. Children who succeed in such settings have learned to live and work reasonably efficiently with their limitations in vision. Evidently, parents provide a good deal of strong support, help and encouragement to children who succeed with such little specially planned help. Very little is known about the relative success of this procedure in comparison with the more structured types of provisions which follow. Undoubtedly this arrangement will be most effective for older children, those with mild impairments, for late blinded individuals, and for those who have excellent previous foundations in more extensive services.

The itinerant teacher, or contact plan, (Sibert, 1960) provides periodic direct service to visually limited children and indirect service to the children through their cooperating classroom teachers and other personnel who participate in the educational program. This plan was pioneered for the partially seeing by Frederika Bertram in California in 1938 and has had a rapid growth since that time for both partially seeing and blind children. Such a plan is possible and practical for visually limited children in ways in which it may not be for other types of exceptional children. This is true because fewer content and methodological modifications are necessary. In fact, such plans when effectively implemented are characterized by good general educational procedures which enhance the effectiveness of education for all children. The direct service by the itinerant teacher includes tutoring and remedial help when needed, instruction in the use of special equipment and materials, and counseling in educational, personal, social and vocational problems. Indirect services by the itinerant teacher include the preparation of specialized materials for use by cooperating classroom teachers, consultation with teachers, and educational planning with the personnel of the school where the child is enrolled. The itinerant teacher plan has been more widely used for partially seeing children but has become increasingly popular in the education of blind with seeing children in recent years. The itinerant plan seems most feasible for visually limited children at the secondary level, especially when the child has had an earlier firm foundation in programs providing more extensive services such as the resource teacher plan.

The resource teacher plan is that in which the child is enrolled in the regular classroom and does virtually all of his work with the regular class. This is often called the resource room plan, which was described in chapter 1. The present author prefers the resource teacher plan because the emphasis should be on the teacher rather than on the room where she functions. The child goes to the resource teacher in the special room she maintains only for special help and materials. The resource teacher, like the itinerant teacher, provides both direct and indirect services to the child and his teachers, but on a more regular and full time basis than the contact teacher. Resource teachers typically serve not more than 12 partially seeing children or 8 blind children or some combination of the two types of children. While programs providing resource teachers serving both partially seeing and blind children have been criticised, they remain a frequent, successful practice in many school systems. The resource teacher plan is probably the most common type of administration provision for educating visually limited children with their normally seeing peers.

The cooperative plan is that in which the child is usually enrolled in the special classroom, does his close eye work (partially seeing) or reading and writing in braille (blind children) with the help of the special teacher in a special classroom setting (described in chapter 1). The visually limited children participate with their seeing classmates in the regular classroom in those activities not requiring special conditions or activities. While the cooperative plan has generally diminished in popularity with educators of the visually limited, some of its characteristics are often used in conjunction with the resource teacher plan, and indeed usually neither program is purely one or the other. Some children may need the more extensive services of a cooperative arrangement until their basic skills of reading and mobility are firmly established. As they become more proficient in these skills they can function effectively with the less comprehensive help characteristic of the resource or itinerant plan.

The special class plan is that in which the visually limited children receive all of their instruction with a special teacher in a "self-contained" class. While the children participate in out-of-class school activities with their seeing peers, their instruction is centered in their own special classroom unit.

The residential school plan is that in which a self-contained educational program is operated solely for visually limited children. Historically, this plan is the oldest for the visually limited. The residential school has provided largely for blind rather than partially seeing children, although many partially seeing children are enrolled, especially from rural settings where local provisions have not been made, or when for unique economic, social, or personal reasons the child is not likely to succeed in local schools. The residential school provides a complete educational and boarding school program with courses of study paralleling those of the states in which they are established. Such schools for the visually limited are in marked contrast to residential facilities for the retarded. They are not custodial and do not entail legal commitment of the children. They function for children only on a school-calendar-year basis. Their major, if not sole, function is education in contrast to welfare. Chapter 1 has indicated the extent to which states have been committed to the residential school plan for visually limited children. While it has been noted that the residential provisions are largely for blind children, many of them are named "braille and sight-saving schools," or "schools for the visually handicapped," and do enroll rural or underprivileged partially seeing youth. Lowenfeld (1959) has listed four groups of children for whom residential programs may be considered most appropriate.

They are (1) blind children for whom no local services are available, (2) blind children whose families do not provide desirable places for them, (3) blind children who for environmental reasons or reasons within the children themselves are not in a condition for local school placement, and (4) blind children whose parents believe the residential school is a better placement for their child.

Two outstanding state plans previously cited merit further special consideration in this treatment of administrative plans for the education of visually limited children. They are the New Jersey Plan and the Oregon Plan. In the 1800s when many states were establishing residential facilities for education of blind children, the state of New Jersey chose to provide for its visually limited children primarily in regular public schools and since 1910 (Taylor, 1959) has implemented this plan. The New Jersey plan utilizes all of the administrative provisions discussed above, supplementing its own day public school provisions by utilizing residential programs in other states to supplement its services for children with special needs or problems. The plan is characterized by central, flexible programming to meet the individual needs of children through a commission for the blind. The commission provides continuous service to the blind from the preschool years into old age.

The Oregon Plan provides the most extensive and detailed cooperative plan between day and residential school services. The Oregon residential school provides its services to children until they have acquired their basic skills after which they enroll in local day school programs where continued special help is available for their education. This arrangement is also characterized by flexibility in planning to meet special, individual needs. As needs indicate, a child may shift from one aspect of the program to the other. Other states, notably California, have adopted plans similar in features but implemented through different administrative arrangements.

## EDUCATIONAL PROVISIONS

Of more basic concern than administrative plans is what happens in educational programs for visually limited children. It has frequently been said that the content and methods of instruction for both the blind and the partially seeing are the same as those for seeing children and that only the media differ—braille, audio and tactual aids, and large type. In general, this is true. The visually limited have the same needs for basic mastery of the skill subjects (the three R's); they also need social studies, science, English, and so on; the methods for good teaching in these subject matter areas are essentially the same as those for normal children. However, effective programs for the visually limited must provide additional emphases. Chief among these is a focus on enabling the visually limited child to function effectively in coping with his environment, both physical and social, through his remaining vision or his other senses or both, and living in harmony with his associates.

Since attitudes of acceptance toward visually limited children play an extremely important part in the personal, psychological, social, and vocational adjustment of these children, they must be enabled to elicit positive attitudes toward themselves from people in their environment. To effect this, the educational program must provide unique opportunities for learning to get around comfortably and effectively in the environment (being mobile and oriented), for learning to acquire efficiently both academic and nonacademic skills, and for learning to relate successfully to the total social environment.

For the blind child, developing mobility, orientation, and effective skills for living is something like the "Kingdom of God." It should be "sought first" and other things can be "added unto" it. The blind child who can play Chopin flawlessly but can't find the piano efficiently is unlikely to elicit favorable attitudes toward himself when away from the piano. In the past, educational programs for the visually limited have often failed to recognize or to cope adequately with this problem. Fortunately, there is a great deal of current interest in this important area. Some educational programs, The Seeing Eye, the Veterans' Administration, Vocational Rehabilitation, and the American Foundation for the Blind have led the way. The AFB has promoted several short summer courses for teachers in orientation and mobility. The Seeing Eye Dog Guide program has financed workshops, promoted research, and provided consultative services. Boston College (Mobility, 1960) has recently developed a preparation program and a new career title for "peripetologists" (orientation and mobility instructors). In 1961, Western

Michigan University instituted another course in this vital area. Some classical research, for example, on obstacle perception (Ammons et al., 1953) provides a base on which to build. It indicates that obstacle perception can be learned and that audition is a necessary and sufficient condition for obstacle perception. Some recent research (Garry and Ascarelli, 1960) contributes additional information suggesting that specific attention to the development of spatial perception and training in spatial relations skills can be productive of more effective mobility and orientation in blind children. Research (Finestone et al., 1960) conducted at the Research Center of the New York School of Social Work, Columbia University, on *The Demand for Dog Guides and the Travel Adjustment of Blind Persons* provides useful information. The research was conducted on adults but has implications for children and their educational programs. Among major findings, the research report shows that most of the blind adults studied had a lower than necessary level of travel performance; were dissatisfied with their performance; had no active plans for improvement; were not deliberate or purposeful in their choice of mode of travel; and had usually not had travel training of any duration or quality. Hopefully, more research in the future will provide much-needed additional information.

The goal of programs of mobility and orientation for blind children is an optimum degree of independent functioning by the individual. The programs are designed to help the individual attain the ability to cope with his environment effectively without sight in terms of his developmental level. The problem is greater than enabling him merely to "navigate" or travel. The program should promote his effective interaction with his total environment and thus requires development of acceptable skills in dressing, eating, interpersonal relations, and moving about in the immediate as well as peripheral environment. This broader conception of orientation and mobility has too often been neglected for a program primarily characterized by emphasis on travel from one place to another.

With regard to the travel aspect of mobility for the blind, the methods used may be enumerated. Some blind persons, especially those who retain small degrees of useful vision (so-called travel vision) can navigate without assistance except in unusual circumstances (such as snowy weather or heavy traffic). Some youth and adults find the cane useful as an aid to mobility and orientation—but young children do not. Emphasis for young children needs to be placed on "precane" skills. As a rule of thumb, the age at which a child should learn to use the cane is that age at which he wants to extend his environment beyond very familiar territory. Special techniques have been developed and can be taught for the effective use of the cane in mobility.

The use of a dog guide as an aid to mobility is effective for a limited number of blind persons. Exploitation of the dog-guide movement for fund-raising and human interest has led to the erroneous impression that virtually all blind people can utilize dog-guides. Contrary to popular opinion, the dog does not guide the individual to a destination, but only assists him in avoiding immediate obstacles or dangers. The blind person must direct the dog to the desired destination. Probably not more than 5 percent of the blind find dog-guides acceptable or satisfactory. Personal, social, and employment reasons limit the number. Dog-guides are not provided for children and, as in the case of "precane" skills, "precanine" skills should be emphasized with school-age pupils.

An acceptable and common mobility aid for the blind is the sighted guide or companion. Nothing provides "eyes for the blind" so well as a sighted person. Training and practice help both the guide and the guided to have a compatible, comfortable working relationship in which overdependence of neither is indulged. The goal of all mobility instruction for the blind child is independent functioning. Personal safety, and personal and social acceptability are paramount considerations in the mode of mobility to be utilized.

The educational program for the visually limited must also emphasize the development of meaningful concepts. French (1932) in his insightful and scholarly book *From Homer to Helen Keller* suggested some special emphases for methods in the education of the blind that still have cogency today. He stressed the urgent need for physical development, for "activity," for the "corrective of concreteness, (and) of objectivity," and for stimulation. He said:

> The chief intellectual problems are those of securing concreteness in the thinking processes and thought products of the blind and of orienting the mind, that is, of giving it its location and directions both in the world of thought and in the world of objective reality. Closely bound with

this is the important problem of immediate physical orientation. Both the physical and mental condition of the blind demands vastly increased activity, which means far more than a mere physical or mental gymnastic. (p. 25).

French also pointed out that teachers of the blind have too often forgotten that the *word* is never an adequate symbol for the entity, phenomenon, process or idea, that it symbolizes. Cutsforth (1951), Lowenfeld (1955) and many others have made these and similar points. Surely an extremely important emphasis in educational programs for the visually limited must be the development of accurate and real concepts—concepts accurate and real to the child himself, which avoid verbal unreality.

Another emphasis that characterizes special educational programs for the visually limited in addition to the general educational program is in the area of communication skills. An extremely important communication tool for blind children is braille. In 1829, Louis Braille (Roblin, 1955) then a young student of the Paris School for the Blind adapted to the needs of the blind a military code for night communication (*ecriture nocturne*). The adaptation was first called sonography, and later braille. No more efficient and useful means of reading and writing for the personal use of the blind has yet been found. The 63 possible combinations of six raised dots in the braille cell $\begin{smallmatrix} 1 & \bullet & \bullet & 4 \\ 2 & \bullet & \bullet & 5 \\ 3 & \bullet & \bullet & 6 \end{smallmatrix}$ can be used to present for the independent use of the blind virtually any literary, musical, numerical, or scientific material that can be presented in print. There is no other efficient medium for which this claim can be made. Since each braille cell requires a quarter inch of line space, many space saving features have been added to Braille's original code in the form of signs, abbreviations, and contractions. To illustrate, the word "knowledge," if spelled letter for letter in braille would require 2.5 inches of line space. To save space, "knowledge" is always represented in braille by the letter "k" $\begin{smallmatrix} 1 & \bullet & \bullet \\ & \bullet & \bullet \\ 3 & \bullet & \bullet \end{smallmatrix}$, dots one and three standing alone, requiring only one half inch and saving two inches of space.

Special notation systems provide for the presentation of mathematics in braille making it possible for the blind child to do his arithmetic on the braille writer. Notation systems for scientific symbols have also been developed. Music notation in braille makes it possible to provide musical scores for any instrument or vocal music. In fact, there is some evidence that Louis Braille's original intention was to provide a tactual medium of music notation. A more highly contracted or abbreviated form of braille is useful as shorthand for the blind stenographer or the college student note-taker.

Several important points about reading and writing in braille should be stressed. Because braille has some attributes of a "code," people are frequently misled into treating it as a code rather than as a complete reading and writing medium. Faulty and damaging attitudes may derive from this thinking. Reading and writing (Ashcroft, 1960) in this medium require essentially the same functions as any other reading and writing, that is, obtaining and conveying meanings. As such, the same principles which apply to teaching and learning reading and writing in print apply to developing these skills in braille. Many children have needlessly developed problems with this medium because of disdainful or critical attitudes toward it on the part of their teachers. Such attitudes seem to be derived from lack of knowledge about the medium, the bulkiness of braille, and the slower speed of tactual reading. One recent effort (Ashcroft, 1961; Ashcroft and Henderson, 1962) is aimed at enabling teachers to learn braille more quickly and easily. This programmed instruction in braille, researched on teachers in preparation, has proved successful both in learning braille reading and writing, and in developing more positive attitudes toward braille on the part of teachers by facilitating their learning to use it.

Instruction in reading in braille proceeds parallel to that of reading for seeing children. The kindergarten and a large part of the first grade are used to develop readiness. As with print reading, a mental age of 6 to 6.5 is thought to be needed for a successful beginning. The methods of teaching reading in braille are very comparable to those of teaching reading in print. In the primary grades the braille reading pupil is not at a great disadvantage in speed as compared to his sighted peer. It is at the point where emphasis shifts from largely oral to mainly silent reading that the unfavorable comparison in rate between ink print and braille readers becomes apparent. The braille reader is not disadvantaged in "aural", or "talking book," reading.

Enlarged print is a necessary medium for most partially seeing pupils. Enlargement of print can be achieved in several ways. The simplest and most efficient way is to bring the print closer to the eyes. Because of traditional attitudes, bordering almost on superstitition growing out of the assumption that holding reading material close damages vision, it is disturbing to many people to see individuals holding reading material very close to the eyes. Most ophthalmologists assure us that this is an ungrounded fear and that children may safely be allowed to hold reading materials where they need to. Unfortunately, this approach to enlargement of print is not adequate for many partially seeing children.

Optical magnification is a second way of enlarging print. Conventional glasses, plain, illuminated, and projection magnifier devices, and special lenses (both contact and those in conventional frames) for very low vision may be used for this purpose. Several optical companies specialize in providing a great variety of such specialized magnifying devices, catering to the individual needs of people with a wide range of vision problems. Microscopic and telescopic lenses (Mann, 1961) are among some of the recent developments. One particularly interesting application is the use of contact lenses along with special lenses in conventional glass frames to provide a telescopic arrangement. Recently, federally subsidized low-vision optical aids clinics have been established to provide extensive diagnostic services and very special corrections for persons with extremely small degrees of remaining vision (well below 20/200). The success of these provisions seems to depend on extensive diagnosis, good rapport between the specialist and patient, repeated fittings over a period of time, counseling and guidance, and the motivation to learn, adapt to, and to see with these aids. Again, however, low-vision aids are not a panacea.

A third method of providing enlarged print is to print reading material with large sized type (Eakin and McFarland, 1960). Type is measured in points, with 72 points to the inch. Thus a letter an eighth of an inch high would be roughly 9-point type. The typical school text other than for the primary grades will usually be in at least

10-point type. Primary texts, like books for the partially seeing, will be in 12-, 14-, 18-, or up to 24-point type. Books for the partially seeing produced by the American Printing House for the Blind are produced in 18-point type. Similar books from Stanwix Publishing House are produced in 24-point type.

It is important to realize that all of these means of enlarging print reduce the effective field of vision or the "eye-span" (the number of words or letters that can be read with one "eye-stop" or saccadic eye movement). It is therefore necessary to find the optimum type and degree of enlargement (neither too large nor too small) for the particular individual and his unique vision characteristics. It is also necessary to realize that enlargement of any kind does not solve all of the reading and educational problems of partially seeing pupils. Some misguided educators and lay persons have assumed that it is only necessary to provide enlarged materials to meet all the educational needs of the partially seeing. It is hoped that this brief discussion will contribute to correcting some of this erroneous thinking.

Few sources of materials for reading in braille or large type are available. These sources are unable to provide the wealth of materials available to normally seeing children. The materials that are available are extremely expensive. This entails another unique provision by specialized educational programs for the visually limited. It is necessary for the teacher to obtain or prepare reading and other educational materials comparable to those used by normally seeing children. This is done by the teacher herself either preparing braille or large type materials, or recorded on tape or disc versions of these materials, or by developing volunteer services for these purposes (getting community persons to transcribe the materials). This latter procedure requires the teacher to teach volunteers the skills of brailling, typing, or recording these materials. Many educational programs throughout the country have developed elaborate arrangements for accomplishing these purposes.

Audio aids provide an additional source of educational materials, supplement scarce reading materials, and provide enrichment for educational programs. Some specialized materials are available for this purpose from such sources as the American Printing House which produces catalogs of talking book records (phonograph records which play at 33⅓ rpm), and recorded educational aids to learning (educational tape recordings). Excellent commercial recordings have recently become increasingly available. Volunteer transcribers supplement these sources. While some attention has been given to the development of listening skills and some research (Nolan, 1960) has been done on audio aids, much more should be done on this important opportunity for learning so especially significant for the education of the visually limited. A recent study (Bixler et al., 1961) indicated that sixth, seventh, and eighth grade blind children comprehend auditory material in literature and science at 225 and 275 words per minute respectively without significant loss in comprehension. These auditory rates are in marked contrast to the approximate rate of 90 words per minute for reading in braille reported for high school students.

Tangible aids such as relief maps and globes, concrete arithmetic materials, and a wide variety of models—all useful in the education of any child, are of special usefulness to the visually limited. In addition to special and commercially available tangible aids and apparatus, creative teachers provide many unique aids which have special significance for the visually limited. Equipment and teacher aids for the partially seeing are regularly listed by the National Society for the Prevention of Blindness. *Pamphlet 302* published in 1962 provides for a recent listing.

A unique emphasis of special educational programs for the visually limited is centered in the provision of an optimal visual environment for learning. In effect, programs for many of these children might well be called "sight development", or "sight utilization", programs, With the appropriate increasing emphasis on use of residual vision and the importance of "learning to see," the visual environment assumes growing importance. Fortunately, recent school construction, lighting, and furnishing have developed along lines earlier prescribed for good educational facilities for the partially seeing. Therefore they provide the basis for development of a good visual environment. Special attention needs to be given to control of levels of illumination, appropriate reflectance values on walls, ceilings, floors, furniture, and chalk boards; reduced glare, and appropriate light contrasts between work and background surfaces.

The foregoing brief treatment of education touches lightly only a few of many points that might be made. By way of summary, it may be said that great expectations may be held for the education of the visually limited if they are provided adequate interest and attention, prepared personnel with wholesome attitudes, and needed educational settings, equipment and materials.

## Research

Demographic, psychological, and educational research on the visually limited has been fairly extensive. Research has been encouraged by such agencies as the National Society for Prevention of Blindness where the best of statistical information on etiology and classification, such as Kerby's data, are available. The American Foundation for the Blind has encouraged research on many facets of the field from appliances for the blind to aspects of rehabilitation. A recent publication (Graham, 1960) reviews the present status and future of research. The Perkins School has encouraged research for many years, notably that of Dr. S. P. Hayes, already cited in connection with psychological and achievement testing of blind and partially seeing children. Since 1953 the American Printing House for the Blind has maintained a department of educational research where attention has been devoted to educational problems of the visually limited. The research on the visually limited has been reviewed periodically in the *Review of Educational Research* (Ashcroft, 1959), and other publications. In spite of this apparent extensive interest in research there are repeated pleas for more and better research in this area. The pleas are well justified for much remains to be known about the education of these children and their psychological, social, and other characteristics.

There are promising trends suggesting that additional research will be forthcoming. The appointment of a specialist on the visually handicapped in the U.S. Office of Education Section on Exceptional Children and Youth will encourage increased research efforts. Other federal agencies as well as the national agencies mentioned are also encouraging additional research. There is no dearth of questions to be studied. The crucial shortage is in competent and interested professional personnel who can put the questions in researchable terms, and design and carry out the experimentation to obtain the answers.

## Summary

Important trends in the education of the visually limited are apparent in connection with each of the major topics dealt with in this chapter. Trends have been suggested with respect to definitions for educational purposes of both the blind and the partially seeing. National study has been devoted to this topic and the fruits of this group thinking should soon be evident in practice. The emphasis is certain to be on more functional definitions of children needing services. Hopefully it will result in flexible planning which takes into account whether special services are needed for children who can make optimum progress in regular classrooms where individual needs are served.

Prevalence of visually limited children in need of special education will hopefully be reduced by continued progress in prevention of blindness, optical aids, restoration of sight, and amelioration of serious eye problems. At the very least it can be hoped that only general population growth will maintain present prevalence levels.

More and better information is becoming available about the physical, mental, social, and emotional characteristics of the visually limited. Growth in research in the future should provide much better information on which to base appropriate educational programs. Better attitudes toward exceptional children, better prepared teachers for their education, and better facilities for their programs are all contributing to giant strides forward in educational programs.

National, state, and local resources, both public and private, are improving in their constructive contributions to satisfy the needs of the visually limited. As these trends develop and are implemented to the benefit of visually limited children we can revise the adman's slogan and say "Products are our most important sign of progress."

## CHAPTER REFERENCES

American Foundation for the Blind. *The Pine Brook Report: National work session on the education of the blind with the sighted.* New York: Amer. Found. Blind, No. 2, 1954.

————. *Itinerant teaching service for blind children.* New York: Amer. Found. Blind, 1957.

————. Problems and trends in the education of blind children and youth. *Concerning the education of blind children.* New York: Amer. Found. Blind, Educ. Series No. 12, 1959.

————. *A teacher education program for those who serve blind children and youth.* New York: Amer. Found. Blind, 1961a.

————. *Guidelines for the coordination and distribution of educational materials for blind children.* New York: Amer. Found. Blind, 1961b.

Ammons, Carol E., Worchel, P. W., & Dallenbach, K. M. Facial vision. *Amer. J. Psychol.,* 1953, **66**, 519–523.

Ashcroft, S. C. The blind and partially seeing. *Rev. educ. Res.,* 1959, **29**, 519–528.

————. Errors in oral reading of braille at elementary grade levels. Unpublished doctoral dissertation, Univer. of Illinois, 1960.

————. Programmed instruction in braille. *Inter. J. Educ. Blind,* 1961, **11**, 46–50.

————, & Henderson, Freda. *Programmed instruction in braille.* Pittsburgh: Stanwix House, 1962.

Bateman, Barbara Dee. Reading and psycholinguistic processes of partially sighted children. Unpublished doctoral dissertation, Univer. of Illinois, 1962.

Bixler, R. H., Foulke, E., Amster, C. H., & Nolan, C. Y. *Comprehension of rapid speech, Part I.* Louisville, Ky.: Univer. of Louisville, 1961. (Cooperative Research Project 1005)

Cowen, E. L., Underburg, Rita, Verrillo, R. T., & Benham, F. G. *Adjustment to visual disability in adolescence.* New York: Amer. Found. Blind, 1961.

Cutsforth, T. D. *The blind in school and society.* New York: Amer. Found. Blind, 1951.

Eakin, W. M., & McFarland, T. L. *Type, printing, and the partially seeing child.* Pittsburgh: Stanwix House, 1960.

Farrell, G. *The story of blindness.* Cambridge, Mass.: Harvard Univer. Press, 1956.

————. Snellen and the E chart. *Sight saving Rev.,* 1958, **28**, 96–99.

Finestone, S., Lukoff, I., and Whiteman, M. *The demand for dog guides and the travel adjustment of blind persons.* N.Y.: Research Center, Columbia Univer., The New York School of Social Work, 1960.

Frampton, M. E., & Karney, Ellen. *The residential school.* N.Y.: The New York Institute for the Education of the Blind, 1953.

French, R. S. *From Homer to Helen Keller.* N.Y.: Amer. Found. Blind, 1932.

Garry, R. J., & Ascarelli, Anna. Teaching topographical orientation and spatial orientation to congenitally blind children. *J. Educ.,* 1960, **143**, 1–48.

Graham, M. D. Social research on blindness. New York: Amer. Found. Blind, 1960.

Hathaway, Winifred. *Education and health of the partially seeing child.* (4th ed.) New York: Columbia Univer. Press, 1959.

Hayes, S. P. Measuring the intelligence of the blind. In P. A. Zahl (Ed.), *Blindness.* Princeton, N.J.: Princeton Univer. Press, 1950.

Hurlin, R. G. Estimated prevalence of blindness in the United States and in individual states. *Sight saving Rev.,* 1962, **32**, 162–165.

Johnson, Isabel. *A blind child becomes a member of your class.* New York: Amer. Found. Blind, Educ. Series No. 14, 1961.

Jones, J. W. The blind child in school. *Sch. Life,* 1961a, **43**, 7–10.

————. *Blind children: Degree of vision, mode of reading.* Washington, D.C.: Government Printing Office, 1961b.

Kerby, C. E. Causes of blindness in children of school age. *Sight saving Rev.,* 1958, **28**, 10–21.

Kirk, S. A. *Educating exceptional children.* Boston: Houghton Mifflin, 1962.

Livingston, J. S. Evaluation of enlarged test form used with the partially seeing. *Sight saving Rev.,* 1958, **28**, 37–39.

Lowenfeld, B. Psychological problems of children with impaired vision. In W. M. Cruickshank (Ed.), *Psychology of exceptional children and youth.* Englewood Cliffs, N.J.: Prentice-Hall, 1955. Pp. 214–283.

————. The role of the residential school in the education of blind children. *Concerning the education of blind children.* New York: Amer. Found. Blind, Educ. Series No. 12, 1959.

Mann, J. W. Optical aids service and its implications for education. *New outlook for the blind*, 1961, **55**, 65–67.

Meyerson, L. The visually handicapped. *Rev. educ. Res.*, 1953, **23**, 476–491.

Mobility and orientation—a symposium. *New outlook for the blind*, 1960, **54**, 77–94.

Murphy, A. T. Attitudes of educators toward the visually handicapped. *Sight saving Rev.*, 1960, **30**, 157–161.

National Society for Prevention of Blindness. *Visual screening, a guide for eye inspection and testing visual acuity.* New York: National Society for Prevention of Blindness, 1961. (Publication 180).

————. *Some suggested sources of equipment and teacher aids for partially seeing children.* New York: National Society for Prevention of Blindness, 1962. (Pamphlet 302).

Nolan, C. Y. *An overview of the educational research program at the American Printing House for the Blind.* Proceedings of 1960 convention of American Association of Instructors of the Blind.

Roblin, J. *The reading fingers—life of Louis Braille.* New York: Amer. Found. Blind, 1955.

Schlaegel, T. F. The dominant method of imagery in blind as compared to sighted adolescents. *J. genet. Psychol.*, 1953, **83**, 265–277.

Sibert, Katie N. Instructional materials and procedures for the partially seeing. *Sight saving Rev.*, 1960, **30**, 162–165.

Taylor, Josephine L. The itinerant teaching program for blind children. *Concerning the education of blind children.* New York: Amer. Found. Blind, Educ. Series No. 12, 1959.

Terry, T. L. Extreme prematurity and fibroplastic overgrowth of persistent vascular sheath behind each crystalline lens. *Amer. J. Ophth.*, 1942, **25**, 203–204.

Villey, P. *The world of the blind.* London: Duckworth, 1930.

## ADDITIONAL REFERENCES

Abel, Georgie L. The education of blind children. In W. M. Cruickshank & G. O. Johnson (Eds.), *Education of exceptional children and youth.* Englewood Cliffs, N.J.: Prentice-Hall, 1958. Pp. 295–298.

Bertram, Fredericka M. The education of partially sighted children. In W. M. Cruickshank & G. O. Johnson (Eds.), *Education of exceptional children and youth.* Englewood Cliffs, N.J.: Prentice-Hall, 1958. Pp. 265–294.

Cholden, L. S. *A psychiatrist works with blindness.* New York: Amer. Found. Blind, 1958.

Gowman, A. G. *The war blind in American social structure.* New York: Amer. Found. Blind, 1957.

Graham, M. D. *Social research on blindness.* New York: Amer. Found. Blind, 1960.

Henderson, F. *Structure and function of the eye, a handbook for nurses and teachers.* San Francisco: Gutenburg Press, 1957.

Irwin, R. B. *As I saw it.* New York: Amer. Found. Blind, 1955.

Lende, Helga. *Books about the blind.* New York: Amer. Found. Blind, 1953.

### REFERENCES FOR PARENTS

American Foundation for the Blind. *Aids for the blind.* New York: Amer. Found. Blind, 1957.

————. *Is your child blind?* New York: Amer. Found. Blind.

————. *Library service for blind persons.* New York: Amer. Found. Blind.

————. *What every person should know about blindness.* New York: Amer. Found. Blind.

Eaton, A. H. *Beauty for the blind and sighted.* New York: St. Martin's Press, 1959.

Kellogg, Alicia W. *The art of seeing with little sight.* New York: National Society for the Prevention of Blindness.

Lowenfeld, B. *Our blind children.* Springfield, Ill.: Charles C Thomas, 1956.

Middlewood, Ester L. *A child though blind.* New York: Amer. Found. Blind, 1954.

Moor, Pauline M. *A blind child too can go to nursery school.* New York: Amer. Found. Blind, 1952.

————. *Toilet habits: suggestions for training a blind child.* New York: Amer. Found. Blind.

National Society for the Prevention of Blindness. *Signs of eye trouble in children.* New York: National Soc. Prevention Blindness, No. 351.

————. *Education of partially seeing children—a committee report*. New York: National Soc. Prevention Blindness, No. 149, 1952.

————. *Education of partially seeing children in school systems*. New York: National Soc. Prevention Blindness.

————. *Eyes for the future*. New York: National Soc. Prevention Blindness, No. 351.

————. *Some suggested sources of equipment and teacher aids for partially seeing children*. New York: National Soc. Prevention of Blindness, No. 159.

Norris, Miriam, Spaulding, P. J., & Brodie, F. A. *Blindness in children*. Chicago: Univer. of Chicago Press, 1957.

Wood, Maxine. *Blindness—ability, not disability*. New York: Amer. Found. Blind, Public Affairs Pamphlet No. 295, 1960.

# RESOURCES

Resources for the visually limited are probably more extensive than for any other handicapped group in spite of the fact that the group is the smallest. A partial listing of the resources follow. Like any such listing it is of necessity selective and limited.

## FEDERAL AGENCY RESOURCES

The Library of Congress Division for the Blind since 1931 has provided free (including postage) reading materials to the blind and partially sighted (legally blind) in the form of braille, talking books, and tape recordings. Its materials are distributed through 31 regional libraries.

The National Institute of Neurological Diseases and Blindness conducts research on ophthalmology in addition to other neurological and sensory areas.

The U.S. Office of Education employs a specialist in the education of visually handicapped children. The specialist provides consultative and other services to all programs for the blind and partially seeing.

The U.S. Office of Vocational Rehabilitation has a special division of services to the blind, which provides service to postschool youth.

## NATIONAL VOLUNTARY RESOURCES

In 1879, the 45th Congress of the United States passed the Act to Promote the Education of the Blind. This act set aside a perpetual fund for the purpose of aiding the education of the blind through the production of educational materials at the American Printing House for the Blind. Continuously and increasingly since, the education of the visually limited has been assisted through the provision of educational materials furnished to legally blind children on a per capita basis. Subsequent revision and expansion of the program has increased the appropriation, liberalized the provision for the assistance of visually limited children educated anywhere in the United States, and expanded the types of materials and equipment to include large-type books, record reproducers, records and tape recordings, raised maps and globes, tangible arithmetic aids, and any material or equipment manufactured, modified, developed, or processed at the American Printing House.

Recent efforts to expand and liberalize these provisions even further have been directed toward making them available to a greater number of partially seeing children, to subsidizing the purchase of supplies from other sources, and to increasing the amount of financial subsidy for these purposes.

The American Printing House is a private Kentucky corporation directed by a vice president and general manager at its headquarters, 1839 Frankfort Avenue, Louisville. It publishes catalogs of braille, large-type and talking books, educational tape recordings, tangible apparatus, braille music, and numerous periodicals such as the *Reader's Digest* in both braille and talking book form and *Newsweek* in talking book form. The Printing House also keeps a Union Catalog of Volunteer Brailled Books and carries on a program of educational and technical research.

The American Foundation for the Blind has a distinguished history as a resource in the education of the visually limited. It has led efforts for constructive legislation; implemented, encouraged, and supported, research in education, psychological and social factors, and on technological developments. It has provided consultative services and scholarship funds to begin, to supplement, and to encourage educational and teacher preparation programs. The foundation employs an executive director and numerous specialized personnel at its headquarters at 15 West 16th Street, New York 11, New York. Among its publications are the *New Outlook for the Blind* (monthly), the *Braille and Talking Book Review,* and monographs on education, research, and legislation. It provides legislative analysis and reports and provides a directory of agencies and services for the blind.

The National Society for the Prevention of Blindness employs a consultant in the education of the partially seeing and provides extensive literature about the education of these children. It encourages the preparation of teachers through courses, workshops, and scholarships. The society promotes research on blindness and its prevention. It carries on a broad program of public education through its national headquarters and local society affiliates. An executive director heads the society, which has its offices at 16 East 40th Street, New York 19, New York. Among its publications are the *Sight Saving Review* (quarterly), the *Wise Owl,* the *Newsletter,* Snellen vision screening materials, and pamphlets and reprints of journal articles.

Among many other national resources are the following: The Council for Exceptional Children (CEC) a division entitled the Council for Teachers of Partially Seeing Children, which holds section meetings at national and regional conventions of the parent council and publishes a *Newsletter* for teachers of the partially seeing.

The American Association of Instructors of the Blind is a professional organization of teachers of the visually limited. It holds biennial conventions for which it publishes extensive proceedings. It also publishes the *International Journal on the Education of the Blind* (quarterly) and the *Fountainhead,* a monthly newsletter. The association affairs are handled by an executive secretary from its headquarters at 2363 Spring Street, St. Louis 10, Missouri. The association also encourages research and provides scholarships for teacher preparation.

The Perkins School, Watertown 12, Massachusetts; The Royer-Greaves School, Paoli, Pennsylvania; and the Hadley Correspondence School, Winnetka, Illinois are three schools that provide specialized national services. Perkins is noted for its research, teacher-training, services to the deaf-blind, and its educational equipment and materials. Royer-Greaves is known for its services to the mentally retarded and other multi-handicapped children. Hadley provides a wide range of home study courses by correspondence to the blind and deaf-blind.

The Stanwix Publishing House, 3020 Chartiers Avenue, Pittsburgh 4, Pennsylvania, publishes many materials in large type and has done research on type size and format of texts for partially seeing children.

Among other national resources are the Recordings for the Blind, Incorporated; the Delta Gamma Foundation; Lions International; and the National Braille Club.

For an extensive list of such resources the reader should see the Directory of Agencies Serving Blind Persons in the United States and Canada of the American Foundation for the Blind and publications of the National Society for the Prevention of Blindness.

## SELECTED 16MM SOUND FILMS

*Betty sees a bird.* 20 min, black & white. National Society for Prevention of Blindness, 16 East 40 Street, New York 16, New York. Film shows how to train teachers and volunteers in vision-screening.

*Johnny's new world.* 20 min, color. National Society for the Prevention of Blindness, 16 East 40 Street, New York 16, New York. Deals with teacher observation and detection of children's eye problems.

*A fair chance for Tommy.* 11 min, black & white. National Society for the Prevention of Blindness, 16 East 40 Street, New York 16, New York. The story of a partially seeing pupil enrolled in regular grades in public day school showing essential services rendered by resource and itinerant special teachers of the partially seeing.

*Glaucoma.* 22 min, color. National Society for the Prevention of Blindness, 16 East 40 Street, New York 16, New York. Emphasizes early signs of glaucoma, and explains acute and chronic aspects of the condition.

*Crossroads at 4.* 13 min, color. National Society for the Prevention of Blindness, 16 East 40 Street, New York 16, New York. Dramatic discovery of a young boy's latent amblyopia.

*It's up to you.* 12 min, color. National Society for the Prevention of Blindness, 16 East 40 Street, New York 16, New York. Industrial eye safety message including eye surgery sequence.

*Toward tomorrow.* 42 min, black & white. American Foundation for the Blind, 15 West 16 Street, New York 11, New York. A series of sequences on nine totally blind preschool and school age children taken in children's own homes or in the school they are attending.

*First steps in clay modeling.* 15 min, black & white. American Foundation for the Blind, 15 West 16 Street, New York 11, New York. Shows one approach to plastic art instruction with a blind child.

*The Perkins story.* 40 min, color. Campbell Films, Saxton River, Vermont. The film tells the story of the Perkins School for the Blind in terms of the children, their experiences, and their problems.

*The long cane.* Part I, 32 min, part 2, 34 min. U.S. Veteran's Administration, Visual Aids Services, Washington 25, D.C. These films were made on indoor (Part I) and outdoor (Part II) mobility instruction for blinded veterans. They are useful to show teachers the importance and complexity of mobility instruction.

## CHAPTER 9

# Crippled and Neurologically Impaired Children

MARGUERITE WILSON

Children with neurological and nonsensory physical impairments have a wide variety of disabilities which may make some type of special education provision necessary. Many pupils present a major challenge to education because of their multiple exceptionalities. In the past, crippling and chronic health problems in children frequently resulted from a postnatal infection. Typical examples were poliomyelitis, osteomyelitis, and tuberculosis. While such conditions could be severe and long term, they usually did not result in multiple disabilities including brain injury. Medical advances have created more effective ways of preventing and treating these contagious diseases. At the same time, other advances have resulted in saving the lives of many more children with severe congenital impairments than formerly, a striking example being the cerebral palsied. A number of these boys and girls have learning, perceptual, visual, and hearing problems as well as a crippling condition. To serve them effectively in school, teachers must draw upon the information presented in the previous chapters as well as this one.

Neurological impairments occur in a growing number of congenitally disabled children. Furthermore, brain injury frequently creates problems of learning for the pupil resulting in a special challenge for the teacher. However, some neurological disorders are not typically classified as either a crippling or special health condition. An example is aphasia (a language disorder due to brain injury) which was discussed by Hull in his chapter on the speech impaired.

Since we are concerned here with the educational rather than the medical aspects of the field, we have chosen to group together all children with nonsensory physical impairments whether they were accompanied by a neurological damage or not, and whether they resulted in a crippling or a chronic health condition. This has been done because such pupils are usually placed in the same special education setting. These most frequently include hospital and homebound programs, and special schools and classes for the non-sensory physically impaired. Even though children with widely diverse impairments may be taught by the same teacher or enrolled in the same program, frequently they require very different curriculum and teaching procedures. It cannot be stressed too strongly here and throughout the chapter that many children classified as crippled or chronic health cases from a medical point of view, do not present a special education problem because they can make adequate progress in the regular grades. Too often in the past they have been placed on homebound instruction or in a special school or class because of a transportation problem, or a disfiguration which was disturbing to others. This practice is being overcome. Special education placement is only justified when an unusual education need exists which cannot be met by the regular school program. Remarkable medical advances have reduced the prevalence of nonsensory pupils—for special education purposes—more than any other, while at the same time making it among the most complex.

## Classification

Many educators have divided into two groups children with non-sensory physical impairments which may or may not be accompanied by neurological damage. This classification has a physical rather than an educational basis. The first, often called the crippled, have muscular or skeletal deformities which in many cases are apparent to the casual observer. They may wear braces or prosthetic devices such as artificial limbs, or they may go about with the aid of crutches or wheel chairs. The second group have disabilities that are not so readily recognized. They have a variety of chronic health ailments which confine them to bed for relatively long periods of time or curtail their activity either periodically or chronically.

In the past, children in these two categories have been described by a variety of names. An excellent example of the divergency of nomenclature used in referring to classes for these children is provided by a UNESCO workshop report, *Statistics on Special Education* (1960). Crippled children are designated as the orthopedically handicapped or the motor impaired. The other subgroup is called children with special health problems, chronic health conditions, low vitality, or poor general health; other terms used in referring to them are the delicate, chronically ill, and physically weak. Some types of illness have also been classified separately for special education purposes. Thus we have had separate classes provided for cardiacs, epileptics, diabetics, asthmatics, the tubercular, and the cerebral palsied.

It is because of these difficulties of classification that it seems wise to avoid ambiguous titles for either the general category or the subgroupings within it and to discuss these exceptional children in terms of the kinds of problems which they present to the administrator or teacher who attempts to provide adequately for their education. It is evident that the educator is interested less in the physical aspects of the child's condition than he is in the manner in which it will affect his functioning in a learning situation. This does not mean that etiology or medical diagnosis is to be ignored or that a complete assessment of the physical condition is not essential in the identification and classification of these exceptional children. However, the emphasis here will be upon those aspects of physical impairment which have definite implications for the educator. Therefore, the children in this heterogeneous group will be discussed in this chapter under three categories: (1) those who have muscular or neuromuscular handicaps which significantly limit their ability to get about, sit in the classroom, or manipulate the materials required for learning; (2) those with skeletal deformities which also affect ambulation, posture and hand use in school work; and (3) those who have disabilities which result in reduced efficiency in school work because of temporary or chronic lack of strength, vitality, or alertness.

## Prevalence

The difficulties that are encountered when an attempt is made to determine the number of children with nonsensory physical impairments who need special education have been indicated by Dunn in chapter 1. He pointed out the limitations of medical frame of reference upon which prevalence figures for children with crippling and chronic health problems has often been based and emphasized that such figures have little usefulness for educational purposes. He cited the most recent U.S. Office of Education estimates of 2 percent for the group, with 1 percent classified as crippled, and 1 percent as chronic health problems. The Dominion of Canada Bureau of Statistics use a sharply reduced estimate of 0.47 percent for the total group, with 0.1 per cent crippled and 0.37 as chronic health problems. Not many years ago, it was common to see a prevalence figure of 2 percent for both the crippling and chronic health categories. The newer statistics, particularly the Canadian ones which are probably more accurate, represent a sharp reduction and are certainly more realistic figures for the educator who is planning school facilities than could be determined by examining prevalences for the separate handicapping conditions described next, based upon medically significant disabilities, since substantial percentages of the children so impaired are able to attend regular school. Instead of citing numerous prevalence figures for the various conditions or groups of conditions considered in this chapter, the discussion will emphasize relative proportions of each type of impairment that might be expected in an educational setting.

## Characteristics

It is not appropriate here to become preoccupied with defining and describing all of the diseases and other conditions which result in neurological and nonsensory physical impairments in children.

The teacher who is planning to become a specialist in this area should have detailed courses dealing with the medical aspects of crippling and chronic health conditions. Others who are interested will find references at the end of the chapter where further information can be obtained. However, if an educator is to provide adequate special education programs he should have some knowledge of the types of problems with which he will need to deal. Therefore, the principal characteristics of those handicapping conditions which will probably be his main concern will be discussed briefly, and the implications for education indicated.

## MUSCULAR OR NEUROMUSCULAR IMPAIRMENT

The impairments of children which are manifested by muscle weakness, paralysis, or incoordination are generally most accurately designated as neuromuscular conditions, since the difficulty usually originates in nerves which innervate the muscles rather than in the muscles themselves. Nerve damage may result from infection or injury at any time during an individual's life, or degeneration may take place without any known cause. Muscle deterioration (atrophy) may result from lack of use of the extremities. Because of the frequent involvement of the nervous system, children in this classification present the most difficult educational problem of any of the subgroups in this area of exceptionality.

*Progressive muscular dystrophy* is a term used for several forms of disease that are characterized by a gradual degeneration and wasting of muscles. There is often an apparent enlargement of muscles which in reality is a displacement of muscle tissue with fatty and connective tissue. Though the exact cause of the disease is not known, theories of etiology include faulty metabolism which results in lack of nutrition to muscles, a malfunction of endocrine glands, or a deficiency of peripheral nerves. The disease may result in slow deterioration of the muscles, often with temporary periods of remission, and in the juvenile types may result in early death, often in the teens. Both psychologically and physically the child with muscular dystrophy is benefited by being allowed to participate in normal activities as long as possible.

*Multiple sclerosis* is similar to muscular dystrophy in that it is also a progressive degenerative disease involving the muscles. However, there are additional symptoms such as spasticity of the extremities, tremors, unsteady gait, visual and other sensory complications which usually develop as a result of the damage to nerves. Patches of hardening or scarring (sclerosis) are scattered over the nervous system, including the brain and spinal cord as well as peripheral nerves. While there is no known cure and severe disability eventually occurs, there may be spontaneous remissions or partial recoveries. The disease may begin in late childhood but it is more common in adults.

*Poliomyelitis* (or infantile paralysis) is undoubtedly the most publicized and best known of the diseases which cause muscle weakness or paralysis. Although paralysis of muscles is the consequence of the disease, it is the nerve cells in the gray matter of the spinal cord which are damaged by the polio virus. In case of complete destruction of cells a return to usefulness of the affected parts of the body depends on utilization of other muscle groups. Thus, some improvement may be seen in children returning to school after an attack of polio. A significant reduction in the prevalence of postpolio disabilities has been brought about by the use of polio vaccines which is conservatively estimated to be effective in preventing paralysis in 70 percent of the cases (Preizler, 1959).

The majority of children with the three types of neuromuscular involvement described can attend regular classes because their intellectual capacity is not impaired by the disease, though there may be severe problems of personal adjustment involved. Therefore, the school problem is mainly one of adjusting physical facilities to compensate for the handicap, and providing counseling services when needed. However, providing an education for the child who has had polio may become less complex since the impairment may become less severe with time. In advanced cases of both muscular dystrophy and multiple sclerosis, due to the progressive nature of the conditions, the child's ability to learn may be considerably diminished.

*Spina bifida* is a congenital developmental condition in which there is a defect of closure of the bony spinal canal. As a result there is usually a protrusion of the spinal cord through this gap. This causes varying degrees of paralysis in the lower extremities as well as the lower abdominal organs. It may be accompanied by other abnormalities of the skeletal system or by hydrocephalus (see chapter 3). In many cases the defect may be treated surgically and although normal function is not always possible the child is enabled to get about with the aid of crutches or braces. Hand and arm use are usually good. Unless the hydrocephalic condition causes mental retardation, mobility and possible lack of bowel and bladder control will be the principal problems to be solved in a school situation.

*Cerebral palsy* cannot be considered a disease in the usual sense of the word. Rather, the term is used to designate a number of types of neuromuscular disabilities which are characterized by disturbances of voluntary motor function, especially of the extremeties and are the result of damage to the brain. The manifestations of the disorder differ according to the site and extensiveness of the lesion and may vary from extremely mild motor incoordination to virtually complete helplessness. A number of types of cerebral palsy have been identified. Classification is generally based on the particular kind of motor involvement, but there are also a number of systems which use other criteria, such as degree or location of physiological impairment (Crothers and Paine, 1959; Minear, 1956; Perlstein and Barnett, 1952). More widely accepted categories will be used here; spasticity, athetosis, ataxia, rigidity, and tremors. These types of cerebral palsy, the principal area of the brain lesion, and the major motor manifestations of each are shown in Table 9.1. While the various types can generally be identified by these characteristics numerous mixed conditions also occur, making accurate differential diagnosis and classification difficult.

Since the injury is seldom confined to a specific, limited area of the brain, secondary impairments are the rule rather than the exception. Mental retardation, sensory, and other defects are found in a considerable number of cases. Certain kinds of defects are more prevalent in one type of cerebral palsy than another. The percentage of children with secondary handicaps as found in a study made in New Jersey (Hopkins et al., 1954) is given in Table 9.2.

It will be seen that approximately one half of the children had IQ's below 70, with a considerably higher figure for the rigidity and ataxic types than for the spastic and athetoid. Sensory defects also differed widely. Over half of the spastic group had speech problems but nearly 90 percent of the athetoids had this defect. Almost one third of the total group had seizures and only a slightly smaller percent had defects of vision. Lack of definite hand dominance which may contribute to difficulty in learning to read and

TABLE 9.1 *Classification of types of cerebral palsy with principal area of brain lesion and major motor manifestations.*

| TYPE | PRINCIPAL AREA OF BRAIN LESION | MAJOR MOTOR MANIFESTATIONS |
|---|---|---|
| Spasticity | Motor cortex and pyramidal tracts | Involuntary contraction of affected muscles when they are suddenly stretched — called stretch reflex—resulting in tenseness and difficult, inaccurate voluntary motion |
| Athetosis | Basal ganglia and extrapyramidal tracts | Involuntary contraction of successive muscles resulting in marked incoordination and almost constant motion of the extremities |
| Ataxia | Subcortical, probably in cerebellum | Incoordinated movement, impaired balance and sense of orientation in space |
| Rigidity | Diffuse | Widespread continuous muscle tension or "lead-pipe" stiffness. |
| Tremor | Basal ganglia | Rhythmic, involuntary, uncontrollable motions limited to certain muscle groups |

write (Harris, 1961) was found in about one fourth of the children studied. Other conditions are also common among children with cerebral palsy. A larger proportion of them than among children generally are left-handed. Coupled with poor coordination and lack of eye-hand coordination, this added deviation causes difficulty. In a recent survey of teachers of the cerebral palsied, hand and eye coordination was listed next to speech as a major problem in school (Geer and Wolfe, 1960).

TABLE 9.2 *Secondary handicaps in various types of cerebral palsy.*

| TYPE | PERCENT OF EACH TYPE IN TOTAL GROUP N 1406 | IQ BELOW 70 N 933 | VISION N 1297 | HEARING N 1293 | SPEECH N 1224 | SEIZURES N 1265 | LACK OF HAND DOMINANCE N 1224 |
|---|---|---|---|---|---|---|---|
| | | | PERCENT WITH DEFECTS | | | | |
| Spastic | 45.9 | 44.1 | 27.3 | 7.2 | 52.0 | 28.2 | 19.1 |
| Athetoid | 23.7 | 40.9 | 20.4 | 22.6 | 88.7 | 20.8 | 36.1 |
| Rigidity | 12.6 | 66.3 | 29.0 | 13.7 | 72.2 | 41.9 | 18.0 |
| Ataxic | 10.8 | 70.5 | 42.7 | 18.4 | 85.3 | 36.3 | 32.9 |
| All groups | | 49.0 | 27.6 | 13.3 | 68.0 | 29.2 | 24.7 |

*Source:* Hopkins, T. W., Bice, H. V., & Colton, Kathryn C. *Evaluation and education of the cerebral palsied child.* Washington, D.C.: Council for Except. Child., 1954.

As cerebral palsy is the result of brain damage many of these children demonstrate characteristics of the Strauss syndrome described in chapter 2. Some have tactual and kinesthetic impairment in perceiving shape, weight, or texture (Woods, 1957). Others have disturbances of spatial orientation and judgment (Dunsdon, 1952). Cruickshank, Bice, and Wallin (1957) demonstrated that children with cerebral palsy often have greater difficulty discriminating figure and background than do normal children. Dolphin and Cruickshank (1951) found problems of conceptualization as evidenced by tendencies on the part of the children studied, to give more concrete than abstract responses, and to make fewer relevant associations when presented pictures which told a story.

The large number of children with cerebral palsy who are mentally retarded has been indicated. In fact about 50 percent obtain IQ scores below 70. While there are some children who have above average intelligence, studies generally substantiate the findings of the New Jersey study in which only 23 percent of the group fell in the borderline dull range and 28 percent were average or above. Though there are many arguments which could be presented against assessing the intellectual potential of severely impaired cerebral-palsied children with the same instruments that are used with normal children on the grounds that such a practice is discriminatory, there is much to be said in favor of the position stated by Allen that "evaluating the cerebral palsied in terms of the picture of the nonhandicapped group eventuates in a more realistic appraisal of strengths and weaknesses as these traits enter into the individual's everyday life" (Allen, 1960, p. 203). These are indeed, as Allen concludes, "the hard facts of life." While the creative psychologist uses every possible technique to determine the potentialities of each cerebral-palsied pupil, it is important to know how he performs intellectually in comparison with the total school population. Thus, the educational problem becomes one not only of adapting the program to the multiple physical and psychological disabilities of the cerebral-palsied child but also in many cases of adjusting it to the level of slow learning, educable mentally retarded, and trainable children—a fact which some teachers of the cerebral palsied refuse to accept. Because the problem of providing an adequate education for children with cerebral palsy is a much more complex one than for children with any of the other conditions in this area of exceptionality, major emphasis will be given to it in later discussions of educational provisions.

## SKELETAL DEFORMITIES

Skeletal impairments in children affect primarily the upper and lower limbs, spine, and joints. Such disabilities may handicap a child in walking, sitting, standing, or using his hands. They may be congenital, a condition with which the child is born, or acquired as a result of infectious disease, developmental disorders, or accident. Abnormalities of the foot and ankle are the most common of the congenital type. *Clubfoot,* a condition in which one or both feet are turned downward and inward at the ankle, occurs most frequently. It accounts for 25 percent of the congenital anomalies seen in crippled children's clinics, and 75 percent of those involving the feet.

*Congenital dislocation of the hip* ranks next in frequency. In this defect the head of the femur or thigh bone is displaced in the hip socket. If this condition is uncorrected permanent crippling and irreversible changes in bone growth result. Early recognition and prompt correction of both this impairment and clubfoot have been successful to the extent that these abnormalities are seldom seen by the average person except in the very young (Boyd, 1956). Therefore, they are rarely a school problem.

*Scoliosis,* a lateral curvature of the spine, may be congenital, but is also acquired as a result of poor posture, disease, or injury. Shands (1959) reports that in a recent survey in Delaware 19 of every 1000 of the population over 14 years of age had this disability to some degree. It is among the 20 most common conditions found in a recent survey of children in special education programs for nonsensory physically handicapped children in the State of Illinois, though it accounted for only 1.2 percent of the total number (Boyles and Calovini, 1960).

A number of acquired deformities of bones and joints, their cause, and characteristic features are shown in Table 9.3. While these conditions account for a comparatively small percentage of the total number of children with nonsensory impairment who are in special education programs, they occur frequently enough to be of concern to the educator. Implications for education can be found in

TABLE 9.3 *Acquired conditions causing impairment to bones and joints.*

| CONDITION | CAUSE | CHARACTERISTIC FEATURES | TREATMENT |
|---|---|---|---|
| Tuberculosis of bone and joint | Tubercule bacilli | Affects mostly spine, then hip and lower extremities; formation of tubercules destruction and disintegration of bone; symptoms of pain, swelling, muscle spasm and muscle atrophy | Antibiotics – streptomycin and isonizid; well-balanced diet, with high vitamin content; rest, immobilization of affected part |
| Osteomyelitis | A pyogenic or pus-forming organism | Affects mostly long bones, usually in lower extremities; acute inflammatory symptoms – pain, fever, generalized weakness; swelling, tenderness of affected area; draining sinuses, destruction of bone | Antibiotics, blood transfusions; caloric diet, vitamins; surgical removal of dead bone; protection from injury |
| Pyogenic arthritis | A pus-forming organism | Inflammation of joints; fever, pain | Antibiotics or sulfonamides; hot or cold applications, rest with some motion |
| Rheumatoid arthritis | Unknown; tendency to be familial | Joint pains, swelling, stiffness; later muscle atrophy and joint deformity; severe weakness and fatigue | Rest with supervised exercise and massage; relief from anxiety and worry; well-balanced diet; treatment of local infections; ACTH and cortisone therapy |
| Legg-Perthe's disease (Coxa plana) | Probably a circulatory disturbance caused by injury or strain | Flattening of head of femur or hip bone; destruction of bone tissue; pain, muscular spasm; limping | Rest from strain or weight-bearing; bed rest until evidence of repair and no pain or muscle spasm |

*Source:* Shands, A. R. *Handbook of orthopedic surgery.* (5th ed.) St. Louis, Mo.: Mosby, 1959.

treatment procedures and occurrence. Only those treatment practices which specifically affect the kind of educational provisions for children with these conditions are included in the table.

All of these conditions are commonly found in school-age children particularly at the elementary grade levels. In recent years many of the diseases listed in the table have decreased because of increasingly effective medical treatment. The incidence of tuberculosis has been markedly reduced, and osteomyelitis has been so successfully controlled by antibiotics that severe cases of it among children are rarely found today.

*Bone cysts and tumors* should also be mentioned as a cause of crippling. Typically, a bone cyst is a slow growing, bone-destructive lesion near one end of the shaft of a long bone. Tumors are growths which may be either benign or malignant. Early diagnosis and treatment can often prevent serious deformities from these conditions.

*Accidents* are the cause of considerable crippling among children. Though the accidental death rate in the United States has actually decreased in the past few years, (U.S. Department of Health, Education and Welfare, 1958) the rate of reduction is only about one third that of the other main causes of death. In 1957, accidents were the major cause of death in the age group from 1 to 34 years of age, resulting in 6 percent of all deaths. For every one of these deaths there were 100 injuries (McClave and Shaffer, 1957). Not all of these cause damage directly to the skeletal system, injury to nerves and muscles often leads to subsequent crippling. Injuries that result in lack of adequate motion, or in the absence of upper extremities are the most handicapping for school work. In addition to such permanent, severe impairments which may necessitate modifications of school programs, services must also be provided to accident victims during periods of convalescence.

#### CHILDREN WITH LIMITED STRENGTH, VITALITY, AND ALERTNESS

Physical conditions that are characterized by greatly reduced strength, vitality, or alertness, which limit the ability of a child to perform at a maximal level of efficiency in school are often the reason for placement in special education facilities. These conditions may be caused by infectious diseases that are permanently disabling or that make necessary long periods of bed rest and convalescence, and by congenital or developmental impairments that have similar results. Other conditions such as diabetes and epilepsy may cause recurrent, often brief, periods of inadequate functioning.

*Heart conditions,* which are either congenital or acquired, are among the commonest causes of death and disability in children as well as in the total population. Of these, congenital heart disorders account for approximately 40 percent of all organic heart diseases in children (Spekter, 1955). Defects may be either in pulmonary blood vessels leading to or from the heart or in the walls of the heart itself. The development of dramatic operations to correct these defects has received a great deal of publicity in recent years, and many children who would otherwise have died early or have been limited in their activity throughout life have been enabled to live normal lives.

*Rheumatic fever* is a chronic infection of the connective tissues of the body, affecting the joints, heart, and blood vessels. It has been responsible for a great deal of the acquired heart disease in children. The specific cause of this disease is unknown, but in most cases it follows a streptococcus infection. The heart damage, which often is the consequence of recurrent attacks of rheumatic fever, has been greatly reduced by the prevention of infection through regular treatment with penicillin and other antibiotics over a period of years. Berman (1959) reports that before the days of antibiotics there was a rather consistent rate of recurrence of the disease in about 20 percent of the cases. In some instances it ran as high as 50 percent. The rate has now been reduced to 1 or 2 percent. The prolonged bed rest formerly prescribed for rheumatic fever patients has also been modified. A recent study (Lendrum et al., 1959) of 368 of these children resulted in the conclusion that as far as the heart was concerned, prolonged bed rest and restriction of activity were unnecessary. Furthermore, the economic burden on the family and the psychological damage to the child could be largely avoided by earlier return to more normal living. However, it is important that the advice of the physician be followed in each individual case.

*Pulmonary tuberculosis* is a low vitality disease that has been of concern to the special educator because of the required restriction of activity and long periods of convalescence which have been a part of the treatment. This disease is the lung infection associated with the term tuberculosis in the minds of laymen, with the well-known symptoms of tiredness, chest pains, cough, fever, and loss of weight. Here, too, the outlook has changed appreciably in the last decade. Not only has the prevalence of the disease decreased but children are also returning to school sooner after infection because of increasingly effective treatment. Consequently, day classes for the tubercular which were common some years ago have virtually disappeared in most areas. The majority of the children who cannot attend regular school are taught in sanatoria or in hospital and home teaching programs. Even here the period of time during which they need special education services is not as long as formerly.

While some health conditions such as tuberculosis and rheumatic fever are on the decrease, a number of other diseases are assuming a relatively more important position in special education programs. Among these are *nephritis, infectious hepatitis* and *infectious mono-nucleosis*. These diseases are not related but they have certain aspects in common which warrant their being discussed together. The causes and distinguishing features of each of these are presented in Table 9.4. It will be noted that these diseases have several similarities both in general symptoms and in treatment. All of them require periods of bed rest or reduced activity during which time a program of instruction in school subjects should be provided.

Children with *leukemia* and other forms of *cancer* may also need special education services. Cancer in children is often congenital or has its onset during the early years, and is generally a more acute and rapidly progressive condition than it is with adults. Leukemia, sometimes called "cancer of the blood," may be either chronic or acute. Presently, there is no known cure, though much research on etiology and cure is being conducted. In the meantime, treatment is aimed at keeping the child comfortable, interesting him in the world around him, and prolonging life as long as possible.

Three other unrelated conditions are found fairly frequently on lists of handicapping disabilities. *Asthma* and *other allergic conditions* result in respiratory difficulties which may interfere with a

TABLE 9.4 *Infectious diseases resulting in lowered vitality.*

| CONDITION | CAUSE | CHARACTERISTIC FEATURES | TREATMENT |
|---|---|---|---|
| Nephritis | Unknown; often preceded by a streptococcal infection | Puffiness about eyes and other parts of body; vomiting, fever, loss of appetite; anemia, high blood pressure with headache, drowsiness, often convulsions; possible damage to kidneys, and enlargement of heart | Bed rest and curtailment of activity; antibiotics |
| Infectious hepatitis | Virus spread by direct contact or through contaminated food and drinking water | Fever, loss of appetite, feeling of weariness, nausea, abdominal pain, headache; jaundice, bile pigment in liver; enlargement and tenderness of liver | Reduction of discomforts of pain and fever; dietary regulation; bed rest until liver functioning is normal |
| Infectious mononucleosis | Probably a virus; method of transmission uncertain | Fever sore throat, chills, headache, abdominal pain; initial enlargement of lymph nodes; body rash and occasional jaundice; possible involvement of central nervous system | Reduction of discomforts; rest and restriction of activity |

*Source:* Spekter, L. *The pediatric years.* Courtesy of Charles C Thomas, Publisher, Springfield, Ill., 1955.

child's school performance. *Malnutrition* can decrease strength and alertness. *Hemophilia* is limiting to a child because of the danger of accidents which might start the excessive bleeding characteristic of this disease. However, it is only in extreme cases of disability that special education is necessary for children with these impairments.

*Epilepsy* (or seizures) is a major chronic health condition which can affect the alertness, vitality, and mental health of a child in a manner and to a degree that may severely lessen his ability to function in a regular school situation. Epilepsy is much more common among children than is usually assumed. In fact it is estimated that one family in 50 has a member afflicted by epilepsy. There are more cases of epilepsy than of cerebral palsy, polio, muscular dystrophy, multiple sclerosis, and tuberculosis combined. Thousands of cases go unrecognized and untreated. In some cases, seizures are a symptom of a physical disorder such as injury to the brain, or are associated with acute infections and fever. Such seizures are sometimes called *symptomatic* epilepsy in contrast with *idiopathic* epilepsy, a condition in which there are repeated seizures without a known cause.

There are several types of epilepsy, and numerous names have been applied to some of the varieties. The two most common are *petit mal* and *grand mal*. A third type, *psychomotor* epilepsy, is less well known. The individual with this type goes through a brief period of automatic behavior during which time his actions may appear to be purposeful but in reality are irrelevant to the situation. He may even act violently and upon recovery from the attack will not remember what he has done. Such an attack may be passed off as "bad" behavior or a temper tantrum.

In *petit mal* the child loses consciousness for a few seconds but does not fall. His eyes may roll up or there may be a rhythmic blinking of the eyelids. He drops things, appears to be staring straight ahead, or stands still, unaware of what is going on around him. The teacher often thinks he is not "paying attention." He quickly recovers and goes on with what he was doing. If he is reading aloud, he will stop for a few seconds and then go on with the passge. As a rule this does not inconvenience him or anyone else to any great extent. However, if such seizures occur frequently the child is apt to lose the thread of a lesson and be handicapped by gaps in continuity. The teacher should watch for signs that indicate a child is having a seizure and repeat directions he may have missed or check to see that he has understood what was going on in the class.

A child who has *grand mal* seizures loses consciousness and falls rigidly to the floor. This is often preceded by a strange sensation known as an aura, and by a shrill cry. His muscles first tighten, then, accompanied by salivation, twitching and tremors may follow. Then comes the coma, or deep sleep or stupor. A seizure may last as long as a minute or two, and when he recovers he may be dull or disoriented. He may want to sleep for some time. Consequently, his school program is interfered with and normal progress impaired. When such a seizure occurs the teacher should not attempt to stop the attack. Instead, he should (1) ease the child to the floor, and (2) see that he is not apt to injure himself by striking furniture or sharp corners while in convulsions. Turning the child's head to one side and carefully placing, but never forcing, a folded handkerchief or similar soft object between the back teeth is sometimes advised. Do not use a pencil or other solid object or the teeth and gums may be injured. Other than these procedures there is nothing a teacher need do aside from providing a place for the child to sleep if he wants to when the seizure is over. Some individuals with this type of epilepsy often have an aura far enough in advance of a seizure that they can get to a place to lie down before losing consciousness.

A grand mal seizure need not be too disturbing for the other children in a classroom if they are prepared for it. If a seizure occurs during a class period, some explanation to the students will be necessary, but their attitude toward the situation will be largely a reflection of the teacher's. The teacher should help them to accept it calmly and to understand that there is nothing contagious or harmful about the convulsion that would mar their association with the epileptic child.

If a teacher is to remain calm during a seizure and properly manage the situation then and during the rest of a child's school life there are several points of which he should be aware. (1) Seizures alone are rarely a cause of death and there is no danger of a child choking on or "swallowing" his tongue. (2) Mental deterioration from repeated seizures over a long period of time is very infrequent, and children with epilepsy fall within the same range of intelligence as do other children. (3) The personality disorders which sometimes accompany epilepsy are as much a consequence of social stigma and the frustrating environment as they are constitutionally determined (Tizard, 1962).

When a teacher has a pupil who is susceptible to seizures in his class he should know: (1) what kind of seizure the child has, (2) the first aid procedures needed, (3) the medication the child is receiving, and (4) what restrictions the physician has ordered. The teacher may provide an invaluable service by reducing stress and anxiety for the pupil. Also he may need to encourage the epileptic youth to take the prescribed medication carefully and regularly, and to follow his ketogenic (high fat and carbohydrates) diet if he is on one.

Though the majority of the children with this condition can attend regular school, measures to control epileptic seizures are still not effective enough to make this possible for all of them. Spekter (1955) states that with anticonvulsive drug therapy, 50 percent of all epileptics can be entirely seizure free, and another 25 percent are improved. He adds that with guidance 80 percent can engage in competitive work without danger. In fact, normal activity and exercise may actually reduce the frequency of seizures, though extremely hazardous pursuits are better avoided. Educators and employers should be aware of these facts and allow persons with epilepsy to lead a "normal" life.

*Diabetes* is another condition which may result in a pupil losing alertness and vitality. However, it creates a quite different educational problem than does epilepsy. Diabetes mellitus, the type ordinarily associated with the general term, is a metabolic condition in which there is insufficient insulin produced by the pancreas to enable the body to utilize adequately glucose, or sugar. It cannot be cured but can be controlled through a balanced regime of diet, exercise, and insulin treatment. The child with uncontrolled diabetes is listless, inattentive, restless, and irritable. He may be accused by the teacher of being lazy. In the initial stages of the disease it may be necessary to hospitalize the child until a treatment program has been worked out. Once this has been established a child can participate in normal activities, and perform his school tasks without interference or inconvenience. The teacher should be informed of the prescribed routine and be aware of the consequences if the child fails to eat promptly, neglects the insulin, or over-exercises. He may go into insulin shock, becoming dizzy and light-headed, suffer abdominal pain, and show other diabetic symptoms described. A piece of candy, lump of sugar, or orange juice will often quickly restore him to normal. Most diabetic children are taught to care for themselves. The teacher need only be prepared to help him with unexpected crises. There is usually no reason why these children should need special placement of any kind.

## Educational Programs

### CURRENT TRENDS THAT AFFECT
### EDUCATIONAL PROVISIONS

The problem of providing special education for children with non-sensory physical impairments is quite different today from what it was 20 or even 10 years ago. The major change has been in the relative numbers of children with various handicapping conditions for whom special services must be provided. The decrease or increase in the prevalence of certain of these conditions, as well as changing philosophy in their management, have been discussed briefly in the previous section and in chapter 1. For the purpose of getting a total picture of the situation which will be useful in planning educational programs a summary of these changes should be helpful.

1. There has been a marked decrease in crippling conditions which are the result of infectious disease. This is particularly true of poliomyelitis and osteomyelitis, but also applies to such conditions as tuberculosis of the bones and joints, arthritis due to infection, and other conditions resulting from contagious diseases.

2. There has been an increase in the number of children born with congenital defects. At the same time, because of the early correction of many deformities and the development of effective

prosthetic devices, a great number of these conditions are no longer handicapping among school-age children.

3. Improved medical procedures have resulted in the saving of many children with multiple handicaps at birth who otherwise would not have survived.

4. Impairments due to accidents of various kinds have increased.

5. Changes in treatment procedures of children with congenital heart conditions, rheumatic fever, and a number of handicapping conditions due to infection have resulted in less restriction of activity and earlier return to normal living.

An example of the extent to which these changes are reflected in special education programs is shown in surveys of the number of children in such programs in the State of Illinois, exclusive of Chicago, made in 1954 and 1960 (Boyles and Calovini, 1960). A comparison of the results of the surveys of these two years is presented in Table 9.5. The 10 most prevalent conditions are listed according to their rank order in 1960, with the number of students with each disability. These figures are compared with those of the 1954 survey, and the decrease or increase over the six-year period is given in column three. Also shown in the table are the percent of increase or decrease for each condition. In order to give a slightly different picture of the situation, the table shows the percent of the total group which each condition represented in each year and the change in percent of the total group betwen 1954 and 1960.

One fact that is evident from the table is that from 1954 to 1960 there was a 6 percent decrease in the number of children in special education programs in this area of exceptionality, in spite of the rapid population increase. The large decrease of 36 percent for rheumatic fever and 57 percent for poliomyelitis, with even larger increases in accidents and postoperative cases of 50 and 77 percent respectively are particularly striking by comparison with this over all decrease. It is also interesting to note that while rheumatic fever, accidents, poliomyelitis and cerebral palsy combined accounted for 63.5 percent of the total group in 1954, they represent only 49.9 percent of the group in 1960.

While surveys of programs in other geographic areas might show slightly different results as far as details are concerned there is

TABLE 9.5  Students enrolled in programs for physically handicapped children in Illinois (exclusive of Chicago) in 1954 and 1960. (Percent of change 1954–1960 and percent of total group for each year.)

| CONDITION | NUMBER 1954 | NUMBER 1960 | CHANGE 1954–1960 | PERCENT CHANGE 1954–1960 Inc. | PERCENT CHANGE 1954–1960 Dec. | PERCENT OF TOTAL GROUP 1954 | PERCENT OF TOTAL GROUP 1960 | CHANGE IN PERCENT OF TOTAL 1954 Inc. | CHANGE IN PERCENT OF TOTAL 1960 Dec. |
|---|---|---|---|---|---|---|---|---|---|
| Rheumatic fever | 559 | 354 | 205 | | 36 | 23.2 | 15.8 | | − 7.4 |
| Accidents | 221 | 331 | 110 | 50 | | 9.2 | 14.7 | 5.5 | |
| Cerebral palsy | 277 | 235 | 42 | | 15 | 11.5 | 10.5 | | − 1.0 |
| Poliomyelitis | 471 | 201 | 270 | | 57 | 19.6 | 8.9 | | −10.7 |
| Postoperative | 65 | 115 | 50 | 77 | | 2.7 | 5.1 | 2.4 | |
| Cardiac | 71 | 79 | 8 | 11 | | 2.9 | 3.5 | 0.6 | |
| Nephritis | 52 | 76 | 24 | 46 | | 2.2 | 3.4 | 1.2 | |
| Mononucleosis | 15 | 64 | 49 | 327 | | 0.6 | 2.8 | 2.2 | |
| Muscular dystrophy | 52 | 49 | 3 | | .06 | 2.2 | 2.2 | 0.0 | |
| Hepatitis | 30 | 48 | 18 | 18 | | 1.2 | 2.1 | 0.9 | |
| Others | 590 | 695 | 105 | 17 | | 24.5 | 30.9 | 6.4 | |
| All groups | 2403 | 2247 | 186 | | 6 | | | | |

Source: Boyles, Iva J., & Calovini, Gloria. Statistical report–physically handicapped children in Illinois. Springfield, Ill.: Office of Superintendent of Public Instruction, 1960.

evidence that the over all situation would be much the same. As a consequence of the trends which are apparent in recent years, educators who are considering special programs for children with crippling and chronic health problems would do well to plan for: (1) more adequate provisions for children with cerebral palsy, and other neurological impairments, and those with multiple handicaps; (2) fewer facilities for children with crippling conditions which do not involve the central nervous system, or are the result of infectious diseases; and (3) more comprehensive evaluation and counseling service for children who can receive an adequate education in regular classes without endangering their health.

# Administrative Provisions

## PROBLEMS OF PLACEMENT

The exceptional children who need special education services because of neuromuscular impairment, skeletal deformities, and reduced vitality are provided for in hospital classes, home-bound programs, and special schools and classes. As has been indicated in the discussion on characteristics of the various nonsensory impairments, a great many children with disabilities of this type will not need special facilities. With some modifications of physical facilities and equipment their educational needs can be adequately met in regular classrooms. Regular class placement is possible because:

1. They have no impairment of intellectual functioning and can learn through the same procedures as children without disabilities. Therefore, specialized teaching methods are not necessary except for those whose physical impairments are complicated by difficulties of learning resulting from neurological damage.

2. They require no drastic curriculum revisions. Certain adjustments in programs of study may need to be made, particularly in those cases in which the disability is permanent and will greatly influence future vocational and social competency. Lack of normal experiences, absence from school, and the necessity of functioning at reduced speed may extend the amount of time required to complete prescribed courses. A rigid, inflexible curriculum will certainly

fail to meet the needs of these students, but there is no reason why ingenuity and flexibility on the part of teachers and administrators cannot result in satisfactory solutions to many of their school problems.

3. When stated in broad terms, the goals of education are essentially the same for handicapped as for nonhandicapped students. These goals may also need to be modified for a particular child on the basis of his physical condition and the extent to which it will continue to be a limiting factor in their attainment. However, education is aimed at assisting the pupil to achieve the fullest measure of self-realization of which he is capable and to become a contributing member of society to the limits of his capacity regardless of where he may be along the continuum of physical and mental capabilities.

*Changes in physical facilities* in regular school buildings that can be made to compensate for physical impairments include modifications in buildings such as: (1) a short ramp up a number of steps to enable children in wheelchairs or on crutches to enter the building; (2) addition of a hand bar by a drinking fountain, in a toilet stall, or near a section of blackboard; (3) the removal of desks to make room for a wheelchair; (4) modification of furniture to provide for the comfort of a child with braces; or (5) rubber mats over slippery sections of floor. Other building features designed to ensure the safety of handicapped students are discussed by Graham (1961) and Connor (1962). Within the classroom the problems of the child with poor hand coordination may be solved by such simple procedures as: (1) taping paper to the desk, (2) devising some means of keeping pencils and crayons from rolling to the floor, and (3) providing book-holders or mechanical pageturners.

In buildings of more than one story, and particularly in secondary schools in which students change classes frequently, the problem is somewhat complicated. In some cases transfer of a student to another building or a change in scheduling may solve the difficulty. Larger school districts can usually plan at least one regular school building with ramps or elevators to which handicapped pupils can be transported. Minor adjustments in buses can be made to accommodate wheelchairs and crutches, and to assist students in getting off and on.

It is evident that with good planning and little expense many children who would otherwise need special education services can be educated in normal classroom situations. Even if the only consideration were a financial one such adjustments would be worthwhile. However, the welfare of the students is of greater concern. It is generally agreed that a physically impaired child is better off in a regular classroom if it is possible to make adequate provisions for him there and he is reasonably well accepted. When this cannot be done, a special educational placement is indicated.

A number of criteria for placement in a special program should be taken into consideration in determining where a particular child will receive his education. Special education facilities should be provided when:

1. The child has specific difficulties of learning which make it necessary for a teacher to employ methods and materials that are not used in regular classroom teaching.

2. The child needs some kind of special equipment or adjustment of physical facilities which it is impossible to make in a regular classroom. This reason for special placement should not be used freely without careful consideration of all alternative possibilities.

3. The needs of the child are such that he requires a disproportionate amount of the teacher's time and attention with the result that other children in the room are seriously neglected. This problem, too, should be thoroughly studied and not be used as an excuse for special placement by teachers and administrators who do not want to be bothered by a handicapped child in the room. Often the guidance of a consultant can help to solve this difficulty in a manner that will be satisfactory to everyone concerned.

4. The child requires some type of therapy or treatment which can be provided only in a special facility.

5. The child's physical impairment causes emotional problems which are so severe in nature that placement in a special class is desirable. A smaller number of children, or more individual attention, may be the solution. There are also situations in which rejection by his classmates creates an emotional condition which makes segregation preferred. Often placement for this reason can be temporary, and the child can gradually be helped to adjust to

more normal situations. Furthermore, other children in the class can be helped to understand the handicapped child. Materials such as the pamphlet sponsored by the then National Foundation for Infantile Paralysis (1956) will be of assistance to the teacher in this respect.

It becomes apparent that placement of a child in a special program cannot be made on the basis of one criterion alone. The decision must be the result of a careful evaluation not only of the child's capabilities, needs, and limitations, but also of the possible arrangements which are available to him.

## TYPES OF SPECIAL EDUCATION PROGRAMS

The types of special education programs that are provided for children with nonsensory physical impairment have been discussed in general terms by Dunn in chapter 1. However, it seems advisable here to enlarge upon some of the aspects of these programs as they relate to the children in this classification.

*Special day schools or classes* are generally provided for those children whose physical impairment does not confine them to home or hospital but is severe enough to make it impossible for them to attend regular schools. Special schools enroll children with many handicapping conditions, though often classes within the school may be composed of students with only one type of disability. The Boettcher School in Denver, Colorado, is an example of this kind of facility. In a building especially designed for handicapped children, with ramps, elevators, rooms for resting and other special equipment, classes are held for children with severe heart conditions, cerebral palsy and other crippling conditions. Other special schools such as the Neil School in Chicago (Mullen, 1957) include nonhandicapped as well as handicapped students. Students are transported to these schools, which may be under the administration of one school district or of a number of districts working cooperatively. Schools such as these have the advantage of being able to concentrate specialized personnel and equipment in one place, thus making medical, therapy, and other services more readily available. Some of their disadvantages were discussed in chapter 1.

A *special class* or a unit of several classrooms in a regular school building is increasingly favored over a separate school for children with crippling or chronic health conditions who are unable to attend regular school. With this type of arrangement the handicapped pupils can participate in many learning activities with their nonhandicapped peers and still have the advantages of specialized equipment. For some children, such as those crippled by polio or recovering from extensive surgery, placement in the special class is only a temporary assignment until they have become adjusted to a school situation. Other children will spend most or all of their school lives in the special facility.

The classroom and equipment provided for these children should be designed to allow for freedom of movement and independent living. Some features to be considered are: (1) wide doorways, (2) nonskid floors, (3) handrails, (4) rounded corners, and (5) protected coat hooks. Play areas, toilet facilities, and drinking fountains should be planned to accommodate wheelchairs and crutches. Within the room, desks and other furniture should be planned with the handicaps of the children in mind and be flexible enough to be adapted to various individual needs. Regular school furniture can sometimes be modified by: (1) adjusting seats to turn to the side so that a child with braces can sit more easily, (2) providing foot rests, (3) adding hinged extensions to the desk with a cut-out for the child that has poor sitting balance, and (4) eliminating protruding parts over which a child might trip. For children with special problems of sitting or standing, equipment such as special adjustable chairs, stand-up tables, stabilizers, or cut-out tables may have to be provided. Further information and descriptions of such equipment may be found in the references, particularly those that deal with the education of children with cerebral palsy.

The number of children in a special class will depend on the severity of their disabilities. Eight children who are severely handicapped may constitute a class load, while as many as 10, or 12, less handicapped children can be managed in one class. Because of the difficulties of handling these children and the need of helping them with toileting, eating, and other self-care activities the teacher of a class of severely impaired children is usually assisted by an attendant.

*Auxiliary services* such as physical, occupational, or speech therapy are provided for students who need them. The availability of these services is one of the main reasons for placing children in special classes. In some states the State Department of Health or Education cooperates with the school administration in financing these programs. In other instances the responsibility is left entirely with the local schools.

*Classes for children with cerebral palsy* make up a large percentage of the special classes for children with physical impairments. Such classes continue to increase as the unique educational needs of cerebral palsied children are recognized, and problems arise which are different from those encountered with other groups of students. These problems justify additional discussion of this specific type of special class.

Determining the best school placement of children with cerebral palsy is by no means a simple matter since they cannot be treated as a homogeneous group. Those individuals with mild physical impairment and normal intelligence will usually be able to attend regular school. Others with mild motor involvement but more severe impairment of intellect, vision, or hearing will be best provided for in classes for the mentally retarded, visually, or auditorially handicapped. For the remainder, a number of criteria for special class placement have been proposed. Denhoff and Holden (1955) list several factors determining school adjustment. In suggesting regular class placement for children with mild physical handicap and average intelligence, they add that good family relationship is an important factor. Special classes are recommended for two groups: those with (1) moderate handicap, borderline or average intelligence, and fair family situation; and (2) severe physical handicap, good relationships with a home teacher, average to borderline intelligence, and good-to-fair family situation. Schonell (1956) states that special schools and classes should function in three different ways for three groups of children. She suggests that: (1) the intelligent less physically handicapped but educationally retarded child be placed temporarily in special classes for remedial work, then placed in a regular class; (2) moderately physically handicapped attend a special class, mainly for physical treatment; (3) severely impaired children be educated in special classes all their lives.

It is evident that educational placement for the cerebral palsied child must depend on many factors. Dunsdon (1952) warns against determining selection or rejection for a class on the basis of purely medical criteria. Neither should a child be denied a chance for an education on the basis of an intelligence test alone if there are other indications that he is capable of doing school work. Poor communication and coordination make accurate evaluation of many children extremely difficult. Trial placement is sometimes the only means of ascertaining how well a child will be able to learn. Decisions should be made on the basis of what education can mean to a child in the realization of his potential capacity.

The administrator who plans special classes for children with cerebral palsy should: (1) see that provisions are made for extensive appraisal of their mental as well as physical potential; (2) set up a screening committee representing the various disciplines concerned to evaluate available information and make recommendations for placement; (3) employ the services of consultants who understand the problems of the cerebral palsied child to plan curriculum; (4) provide the needed physical facilities; (5) make some arrangements for auxilliary physical, occupational, and speech therapy services; (6) employ a well-qualified teacher with training in the education of children with neuromuscular impairment and (7) arrange for adequate supervision and coordination of the program. Though these requirements may seem excessive they are justified because many children with cerebral palsy can make considerable improvement, and early, adequate attention to their needs may enable them to attend regular school in their later years.

The *homebound program* is designed to provide continuing educational experiences for children who cannot attend school. Children who are taught in this type of special education program fall into two general categories: those who are forced to remain at home for variable periods of time because of a long-term disease or handicapping condition, accidents, or operations, but who will be expected to return to regular school eventually; and those who have some chronic disability that is severe enough to prevent their ever leaving home, even to attend a special class. Though many states exclude children other than those in these two groups from homebound programs, in some school districts where there are few or no special facilities for the mentally or emotionally handicapped, these children are often taught at home even though this is a less desirable arrangement than classes suited to their particular needs. This situation also exists in sparsely settled rural areas where the problem of transporting students great distances makes special classes impractical. Thus the types of handicapping conditions found among the students on the home teacher's roll are apt to vary according to the special education facilities available and the area in which the children live. One safeguard to prevent

TABLE 9.6 *Groups of major disabilities of high school homebound students in New York City, by numbers and percentages in 1959.*

| MAJOR DISABILITY | NUMBER | | | PERCENT | | |
|---|---|---|---|---|---|---|
| | M | F | Total | M | F | Total |
| Emotional | 110 | 70 | 180 | 28 | 21 | 25 |
| Orthopedic | 88 | 72 | 160 | 23 | 21 | 22 |
| Neuromuscular and neurological | 75 | 63 | 138 | 19 | 18 | 19 |
| Heart | 27 | 41 | 68 | 7 | 12 | 9 |
| Upper respiratory | 31 | 35 | 66 | 8 | 11 | 9 |
| Gastro-intestinal | 12 | 12 | 24 | 3 | 4 | 3 |
| Blood and blood-forming diseases | 15 | 8 | 23 | 4 | 2 | 3 |
| Other and unclassified | 29 | 40 | 69 | 8 | 11 | 10 |
| Totals | 387 | 341 | 728 | 100 | 100 | 100 |

*Source:* Jenkins, Shirley. Some characteristics of homebound adolescents in New York City. *Except. Child.*, 1960, **27**, 175–182.

placing children in the homebound program who could be at school is to require a statement from the physician to the effect that the pupil is unable to attend school, and needs homebound instruction.

In a recent study of homebound adolescents in New York City (Jenkins, 1960) information was compiled on the number of major disabilities among the students of junior and senior high school age who were receiving home instruction. Ages of the group ranged from 12 to 21 years. Table 9.6 summarizes the types of impairments that were found. It will be noted that approximately one fourth of these students were being taught at home because of emotional disability. A slightly fewer number had orthopedic conditions, while neuromuscular and neurological impairments ranked third. In comparing the ranking of these two latter groups with the figures cited for the number of students in the total program for the nonsensory physically handicapped in Illinois (Table 9.5) it is evident that if similar groupings were made here, there would be fairly close agreement in the two studies. It should be taken into consideration that the New York study included only junior and senior high school students. A higher prevalence of some disabilities is found among elementary age pupils. This fact is particularly true of rheumatic fever and poliomyelitis, as well as of most of the infectious and developmental conditions cited in Table 9.3 and Table 9.4. An additional point should be noted. In some school districts, students who are expectant mothers are taught at home.

The length of time that a student might be expected to be enrolled is one factor which needs to be considered in planning the homebound program. A minimum time is set by some districts and regulations state that schooling will be provided only for those who might be expected to be absent from school for a longer period of time than this. This lower limit is often three months, while in other cases six months is the cutoff point. In the New York study cited above it was found that approximately half of the pupils with neuromuscular and neurological disabilities had been in the program for two years or longer, while in the orthopedic group this was true of only about 15 percent.

The class load of the teacher of the homebound is of concern to the administrator. If a teacher spends one hour of each school day with each pupil, five or six students would be a maximum case load. In some instances pupils are visited only two or three times a week and the number of students handled by one teacher is doubled. Travel time must be taken into consideration and consequently the farther the teacher has to travel in a day the fewer the number of students she can handle. In this case, states may also set minimum and maximum limits for number of students and the amount of time spent in instruction. In a survey of programs for the homebound (Simches and Cicenia 1958) it was found that of 33 states, 11 set a minimum and maximum time per pupil, while 4 had no limits. Some states specify five hours of teaching a week for each student, while others merely state that 50 minutes of individual instruction constitutes a day's attendance for purposes of financial support on the basis of average daily attendance. Home instruction is sometimes permitted on Saturdays and during the summer, particularly in cases in which a student needs to have extra teaching in order to continue with his class. In this study, 79 percent of the states reported that teachers of the homebound do not work longer hours than classroom teachers. In 59 percent of the states, travel time was included in the number of hours a teacher worked while in 31 percent it was not. The amount of time spent in travel was not given.

The *hospital teaching program* has as its obvious purpose the continuation of a sequential school experience during the time a child is in the hospital. It is generally administered by the officials of the school district in which the hospital is located and the teacher is employed by them. Some hospitals conduct programs which are entirely under their jurisdiction. If a hospital is small the teacher may be employed on a part-time basis, or may serve more than one hospital. In small communities children in the hospital are sometimes taught by a teacher of the homebound, who then continues with the same children while they convalesce at home. In large urban areas where there are many teachers, a well-organized program is established with a supervisor to coordinate curriculum, assist with scheduling, provide needed equipment, and help teachers with other problems.

The daily class load of the hospital teacher is more variable from day to day than that of the teacher of the homebound. This is increasingly true as the length of time spent by patients in the hospital decreases. The variability will be found not only in numbers but also in age range and types of disability. Some illnesses such as poliomyelitis are seasonal. Therefore, at certain times of the year there may be fewer children to be taught than at other times. School-age children are more apt to be hospitalized for surgery during vacation time. Thus, there are periods when the age of students will vary. It is not feasible to be constantly changing hospital teachers either during times when there are fewer children to teach or when the majority of the students shift from primary grades to secondary level. Consequently, the teacher must be prepared to handle a wide variety of grades and subjects. The number of students he can manage at one time will depend upon: (1) the variability in the age of the patients, (2) the types and degree of disabilities among them, (3) the variation in the amount of schooling they have had, and (4) the facilities in the hospital for group teaching.

One of the advantages of hospital teaching over the home-bound program is the opportunity which the students have of learning in group situations. Physicians emphasize the importance of helping the child to "develop a feeling of independence and trust in himself and in his own health" through companionship with other children of his own age (Spekter, 1955, page 114). In a study of group work with hospitalized children, Albee (1955) concluded that the greatest value of group activity was to provide for the child reassurance about his condition and an opportunity to discharge tension. The satisfaction which parents have from knowing that their child is happy and contented with other children is of additional value.

## Instructional Provisions

As has already been indicated, many children with non-sensory physical impairments will not require *special teaching methods* even though they may need to be placed in special schools or classes. Nor will the basic curriculum of the regular class need to be revised to any great extent other than to adapt it to the rate of progress and ultimate goals of each individual student. Adaptation of teaching materials and equipment to the physical capabilities of pupils has been discussed previously. When the required adjustments in physical facilities have been made further modifications in the educational program are not necessary. Therefore, since with a few exceptions, instructional provisions are essentially the same as those for average or "normal" children, they need not be discussed in detail.

The major exception to this generalization is in the case of *children with neurological disorders,* particularly those with cerebral palsy. Methods of educating neurologically impaired or brain-injured children who are mentally retarded have been discussed by Dunn in chapter 2. Similar procedures are used in teaching brain-injured children who have normal or nearly normal intelligence and little or no muscular involvement. A study aimed at developing teaching methods for brain injured children recently conducted in Montgomery County, Maryland (Cruickshank et al., 1961), resulted in useful suggestions on both diagnosis and procedures. The recommendation is made that in teaching reading the exact nature of the perceptual problem be identified by determining whether the child has the ability to perform such tasks as: (1) distinguishing form and color, (2) recognizing spatial relationships, (3) differentiating between high and low or loud and soft sounds, (4) seeing a picture as a whole, or (5) following simple directions. Training is then given in those areas in which the child is deficient. While any child must acquire these skills before learning to read, in the case of the brain-injured child inability to perform them may be evidence not of sensory defect or delayed maturation, but rather of a lack of ability to perceive and interpret sensory impressions. Though there is little conclusive evidence on whether or not it is possible to improve appreciably the powers of perception through training, a number of methods have been tried with some success. Kephart (1960) suggests procedures in: (1) chalkboard training, including problems in directionality, tracing, copying, and the use of templates; (2) sensory-motor training in walking, balancing, bouncing, and rhythm; (3) ocular control; and (4) form perception.

Conceptual, as well as perceptual difficulties, found in these children will necessitate using special methods of teaching. Particular attention may need to be given to help pupils in advancing beyond the concrete stage of learning, in arriving at generalizations, and in seeing broad relationships. Learning experiences which will help to accomplish these goals include: (1) arranging objects in suitable categories, (2) deciding which items are relevant to a certain situation, or (3) matching objects on the basis of specific relationships. These skills are vitally important in learning to read and should be acquired as part of the readiness program.

Problems in concept development lead to difficulties in learning arithmetic which are similar to those encountered in reading. A great deal of experience with number concepts in concrete situations before proceeding to the abstract stage of number symbols is essential. Most courses of study in arithmetic have moved in this direction in recent years and a wealth of material is available. The "arithmetic tangibles" put out by a number of companies and the structural arithmetic kits (Stern, 1949) are helpful in building concepts of size and number through manipulation. Kinesthetic aids such as cut-out or sandpaper numbers which can be felt are recommended. Colors can be used to emphasize configurations and aid perception. Dolphin and Cruickshank (1951) suggest the use of puzzles and manipulative devices as aids in overcoming disassociation, distractibility, and disinhibition in brain-injured children as well as in the conceptualization of arithmetic. They also state that film strips, slides, and motion pictures are useful in this respect. Several sources from which valuable help and suggestions on teaching materials can be obtained are given at the end of the chapter.

## THE CEREBRAL PALSIED

Children with cerebral palsy may have the learning difficulties of the brain-injured child added to the basic problem of muscular coordination and secondary sensory and mental impairment. Thus, their educational problem is particularly complicated. It is especially vital for these children that the goals of education and the curriculum be continuously reappraised for each pupil. Otherwise, because the educational process is so complex, valuable time is apt to be wasted on unnecessary courses and unproductive procedures. During the early years of life it may be impossible to determine the extent to which a child will be able to overcome his handicap and live a normal life in adulthood. Nevertheless, it is important to scan the future from a realistic point of view and to prepare each individual for the fullest life of which he is capable. Careful appraisal of potential is especially necessary when pupils reach secondary school where decisions regarding future schooling and vocational possibilities must be made. Curriculum content will depend to a great extent upon what the student is going to be able to do with his education when he leaves school. Recommendations for planning curriculum and instruction, based on a study made of classes for children with cerebral palsy (Wrightstone et al., 1954), emphasize enrichment of experience through: (1) close integration with the life of the school (2) stimulation of interests and creative guidance in leisure activities, (3) development of pupil initiative and leadership, (4) wide experience in the community, (5) extensive utilization of school and public libraries, (6) development of a program of physical activities. Such enrichment of experience is difficult to provide for children who, without a great deal of assistance, cannot browse through the library, take a nature walk, visit the fire department, participate in the student council, or plan a school program, but with the cooperation of teachers, principals, therapists, parents, and volunteer workers these activities can be a part of the school program of children with handicaps as they are for nonhandicapped pupils. Without broad experience the formal school subjects will have little meaning. Therefore, educational planning for children with cerebral palsy should begin early. It is advisable to bring some children into a group situation as early as three years of age. Haeussermann (1956) suggests an early readiness program which is designed to: (1) stimulate interest and curiosity, (2) provide for meaningful experience, (3) increase language comprehension, (4) develop satisfactory perception, and (5) build toward independence. The readiness period may extend over a number of years until the children are prepared socially, emotionally, physically, and mentally for learning.

*Methods of teaching the basic tool subjects* should emphasize meaningful materials. While this is true of arithmetic, writing, and other language arts, the importance of useful reading skills for the child with cerebral palsy can scarcely be overemphasized. Reading for pleasure, for stimulating creative thinking, and for the purpose of keeping in touch with the world can mean much to the person who has limited opportunity for first-hand experience. However, secondary handicaps such as intellectual and perceptual problems which accompany cerebral palsy make the acquiring of these skills a difficult task.

It is sometimes advisable to teach reading to cerebral palsied children by methods that minimize the amount of muscular coordination involved, and therefore focus on silent reading. Extensive oral reading employed in beginning programs for normal children may be an added burden to the child with severe problems in speaking. A teaching guide by Loviner and Nichols (1956) outlines procedures for teaching reading by the nonoral method so that no effort need be expended by the child on vocalization. The kinesthetic sense can be utilized in supplementing visual and auditory impressions, and children whose motor involvement is not too severe can learn to read words through tracing them. Colored felt pens are useful for this purpose because the color gives added clues.

Adequate *language and speech development* is important for cerebral palsied children. Inability to communicate with others is extremely frustrating and can lead to increased tension which further aggravates the physical problems of these children. The acquiring of understandable speech is a long and tedious task in many cases and for some children will never be accomplished. Westlake (1951) proposes a system of speech training that proceeds through three phases: (1) psychological and social readiness for speech, (2) physiological readiness for speech, (3) direct training of speech. The first of these stages involves guiding the language development of the child through wide experience, building an awareness of self and of speech, and cultivating an interest in persons and things. The second phase is aimed at developing the muscular readiness for speech through exercises in breathing, phonation, chewing and closing the mouth, elevating the tip of the tongue, and swallowing. The direct speech training is the direct application of the levels of readiness achieved in the first two stages.

While formal speech therapy must be done by a trained therapist, the classroom teacher can accomplish a great deal (see chapter 2). Games and exercises which stimulate auditory discrimination or the production of specific sounds can be a part of the daily schedule or can be incorporated into lessons in spelling, phonics, reading, and other subjects. More detailed information on speech development will be found in the references.

When good speech is not possible communication through some form of written language becomes extremely important. If the cerebral palsied person can learn to carry on conversation with others, tension will be considerably relieved. A "conversation board" containing pictures of common objects for the child who has not yet learned to read and the letters of the alphabet for the older child is a useful device. By merely pointing to the proper item the child can make himself understood. Older nonoral students get a great deal of satisfaction from learning the Morse code and using this means of communicating with the teacher and other pupils by blinking their eyes or tapping on the desk for dots and dashes.

Handwriting is difficult for many children with cerebral palsy. Bachmann and Law (1961) studied a method for teaching manuscript writing which shows promise. The writing period followed rest when the children were most relaxed. Techniques used included: (1) activities in space orientation, (2) coloring within lines, (3) tracing, and (4) using word boxes with pictures. Adaptations must often be made in the regulation school materials and equipment in order to enable a child to write. Children who cannot hold an ordinary pencil may be able to manage one which has been built up with tape or inserted in a plastic or rubber holder. Electric typewriters can be fitted with a plastic guard with cutouts for keys and bars. Thus a child who does not have the coordination to get his fingers in the proper place is sometimes able to use a piece of dowel to which a handle has been attached for this purpose.

*Teaching materials* must be adapted to the needs of individual students on the basis of their physical problems as well as the perceptual and other learning difficulties of cerebral palsied children. Pupils in pre-academic classes will learn to match colors and shapes, distinguish between objects of different sizes and textures, or develop concepts of number through manipulative games and devices which develop eye-hand coordination. Some of the materials than can be made or obtained commercially are: (1) peg boards, (2) snap blocks, (3) lock boxes, (4) coordination boards, (5) take apart toys, (6) color cones, (7) jumbo beads, and (8) puzzles. Many variations of these materials will need to be devised to increase motivation and minimize boredom. Dorward (1960) has developed easily constructed teaching materials for number and reading readiness which help in the development of muscular control and coordination.

The *physical aspects* of the total educational situation assume major importance for children with cerebral palsy. Physical development should always go along with academic and social growth if the student is to make adequate use of his education. It is useless, if not actually inhuman, to educate the mind of a child to the neglect of his body, so that at the completion of his schooling he is unable to utilize his learning either for his own satisfaction or for making a living. The alert, imaginative teacher can find many ways to develop physical coordination at the same time that academic learning is going on. Special equipment can be devised with the assistance of the physical or occupational therapist so that training begun in the therapy sessions can be carried over into the classroom. In order to cooperate fully with therapist in carrying out a consistent program the teacher should understand the purposes and general procedures used in therapy. Therapists should also be aware of the educational goals of the school and cooperate in working toward their attainment.

The *physical therapist* is concerned primarily with the development and maintenance of bodily posture and mobility. With some children he may concentrate on relaxation to allow for voluntary body movement, while with others the problem may be to develop muscle tone and strength. Research has not yet established the value of physical therapy in the correction of the neuromuscular impairments of all cerebral-palsied individuals, nor of the relative effectiveness of the various methods. However, experience has shown that many persons benefit from regular therapy treatments. Concepts of neuromuscular disorders have gone through radical changes in recent years and it is probable that physical medicine may soon be able to provide more concrete help in the management of the incoordination of cerebral palsy for both therapists and teachers (Lamm, 1960).

The *occupational therapist* concentrates on the development of the self-help skills of dressing, grooming, and feeding that will increase the child's independence as well as those abilities that are necessary for school work, such as writing, drawing, and typewriting. Though he is not concerned entirely with the improvement of hand skills, much of his emphasis is upon the finer motor abilities. While vocational training as such is not a part of the program of the occupational therapist, he tries to develop many of the skills that might be useful in later, more specific, training.

These therapists always work under the direction of a doctor and can assist the teacher in carrying out his recommendations for the physical comfort and development of the pupils. A child will work more effectively in a classroom if he is comfortable, if correct sitting or standing posture are maintained, and if he is able to have maximum hand use. Through close cooperation with therapists the teacher receives guidance in managing the child who should work part of the day in a standing position to develop leg and trunk strength and coordination, or who will benefit by restrainers to control involuntary motions and improve his hand use.

## THE HOMEBOUND

The teacher of children who are confined at home must be both flexible and versatile for he will encounter a variety of situations to which he will need to adapt. He will teach children with widely different educational backgrounds and with many kinds of disabilities and will have to know something of the limitations each imposes upon a child. He will go into many types of homes, some of which provide an atmosphere that is conducive to learning, others which have the opposite effect. Perhaps the best preparation he can have for his task is breadth of teaching experience and skill in public relations.

*Curriculum* for the homebound child will vary to some extent for each individual, but in the main will not differ drastically from that of the regular student. The physical condition of the pupil will have some effect upon the school activities, and the medical prognosis will largely determine the long-term educational goals. For the group of children who will return to school after periods of home instruction, one of the principle objectives of home teaching is to enable them to progress through the regular grades at the same rate as their classmates. This is of great concern to most children. Often a child's recovery is impeded by worry over "getting behind" or "not being promoted." There is real therapeutic value in the confidence which comes from knowing that normal academic progress is being made. Regular instruction not only helps to reassure the child but also adds variety and purpose to the long hours of sitting or lying in bed. Such constructive activity is recognized by physicians as a valuable aid in shortening the period of convalescence. To accomplish the goals of the home teaching program for these children, the teacher needs to keep in close touch with each child's regular classroom. Lessons will follow rather closely the general curriculum of the school. In most cases the same textbooks and materials are used, and assignments and experiences parallel as much as possible those of other pupils in the child's grade.

The permanently disabled, severely impaired student who may never be able to attend a classroom presents a somewhat different problem. Here the aim is to provide educational activities that will enable him to develop to the maximum of his capabilities despite his handicap. Breadth of experience is desirable, but keeping abreast of the regular school curriculum is of secondary importance. Teaching that will help him to acquire skills in reading, listening, and communicating, to exercise his creative powers and to enjoy the natural world around him, may be more vital to his future happiness than more purely academic learning. For some of these children, economic self-sufficiency may never be entirely possible. However, independence in self-care, usefulness around the home and some degree of self-support are realistic goals. To attain these goals requires a careful evaluation of each child's physical and mental potentialities. Such evaluation should be made by the physician, psychologists, therapists, teachers and other professional personnel. Vital information should then be interpreted to the teacher so that he can plan his program in accordance with the findings and recommendations. In the light of the child's future possibilities and problems, as well as his present condition, the home teacher will then plan an educational program that will provide for him the greatest development now, and the most satisfaction in the future.

One of the problems of the teacher of the homebound is the *scheduling* of pupils. Generally he spends an hour a day with each student. In other situations he sees each pupil for periods of from one and a half to two hours three times a week. Sometimes older pupils are able to work independently and can be given long-term assignments, then can be seen less often. The distance the teacher must travel between teaching sessions will determine to some extent the kind of program which he plans and the amount of time he can spend with each pupil.

*Teaching materials, textbooks, and equipment* are many times a difficult problem. A teacher may often feel that he needs a small truck to get his supplies from place to place. He will also find that careful planning is necessary so that he will have everything he needs. For him there is no sending to the supply room for more paper. One of the limitations of the program is that materials such as large maps and charts, science equipment, sets of encyclopedias, and other reference material are difficult to transport and cannot easily be brought into the home. Therefore, instruction is often limited to the textbook, and the curriculum is confined to the academic subjects. There is usually neither time nor facilities for teaching art, music, or crafts though these would be of great value to the students.

Many school districts have an office for home teachers and a central source of supplies from which all of them may draw. In some cases large equipment such as projectors and film may be provided by an audio-visual department and delivered directly to a home when needed by the teacher. In other instances a teacher is responsible to the principal of the school in the district where his students live, and he requisitions supplies through him. Lines of responsibility and authority, as well as procedures for getting teaching materials, should be carefully defined for teachers in the program so that they will know specifically where to go for help with various kinds of problems. The beginning teacher of the homebound often feels that he has been cut loose from all support and left to his own resources. This is especially true in smaller districts where adequate supervision is lacking. Thoughtful administrative planning can largely overcome these difficulties.

One problem with which the teacher of the homebound must be prepared to cope is that of *parent relations*. Without a good teacher-parent relationship, the home teaching program is seriously handicapped. A teacher finds himself in a very special relationship with the child's mother, in particular, which is quite different from that in any other teaching situation. The mother has the care of the ill child all day so she is often weary and anxious, and wants reassurance and advice. The teacher is sometimes caught in a difficult position as a result of the need to give some support to the mother without robbing the pupil of the time and attention that should be his. It is important for him to have the friendly cooperation of the mother in providing a quiet place, and following through on assignments left for the child. This may be managed without devoting a major proportion of time to the mother's problems, yet not antagonizing her by curt refusal to discuss hers or the child's problems. Some teachers set aside a little time on a regular basis for counseling sessions with the mother. But this must be kept to a minimum. The teacher may need a great deal of tact, patience, and understanding to maintain an atmosphere which is conducive to the best interests of everyone concerned.

No mention has been made thus far of *teaching methods* for the homebound. The reason for this is that with few exceptions there are no special teaching procedures or devices which are peculiar to these students. Many activities which provide motivation for learning and enrich the experience of pupils in regular classrooms can be used successfully in teaching the homebound. These include crafts, puppetry, educational games, science experiments, collections and nature projects (Rooke, 1962). Some children will have conditions which complicate their learning problem to such an extent that specialized methods of teaching will be necessary. These methods have been discussed in the section on special classes. In general, however, the same type of individualized instruction which is applicable with normal children is quite adequate to meet the needs of the homebound child. The individualization of learning is one of the advantages of home teaching, though home instruction is certainly not an adequate substitute for those students who can participate in a classroom. Children taught individually are deprived of the social contacts with their peers which are important to the development of well-rounded personalities. In addition to social isolation, there is the major problem of meeting the child's recreational needs. There will always be children who will have to be taught at home, but every effort should be made to provide more adequate facilities for those who can take advantage of them.

A number of *supplementary aids* which can make home teaching more effective and interesting for the pupil and easier for the teacher have been developed in recent years. Educational television has now progressed in many areas to the point where it can be a valuable asset. Though radio programs are now more limited in scope than formerly, there are still possibilities here for enriching the curriculum. Correspondence courses also can be used to supplement teaching or used as a method in themselves where personal visits by a teacher are not feasible.

One method which is increasing in use is the home-to-school telephone. The shut-in child is provided with an electronic communications unit which enables him to speak to the teacher and students in the regular classroom. Through another unit which can be moved about the school room, he is able to hear what is being said. Thus, with the flip of a switch, the child at home becomes a participant with his classmates. Richards (1957) stated that in 1957 this method was being used successfully in more than 46 states and territories. Handbooks of instructions and suggestions for teachers and administrators, parents, and physicians are provided by both the telephone companies and the suppliers of the units. Schuchman (1957) surveyed 33 states and reported that in those in which home-to-school telephones were used, their use was confined principally to grades nine to twelve and sometimes only to certain subjects such as foreign languages. However, one school district planned to set up teaching by telephone as the sole type of home instruction. This method is better adapted to the older students and is not recommended below the fourth grade. Younger children have difficulty visualizing the classroom situation and identifying with it. An IQ of 90 is also suggested by Richards as a minimum level of intelligence for students taught in this way. The home-to-school telephone does not take the place of the home teacher but can add to his effectiveness and may make it possible to reduce the amount of time he spends with the pupil. The method is particularly useful in sparsely settled areas where much of a teacher's time would be spent in traveling from one student to another.

Another medium which has very intriguing possibilities for home instruction is the teaching machine. Present speculations over whether or not machines will replace teachers need be of little concern in this instance. When the teacher can spend only an hour a day with each student, a device which can take over for him the rest of the time has definite advantages. Contrary to much public opinion, teaching machines are not mere "gimmicks" to fascinate the student and relieve the teacher. On the contrary the programs of study used are painstakingly designed on sound psychological principles to facilitate learning. A child can progress through a lesson at his own rate, skipping those areas in which he is already proficient and spending more time on his deficiencies. Instruction can be truly individualized. Experience has shown that many times students are able to learn faster and more efficiently in this way than in the classroom. The home teacher will not be replaced by the machine but will still be important in personalizing the situation. However, in his absence the student can continue to learn new material and check his own progress. Machines are being developed which are inexpensive to buy and in which teacher-developed materials can be used. The preparation of the lessons or program to be used in the machine is the greatest problem. Initially this requires a great deal of time and effort, but once prepared the programs can be used over and over again with different students. It will undoubtedly be some time before commercially prepared programs are available in many subjects and levels of difficulty, but this should not deter teachers and administrators from experimenting with this interesting teaching medium. It is ideally suited to individual instruction.

Finally, some consideration should be given to the steps needed for returning a homebound student to school. This is frequently difficult, especially when the pupil has never attended school or has been at home for a number of years. A number of conferences between the regular and homebound teachers are usually desirable, before and just after the student enrolls at school. In a departmentalized program, a conference of the various teachers who will be instructing the student is suggested. The regular teachers will need to make special effort to help the pupil become socially integrated and accepted by his school peers.

## THE HOSPITALIZED

The teacher of hospitalized children has many problems which are the same as those of the teacher of the homebound. Essentially the same type of children are encountered by both since obviously many of the students will move from the hospital into their homes for convalescence. However, the child in the hospital is apt to be more physically ill and emotionally upset than the one who is recovering at home. Hospitalization is a traumatic experience for a great many children. Gofman and others (1957) have reported on the emotional response to hospitalization. They cite studies which indicate that from 20 to 50 percent of all children showed behavior changes, including regressive behavior, speech disturbances, and greatly increased dependency and negativism that lasted from several months to three or four years after leaving the hospital. One of the ways suggested for preventing such emotional disturbances is to have the children continue with a school program which is as normal as possible. While providing such a program, the teacher must be prepared to recognize and deal with the emotional problems as they arise. As a rule, these problems decrease in both frequency and severity with the age of the child, but occasionally even the teen-ager needs support and reassurance from the teacher. He must be able to give the child a feeling of security and adequacy without becoming overly solicitous and too sympathetic.

The *educational objectives and curriculum* for hospitalized children may differ widely. The teacher will work with some pupils during short stays in the hospital when no systematic, long range program is possible. The primary purpose here is to maintain the continuity of the child's regular school program while at the same time bolstering his morale by allaying his fears about himself, occupying his time with purposeful activity, and bringing him into group situations with other students. There are other children who have chronic disabilities or who need long-term corrective surgery, and may spend a major portion of their early school years in the hospital. The objective for them will be quite different. They will need a varied and broad curriculum which will provide educational experiences that can compensate for limited opportunity to explore the world in which they live.

*Methods of teaching* in the hospital are similar to those used in home teaching in that they differ little from good methods which are employed in regular classrooms, again with the exception of the specialized procedures necessary in teaching children with neurological damage. Though the students can work in groups on units in the various subject matter areas, much of the instruction in skill subjects will have to be individualized because few of the pupils will be at the same level of achievement.

The hospital teacher faces problems of scheduling instruction which are complicated not only by the factors of shifting population, varying age groups, and individual needs, but also by the necessity of fitting the teaching into the hospital routine. The child is hospitalized for medical treatment, and the teacher needs to realize that clinic and therapy sessions, medications, and other such procedures have first call on his time. This adds to the complex problem of maintaining a semblance of continuity in the school program but it is a situation which must be accepted and planned for accordingly. The teacher should work in close cooperation with doctors, nurses, therapists, and other professional personnel and be kept well informed of the child's condition, progress, needs, and capabilities.

*Supplies and equipment* are often not the problem that they are in home teaching. An increasing number of modern hospitals have specially designed and equipped classrooms and storage facilities. Libraries, small stages for performances, movie and slide projectors, and play equipment contribute to a varied and rich curriculum. Ambulatory children can be brought into the classrooms for group instruction and for socialization through music, arts, crafts, story telling, and dramatic play. Occupational, speech, and recreational therapists are usually available to assist in planning or providing materials for these activities. Thus the hospital program can be as full and diversified as that in the regular school. However, in other situations which are less ideal there may be no central schoolroom, and storage and availability of supplies become more of a problem. Even with classroom space not all children can be moved and some must be taught in their rooms or wards. Then teaching materials must be moved to the bedside, and the curriculum becomes more limited, though even when bedside teaching is necessary small groups can be formed by moving beds and activities can be engaged in together. Since children are usually placed in wards on the basis of approximate age level, this presents no problem. The imaginative teacher can provide many activities which will enrich the school program.

The teacher's *relationship with parents* is quite different from that of the teacher of the homebound since generally he will have few direct contacts with them. If he meets the child's parents at all it is usually only briefly and casually. He is not apt to become involved in the parents' problems or feel called upon to give them advice and support. However, he does need to be aware of the possible effect which the parents' anxiety, over-solicitousness, or uncertainty may have upon the child and his performance.

In hospital teaching close cooperation with the pupils' regular schools is desirable but not always possible. Instruction must frequently be given to children from widely scattered and divergent school districts. It is often impossible for the teacher to be well acquainted with the courses of study, textbooks, or school experiences that have been provided for each of his students. He may have access to very little information about each child's potential, achievement level, or school background. In such a situation he will have to make decisions as to what to teach and which materials and textbooks to use on the basis of the information he can gather himself. Therefore, he needs to have some skill in educational diagnosis so that he can determine a child's present level of functioning and plan a program based on his needs and capabilities. The teacher's job may be complicated, full of uncertainty, and sometimes frustrating, but it is also varied, challenging, and rewarding.

## Summary

Children with crippling and chronic health conditions have been grouped together as those having nonsensory physical impairments, since they are usually not separated in terms of school placement. They are an extremely heterogeneous group in the varieties of disabilities which are represented but they can be classified in three categories on the basis of the type of defect that will determine the adjustments which must be made in their school programs: those with (1) muscular or neuromuscular impairments, (2) skeletal deformities, and (3) reduced strength, vitality, or alertness.

Every effort should be made to place these children in the regular classroom where they will have the opportunity to grow up in the world of the nonhandicapped in which they will spend the majority of their lives. However, when they are confined to home or hospital, need extensive modifications in physical facilities, must have regular auxiliary services, or require teaching methods that are not used in regular schools, special education provisions must be made for them in homebound or hospital teaching programs, or in special schools and classes. No matter where they receive their schooling the aim of education for them remains the same, namely to attain the highest possible degree of self-realization and usefulness to society of which they are capable.

In attempting to reach this goal it is important to remember that it is not the physical facilities or equipment which make a good program. In fact, there is a real danger that special provisions for children with nonsensory physical impairments may be made too specialized, and that students may become so surrounded with "gadgetry" designed to make things easier for them that they never learn to cope with the world outside the classroom walls. More vital to the realization of each child's goals than his physical environment is the attitudinal climate in which he learns. The determining factor is not where the child is but how he and others think and feel about him. He can become dependent and insecure, or be rejected and isolated in any type of program. The school has not fulfilled its responsibility to the physically impaired pupil until it has helped him to accept himself as he is, to view his assets and limitations realistically, to strive for goals that are attainable, to develop independence in thought and action, and to find a place for himself among his peers. Nor has the school accomplished its purposes unless it has assisted those with whom the child associates—his classmates, parents, neighbors, teachers—to accept him as a worthy individual and to see beyond his defect to the person that is there. This is the challenge and the opportunity of the special educator.

## CHAPTER REFERENCES

Albee, Constance J. Group work with hospitalized children. *Child.*, 1955, **2**, 217–221.

Allen, R. M. Intellectual evaluation in cerebral palsy. *Except. Child.*, 1960, **27**, 202–204.

Bachmann, Winnie, & Law, Kay. Manuscript writing with the cerebral palsied child. *Except. Child.*, 1961, **27**, 239–245.

Berman, B. B. The prevention of rheumatic fever recurrence. *Ill. Med. J.*, 1959, **116**, 255–256.

Boyd, H. B. Advances in conquering crippling. *Crippled Child.*, 1956, **35**, 4–7.

Boyles, Iva J., & Calovini, Gloria. *Statistical report—physically handicapped children in Illinois*. Springfield, Ill.: Office of Superintendent of Public Instruction, 1960.

Connor, Frances P. Safety for the crippled child and child with special health problems. *Except. Child.*, 1962, **28**, 237–244.

Crothers, B., & Paine, R. S. *The natural history of cerebral palsy*. Cambridge, Mass.: Harvard Univer. Press, 1959.

Cruickshank, W. M., Bentzen, F. A., Ratzburg, R. H., & Tannhauser, Mirian T. *A teaching method for brain-injured and hyperactive children*. Syracuse, N.Y.: Syracuse Univer. Press, 1961.

————, Bice, H. V., & Wallin, N. E. *Perception in cerebral palsy*. Syracuse, N.Y.: Syracuse Univer. Press, 1957.

Denhoff, E., & Holden, R. H. Understanding parents: One need in cerebral palsy. *Cerebral Palsy Rev.*, 1955, **16**, 9–11.

Dolphin, Jane E., & Cruickshank, W. M. Pathology of concept formation in children with cerebral palsy. *Amer. J. ment. Defic.*, 1951, **56**, 386–392.

Dorward, Barbara. *Teaching aids and toys for handicapped children*. Washington, D.C.: Council for Except. Child., 1960.

Dunsdon, Marjorie I. *Educability of cerebral palsied children*. London: Newnes Educational Company, 1952.

Geer, W. C., & Wolfe, W. G. *Education of the cerebral palsied in the South*. Atlanta, Ga.: Southern Regional Education Board, 1960.

Gofman, Helen, Buckman, Wilma, & Schade, G. The child's emotional response to hospitalization. *Am J. Dis. of Child.*, 1957, **93**, 157–161.

Graham, R. Safety features in school housing for handicapped children. *Except. Child.*, 1961, **27**, 361–364.

Haeussermann, Elsie. Fundamental problems in the formulation of the reading program for children with cerebral palsy. *Cerebral Palsy Rev.*, 1956, **17**, 192–196.

Harris, A. J. *How to increase reading ability*. New York: Longmans, 1961.

Hopkins, T. W., Bice, H. V., & Colton, Kathryn C. *Evaluation and education of the cerebral palsied child*. Washington, D.C.: Council for Except. Child., 1954.

Jenkins, Shirley. Some characteristics of homebound adolescents in New York City. *Except. Child.*, 1960, **27**, 175–182.

Kephart, N. C. *The slow-learner in the classroom.* Columbus, Ohio: Charles E. Merrill, 1960.

Lamm, S. S. A new concept of the significance of hypertonus in cerebral palsy. *Amer. J. dis. Child.*, 1960, **100**, 27–29.

Lendrum, Bessie L., Simon, A. J., & Irving, M. Relation of duration of bed rest in acute rheumatic fever to heart disease present 2 to 14 years later. *Pediatrics*, 1959, **24**, 389–394.

Loviner, Della G., & Nichols, Edith C. *The cerebral palsied child goes to school.* Columbus, Ohio: Ohio Society for Crippled Children, 1956.

McClave, C. R., & Shaffer, T. E. Accidents, injuries and children. *Pediat. Clinics of North America*, August, 1957, 635–647.

Minear, W. L. A classification of cerebral palsy. *Pediatrics*, 1956, **18**, 841–852.

Mullen, Frances A. Chicago opens a new school for the physically handicapped. *Except. Child.*, 1957, **23**, 296–299.

National Foundation for Infantile Paralysis and Citizenship Education Project. *Understanding the disabled.* New York: Columbia Univer., Teacher's College, 1956.

Perlstein, M. A., & Barnett, H. E. Nature and recognition of cerebral palsy in infancy. *J. Amer. Med. Assoc.*, 1952, **148**, 1389–1397.

Preizler, J. Vaccine effectiveness in prevention of poliomyelitis. *Wisconsin Med. J.*, 1959, **58**, 489–491.

Richards, J. A. *How to teach shut-in students by telephone.* New York: Executone Inc., 1957.

Rooke, M. L. Aids for home and hospital teaching. *Except. Child.*, 1962, **28**, 261–265.

Schonell, F. E. *Educating spastic children.* Edinburgh, Scotland: Oliver and Boyd, 1956.

Schuchman, L. Current practices in administering home teaching. *Except. Child.*, 1957, **23**, 246–253.

Shands, A. R. *Handbook of orthopedic surgery.* (5th ed.) St. Louis, Mo.: Mosby, 1959.

Simches, R. F., & Cicenia, E. F. Home teaching provisions at a state level. *Except. Child.*, 1958, **25**, 11–15.

Spekter, L. *The pediatric years.* Springfield, Ill.: Charles C Thomas, 1955.

Stern, Catherine. *Children discover arithmetic: An introduction to structural arithmetic.* New York: Harper & Row, 1949.

Tizard, Barbara. Personality of epileptics. *Psychol. Bull.,* 1962, **59,** 196–210.

UNESCO Workshop Report, *Statistics on special education.* Paris: United Nations Education, Scientific, and Cultural Organization, 1960.

U.S. Department of Health, Education and Welfare. *Background on the nation's health—1959.* Washington, D.C.: Dept. of Health, Education and Welfare, 1959.

————. *Summary of health and vital statistics.* Washington, D.C.: Dept. of Health, Education and Welfare, 1958.

Westlake, N. *A system for developing speech with cerebral palsied children.* Chicago: National Society for Crippled Children and Adults, 1951.

Woods, Grace E. *Cerebral palsy in childhood.* Bristol, England: John Wright & Sons, 1957.

Wrightstone, J. W., Justman, J., & Moskowitz, Sue. (Eds.) *The child with orthopedic limitations.* New York: Board of Education of City of New York, Bureau of Educational Research, No. 33, 1954.

## ADDITIONAL REFERENCES

Barker, R. G., Wright, Beatrice A., & Gonich, Mollie R. *Adjustment to physical handicap and illness: A survey of the social psychology of physique and disability.* New York: Social Science Research Council, 1953. (Bull. 55)

Bridge, E. *Epilepsy and convulsive disorders in children.* New York: McGraw-Hill, 1949.

Cardwell, Viola E. *Cerebral palsy, advances in understanding and care.* New York: North River Press, 1956.

*Cerebral palsy equipment manual.* Chicago: National Society for Crippled Children and Adults, 1950.

Cruickshank, W. M., & Raus, G. M. *Cerebral palsy: Its individual and community problems.* Syracuse, N.Y.: Syracuse Univer. Press, 1955.

Denhoff, E., & Robinault, Isabel P. *Cerebral palsy and related disorders.* New York: McGraw-Hill, 1960.

Illingworth, R. S. *Recent advances in cerebral palsy.* Boston: Little, Brown, 1958.

Kessler, H., *Rehabilitation of the physically handicapped.* New York: Columbia Univer. Press, 1947.

Lennox, W. G., & Lennox, Margaret A. *Epilepsy and related disorders.* Boston: Little, Brown, 1960.

Lofquist, L. H. *Vocational counseling with the physically handicapped.* New York: Appleton-Century-Crofts, 1954.

Mackie, Romaine P. *Crippled children in American education,* 1939–1942. Contributions to Education, No. 913. New York: Bureau of Publications, Columbia Univer., Teacher's College, 1945.

————. *Crippled children in school.* Washington, D.C.: Government Printing Office, 1949.

————, & Fitzgerald, Margaret. *School in the hospital.* Washington, D.C.: Government Printing Office, 1949.

Martmer, E. E. (Ed.) *The child with a handicap.* Springfield, Ill.: Charles C Thomas, 1959.

Mecham, M. J., Berko, M. J., & Berko, Frances G. *Speech therapy in cerebral palsy.* Springfield, Ill.: Charles C Thomas, 1960.

National Foundation for Infantile Paralysis and Citizenship Education Project. *Understanding the disabled.* New York: Bureau of Publications, Columbia Univer., Teacher's College, 1956.

Perrin, Lois. *Recreational activities for crippled children.* Iowa City, Iowa. State Services for Crippled Children, Univer. of Iowa, 1944.

Plank, Emma N. *Working with children in hospitals.* Cleveland, Ohio: Western Reserve Univer. Press, 1962.

*Realistic educational planning for children with cerebral palsy.* New York: United Cerebral Palsy Assoc., 1953. (Pam. No. 2, 3, 4)

Rich, Mildred K. *Handcrafts for the homebound handicapped.* Springfield, Ill.: Charles C Thomas, 1960.

Taylor, Edith M. *Psychological appraisal of children with cerebral defects.* Cambridge, Mass.: Harvard Univer. Press, 1959.

*Teaching aids for children with cerebral palsy.* Albany, N.Y.: Bureau Handicapped Children, Division of Pupil Personnel Services, New York State Education Department, 1956.

Wright, Beatrice A. *Physical disability—a psychological approach.* New York: Harper & Row, 1960.

Wright, G., Gibbs, F., & Linde, Shirley M. *Total rehabiltation of epileptics —gateway to employment.* Washington, D.C.: Office of Vocational Rehabilitation, 1962.

## REFERENCES FOR PARENTS

Abbot, Marguerite. *Cerebral palsy—its scope and management.* New York: Public Affairs Committee, 1956.

Alpha Chi Omega. *Toy book: self-help toys to make for handicapped children.* Indianapolis, Ind.: Alpha Chi Omega Fraternity, 1960.

*Child welfare services: how they help children and parents.* Washington, D.C.: Children's Bureau, Dept. of Health, Education, and Welfare, 1957.

*Children with special health problems: Educational adaptations in school, home, and hospital.* New York: National Tuberculosis Association, 1953.

Haring, N. G. *Educating children who have epilepsy.* Washington, D.C.: Federal Association on Epilepsy, 1959.

Forster, F. M., & Smith, G. B. *Modern concepts of epilepsy.* Washington, D.C.: Georgetown Univer. School of Medicine, 1956.

McMullin, Margery D. *How to help the shut-in child.* New York: Dulton, 1954.

Phelps, W., Hopkins, T. W., & Cousins, R. *The cerebral palsied child: A guide for parents.* New York: Simon & Schuster, 1958.

Rogers, Gladys G., & Thomas, Leah. *Toys, games and apparatus for children with cerebral palsy.* Chicago: National Society for Crippled Children and Adults, 1949.

*Services for children with cerebral palsy.* New York: American Public Health Association, 1955.

*Small business enterprises for the severely handicapped.* Washington, D.C.: Office of Vocational Rehabilitation, 1955.

Ware, E. Louise. *Mental health for the orthopedically handicapped child.* New York: Association for Aid of Crippled Children, 1947.

Yahraes, H. *Now—a brighter future for the epileptic.* New York: Public Affairs Committee, 1954.

# RESOURCES

Additional information on specific handicapping conditions, educational procedures, materials and equipment, and general management of children with nonsensory physical impairment can be obtained from numerous public agencies. The services provided by the U.S. Office of Education and the U.S. Vocational Rehabilitation Administration have been discussed in chapter 1. Another agency under the U.S. Department of Health, Education and Welfare that furnishes material on various diseases is the U.S. Public Health Service. Health statistics as well as pamphlets describing the diseases are available free or at a small cost. The Council for Exceptional Children mentioned in chapter 1 has a division known as the Association of Educators of Homebound and Hospitalized Children.

Several private health agencies are concerned with a broad range of handicapped children. The National Society for Crippled Children and Adults is a major example. It publishes monthly magazines, the *Crippled Child,* the *Easter Seal Bulletin,* and *Rehabilitation Literature,* a journal of abstracts, book reviews, and digests. It also maintains a library service and makes available reprints, pamphlets, books, and listings of films. Other agencies that have similar materials for distribution are the Association for the Aid of Crippled Children and the American Public Health Association.

In recent years there has been a tremendous growth of agencies that are concerned with research and education of the public on a specific disabling condition. Perhaps the best known of these are the National Foundation, which has extended its area to include birth injuries and congenital deformities as well as infantile paralysis, the National Tuberculosis Association, the American Heart Association, and the American Cancer Society. Other such organizations are United Cerebral Palsy, the National Multiple Sclerosis Society, Muscular Dystrophy Associations of America, the National Epilepsy League, the Federal Association for Epilepsy, the American Diabetes Association, and the Arthritis and Rheumatism Foundation. These and other groups that are well known through their fund drives distribute free or inexpensive material which is useful to educators and parents. Two magazines on cerebral palsy are published: *Cerebral Palsy Review* in the United States, and *Developmental Medicine and Child Neurology,* in Great Britain. Booklets on health problems can also be obtained from a number of insurance companies.

Two publications of the American Medical Association give valuable information. *Today's Health* is written to appeal to the lay person, while the *Journal of the American Medical Association* is designed for the profession. Other medical publications that provide more technical references are: *Journal of Diseases of Children, Journal of Chronic Diseases, Journal of Infectious Diseases, Epilepsia, Neurology, Journal of Bone and Joint Surgery,* and *Pediatrics.* The *American Journal of Physical Medicine, Physical Therapy Review, American Journal of Occupational*

*Therapy, Canadian Journal of Occupational Therapy, Archives of Physical Medicine and Rehabilitation,* and *American Archives of Rehabilitation Therapy* give professional information on therapy and rehabilitation.

## SELECTED 16 MM SOUND FILMS

*A day at Washington Boulevard School.* 20 min, color. Bailey Films, 6509 DeLongpre Avenue, Hollywood 28, California. School services for mentally retarded—physically handicapped children in a Los Angeles elementary school.

*The cerebral palsied child.* 29 min, black & white. National Educational Television Film Service, Indiana University, Bloomington, Indiana. Presents the three major types of cerebral palsy and the special problems and needs they present.

*Boy in storm.* 25 min, black and white. National Epilepsy League, 208 North Wills Street, Chicago 6, Illinois. Depicts medical and social aspects of epilepsy.

*Deadline 53 minutes.* 30 min, black & white. United Cerebral Palsy, 321 West 44 Street, New York 36, New York. United Cerebral Palsy program of education, research, and rehabilitation services.

*These are our children.* 18 min, color. United Cerebral Palsy, 321 West 44 Street, New York 36, New York. Shows how cerebral palsied children are taught to help themselves in Schenectady, New York.

*Camp cheerful.* 15 min, black & white. National Society for Crippled Children, 2023 West Ogden, Chicago 12, Illinois. Shows a residential camp in Ohio for crippled children.

*Reach for tomorrow.* 26 min, black & white. National Society for Crippled Children, 2023 West Ogden, Chicago 12, Illinois. Shows range of services in Easter Seal treatment centers nation-wide.

*Cerebral palsy: methods of ambulation.* 20 min, color. National Society for Crippled Children, 2023 West Ogden, Chicago 12, Illinois. Shows teaching preschool cerebral palsied children to roll, crawl, kneel, stand, and finally to walk.

*The valiant heart.* 27 min, black & white. Motion Picture Library, American Medical Association, 535 West Dearborn Street, Chicago 10, Illinois. Case history of an eight-year-old rheumatic fever victim.

*Loretta.* 28 min, black & white. National Foundation, 800 Second Avenue, New York 17, New York. How a young couple learn how to deal hopefully with their first child born with a birth defect.

*Nursing in rehabilitation of paraplegics.* 25 min, black & white. National Paraplegia Foundation, 432 Park Avenue South, New York 16, New York. The topic describes the film.

*First steps.* 11 min, black & white. International Rehabilitation Film Library, 701 First Avenue, New York 17, New York. Shows work for the physically handicapped provided at special centers all over the world.

## CHAPTER 10

# Exceptionality and Adjustment

SAMUEL C. ASHCROFT

Americans are frequently accused of worshipping the normal or average. It has been said that a cult of conformity has developed in our culture and that we seem to "seek security in the bosom of the majority." Beatrice Wright (1960) has cited an apt phrase to illustrate one aspect of this reaction as it applies to individuals with physical impairments. Impaired individuals frequently "idolize normal standards." Perhaps all of us should be less concerned about such normality, conformity and security and recall the comment of Thoreau (1910) in *Walden* where he said "If a man does not keep pace with his companions, perhaps it is because he hears a different drummer. Let him step to the music which he hears, however measured and far away." Nevertheless, normality, security and good adjustment are highly prized in our cultures. Social and personal adjustment are seen by the schools both as ends or objectives of education and as means of facilitating the attainment of other educational aims. Frequently, adjustment is defined (both culturally and educationally) as conformity to group standards. Those who do not or cannot conform may often be considered maladjusted. Thus, to the casual thinker, it will seem just common sense to assume that it is virtually impossible for an exceptional child to be well adjusted. Furthermore, such common sense thinking suggests that the greater the exceptionality the greater the deviation from the "idolized normal standard" and the more difficult it will be for persons with exceptionalities to obtain or maintain good adjustment.

In common sense terms, the "genius" is expected to be more maladjusted than average children, often being considered an "oddball," or at least a "bookworm," "egghead," or "non-conformist." Another widely held common sense notion is the "happy little moron theory" that assumes the retarded have relatively few adjustment problems because they don't have to come to grips with many of life's complexities. Similarly common-sense generalizations are often expressed about the physically disabled. In terms of common sense, the severely impaired are assumed to have more serious adjustment problems than those mildly impaired. The hard of hearing are expected to be better adjusted than the deaf; the partially seeing better adjusted than the blind; the ambulatory cripple better adjusted than the wheelchair case. In other words, common sense suggests that the degree of maladjustment will be a relatively simple function of the degree of deviation from normal or the degree of impairment. From the standpoint of common sense it will seem that an index of deviation from normal on some mental or physical dimension, such as represented by an intelligence test score (IQ), an audiometric test (audiogram), a vision test report (visual acuity rating), or a medical specialist's report will also be an index of adjustment. Common sense also suggests an order of adjustment potential among different handicaps. Blindness is often thought to be the worst catastrophe which could happen to an individual and therefore the most difficult to accept.

As we will see in an examination of the topic at hand, common sense alone fails to provide an adequate basis for understanding and dealing with adjustment to exceptionality. Common sense notions about adjustment of exceptional children frequently fail to be validated by careful research. Numerous research studies have had as their orientation for the study of adjustment such common sense notions as have been suggested. Many others have been undertaken to examine the validity and fruitfulness of such common sense notions. Complex and sophisticated theories of behavior, of personality and of personal adjustment have been examined for promising leads to understanding adjustment of exceptional children as alternatives to the common sense approach. A variety of interpretations of theories have been made to provide more scientific and parsimonious explanations of adjustment characteristics, to predict adjustment, and to control adjustment processes. As a result, there are extant numerous theories. We will examine the status of our knowledge with respect to the body of information accruing from such theorizing, study, and research.

Since this text is written largely by educators and is directed primarily to school personnel, this chapter is similarly written and oriented. One of its chief aims is to introduce the educator to the topic of exceptionality and adjustment and to provide an orientation in this interesting and challenging area.

## Adjustment Defined

Adjustment can be defined in many ways. For purposes of this discussion, it is defined as *a continuous process of maintaining harmony among the attributes of the individual and the environmental conditions which surround him.* It involves the fulfillment of potential for a personally and socially satisfactory life. Though this is a general definition, it includes enough essentials for the purposes of this discussion. Several points should be noted about the definition. First, that there is nothing unique in it with reference to exceptional children. Furthermore, no differentiating aspect is necessary or desirable since it is commonly accepted in this field that the broad educational goals (such as those of the Educational Policies Commission) for exceptional children are the same as those for all children. This definition stresses that adjustment is a continuous process rather than a static goal to be strived for or reached. The definition suggests that characteristics of the individual will be determinants of adjustment, but that environmental factors will also have their influence. It suggests that the individual's potential and characteristics are inborn, but are also modified through experience, and that effective adjustment will involve both personal and social criteria and value judgments.

The foregoing introduction and this definition serve as points of departure for the remainder of the chapter. We review briefly some studies concerning the adjustment of exceptional children;

we examine briefly some of the theories that have been utilized to orient research and to understand the problems; and we make some suggestions for dealing with exceptional children from the standpoint of understanding and facilitating their adjustment in educational settings.

The body of information and knowledge about adjustment, psychological aspects, social factors, and the personal-social characteristics of exceptional children is large enough to justify complete books. Among those which are available, are: Barker et al. (1953), Cruickshank (1955), Garrison and Force (1959), Louttit (1957), and Wright (1960). Each of these books brings together extensive information and in some cases critical reviews on psychological characteristics and adjustment. They merit serious study by the scholar interested in the field. The information and studies cited in each of the areas of concern in this text are only suggestive of the kinds of information more fully available in such sources as those mentioned.

## Adjustment Problems

## According to Exceptionality

### GIFTED CHILDREN

The chapter on the gifted in this text has pointed to the fallacy of the once widely held "common sense" idea that intellectual superiority is related to social and emotional maladjustment. As Lucito has pointed out, many studies, both recent and long past, have refuted this notion. These studies suggest that, as a group, the gifted achieve above average social and emotional adjustment both from a personal and interpersonal standpoint.

Miriam Goldberg's review (1958) was an attempt to compare recent research on the gifted with that of the past. With regard to social and personal adjustment, she noted that the gifted:

... are successful in sports, better satisfied with their peer relations than are average youngsters, more confident, and aware of their above-average ability ... high school boys were found ... to rate higher on behavioral controls; were less apt to show lability of mood, social delinquency, carelessness and impatience, especially in matters requiring long term personal investment of an intellectual nature. (p. 151)

The classic study of the gifted, a long-term comprehensive longitudinal study by Terman et al. (1925–1959), has resulted in a composite portrait of a hypothetical gifted child. This study supports the view of good adjustment almost universally attributed to the gifted by researchers. However, Terman and Oden (1947) note that:

Gifted children do not fall into a single pattern but into an infinite variety of patterns. One can find within the group individual examples of almost every type of personality defect, social maladjustment, behavior problem, and physical frailty; the only difference is that among gifted children, the incidence of these deviations is, in varying degrees, lower than in the general population. (p. 57)

Gallagher and Crowder (1957) observed that the gifted children in their study had superior social popularity, few negative personality characteristics and favorable ratings by teachers on most aspects of behavior. However, they noted problems in motivation and intellectual flexibility (some children restricted their intellectual activity to insure social status). They also noted that some minor personal problems tended to reduce the potential for good adjustment. Gallagher and Crowder's findings were in accord with Terman's portrait, suggesting that no general statement without many exceptions could be made concerning the group.

Gallagher's valuable analysis of research (1960) points out that it is not clear that high intelligence *causes* social acceptance. He raises questions regarding the source, dynamics and effects of achieving social adjustment. One of the most crucial of these questions is whether good adjustment may really be due more to socioeconomic factors than to giftedness.

Hollingworth (1942) has been among the most pointed in noting adjustment problems of very bright individuals. She has suggested that extremely gifted individuals (170 IQ and above) may be so intellectually above average that they are not understood by people in general and that perhaps the optimum range of intelligence for social adjustment lies between 130 and 150 IQ. This type of assumption bears an interesting parallel to the common sense notions referred to earlier. Hollingworth (1931; 1936) has noted "learning to suffer fools gladly" as one adjustment problem for the gifted. She also cited problems related to tolerating routine, unchallenging school work and undue pressure to conform to school conventions. Such pressure may encourage idleness, and distaste for school. Additional problems may result from pressure to adjust to older, less bright classmates and from the difficulty to find adequate play opportunities and activities. Precocious concerns with philosophical and religious issues may cause adjustment difficulties. In the context of this chapter where adjustment of the gifted is considered along with the adjustment of other exceptional children, it is interesting to consider another problem area mentioned by Hollingworth. It is the problem of physique and its relationship to social and personal adjustment. As we will see in our consideration of the relationship of adjustment to body type, physique, and somatopsychological theory, physical characteristics may have a significant bearing on adjustment for the impaired. For the gifted, their usually better developed physique, even though it deviates in the positive direction from that of their chronological agemates, often leaves them at a physical size disadvantage in association with their mental age peers with whom they may be associated in school and may have implications for adjustment.

Kirk (1962) has written an introductory text around the unifying theme of the exceptional child's growth and development deviations or discrepancies from normal. He applies this concept in his consideration of the gifted. He analyzes deviations in growth and adjustment from the expectancies held for average children and discrepancies from expectations for growth within the individual child—that is, uneven growth in the different developmental areas. For the gifted these deviations and discrepancies are largely positive in direction or remain in the above average range, nevertheless they may have a unique impact on adjustment in both school and society.

## MENTALLY RETARDED CHILDREN

In marked contrast to the above-average adjustment of the gifted as a group, the group adjustment of the mentally retarded has been seen as a virtual "mirror image" in the below average direction.

Most definitions of the mentally retarded include either implicitly or explicitly a criterion of social inadequacy or incompetence. The *Manual on Terminology and Classification in Mental Retardation* (Heber, 1961) documents this point. In virtually every curriculum guide or statement of goals for the education of the retarded, personal-social adjustment objectives rank high (Stevens, 1958).

Many factors complicate the achievement of adequate personal and social adjustment for the retarded. As noted by Dunn in chapter 2, one of the characteristics of a child most difficult to accept by a teacher is scholastic ineptness. As he points out, the very central characteristic of the retardate is his learning difficulty, thus making it very difficult for him to gain genuine acceptance from the typical teacher. Attaining adequate personal and social adjustment is difficult in a climate where one's basic characteristics do not find acceptance.

Even more basic in the life of the retarded child are parental reactions. Farber's sociological research (1960) shows that the presence of a markedly retarded child may have a profound and serious effect on parents and family. Marital integration and other children in the family are affected by the presence of a retardate and the effects vary according to the sex and birth order of the child, the social class position of the family, and their religious affiliation. Farber suggests that three "game-theory" type reactions are characteristic of families of retardates. In the "child-centered" home the family reacts by centering its activities primarily in the functions of its normal children. In the "home-oriented" family a pleasant home life for all members becomes the focal point. For the "parent-oriented" family, the value emphasis is on achievement, the development of social skills, and the attainment of personal growth. Studies like those by Farber provide useful insights for our understanding of the personal and social adjustment of exceptional children. Similar studies are needed in other areas of exceptionality and the application of unique behavioral science tools such as "game theory" may prove especially helpful.

Analysis of family integration such as that cited has special implications since retardates tend to be able to tolerate less social pressure than normal children. While their reactions to emotional stress are presumed to be much like those of normal children in kind, they tend to differ in degree. Foale (1956) pointed out that as compared to normal adolescents, the retarded show twice as many psychoneurotic reactions, and can tolerate less anxiety and stress. However, evidence does not support the "common sense" assumption that mentally retarded children are necessarily predisposed to delinquent and criminal behavior (Blatt, 1960). Jordan (1961) has devoted a chapter in his book to the family, considering the impact of retardation on family life and what can be done about it through guidance and counseling.

The age at which the retarded are placed in appropriate learning situations where they can achieve success may have an important bearing on adjustment since retardates often have had failure experiences in the regular grades and may have learned maladaptive behavior (Cromwell, 1961). The retardate may not be utilizing the potential he has because of having learned faulty modes of reaction in response to these frequent failure experiences. This may well account for the observation that the more severely retarded often exhibit better adjustment than those less severely retarded, since they are not placed in the regular grades and expected to achieve at the same level as their agemates. The more seriously handicapped are likely to be identified early and to have fairly realistic expectations made of them. The mildly retarded who were earlier assumed to be essentially normal may have special adjustment problems because of unrealistic expectations that were held for them.

Kirk (1954) in writing on counseling for the psychological acceptance of retardates has said, that lack of acceptance on the part of the professional person often results in a discrepancy between the retardates' capacity to perform and level of aspiration that one sets for them, leading to frustration and inadequate adjustment.

## THE EMOTIONALLY DISTURBED

## AND SOCIALLY MALADJUSTED

This group of children is exceptional primarily because of deviating or maladaptive behavior, although many emotionally disturbed children may be exceptional in other ways as well. Their emotional disturbance is evidence of a serious adjustment problem, but it gives rise to, or is associated with, secondary adjustment problems.

Furthermore, emotional disturbance serious enough in and of itself to constitute exceptionality is found frequently associated with other impairments or deviations. In the case of such multihandicapped children, they tend to be characterized by the exceptionality which seems to be basic or more crucial in terms of its educational consequences.

With regard to the problems of emotionally disturbed children, Kanner (1957) has cited a specially critical issue when he said: "We are barely beginning to realize the extent of emotional penetration into 'otherwise unimpaired intelligence'." The problems of pseudo-feeblemindedness seem to represent the extreme case in faulty adjustment—the point at which adjustive behavior is so maladaptive that the person appears as if he were mentally retarded though there is reason to believe he has the basic intellectual capacity to function more normally.

The teacher with a background of standard teacher preparation and experience in the regular classroom, will tend to feel that he is most familiar with and has had occasion for more contact with this group of exceptional children than perhaps any other. A classic study of some time past (Wickman, 1928) indicated that regular classroom teachers by contrast with mental health clinicians were inclined to be more sensitive to aggressive behavior than to withdrawing behavior (considered more serious by mental health clinicians) and thus tended to fail to identify many cases of children with potentially serious emotional problems. Subsequent research suggests marked improvement in this regard. The study reported by Bower (1957) indicates that teachers now may be very much like clinicians in their sensitivity to withdrawal behavior as well as aggressive behavior. This study is instructive on several other points with regard to these children. It was concerned with early identification of the emotionally disturbed so as to determine if identification by regular classroom teachers was feasible and if information ordinarily available or easily obtained in the classroom might be used for the purpose. Here are some of the findings. At least three children in each average classroom could be regarded as having emotional problems sufficiently serious to warrant special help. The differences between the disturbed children and their peers seemed to increase with grade level; as Bower put it: "The rich get richer while the poor get poorer." The children studied were found to be accurate identifiers of emotionally disturbed peers. The disturbed children scored low on group tests of intelligence, but were near average on individual intelligence tests. On standardized achievement tests they scored low in reading and arithmetic and the differences from their normal peers increased in the later grades. On personality inventories they showed less satisfaction with themselves than did others in the class. Emotionally disturbed children were found to come from homes not essentially different in socioeconomic level from those of other children. The teachers in this study had available to them only information they could obtain easily, without infringing upon time needed for other purposes, which could be interpreted without extensive specialized training. The information found most useful for differentiating the emotionally disturbed consisted of scores on group tests of intelligence, achievement, and personality; a classroom sociometric device; age-grade and attendance information; the teacher's own ratings of physical and emotional status; and a rating of socioeconomic background.

It is encouraging to realize the possibilities from this study that could sharply reduce the "extent of emotional penetration into 'otherwise unimpaired intelligence'" about which Kanner speaks. Among these possibilities is that teachers using readily available information may identify very early those children with emotional problems or potential for developing them. While to identify the problems is not to solve them, it is a first and necessary step. In their review of research on *Emotional Factors and Academic Achievement*, Bower and Holmes (1959) note an encouraging increase in the research study of the relationship between emotional factors and school success which should lead to knowledge of how to prevent and ameliorate the problems.

For too long, it has been assumed in common-sense terms that a single factor such as a physical problem, a home situation, temperament, or undue pressure for school achievement was responsible for emotional maladjustment. In fact, it has almost been routinely accepted, for example, that undue pressure for scholastic attainment is an important cause of emotional maladjustment. A recent study by Wilson (1959) found no significant differences among third graders who were subjected to the stress of heavier requirements for academic achievement as compared with other children. This study is cited not to disprove that scholastic pressure may be a cause of emotional disturbance but rather that our common-sense notions about adjustment problems and their sources need intensive examination and study. Such research documents further the well known but frequently neglected principle of multiple causation; *adjustment problems seldom, if ever, have a single simple cause.*

## THE SPEECH HANDICAPPED

Children with speech disorders have been studied to determine whether their speech problems were a result of difficulties in adjustment, or whether the adjustment problems were the source of the speech difficulty. Many speech problems are suspected of having their origin in psychological factors. As Hull has pointed out in chapter 6, while probably the most important factor related to the development of normal speech is the integrity of the total biological system, research has shown that intelligence, emotional status, and environmental elements affect it also. He went on to indicate that psychological aberrations such as withdrawal and overt hostility have been observed in children with severe speech disorders, but that it is difficult to differentiate which is cause and which effect; that is, whether the speech problem was caused by, or causative of the psychological problem.

As suggested in Van Riper's (1954) commonly accepted definition of the speech disordered, one criterion of defective speech is maladjustment, whether cause or effect. Some investigators have concluded that a relationship exists between such speech problems as articulation disorders and adjustment problems. Disturbed family relationships are presumed by some researchers to be an important factor but others question their importance.

Personality theories regarding the genesis of stuttering have been considered along with constitutional and developmental theories. Rotter (1954), for example, has suggested that stuttering develops as a symptom of otherwise unmet needs for security or approval or to avoid embarrassment or failure. A psychoanalytic conception of stuttering has been developed. In terms of such theory, the motivation to stuttering is unconscious and is related to arrest in libidinal development at an oral stage. Unique personality patterns have been sought among stutterers by a number of investigators. A review of such studies using projective techniques of personality assessment produced little evidence that such patterns exist, either as cause or effect (Sheehan, 1958). A recent review of research on the speech handicapped (Murphy, 1959) cites other reviews pointing up inadequate sampling, lack of adequate controls, faulty measuring instruments, inappropriate statistical analyses, and over generalizing from results.

Whether the etiology of speech disorders is presumed to be of organic or other origin, investigators and specialists almost universally point out the need for such intervention as environmental modification, counseling, or the modification of attitudes to bring about speech improvement and to reduce adjustment problems.

The research evidence available on children with speech problems, incomplete as it may yet be, seems to show that personality and adjustment problems are somewhat more frequent among the speech disordered and are related to speech problems (either as cause, or effect, or a complex combination of both). The safest present generalizations seem to be that no unique type of personality adjustment problem is either causative of, nor resultant from, speech difficulty. Personality and adjustment problems are similar in kind to those of children with normal speech. Individual adjustment and personality vary greatly among children with speech problems.

### THE DEAF AND HARD OF HEARING

A hearing loss is assumed to have especially crucial implications for personal, social, and emotional adjustment because it affects communication and because communication is so distinctly a social process. Normative studies of the deaf, such as Gesell's (1956) purport to show that the deaf are retarded in all areas of development, and especially so in social and emotional adjustment. As Wooden points out in his chapter on the hearing impaired, language contributes importantly to social efficiency, to other's judgments about us, and to our roles in life. As the study by Quigley and Frisina (1961) suggests the environment of the deaf has an important effect on their psychosocial adjustment. Myklebust (1960) has indicated that, "It is in social maturation that the handicap of deafness is most apparent." As previously cited by Wooden, Elser (1959) studied the social position of hearing handicapped children nine to twelve years old in regular classes. His findings suggested that children with greater hearing losses and those who wore aids were better accepted than those with less-severe hearing losses. As a group the hearing handicapped were not as well accepted as their almost normally hearing classmates. The hearing handicapped were seldom rejected because of hearing or speech problems but for aggressive and unacceptable behavior. It is noteworthy that the mildly hard of hearing appeared to have greater personal adjustment difficulties than the more-severely hearing impaired, suggesting that the former may be under greater pressure to conform to the standards of the normally hearing world.

Myklebust (1960) suggests that there is probably no more important factor than isolation in the emotional adjustment of the hearing impaired. He contends that the deaf child's psychological organization is different from the normal and that this occurs because the deprivation in the distance sense (hearing) causes a "shift" or difference in the integration of experience. From a study of 830 children in educational programs for the deaf by use of the Drawing of the Human Figure Test, Myklebust stated, "The most forthright conclusion from this investigation is that a relationship was found between deafness and personality adjustment." (page 176). In addition to the changed psychological organization or shift already mentioned, Myklebust noted evidence of emotional disturbance.

Several authorities have pointed up especially critical limitations on the research in this area. DiCarlo (1959) in reviewing educational research pointed out that "Research in education and rehabilitation needs to be aimed more toward basic considerations. It has neglected problems of methodology." An extensive analysis and summary of results of research on the personality and adjustment of persons with impaired hearing is provided by Barker and others (1953). The highlights of their findings include the following: the methods and instruments used in most of the research tended to be inadequate and the findings were therefore unreliable. Nevertheless the research tends to show that children with impaired hearing were less well adjusted, less stable emotionally, and more neurotic than normally hearing children. Children in residential schools appeared to be less socially mature than children with normal hearing, but this may be altered by previous preschool group experience. Children who attend day school programs show differences but these may be due to selection factors or to the difference in environments, but this is unknown (Quigley and Frisina, 1961). Findings also suggest that children with impaired hearing appear to behave more rigidly and to have more fears than children with normal hearing. Indices of adjustment have not been found to be significantly correlated with the degree or duration of the hearing loss, with age at onset, chronological age, or time spent in speech-reading instruction. Better adjustment tends to be associated with intelligence, full use of residual hearing with aids, and with the presence of other deaf members in the family.

## THE VISUALLY LIMITED

Introducing the conclusions of a thorough investigation of studies of personal and social adjustment of the visually limited, Meyerson (Barker et al., 1953) wrote: "Very little systematic research on the social behavior and personality of the visually handicapped has been done, and much of what has been attempted has been caught in the snare of methodological difficulties." In their careful analysis of fifteen studies of personality in the visually limited, it was noted that six studies showed greater maladjustment for the visually handicapped when compared with seeing groups, but in nine others, those with vision problems did not consistently score significantly below seeing control subjects. Furthermore, some different studies using the same tests reported markedly different results.

While Meyerson concluded from his review of the literature that "probably the most impressive fact yet discovered about the psychology of the blind is the relatively small amount of personality disturbance that accompanies it," there can be no doubt that visual limitations complicate life adjustment. Blind and partially seeing individuals must learn to cope with their environment and be mobile in it with restricted vision. A wide range of personal-social adjustment patterns are found in such individuals, but adequate evidence is available to indicate that no simple relationship exists between degree of vision loss, age at the onset of loss, or any specific characteristic of the vision problem and the degree or quality of adjustment. As we shall see in the study discussed later (Cowen et al., 1961), there is in fact reason to suggest that an inverse relationship exists between adjustment and degree of remaining vision.

Finding vision characteristics inadequate as a predictor of adjustment, many investigators have turned to environmental variables for information. Sommers (1944) interviewed parents of visually limited children and questioned the children themselves to study the influence of parental attitudes toward the visual conditions and adjustment problems. She found parental attitudes apparently shaped by four reactions to the impairment in their children: fear, guilt, punishment, and disgrace. The parents exhibited five types of response to their children: acceptance, denial, overprotection, disguised rejection, and overt rejection. Sommers concluded that the child's adjustment and reaction to his own impairment was shaped by the way in which his parents reacted.

In a more recent study (Cowen et al., 1961) questioned Sommers' conclusions and the direct relationship between adjustment and parental attitude which she ascribed. In their long-term study, they compared the adjustment of visually limited adolescents living at home but attending day school with that of residential school students. Comparisons were also made between these groups and comparable sighted adolescents. Attempts, not fully successful, were made to avoid many of the methodological problems that have vitiated other studies through the development of special test instruments, and the use of equated experimental and control groups. The study neither showed differences in adjustment between the groups, nor did it indicate a significant relationship between degree of visual loss and adjustment, except to suggest that the partially seeing tended to have greater adjustment difficulties than the blind. The study did not reveal the direct relationship between adjustment and parental reaction which Sommers found. The authors cite as the most important contribution of their study its challenge to the belief that there is a direct relationship between visual disability and maladjustment. They emphasize the fact that there is considerable overlap in adjustment between visually disabled and sighted adolescents rather than a sharp difference between the groups. The partially seeing may have more adjustment difficulties than do the blind—a parallel to what may be happening in the case of hearing loss. Ashcroft (1959) noted in a recent review of research that few studies of the adjustment and psychological characteristics of the partially seeing have appeared. He pointed out that some deviant modes of personality adjustment attributed to the partially seeing seemed inadequately supported by available data.

## PUPILS WITH NONSENSORY PHYSICAL IMPAIRMENTS

In a review of research on crippling and special health conditions, Connor and Goldberg (1959) said: "Handicapped and non-handicapped persons have been compared to determine whether a particular disability precipitates a unique personality pattern. In general, deviations from the normal, due to the handicap itself, have been negligible" (p. 477).

In their critical review and analysis of research on crippling, Barker and his associates (1953 pp. 63, 64) reached such conclusions as the following: "Physically deviant persons are not a homogeneous group psychologically. Physique (in this case a physique in part characterized by crippling) is only one factor in an extensive context of environmental and personal conditions acting together to create the particular life situations of the person".

In spite of these statements, there can be no doubt that crippling and special health conditions pose unique adjustment problems. Force (1956) examined the acceptance and integration of physically handicapped children and compared them with nonhandicapped children in regular classrooms. He found the physically handicapped less well accepted than normal children in integrated classes; that physical integration does not necessarily achieve psychological integration; and that various kinds of handicaps have different social values. Children having cerebral palsy or visual disabilities were the least well accepted. The handicapped children studied were less accurate than normals in their guessed status as friends of others.

Elsa Miller (1958) studied four groups of crippled children and their parents. She concluded that children with milder handicaps often appeared to have more severe adjustment problems arising from disturbed parent-child relationships than did children with more severe handicaps. Melba Miller (1953) studied 165 children with cerebral palsy and concluded that 23 percent were emotionally maladjusted demonstrating such symptoms as bedwetting, hyperactivity, aggressiveness, withdrawal, speech and language problems, temper-tantrums, and others. Her subjects scored low in self-adjustment as measured by personality tests.

Bice (1954) classified parental attitudes (reflected in quotations by them) toward their cerebral palsied children and concluded that three fourths of them were negative. The quotations revealed a range of attitudes from those symbolized by wishes of death for the child to mildly rejecting statements.

Shere (1956) studied 30 pairs of twins one member of each pair being cerebral palsied, and one noncerebral palsied. She observed parent-child behavior in the homes to determine if parents exhibited different behavior toward the cerebral palsied child from that toward the noncrippled sibling. Shere found better parent-child adjustment with the palsied twins, than with the normal twin. Parents tended to be less sensitive to the problems of the noncerebral palsied child. From a mental health standpoint, parents' reactions were generally better to the noncrippled child. In general the cerebral palsied child exhibited better behavior from a mental health point of view than did the noncrippled twin who used more attention getting devices. The study suggested, in Shere's own words, ". . . that the condition of cerebral palsy can be more harmful to the social and emotional development of the noncerebral palsied child than to his cerebral palsied twin" (p. 206).

We have been able to review a few of many studies about the adjustment of the various types of exceptional children who are the topic of this text. Even these few may suggest, as Olson (1959) has observed, that "A child tends to produce in his behavior anything that the culture demands, if it is in his repertory of possible responses." Exceptional children may forcefully illustrate that they have within their "repertory of possible responses" remarkable potential for adjustment. This may gain additional meaning for those who work with exceptional children when we realize that even the physically healthy child can become maladjusted due to unfavorable factors in the environment. If it is true that the reaction of the social environment to impairment may be the major source of maladjustment in the child, then our task is to shape the reactions of the environment. Manipulating and shaping the environment is a difficult task but the special educator must rise to the challenge. There is hope of success if we realize that perhaps the most profound and important impact on the environment may be effected by assisting exceptional children to obtain the knowledge, skills, and confidence which will enable them to elicit or evoke favorable attitudes from the environment. Cutsforth's (1951) book put the problem very well when he suggested that the task facing the educator is that of reshaping the training of exceptional children to enable them to live in harmony with themselves and in mental and social comfort in society.

To integrate more concisely some of the findings from the types of studies reviewed, the following list presents observations which seem to have probability of reasonable accuracy.

1. Poor adjustment is not always associated with exceptionality.
2. A wide range of adjustment and a great variety of adjustment patterns exist among exceptional children.
3. Unique personality types are not specifically associated with particular exceptionalities or handicaps.
4. The degree of adjustment is not necessarily related to the degree of exceptionality; in fact, there is some evidence that a minor degree may be more traumatic psychosocially than a marked degree of a particular exceptionality.
5. Exceptional children tend to meet more negative than positive attitudes from people in their environment, even their own parents. Such negative attitudes are not necessarily elicited by the exceptionality but are likely to be associated with the behavior of the exceptional child.
6. As a group, exceptional children are likely to be less well adjusted than a group of their otherwise normal peers.
7. Many of the adjustment problems associated with exceptionality have their source more in environmental factors than in the condition of exceptionality in and of itself.

8. Deviation from normal, impairment, disability, and handicap are not synonymous terms or labels. One can deviate without being impaired. Impairment does not necessitate abnormal deviation. An impairment need not constitute a disability until it interferes significantly with behavior. A disability need not but may result in a handicap if behavior and conditions require it. A handicap is not an absolute but rather a relative attribute dependent upon a variety of factors.

## Theoretical Contributions

The foregoing sampling of research on the adjustment of exceptional children makes the reader aware that common sense is inadequate to explain fully the complexities of the problems. With this awareness comes an appreciation of the need for more study and of the importance of contributions from the behavioral sciences. While probably all the behavioral sciences have some contributions to make, especially pertinent contributions come from such disciplines as clinical psychology, social psychology, sociology, physiology, psychiatry, and anthropology. In addition, help is promised from such areas as biochemistry, biophysics, mathematical biology, cybernetics, microbiology and others. Historically, the special educator's best help with respect to problems of adjustment in the personal and social life of exceptional children has come from psychology, and more recently from sociology. The educator seeks both general and specific information which will be of help to him in understanding better the characteristics of exceptional children as groups and as individuals. The educator has sought contributions from these disciplines to help him plan effective educational programs. They provide him with information regarding the intellectual potential of his subject, about how learning takes place, about social maturity, personality and individual and group relationships. The following section provides an introduction and orientation to some of the specialized theories that have been developed. It deals primarily with specialized theories or specialized applications of theory and does not deal with the general application of standard psychological or sociological theory or child development principles.

The reader is expected to have such background or to obtain it elsewhere.

Many scientists have said in other ways what Hebb (1958) has put very succinctly and with great implications for the study of exceptional children: "A man who constructs a theory is certainly trying to hit on the truth, but the function of theory is better seen, perhaps, if we regard it as a sophisticated statement of ignorance: 'sophisticated,' because the ignorance is put in a form that shows us how to go about decreasing it." There can be no doubt that in the area of personal-social adjustment of exceptional children we have abundant "sophisticated ignorance" as well as unsophisticated ignorance for we have many common-sense notions, numerous theories, theoretical frameworks, and theoretical positions. Though theory shows us something of how to go about decreasing our ignorance, much progress is yet needed. A few of the special theories follow.

## PHYSIQUE THEORY

Earliest attempts to account for differences in individual behavior had their basis in attempts to relate the behavioral differences to physical characteristics observed among people. Hippocrates, renowned Greek physician, classified personality types in terms of the four humors of the body. Among the better known of more recent work along this line is that of Sheldon (1949) who attempted to relate personality and behavioral characteristics to three general body types. He classified individuals as ectomorphs (lean body type dominated by development of the nervous system and a sensitive, intellectual, and aloof personality), mesomorphs (rectangular body-type dominated by bone and muscle development and an energetic, aggressive personality) and endomorphs (soft, round body-type dominated by visceral organ development and a sentimental, social, pleasure-seeking personality).

The Gluecks (1956) studied the relationship between physique and delinquency, a possibility suggested long ago by Lombroso and early anthropologists. Utilizing Sheldon's early work, they distinguished four types of delinquency potential in terms of body types. They also found differences in body types between delinquents and nondelinquents. The delinquents tended to be mesomorphic. However, they also found delinquency associated with intelligence, educational retardation, negative attitudes toward school and other factors. As Olson (1959) has pointed out, "The attempt to ascribe large areas of social failure, such as crime and delinquency, to one set of factors or to a group of factors has been without success." That is, while such factors as those studied by the Gluecks may be related or correlated, it cannot be assumed with confidence that they are individually causative. Schilder (1950) who has done much work on body types as a factor influencing adjustment in the exceptional has theorized in terms of the body image or the individual's own conception of the body-self. Schilder's thinking suggests that the social and vocational behavior that seems appropriate to the exceptional individual in terms of the mental image he holds of his body is thwarted because of its discrepancy with the actual distortion of his body structure. Bender and Silver (1948) have elaborated this idea and pointed to the conflict growing out of the discrepancy between the mental image of the body and the actual body condition as the source of excessive emotional phantasy and delusional behavior.

## PSYCHOANALYTIC THEORY

Adler's (1917) thinking provides a bridge between those who center attention in body type and those whose central concerns are more exclusively psychological. Adler's book (1917), *Organ Inferiority and Its Psychical Compensation* has done much to influence thinking about adjustment among the exceptional. Adler became dissatisfied with Freudian emphasis on sexual energies, gratification and power as the driving forces in human behavior. As a result he developed the school of individual psychology which held that man's basic motive is to belong to and have status in his group. He reasoned that because we aspire to this belonging and status goal we develop in childhood inferiority feelings and adopt a particular style of life to achieve our goals.

The style of life involves compensation or overcompensation for an inferiority "complex," and this may result in maladjustive or neurotic behavior. In this frame of reference, any physical impairment results in extreme feelings of inferiority which in turn results in compensatory behavior. Many of Adler's followers have taken the view—and have presented data interpreted to support it—that physical impairment should be accompanied by inferiority feelings and compensatory behavior. They see such feeling and behavior as growing out of the unfulfilled or thwarted drive for power. The resulting efforts to compensate may or may not lead to maladjustment. In this connection, Cutsforth (1948) has said "The attempt to compensate for the feelings of inadequacy drives the individual at times to the achievement of successes, but never to personality adjustment." It should be noted that these feelings have their source in social relations and the development of a personal "style of life" for a particular set of circumstances or the individual's perception of those circumstances. Therefore they may not be directly or even primarily related to impairment or deviation alone. That is, environmental conditions may be as crucial as physical disability in influencing the development of a style of life.

Students and followers of Freud have made a number of more orthodox applications of Freudian theory to the adjustment of the exceptional. It should be remembered that in Freudian terms unconscious and irrational influences from childhood experience are important motivators and determinants of behavior and adjustment. The driving force in man is seen primarily as the desire for a broadly conceived sexual gratification, a concept which Adler found unsatisfactory. Freudians see early childhood experiences as the point of origin of personality difficulties, largely because of conflict between unconscious drives and social prohibitions on their satisfaction. They believe that the pleasure principle or drive is an important influence in determining behavior but that good adjustment is attained when the individual recognizes the reality principle. Those who analyze the adjustment of exceptional individuals from this standpoint see an impairment as influential in arresting progress toward this reality principle.

Barker et al. (1953) have cited Meng among the Freudians as having treated the problems of physical disability most extensively. Barker's analysis of Meng's work leads to the conclusion that "although some factors in the environment of a crippled person often tend to produce distortion, other factors operate at the same time to lessen the probability of its occurrence." Among the factors which Meng has proposed as accounting for the psychological effects of physical disabilities (Barker et al., 1953) were: (1) Narcissistic (self-love) satisfaction deriving from pain and uniqueness, (2) lack of normal play and expressive actions due to exceptionality, (3) cathexis (investing mental and emotional energy in an idea or body part) to a disabled part, (4) unrelated anxieties transferred to bodily handicap, (5) blame of parents and feelings of guilt and hostility toward parents, (6) dependent, demanding, or apathetic behavior deriving from an oversolicitious and overprotective situation, (7) retaliatory behavior for "unjust" treatment by nature.

## SOMATOPSYCHOLOGY

Dembo et al. (1948) have developed a theory of mourning or misfortune in an attempt to understand and explain adjustment among the physically disabled. They propose that the psychological shock reaction to the recognition of physical impairment involves a period of mourning comparable to that of the bereavement felt at the loss of a loved one. The disabled individual is seen as requiring a period of mourning in which he evaluates the losses entailed by his impaired condition in comparison with normality. At this stage he concentrates on the loss aspects of his situation and idolizes normal standards to the exclusion of almost all else. The individual then reaches a stage in which he has exhausted this activity as a source of satisfaction. He then begins to change and enlarge his value system to find positive possibilities and new values that are still available to him despite his impaired condition. Only then can he go on to an adjustment in terms of new found values, such as the fact that he can be mobile in a different way; he may find pride in deploring self-pity; he may make a more healthy comparison of his condition with that of those worse off; he may find a new involvement and challenge in life. Blank (1957) and Cholden (1958) have applied this thinking to adjustment to blindness and see mourning as a required phase in the adjustment process for the newly blinded. This rationale suggests that persons with a congenital impairment may have somewhat different problems of adjustment than those confronting persons whose impairment is acquired.

Somatopsychological theory of adjustment to physical handicap perhaps fits the Hebbian observation on theory construction better than any considered in connection with the exceptional since it is one of our most "sophisticated statements of ignorance" in this field. It represents a valiant effort to "put our ignorance in a form that shows us how to go about decreasing it." Barker wrote that:

Somatopsychological research has been on the scientific frontier where technical precision, experimental rigor, and theoretical sophistication have been impossible. Nevertheless, much has been learned (p. 66). Somatopsychology is ... the relations between social behavior, and personality and normal and pathological variations in physical size, strength, motor ability, sensory acuity, and health. (Barker et al., 1953)

In the preface to this work it is noted that "The state of our knowledge of these matters is little above the level of folklore in many respects, and in others that which is known has very limited circulation." (preface, 1st edition, p. 7)

Meyerson (Cruickshank, 1955) provides some concepts for somatopsychology which he believes help in understanding the behavior of the physically handicapped. In his chapter, he gives credit to Lewin, and Barker and associates on whose thinking he draws heavily. The two concepts which Meyerson presents as a new way of thinking about somatopsychology are (1) new psychological situations, and (2) overlapping psychological roles. To understand these concepts the "life-space" of an individual must be conceptualized as his total perceived continuous interaction with his environment. Examining the individual's life space at any momentary point in time reveals familiar (or old) and unfamiliar (or new) life (psychological) situations. Through experience, the person has become familiar with, and more or less comfortable in, the old situations. Thus these have largely positive attraction (valence) for him—though some have negative attraction. There are also new situations which are relatively unknown and these have largely negative but also some positive valences.

The adjustment of the individual in terms of these concepts would be analyzed by examining his adaptation to familiar situations—the harmony he has achieved among his personal attributes and the environmental conditions he faces. His exceptionality is assumed to have limited or unfavorably influenced his experience or both and thereby impeded his adequate mastery of many life situations. The exceptional individual's experience is likely to be limited by his sensory impairment, by a reduction in his ability to get about and to participate in normal life experiences, or by having had such experiences so infrequently that they have limited value. The limitations on experience or lack of them deprives the individual of the "tools" to reach his goals and constitutes barriers to new achievement or to new levels of adjustment. New interests, activities or efforts comprise essentially "new" psychological situations or overlapping situations (which have some attributes of both new and old situations). Since the individual does not have the knowledges and skills needed to cope with such situations he does not know how to achieve his goals nor to conquer the barriers through efficient action. He must therefore resort to trial and error behavior, complicating his adjustment. In chapter 7 Wooden has outlined the three possible adjustment patterns open to those with disabilities developed by Meyerson in light of this theoretical rationale.

Beatrice Wright (1960) in an assessment of the field of somatopsychology has attempted to make generalizations on some of the broad areas wihch have captured the interest of investigators. She has noted such points as follow:

1. There is no substantial indication that persons with impaired physique differ *as a group* in their *general* or *overall adjustment.*

2. There is also no clear evidence of an association between types of physical disability and particular personality characteristics.

3. Although personality patterns have not been found consistently to distinguish disability groups as a whole, certain behaviors have been found rather directly connected with the limitations.

4. Studies of individuals convincingly indicate that physical disability has a profound effect on the person's life.

5. Public verbalized attitudes toward persons with disabilities are on the average mildly favorable.

6. The attitudes of parents toward their children who have a disability tend to the extreme more often than toward their nondisabled children. . . .

7. What evidence there is on attitudes of persons toward their own disabilities suggests that these attitudes vary widely, have little

relation to the degree of disability in massed data, are related to personality characteristics existing prior to the disability, and are influenced in the direction of acceptance via change in the person's value system. (pp. 373–377).

## NEUROPHYSIOLOGICAL THEORY

There has been increasing interest in the application of neurophysiological theory to problems of behavior and adjustment. Hebb (1958) has theorized that thought processes upon which behavior is based are built up in reverberating circuits in cell assemblies within the brain and nervous system. Behavior therefore has a neurological and perceptual foundation. Organized behavior is possible only with adequate sensory guidance, and adaptation to the environment can only be effective under such conditions. Emotional disturbances, fear, and other adjustment problems introduce disruption of time relations in neuronal activity in the cerebrum. Any disruption in the development or organization of cortical activity may lead to adjustment problems. From comparative studies on primates, Hebb has suggested that sensory deprivation in early visual or other sensory experience may produce grossly atypical later behavior in the sense modalities. The application of Hebb theory has been more specific with respect to learning disability in the mentally retarded and neurologically damaged since cell assemblies are not properly formed or are disrupted. Implications of this theory for improved education for such children are provided by Benoit (1960).

## LEARNING THEORY

Learning theory may be applied to the adjustment process in many ways. Cromwell (1961) has listed seven fundamental principles from learning theory that seem to have special implications for adjustment among the mentally retarded, but also among the gifted and other exceptional children. The seven points may be summarized as follows:

1. Positive reinforcement (reward) will increase the probability of behavior occurring while negative reinforcement (punishment) will reduce it.

2. Positive reinforcement will tend to develop goal-directed behavior while negative reinforcement will tend to develop avoidant or defensive behavior.

3. Immediateness of reward facilitates learning of desirable behavior.

4. Partial or irregular reinforcement may promote learning as well as regular reinforcement.

5. The way in which a child conceptualizes reinforcement is very important. That is, understanding the reason for reinforcement may be more important than the amount of reward or punishment.

6. Reinforcement must be consistent. That is, it cannot be positive at one time and negative at another for the same behavior.

7. Positive reinforcement should consistently be given to the individual as a person and not just in response to the behaviors that are to be established.

### FUTURE THEORY

It is possible that new directions in theory may be fruitful. Psychology has traditionally concerned itself with concepts centered in the fulfillment of inherent or acquired needs, the reduction of physiological or psychological tensions, and the maintenance of equilibrium or psychological homeostasis. Maslow (1955) has described these approaches as "deficiency motivation," and pointed out that there is a preoccupation with this type of thinking. Such a framework seems to have a natural and logical appeal as an orientation for the study of exceptional children since they are almost universally viewed as being "deficient"—as being motivated or driven by unmet needs even more than so-called "normal children." Increasingly, attention is being given to what Maslow (1955) and other behavioral scientists have called "growth motivation." Growth motivation is characterized by terms such as self-actualization, self-realization, creative capacities and tendencies, self-acceptance, constitutional potentialities and others. These terms are tending to replace "needs" motivation and they provide new leads to understanding how behavior is motivated. New understandings of the adjustment of exceptional children may result if more attention is given to what the exceptional child has, rather than what he lacks. Successful teachers of exceptional children have learned the value of working with children in terms of what they have. In fact, it is well accepted that many of the effects of exceptionality seem to result because the child is reacted to almost exclusively in terms of his exceptionality. He thereby learns to make the deviation the central feature of his way of life. Thus the child learns to conform to the stereotype that conditions the reactions of others to him.

Perhaps newer theory and thinking will lead us to increased attention on positive factors in research efforts. In all areas of exceptionality there are individuals who have "made the grade" in adjustment. We should study these individuals and the factors that contributed to their success.

## Recommendations for Teachers

One purpose of this chapter has been to cause the reader to question sole reliance on a common-sense approach to understanding the adjustment of exceptional children. Unfortunately, research and theory have yet to provide enough unequivocal answers needed for complete understanding without resort to common sense. We have noted many criticisms of the research that has been done. The reader should be sensitive to the need to be a critical consumer of research on adjustment. As such he will need enough knowledge of measurement, statistics, and research methodology to read the research literature intelligently. The difficult challenge presented is to make sound judgments regarding what is good and useful from common sense thinking and what is adequately derived through sound research.

The following recommendations for teachers seem to be in accord with sound research, with principles of good mental health, and with the results of successful experience in working with exceptional children.

1. Exceptional children need information, knowledge and skills that will enable them to cope adequately with life in their unique circumstances. Competence to deal with the vocational and social tasks of life will promote adjustment by enabling the individual to elicit positive attitudes from those with whom he lives and works.

2. Educational programs have as *one* ultimate goal—the optimum adjustment and integration of the exceptional child. The physical placement of an exceptional child in a normal setting neither guarantees his acceptance nor his integration with his classmates. The child must be helped to develop the attitudes and skills that will promote his acceptance and integration.

3. Theory and research primarily provide information about exceptional children *as groups.* Ultimately, we must deal with the exceptional child as an individual. Knowledge from theory and research must supplement the experience derived from personal contacts in individual work with children to promote good adjustment.

4. The exceptional child, like all others, is sensitive to the attitudes he meets in those with whom he lives and works. His own attitudes toward himself and others are built and shaped in response to the treatment accorded him. Realistically positive attitudes are essential.

5. Since behavior and adjustment can be so profoundly affected by environmental factors, the teacher must systematically strive to create an emotionally accepting school environment for each child.

6. The exceptional child can be cruelly rejected, or can feel thus rejected, as much or more as a result of the ignorance (stereotyped attitudes and prejudices) of others as from malice. Information about exceptional individuals must be widely available to dispel such ignorance. The teacher must be accurately informed and disseminate accurate and objective information.

7. The exceptional child needs to grow in independence. The teacher should not do for the child anything he can do for himself that will promote his growth toward a reasonable degree of independent functioning.

8. Open channels of communication and clarity of understanding among parents, faculty and administration are important to the adjustment of the exceptional child. The teacher should facilitate such communication as a means of promoting the child's adjustment.

9. The teacher should examine his own motives in working with exceptional children. Teachers who are motivated to work

with exceptional children to fill their own unmet needs are unlikely to be effective in working with such children.

10. The temptation to exploit exceptional children for the admiration of the public must be resisted. This is often difficult because of the natural appeal of the unusual or handicapped child.

11. The teacher must attempt to differentiate the realistic or irreducible limitations of the impairment from those associated effects which may result from overprotection, overindulgence or excessive sympathy.

12. Since exceptionality has different meanings and values to different people, the teacher should attempt to clarify its meaning for herself, for the child and for others in the child's environment.

13. The teacher's role is primarily that of educator rather than therapist. The teacher must operate within the limits of his own understanding and seek specialized help from those specialists in other disciplines who have unique complementary and supplementary assisting roles to play.

14. The exceptional child needs the security of clearly defined behavioral limits. Neither extreme permissiveness nor rigid autocracy provide an optimum climate for these children.

15. The exceptional child must be treated attitudinally in terms of what he has and not in terms of what he lacks. This is in contrast to educational treatment and planning which does need to be in terms of what the child lacks with regard to information, knowledge and skills. Again, however, educational planning should capitalize on what the child has with which to work.

## Summary

The attainment of satisfactory social and personal adjustment ranks high among the goals for exceptional children in the schools. This goal is realized for many exceptional children but inadequately achieved for others] Extensive attention has been given to exploring the dynamics of adjustment of such children. The research which has been done provides much useful information, both on adjustment and on research methodology. Among such findings on adjustment are the following. Exceptional children tend to have more adjustment problems than do normal children. Nevertheless, it is evident that a wide range of potential for adjustment prevails among individuals with exceptionalities of all types. No simple one-to-one relationship exists between poor adjustment and degree of deviation on mental, physical, or social continua. Efforts to understand adjustment in terms of a single factor seem to contribute little useful information. Evidence indicates that environmental factors interacting with physical or mental deviation have a profound and complex relationship to adjustment. Findings like these encourage school personnel to an optimistic view of each child's prognosis for satisfactory adjustment, but focus their attention on the need for awareness of the problems which may face many exceptional children. Thus, educators realize the importance of developing school settings in which each individual's adjustment potential can best be realized.

Research and experience suggest many things that can be done to promote good adjustment. Teachers themselves need to have positive attitudes toward exceptional children. They need to provide a classroom climate conducive to the development in children with deviations of more positive feelings about themselves and their life situations. In this regard, teachers can facilitate exceptional children's acquisition of knowledge, skills, and attitudes that enable them to evoke more positive reactions from people in their environment. Teachers can also interpret exceptional children to school and society, thus bringing about more acceptance.

In addition to information about the dynamics of adjustment, previous research has been fruitful in developing improved methodology for studying this field. Better tools such as tests, rating scales, and observational methods have been and are being developed. Sounder criteria for selecting the subjects for research have been proposed. We have learned to limit our generalizations about adjustment to conclusions justifiable in terms of the research that has been done. We have come to realize that sound research should be based on theory rather than being guided alone by common sense speculations.

Finally, this last chapter, and the book as a whole, reveal that the education of exceptional children is still a developing and growing field. As special educators, the authors believe there is a substantial body of knowledge and some proven methodology to put into practice, but a tremendous potential yet to be fulfilled. The progress which has been made in the century and a half of special education's history and the possible future gains seem related to western societies' unique cultural, social, and political ideas. Such ideals are well epitomized in a statement by Jefferson who said, "We must dream of an aristocracy of achievement arising out of a democracy of opportunity." This book is one effort to promote the attainment of this ideal in education and adjustment for exceptional children in the schools of today.

## CHAPTER REFERENCES

Adler, A. *Study of organ inferiority and its psychical compensation: a contribution to clinical medicine.* New York: Nervous and Mental Disease Publ., 1917.

Ashcroft, S. C. The blind and partially seeing. *Rev. educ. Res.,* 1959, **29**, 519–528.

Barker, R. G., Wright, Beatrice A., Meyerson, L., & Gonick, Mollie R. *Adjustment to physical handicap and illness: A survey of the social psychology of physique and disability.* (2nd ed.) New York: Soc. Sci. Res. Council, 1953. (No. 55)

Bender, Lauretta, & Silver, A. Body image problems of the brain damaged child. *J. soc. Issues,* 1948, **4**, 84–89.

Benoit, E. P. Application of Hebb's theory to understanding the learning disability of children with mental retardation. *Training School Bulletin,* 1960, **57**, 18–23.

Bice, H. V. Some factors that contribute to the concept of self in the child with cerebral palsy. *Ment. Hygiene,* 1954, **38**, 120–131.

Blank, H. R. Psychoanalysis and blindness. *Psychoanal. Quart.,* 1957, **26**, 1–24.

Blatt, B. Some persistently recurring assumptions concerning the mentally subnormal. *Train. sch. Bull.,* 1960, **57**, 48–59.

Bower, E. M. A process for identifying disturbed children. *Child.* 1957, **4**, 143–147.

——, & Holmes, J. Emotional factors and academic achievement. *Rev. educ. Res.,* 1959, **29**, 529–544.

Cholden, L. *A psychiatrist works with blindness.* New York: Amer. Found. Blind, 1958.

Connor, Frances P., & Goldberg, I. I. Children with crippling conditions and special health problems. *Rev. educ. Res.*, 1959, **29**, 471–496.

Cowen, E. L., Underberg, Rita P., Verrillo, R. T., & Benham, F. G. *Adjustment to visual disability in adolescence.* New York: Amer. Found. Blind, 1961.

Cromwell, R. L. Selected aspects of personality development in mentally retarded children. *Except. Child.*, 1961, **28**, 44–51.

Cruickshank, W. M. (Ed.) *Psychology of exceptional children and youth.* Englewood Cliffs, N.J.: Prentice-Hall, 1955.

Cutsforth, T. D. Personality crippling through physical disability. *J. soc. Issues*, 1948, **4**, 62–67.

———. *The blind in school and society.* New York: Amer. Found. Blind, 1951.

Dembo, Tamara, Ladieu, Gloria, & Wright, Beatrice A. Social-psychological rehabilitation of the physically handicapped. Final Report, Army Research and Development Board, Office of the Surgeon General, War Department W-49-007-MO-325, Sup. 5, April, 1948.

DiCarlo, L. M. The deaf and hard of hearing. *Rev. educ. Res.*, 1959, **29**, 491–518.

Elser, R. P. The social position of hearing handicapped children in the regular grades. *Except. Child.*, 1959, **25**, 305–309.

Farber, B. Family organization and crises: Maintenance of integration in families with a severely mentally retarded child. *Mon. Soc. Res., Child. Dev.*, 1960, No. 75.

Foale, Martha. The special difficulties of the high grade mental defective adolescent. *Amer. J. ment. Defic.*, 1956, **60**, 867–877.

Force, D. G. Social status of physically handicapped children. *Except. Child.*, 1956, **23**, 104–107.

Gallagher, J. J., & Crowder, Thora H. Adjustment of gifted children in the regular classroom. *Except. Child.*, 1957, **23**, 306–312, 317–319.

———. *Analysis of research on the education of gifted children.* Springfield, Ill. Office of the Superintendent of Public Instruction, 1960.

Garrison, K. & Force, D. *The psychology of exceptional children.* 3rd Edition. New York: Ronald Press, 1959.

Gesell, A. The psychological development of normal and deaf children in their preschool years. *Volta Rev.*, 1956, **58**, 117–120.

Glueck, S., & Glueck, Eleanor. *Physique and delinquency.* New York: Harper & Row, 1956.

Goldberg, Miriam L. Recent research on the talented. *Teachers College Record*, 1958, **60**, 150–163.

Hebb, D. O. *A textbook of psychology.* Philadelphia: Saunders, 1958.

Heber, R. F. A manual on terminology and classification in mental retardation. *Monogr. Suppl. Amer. J. ment. Defic.* (2nd ed.) 1961.

Hollingworth, Leta S. The child of very superior intelligence as a special problem in social adjustment. *Ment. Hygiene,* 1931, **15**, 3–16.

———. *The development of personality in highly intelligent children.* Washington, D.C.: NEA Fifteenth Yearbook Dept. Elem. Sch. Prin., 1936.

———. *Children above 180 intelligence quotient, Stanford-Binet.* New York: Harcourt, 1942.

Jordan, T. E. *The mentally retarded.* Columbus, Ohio: Merrill, 1961.

Johnson, G. O. A study of the social position of mentally handicapped children in the regular grades. *Amer. J. ment. Defic.,* 1950, **55**, 60–89.

Kanner, L. Emotional disturbances simulating mental retardation. *Pub. Hlth. News,* 1957, **38**, 313–332.

Kirk, S. A. *Counseling for psychological acceptance of disability.* Washington, D.C.: U.S. Dept. of Health, Educ. & Welfare, Rehab. Service Series, 1954.

———. *Educating exceptional children.* Boston: Houghton Mifflin, 1962.

Louttit, C. M. *Clinical psychology of exceptional children.* (3rd ed.) New York: Harper & Row, 1957.

Maslow, A. Deficiency motivation and growth motivation. In Jones, M. R. (Ed.) *Nebraska symposium on motivation.* Lincoln, Nebraska: Univer. of Nebraska, 1955.

Miller, Elsa A. Cerebral palsied children and their parents: A study in parent-child relationships. *Except. Child.,* 1958, **24**, 298–302.

Miller, Melba. An investigation of secondary defects potentially affecting the educability of children crippled by cerebral palsy. Unpublished doctoral dissertation, Univer. of So. Calif., 1953.

Murphy, A. T. The speech handicapped. *Rev. educ. Res.,* 1959, **29**, 533–565.

Myklebust, H. R. *The psychology of deafness.* New York: Grune & Stratton, 1960.

———, & Burchard, E. A study of the effects of congenital and adventitious deafness on the intelligence, personality and social maturity of school children. *J. educ. Psych.,* **36**, 321, 1945.

Olson, W. C. *Child development*. (2nd ed.) Boston: Heath, 1959.

Quigley, S. P., & Frisina, D. R. *Institutionalization and psycho-educational development of deaf children*. Washington, D.C.: Council for Except. Child. Research Monogr., 1961.

Rotter, J. B. *Social learning and clinical psychology*. Englewood Cliffs, N.J.: Prentice-Hall, 1954.

Schilder, P. *The image and appearance of the human body*. New York: Int. Univer. Press, 1950.

Sheehan, J. G. Projective studies of stuttering. *J. Speech Hearing Disord.*, 1958, **23**, 18–25.

Sheldon, W. H. *Varieties of delinquent youth: An introduction to constitutional psychiatry*. New York: Harper & Row, 1949.

Shere, Marie O. Socioemotional factors in families of the twin with cerebral palsy. *Except. Child.*, 1956, **22**, 197–199, 206–208.

Sommers, Vita S. *The influence of parental attitudes and social environment on the personality of the adolescent blind*. New York: Amer. Found. Blind, 1944.

Stevens, G. D. An analysis of the objectives for the education of children with retarded mental development. *Amer. J. ment. Defic.*, 1958, **63**, 225–235.

Terman, L. M., et al. *Genetic studies of genius*. Stanford, Calif.: Stanford Univer. Press, 1925–1959. 5 vols.

Terman, L. M., & Oden, Melita H. *The gifted child grows up*. Vol. IV. Genetic studies of genius. Stanford, Calif.: Stanford Univer. Press, 1947.

Thoreau, H. D. *Walden*. New York: Thos. Y. Crowell, 1910.

Van Riper, C. *Speech correction: Principles and methods* (4th ed.) Englewood Cliffs, N.J.: Prentice-Hall, 1954.

Wickman, E. K. *Children's behavior and teacher's attitudes*. New York: Commonwealth Fund, 1928.

Wilson, J. A. Achievement, intelligence, age and promotion characteristics of students scoring at or below the tenth percentile on the California test of personality. *J. educ. Res.*, 1959, **52**, 283–292.

Wright, Beatrice A. *Physical disability—a psychological approach*. New York: Harper & Row, 1960.

# AUTHOR INDEX

# SUBJECT INDEX

Talking books, 449
Tangible aids, 451
Teacher counselors, 254
Teachers
  of exceptional children, 3–4
  of crippled and neurologically
    impaired, 495–497, 504–505
  of educable mentally retarded, 86,
    108–112
  of emotionally disturbed and
    socially maladjusted, 273–275
  of gifted, 228–229
  of trainable mentally retarded,
    149–150, 157–161
  of visually limited, 436–439
Teaching (*see* Education)
Teaching-by-telephone, 506
Teaching machines, 506
Tectorial membrane, 356, 357
Tests
  delinquency, 264
  intelligence, 58–64, 75–76, 247
  personality, 246
  projective, 247
Texas Education Agency, 374
Texas School for the Deaf, 374
Thematic Apperception Test, 247
Therapeutic education, 254–256
Therapy
  drug, 481
  occupational, 501
  physical, 501
  speech, 499
Trainable mentally retarded children,
    9, 129–178, 526–528
  achievement, 130–131
  adjustment, 526–528
  behavior, 141
  characteristics, 134–141
  classification, 134–140
  clinical types, 139
  curriculum
    early approaches, 142–146
    present day approaches, 147–151
  defined, 130–131
  diagnosis (*see* identification)
  employment of (*see* postschool
    adjustment)
  enrollments, 20
  family adjustment, 167–169
  films, 177–178
  identification, 132–133
  Illinois study, 151–152
  lesson areas, 147–149
  Michigan study, 152
  Minnesota study, 151
  New York study, 152–153

  parents of, 167–169
  postschool adjustment, 163–166
  prevalence, 131–132
  references
    additional, 175–176
    chapter, 171–174
  residential schools, 143–146,
    161–163
  resources, 176
  San Francisco study, 153–154
  school aims, 142
  school programs for, 142–163
    administrative provisions,
      129–130, 143–146, 151–163
  sheltered workshops, 166
  special day classes, 129–130,
    151–161
    admission to, 155–157
    arguments for and against,
      157–161
    effectiveness of, 151–155
    exclusion from, 156
    growth, 129
    research on, 151–155
  special day schools, 160
  summary, 169–171
  teachers, 149–150, 157–161
  teaching principles, 149–151
  Tennessee study, 153
  vocational adjustment (*see*
    postschool adjustment)
Transient situational personality
    disorders, 249
Tremors (*see* Cerebral palsied
    children)
Tuberculosis, 474, 476–477
  bone and joint, 474
  pulmonary, 476–477
Tumors, 429, 475
Tuning forks, 346
Tympanic canal, 355, 356
Tympanic cavity, 353–354
Tympanic membrane, 353–354
Types of special education programs
    (*see* Administrative provisions
    for special education)

UNESCO, 9, 19, 58, 73, 465
Unit method, 103–105
United Nations, 263, 264, 268, 269
U.S. Census of population, 268
U.S. Children's Bureau, 269, 271, 409
U.S. Department of Health,
    Education, and Welfare, 49,
    409, 475
U.S. Justice Department, 262, 263